M000118897

SANTA BARBARA
BARBARA
& THE CENTRAL COAST

MICHAEL CERVIN

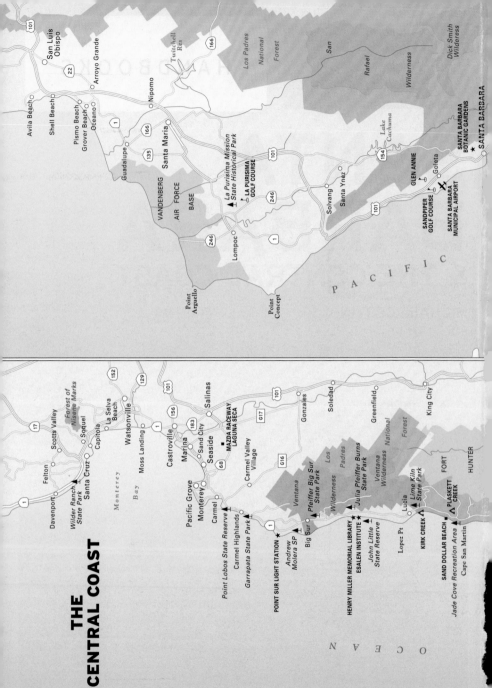

THE
CENTRAL COAST

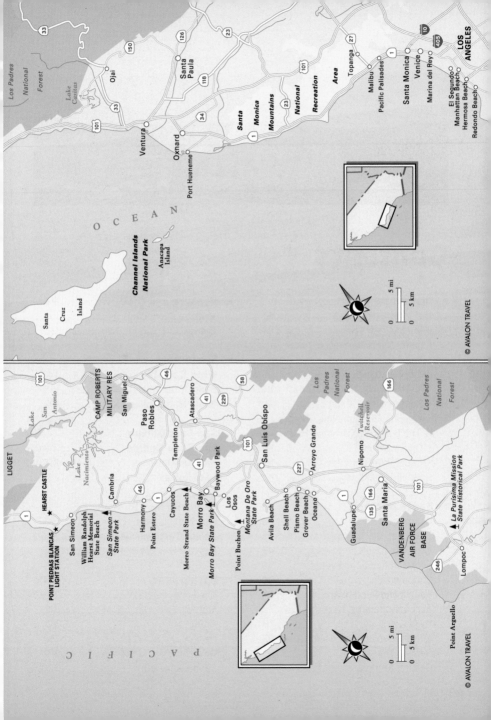

Contents

Discover Santa Barbara & the Central Coast

Little more than 30 years ago, California's Central Coast – with mid-sized cities like Ventura, Santa Barbara, and San Luis Obispo, and smaller towns like Ojai, San Simeon, Paso Robles, Cambria, and Solvang – was nothing more than a loose aggregate of beachside towns, tract housing, mom-and-pop eateries, and lone motels. There were few reasons to visit, unless you were looking for an idyllic stroll along the Pacific Ocean or among the gentle rolling hills of the rural valleys. But within three decades, Santa Barbara, Ventura, and San Luis Obispo Counties have morphed into tourist destinations filled with high-end real estate, world-class vineyards, exceptional restaurants, and vibrant sporting events, and are now viewed as representations of the quintessential California dream.

Situated on a narrow shelf 26 miles long and sandwiched between the Pacific Ocean and Los Padres National Forest, Santa Barbara is blessed with a nearly perfect and consistent climate and stunning vistas of the nearby mountains and ocean.

Ventura and Santa Barbara, less than 90 miles from Los Angeles, are a day-tripper's delight, and the wine regions of both counties can be accessed on a day trip – or even better, make a superb weekend getaway. Charming and unpretentious San Luis Obispo, not yet influenced by the megacities, is great for a true small-town beach experience.

The Central Coast wine industry has been a driving force in making this region into a destination. The sheer number of wineries is staggering: There are more than 400 of them here, with more starting up all the time. Whereas regions like Napa and Sonoma took decades to understand their soils, microclimates, preferred rootstock, and clones, the learning curve on the Central Coast was truncated, affording greater opportunities for innovative winemakers in less time. The Central Coast is also one of the last refuges for maverick farmers, risk-taking winemakers, and independent business owners.

California's Central Coast makes up the best of California: beautiful ocean drives, copious sun, deserts, pine-studded mountains, excellent wines, locally owned businesses, diverse outdoor activities, discernable architectural identities, and an intriguing history, all within a three-county area that's less than a three-hour drive from boundary to boundary.

Planning Your Trip

▶ WHERE TO GO

Santa Barbara

Sandwiched between the sparkling Pacific Ocean and the rugged Los Padres Mountains, Santa Barbara is the quintessential California getaway. Surrounded by undeniable physical beauty, the city provides many waterfront sights, including the popular Stearns wharf and the cove-like Leadbetter beach, a city favorite. Wine-tasting, dining, and shopping amidst breathtaking Spanish architecture abound on the city's main artery, State Street, and in the surrounding neighborhoods. The city also boasts museum gems that highlight the city's rich Native American, Spanish, and Mexican history and culture, as well as a flourishing arts scene evident in the multitude of art galleries and top-notch performing-arts venues.

Ventura and Ojai

Ventura is a throwback to what the coast was like 30 years ago, and it's surprising that it hasn't changed much. The surf vibe is strong here, with a vibrant commercial district and an up-and-coming arts community. The county is home to a dozen wineries and an increasing number of outstanding restaurants. It's also the base to get to the Channel Islands National Park; Anacapa Island, which is a mere 12 miles offshore, is an easy and awe-inspiring day trip. Ojai, by contrast, is a left-of-center small town that attracts artists and those seeking an off-the-beaten-path experience. It's also a spiritual hub, claiming many meditation and yoga retreat centers. Nearby Lake Casitas offers camping and water activities in a remote mountain setting.

Santa Barbara Wine Country

Small towns featuring intimate wine-tasting rooms punctuate the Santa Barbara wine country region. Unlike any other town on the Central Coast, quaint Solvang features sights that explore Danish heritage and a

one of the many coves at the Channel Islands

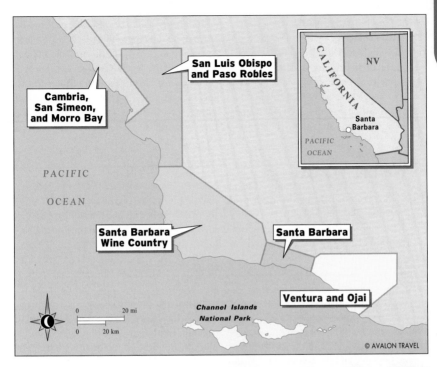

multitude of tasty Danish bakeries and restaurants. Santa Ynez boasts scenic wine roads and excellent wineries in a quiet setting. Los Olivos is a one-stop shop for all things wine, with the don't-miss biodynamic Beckmen Vineyards; and in Santa Maria, the gateway to wine country, you can visit the Mission La Purisima Concepcion de Maria Santisima, one of the most beautiful and authentic missions in Central California.

San Luis Obispo and Paso Robles

Slow-paced coastal town San Luis Obispo beckons with a beautiful downtown fronted by Higuera Street, an ideal spot for creekside dining and strolling. Nearby, the historic Madonna Inn is the perfect place to stop for lunch or dinner and marvel at the over-the-top decor. A short day trip from San Luis Obispo is Paso Robles, the hub of the most exciting wine industry area

Paso Robles is the heart of the wine industry in San Luis Obispo County.

in all of California, with access to more than 200 wineries that have made their home along the languid and scenic Highway 46.

Cambria, San Simeon, and Morro Bay

The largest draw for this slice of craggy beach is the opulent, impressive, and outlandish Hearst Castle, but that's certainly not all there is to see here. The rugged beauty of Cambria and San Simeon's coastline provides many recreational activities, including strolls along the stunning Moonstone Beach boardwalk, excellent hiking trails in the Montana de Oro State Park, and a trip to the base of the ancient dormant volcano Morro Rock. Cambria's village area draws a crowd for its local storefronts featuring antiques, local artwork, and a variety of unique gifty items, as well as its excellent and cozy restaurants.

▶ WHEN TO GO

During the summer months, the weather can be hit or miss. The "June gloom" is a reality, with the marine layer covering the area until as late as 4 P.M. The beaches and the islands are often blanketed in fog. There are certainly days when it's warm and postcard perfect, but these are the exception and not the rule. During this time the crowds are larger, the lines are longer, parking is more expensive, and services can be rushed because everything is operating at capacity. This is especially true of the smaller towns like Los Olivos, Cambria, Solvang, and Morro Bay, simply because of their small size. However the majority of events and festivals happen during the summer months, and draw many visitors to the area.

The coast is at its best March–May and October–December. During the spring, after the winter rains, the land has been replenished and the hillsides are verdant green. In fall, the crowds have thinned and there isn't the frenetic pace of the busy summer months. At both times of year it's warm, not hot, and the skies are clear.

Hearst Castle

Explore Santa Barbara & the Central Coast

▶ THE FIVE-DAY BEST OF SANTA BARBARA AND THE CENTRAL COAST

These five days of bliss will get you to many of the high points on the Central Coast. This itinerary is not designed for a leisurely pace, but you will definitely see a lot and get the best possible overview of all that the region has to offer. The Central Coast covers three different counties; it's possible to use Santa Barbara as a base from which to fan out south to Ventura or north to San Luis Obispo, which can be accomplished in single day trips. To fully explore the Central Coast,

though, it's best to use each county as a one- or two-day base if possible.

Day 1

Start your first day in the city of Santa Barbara with breakfast at Renaud's Patisserie and Bistro to make certain you get the best croissants in town. From there head over to the Old Mission Santa Barbara, and do the self guided tour. Plan for a little time to walk across the street and

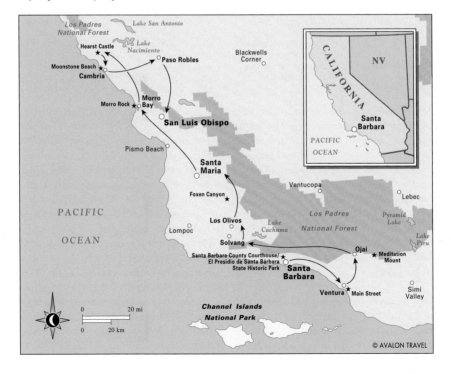

© AVALON TRAVEL

BEST BEACHES

- **The Rincon,** Ventura County: This stretch of beach and rock abuts the highway and the mountains. It's the undisputed surfing capital on the Central Coast.

- **Butterfly Beach,** Santa Barbara: Located near celebrity-infested Montecito, this dog-friendly beach has mild breaks perfect for kids.

- **Leadbetter Beach,** Santa Barbara: Surfing, beach volleyball, nearby eateries, a bike path, picnic and grassy areas, easy access for kayaking – you name it, this beach has it, all inside a protected cove. It's classic Santa Barbara.

Leadbetter Beach

- **Jalama Beach,** northern Santa Barbara County: Remote and secluded Jalama Beach has all the amenities you'll need, including food, RV hook-ups, picnic tables, and barbecue grills. The drive to reach this seldom-visited beach is half the adventure.

- **Pismo Beach,** San Luis Obispo: Pismo Beach has low and flat sand with dunes to the south and cliffs to the north. Take a break from the beach to sample the locals' favorite clam chowder, then check out the surfers near the pier, the beach's focal point.

- **Moonstone Beach,** Cambria and San Simeon: Sea lions drape across the rugged malformed rocks at this beach, the best place for tide-pooling in the area. There's also a nearly mile-long boardwalk on the bluffs with occasional beach access.

- **Morro Strand State Beach,** Morro Bay to Cayucos: Morro Strand is really a vast park – six miles of low flat sandy beach from Morro Bay to Cayucos. You can walk, run, or stroll while keeping sight of Morro Rock.

over the lawn to see the 1,000 varieties in the rose garden. Meander down to The Santa Barbara County Courthouse and explore the Sunken Gardens, and get your photo op in the clock tower with its expansive views of red-tile roofs, the ocean, the mountains, and downtown. Walk from there to State Street to Sullivan Goss: An American Gallery and admire the art, then lunch at Arts & Letters Café in the quiet courtyard with a three-tiered Spanish fountain directly behind the art gallery.

Head down State Street to explore the shops and stores and swing into El Presidio de Santa Bárbara State Historic Park to stand in the birthplace of the city. Across the street is El Cuartel, the second oldest building

in California and the only remaining original section of the presidio from the late 1700s. As you continue down State Street, walk through El Paseo or La Arcada Court, two historic and quintessential Santa Barbara paseos. Head to the waterfront and rent a surrey or bike and roll down the coast along Cabrillo Boulevard all the way to the Andre Clark Bird Refuge, then circle back and drop off the bike.

Go for an early dinner at Opal Restaurant and Bar for a good introduction to Santa Barbara's culinary scene. Then walk a few doors down to the Arlington Theatre to see what's on the screen or on stage and also to view its unique Spanish interior. Stop by Live Culture in the Paseo Nuevo mall for a bit of live music and a late-night snack or a nightcap.

Knapp's Castle

Day 2

From Santa Barbara, drive 20 minutes downcoast to Ventura. Start with breakfast at My Florist, then take a walk along C Street to watch the surfers, all the while keeping an eye out for dolphins or whales. Walk back to Main Street and check out the stores. Go for lunch at Yolanda's Mexican Cafe for some of the best Mexican food in town.

Right after lunch, drive Highway 33 up to Ojai to browse the art galleries and diverse shops including Ojai's best gallery, Primavera Gallery. Drive the short distance out to Meditation Mount for a great view of the Ojai Valley. Return to town and head back along Ojai Avenue to experience the Pink Moment as the sun sets over the Topa Topa mountains. Dine at Suzanne's Cuisine and spend the night in Ojai, at Su Nido Inn & Suites or the Blue Iguana Inn.

Day 3

Get up early and drive Highway 150 to connect with Highway 101 north, and make your way towards Solvang. On your way check out Knapp's Castle for what is arguably the best views of the ocean, the Santa Ynez Valley, and Lake Cachuma. Once in

Solvang stop at Mortensen's or one of the other Danish bakeries for local sweets and coffee. Explore shops like the Solvang Antique Center and Jule Hus and swing by the Elverhøj Museum of History and Art to gain an understanding of the historical significance of Solvang.

From there, a short five-minute drive gets you to Los Olivos, but not before a brief stop at Mission Santa Inés, which will be on your right on the way out of Solvang. Once in Los Olivos have lunch at Patrick's Side Street Café or Panino's, then sample a few wineries. Stop at Carina Cellars and Stolpman Vineyards to taste killer syrah and viognier.

Leave Los Olivos and take the Foxen Canyon route, a back-roads drive past vineyards and farms that weaves its way towards Santa Maria. There are a few tasting rooms along the way should the mood strike you. On your way back stop by the Far Western Tavern in Guadalupe for a later dinner of steaks grilled over red oak, then stay the night at the historic Santa Maria Inn.

Day 4

Leave early and drive the coastal route to

Santa Barbara's waterfront

Morro Bay, just about an hour from Santa Maria, and head to the Embarcadero for a brief walk along the waterfront out to Morro Rock. Grab a lunch of fish tacos at Taco Temple just north of downtown Morro Bay, and continue on Highway 1 towards Hearst Castle, a 30 minute drive, for an afternoon tour, which will take about two hours.

Heading back to Cambria, stop at Moonstone Beach and meander the boardwalk. Then head into Cambria and check out the unique local shops and have dinner at either the Black Cat Bistro or Robin's. Spend the night on beachfront property at Best Western Cavalier Oceanfront Resort in San Simeon, or head to the peace and quiet and quaint vibe of the Olallieberry Inn in Cambria. To round out the evening, head over to the Cambria Pines Lodge for live music in front of the fireplace.

Day 5
Grab a buttery croissant and coffee at the French Corner Bakery or something more substantial at the Cambria Pines Lodge, and then drive toward Paso Robles on Highway 46. As you get to about the halfway point before reaching Paso Robles, turn left on Vineyard Drive. Don't worry if you're not a wine person—this drive is fetching in itself. Take Vineyard Drive to Adelaida Road, and then turn right past mature oak trees and panoramic views towards the coast. The drive deposits you in downtown Paso Robles. If you like wine, swing by Edward Sellers Vineyards for killer Rhône-style wines before or after you have lunch near the town square at Berry Hill Bistro or Artisan. Then stroll through the City Park and take a peek in The Paso Robles Historical Museum.

Hop on Highway 101 to San Luis Obispo. Once you arrive, explore Higuera Street, and make sure to seek out Bubblegum Alley. Check in to the Madonna Inn, then head to the Gold Rush Steakhouse on the premises to enjoy a nice steak dinner and maybe some dancing while lounging in their signature pink booths.

▶ WINDING THROUGH WINE COUNTRY: THE BEST ONE-DAY WINE TOURS

Santa Barbara Wine Country
Get up early and make the short drive to Solvang from Santa Barbara, via the San Marcos Pass, Highway 154. Watch out for deer, wild turkeys, red-tailed hawks, cattle, and possibly even a bald eagle as you cruise to Solvang. Once you get to Solvang, grab a pastry from one of the bakeries and then stop at Presidio Winery in downtown for some biodynamic wines. From there you can easily walk to the D'Alfonso-Curran Wine Group just up the street for their unusual wines like grenache blanc. Then walk over to Mandolina and sample their Italian varieties including dolcetto. For lunch, walk over to The Chef's Touch for a salad or sandwich.

Then drive to Los Olivos for a sampling at Carhartt, the smallest tasting room in the county. Drive Foxen Canyon Road to Curtis Winery. Take Foxen Canyon all the way to

Take San Marcos Pass into Santa Barbara wine country.

Kenneth Volk Vineyards for some of the most unusual and rare wines you'll ever taste, such as negrette.

Head back down Highway 101 and cut through Ballard Canyon for a final stop at Rusack Vineyards. Take Ballard Canyon directly back into Solvang for a night's rest at Hadsten House, where you can have dinner and enjoy their hot tub.

Ventura and Ojai

Start your day at small family-owned Cantara Cellars near Camarillo, the farthest point south, then work back towards Ventura with a stop at Rancho Ventavo Cellars and their beautifully restored early-1900s tasting room in Heritage Square. Save a little time to explore Heritage Square. From there, completely shift gears and go to Herzog Wine Cellars for kosher wines and a wine tour in their massive complex.

Drive back to Ventura for a fresh, organic lunch in a converted train at The Sidecar, then make the short drive toward Ojai and visit Old Creek Ranch Winery on the way up Highway 33. Check out the original winery's old ruins behind the tasting room. Arriving in Ojai, park behind the Arcade and head over to

Casa Barranca to sample their organic wines while sitting in Craftsman-style chairs. Cross the street to relax at Libbey Park, then finish off with a Mediterranean dinner at Azu a few blocks down before crashing at Su Nido Inn & Suites.

San Luis Obispo

This day is laid out as a big loop. Starting from downtown, drive out to the Edna Valley via Tank Farm Road, which turns into Orcutt Road. This is a little longer back road past the

There are many wine tasting rooms in Santa Barbara that are just a block from the ocean.

ON A MISSION

Old Mission Santa Barbara

The Spanish missions along the Central Coast are an integral part of the history, culture, and architecture of the region, and they defined the cities that grew up around them. Though their effects may have waned over the years, a proper understanding of the history of the Central Coast should include a visit to some of following Central Coast missions.

· **Mission San Buenaventura,** Ventura: This mission was established in 1782 and was one of the most prosperous of the missions in the area. Still an active church today, it's integrated into daily life in downtown Ventura, located right on Main Street.

· **Old Mission Santa Barbara,** Santa Barbara: Known as the Queen of the Missions, this mission is visited by more people than any other on the Central Coast. The views from the front steps are spectacular.

· **Mission Santa Inés,** Solvang: Tucked behind Solvang, Mission Santa Inés is the least crowded with visitors of the missions in the area. Also an active church, it has views to a small valley below.

· **Mission La Purisima Concepcion de Maria Santisima,** Lompoc: The most uniquely designed of the missions, Mission La Purisima Concepcion de Maria Santisima was founded on December 8, 1787, and is now operated as a state park. It's also the

most authentic mission, with historically correct gardens and stables.

· **Mission San Luis Obispo de Tolosa,** San Luis Obispo: This mission was founded in 1769 in part because there were ample food resources in the area for soldiers. Now a central part of downtown San Luis Obispo, it's folded into the fabric of the town with festivals in the plaza in front of the mission, right next to the creek.

· **Mission San Miguel,** San Miguel: Mission San Miguel has been fraught with historical underpinnings; 11 people were murdered here in the 1840s, and a 2003 earthquake nearly destroyed it. Restoration efforts continue, and this mission has one of the most decorated chapels in all of the Central Coast.

Roblar Road near Los Olivos in the Santa Ynez Valley

dormant volcanoes, but is a preferred drive over Highway 227 because you see more of the valley as the road rises and falls, with views of the impressive vineyards.

Stop at Saucelito Canyon Vineyard to start your day of tasting with old-vine zinfandel that is sourced from their historic 1880 vineyard. You'll also pass Edna Valley Vineyards; stop in if you have time. Otherwise, head west through Price Canyon, which will place you in Pismo Beach. Explore the waterfront if you wish and grab fish-and-chips and clam chowder at Splash Cafe.

Then make your way upcoast to Avila Beach and visit Wood Winery at the boardwalk. After your tasting there, walk the pier and bask in the gentle vibe of this little bay.

As you head back toward Highway 101 deviate left to stop at Salisbury Vineyards'

historic tasting room and take a look at their rotating art gallery. Just up the road you can finish a full day of wine-tasting at Per Bacco Cellars with pinot noir and petite sirah. Have a relaxing Asian-influenced dinner at Chow in San Luis Obispo.

Paso Robles

This is a vast region, separated geographically by Highway 101. There are differences in temperature, soil, and growing conditions here, and a well-planned day trip allows you to taste these differences. Start by heading to Hunt Cellars on the west side of Highway 46, talk with Uncle Willie in the tasting room, and try their plush, velvety wines, specifically the sangiovese and zinfandel. Take Vineyard Drive up to the exceptionally sleek and cool-looking Denner Vineyards to enjoy their exceptional Rhône wine with views to the vineyards. Then drive back down Vineyard Drive (the way you came), which will place you at the Donati Vineyard.

Head back into downtown Paso Robles for lunch at Villa Creek, then check out Edward Sellers just around the corner for their beautifully delicate Rhône wines.

Hop across to the east side of Highway 46 to Eberle Winery. Go for one of their tours, which include the caves and winery. Then head west to see the mammoth art sculptures and wines at Sculpterra Winery. While you are there, taste the pistachios they grow on the property.

Once you circle back to downtown Paso Robles it will be nearly time for dinner, so swing by Artisan for some wine country cuisine. If you still want to try more local wines, walk the three blocks over to the Pony Club Bar at the Hotel Cheval and see what local wines they are pouring that night.

▶ COASTAL ADVENTURES

There's far too much to do, see, and explore on the Central Coast to spend all your time inside. The following activities are some of the best ways to experience the sun, sea, mountains, and islands on the Central Coast.

Hiking

The city of Santa Barbara has some of the best hiking experiences around, in part because the views from the mountains extend throughout the city, across the ocean, and out to the islands. Whether hiking near the coastal bluffs or up nearly 4,000 feet to the mountain ridges, you'll have expansive and breathtaking views. Seven Falls has an elevation gain of 600 feet over a two-and-a-half-mile path that follows Mission Creek north of the Santa Barbara Mission and will put you through canyons and natural water pools. Rattlesnake Canyon (Los Conoas and Rattlesnake Bridge) is a perennial favorite where you'll gain 1,000 feet in 3.5 miles, with great views to the ocean.

For something less taxing, try the easy hike at Oso Flaco Lake in the northern part of Santa Barbara County near Guadalupe; it's a two-mile round-trip passing over the lake and out to forlorn sand dunes at the water's edge. Also fairly easy, near Cayucos in San Luis Obispo County, is the Estero Bluffs, a four-mile stretch of bluffs with ocean access down craggy rocks and views across Cayucos to Morro Bay and Morro Rock.

Kayaking

The best kayaking hands down is at the Channel Islands, just off Ventura. The islands are incredibly diverse and the volcanic formations, sea caves, small coves, and beaches are perfect to make you feel like an explorer yourself. Blue Sky Kayak Tours can take you to parts of Santa Cruz Island that other companies cannot access, so you'll see up close the rich geologic beauty of these islands. Go for a day or up to a week with a trained guide who knows the cool spots for picnicking and kayaking.

Ventura has some of the best surfing spots in the area.

SMALL-TOWN GEMS

Sure, the big cities get all the attention, but the smaller towns peppered across the Central Coast have a charm all their own, and hold some hidden gems worthy of a visit.

- **Ojai** in Ventura County is the undisputed center for spiritual renewal. You'll feel relaxed the moment you enter the valley; stay to experience the Pink Moment, when the setting sun illuminates the town in a soft dusty-rose hue.

- **Solvang** in the Santa Ynez Valley is the Danish capital of America, and it looks unlike any other town. Sure, tourists flock here for Danish pastries and now wine-tasting, but they also come to experience the Elverhøj Museum of History and Art, which explores Danish history, and the very cool Motorcycle Museum.

- **Carpinteria** in Santa Barbara County has long been regarded as a great family-oriented beachfront area. That's still true, but Linden Avenue also offers a sophisticated culinary scene that elevates this small town above the norm.

- **Avila Beach** in San Luis Obispo County is a family-friendly beach town that was cleaned up and redesigned after a devastating oil spill. The town has been reborn, and its beach is a family favorite because of the protected cove setting and the swing sets that face the ocean.

- **Los Olivos** is small but important. The railroad ran through here in the 1880s, right where Highway 154 is now, allowing for commercial expansion into the Santa Ynez Valley. Mattei's Tavern, the original stop, still serves guests today, as do the wine-tasting rooms that have supplanted the old Western stores.

- **Cayucos,** between Morro Bay and Cambria, feels like it's been left behind as the rest of the world has progressed. It's a classic beach town, with a walkable downtown and wide friendly beaches. Make sure to visit the Brown Butter Cookie Company and browse the antiques stores. There's no rush when you're in Cayucos.

Surfing

If you are a surfer looking for those perfect surfing conditions, Ventura is the place to be, with notable surf spots like The Rincon, Ventura's most famous surfing landmark, and easily accessible low breaks at C Street (the nickname for California Street, near Surfers Point at Seaside Park), all with amazing views of the Channel Islands.

Boating

Santa Barbara provides the best backdrop for getting out on the water on a sailboat, powerboat, personal watercraft, or sunset cruise. You can hug the harbor or go full tilt all the way to the Channel Islands. And best of all, you have the city itself, set against the mountains, as a backdrop.

Kayaking the coast is the best way to intimately explore the sea.

Boating is a fantastic way to see the Central Coast.

Located in the Santa Barbara harbor, Sunset Kidd Sailing offers private charters on their 41-foot sailing yacht or join a bird-watching or whale-watching cruise on a 75-foot high-speed catamaran with Condor Cruises.

Scuba Diving

If you dive, you must get to the Channel Islands. Anacapa and Santa Cruz are the closest islands and offer the best visibility and variety of things to see, including sharks, seals, dolphins, lobsters, and stunning kelp forests. These can be done as day trips or you can pull an overnight and hit up multiple islands. *Peace Boat* sets out from the Ventura harbor and runs dive trips with a certified divemaster on board and a well-trained staff.

Biking

You can't beat San Luis Obispo for biking trails. The best spot to hit the trails is at Montana de Oro State Park. You can bike on the asphalt on Pecho Valley Road, the main road through the park, or get off-road with a maze of single- and double-track fire roads like the moderate Barranca Trail Loop, the strenuous Hazard Peak Trail, or the coastal Bluff Trail at Spooner's Cove, all of which intertwine through 8,000 acres of pristine land. There are great elevation gains, flat scrub areas, coves, cliffs, and trails to the ocean.

Dolphins are often spotted off shore.

SANTA BARBARA

Santa Barbara's laid-back vibe, inspired by endless waves and eternal sunshine, is complemented by great shopping and recreational opportunities, world-class wine-tasting, and breathtaking Spanish architecture. The city has been referred to as "America's Riviera"—and with good reason. It has an enviable setting, nestled between the Pacific Ocean and the mountains, and incredible views of both—plus fantastic weather. It's an idyllic spot—so much so that if you stay long enough, you probably won't want to leave.

Most tourists enjoy Santa Barbara's idyllic setting and mellow mood along the city's popular waterfront and State Street, but this city of roughly 120,000 people also offers a wealth of cultural, architectural, and historical treasures. Fiercely proud of its heritage, Santa

Barbara has a history that extends back to the Chumash Indians' habitation of the area more than 10,000 years ago. The city is also committed to maintaining a unifying architectural theme of whitewashed authentic adobe and adobe-looking buildings capped with red-tile roofs that stand out against the blue skies—it's no surprise that the National Trust for Historic Preservation named Santa Barbara a Distinctive Destination in 2009. The mission, superb Moorish-influenced county courthouse, historic Spanish and Mexican adobes, and the handsome State Street corridor with its vine-covered walls and mature trees shading brick sidewalks all combine to give you a unique experience among American cities.

The city inspires physical activity and healthy living: With copious sunshine, wide

HIGHLIGHTS

(El Presidio de Santa Bárbara State Historic Park: Though much of it has been rebuilt, two sections of the early fort the Spanish built here to defend their territory still stand. El Cuartel, an original adobe, is the second oldest building in the state of California. This is the birthplace of Santa Barbara (page 26).

(Santa Barbara Historical Museum: Housing an impressive array of artifacts from Santa Barbara's varied history, this little gem of a museum provides the best visuals of the last 600 years (page 30).

(The Santa Barbara County Courthouse: This building offers the definitive Santa Barbara experience, with Spanish and Moorish architecture, California history, and views of the city, mountains, oceans, and islands from a stunning building rightly called the most beautiful public building in America (page 32).

(Stearns Wharf: Stearns Wharf is the most visited landmark in Santa Barbara, a classic pier with restaurants, shopping, and killer views of the city (page 36).

(The Santa Barbara Harbor: The harbor is home to fresh fish hauled in daily, the Santa Barbara Maritime Museum, the best sea-

food restaurant in the city, and the long breakwater wall (page 37).

(Old Mission Santa Barbara: Known as the Queen of the California missions, this intricately painted church has some of the most lush grounds and landscaping of any mission, making it a routine stopping point (page 38).

(Lotusland: The sheer diversity and immaculate arrangement of the plants, trees, and every other form of flora and fauna at this estate creates a botanical wonderland (page 41).

(Casa del Herrero: This 11-acre estate is an incredible example of Spanish Colonial Revival architecture from the early 20th century. The building is in its original pristine condition, with mesmerizing interior detail (page 42).

(Knapp's Castle: A magnificent 1920s seven-building estate burned to the ground in 1940, leaving only forlorn stone outcroppings above the Santa Ynez Valley. The stark beauty compels locals, tourists, and photographers to visit and imagine what once was (page 43).

(Leadbetter Beach: There's no better beach in all of Santa Barbara. Others are larger, but this cove-like beach, flanked by a point and the harbor, has everything you could want, including great views (page 46).

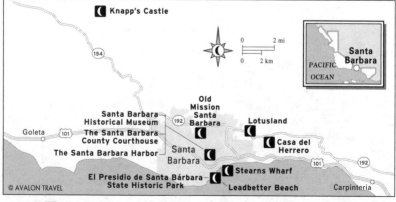

LOOK FOR (TO FIND RECOMMENDED SIGHTS, ACTIVITIES, DINING, AND LODGING.

SHAKEN, NOT STIRRED: SANTA BARBARA'S SEMINAL EARTHQUAKE

At 6:44 A.M. on June 29, 1925, all was fine and quiet on the streets of Santa Barbara. Less than two minutes later, 30 square blocks of the downtown core had been severely damaged; the Sheffield Dam had failed, plunging water into the city center; a two-acre parcel just west of the city sunk nearly a foot; the waterfront road sustained cracks larger than 12 inches wide; and 13 people were dead. The magnitude 6.8 quake was felt as far south as Anaheim, 130 miles away, and 120 miles north in Paso Robles. Much of the city's sub-standard construction failed, and parts of commercial buildings on lower State Street, built on landfill, collapsed quickly. Brick buildings and wood construction shattered miserably, and some storefronts dissolved so that you could see directly into the buildings.

Architect Julia Morgan was in Santa Barbara that fateful day. She had arrived early that morning, blueprints in hand, to meet with the building committee regarding a potential project. As she waited for the streetcar to take her up State Street, the earthquake struck. As she fell to her knees, she saw clouds of dust envelop the downtown thoroughfare, and she grabbed a gunny sack from a nearby ice wagon to protect herself. She spent a good part of that morning viewing the damage, observing which buildings had best survived and taking copious notes. The experience made her even more keenly aware of the urgent need for reinforced buildings in her own work (Hearst Castle is well reinforced with rebar).

The city faced destruction totaling about $8 million, a staggering sum by mid-1920s standards. Had the quake struck later in the morning, as citizens were on their way to work, the death toll would have been much higher. Unlike San Francisco after the 1906 quake, Santa Barbara didn't have fires to contend with, and therefore the damage was fairly limited. But the earthquake gave the city a chance to reinvent itself, and encouraged the enforcement of stricter building codes to withstand the onslaught of what Mother Nature can dish out.

roads, lots of warm sandy beaches, and challenging mountain trails, it's the kind of environment where getting outside is so easy that simply being in Santa Barbara is equated with being out-of-doors. There are no excuses not to walk, jog, hike, surf, run, bike, dive, or play. Surfing is a favorite activity here, with eager surfers dotting most of the coastline. And along the waterfront, a paved path allows anyone on two feet, two wheels, or anything else that moves to enjoy the coastline alongside grassy areas with palm trees gently tottering in the breeze. At least five farmers markets held every week make healthy produce abundant and accessible to all residents.

To both residents and visitors, Santa Barbara seems almost like a dream. Its natural beauty and great weather, plus stunning geography, creative restaurants, local culture, rich history, a thriving wine industry, and unique festivals, all bookended by the mountains and ocean,

make this prime spot enviable beyond belief. When I travel and people hear that I'm from Santa Barbara, the response is predictable: They smile widely, nod knowingly, and say, "Oh, that's a nice place."

HISTORY

Prior to the arrival of the Spanish on these lands in the mid-1500s, about 20,000 Native American Indian Chumash lived between Malibu and San Luis Obispo, and on the Channel Islands, in self-sustaining and autonomous communities. There are still cave paintings, made by the Chumash in order to write their own stories, scattered throughout the Central Coast region. In 1542 Juan Rodríguez Cabrillo sailed into the Santa Barbara Channel and, contrary to popular belief, didn't drop anchor near the mainland. He landed his ship at the Channel Islands, having never set foot in what is now Santa Barbara. But he put up a Spanish flag and claimed the

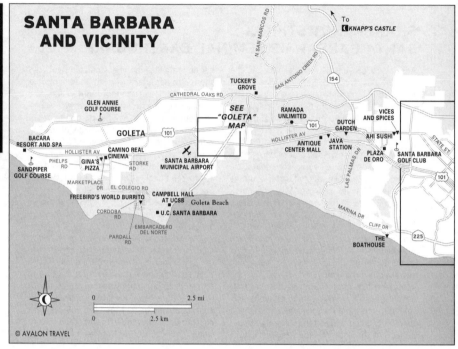

SANTA BARBARA AND VICINITY

region for Spain. It was Sebastián Vizcaíno, a cartographer for the Duke of Monte Rey, who landed in the Santa Barbara harbor 60 years later on December 4, 1602, which happened to be the feast day of Saint Barbara. The flag was officially planted and Santa Barbara was put on the map for the first time. But living on land claimed and named by Spain didn't really affect the Chumash Indians in the least—until the arrival of Spanish missionaries in the mid-1700s.

Spain, in need of defensible positions along the coast to secure its newly claimed territory, established the very first presidio, a ramshackle wood structure, here on April 21, 1782. The formal presidio, or fort, was constructed beginning in 1784, followed closely by the Santa Barbara mission in 1786. Spain effectively ruled the region until the early 1820s, when Mexico fought for and won its independence from Spain. But Mexico's rule was short-lived, as the United States then declared war on Mexico in 1846 in order to expand its territories.

With the discovery of gold in Northern California in 1849, easterners came west, and many of those looking for a new life ended up in Santa Barbara. The city's mild climate also began to draw people to the coast for health reasons. In the late 1880s Santa Barbara was considered a health resort, and reports of the day promoted the healing environment of the city's natural springs and mild climate. Of course the arrival of the railroad in 1887 also helped the city grow. Many wealthy East Coast industrialists who could afford second homes on large swaths of land built estates in Montecito, just outside the city. But even at this point, though there were large and impressive hotels like the Potter and Arlington that catered to the elite, the city was still relatively small. The 1925 earthquake decimated parts of Santa Barbara, and the fortuitous opportunity to reinvent the city is considered a seminal moment in its evolution. The city fathers viewed this "blank canvas" as a blessing and called upon the town's

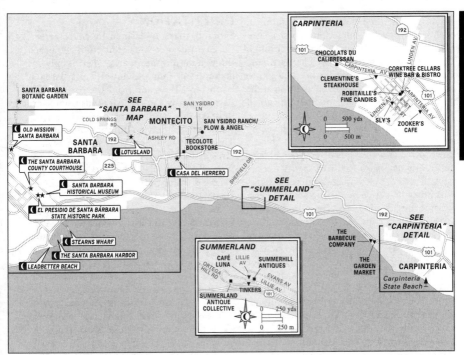

original Spanish and Mexican influences to create a definable identity, still evident in the downtown of today. But even post–World War II, Santa Barbara was considered a sleepy little beach community, and not the tourist destination it is now. There were iron oil derricks all along Summerland's beaches, and they blighted the Mesa. Property values plummeted when a Japanese submarine fired a shell at the coast. Additionally, since there were few viable businesses here, land was cheap. But it wasn't long before that started to change. More people began to recognize all that the area had to offer and the demand increased. The real estate market began to grow exponentially in the early 1990s.

Part of Santa Barbara's appeal is the fact that its natural boundaries, created by the ocean and the mountains, leave little possibility for urban sprawl. (It's interesting to note that the tallest building is still only a mere eight stories, and there's just one at that height.) Preservationists have long held power here and have kept unbridled growth in check in order to control the city's overall visual theme. Considering the area's limited building potential, it's no wonder that land became a hot commodity. And its strong agricultural components, most notably the wine industry, avocados, broccoli, and strawberries, mean Santa Barbara is assured of being a desirable location for a long time to come.

PLANNING YOUR TIME

Santa Barbara is fairly compact and can easily be enjoyed in a weekend, but to fully explore the city you'll need at least three or four days, especially if you want to enjoy water activities, hiking, or cycling. If you're the meandering type, the waterfront and State Street will suit you fine and can be explored in a weekend.

The ideal time to visit is from March to May, when everything is pristine after the mild winter rains. The temperatures are still moderate, the views are crystal clear, and the air is fresh and crisp. The June gloom kicks off summer, with lots of fog that sometimes doesn't burn off until early afternoon. October through December is also a great time. There are more chances of rain then, but it's not unusual to be able to spend Thanksgiving weekend at the beach, playing in the water and burning off all those calories.

The city's grid layout makes sightseeing easy; the majority of sights are within 12 blocks downtown, so walking is often preferable to constantly having to find parking. If you are an early riser, it's recommended to get to sights when they first open in order to avoid crowds. Everything gets progressively more crowded as the day wears on, but the early mornings, and even as late as 10–11 A.M., are reasonably crowd free. Many visitors stay downtown or by the waterfront, and the city is an easy base for the sights you'll need to drive to, such as the mission, Montecito, and Carpinteria. Even the Santa Ynez Valley is only a 30-to-40-minute drive, and is a great day trip. If you head to the valley for the day, drive up via the San Marcos Pass (Highway 154) over the mountains and return to the city via Highway 101 along the coast, or vice versa. That way you get the best of everything—mountains with killer views, and lots of ocean and ranch land.

ORIENTATION

Santa Barbara is defined by State Street, the main drag, which runs from the beach through the downtown area. There is only one major artery into and out of Santa Barbara, Highway 101. Aside from the San Marcos Pass (Highway 154), which heads from Santa Barbara over the mountains and into the Santa Ynez Valley, no other roads lead here. This can be a problem every once in a while: Fires can shut down Highway 101, leaving Santa Barbara isolated from its neighbors. If there is a major traffic accident, there simply are no alternate routes.

Aside from that, getting around Santa Barbara is easy, as the city is laid out in a classic grid pattern. State Street does get congested during summer months; unless you enjoy sitting in your car and inching your way along, it's best to use other arteries on the weekends. The first street east of State Street is Anacapa, which runs one way to the ocean. Chapala, the first street west of State Street, runs one way towards the mountains. These two streets allow for quick travel through the city.

Though State Street is not a lengthy street, the 400–600 blocks have become known as "Lower State" and you will hear people refer to this often.

Sights

Santa Barbara is a visually appealing city surrounded by extreme natural beauty. Many visitors come here for the coastline, but also for the historical missions, the museums, and the amazing architecture, such as the Spanish buildings with wrought-iron rails and wooden porches and copious colorful tile work, or buildings from the 1880s with their Western feel, or even the 1940s influence on structures with an industrial motif.

DOWNTOWN

Downtown Santa Barbara covers about 12 blocks. It is a pedestrian-friendly area with more

than enough places to grab a bite, get more cash at a bank, or step inside a store to find something of interest. There are even plenty of combination trash cans and recycle bins (the dark green ones). What are lacking, however, are restrooms. Surprisingly, there is only one public facility (914 State St., next to Borders), and many businesses will not allow non-customers to use theirs.

◖ El Presidio de Santa Bárbara State Historic Park

El Presidio de Santa Bárbara State Historic Park (123 E. Canon Perdido St., 805/965-0093, www.sbthp.org, daily 10:30 A.M.–4:30 P.M.,

BUILDING A BETTER BRICK: ADOBE CONSTRUCTION

Santa Barbara's early Spanish settlers found a landscape devoid of trees, where lumber was almost non-existent-hard to believe considering the incredible population of trees in the area today. The settlers' answer for building the new town was the very earth beneath their feet. They made adobe bricks by digging a pit, into which clay-like soil and water were added. Once the mixture was smooth, straw and sand were added to bind and strengthen the adobe.

Obtaining the correct proportions of soil, water, straw, and sand was crucial to prevent the bricks from crumbling. The mixture was poured into wooden forms to create bricks, then set aside to dry in the sun. Depending on the size of the bricks, which averaged 50-60 pounds, they could take as many as 30 days to thoroughly dry. As many as 5,000 bricks would typically be used to create even a modest one-room structure. Adobe walls were thick by modern standards, usually about two feet for smaller buildings. To give the walls greater strength they were covered with a coating of sand and mud. The walls were then sealed with a plaster made of lime mixed with sand and water. As the mixture dried it hardened, forming a protective coating. The finished adobe was cool in the summer, warm in the winter, and proved to be quite durable.

Santa Barbara's historic adobes have survived most of the earthquakes over the last 200 years. But the influx of Americans predominately from the east coast to Santa Barbara after 1850 caused a decline in the popularity of adobe construction, as the new residents wanted houses that reminded them of their wood-framed homes they had recently abandoned. In some cases the adobe structures were covered with wood siding, or they were simply torn down. There are some 300 adobe structures still standing in the county, proving that the original construction methods were sound.

closed major holidays, $5 adults, $4 seniors, admission includes Casa de la Guerra) can rightfully be called the birthplace of Santa Barbara. The presidio, as it's referred to, was founded on April 21, 1782, and was the last in a chain of four military fortresses built by the Spanish along the coast of California. The whitewashed buildings were constructed of sun-dried adobe bricks laid upon foundations of sandstone boulders. Timbers from the Los Padres forest supported roofs of red tile. The buildings of the presidio form a quadrangle enclosing a central parade ground, and the whole structure is surrounded by an outer defense wall with two cannon bastions. The most prominent building was and still is the chapel, Santa Barbara's first church for its townspeople (the Christianized Chumash Indian population worshipped at the mission). Today, only two sections of the original presidio quadrangle remain, and both are within the state park: El Cuartel, the family residence of the soldier assigned to guard the western gate into the Plaza de Armas, and the Canedo Adobe, named after the presidio soldier to whom it was deeded when the presidio became inactive.

Though much has been reconstructed at the presidio, El Cuartel (the second oldest building in California, dating from 1782), right across the street from the chapel, is a great example of living architecture; it's the type of historic building that can be accessed by the public, touched, and experienced. The massively thick walls still stand as they have for more than two hundred years, with only cosmetic touch-ups to the plaster that covers the original adobe bricks. El Cuartel is small, with tiny doors and windows reflective of the time, but it's awesome to stand in the spot where Santa Barbara was first formed, and feel the connection to history. The presidio is just a block off State Street downtown and can easily be worked into your downtown sightseeing plans.

SANTA BARBARA

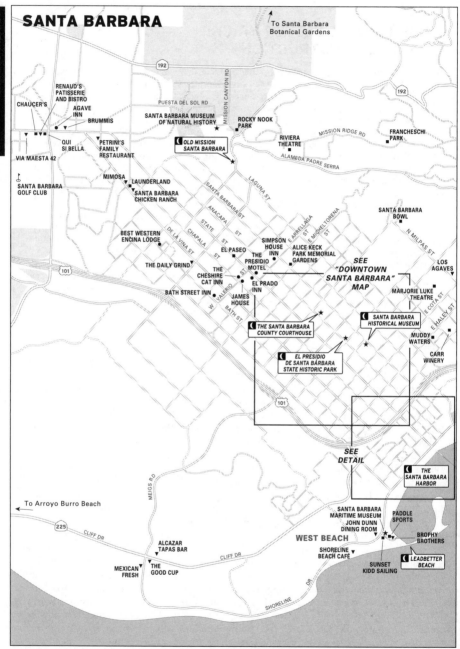

SANTA BARBARA

To Santa Barbara Botanical Gardens

192

RENAUD'S PATISSERIE AND BISTRO

CHAUCER'S

AGAVE INN

BRUMMIS

PUESTA DEL SOL RD

SANTA BARBARA MUSEUM OF NATURAL HISTORY

ROCKY NOOK PARK

192

FRANCESCHI PARK

QUI SI BELLA

PETRINI'S FAMILY RESTAURANT

VIA MAESTA 42

MIMOSA

LAUNDERLAND

SANTA BARBARA CHICKEN RANCH

SANTA BARBARA GOLF CLUB

OLD MISSION SANTA BARBARA

RIVIERA THEATRE

MISSION RIDGE RD

ALAMEDA PADRE SERRA

MISSION CANYON RD

LAGUNA ST

SANTA BARBARA ST

ANACAPA ST

STATE ST

CHAPALA ST

DE LA VINA ST

E ARRELLAGA ST

E MICHELTORENA ST

N MILPAS ST

SANTA BARBARA BOWL

BEST WESTERN ENCINA LODGE

EL PASEO

SIMPSON HOUSE INN

THE DAILY GRIND

THE PRESIDIO MOTEL

THE CHESHIRE CAT INN

EL PRADO INN

ALICE KECK PARK MEMORIAL GARDENS

SEE "DOWNTOWN SANTA BARBARA" MAP

LOS AGAVES

MARJORIE LUKE THEATRE

BATH STREET INN

JAMES HOUSE

W VALERIO ST

BATH ST

THE SANTA BARBARA COUNTY COURTHOUSE

SANTA BARBARA HISTORICAL MUSEUM

E COTA ST

E HALEY ST

MUDDY WATERS

EL PRESIDIO DE SANTA BARBARA STATE HISTORIC PARK

CARR WINERY

101

SEE DETAIL

THE SANTA BARBARA HARBOR

To Arroyo Burro Beach

MEIGS RD

225

CLIFF DR

ALCAZAR TAPAS BAR

CLIFF DR

SANTA BARBARA MARITIME MUSEUM JOHN DUNN DINING ROOM

PADDLE SPORTS

WEST BEACH

BROPHY BROTHERS

MEXICAN FRESH

THE GOOD CUP

SHORELINE BEACH CAFÉ

SUNSET KIDD SAILING

LEADBETTER BEACH

SHORELINE DR

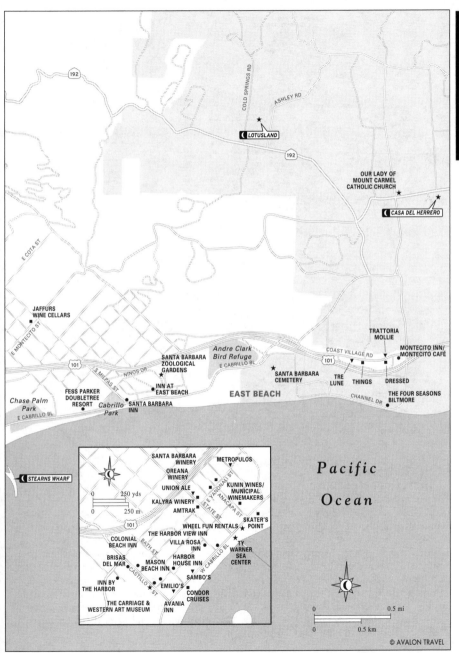

© AVALON TRAVEL

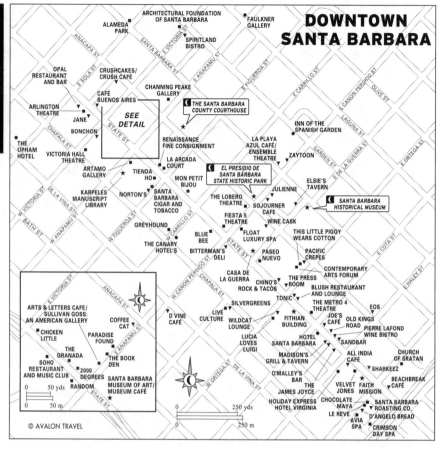

◖ Santa Barbara Historical Museum

The Santa Barbara Historical Museum (136 E. De La Guerra, 805/966-1601, www.santabarbaramuseum.com, Tues.–Sat. 10 A.M.–5 P.M., Sun. noon–5 P.M., free, donations accepted) houses a beautiful and comprehensive collection of historical artifacts covering the last 600 years of local history, including an 1813 Peruvian mission bell, a three-foot tall hand-painted wood carving of Saint Barbara, and an exquisitely carved ornate 15-foot Tong shrine from the days when Santa Barbara had a thriving Chinatown.

There are also Chumash, Spanish, and Mexican period garments on display, as well as guns, swords, and working tools.

The entry foyer hosts rotating exhibits that feature anything from important local artists to designer Kem Weber's industrial work and furnishings from his time spent teaching art and design in Santa Barbara at a his own small studio. The museum, which also has a small gift store, is one of the great jewels of the city, and a visit is nearly mandatory for anyone who desires an understanding of the multilayered history of this area.

© MICHAEL CERVIN

Casa de la Guerra is one of the oldest homes in Santa Barbara. It was the center of cultural and political life.

Faith Mission

In 1889, the Faith Mission (409 State St.) opened its doors to convert young men "from their erring ways." Good intentions, however, didn't allow the occupants to stay put for too long, and the building became a hotel in 1931. Most recently it was a sushi joint, with pool tables and stiff drinks that might have deeply offended the original owners. (Well, that and the fact that the building sits two doors up from an adult bookstore.) These days the building is vacant, but its former glory is still evident. Often overlooked, it's the only intact 19th-century commercial facade in downtown. The two-story building was constructed of brick masonry, with an elaborate stamped metal veneer applied on the front, making it unlike any other building in all of Santa Barbara County.

Doremus Stone Pine Trees

When driving or walking along the 300–800 blocks of East Anacapa, you're not likely to look up, but you should. The Doremus Stone Pine Trees, so named for Agustus Doremus, the

city's first parks superintendent, were planted between 1908 and 1929 and form an incredible canopy shielding the street from the sun and sky. Vast in their reach, sublime in their simplicity, the 60-foot trees are worth checking out as you drive or, preferably, walk down the street. They are, unfortunately, one of those sights that few people ever notice.

Fithian Building

When tooling along State Street, you'll pass the Fithian Building (629 State St.), and you may not think much of it, as it seems like just another storefront. But do yourself a favor and enter the double doors and go to the top of the stairs. You'll be treated to a beautifully restored turn-of-the-20th-century interior, complete with original hardwood floors, narrow offices, and doorways with transoms in each office. The exterior of the building, originally built in 1895, does not do justice to the interior. Now holding the offices of architects and designers it's a blast from the past and worth a few minutes to see how much has changed.

The Santa Barbara County Courthouse has Spanish and Moorish design elements.

© MICHAEL CERVIN

Casa de la Guerra

Casa de la Guerra (15 E. De La Guerra St., 805/965-0093, www.sbthp.org, Sat.–Sun. noon–4 P.M., $5 adults, $4 seniors, includes admission to Presidio) has been at the heart of Santa Barbara's history since its construction 1819–1827 by the fifth presidio commandant, Don Jose de la Guerra. Among Santa Barbara's wealthiest and most influential citizens, the Spanish-born commandant stood out as the patriarchal figure to whom the entire community looked for protection and assistance. Casa de la Guerra was the social, political, and cultural center of the pueblo of Santa Barbara. That legacy survived with the political activity of de la Guerra's son, Pablo, during the early years of California's statehood. Don Pablo served as a state senator and as lieutenant governor of the state; prior to statehood he was a local judge. In 1874 the first city hall was constructed opposite the Casa in Plaza de la Guerra. In 1922 El Paseo was designed and built around the Casa. When the first Old Spanish Days Fiesta was held in 1924, parties, dances, and teas in honor of the members of the early families were held at Casa de la Guerra in the large courtyard where you can walk today. Following the devastating 1925 earthquake, the Casa and El Paseo served as models for rebuilding parts of downtown. It may seem a simple structure, but

it serves as a reminder of the vast importance of Santa Barbara's heritage. A visit lets you see the rooms that were, at the time, some of the nicest and most ornate around, though by today's standards they seem a little crude. Unless you're a history buff, a self-guided tour of the site is sufficient, though they do offer hour-long guided tours by appointment only.

The Santa Barbara County Courthouse

Covering an entire city block, the still-functioning Santa Barbara County Courthouse (1100 Anacapa St., 805/962-6464, www.sbcourts.org, free docent-led tours Mon.–Sat. at 2 P.M., additional free docent-led tours Mon., Tues., and Fri. at 10:30 A.M.) is a stunning example of Spanish and Moorish design. William Mooser designed this courthouse to replace the earlier 1872 version, a colonial-looking thing with a massive domed cupola. When the courthouse was completed in 1929, it was unlike anything in the city. Lush grounds including the copious lawn and Sunken Gardens lay the foundation for the sandstone building with arabesque windows, archways, hand-painted wood ceilings, walls with intricate designs, and pueblo tile inlays nearly everywhere flashing brilliant colors and native designs. Of particular note is the Mural Room, once used by

SANTA BARBARA: AN ARCHITECT'S CANVAS

It's no wonder that many prominent architects have used Santa Barbara's stunningly beautiful topography as a backdrop for their own inspired creations. Julia Morgan, best known as the sanity behind Hearst Castle, designed several buildings in town, two of which survive today. Her first commission was for a 3,000-square-foot ballroom for the Montecito estate The Peppers, completed in 1917, which made use of redwood, mahogany, and oak, and featured a magnificent fireplace. In 1918, she designed a tuberculosis clinic for children on North San Antonio Road. In 1925, she was hired to design the **Margaret Baylor Inn** (924 Anacapa St.). Today, as the **Lobero Building**, it holds a variety of offices. The **City Gymnasium** (102 E. Carrillo St.) was badly damaged in the 1925 earthquake, and Morgan was retained to design a new one. She placed handball and tennis courts on the roof, and her Spanish Colonial Revival concept fitted in nicely with the city's new architectural guidelines for the downtown area. The building is a City Structure of Merit.

Other prominent architects were also active in the area. Frank Lloyd Wright built two residential homes here. Kem Weber, the post-WWI industrial designer, created the **Church of Religious Science Reading Room** (1301 State St.). Myron Hunt, best known for his Rose Bowl and Huntington Gardens, both in Pasadena, was the creative brains behind **La Arcada Court** (1114 State St.) and the **Santa Barbara Public Library** (40 E. Anapamu), whose beautifully detailed original entrance facing Anapamu is, sadly, no longer used.

Greene and Greene, the ultimate Craftsman designers, also from Pasadena, designed a gorgeous dark shingled residence, the **Nathan Benz Residence** (1741 Prospect Ave.), near the Mission in 1911. Local legendary architect George Washington Smith designed over 80 residences and commercial buildings in the city, not to mention other buildings across the nation. Undoubtedly Smith, more than anyone else, is associated with the Spanish Colonial Revival architecture that has made Santa Barbara famous. Most notably, Smith worked on **Casa del Herrero** (1387 E. Valley Rd.), which is a National Historic Landmark, and the redesign of the **Lobero Theatre** (33 E. Canon Perdido).

the county board of supervisors. The huge room is covered in a mural depicting the early Chumash Indians and following the history of the area leading up to California statehood. All tours of the building meet in the Mural Room and are approximately one hour.

The clock tower, known as **El Mirador,** juts out of the top of the courthouse, making it one of the tallest structures in the city, though the tower is a mere 85 feet tall. But it is here that you'll get the best views of downtown, the mountains, and the ocean from a downtown perspective—it's a must for photo ops. Take the elevator to the 4th floor. Once there, a dozen steps lead up and out to the platform. You'll be thrilled at the red-tile roofs splayed out in front of you on the nearby buildings. There are placards describing points of interest in each direction so you can easily get your bearings. You don't need the formal tour to

appreciate the sheer beauty and craftsmanship of the building, but it will give you more specific information. Ironically, the courthouse doesn't meet the county's current building codes and standards, and could never be approved for construction today.

Karpeles Manuscript Library
The Karpeles Manuscript Library (21 W. Anapamu, 805/962-5322, www.rain.org, Wed.–Sun. noon–4 P.M., free) might sound a tad dry as a sightseeing stop. But manuscripts come in many forms, and the two-story building, which is expectedly quiet inside, houses some of the earliest writings from 1,400 B.C., plus artifacts like stone carvings. There are also original documents, letters, and sections of diaries. It may not take long to view the works represented, but it is nonetheless impressive to see how the written word has carried civilization

forward. There's a small rotating art exhibit on the 2nd floor to round out the offerings.

Santa Barbara Museum of Art

See the power of the visual arts at the Santa Barbara Museum of Art (1130 State St., 805/963-4364, www.sbmuseart.org, Tues.– Sun. 11 A.M.–5 P.M., $9 adults, $6 seniors and students, free children under 6, free Sun.). Santa Barbara has one of the most impressive art museums and best collections for a community of its size. Two stories of rotating exhibits always keep the public intrigued; the museum showcases abstract, post-modern, and much more in a large diversity of media, from print to photography. Of particular note is their collection of Asian art. At the museum's inception in 1941, 19 Chinese robes were donated to the museum, which encouraged the donation of more Asian works. Today the Asian collection consists of over 2,600 objects spanning a period of 4,000 years, including 19th-century Japanese woodblock prints. Admission is free to everyone on Sunday, though a donation is suggested.

Santa Barbara Cemetery

The Santa Barbara Cemetery (901 Channel Dr., 805/969-3231, daily 8 A.M.–5 P.M.) may not seem like a normal sightseeing stop. But the cemetery is on the best piece of land around, high on a bluff overlooking the Pacific Ocean, with pristine views to the mountains. As cemeteries go, it is flat-out beautiful. The land has been used as a burial ground since 1867, and many notables from Santa Barbara history are buried here. There's even a 200-page hardcover book on the cemetery's history, called *The Best Last Place*. Such is the dedication of Santa Barbara natives and their love of local history. A short walk across the thin grass amid palm trees and headstones might give you a new perspective on life.

The Carriage & Western Art Museum

The little-known Carriage & Western Art Museum (129 Castillo, 805/962-2353, www.carriagemuseum.org, Mon.–Fri. 9 A.M.–3 P.M.,

---

PEARL CHASE: A WOMAN WITH VISION

It seems in every town, there's someone who makes it their mission to force the idea of preserving history while everyone else is in a hurry towards the future – and it's a good thing. It is impossible to overstate the contribution Pearl Chase has made to Santa Barbara; simply put, she is one of the reasons that the city looks the way it does. She also founded the local chapter of the American Red Cross, the Community Arts Association, and the Santa Barbara Trust for Historic Preservation. She was selected Woman of the Year by the *Los Angeles Times* in 1952, and was chosen Santa Barbara's first Woman of the Year in 1956. Her reputation as a preservationist was acknowledged by the National Trust for Historic Preservation, which awarded her their highest honor in 1973. It is because of Chase that the **Moreton Bay Fig Tree** (Chapala and W. Montecito Streets at the train station) was never cut down and remains the single largest of its kind in the United States, measuring a whopping 38 feet in circumference.

Today her fierce determination has taken shape as the **Pearl Chase Society** (www.pearlchasesociety.org), an all-volunteer organization that continues her legacy of preservation and historical and cultural awareness by sponsoring lectures, trips to various historically significant sites around town, and a continuing education agenda to remind people that it's because of people like Pearl Chase that Santa Barbara has the identity it does.

---

docent tours Sun. 1–4 P.M., free) is home to over 70 different horse-drawn carriages, most constructed 1850–1911; many of these beautifully restored carriages are used during the annual Fiesta parade in August. There are also hand-tooled saddles, including ones belonging to celebrities like Clark Gable, former president Ronald Reagan, Jimmy Stewart, and

© MICHAEL CERVIN

The Santa Barbara Cemetery has great views of the ocean and is one of the quietest places in the city.

Will Rogers. There's also more tack than you'll know what to do with, but serious equestrian fans will be in heaven. The museum is one block from the beach.

Chase Palm Park

Chase Palm Park (along Cabrillo Blvd. from East Beach to Stearns Wharf), named for community activist Pearl Chase, is comprised of two grassy areas bisected by Cabrillo Boulevard. On the city side of the street there is an outdoor music pavilion, carrousel, children's playground, and plenty of well-tended paths for ambling, as well as a lovely pond that gives this place a unique charm. On the harbor side there is a long trail for cycling and in-line skating, a skateboard park, and plenty of beach access. The long stretch of grass hosts soccer, Frisbee, and dancing for whomever gets there first.

Santa Barbara Zoological Gardens

In the early 1960s a group of locals decided the area needed a zoo, and with little more than time in one hand and a hammer in the other,

they built the Santa Barbara Zoological Gardens (500 Niños Dr., 805/962-5339, www.santabarbarazoo.org, daily 10 A.M.–5 P.M., Thanksgiving and Christmas Eve 10 A.M.–3 P.M., closed Christmas, $11 adults, $9 seniors and children 2–12, free children under 2, $4 parking) on 30 acres of prime real estate overlooking the ocean. Even today the small and intimate zoo looks old-fashioned in some ways, but it is a testament to how citizens can band together for a common cause. The zoological garden sits on the old estate of Lillian Childs, a wealthy woman who built lush gardens, and in fact many of the trees at the zoo date back to the 1920s when they were first planted. Childs allowed hobos to routinely camp on her property and they built a ramshackle village on what is now the parking lot.

Part of the beauty of this zoo is that the displays are small enough that you can see the animals up close. It has been described as the Audrey Hepburn of zoos, "small but sophisticated." They also brag that this zoo is the only one where the lions have views of beach

© MICHAEL CERVIN

flamingos at the Santa Barbara Zoological Gardens

city, and the birds certainly love the open water and reeds, but the spot is sandwiched between busy Cabrillo Boulevard, the 101 freeway, and the train tracks. Yet in the early mornings, as the mist rises from the lake, it's a beautiful ghostly sight to behold.

Directly across from the refuge on a small hill above the shore is an old mansion, uninhabited for 30 years. There are caretakers on the property, however, as there have been for three decades. The owner, Huguette Clark, donated money to the city to excavate and create this salt water bird refuge, and had it named after her younger sister who died as a child.

OCEANFRONT

Santa Barbara's oceanfront is defined by Cabrillo Boulevard, which follows the shore line and includes Stearns Wharf and the harbor. With the exception of the wharf and harbor there are no business or shops on the beach side of the street. This undeveloped sandy, grassy area lined with palm trees has helped to create an idyllic setting that people find intoxicating and typically Californian. On clear days the islands hug the horizon and the sounds of the crashing surf, the gulls, and people milling about create a relaxing experience.

This four-mile stretch incorporates Stearns Wharf, the harbor, hotels, and shops; the concrete bike path stretches past the zoo and a number of beaches and is the main access route to the areabesides Cabrillo Boulevard. Rent a bike, a tandem bike, or a four-person surrey at **Wheel Fun Rentals** (23 E. Cabrillo Blvd., 805/966-2282, www.wheelfunrentalssb.com, daily 8 A.M.–8 P.M., $8–35 per hour depending on vehicle) and meander the path from Leadbetter Beach at the west end to the zoo in the east. It's actually a lot of fun, even though the surreys seem to have a mind of their own and steering is sometimes challenging. Or use the path as many other people do to stroll, run, or in-line skate while basking in the sunshine.

◖ Stearns Wharf

Stearns Wharf (intersection of State St. and Cabrillo Blvd., www.stearnswharf.org, parking

volleyball. True enough, but so do the giraffes. The zoo features beautifully landscaped gardens and gentle grassy slopes and views to the ocean and the mountains. A small train takes little kids—and big ones—around the perimeter, where you can see condors, bald eagles, and an exhibit focusing on the adorable miniature Channel Islands fox and other native animals and plants from the Channel Islands and surrounding mountains.

From the zoo, there are also views to the **Andre Clark Bird Refuge** (1400 E. Cabrillo Blvd., 805/564-5418), a 42-acre salt marsh with a few tables around the perimeter. This is an excellent spot to see white pelicans, black-crowned night herons, egrets and bushtits, grebes and mallards. Once considered a spot to place the harbor, the natural water area was quickly forgotten because early yachts wouldn't have fit inside. With the word refuge in the title, the place sounds like a respite from the

HOLLYWOOD NORTH

Though the film *Sideways* placed Santa Barbara squarely on the moviemaking map, it comes as a surprise to most people that Santa Barbara was the main filmmaking hub before Hollywood took the eventual crown. Between 1910 and 1921, the Flying A Studios, originally located on Mission between State and Chapala Streets, housed the largest film studio in America. Known as the American Film Company, it produced some 1,200 films in Santa Barbara during that brief time, mostly Westerns due to the rugged backcountry. The remoteness of Santa Barbara, however, and the appeal of the growing metropolis of Los Angeles made the decision to move south an easy one for production companies.

But even recently, Santa Barbara has provided the backdrop for films and TV shows. *Seabiscuit, It's Complicated, Pirates of the Caribbean: At World's End*, and *L.A. Story* are just a few of the major films made in the county. Much earlier, Cecil B. DeMille's early epic *The Ten Commandments* was filmed here in 1923. TV shows like *Monk, The Bachelor, Top Chef, Psych*, and *Curb Your Enthusiasm* have all shot episodes here, too. With the rise of the Santa Barbara International Film Festival held each February, Santa Barbara has once again solidified its relationship with film and television.

$2.50/hr, first 90 mins free with validation) is Santa Barbara's most visited landmark. Santa Barbara has no natural harbor and the shifting sands prohibited large ships from docking here; the wharf was built in 1871 to allow ships to off-load supplies for the bourgeoning town. The wharf, which used to extend much further into the ocean than it does currently, has burned completely twice and has been destroyed by storms. The current iteration, scaled back in size, is a favorite for tourists. Frankly, there are a lot of typical tourist shops selling seashells, small personalized license plates, and gift items you can find most anywhere, which has nothing to do with Santa Barbara in the least, but if you walk to the end you get some of the best views back to the city. There are no railings at the end of the wharf, so keep an eye on little ones.

In addition to the views, there are a few restaurants, an ice cream store, and the **Ty Warner Sea Center** (211 Stearns Wharf, 805/962-2526, www.sbnature.org, daily 10 A.M.–5 P.M., $8 adults, $7 seniors and teens 13–17, $5 children 2–12), which is a two-story building devoted to giving you a better understanding of how our oceans work. When you first enter you'll notice the full-size replica of a blue whale hanging from the ceiling. There are touch tanks on the lower level and staff to answer questions and discuss why you should pet the starfish, how sealife coexists with humans, and other educational ideas. As you move upstairs you come eye to eye with the blue whale, giving you an idea of how massive these creatures really are. There's also a very beautiful little exhibit, nicely backlit, showing jellyfish and how these supple, graceful creatures impact our oceans.

◖ The Santa Barbara Harbor

The Santa Barbara harbor (the intersection of Cabrillo and Harbor Way) is home to about 1,100 sailing vessels, a few stores and restaurants, and a museum. It's a short walk from Stearns Wharf and is the eye candy most people expect to see when visiting. One of the best parts of the harbor is the long breakwater wall, often with colorful flags flying in the wind. It's a great walk and terminates on a sand spit, which you can access at low tide. At high tide and during storms the breakwater is constantly hit by crashing waves that splash over the wall; half the fun is trying to outrun them. There's minimal shopping at the harbor, but you can buy fresh fish every day of the week and smell the catch as it's hauled in.

Interestingly, the area where the harbor is positioned today is not a natural harbor at all, but was built in the 1920s when millionaire Max Fleischmann (of Fleischmann's yeast) wanted a protected place to moor his yacht and ponied up a lot of money to build the breakwater. Unfortunately, the shifting sands under the water need to be constantly dredged, at a huge cost to taxpayers, to allow boats to enter the harbor, and you'll usually see the rather unsightly dredging equipment sitting near the sand spit.

While at the harbor, stop in to the **Santa Barbara Maritime Museum** (113 Harbor Way, 805/962-8404, www.sbmm.org, Thurs.–Tues. 10 A.M.–5 P.M., $7 adults, $4 seniors, students, and active military, free military in uniform, free to all third Thurs. of month), which is housed in a 1940s naval building. Inside the two-story structure are exhibits on surfing and shipwrecks and a full-length *tomol,* a wood canoe the Chumash used to cross between the mainland and the islands. There are rotating exhibits with the sea as a common theme as well as lectures and special screenings in their upstairs theater.

THE MISSION AND THE RIVIERA

One of the older parts of the city, the Riviera sits in the foothills where the mountains cascade down to the lowlands. The area is studded with oak trees and natural waterways and was obviously chosen as a place to build homes because of the views. The main draw of the area is the Old Mission Santa Barbara, but it is also home to the Santa Barbara Botanic Garden, great hiking opportunities such as the popular Rattlesnake Canyon trail, secluded parks like Franceschi Park, and estates from the 1920s. Some of the estates here, including Lotusland and Casa del Herrero, can be accessed by the public.

◖ Old Mission Santa Barbara

More closely associated with Santa Barbara than any other landmark, Old Mission Santa Barbara (2201 Laguna St., 805/682-4713, www.santabarbaramission.org, daily 9 A.M.–5 P.M., self-guided tours $5 adults, $4 seniors, $1 children 6–15) was founded on December 4, 1786 (the Feast of Saint Barbara). Originally there were no plans to place the mission on this spot, but after considering the proximity to a fresh water

THE FROG WALL

About 1986 or so, a woman noticed a plastic frog on the sandstone wall across the street from her house. For reasons even she's not sure about, she added another frog to the niche and attached wall that runs about 70 feet long. Days later, another frog appeared. Over time other people, mainly those in the neighborhood taking a walk, brought frogs in one form or another to place on the wall on Paterna Road on the Riviera. The wall, also called the frog shrine, is now home to hundreds of frogs, be they plastic, ceramic, metal, small, large, or otherwise. There are clocks, PEZ dispensers, stuffed frogs, pillows, potholders, frogs getting married, frogs praying, and frogs being frogs. To this day, no one knows who left the first frog or why. If you go, bring along a frog to leave – and take nothing with you. The frog wall is for everyone to enjoy and to add to. If you take something, may the wrath of Kermit be upon you! To get there, take Alameda Padre Serra up from the mission and turn left onto Alvarado. Head straight, passing the El Encanto Hotel (under construction) on your left. Don't go down the small hill, but head straight, and as you pass the intersection turn right on Paterna. The frogs are on the left a few hundreds yard down the road.

© MICHAEL CERVIN

© MICHAEL CERVIN

Still an active church, the Old Mission Santa Barbara has held its ground for more than 225 years.

source, namely Mission Creek, and the defensible position of being able to view the ocean in time to spot unfriendly ships approaching, it was decided the area was ideal. As you stand on the church steps you immediately understand the importance of this location. Still an active church, this has been a gathering spot for over 225 years.

Though visually striking, it is one of the least authentic looking of the missions, and what you see today is the culmination of decades of restorative efforts. The original adobe church was a simple structure that was enlarged two times to accommodate the growth of the Chumash Indian population and the settlers in the area. The fourth and current iteration was built in 1820. The 1925 earthquake inflicted major damage on the mission, and the east bell tower was almost completely destroyed while its twin tower sustained serious injury. Restoration efforts began in May 1926, but within 10 years signs of further problems began to appear. Cracks emerged in the mission towers and facade, and the conditions

continued to worsen so that by 1949 it was apparent that something desperately needed to be done. Studies revealed that chemical reactions inside the concrete were fatally weakening the material, rendering the building unsafe. Drastic action—nothing less than a total reconstruction of both towers and the church facade—was called for. Work began early in 1950 and continued until the summer of 1953.

Around back of the mission is the Huerta Project, where about 10 acres of *huertas,* or gardens, were originally established so that there would be food for everyone living at the mission and presidio. Considered a living museum, the garden today has a variety of fruit trees, grapevines, herbs, and edible plants, all consistent with what would have been grown in mission times. Across the lawn is the rose garden, where over 1,000 different varieties are growing. As you walk across the street, consider that this is where some of the grapevines were planted.

The **Mission Museum** offers a docent-guided tour Thursday–Friday at 11 A.M. and Saturday at 10:30 A.M. Admission is $8 and

Tucked behind the Old Santa Barbara Mission, the Santa Barbara Museum of Natural History is home to a 72-foot blue whale skeleton.

© MICHAEL CERVIN

the 90-minute tour allows a maximum of 15 people. You cannot see the church unless you pay for a guided or self-guided tour. Should you decide on a self-guided tour, you'll first come across the interior courtyard, where a center fountain is encircled by palm trees. Following the signs you then come upon the cemetery with a handful of headstones and crypts and a beautiful Moreton Bay fig tree planted about 1890. From there it is a few steps into the church. This is the most decorated of the mission interiors, with lots of vibrant stenciling surrounding the doors and altar and a complete painted wainscoting. Large paintings flank both walls; near the formal entrance is a small gated room wherein is the only original altar and tabernacle in the entire mission chain, dating from 1786. After leaving the church you'll enter the museum section, which houses old photographs of the mission from the 1880s and a few vestments and artifacts from the early services. There's also a side room that shows how a typical kitchen looked during the mission's heyday as well as other exhibits dealing with how they constructed the mission and the tools of the times.

Santa Barbara Museum of Natural History

The Santa Barbara Museum of Natural History (2559 Puesta del Sol, 805/682-4711, www.sbnature.org, daily 10 A.M.–5 P.M., closed major holidays, $10 adults, $7 seniors and teens, $6 children 3–12) sits just above and over Mission Creek and a stone's throw from the actual mission. The first thing you notice when you arrive is the skeleton of a 72-foot blue whale right out front. The collection of buildings, again with a Spanish theme, abuts the creek, and plenty of old oak trees cover the property. The museum is small but spread out with exhibits on early Chumash life including crafts, a small nature trail, a planetarium, sections devoted to vertebrate and invertebrate zoology, and even a small fossil dig for kids. It's not a lengthy stop, but it certainly gives an overview of the area.

© MICHAEL CERVIN

The topiary is just part of the magnificence of the stunning Lotusland.

Santa Barbara Botanic Garden

Santa Barbara Botanic Garden (1212 Mission Canyon Rd., 805/682-4726, www.sbbg.org, daily 9 A.M.–6 P.M., closed major holidays, $8 adults, $6 seniors and teens, $4 children 2–12, guided tours weekdays at 2 P.M., weekends at 11 A.M. and 2 P.M.), or the Garden as it is simply known, is 78 acres of pristine wilderness where redwood trees grow in a shaded creek, and oaks fan out everywhere. The garden was founded in 1926 to showcase the rich diversity of western plants. By 1936 this emphasis had narrowed to plants native to the state of California, and now includes northwestern Baja California and southwestern Oregon, which are part of the California Floristic Province. There is a rich diversity represented here, including part of the original mission aqueduct that fed the mission with clean water from the mountains. Today there are nearly six miles of walking trails and over 1,000 species of plants, and their library contains over 15,000 volumes of works related to the disciplines of botany and horticulture. They have a gift shop and you can purchase plants directly from them.

❰ Lotusland

To enjoy the beauty of nature, albeit in a methodically constructed way, visit Lotusland (695 Ashley Rd., 805/969-9990, www.lotusland.org, tours Wed.–Sat. at 10 A.M. and 1:30 P.M. mid-February–mid-November, $35 adults, $10 children 5–18), 37 acres of the most well-manicured and lovingly tended gardens you will probably ever see. Given that Lotusland is a public garden operating in a residential neighborhood, reservations are mandatory; tours are docent-led and average just under two hours. There was a commercial nursery on the land in the 1880s, and the garden was last owned by Madame Ganna Walska, a Polish opera singer in the 1920s, who routinely arranged her vast collections of plants into bold color schemes and unusual shapes. For over four decades she constantly tinkered with her gardens. After Walska's death in 1984 her estate, Lotusland, so named because of the lotus flowers on the property, became a nonprofit.

It is one thing to visit a botanical garden, and yet another to wander here, through the

© MICHAEL CERVIN

Our Lady of Mount Carmel Catholic Church features Pueblo Revival architecture.

moonscape barrenness of the cactus gardens, to the topiary garden, to the serenity of the Japanese garden, to the olive allée and the formal English-styled gardens. Lotusland is that rare stop where you feel you could stay forever—in fact, one of the staff gardeners has been there for over 30 years. It is truly an awe-inspiring place and is nearly overwhelming in its botanical diversity and beauty. Bring a jacket, as it can get brisk in the many areas that are so heavily wooded that you can't see the sun. The wide walking paths easily accommodate wheelchairs.

Casa del Herrero

At first glance the entrance to Casa del Herrero (1387 E. Valley Rd., 805/565-5653, www.casadelherrero.com, docent-led 90-min. tours Wed. and Sat. 10 A.M. and 2 P.M., $20 adults and children 10 and up, reservations mandatory), the "house of the blacksmith," seems like just another Spanish facade in a town overrun with seemingly thousands of Spanish-style houses.

But the moment you cross the threshold and enter the lobby, you'll see the Tibetan 18th-century wood ceiling and know you're in another world. Designed by owner George Fox Steedman and architect George Washington Smith, it was completed in 1925. The estate, essentially unchanged from its original state, is Spanish Colonial Revival architecture at its best. The house is included on the National Register of Historic Places and is a National Historic Landmark. The amount of detail is overwhelming: From intricate tile work and hand-carved door surrounds to authentic Spanish antiques, it is a precise expression of interior design. Steedman traveled throughout parts of Europe searching for interiors to embellish his home, and in fact he had the house altered to fit the doors and windows he purchased. Though it is ornate and elaborate, the amazing thing is the sense of proportion throughout the home. Steedman also commissioned local artist Channing Peak to provide a western flair to some of the original art.

© MICHAEL CERVIN

ruins of Knapp's Castle

Our Lady of Mount Carmel Catholic Church

Just down the road from Casa del Herrero is Our Lady of Mount Carmel Catholic Church (1300 E. Valley Rd., 805/969-6868, www.olmc-montecito.com, daily 8 a.m.–6 p.m.), which deviates from the mission feel of the churches in the area. The working Catholic church was built in its present capacity in 1936, upgraded from a working parish started in 1856. The unique architectural style was patterned after the Pueblo Indian missions built in New Mexico and Arizona as early as the 17th century. Typifying the handiwork of the Chumash Indians are the uneven window openings and irregularly plastered walls. The wood floors and rustic feel of the church, both inside and out, make it a unique and different house of worship and worth a peek inside.

◖ Knapp's Castle

The lonely burned remnants of a seven-building complex sit on a precipice overlooking the Santa Ynez Valley. In 1916 George Owen Knapp, founder of Union Carbide company, which has become a behemoth chemical monopoly, purchased a 160-acre parcel including this ridgeline. He set out to construct what he called the Lodge at San Marcos, not really a castle at all. He wanted a more rustic home in contrast to his manicured and immaculate 70-acre Arcady estate in the tony Montecito area. The laborious efforts to build the lodge took many years, given the relative isolation of the property and the difficulty in hauling materials into the mountains. In 1940, Frances Holden bought the property from Knapp, no doubt looking forward to many years of peace and quiet in the remote home, but just five weeks later the entire property was destroyed by a forest fire. Today only the massive sandstone foundations, fireplace pillars, walls, and arches looking out to the valley remain intact. It is hauntingly beautiful and rugged, and often only the whisper of the wind through the trees can be heard. The parcel is still privately owned but open to the public. To access it, turn onto East Camino Cielo at the top of the San Marcos Pass and drive exactly three miles. On your left will be a rusted gate. From there it's about a 10-minute walk to the property. As you slowly descend off the road you'll begin to see the tops of the chimneys, standing guard like sentinels in the distance. Knapp's Castle is a popular place for photo shoots (especially for weddings) and picnics, and has amazing views. It's impossible to get a bad photo here—good news for any shutterbug.

Beaches

People flock to Santa Barbara's beaches, which are generally long and flat. Water temperatures in the summer are generally about 61 degrees, and cool down to about 58 degrees in the winter months. At low tide you can clearly see the rocks hidden under the waves, which makes for great tide pooling. Due to several creeks running into the ocean, and the inability to keep the creeks clean and free from debris and waste, there are occasional closures at some beaches. These are posted on the beaches should they occur. Aside from that, swimming in Santa Barbara is a safe endeavor. There are lifeguards during peak summer hours, but they disappear once the crowds do. At Goleta Beach in particular, and occasionally at West, East, and Leadbetter Beaches, you might see bulldozers scooping sand back into the ocean. It's a peculiar sight, but they do this to keep the beaches from eroding too much.

East Beach

East Beach (Cabrillo Blvd. at Milpas, daily sunrise–10 P.M.) is so named because it is east of Stearns Wharf. It's all soft sand and wide beach. There are a dozen volleyball nets in the sand close to the zoo (if you look closely you can see the giraffes and lions), and it has all the amenities a sun worshipper could wish for, like a full beach house, snack bar, play area for children, and a path for biking and in-line skating. The beachfront has picnic facilities and a full-service restaurant at the East Beach Grill. The **Cabrillo Pavilion Bathhouse** (1119 East Cabrillo Blvd.), built in 1927, offers showers,

© MICHAEL CERVIN

Arroyo Burro Beach

THE SANTA BARBARA CHANNEL, A WATERY GRAVE

The Channel Islands seem a peaceful place when viewed from shore, but the channel that separates them from the mainland is notoriously dangerous. A section known as Windy Lane is just that, known for fierce winds. During the early 1900s, the most economical way to move cargo was by ship, and California's waters were inundated by steamers moving goods and passengers up and down the coast. One steamship, the *Santa Rosa,* an ironclad launched in Pennsylvania in 1884, was a veteran of California waters. But its years of faithful service would come to a tragic end on a gloomy night in July 1911. On July 6, the *Santa Rosa* was heading south on its usual route from San Francisco to San Diego. It carried 200 passengers who were all aware that the coast could be hazardous due to the possibility of high seas or fog, but it was Point Conception, where the coastline makes a sharp change in direction from north-south to west-east, that presented a unique danger. Ships must make the course correction to follow the coastline and avoid the shoals of San Miguel Island, thereby steering safely into the Santa Barbara Channel. At the turn of the 20th century, captains had only a series of three lights to guide them through this part of the trip, at Point Sur, Point Sal, and Point Arguello. The gloom of a foggy night could render these lights nearly invisible, as on this night when the crew missed the Point Sal beacon and the course adjustment was not made. In the early morning hours of July 7, the *Santa Rosa* ran aground near the outlet of Honda Creek, just north of Point Arguello. The ship was approximately two miles off course. At first, the seas were calm and the ship appeared largely undamaged. But by late afternoon the high tides had arrived, along with strong winds and growing waves.

The high surf, instead of freeing the ship, began to wreak serious havoc. A particularly large wave eventually lifted up the ship, then smashed it down on the rocks. The *Santa Rosa* broke in two and frantic evacuation efforts began, with rescue ships standing by. The high seas created dangerous conditions, overturning life rafts, snapping lifelines, and shredding life nets. Four crewmembers died in the cold, unforgiving waters and dozens were injured. The ship was a total loss. Most of the cargo ended up at the bottom of the Pacific, including two automobiles. The remains of the ship still lie just off Honda Creek near the surf line.

The resting place of the *Santa Rosa* would once again become the site of a maritime tragedy 12 years later. In September 1923, one of the greatest peacetime disasters in the history of the U.S. Navy took place, when seven destroyers ran aground at the rocks of Honda Creek.

Most notably, however, the *Winfield Scott* departed San Francisco on December 1, 1853, with a full load of passengers and a shipment of gold bullion. Choosing the Santa Barbara Channel rather than a passage outside the islands in an effort to save time, Captain Simon F. Blunt entered the channel as fog developed. Evidently attempting to steam between Anacapa and Santa Cruz Islands, the *Winfield Scott* ran directly into Anacapa Island at full speed. No one was injured, however, and passengers hastily built makeshift accommodations on the island, where they waited until the *California* plucked them from the beach on December 10 and took them south towards Panama.

In all, more than 30 major cargo ships and countless smaller ships have ended their runs in the channel, making it clear the channel is not to be toyed with.

© MICHAEL CERVIN

volleyball nets at East Beach

lockers, a weight room, a single rentable beach wheelchair, and volleyball rental.

West Beach

West Beach (Cabrillo Blvd. and Chapala St. btwn. Stearns Wharf and the harbor, daily sunrise–10 P.M.) is an 11-acre beach offering a picturesque sandy area for sunbathing, swimming, kayaking, windsurfing, and beach volleyball. Large palm trees and a wide walkway and bike path make this beachfront area a popular tourist spot. Outrigger canoes also launch from this beach.

◖ Leadbetter Beach

Leadbetter Beach (Shoreline Dr. and Loma Alta, daily sunrise–10 P.M.) is the best beach in Santa Barbara. There's a long, flat beach and a large grassy area; Leadbetter Point is the demarcation line for the area's south- and west-facing beaches. The nearly sheer cliffs suddenly rise up from the sand and trees dot the point. The beach, which is also bounded by the harbor and breakwater, is ideal for swimming because it's fairly protected, unlike the other flat ocean-facing beaches.

Many catamaran sailors and windsurfers launch from this beach, and you'll see occasional surfers riding the waves. The grassy picnic areas have barbecue sites that can be reserved for more privacy, but otherwise there is a lot of room. The beach and park can get packed during any of the many races and sporting events held here. There are restrooms, a small restaurant, and outdoor showers. Directly across the street is Santa Barbara City College. If you enter the stadium and walk up the many steps, you'll get some terrific views of the harbor, plus a mini-workout.

Arroyo Burro Beach

Arroyo Burro (at Cliff Dr. and Las Positas, daily sunrise–10 P.M.), which is known locally as Hendry's, sits at the mouth of Arroyo Burro Creek. This dog-friendly beach is a popular spot for surfers and the occasional kayaker or scuba diver. With a restaurant on-site and a small grassy area for picnics, plus restrooms and outdoor showers, it's very popular with locals and far removed from the downtown beaches, though it can still become very crowded on

© MICHAEL CERVIN

Leadbetter Beach

summer days. At peak times when the parking lot is full, there's no other parking around. It's flanked by large cliffs, one of which holds the **Douglas Family Preserve,** still known locally as the Wilcox Property. The 70-acre eucalyptus-studded dog-friendly preserve is popular with locals, but few tourists even know about it. The parcel was to be a planned housing development, but this concept was thwarted when a grassroots campaign raised awareness of the property and the potentially destructive development. Money to purchase the property was limited until actor Michael Douglas gave a substantial gift, enabling the parcel to remain undeveloped. He then named it after his father, actor Kirk Douglas.

Butterfly Beach

Butterfly Beach (Channel Dr. across from the Four Seasons Hotel, Montecito, daily sunrise–10 P.M.) is accessed by a handful of steps leading to the narrow beach. Many people come here hoping to catch a glimpse of a celebrity from nearby Montecito, but chances are that won't happen. Butterfly is the most west-facing beach in Santa Barbara, meaning that you can actually see the sun set over the Pacific here. To find it, take Highway 101 to Olive Mill Road in Montecito (a few minutes south of Santa Barbara). At the stop sign, turn towards the ocean (away from the mountains) and follow it a quarter of a mile along the coast. Butterfly Beach is on your left. The beach is packed on most weekends and often on weekdays too, and parking is limited. Park on either side of the street along the beach or drive up Butterfly Road and park in the nearby neighborhoods. Bring your lunch, water, and sunscreen—there are no public facilities at this beach. Dogs roam freely here.

Carpinteria State Beach

Carpinteria State Beach (5361 6th St., Carpinteria, 805/684-2811, daily 7 A.M.–sunset, no day-use fees, camping fees $20–100 per night) has designated itself the "world's safest beach." Whether that's an understatement or not, this beautiful wide, flat beach is definitely a favorite for locals and tourists. With plenty of

Linden Avenue in Carpinteria is the gateway to Carpinteria State Beach.

campgrounds, picnic tables, outdoor showers, RV hookups, telephones, and a short walk to Linden Avenue, where there are lots of restaurants, shops, and a grocery store, you'll have everything you need, all within walking distance. Parts of the campgrounds are tree lined but right next to the train tracks; passing trains might wake up light sleepers. Aside from that, there is a great sense of community with the campers here.

Goleta Beach

At the base of the University of California, Santa Barbara, campus, Goleta Beach (5986 Sandspit Rd., daily sunrise–10 P.M.) is popular for its picnic tables, barbecue pits, horseshoes, multiple restrooms, and fishing opportunities. The grassy area is partially shaded by trees and there's also a small jungle gym for the kids. The pier is popular for fishing and the low breaks make this an easy entry for kayakers. You can also launch small boats from the pier on weekends only, when they have a crane that lowers boats into the water (there is no launch ramp directly into the water). On the mountain-facing side along the bike path are a few platforms for viewing birds in the slough that runs behind the beach.

Refugio State Beach

Refugio State Beach (10 Refugio Beach Rd., Goleta, 805/968-1033, www.parks.ca.gov, daily 8 A.M.–sunset) is a state park with a small strip of grass that abuts the water. It offers excellent coastal fishing, snorkeling, and scuba as well as hiking, biking trails, and picnic sites. Palm trees planted near Refugio Creek give a distinctive look to the beach and camping area. With one and a half miles of flat shoreline, Refugio is located 20 miles west of Santa Barbara on Highway 101 at Refugio Road.

El Capitán State Beach

Near Refugio State Beach is El Capitán State Beach (off Hwy. 101, 17 miles west of Santa Barbara, 805/968-1033, www.parks.ca.gov, daily 8 A.M.–sunset); if you take Highway 101 north about 15 minutes from downtown you will see the El Capitán signs. At the bottom of the exit, turn left and go under the bridge. The road will take you right into the park. El Capitán State Beach offers visitors a sandy beach, rocky tide pools, and stands of sycamore and oak trees along El Capitán Creek. It's a perfect setting for swimming, fishing, surfing, picnicking, and camping. A stairway provides access from the bluffs to the beach area. Amenities include RV hookups, pay showers, restrooms, hiking and bike trails, a fabulous beach, a seasonal general store, and an outdoor arena. Many of the camping sites offer an ocean view.

Wineries

The wines in Santa Barbara County have been receiving very favorable scores and write-ups in the national press. The area is predominately known for pinot noir and chardonnay, but with so many diverse microclimates, there are over 50 different types of grapes planted here. This means you can find traditional varieties like cabernet sauvignon, merlot, sauvignon blanc, and syrah, but you will also find sangiovese, dolcetto, viognier, cabernet franc, malbec, and many others.

Not all wine-tasting is done surrounded by vineyards. On the Urban Wine Trail (www.ur-banwinetrailsb.com) you can sample some of the county's best wines without even seeing a vine. Near Lower State Street, a block from the beach, you can walk to six tasting rooms. Visiting others that are part of the trail will require a little driving. Recently passed legislation means that some, but not all, wineries now offer wines by the glass in addition to wine-tasting, so if you sample something you like, you can purchase a glass to enjoy on the spot or a bottle to take with you.

Kalyra Winery

Kalyra Winery (212 State St., 805/965-8606, www.kalyrawinery.com, daily noon–7 P.M.) is famous for having been featured in the movie *Sideways*. This tasting room, their second, wasn't in the film, but you can still sample their California and Australian wines made by Mike Brown, an avid surfer and Aussie. There's a tribal feel to the interior, with a thatched roof over the tasting bar, and the vibe is relaxed. They started out making sweet wines, of which they still offer quite a few, but Kalyra has a broad portfolio.

Santa Barbara Winery

Once you're done at Kalyra Winery, walk a block down Yannonali Street to Santa Barbara Winery (202 Anacapa St., 805/963-3633, www.sbwinery.com, daily 10 A.M.–5 P.M.), which is the oldest winery in the county, started in 1962. Their chardonnay is delightful

and truly expresses a Santa Barbara character with its bright citrus notes. They produce a lot of wine in varieties including pinot noir, sangiovese, sauvignon blanc, and many others. If you are looking to sample a diverse array of wines, this is your best stop. The tasting bar is just a few feet from the barrel room, and there's a good-sized gift shop too.

Oreana Winery

Across the street from Santa Barbara Winery is Oreana Winery (205 Anacapa St., 805/962-5857, www.oreanawinery.com, daily 11 A.M.–5 P.M., tasting fee $10), an old tire store converted for use as a winery. The interior retains its warehouse feel with a tasting bar up front and the production facility in the back. You'll find syrah, cabernet sauvignon, chardonnay, verdelho, and others. Many of the wines are priced under $20. It's a laid-back vibe here, with lots of light coming in and a friendly staff.

Kunin Wines and Westerly Vineyards

Another block towards the beach you'll find the shared space of Kunin Wines and Westerly Vineyards (28 Anacapa St., 805/963-9696, www.kuninwines.com and www.westerlywine-yards.com, daily 11 A.M.–6 P.M., Kunin tasting fee $10, Westerly tasting fee $8). Seth Kunin, a surfer, styles his wines after the Rhône Valley varieties from southern France, like syrah and viognier. The tasting room, a sleek interior with a minimalist approach, is a small space within eyesight of the beach; it can get crowded on summer days—and for good reason. His wines are smooth and very drinkable, and it's easy to enjoy your time here. The Westerly lineup consists of merlot, syrah, and sauvignon blanc. The beauty of this double whammy is that you can get a very good understanding of Santa Barbara wines as you visit two wineries in one place.

Municipal Winemakers

Located just behind Kunin Wines and

Westerly Vineyards is the newest addition to the scene, Municipal Winemakers (28 Anacapa St., 805/931-6864, www.municipal-winemakers.com, Sat.–Sun. 11 A.M.–6 P.M., tasting fee $10), in an unpretentious small space with an even smaller deck. The inside is all rough wood ceilings and plain walls, with a four-top table and standing room at the bar. This is a weekend venture for owner Dave Potter, who will be there to answer your questions and pour his wines. The offerings are Rhône wines including grenache, syrah, and a sparkling shiraz.

Carr Winery

Carr Winery (414 N. Salsipuedes St., 805/965-7985, www.carrwinery.com, daily 11 A.M.–5 P.M., tasting fee $10) has a focus on small lots of syrah, grenache, cabernet franc, and pinot noir. The tasting room is in a WWII Quonset hut, with a bar up front and tables in the back. Thursday–Saturday 5 P.M.–midnight they open their wine bar, which features live music and appetizers and wines by the glass. It's run by another surfer-winemaker, and you'll see surfboards placed around the tasting room. There's a much younger crowd here, eager to sample some excellent wines and enjoy life.

Jaffurs Wine Cellars

Craig Jaffurs of Jaffurs Wine Cellars (819 E. Montecito St., 805/962-7003, www.jaffurswine.com, Fri.–Mon. 11 A.M.–5 P.M., tasting fee $10) has been an avid surfer for decades, and he equates wine to surfing. "The joy I get surfing is the same joy I get walking through a vineyard, or tasting barrel samples," he says. His seven different syrah and petite sirah are excellent, and his downtown location is all by itself on a small street. Once the doors are rolled up, the public comes in eagerly to taste beautiful wines.

Wine Cask Tasting Room

The Wine Cask Tasting Room (813 Anacapa St., 805/966-9463, www.winecask.com, daily noon–6 P.M., tasting fee $12) is a consortium of sorts. It used to be a wine shop and now hosts wine-tastings each day. The various winemakers are all producers who make small amounts of wine and who may not have their own tasting room. It's an eclectic offering, featuring the wine of Doug Margerum, the co-owner of the Wine Cask, who makes wines under his own name as well as consults for many smaller producers in the area. These tend to be whites like sauvignon blanc and high-end reds like cabernet sauvignon, merlot, and syrah.

Entertainment and Events

Though people flock to Santa Barbara to be outside, there's plenty to do inside as well. In bars, clubs, and theaters, Santa Barbara has its own brand of action when the sun goes down. The area is also home to a lively roster of festivals and events year-round.

NIGHTLIFE

Every city needs its watering holes, and Santa Barbara is no different. Plenty of bars clog a two-block-long section of State Street; a few more hug the side streets. But this is nothing new: Of the very first 50 business licenses issued by the city in 1850, 32 were for saloons.

Many bars have small dance floors, but there are very few actual dance clubs. Nightlife in town is often criticized as seeming amateurish compared to Los Angeles, New York, or any other major city. But that's exactly the point: Santa Barbara is not a major city, and the club experience here is very different. It's not trendy and flashy, though some may want it to be.

Dance Clubs

There are a few dance clubs in town, most notably **Wildcat Lounge** (15 W. Ortega St., 805/962-7970, www.wildcatlounge.com, daily 4 P.M.–2 A.M.), which has red glitter vinyl

FAMOUS SANTA BARBARA MUSICIANS

There is a rhythm to the ocean waves on the coast – it just might be why so many musicians claim Santa Barbara as their home. Before **Katy Perry** kissed a girl and shot to the top of the charts, the pop star was singing in local churches and taking dancing lessons downtown. Perpetual laid-back dude **Jack Johnson** always sells out his shows at the Santa Barbara Bowl, in part because he makes everything seem so easy and relaxed. **Toad the Wet Sprocket** came into being in 1986 while the members were attending San Marcos High School; they worked diligently towards releasing their first album just three years later. **Kenny Loggins** has long been a staple of the area, lending his name and concerts to charities and benefits, and the post-grunge band **Dishwalla** also hails from the city. Soft-core ska-punkers **Mad Caddies** have been rollicking as a solid seven-piece band since they officially formed in Santa Barbara in 1995; their *Rock the Plan* CD was recorded here.

booths, a fiber-optic dance dome, and a hip retro feel. It's one of the more popular dance clubs in town and has a crowded outdoor patio. There's a divergent mix of people who show up at the Wildcat, though the crowd is mainly younger, all looking for a good time. There have been some cases of dosing (slipping a drug into someone's drink) here; nothing's been reported for a long time, but it's still wise to keep an eye on your drink. Otherwise, dance and have fun at one of the city's oldest clubs.

Sophisticated **Tonic** (634 State St., 805/897-1800, Thurs.–Sat. 8 P.M.–2 A.M.) really begins to rock its two dance floors after midnight. There tends to be a line to get in and the drinks are pricey, but the space looks and feels akin to an actual club and not merely a revamped bar.

Eos (500 Anacapa St., 805/564-2410, www.eoslounge.com, Tues.–Wed. 8 P.M.–close, Thurs.–Fri. 5 P.M.–close, Sat. 8 P.M.–close) aims to be Santa Barbara's premier nightlife destination. The unique atmosphere blends the feel of a Mediterranean beach club with sleek furnishings and both indoor and outdoor spaces. The crowd tends to be younger, mid-20s and under, and well dressed, and the club is off State Street and doesn't get as many intoxicated walk-ins. It's a bit trendier than other spots and is a great place to see and be seen.

Bars

In the 400–600 blocks of State Street you'll find the majority of Santa Barbara's bars. Frequented mainly by college students, the area has become a hot spot on weekends for flitting in and out of as many bars as possible, while taking advantage of cheap drink specials. This has become known as the State Street Crawl, that slow, methodical negotiating of bars and clubs. It's worth remembering that any bar in Santa Barbara leans towards mellow on the weeknights and rowdier on the weekends. All bars close at 2 A.M. and this is often when trouble occurs, especially on weekend nights; fights are common enough as far too many intoxicated people converge on the streets at the same time. It's best to be back at your hotel long before that.

At **Madison's Grill & Tavern** (525 State St., 805/882-1182, www.madisonssb.com, Mon.–Sat. noon–2 A.M., Sun. 11 A.M.–2 A.M.), the food is typical bar fare, and the fact that it's served by a sexy all-girl waitstaff in umpire uniforms won't make it taste any better. But this spot is packed during playoff games, and over 20 flat screens means you won't miss a second of your favorite team's action. The drinks are inexpensive and they offer lots of two-for-one specials to keep you in your seats.

Joe's Café (536 State St., 805/966-4638, Thurs.–Sat. 11 A.M.–1:30 A.M., Sun.–Wed. 11 A.M.–11 P.M.) undeniably serves the stiffest drinks in town. A renovation to the interior has produced an old-school feel to the place, harkening back to its 1920s origins. It gets packed here on weekends, and the bar and restaurant has found new life. It's also the only place on

SANTA BARBARA'S SOAP OPERA

Soap operas have been a staple of daytime television since their inception. Ah, the troubled lives of other people, the cheating, the back-stabbing, name-calling, the scheming, the... well, you get the idea. One of the shortest lived, but extremely successful, soaps was called simply *Santa Barbara*. Lack of creativity notwithstanding, the show ran on NBC for a (relatively) brief nine years and centered on the wealthy though emotionally challenged Capwell family, who used Santa Barbara for their personal playground. Though not overly successful in the United States, the show's overseas fan base was huge and it aired in more than 40 countries. It went on to eventually win 24 daytime Emmy Awards and 18 *Soap Opera Digest* Awards.

State Street where you'll see a neon sign advertising the joint.

The James Joyce (513 State St., 805/962-2688, daily 10 A.M.–2 A.M.) offers free darts and free peanuts, and the Guinness comes quickly from the tap. There is a great selection of other beers and whiskey as well. The walls are lined with photos of, we assume, Irishmen, and the tin ceiling and rugged feel of the place, not to mention the nice fireplace, means that there's usually an older crowd here. A small dance floor in the back doesn't get much use, but the wood bar is a classic drinking spot.

Old Kings Road (532 State St., 805/884-4085, www.oldkingsroad.com, daily noon–2 A.M.) is as close as you'll get to a British tavern on the Central Coast. It's not filled with as many college-age kids and tends to be less rowdy, but that should not suggest a quaint, quiet gentlemen's tavern. Wednesday is quiz night, a very popular trivia time, and when darts are flying, it's boisterous. The look and feel is fairly authentic inside this small bar.

O'Malley's Bar (523 State St., 805/564-8904, daily noon–2 A.M.) has a giant-screen TV and draws big crowds for fight nights. There are plenty of other smaller screens ringing the perimeter of the bar. The only drawback is that no food is served, but they have no problem with patrons bringing in their own grub from one of the many establishments that line State Street. The antique bar at O'Malley's looks like a bar should look—wooden, thick, substantial, and well-worn.

The **Sandbar** (514 State St., 805/966-1388, www.sandbarsb.com, Mon. 3 P.M.–close, Tues.–Fri. 11:30 A.M.–close, Sat.–Sun. 11 A.M.–close) is a kind of rustic tequila bar with big cushioned love seats and chairs and 20 different tequilas available by the shot. The interior is small and most people crave the patio fronting State Street, as that's where the action is. But you also might want to stay inside with the 20 plasma TVs and chow down on south-of-the-border food.

Sharkeez (416 State St., 805/963-9680, Mon.–Fri. 11 A.M.–2 A.M., Sat.–Sun. 9 A.M.–2 A.M.) is a sports bar on steroids, with plenty of energy and testosterone. Their cluttered, hyperactive decor includes every kind of plastic pennant there is, plus flags, jerseys, and any other sports paraphernalia under the sun tacked to the wall. It's a loud, crazy place, with people drinking far too early in the morning, but if that's your thing, it's one of the only bars open before noon.

Elsie's Tavern (117 E. De La Guerra, 805/963-4503, Mon.–Thurs. noon–2 A.M., Fri.–Sun. 4 P.M.–2 A.M.) is an old garage that was turned into a tavern. There is a funky room with abandoned couches as you first enter, and as you make your way to the back the space opens up with a bar and pool table. It's low-key here: No one is trying to really impress anyone, and the place has an almost lonely feel to it. Rotating shows of local art hang on the walls, and though this is close to downtown, it's a world away.

Located behind the *Santa Barbara News-*

Press building is **The Press Room** (15 E. Ortega, 805/963-8121, daily 9 A.M.–6 A.M.), a little English bar with a great jukebox, stiff drinks, British pints, and a fine selection of whiskies. Game nights get noisy and crowded, like at any bar, but this spot is usually chill enough for conversation and without the typical on-the-prowl types who make some bars uncomfortable. Posters of British bands like The Who cling to the old walls, and it's also still on the inexpensive side.

Pool Halls

While there are a few single pool tables scattered about town in various bars, the only actual pool hall is **Don Q Family Billiard Center** (1128 Chapala, 805/966-0915, daily noon–2 A.M.). A dozen tournament tables fill the large spot, and there is enough room to play. This is not the hustle crowd but a smattering of good players and beginners. There's Wi-Fi, a small bar, and loud music as well. The place could use a coat of paint to freshen the interior, but since it's the only pool hall in town you can easily just focus on your game.

Live-Music Venues

Though Santa Barbara is home to a handful of well-known musicians, live music here is a small scene. Yes, there is always some guy with a guitar playing in a corner somewhere, but we're talking actual bands here. One of the better spots is **Velvet Jones** (423 State St., 805/965-8676, www.velvet-jones.com, daily 8 P.M.–close), which offers live music seven nights a week, much of it up-and-comers from the Los Angeles area. The space isn't going for looks, but it does go for hard rock, ska, hip-hop, and anything other than popular and middle-of-the-road music. They have a tiny kitchen and you can get hot dogs and pizza, but that's it. A small interior balcony and medium-sized dance floor gives you space so you're not crammed in, and a small gated front patio lets you cool down before you heat up again.

Live Culture (11 W. De La Guerra, inside Paseo Nuevo Mall, 805/845-8800, www.liveculturelounge.com, Sun.–Thurs.

Arlington Theatre

11 A.M.–10:30 P.M., Fri.–Sat. 11 A.M.–midnight) is a wine bar, restaurant, yogurt stop, and yes, live music venue. The musicians, usually just one to three people, perform on a small, elevated stage near the bar, which makes more room for patrons. You won't hear many full bands—there just isn't space—but this is a great place for the wine crowd on a weekend night.

Muddy Waters (508 E. Haley, 805/966-9328, Mon.–Sat. 6 A.M.–6 P.M.) has the distinct look of an unsupervised dorm room; it's unkempt and laid-back, but it works. Local musicians, mostly playing alternative music, use this as a spot to work out their new songs, and local art hangs on the walls. The have open mic nights as well. Coffee drinks, a few brews, and simple sandwiches and Wi-Fi are on offer, but note that they only take cash. On scheduled performance nights the venue will stay open later, so call ahead for extended hours.

SOhO Restaurant and Music Club (1221 State St., 805/962-7776, www.sohosb.com, daily 6–10 P.M.) is the premier midsized venue in town. There's live music seven nights a week, and every Monday is jazz night. SOhO has seen its share of well-known performers, including David Crosby, Kenny Loggins, Rickie Lee Jones, Jimmy Cliff, the Mad Caddies, Acoustic Alchemy, and many others. The 2nd-floor outdoor patio is a prime spring and summer location to enjoy tunes under the stars. They also have a full bar and restaurant.

The outdoor **Santa Barbara Bowl** (1122 N. Milpas, 805/962-7411, www.sbbowl.org), with just over 4,500 seats, is an intimate venue that brings in big A-list talent. It was originally built in the 1930s, but a renovation has greatly expanded the facilities. From its hillside location you can see the ocean and dance away under the stars. There is no larger or more preeminent music venue in town, and certainly for live music, this is the most beautiful.

PERFORMING ARTS

Santa Barbara has always fancied itself as a cultural hub on the Central Coast, but for a long time there was no real theater district. That has now changed. The venues in Santa Barbara, and the fact that top talent can command big bucks here, makes this a stopping point for many performing artists, bands, celebrities, and occasionally comedy tours and dance troupes, which is impressive for a town of its size.

The Granada (1216 State St., 805/899-3000, www.granadasb.org) reopened in 2008 after a $20 million expansion and renovation. The theater, built in 1924, has been given new life, with state-of-the-art sound and light systems and locally created wrought-iron chandeliers and railings. The stage is beautifully detailed and now reflects the show palaces of a long gone era. But like many theaters, the seats are still too cramped. Broadway shows and dance and music events are the order of the day here.

Arlington Theatre (1317 State St., 805/963-4408, www.thearlingtontheatre.com) has the coolest interior of any theater in town. Used for film (the Santa Barbara Film Festival uses this as their main screen) as well as lectures, dance, music, and most anything, it is classic

Santa Barbara. The entrance is a long covered atrium with painted arches, and a large fountain out front and a sweeping spire atop a red-tile roof. The Spanish theme continues inside the theater, which was designed to look like the courtyard of a Spanish village, with walls that look like buildings featuring balconies, red roofs, stairways, and porches. It's the best place to see a movie or show.

The Lobero Theatre (33 E. Canon Perdido, 805/966-4946, www.lobero.com) is the oldest continuously operating theater in California. The space is perfectly intimate and ideal for spoken word, lectures, theater, and dance. They have a roster of music acts as well, but the sound system has never been clean enough for pinpoint acoustics, in spite of the small space. Be sure to check out the hand-painted coffered ceiling. Originally built in 1873, then rebuilt in 1924, the theater has a great sense of history, which seems to be reflected in the works presented here: original, thought provoking, and just out of the norm.

Campbell Hall at UCSB (574 Mesa Rd., 805/893-3535, www.artsandlectures.ucsb.edu) may be located on the campus of the university, but this semi-formal space brings in some great talent and under-the-radar shows and is ideal for intimate performances, be that John Cleese in a one-man show, drummers from Japan, dance, or even film. It's a near perfect venue—small but intimate, technologically advanced but comfortable.

Ensemble Theatre (914 Santa Barbara St., 805/965-5400, www.ensembletheatre.com) is the city's best-known live theater venue, producing five shows each year. The theater is even more of an enviable space for its ability to pull in some well-known talent from Hollywood. The theater has a capacity of 140, ensuring you won't get a bad seat.

The **Marjorie Luke Theatre** (721 E. Cota St., 808/884-4087, www.luketheatre.org) is that small treasure in a community. Originally built in 1933, it went through a major upgrade and now this 800-seat theater is home to a variety of events including musicals, dance shows, musical acts, and more. Located on the campus of the Santa Barbara Junior High School, it's also their premier—and quite sophisticated—venue for school shows.

The **Victoria Hall Theater** (33 W. Victoria St., 805/730-1038, www.victoriahalltheater.com) was originally built in 1921 and now hosts a variety of performances including theater, film, seminars, and more. The 200-seat theater is home to the Victoria Hall Theater Foundation and operates as a nonprofit. It's a beautiful and intimate space and is right near State Street.

CINEMA

Santa Barbara residents love going to the movies as much as everyone else. But Santa Barbara has actually been *in* a lot of movies, and it was the hub of movie-making before Hollywood became cinema central. Since all of the movie theaters in town are operated by the Metropolitan Theatre Corporation (www.metrotheatres.com), they all have the same pricing, with $9.75 being the high weekend rate.

Mainstream films are best viewed at **Paseo Nuevo** (8 E. De La Guerra Plaza), located at Paseo Nuevo Mall, which has four screens but also proximity to restaurants, bars, and shopping for before or after the movie. The **Metro 4 Theatre** (618 State St.) offers stadium seating and four screens, as does the **Fiesta 5 Theatre** (916 State St.), and they're also right on State Street, convenient for hanging out.

Independent and art-house films are show at just two venues. The **Riviera Theatre** (2044 Alameda Padre Serra) is housed in the old UCSB campus up on the Riviera; it has a single screen but the seats and sound system are not high end. Off Upper State Street is **Plaza de Oro** (371 S. Hitchcock), which has two screens but seats and sound systems that could use a little upgrading.

The single best place to see a movie in the city—or the county, for that matter—is and will always be the **Arlington Theatre** (1317 State St.), with its formal grand entrance and an interior that resembles a Spanish village. They show only one movie here on a large

screen. The seats are old, so check them out before you plop down for two hours.

In Goleta, the **Camino Real Cinema** (7040 Marketplace Dr.) in the shopping mall has five screens and stadium seating. There are several restaurants nearby, including a brewery and the best pizza in town. The smaller three-screen **Fairview Theatre** (225 N. Fairview) shows current releases and is in a strip mall with restaurants within walking distance or a short drive away.

FESTIVALS AND EVENTS

Like every city, Santa Barbara is home to a lot of festivals, some pretty standard and some unique. The city's festivals tend to draw a lot of people from outside the county since Santa Barbara is an ideal weekend getaway.

Year-Round

Once a month, **First Thursday** (downtown, www.downtownsantabarbara.com for downloadable map, first Thurs. of each month 5–8 P.M.) provides an evening of art and culture in downtown Santa Barbara. Nearly a dozen galleries and art-related venues offer free access to visual and performing art and feature attractions such as art openings, live music, artist receptions, lectures, wine-tasting, hands-on activities, and even mobile poetry, where local poets spontaneously recite their works. It's become quite the social scene.

Nite Moves (www.runsantabarbara.com) is a weekly 5K race held each Wednesday May–September. For a small fee anyone can race, as well as participate in the open-water swim. There's food, music, and awards. It starts at Leadbetter Beach as the sun begins to set, climbs for a mile and a half, then returns the same way. It's not flat, but it's also not difficult, and with so many people participating, you probably won't be the slowest in your age group.

Spring

I Madonnari Italian Street Painting Festival (www.imadonnarifestival.com, free) is held at the Santa Barbara Mission every Memorial Day weekend. Adults aren't often encouraged to use chalk to draw on the sidewalk—except at the I Madonnari Festival. The parking lot in front of the mission is transformed from bleak black to more than 200 chalk paintings as artists, many local and some from across the globe, take chalk to asphalt and create beautiful reproductions of classic works as well as original art. The mission comes alive and the lawn is crowded with food vendors, live music, picnics, and the chance to watch surprisingly beautiful art in action. Going for over 20 years, it's the perfect weekend stop if you're in town. Bring a picnic and munch on the lawn or buy food there—either way it's a day well spent.

The stars of **The International Orchid Show** (805/687-0766, www.sborchidshow.org, $12) may seem like just a bunch of flowers, but ask any lover of orchids and they will tell you passionate stories of these plants. Santa Barbara enjoys a mild, Mediterranean climate with temperate nights and soft, ocean breezes, and orchids first took root in Santa Barbara at the turn of the 20th century when wealthy industrialists came to the area's burgeoning spas and resorts to escape harsh, eastern winters. Many of them stayed, building estates and commissioning world-class horticulturists and landscape architects to design elaborate gardens. Exotic orchids became the rage, with mass plantings of Cymbidiums and other unusual species adding prestige to Montecito and Hope Ranch estates. Held since 1945, and with current attendance in excess of 5,000 people, the March orchid festival is most certainly worth a visit. Thousands of unique and in some cases bizarre-looking plants are displayed at the Earl Warren Showgrounds. Experts are on hand to discuss the unusual flowers and there are a large number for sale.

Summer

The **French Festival** (www.frenchfestival.com, free) is a yearly tradition held at Oak Park (at Juniper and Alamar Sts.) each Bastille Day weekend, which for us Americans means mid-July. The festival runs 11 A.M.–7 P.M. and over 20,000 people attend to sample escargots, French onion soup, crepes, and baguettes;

watch cancan dancers; and line up to see the poodle parade, where poodles are dressed in berets and scarves, perhaps even Hermès. There are jugglers, mimes, and more accordion music than you thought possible. Dozens of chefs also attend to showcase their food, French wine, and French water. It's almost like going to France without paying for the airfare. Local French restaurants are here as well. C'est magnifique!

The **California Wine Festival** (www.californiawinefestival.com) is held across from the beach at Chase Palm Park and pulls in some 3,000 folks to sample wines from across California. Local wines are here, yes, but Napa and Sonoma are also well represented, as well as about a dozen breweries. There's plenty of food and live music, and you can't beat winetasting near the ocean. It does get crowded and warm during this July event, which translates into a rowdier crowd.

Woodies at the Beach (www.nationalwoodieclub.com, free) is one of the coolest festivals, held in mid-August. About 100 woodies (wood-bodied vehicles), from cars to trucks to campers and a handful of hot rods, grace the grassy bluffs at Santa Barbara City College overlooking Leadbetter Beach. There's live music, a surfboard raffle, and the chance to examine up close some beautifully restored classic cars. It's all free, and even if it's not your thing it's worth a stop to admire a piece of the past. Plus everyone's wearing Hawaiian shirts and seems so relaxed that you'll easily end up making friends.

The **Solstice Parade** (www.solsticeparade.com, free) started in 1974 as an homage to local artists and a pseudocelebration of the summer solstice and has exploded into a free-for-all of color, costume, political incorrectness, dance, music, and just plain summertime revelry. Think of this as a family-oriented Mardi Gras and you get the idea. Nearly 100,000 people cram the streets to celebrate the longest day of the year with the parade of funky floats and dancing in the streets, and a thousand people end up volunteering in the effort. The after party at Alameda Park is sometimes more fun than the parade itself, with drumming circles, more dancing, food, vendors, two live bands, and people wearing the bare minimum in the July sun. Grab your tie-dyed T-shirt and join in.

Also known as Old Spanish Days, **Fiesta** (www.oldspanishdays-fiesta.org, some events free) is a five-day extravaganza held the first weekend of August, and is Santa Barbara's oldest and best-known festival. Started in 1924 to honor the Spanish and Mexican heritage of the city, Fiesta has blossomed into the second largest equestrian parade in the United States, plus a feast of Mexican food and margaritas, and an opportunity to see lots of dance. There are three *mercados* (marketplaces) around town with tortillas, burritos, tamales, tacos, and more Mexican food. There are also activities for the kids at the *mercados,* like climbing walls, mariachi bands, and carnival rides. During Fiesta the Sunken Gardens at the county courthouse is transformed for a three-night free event known as Las Noches de Ronda (meaning "nights of gaiety"), with a stage where performers from across the globe dance *folklórico,* flamenco, and ballet, and belt out hip-hop and traditional Mexican songs, all under the beautiful evening skies of an August moon. The courthouse, lit up and shining in her magnificence, is a beautiful venue for the free concerts; all you need to do is grab a blanket or chair and a picnic and you're set.

But Fiesta officially kicks off with La Fiesta Pequeña (the "little fiesta"), held at the mission, with dance, local political figures, and a blessing of the mission fathers. It also now includes tribal dances by native Chumash people. There are a number of additional festivities during Fiesta, many of which you need to pay to attend, but the parade, Las Noches de Ronda, and the *mercados* are all free. During the Fiesta festivities, you'll see people walking all over town with baskets of hollowed-out eggs that are painted and filled with confetti; it's typical to crack them over the heads of friends and loved ones and shout out, "Viva la Fiesta!" Many locals flee town during Fiesta, as everything in town changes during the event. Hotel room rates increase, parking is at a premium, and there are cover charges at bars and clubs and lines at restaurants.

Fall

Pier to Peak (www.runsantabarbara.com), a 13.1-mile race, starts at Stearns Wharf and takes you on a point-to-point course up nearly 4,000 feet to La Cumbre Peak in September. Yes, you see much of Santa Barbara, the ocean, the mountains, and the mission, but you may not care as you gasp for air. This is a tough race, but an extraordinarily satisfying one, and the views are part of your reward.

It's fitting that Santa Barbara should have a seafood festival. After all, the Santa Barbara Channel is one of the nation's richest sources of bountiful, sustainable seafood. Lobster, ridgeback shrimp, rock crab, white sea bass, California halibut, yellowtail, salmon, swordfish, thresher shark, spot prawns, and sea urchin all thrive here, and about 100 local anglers catch between 6 and 10 million pounds of seafood annually. Held each October, the **Harbor and Seafood Festival** (805/897-1962, 10 A.M.–5 P.M., free) is a one-day event that brings out local fishermen, food vendors, and craftspeople together with cooking demonstrations and coast guard vessels, all to edify the public about the fish they consume, the water they play in, and the men and women who hit the ocean each day to bring in fresh fish and shellfish. It's all to celebrate the sea and our relationship with it.

The **Avocado Festival** (www.avofest.com, Fri. 4–10 P.M., Sat. 10 A.M.–9 P.M., Sun. 10 A.M.–6 P.M., free) is held each October in Carpinteria. Between 40 and 60 bands perform over the three-day event, and there are arts and crafts, lots of food purveyors, and yes, a guacamole contest. Since the region is the third largest producer of avocados, it only makes sense to celebrate it. This is a family event, free to everyone, and draws in massive numbers of people to bask in the sun and enjoy one of the Central Coast's best fruits.

The *Santa Barbara News-Press* **Half-Marathon** (www.newspress.com/halfmarathon) is the granddaddy of half marathons, having been held for over three decades. The half-marathon course hugs much of the coast, while the 5K race is all flat and all by the water. The early November race offers cooler temperatures. Several thousand people sign up for this, the city's premier race event.

Shopping

SHOPPING DISTRICTS AND CENTERS

The unique thing about Santa Barbara is that even the malls and shopping districts are visually interesting. They are all outdoor malls, but even in the rain they are still fun for hanging out.

Downtown

La Arcada Court (1114 State St., 805/966-6634, www.laarcadasantabarbara.com) was conceived and built in 1926. Vines climb up walls, tiled fountains beckon you to sit around them and engage in conversation, colorful flags hang over the walkway, and local shops and sidewalk cafés encourage you to skip out on your duties. The mall, a paseo of sorts, has entrances on both State and Figueroa Streets. The mall abuts the Museum of Art and the main library is just beyond. It's a small but important escape, a turn off the beaten path to a small wonder and visual delight. You'll notice a few patrons who never move, full-size bronze sculptures—one of which takes up valuable space on a bench! Inside La Arcada you will find three art galleries, a vintage barber shop, a wine shop, and a few restaurants.

Paseo Nuevo outdoor mall, with its ambience of a lazy afternoon, makes shopping fun even if you don't buy anything. The brick pathways meander along, vines climb the white walls, and fountains dispense water. This place took its cues, and its name, from the historic

El Paseo, an outdoor mall built in the 1920s

© MICHAEL CERVIN

SANTA BARBARA ORIGINALS

Santa Barbara has definitely earned some interesting bragging rights as the home of a number of notable products and brands.

Creamy **Hidden Valley Ranch salad dressing** is named for Hidden Valley Ranch in rural Santa Barbara County. Steve Henson created the dressing recipe while living in Alaska before purchasing Hidden Valley Ranch. Cold Spring Tavern was the first restaurant to serve his dressing, and the brand was purchased in 1973 for $8 million. It's gone on to become America's most popular salad dressing choice, and the ranch flavor is a national favorite for chips and dips.

Mr. Zog's Sex Wax was invented in Goleta in 1972 by chemist Nate Skinner and surfer Frederick Charles Herzog III. The brand remains a leading surfboard and snowboard wax producer from its Carpinteria headquarters, and Herzog still resides and surfs in Santa Barbara.

Channel Islands Surfboards (36 Anacapa St.), created by the legendary Al Merrick, is based in Santa Barbara and the boards are used by many professional surfers. The Santa Barbara retail store boasts the largest number of boards shaped by Merrick.

McDonalds' **Egg McMuffin** was invented in 1968 in Santa Barbara by a franchise owner, Herb Peterson, and restaurant chains like **Carrows** and **Sambo's Restaurant** (216 W. Cabrillo Blvd.) also got their start here. The original Sambo's opened in Santa Barbara in the 1950s and, today, it is the only remaining location of the once controversial chain which fell into disrepute during the civil rights movement because of its name and imagery. Sambo's still serves up plenty of food, but the theme has changed. **Kentucky Fried Chicken** has their headquarters in Carpinteria right off the 101 freeway.

Clothing is also big here. Major brands based in Santa Barbara include the **Territory Ahead, Big Dog Sportswear, Deckers** (makers of Ugg, Simple, and Teva footwear), and the powerhouse Global Brand Marketing, makers of **Diesel, Nautica, XOXO,** and **Pony** footwear. **Balance Bar** was created here, and the travel giant **Magellan's** is also based here.

And in 1970, a copy shop located in a minuscule storefront next to a hamburger stand in Isla Vista began catering to UCSB students to photocopy their homework and term papers. That humble beginning became **Kinko's.** The Loughead brothers established the Loughead Aircraft Manufacturing Company here in 1916, which eventually became Lockheed Corporation. And in 1962, a simple no-frills motel opened its doors, charging just six bucks a night. The room rates have changed, but chances are many of us have stayed at a **Motel 6** at some point. The original Motel 6 (443 Corona del Mar) still gives weary travelers an inexpensive place to sleep.

El Paseo across the street. From stores selling knives, candy, or cheese to restaurants and Nordstrom and Macy's, you'll find most everything at two-block-long Paseo Nuevo.

But it was the historic **El Paseo** (1812 State St.) that started it all. Though the complex has lost great tenants and there's little reason anymore to wander inside the true paseo, it's still a beautiful reminder of how Santa Barbara shopping was originally envisioned. Built in 1924, the paseo was the first of its kind in the state. The walkways pass through arched doorways into courtyards with wrought-iron railings and vine-covered walls, giving the feel of a small village in Spain. There are two restaurants inside, a jewelry store, and private offices, so it's no longer a shopper's paradise, but it is worth walking through to see the paseo concept that started it all.

Upper State Street

La Cumbre Plaza (121 S. Hope Ave., 805/687-3500, www.shoplacumbre.com, Mon.–Fri. 10 A.M.–8 P.M., Sat. 10 A.M.–6 P.M., Sun. 11 A.M.–6 P.M.) had a face lift that upgraded this outdoor mall into yet another Spanish-style shopping center. But given that Upper State Street doesn't have too much in the way of architecture, it's a welcome addition. Ruth's

Chris, Tiffany & Co., Sears, and Macy's all share the space with smaller nationally known stores like Lane Bryant, Williams-Sonoma, and See's Candies. It's far less crowded here, being uptown and all; there is ample free parking and it's close to the freeway.

Montecito

Coast Village Road is the main street that runs through trendy Montecito, and though it's small, there are many businesses that vie for attention, predominantly clothing boutiques and small galleries, restaurants, and even a wine shop and liquor store; the street is home to professional offices as well. CVR, as it's called here, is not an inexpensive place to buy anything. But it has a modest village feel to it, cozy and easily walkable, with mature trees shading one- and two-story shops. It doesn't have the traditional Spanish look but instead is an amalgam of different looks, but still pleasant and inviting.

Carpinteria

Carpinteria's **Linden Avenue,** about three blocks from the beach, is aiming to become the next State Street. The offerings are still quite limited, but it's a pleasant place to spend the day. Restaurants, an old hardware store, beachwear boutiques, a bakery, clothing stores, and 100-year-old palm trees share the street. This is a place for strolling and chatting, maybe stopping for a glass of wine, coffee, or a taco along the way.

CLOTHING AND ACCESSORIES

Tienda Ho (1105 State St., 805/962-3643, www.tiendaho.com, Mon.–Sat. 10 A.M.–6 P.M., Sun. 11 A.M.–6 P.M.) has an eclectic collection of Balinese, Moroccan, and Indian fashions and furnishings. The upstairs is mainly blocky wood furniture and deity masks, and the downstairs is packed with diverse women's wear including vivid scarves, wraps, and skirts. There's even a small indoor waterfall near the dressing rooms in the colorful bazaar. They have been in business for more than 25 years and have held their own

amongst corporate chains, while still offering unusual, eclectic clothing.

Blue Bee (913 State St., 805/882-2468, www.bluebee.com, Mon.–Sat. 10 A.M.–6 P.M., Sun. 1–6 P.M.) is a local success story. John Doucette and Marty Bebout decided that Santa Barbara was the place to create a high-end boutique with a wide diversity of designer clothing labels covering the latest trends. They were right: Blue Bee was instantly popular. Their success resulted in additional stores, including menswear store Blue Beatle, Blue Bee Jeans, Blue Bee Shoes, and the more exclusive Honeycomb. Though the prices are high here, no one seems to mind.

Near Lower State, **Lucia Loves Luigi** (21 W. Ortega St., 805/883-1111, www.lucialovesluigi.com, Mon.–Sat. 10 A.M.–5:30 P.M., Sun. noon–5 P.M.) is an intimate shop with cream-colored walls and old hardwood floors where, as its name suggests, you'll find a plethora of sleek designs from Italy, as well as purses, dresses, shoes, and more from other European and American designers. Luigi, an English sheep dog mix, is the store's mascot.

Dressed (1253 Coast Village Rd., 805/565-1253, www.dressedonline.com, Mon.–Sat. 10 A.M.–5:30 P.M., Sun. noon–5 P.M.) and sister store **Ready** (1253 Coast Village Rd., 805/565-0819, www.dressedonline.com, Mon.–Sat. 10 A.M.–5:30 P.M., Sun. noon–5 P.M.) are neighboring boutiques run by well-known local fashionista Susan Pitcher. Both offer formal and casual eclectic clothing as well as high-end clothing by well-established designers.

The stock rotates frequently at **Renaissance Fine Consignment** (1118 State St., 805/963-7800, Mon.–Sat. 10 A.M.–6 P.M., Sun. 11 A.M.–5 P.M.), where you can find fashions and accessories from Chanel, Valentino, and other high-end designers. If couture isn't your thing, there's also a large selection of trendy clothes. The quality is great and many of the clothes have hardly been worn.

CHILDREN'S STORES

Chicken Little (1236 State St., 805/962-7771, www.chickenlittlekids.com, Mon.–Sat.

10 A.M.–6 P.M., Sun. 10:30 A.M.–5:30 P.M.) sells everything for little ones. Should you be visiting town and forget something for the kids—clothes, a car seat, or a game to keep them occupied—you'll find it at Chicken Little, the oldest children's store in the area.

If kids could design a sophisticated boutique shopping experience, **Mon Petit Bijou** (1014 State St., 800/945-0015, www.monpetit-bijou.com, Mon.–Sat. 10 A.M.–6 P.M.) would probably be it. Flush with hardwood floors, two stories, comfy resting chairs, the shop offers loads of high-priced fashions for newborns and younger kids with a decidedly elegant and French flair. There is whimsical furniture, high-end silverware, and engraving services.

This Little Piggy Wears Cotton (8 E. De La Guerra St., 805/564-6982, www.lit-tlepiggy.com, Mon.–Sat. 10 A.M.–6 P.M., Sun. noon–6 P.M.) sells unique clothing, accessories, toys, and books for newborns, kids, and pre-teens. Many of their clothes are made of organic fibers.

ANTIQUES

As the old saying goes, one person's trash is another's treasure, and antiques shopping is more treasure hunt than anything else.

Old Town Antiques (5799 Hollister, Goleta, 805/967-2528, www.antiquesoldtown.com, Mon.–Sat. 10 A.M.–6 P.M., Sun. 11 A.M.–5 P.M.) in Goleta is a collective of 15 dealers and over 5,000 square feet of eclectic items, especially furniture. The pieces here are clean, unusual, and well priced, since it is way off State Street. The inventory rotates regularly, with new merchandise coming in frequently.

Also off State Street is the **Antique Center Mall** (4434 Hollister, 805/967-5700, Mon.–Sat. 11 A.M.–6 P.M., Sun. noon–5 P.M.), with nine rooms packed full of everything you can imagine. Of particular note is a very good selection of mid-century modern by a local dealer who knows her stuff; it's located right at the entrance. There is also a lot of wrought-iron outdoor pieces and statuary, plus furniture, jewelry, and accessories.

Summerland, just south of Santa Barbara,

has become a centralized location for antiques and furnishings. There are a dozen places on or just off Lillie Avenue, Summerland's main drag. The best, and oldest, is the **Summerland Antique Collective** (2192 Ortega Hill Rd., Summerland, 805/565-3189, daily 10 A.M.–5 P.M.). Over 30 years they've amassed over 45,000 square feet of everything you can imagine: Mid-century modern, jewelry, retro, artworks, and garden furnishings, it's all here under one roof.

More expensive, but with some amazing museum-quality items, **Summerhill Antiques** (2280 Lillie Ave., Summerland, 805/969-3366, daily 11 A.M.–5 P.M.) has a lot of French and Asian furniture, accent pieces, tables, and unusual pieces like 17th-century statuary. This is a place for the serious antiques lover.

The aptly named **Things** (1187 Coast Village Rd., 805/845-8411, www.thingsof-montecito.com, Tues.–Sun. 11 A.M.–5 P.M.) is a high-end consignment store with antique furnishings and decorative items like wall sconces and ornamental iron work. The intriguing and visually appealing selection varies, as the store sells merchandise quickly.

BOOKSTORES

Santa Barbara has always been a refuge for the literary types; Sue Grafton and T. C. Boyle are two of the writers who currently keep residences here. Unfortunately, these days most independent bookstores have been replaced by megachains, but there are three die-hard holdouts, all with unique charms.

The Book Den (15 E. Anapamu St., 805/962-3321, www.thebookden.com, Mon.–Sat. 11 A.M.–6 P.M., Sun. noon–5 P.M.) is one of those places that smells a bit musty when you walk in. It's understandable in this case, since this has been a bookstore since 1933. It's great for browsing, with a large selection of used, out of print, and antiquarian books, as well as new titles, housed on floor-to-ceiling shelves packed with books; a rolling ladder is needed to reach the top shelves. But with 1.4 million titles at their disposal, they simply don't have room for them all in this small space.

Chaucer's (3321 State St., Loreto Plaza, 805/682-6787, www.chaucersbooks.com, Mon.–Sat. 9 A.M.–9 P.M., Sun. 9 A.M.–6 P.M.) opened its doors in 1974 and has become the premier independent bookstore in Santa Barbara. The events schedule is busy with book signings by local, regional, and national authors, and there's a huge selection of books from well known to obscure.

Past the Dutch doors, the carpet and beautiful wood bookcases at **Tecolote Bookstore** (1470 E. Valley Rd., 805/969-4977, Mon.–Fri. 10:30 A.M.–5:30 P.M., Sat. 10 A.M.–5 P.M. make it feel more like a library than a bookstore. Intimate and comfortable, it's the oldest bookstore in the county, and is supported by very loyal locals.

Paradise Found (17 E. Anapamu, 805/564-3573, www.paradise-found.net, Mon.–Sat. 10 A.M.–6 P.M.) is for the discerning spiritualist. The metaphysical bookstore also sells aromatherapy products, incense, candles, CDs, cards, and unusual gift items, and offers intuitive readings. The store is small but well laid out, and the staff is friendly. They occasionally have special events such as book signings and aura readings.

ART GALLERIES

Santa Barbara has long been a draw for artists hoping to capture the stunning terrain, landscapes, seascapes, and whitewashed buildings with red-tile roofs. There is a focus in town on plein air, but it is by no means the only form of art represented. Most galleries are bunched in the downtown core and have great accessibility, while a few other galleries dot the outer edges of the city. Beyond that, you're likely to see art hanging, and even artist receptions taking place, in restaurants, salons, offices, and other businesses.

The **Santa Barbara Art Dealers Association** (www.sbada.org) is the ideal place to start. Their map gives the locations of the galleries in town and can help you in your search for a specific style.

Sullivan Goss: An American Gallery (7 E. Anapamu, 805/730-1460, www.sullivangoss.com, daily 10 A.M.–5:30 P.M.) is the most well-known art gallery in town. Owner Frank Goss knows his stuff and hosts constant exhibitions showcasing top talent from across the United States, with an emphasis on the 19th through 21st centuries. Two side-by-side galleries create a large enough space to show oversized works. Sullivan Goss has a number of local artists on its large roster of clients, and also looks to acquire new works.

Decidedly smaller, **Artamo Gallery** (11 W. Anapamu, 805/568-1400, www.artamogallery.com, Wed.–Sun. noon–5 P.M.) has a clear and aggressive focus on abstract expressionism. Shows rotate every 2–3 months, with artists both well known and under the radar from around the globe. Artamo represents an excellent selection of artists working in mixed media, found media, paint, sculpture, and photography.

The **Contemporary Arts Forum** (653 Paseo Nuevo, inside and upstairs at Paseo Nuevo Mall, 805/966-5373, www.sbcaf.org, Tues.–Sat. 11 A.M.–5 P.M., Sun. noon–5 P.M., $5) is, as the name suggests, devoted to contemporary arts, be that visual, media, or performing arts, representing a wide range of artistic attitudes. CAF shows new works of local, regional, national, and international artists in a warehouse-sized space and pushes the envelope with many of their exhibitions. Multimedia exhibits and performance art is common, perhaps confusing, but CAF gives Santa Barbara much-needed exposure to diverse expressions.

The **Faulkner Gallery** (401 E. Anapamu, 805/564-5608, Mon.–Thurs. 10 A.M.–8 P.M., Fri.–Sat. 10 A.M.–5:30 P.M., Sun. 1–5 P.M., free) is one of those places you'd rarely think about going into, and if you didn't know it was there you would walk right past it. Located in a separate room inside the main branch of the public library, there is a large space with art exhibits rotating every few months, and two small side rooms with even more art. There's always something interesting, and everything is for sale at prices lower than those of traditional galleries. Mainly local artists exhibit here, and you just might make a very cool discovery.

The **Channing Peake Gallery** (105 E.

Anapamu St., 1st fl., 805/568-3990, www .sbartscomission.org, Mon.–Fri. 9 A.M.–5 P.M., free) is located on the ground floor of the County Administration building, which seems odd until one learns that the Arts Commission, which runs the gallery and other artistic endeavors around town, is supported by the county government. There are significant works presented on the ground floor, from photography exhibits to art, poetry, and more. And who knows, you might just bump into a county supervisor while you're admiring the work.

The **Architectural Foundation of Santa Barbara** (229 E. Victoria, 805/965-6307, www.afsb.org, Tues.–Fri. 9 A.M.–2 P.M.) is housed in an old Victorian residence and has an attached gallery that showcases the work of local architects and artists. The works tend to have an abstract bent. One exhibit featured all the things that architects use to sketch out ideas when they are not in their offices: napkin, matchbook cover, tablecloth, menu, and other unusual spur-of-the-moment idea pads. In 1989, the Architectural Foundation started the highly successful Kids Draw Architecture program, which provides an opportunity for children to sketch Santa Barbara's famous landmark buildings. The result is a yearly show featuring some excellent works by children. This is one of the few venues where local architects can present not only images of their architectural work, but their artistic side as well.

ARTS AND CRAFTS

The **Sunday Arts and Craft Show** (Cabrillo Blvd. at Chase Palm Park, 805/897-1982, www.sbaacs.com, Sun. 10 A.M.–dusk) is the definitive arts and crafts show, which happens every Sunday at the beach. Over 100 local sculptors, painters, and photographers set up their tables with jewelry, wind chimes, art, vases, and much, much more. The show has been around for over 30 years. It's free to stroll the waterfront, and chances are you'll find something you love.

It's pretty hot at **2000 Degrees** (1206 State St., 805/882-1817, Tues.–Fri. noon–8 P.M., Sat. 10 A.M.–9 P.M., Sun. noon–6 P.M.), the only

place in town where you can paint your own pottery (choose from the naked ceramics on the showroom floor: mugs, plates, vases, etc.), have it kiln–fired, and then take it home. It's pretty cool to have semi-created a unique piece of pottery for your home.

SPECIALTY STORES

Church of Skatan (26 E. Gutierrez, 805/899-1586, Mon.–Sat. 11 A.M.–6 P.M., Sun. 11 A.M.–5 P.M.) is the only skate shop in town. There's a large selection of boards, trucks, shoes, clothing, and advice for the skate crowd, all housed in the old Second Baptist Church. The original hardwood floors and stained-glass windows remain. It's a fitting place of worship for those to whom skateboarding is a religion.

As the name implies, **Random** (1207 State St., 805/966-3257, www.randomstore.com, daily 10 A.M.–9 P.M.) is that weird store where you can find anything: wing nuts, bolts of clothing, weirdo totem poles, books, hangers, most anything that seems like it has no purpose. They buy closed-out merchandise and inventory varies constantly. It's the kind of store that sells that thing you didn't know you needed until you stumbled across it.

There are strict smoking laws in the city, but for 15 years **Santa Barbara Cigar and Tobacco** (10 W. Figueroa St., 805/963-1979, www.santabarbaracigars.com, daily 11 A.M.–6 P.M.) has sold cigars and accessories. This isn't a cigarette store, though they do sell some cigarettes—this is a place for the discerning smoker.

SWEETS

Everyone loves something sweet, and Santa Barbara has offers a small share of confections made right here.

Chocolate Maya (15 W. Gutierrez, 805/965-5956, www.chocolatemaya.com, Mon.–Fri. 11 A.M.–6 P.M., Sat. 10 A.M.–5 P.M.) has an assortment of chocolates from across the globe, including some they make on-site. High-quality playful molded chocolates make great gifts. They'll put together a special chocolate tasting on request.

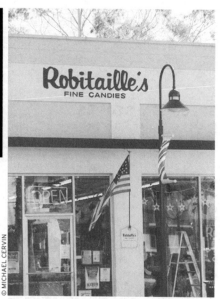

© MICHAEL CERVIN

For over 30 years, Robitaille's thin mints have given sweet tooths something to smile about.

When you enter **Chocolats du CaliBressan** (4193 Carpinteria Ave., Carpinteria, 805/684-6900, www.chococalibressan.com, Mon.–Fri. 10 A.M.–6:30 P.M., Sat. 10 A.M.–5:30 P.M.) you're hit with a heady aroma of chocolate. The shop is run by a French chocolatier, so you're pretty much guaranteed to get fabulous bonbons and truffles to satisfy your sweet tooth.

They offer samples and tours of the chocolate-making process; contact them for details.

Robitaille's Fine Candies (900 Linden Ave., Carpinteria, 805/684-9340, www.robitailles-candies.com, Mon.–Sat. 10 A.M.–5:30 P.M., Sun. 10 A.M.–3 P.M.) has been making and selling chocolates for 40 years, and has been at their Linden Avenue location for over 25 years. Though they carry a of lot of prepackaged items, including sugar-free candies, they are best known for their original thin mints, small multicolored minty discs.

FARMERS MARKETS

Santa Barbara County hosts 11 farmers markets each week. The markets are just as much for socializing as getting lemon basil or torpedo onions. Strolling musicians entertain while local chefs scour the stalls for what they'll serve that evening. Check out www.sb-farmersmarket.org for a complete schedule. The markets occur all over the county, including Goleta, Montecito, and Carpinteria, but the biggest and best are the Saturday-morning **downtown market** (Santa Barbara and Cota Sts., Sat. 8:30 A.M.–1:30 P.M.), which is the largest and most social, and the Tuesday-afternoon **State Street market** (500–600 blocks of State St., Tues. 3–6:30 P.M.). Be advised that the Tuesday market shuts down parts of State Street, and drivers are re-routed through the area.

Sports and Recreation

PARKS

Rocky Nook Park (610 Mission Canyon Rd., 805/568-2461, daily 8 A.M.–sunset) is a great spot for watching Mission Creek wander towards the mission and is covered with, well, rocks. This 19-acre park is a wonderful respite or place for a picnic. It offers barbecue grills, picnic tables, hiking trails, horseshoes, a small playground, and restrooms.

From there you can head up Alameda Padre Serra to **Francheschi Park** (1510 Mission Ridge Rd., daily sunrise–sunset), home to an old dilapidated estate. The house, named for Italian horticulturist Francesco Franceschi, is closed to the public, but the 18-acre grounds are open and offer some of the absolute best views of the city, harbor, and coast, especially at sunset. There's a small parking lot and a few picnic tables, and even a disturbingly dirty bathroom. The view corridor is narrowed by the eucalyptus trees, but it makes a perfect frame for photos.

Elings Park (on Los Positas between Cliff Dr. and Modoc Rd., 805/969-5611, www.elingspark.org, daily 7 A.M.–sunset) is a former landfill and now a 230-acre park that offers activities such as a BMX course, radio-controlled car racing, and paragliding, as well as a soccer field, wedding venues, hiking trails, picnic grounds, and perfect views of the harbor, mountains, and ocean. A number of large events take advantage of the grounds, including the Santa Barbara Beer Festival (www.sbbeerfestival.com), held each October, and the Santa Barbara Bicycle Festival (www.santabarbarabikefest.com) held in June with cross-country, BMX, and downhill courses and races. This is a wonderful gem of a spot. The hiking on moderate hills will take you to some great vistas of both the ocean and mountains.

Skater's Point (Cabrillo Blvd. at Garden St., daily 9 A.M.–sunset) was one of those concepts that people decried when the idea was first floated: A concrete skate park at the beach? Over $800,000 later, it's proved a great success. Skateboards and bikes swoop up and down the ramps covering nearly 15,000 square feet of concrete in full view of anyone who cares to watch. Skater's Point is located just east of Stearns Wharf in Chase Palm Park, and it's fun just to hang out there and imagine yourself doing some of the tricks.

Alameda Park (1400 Santa Barbara St., daily 8 A.M.–sunset) is a wonderful two-block family-oriented picnic and playground spot that hosts the 8,000-square-foot Kids Zone playground, a medieval-looking fort with swings, slides, and climbing equipment. It's close to downtown, and you can usually find plenty of parking and a picnic table if you come early. Don't expect sunbathing here, though, as the trees provide plenty of shade. There are restrooms, a small gazebo, and plenty of open spaces for Frisbee. This park is a centerpiece for many citywide celebrations, such as on the summer solstice.

Just across the street is the **Alice Keck Park Memorial Gardens** (1500 Santa Barbara St. at Arrellaga, daily dawn–dusk), which is one of the city's most beautiful spots. The site used to hold a grand hotel, and Alice Keck Park (that's her name, not the name of the park) deeded the plot of land to the city. Well-tended gardens surround a man-made pond with koi and turtles. Of special note is that the 75 different plant and tree species can be enjoyed by guests with vision or hearing difficulties, as there are Braille signs and audio posts at specific spots to identify what has been planted. The walkway meanders around specialized planting beds that feature low-use water species. It is a labor of love with a message: Beautiful plants don't have to consume lots of precious resources. The park is popular with both student and professional photographers, and every Saturday and Sunday you will find brides vying for position in front of the most beautiful flowers or splash of unique foliage to immortalize their big day. There are no facilities here; you'll have to head across the street to Alameda Park.

Tucker's Grove (805 San Antonio Creek Rd. at Cathedral Oaks, 805/967-1112, www.sbparks.com, daily 8 A.M.–sunset) is officially called San Antonio Canyon Park, as San Antonio Creek runs through it, but it's known locally as Tucker's Grove (which is actually the lower section where the entrance to the park is located). Tucker's Grove is open and sunny, and the lower park is great for families because of its wide-open spaces and relatively flat grounds right next to a large playground. There are lots of picnic tables here, even a vending machine with cold drinks. The upper section of the park, called the Kiwanis Meadow, as the look and feel of a completely different park. From Kiwanis Meadow you can access hiking and riding trails that go all the way to San Marcos Road. For all of Tucker's Grove, there are picnic and barbecue facilities for up to 400 people, playgrounds, volleyball, horseshoe pits, ball fields, hiking, lots of free parking, and restrooms.

Shoreline Park (Shoreline Dr. at La Marina, daily sunrise–10 P.M.) is a long, narrow ocean-side park that offers fabulous views of the harbor, the islands, and the mountains. Scattered parking and picnic facilities, as well as a small playground, make this a popular spot for family gatherings. This is a great park for walking, skating, playing Frisbee, and flying kites as well. Follow the narrow wooden stairs near the restrooms to discover a local secret: a beach and tidal pool area (when the tide is low) that is both private (sort of) and beautiful. You will often see dolphins skimming the surface from here. There is a stationary metal binocular by the bronze whale tail at the west end of the park.

GOLF COURSES

There are only six 18-hole golf courses in Santa Barbara, and a few nine-hole courses.

Rancho San Marcos (4600 Hwy. 154, 805/683-6334, www.rsm1804.com, green fees $79–104), built on the site of the historic 1804 Rancho San Marcos, is a Robert Trent Jones Jr.–designed gem that gracefully saddles the natural topography, meandering amidst a plethora of ancient oaks and preserved traces of 19th-century adobe structures. This par-70 course sits off the San Marcos Pass, just 15 miles from both Santa Barbara and Solvang. It's a course for business types, with a small pro shop and restaurant, but plenty of privacy to close a deal. No denim clothing is allowed.

Forgo the inland for the breathtaking views at **Sandpiper Golf Course** (7925 Hollister Ave., 805/968-1541, www.sandpipergolf.com, daily dawn–dusk, green fees $139–159), one of the most beautiful courses anywhere. Sandpiper is a par 71, which provides expert-level play and terrific views from the bluffs above the ocean. The only oceanfront course between Los Angeles and Pebble Beach, this is a must-play for visitors.

Tucked into the hills with views to ocean is **Glen Annie Golf Course** (405 Glen Annie Rd., 805/968-6400, www.glenanniegolf.com, daily dawn–dusk, green fees $59–74). Part of what makes this par-72 course so beautiful is its natural setting, away from it all in the low hills facing the ocean. In conjunction with Audubon International, this course is one of six in California that supports an Environmental Enhancement Program. Three different habitats provide homes to numerous wild animals

that call the golf course home, so if you go looking for that lost ball, you won't be alone. There is a pro shop and restaurant on-site.

The **Santa Barbara Golf Club** (3500 McCaw Ave., 805/687-7087, www.santabarbaraca.gov, daily dawn–dusk, green fees $40–50) is a par-70 public course sitting on what used to be an airstrip. The course is dotted with eucalyptus trees, and there are peek-a-boo views to the islands. It's a beautiful course and you may forget you're next to the freeway. The greens are a little slow for the avid golfer, but for a municipal course it's one of the best in the region (and priced accordingly).

HIKING

Santa Barbara offers hikes for all difficulty levels in a variety of settings. The best place to start to plan a hike is www.santabarbarahikes.com. Here are some suggestions that will get you outside for some of the city's best views.

Rattlesnake Canyon is one of the more popular hikes and is fairly easy—and no, you probably won't come across any rattlesnakes; it was named for its winding canyon location. It's close to downtown, well marked, and less than four miles long. You'll pass pools and streams and eventually come out at the top of a small hill with panoramic views to the ocean. From the mission, take Mission Canyon Road north to Foothill Road. Turn right and make a quick left onto the continuation of Mission Canyon Road. After about half a mile, make a sharp right at Los Conoas, which will take you just over a mile to Rattlesnake Bridge, an old stone bridge over the creek. Park in one of the pullouts. The trailhead is here, clearly marked.

Seven Falls has an elevation gain of 600 feet over a two-and-a-half-mile path that follows Mission Creek through a gorge and across small waterfalls and deep pools, over boulders and sandstone rocks. It's a moderate hike, and in season when the creek flows unabated the trail is alive with the sounds of water. To access the trail, from the mission take Mission Canyon Road north to Foothill Road. Turn right and make a quick left onto the continuation of Mission Canyon Road. The road divides—veer left up the hill; you'll be on Tunnel Road at this point. It's about a mile drive before the road ends. Park there and walk to the end of Tunnel Road, staying on the pavement. You'll pass a gate and the road splits off about a half mile up—stay left. You'll cross a wooden bridge over Mission Creek, with Fern Canyon Falls right below you. At just under a mile the road ends at a trail split. The right fork is a fire road, so take the left fork, the Jesusita Trail, which drops into Mission Canyon. Once you cross the next creek you'll take the narrow path to the right, which runs up the west side of the canyon. This is not a very well-maintained trail and requires scampering over boulders, but you'll soon come upon the waterfalls and pools.

BIKE TRAILS

Off road, on major streets, by the beach—anywhere you go in town you'll see someone on a bike. From flat beachfront rides to tough mountain roads, there is something for every skill level. Lance Armstrong used to train in the mountains here, and there are hard-core cyclists everywhere. Regardless of your skill level, when you come up behind another cyclist always call out "on your left" to alert him or her to move over to the right. Contact Traffic Solutions (805/963-7283, www.trafficsolutions.info) to obtain a copy of the free and most excellent Santa Barbara County bike map. If renting, consider a mountain bike over a touring bike; the slightly beefy tires are perfect for getting off road and even riding on the sand. Yes, you'll have a slower pace, but you'll be able to go anywhere the mood strikes you.

The Foothill Route, also known as Highway 192 or Cathedral Oaks, alternates between narrow stretches of road around Mission Canyon to flat wide streets near Winchester Canyon and the beach in Goleta. It's very popular because of its many hills, and you can ride from the beach in Goleta all the way into Ojai. There is a lot of traffic around the Mission Canyon area; as the road climbs it twists and turns and cyclists need to be on the lookout for cars coming around blind curves. Between

Mission Canyon and Goleta, the road widens and takes you past avocado orchards and citrus ranches until it leads into Winchester Canyon by the water.

For the most part, the **Coast Route** bike path hugs the coast near the waterfront, then climbs into a residential area and drops you down near Arroyo Burro Beach. From there the road climbs into Hope Ranch, a beautiful and well-to-do section of Santa Barbara with a stunning number of mature trees. Eventually you hit the Atascadero Bike Path, which shuttles you through low marsh lands before arriving at UCSB. You can continue on through campus to hook up with the Foothill route and make a wide loop, but it's a taxing ride.

RUNNING

Santa Barbara is a great place for runners. You can run on the sand, in the mountains, around downtown, or at tracks overlooking the ocean, and join in weekly runs and meet new friends. The weather here is ideal—even winter isn't that cold—so lace up those shoes and hit the road.

More Mesa is, hands down, the best spot to run. Just under 300 undeveloped bluff-top acres with loads of trails give you views to the ocean and islands and unfettered views to the mountains. It's also relatively isolated. There are a few walkers, other runners, and occasional off-road cyclists, but for the most part you don't pass by too many people. The bluff-top trail inches its way to the cliffs, in some cases within a foot or two. A misstep and you'll plummet 150 feet to the surf below, so keep an eye on the trail. In addition to the views there is beach access via an old stair system built into the cliffs by the eucalyptus trees, and chances are you'll see dolphins, a variety of birds, the occasional whale, and maybe a fox, skunk, or snake. More Mesa is accessed off Patterson in Goleta going south. Patterson turns into Shoreline Road and makes a right curve into Orchid. The trail leading to More Mesa will be on your left at the top of a small hill. Park at the bottom of the hill in either of the two pullouts and walk up.

The **waterfront** is where most people feel

With about 300 undeveloped blufftop acres, More Mesa is the best place to run in Santa Barbara.

they should run, because it all seems flat and easy. And the concrete path is indeed perfectly fine for a 3-to-4-mile out and back, running the length of the ocean and past the zoo towards the bird refuge. It can get crowded in late mornings (as sleepyheads emerge to start their day) and in the afternoons. It's also important to watch out for inline skaters, cyclists, and those driving rented four-wheel surreys, as their steering mechanisms aren't the greatest. As you run by the ocean with towering palm trees swaying gently in the breeze, the blue Pacific crashing near your feet, and islands standing guard in the distance, you can't help but think you're in paradise. There are restrooms and drinking fountains along the way.

Mountain Drive is a 15-mile asphalt road with gentle slopes and turns. And since it's cut into the mountains, you get great views towards the ocean. There are no services, however, as this is a residential area. Park near the Sheffield Dam and head north to Mountain Drive; turn right and begin. Sunday morning, when traffic is the lightest, is the best. Once you get to about two miles you'll see on your

right a mailbox in the shape of a chubby cyclist, whose rear end is where the mail goes. As many have done before, slap his butt, and either head back or continue on.

Hope Ranch, a wealthy enclave of hills and equestrian paths, is stunningly beautiful. Follow the bridle paths most anywhere, past the small lake, under a canopy of oak trees, and out to the bluffs overlooking the ocean. There are no maps, and this residential area is quiet and peaceful. The best plan is to park on Modoc Road near the entrance to the bike path, near Lyric Lane, and simply follow the bike path until you see the trails on you left-hand side. Then, go explore.

WATER ACTIVITIES
Whale-Watching and Sunset Cruises

There is nothing like the thrill of seeing a whale, a pod of dolphins ripping through the surf, or the tranquil simplicity of a sunset cruise. These boats offer a variety of excursions. Most places will offer you another trip if you don't see any whales. But remember, a small break in the water as one of these magnificent creatures takes in air might count as a sighting.

Sunset Kidd Sailing (12 Harbor Way, 805/962-8222, www.sunsetkidd.com, daily 8 A.M.–7 P.M., $40 and up) offers private charters and morning, afternoon, evening, and full-moon cruises on their 41-foot sailing yacht. They can accommodate about 20 people, so it's not a crowded outing, and you're not fighting to get to the sides to see anything. It's a great ship in that on the return to the harbor they generally cut the motor and rig the sails for a quiet return. But remember, this is a sailboat, so there's a lot of up and down movement.

In contrast, **Condor Cruises** (301 W. Cabrillo Blvd., 805/882-0088, www.condorcruises.com, whale-watching $48 adults, $12 children under 12, cruises $25–35) is a 75-foot high-speed catamaran, which means you're tooling across the water quickly, not sailing. This is a more stable ride for those prone to motion sickness. Whale-watching cruises run about two and a half hours. They too offer a full roster of cruises and excursions, including bird-watching trips. Those trips are usually about two hours and have an open bar and light food.

Kayaking

Sitting low in a kayak allows you to really experience the water. Kayaking need not be a strenuous activity, and paddling is not difficult. You can rent kayaks for an hour or longer and explore the coast easily and up close—pack food with you and you can choose a beach for a picnic. All rental places will train you in the simple forms of safety. If you do launch from the harbor and choose to pass the breakwater, a half mile straight out is a green buoy that is usually packed with seals basking in the sun. Make a slow approach, and you can easily get within five feet. Otherwise, just enjoy the coast, but remember that it's easy to paddle out and it's always longer to come back. Winds, currents, and fatigue could mean it ends up being a longer day than you had planned. Always take water and sun protection with you.

There are also companies offering guided tours of the Channel Islands, including some of the sea caves on Anacapa and Santa Cruz Islands. Some of the caves go several hundred feet into the islands and are simply spectacular with their soft color palettes of ochers, blues, and greens. Please note: Do not ever attempt to kayak into a sea cave without a knowledgeable person with you. The surges can easily lift your kayak up and smash you into the roof or sides of the caves. Yes, the caves are enticing, but if you don't know the area and how the surges affect the caves, you're asking for problems.

Paddle Sports (117 Harbor Way, 850/899-4925, www.kayaksb.com, basic kayak rental $25 for 2-hour minimum) has been around for 20 years and has a great staff. You can rent and get trained in both kayaking and paddle surfing. They also rent pedal kayaks so you can save your arms.

The **Santa Barbara Sailing Center** (at the harbor, 800/350-9090, www.sbsail.com, basic kayak rental $10–15/hr) will also take you to the islands or just along the coast. They provide single and tandem kayaks and can provide extensive kayak instruction if you want to get really serious.

Scuba Diving

The Channel Islands offer some of the best dive spots on the western seaboard. The confluence of warm tropical water and cooler waters allows for a large diversity of fish and plant life. The islands are a great day trip, which usually allows for four dives. There are other divers who prefer an ocean entrance, and you'll often see divers enter the surf breaks right off shore. The visibility can be pretty limited, as there is a long shelf here, but on a clear day without much surge you can still find a lot of sealife just 20 yards from shore.

Two places in town will certify or re-certify you. Depending on the length of your visit, you could possibly get certified over a weekend course and then dive solo, but that would take some planning. Both of the companies listed below contract with dive boats. These boats are fully loaded with hot showers, full galleys, a hot tub, breakfast, lunch, and snacks.

As a word of caution, always dive with a fully registered dive boat and divemaster. There are charter boats that will take scuba divers anywhere they want to go, but if trouble strikes an untrained staff cannot respond adequately.

Anacapa Dive Center (22 Anacapa St., 805/963-8917, www.anacapadivecenter.com, Mon.–Fri. 10 A.M.–7 P.M., Sat. 9 A.M.–6 P.M., Sun. 11 A.M.–5 P.M., certification classes $300) offers not only dive certification but also basic swimming lessons as well. Their indoor pool and vast selection of equipment allows them to service most every size individual. They contract with dive boats in both Santa Barbara and Ventura to access the islands and have one-day dive trips up to four-day trips. You can rent anything and everything from them. If you use or want to use Nitrox, they have specialty courses and gear for that as well.

Santa Barbara Aquatics (5822 Hollister Ave., Goleta, 805/967-4456, www.sbaquatics.com, Mon.–Fri. 10 A.M.–6 P.M., Sat.–Sun. 10 A.M.–4 P.M., certification classes $269) also teaches classes for first-time divers and re-certifies divers who've been away from scuba for a long time. They have their own 92-degree indoor pool and use a dive boat out of Ventura for single-day and multi-day dive trips. They also have a small store with wetsuits and a variety of diving gear. They do not offer Nitrox, however.

Surfing

Surfers are a protective lot—they don't want you horning in on their special breaks. Nonetheless, Santa Barbara has many prime surf spots and since the coast extends for more than 50 miles, chances are you will find a spot that suits you. The best time to surf is in the winter and fall is second best. Storms in the North Pacific generate swells as they approach the West Coast, making for strong waves. Spring swells, on the other hand, tend to be wind generated and are therefore often less powerful.

The Rincon is the undisputed king of the surf spots, with a large point break. Rincon straddles Ventura and Santa Barbara Counties and gets insanely crowded. A long right point break with several distinct lineups means that

if you can connect the entire point, it's a ride over a mile long. Exit Highway 101 at Bates Road (going north or south) and park in either the county or the state lot. It fills up quickly, so you may have to park up on Bates.

By contrast, **Leadbetter Point** across from City College offers small fun, easy waves, good for beginners. There are a lot of peaks along this small right point break, which is set below Shoreline Park in a small protected cove. There are outdoor showers and restrooms. Take Cabrillo Boulevard past Stearns Wharf and turn left into the pay parking lot.

Campus Point/Isla Vista Cliffs, a small right point break, is located at UCSB on the eastern edge of the campus at the base of the lagoon. On the western edge of the campus is Devereux Point, commonly known as Coal Oil Point, which is another right break with many peaks. It gets crowded sometimes, as students can simply cross the street from their dorms and hit the waves. You'll also see lots of longboarders and some tar from natural oil upwellings near the aptly named Coal Oil Point. There are outdoor showers and restrooms.

If surfing is new to you and it sounds like fun, or if you just want to brush up on your skills, **Surf Happens Surf School** (1117 Las Olas Ave., 805/966-3613, www.surfhappens.com, by appointment, individual classes $80/hr) will teach you the basics individually, as a couple, or even for a team-building exercise. Group rates drop the price, but it's still dependent on how many people are in your group.

BEACH VOLLEYBALL

There's nothing more "California" than beach volleyball. Beaches in Santa Barbara have nets already in the sand for you, but they are first come, first served. Bring your own ball, or even a badminton set for that matter, and spike, make a kill, and eat the sand, all while getting a tan. If you start to overheat, you're steps away from the water.

East Beach (1400 E. Cabrillo Blvd., daily sunrise–10 P.M.) is the single best spot to play beach volleyball. Located across from the zoo, there is a shady and grassy area near Cabrillo

Boulevard to beat the heat and grab a bench. Plus you have the Cabrillo Pavilion Bathhouse (1118 E. Cabrillo Blvd., 805/897-2680, Mon.–Fri. 8 A.M.–5 P.M., Sat.–Sun. 11 A.M.–4 P.M.), an oceanfront facility that is one of the best-kept secrets in town. Built in 1927, this place is open to the public and has showers, lockers, a weight room, and a beach wheelchair. The on-site East Beach Grill is great for a quick bite to eat.

Just down the shore, **West Beach** (Cabrillo Blvd. between Stearns Wharf and the harbor, daily sunrise–10 P.M.) is an 11-acre picturesque sandy area. There is no shade here for protection, but you are within walking distance to the wharf and across the street from hotels.

Even further down the shore is **Leadbetter Beach** (Shoreline Dr. and Loma Alta, daily sunrise–10 P.M.), which has courts as well. Sandwiched between the Santa Barbara harbor and adjacent to Shoreline Park, which is just up the hill, there are shaded grass areas and picnic tables, and you're next to Shoreline Café for a snack or smoothie to recharge you.

SPAS

"Spa" is a pretty loose term these days, and can encompass a variety of treatments. Many spas focus on gentle pampering, with facials and the like, but not all provide the same services. It's best to know what you're looking for first, then find a spa to meet your needs.

Healing Circle Massage (805/680-1984, www.healingcirclemassage.com, by appointment only, basic one-hour massage $80) is where you go to get the kinks worked out. This isn't fluffy pampering with hot stones while sipping cocktails; this is serious deep-tissue and trigger-point work. Owner Kathy Gruver works on hard-core athletes and anyone with chronic pain–related problems, and specializes in medical and therapeutic massage—not for the faint of heart. In addition to returning range of motion to stressed-out individuals, she also does pre-natal massage, health consultations, Reiki, and Bach flower essences. While many places actually give you a 50-minute massage and call it an hour, at Healing Circle you get a full hour.

Acupuncture, aromatherapy, spa parties, warm seaweed wraps, and waxing are just some of the offerings from **Crimson Day Spa** (31 Parker Way, 805/563-7546, www.crimsondayspa.com, Mon. noon–4 P.M., Tues.–Sat. 10 A.M.–5 P.M., and by appointment, basic one-hour massage $80). The space is uncluttered, with nice touches of decor to suggest relaxation, and they are very professional and have developed a loyal following.

Avia Spa (350 Chapala St., 805/730-7303, www.aviaspa.com, Mon.–Wed. and Fri. 10 A.M.–6 P.M., Thurs. 10 A.M.–8 P.M., Sun. 11 A.M.–6 P.M., basic one-hour massage $100) offers a wealth of services, including tanning beds (both sunless and UV), massage, and salon and spa services like nail and foot care, all housed in a bamboo-accented interior with wood floors and an Asian-inspired decor. They also have their own line of skin-care products.

Float Luxury Spa (18 E. Canon Perdido, 805/845-7777, www.floatluxuryspa.com, Mon.–Sat. 9 A.M.–7 P.M., Sun. 10 A.M.–6 P.M., basic one-hour massage $100) is one of the newest additions to the spa scene, aiming for a day-spa concept, where you can stay for hours. Located downtown, their space is surprisingly large, sleek, and uncluttered. They offer the usual treatments like massage, facials, and the rest, but out back is a beautiful rectangular tiled reflecting pool, a great spot to get lunch or to take a deep breath. Upstairs they have a quiet space, a nearly solid white room with chairs fronting a fireplace; here you can sit and detox.

Le Reve (21 W. Guttierez, 805/564-2977, www.le-reve.com, Mon.–Tues. 10 A.M.–3 P.M., Wed. 10 A.M.–6 P.M., Thurs.–Fri. 10 A.M.–7 P.M., Sat. 9 A.M.–5 P.M., Sun. 10 A.M.–5 P.M., basic one-hour massage $95) is the only green-certified spa in town. If you love lavender, Le Reve ("the dream") offers an aromatherapy massage or body wrap. Located downtown near the freeway, this spa uses Jurlique products, which have plant-based and herbal ingredients such as lavender. They also offer Girls Night Out every Wednesday from 6 to 8 P.M., which starts off with a glass of champagne and chocolate, then it's off to relaxation. They also offer waxing and tinting and a host of other services.

Qui Si Bella (3311 State St., 805/682-0003, www.quisibella.com, Mon. noon–5 p.m., Tues.–Sat. 10 a.m.–7 p.m., Sun. 10 a.m.–5 p.m., basic one-hour massage $80) handles manicures and pedicures, scrubs and facials, in an Italian-designed spa on Upper State Street. They also perform massages and microdermabrasion, and bath soaks in coconut milk. Or, get an ion-cleanse foot bath before your walks on the beach.

Accommodations

Santa Barbara has never been an inexpensive place to stay. Regardless of time of year, weather, even economic downturns, people continue to flock to the area—and they pay for the privilege of hanging out here. Be prepared to spend some cash, and don't expect much negotiating. The bed tax is currently at 12 percent; make sure to factor that into your travel plans and budget. Most properties will require a two-night minimum stay during the peak summer season.

DOWNTOWN

The great thing about staying downtown is that you don't need a car. You walk out your door and you're close to shopping, restaurants, galleries, and bars. On the flip side, weekend evenings can get noisy, and there's a lot of foot traffic on State Street.

Under $200

◖ **The Presidio Motel** (1620 State St., 805/963-1355, www.thepresidiomotel.com, $150–175 d) is several blocks up State and is a very cool motel. The 16 rooms are minimalist, but each one has unique designs created by UCSB students, like abstract stars or a girl holding a parasol as she walks a tightrope above the gaping jaws of an alligator. It's not in the thick of things, but you can still easily access many activities by walking a little farther. They have complimentary beach cruisers so you can explore on two wheels, and an upstairs sun deck from which to watch the happenings on State. A continental breakfast and free Wi-Fi add to the allure. The young owners are dedicated to making the motel a must-stop for those who want something different.

Just a few blocks closer to downtown, the **El Prado Inn** (1601 State St., 805/966-0807, www.elpradoinn.com, $155–175 d) is a family owned three-story hotel built in 1960. The 67 rooms and suites all have nice decor, but are pretty standard. There's a pool and some rooms have views of the mountains. The best part of staying here is the price, which, for Santa Barbara, is a deal. The El Prado is nothing fancy, but they offer good clean accommodations, with continental breakfast and microwaves and refrigerators in the rooms.

At the **Best Western Encina Lodge** (2220 Bath St., 805/682-7277, www.encinalodge.com, $175–195 d), 122 good-sized rooms are decorated with a country motif; the suites are great for an extended stay. Located on a residential street near a hospital, it's an out-of-the-way place and fairly quiet. They have a heated pool, small aviary, free Wi-Fi, and free shuttle service to the airport and train station. It's not really within walking distance to much, so you will probably need a car if you stay here.

$200-300

The super-under-the-radar ◖ **Inn of the Spanish Garden** (915 Garden St., 805/564-4700, www.spanishgardeninn.com, $265–285) is so unknown that most locals don't even know where it is. Tucked off of State Street, this Spanish-style full-service hotel aims for stellar service while keeping a low profile. All 23 rooms are beautifully appointed and have either balconies or patios facing a central courtyard. They have high-end linens and French press coffeemakers, plus generous bathrooms. It's an easy three-block walk to the action, but

© MICHAEL CERVIN

Hip and minimalist, The Presidio Motel distinguishes itself from the Spanish architecture that dominates the city.

you'll love returning to the luxurious beds and deep baths and large showers. It's something of a secret that many celebrities stay here because it's so low-key.

◖ **The Upham Hotel** (1404 De La Vina St., 805/962-0058, www.uphamhotel.com, $220–325 d) is the oldest continuously operating hotel in Santa Barbara, having opened its doors as the Lincoln House in 1871. A Historic Hotel of America, the property has seven buildings, though it feels much more intimate, and is predominantly centered about a garden courtyard. There are smaller rooms, ideal for a busy weekend, or larger rooms with fireplaces for a stay-in weekend. The Upham has an attached restaurant, Louie's, but you're also within walking distance of State Street or a cab ride from the beach. There are varying degrees of antiquity within the hotel, with some rooms from the 1800s and 1920s.

Similar in style is the **Cheshire Cat Inn** (36 W. Valerio, 805/569-1610, www.cheshirecat.com, $159–299 d), which has adopted an Alice in Wonderland theme. The 17 rooms

and cottages in this Queen Anne 1894 building are decorated, though not with the wild, goofy colors you'd expect—there's a more restrained English country feel to the rooms, some of which have fireplaces, hot tubs, and balconies. Full breakfasts are included, as is an evening wine and cheese reception; there's free Wi-Fi and off-street parking. It's quiet here, in spite of being just a few blocks from the action on State Street.

Also quiet is the remarkable **James House** (1632 Chapala St., 805/569-5853, www.jameshousesantabarbara.com, $259 d), a historic 1894 Queen Anne property with only five rooms, nicely appointed with period-style furnishings and hardwood floors. The bathrooms have all been upgraded to more modern amenities, but the rooms will remind you of time gone by. Breakfast cooked by the owner herself is served each morning. People return here again and again for the hospitality, the small number of rooms, the walking distance to much of State Street, and just the thrill of being in a property where time slows down as it does here.

The Upham Hotel, the oldest operating hotel in Santa Barbara, has welcomed guests since the 1870s.

Holiday Express Hotel Virginia (17 W. Haley, 805/963-9757, www.hotelvirginia.com, $205–230 d) is just off State Street with easy access to shopping and dining. The lobby screams Spanish, with its tiled floors and a fountain dead center. Some of the 61 rooms have balconies with partial views to the mountains; a complimentary continental breakfast is served in the lobby or brought to your room. The rooms are nicely appointed and a bit small, and the place dates from 1916. This is a great get-out-and-explore hotel—don't choose it if you plan to stay inside.

If staying inside is part of your plan, then the **Bath Street Inn** (1720 Bath St., 800/549-2284, www.bathstreetinn.com, $160–225 d) might be your digs. A dozen rooms are available, most of which, though beautifully decorated in a French country motif, are a bit small—but then again, this is an old house from the 1890s and rooms were smaller back then. Breakfasts include fresh fruit, house-made granola, and egg dishes. In the afternoons the rooms smell of cakes, brownies, and cookies, which are yours for the taking. Around dinnertime they'll pour you a glass of wine before you search for food. Staff is very accommodating and helpful.

If being right downtown is what you want, the **Hotel Santa Barbara** (533 State St., 805/957-9300, www.hotelsantabarbara.com, $229–249 d) is a good choice—it's directly on State Street, right where the action is. You walk out your door and everything is within walking distance. The 75 rooms are nicely appointed and comfortable, if a tad small for the standard rooms. Copious amounts of tile work inside will give you that Santa Barbara feel. The pillows are either down, feather, or hypoallergenic. There are in-room coffeemakers, but there's also a Starbucks on the premises. There is no on-site gym, but they offer a package with a local gym (that you would need to drive to). They offer a basic continental breakfast.

Over $300

The best selling point of **The Canary Hotel** (31 W. Carrillo, 805/884-0300, www.canary-santabarbara.com, $430–445 d), other than its dead-center location in town, is the rooftop deck with a pool and fireplace. On summer nights you can lounge here for hours under the stars with some pretty excellent views. The smartly designed interiors have a Moroccan feel with Spanish undertones and hardwood floors—it's kind of like a modern-day Casablanca. They have the best access to State Street and all that it offers. The 97 rooms and suites are a little small for the money, but beautifully done. The drawback is that it's across the street from the bus terminal and a gas station, but if you don't look out your window you'll never notice.

The **Simpson House Inn** (121 E. Arrellaga, 805/963-7067, www.simpsonhouseinn.com, $255–475 d) bed-and-breakfast features a total of 16 opulent rooms on an 1874 estate with a well-manicured and formal English garden—you'll feel like you're in another world. A vegetarian breakfast starts the day, afternoon tea and desserts are available midday, and an evening wine-tasting brings it to a close. They offer croquet and a day pass to a local fitness club, and they boast gratuity-free services. Situated on a corner lot in a residential section, it's a short walk to State Street.

OCEANFRONT
Under $200

The **Harbor House Inn** (104 Bath St., 805/962-9745, www.harborhouseinn.com, $149–209 d) is a great little property a half block from the water. They'll loan you beach towels, chairs, and umbrellas for lounging at West Beach, and bikes to ride there. The 17 rooms and studios are surprisingly well appointed, with a more home-like feel than most hotels, and they have a respectable amount of furnishings—the kind you'd find in someone's house. Best of all, you won't break the bank.

With a pseudo-1950 retro flair to their interiors, the **Avania Inn** (128 Castillo St., 805/963-4471, www.avaniainnsantabarbara.com, $175–195 d) is just a block up from the beach in an unremarkable two-story motel building. But the rooms are cool and hip, and you're saving some clams at this 46-room, five-suite pad.

Perhaps the best thing they offer, in addition to standard fare like a simple breakfast and proximity to the beach, is the small redwood spa and heated outdoor pool. They will give you a free morning paper so you can plan your day.

$200-300

(**Santa Barbara Inn** (901 E. Cabrillo Blvd., 800/231-0431, www.santbarbarainn.com, $279–299) is prime oceanfront property. The 69 spacious rooms all have a palm motif, from the bedding to the furniture to actual palm trees inside. Most rooms face the water, with private balconies and sliding glass doors; some face the mountains. There's an outdoor pool and hot tub, and you're literally steps from the beach with unfettered views. The trolley stops directly in front of the hotel, so you can go carless with ease. They provide a continental breakfast each morning and offer free Wi-Fi.

The **Villa Rosa Inn** (15 Chapala St., 805/966-0851, www.villarosainnsb.com, $229–279 d) is deceptive from the outside. The small door in what looks like someone's house a half block from the beach seems nearly hidden, except for the sign. But beyond the door is a beautiful hideaway with a Mediterranean feel and luxurious antiques. The 18 rooms are all vastly different, and it's intimate and very comfortable. All rooms have views—of the ocean, mountains, harbor, or courtyard—though some are constrained and the bathrooms are a little small. They claim they are only 84 steps to the beach. They offer evening port or sherry by the fire and a continental breakfast.

(**Brisas del Mar** (223 Castillo, 805/966-2219, www.brisasdelmarinn.com, $267–297 d) is located just two blocks from the beach. Half of their rooms are larger suites with full kitchens, making this 31-room hotel great for a longer getaway. Though the exterior is Mediterranean, the interiors have knotty pine furnishings and soft tones. There's covered parking, something unusual for most hotels in town, as well as a collection of over 800 DVD, Wi-Fi, an exercise room, continental breakfast, and a gracious staff. There's an outdoor shower by the pool.

The 42 guest rooms at the **Inn by the Harbor** (433 W. Montecito St., 805/963-7851, www.innbytheharbor.com, $225–269 d) are decorated with Spanish Mediterranean–style furnishings, all slightly different. Many rooms feature full-sized kitchens, ideal for budget vacations or extended stays. In addition to a deluxe continental breakfast and afternoon wine and cheese, they serve evening milk and cookies. Bud Bottoms, a local artist who created the bronze dolphins that are at the entrance to Stearns Wharf, created the dolphin sculpture in front of the inn.

If you're growing weary of the Spanish themes, try the **Colonial Beach Inn** (206 Castillo, 805/963-4317, www.colonial-beachinn.com, $235–265 d), which is very thematically different than most places in town. Just two blocks from the beach, it has 23 nicely appointed rooms, some with 15-foot ceilings, that give a nod to southern charm. Rose bushes flank the entrance, and the tiny hot tub—about big enough for two people—is protected by a vine-covered fence so you can have privacy. They offer a continental breakfast and free Wi-Fi, and there's a heated pool.

The **Mason Beach Inn** (324 W. Mason, 805/962-3203, www.masonbeachinn.com, $239–269 d) is a pretty simple whitewashed hotel with 45 rooms that feature standard furnishings. But it's clean, close to the beach and harbor, and right across from the Carriage Museum. It's not fancy, but it is a fine base for accessing the beach and downtown while saving some cash. They offer a heated outdoor pool and hot tub, basic continental breakfast, and free Wi-Fi.

The **Inn at East Beach** (2019 Orilla Del Mar, 805/965-0546, www.innateastbeach.com, $250–275 d), just steps away from the beach and the zoo, is a 33-room hotel offering slightly larger than normal rooms but without all the Spanish trappings and just a hint of retro. From the outside it looks more like an apartment complex, but don't let that fool you. They provide free Wi-Fi, continental breakfast, beach towels, chairs and umbrellas, and even boogie boards. Some of the rooms have fireplaces and there's an outdoor pool.

Over $300

The Harbor View Inn (28 W. Cabrillo Blvd., 800/755-0222, www.harborviewinnsb.com, $325–375 d) has a plum spot at the intersection of State Street and Stearns Wharf. Of course, you pay for such proximity. But this high-end amenity-filled property, wrapped in red-tile roofs and Mexican-tiled stairways and fountains, is classic Santa Barbara. There are 102 rooms and 13 suites, an in-house restaurant, a pool, a spa, and, frankly, all you'd need to make your stay in town wonderful. There are in-room safes, free Wi-Fi, and quick access to the beach and activities.

Not too far down the beach is the **Fess Parker DoubleTree Resort** (633 E. Cabrillo Blvd., 805/564-4333, www.fessparkerdouble-treehotel.com, $410–455 d), a Mission-style spread with four restaurants, an exercise facility, three tennis courts, shuffle board, and a putting green, all just across from the beach. The 360 rooms face either the mountain or the beach; a few face the interior courtyard. Even their small rooms are pretty large, and you can't beat the location if you like being close to the water. They offer a free shuttle to the airport and train station, but charge a fee for parking.

UPPER STATE STREET

Staying just outside the money zone is not necessarily a bad idea. Sure, you don't have the ocean views and are not close to downtown, but if you save some cash on your room you can spend it elsewhere.

Under $200

⚑ Agave Inn (3222 State St., 805/687-6009, www.agaveinnsb.com, $169–189 d) uses the Spanish theme a little differently: Spanish movie posters and brightly colored throws as well as various brightly painted walls are the accents that set this place apart. It's like a bit of modern pop was tossed into each of the 13 rooms, where you'll also find iPod docks. Agave Inn is directly across from a small park and near Loreto Plaza, a small shopping center with a grocery store and restaurants. The freeway is close, as is downtown. Some rooms come with full kitchens, and the inn is a delightful spot, very cool, hip, and simple.

$200-300

Amid the visually unappealing architecture on Upper State Street is the **Best Western Pepper Tree Inn** (3850 State St., 805/687-5511, www.bestwesternpeppertreeinn.com, $225–255), a five-acre locally owned property. The 150-room building is large by Santa Barbara standards, but you're close to the freeway and right across the street from La Cumbre Mall. The private decks and balconies look over a central courtyard where the pool is located. Though the style is somewhat Spanish, it's a more classic hotel interior with standard furnishings. The rooms are large enough but a little dark, as the one window faces the courtyard and you may not want your sliding door open. There are two pools, two hot tubs, and a fitness center. They offer shuttle service to the airport and train station.

GOLETA
Under $200

Ramada Unlimited (4770 Calle Real, Goleta, 805/964-3511, www.sbramada.com, $149–189 d) is a locally owned and operated Ramada, about a 10-minute drive from downtown. The best rooms and suites face the mountains, and every one of the 126 rooms has a small refrigerator, a microwave, and a coffeemaker. Dead center in the hotel, near the outdoor pool, is an amazing tropical lagoon with water lilies, palms, and koi. The rooms are standard, but also less expensive than downtown.

$200-300

Further out in Goleta the **Pacifica Suites** (5490 Hollister Ave., Goleta, 805/683-6722, www.pacificasuites.com, $249–269 d) has 87 suites with separate sleeping and living areas. Some of the interior design are rather boring andformal, but they are large rooms and there is a heated pool and a cooked to order breakfast. There's more of a business clientele here, which means there aren't noisy gatherings and parties.

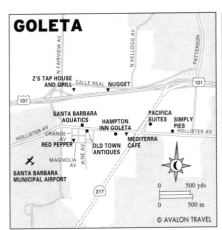

Rooms include microwave and refrigerators, free Wi-Fi and they have a free airport shuttle, even though the airport is five minutes away.

Hampton Inn Goleta (5665 Hollister Ave., Goleta, 805/681-9800, http://hampton-inn1.hilton.com, $229–249 d) is a 98-room hotel located near the heart of Goleta, and within a two-minute drive of Goleta beach. The rooms are a nice size, larger than standard accommodations, and there are in-room coffeemakers. A continental breakfast is included. The hotel tends to attract business travelers, and there is a business center and meeting facilities on-site, as well as a small exercise room, a hot tub, and a smaller pool. The staff is quiet and professional.

Over $300

If money is no object and you want a luxury lodging close to the beach, the **Bacara Resort and Spa** (8310 Hollister Ave., Goleta, 877/422-4245, www.bacararesort.com, from $475) is ideal. It is a 360 room Andalusian-style village of suites and rooms just steps from the crashing surf. Perched on 80 acres of prime Pacific coast shoreline it is also exclusive and expensive, but that is the point. The rooms are large, with sliding doors to views of the ocean. It's all five-star here, and with the multiple restaurants, spa, and even a little shopping on-site, you may not spend a million bucks, but you're sure to feel like a million bucks when you stay here. Amenities include 24-hour in-room dining, personalized voice mail, and free Wi-Fi.

Montecito
$200-300

That Charlie Chaplin founded the **(Montecito Inn** (1295 Coast Village Rd., 805/969-7854, www.montecitoinn.com, $265–285 d) is of no small importance. In the late 1920s Chaplin wanted a getaway from the hectic Hollywood crowd, and so built the inn, more so his friends could escape with him than as an actual inn. These days it's still as charming as it was intended. The 61 rooms are small, the halls even smaller, but that's how life was back then. This is a wonderful historic property; vintage Chaplin posters line the walls, and there's a collection of Chaplin's DVDs to watch in your room. Visitors also have free use of the beach cruisers, or jump into the heated pool or sweat in the exercise room. The hotel is only two blocks from the beach and on Coast Village Road, the heart of the tony Montecito shopping district.

Over $300

There's no place quite like **The Four Seasons Biltmore** (1260 Channel Dr., 805/969-2742, www.fourseasons.com, from $425), which sits just above Butterfly Beach in Montecito and has long held its ground as one of the best

places to stay. It's laid out like a small Spanish village, with lush landscaping including ferns and bright red bougainvillea set against the whitewashed hand-troweled walls creating an almost tropical feel. The rooms continue the Spanish theme with large ornate furniture. You can walk to shopping and restaurants on Coast Village Road, or drive into downtown. In addition to tennis courts and exercise rooms, guests are able to access the exclusive Cabana Club next door, a private club for members and guests only. The Cabana Club's historic 1937 structure was renovated 2005–2008 and now has a post-modern interior. There's a large pool, cabanas, and a play room for the kids, and it has an excellent restaurant where sliding doors on the 2nd floor open up to expansive views of the ocean.

If a mountain retreat is more your style, the **San Ysidro Ranch** (900 San Ysidro Ln., 805/565-1700, www.sanysidroranch.com, from $795) has 41 individually and lushly appointed rustic cottages and suites tucked neatly into the mountains with exceptional ocean views. Rooms range from small and intimate to the 1,300-square-foot Kennedy Cottage, where John Kennedy and his new bride, Jackie, honeymooned in 1953. There are two restaurants on the property and 17 miles of hiking trails. In-room spa services are available, and pets are welcome.

Food

There's a long-standing claim that Santa Barbara has more restaurants per capita than any other place in the United States. That's never been proven, nor disproven, but with everything from taco stands to five-star restaurants, you will definitely find something you like. Touristy places are not always the best choice. There's a lot of average food in town, so seek out the exceptional.

DOWNTOWN

Many restaurants in downtown Santa Barbara have outdoor seating, and it's not unusual to

see long waits on summer nights. Not all places take reservations, but many do—make reservations if you can. Many of the restaurants serve what is loosely labeled "wine country cuisine," which is to say local fresh foods and ingredients used in lighter dishes, not heavily laden with sauces, that pair well with local wines. Specifically, this means fresh fish from the harbor, fresh veggies and fruits from the many local farmers, and locally sourced meats—not processed foods, but foods that are inherently, naturally flavorful.

MARKET FORAYS

Market Forays (805/259-7229, www.marketforays.com, Tues. 3-8:30 P.M., Sat. 8 A.M.-3:30 P.M., $145) is a unique hands-on cooking class – the very cool idea was started by the founder of the local slow-food movement. You spend the day meeting with local fishermen, then spend time at the farmers market, all while obtaining fresh food you will then use to cook an ideal Santa Barbara meal. The point is to get people in touch with farmers and local suppliers, to get to know them and gain an understanding and appreciation for one's food.

Wine Country Cuisine

Opal Restaurant and Bar (1325 State St., 805/966-9676, www.opalrestaurantand-bar.com, Mon.–Thurs. 11:30 A.M.–2:30 P.M. and 5–10 P.M., Fri.–Sat. 11:30 A.M.–2:30 P.M. and 5–11 P.M., Sun. 5–10 P.M., $20) is eternally popular with locals. With fresh pastas, seafood, salads, and steaks, plus a well-rounded wine list with over 300 selections, Opal succeeds every time. The owners have been part of the Santa Barbara dining scene for over two decades, and some of their staff have been with them for nearly as long. The interior is soft yellow tones and dark hardwoods, and the place is noisy, lively, and energetic.

At **Julienne** (138 E. Canon Perdido, 805/845-6488, www.restaurantjulienne.com, Wed.–Sat. 5–10 P.M., Sun. 5–9 P.M., $25), chef Jason West uses vegetables pulled from the ground that day and seafood that's arrived on the dock that morning. The small space with only 12 tables has a bistro feel to it, and the menu rotates as often as every few days, so you often can't come back and order the same thing. The menu is limited, and at first you might think you want more options. But the food (and service) is excellent; be adventurous and let the thoughtfully prepared food work its magic. Things you may have thought you didn't like are masterpieces in the chef's hands.

Arts & Letters Café (7 E. Anapamu St., 805/730-1463, www.sullivangoss.com, lunch Mon.–Sun. 11 A.M.–3 P.M., dinner Wed.–Sun. 5–9 P.M., $18) is sequestered behind the Sullivan Goss Art Gallery, and you need to walk through the gallery to reach the secluded back patio. Once there you'll feel like you're a world away. Try their excellent pumpkin soup, which was written up in the *New York Times,* the smoked-salmon pot stickers, or their very best salad, with warm lamb on top of baby spinach with feta cheese. You'll be looking at beautiful art on the walls, and beautiful food on your plate. You needn't buy any art, but you might be so pleased with your meal that a new painting could be the perfect ending.

Bouchon (9 W. Victoria, 805/730-1160, www.bouchonsantabarbara.com, Sun.–Thurs. 5:30–9 P.M., Fri.–Sat. 5:30–10 P.M., $30) is classic farm-fresh Santa Barbara cuisine, paired with local wines. The small space, with simple country furnishings that belie the complex food, also has an outdoor covered patio. The kitchen excels at most everything it does, including foie gras, venison, and stellar duck breast. You pay dearly for this kind of food and service, but the fresh, flavorful food will leave you hankering for more. The staff knows what Santa Barbara wines pair well with your food.

The **Museum Café** (1130 State St., 805/884-6487, Tues.–Sun. 11 A.M.–5 P.M., $15) is located inside the Museum of Art, and though they are not affiliated with the museum, they make a treasure trove of flavorful food. There's an emphasis on tapas, small plates of one-bite wonders like chicken empanaditas and Spanish potato tortilla, and they are getting busy as the word is spreading about this little jewel. The interior feels more like an upscale cafeteria, but the food relies on spices and seasonings to command your attention. The flourless chocolate torte is rich and decadent, and worth the small amount they charge for it.

Blush Restaurant and Lounge (630 State St., 805/957-1300, www.blushsb.com, daily 11 A.M.–10 P.M., late-night menu Mon.–Sat. 10 P.M.–midnight, $25) is hip, sleek, and very cool inside. Big comfy booths line up against exposed brick walls, and glass balls of light suspended by thin wire give the illusion of stars hanging in mid-air. The long outdoor area has couches and three fireplaces. Fortunately, the food matches the cool ambience. Juniper chicken and a surprisingly excellent and unusual beet carpaccio are some of the creative dishes they have come up with. There's a crowded bar and it gets loud inside, but dining outside on a couch near the fireplace while watching people amble down State Street is a fine experience.

The **Wine Cask** (813 Anacapa St., 805/966-9463, nightly 5:30–9 P.M., $30) has been one of the most influential restaurants in town for over 25 years; it was one of the first to create wine pairings with food. Several years back it was sold to an out-of-town interest who fouled it up tremendously. It was then taken back by the original owner and a new partner, and now it's the flagship restaurant for wine country cuisine that people have always expected, with attentive service and well-executed innovative dishes like pistachio and watercress soup, cassoulet of duck leg confit, pork cheeks and rabbit sausage, and pan-seared salmon.

At **Jane** (1311 State St., 805/962-1311, Mon.–Sat. 11:30 A.M.–2:30 P.M. and 5:30–10 P.M., $17), two interior balconies flank the main dining room, and the vaulted ceilings feature exposed wood beams and an apex skylight. A long communal wood table in the center of the space gives diners a new option. But the coolest spot is the minuscule balcony, with just two tables overlooking State Street. The menu is tried and true formula, with veal scaloppini, turkey sandwiches, and lamb fettuccini, similar to their Montecito eatery, the Montecito Cafe. It can get a tad noisy during the lunch and dinner rush, but it's a cozy, familiar environment and locals have taken to it in droves.

One of the single best spots for alfresco dining is **Pierre Lafond Wine Bistro** (516 State St., 805/962-6607, www.pierrelafond.com, Mon.–Fri. 9 A.M.–9 P.M., Sat.–Sun. 8 A.M.–9 P.M., $20). The interior, with its large plate-glass windows fronting State Street, feels somewhat industrial and lacks a motif, but that doesn't belie the quality of the food. The exterior gated patio allows all kinds of people-watching and is the prime place to be. The food choices are creative, like the grilled Hawaiian escolar, a goat cheese and onion tart, or the chicken chorizo omelet. Since this is owned by the Santa Barbara Winery, you'll see plenty of their wines offered along with a wide selection from around the globe.

Argentinian

Café Buenos Aires (1316 State St., 805/963-0242, www.cafebuenosaires.com, Mon.–Fri. 11:30 A.M.–2:30 P.M. and 5:30 P.M.–close, Sat.–Sun. 11:30 A.M.–3:30 P.M. and 5 P.M.–close, $20) offers food from the owners' home country of Argentina. A central fountain is surrounded by tables on a patio that allows for fresh air and people-watching. On Wednesday evenings, live tango music and dancing fills the patio for those who want to burn a few calories. On weekend nights, Latin jazz takes center stage. The menu offers traditional South American dishes of beef, pork, and fish, as well as vegetarian options. Keeping with the theme, they pour Argentina's most well-known wine, malbec, by the glass and bottle.

French

Petit Valentien (1114 State St., 805/966-0222, lunch Mon.–Fri. 11:30 A.M.–3 P.M., dinner Wed.–Sat. 5–9 P.M., $20) has the feel of a classic neighborhood bistro, a familiar, comfortable place you want to return to. The high ceiling and soft yellow walls taper down to dark wood chairs, bar, and floors, punctuated by granite tabletops. The storefront windows facing the paseo are fully opened up during nice weather, and it feels like you're in Paris. Potato-crusted chicken breast, sautéed frog legs, and delicately breaded and pan-sautéed veal Milanese are some of the standout dishes. The food relies on simple, light sauces, avoiding clumsy and heavy food.

Another delightful spot is the often-overlooked **◖ Pacific Crêpes** (705 Anacapa St., 805/882-1123, www.pacificcrepe.com, Mon.

10 A.M.–3 P.M., Tues.–Fri. 10 A.M.–3 P.M. and 5:30–9 P.M., Sat. 9 A.M.–9 P.M., Sun. 9 A.M.–3 P.M., $18). The interior is laden with French posters, and books line the walls. It's an intimate space, with simple French country decor and indoor and outdoor seating. They use buckwheat as their main ingredient—traditional for crepes in Brittany where the owners are from—hence the brown color. The fillings are as diverse as you could want, and the crepes are surprisingly large. Also be sure to try the french onion soup, escargot, and the wonderful profiteroles. Each Wednesday conversational French classes are held 5:30–7:30 P.M.

Middle Eastern

Zaytoon (209 E. Canon Perdido, 805/963-1293, www.cafezaytoon.com, Mon.–Sat. 11:30 A.M.–9 P.M., Sun. 5–9 P.M., $25) is an amalgam of Middle Eastern foods, from Lebanese wine to Turkish coffee and immensely flavorful tabbouli, hummus, and lamb, all spicy and earthy. This is a lounging spot with plenty of outdoor tables, belly dancers, and hookah. This is not a place for a quick bite to eat, however, as the service can be pretty slow, especially on weekend nights, but it's a great overall experience. There's very little in the way of Middle Eastern food in town; fortunately Zaytoon does it well.

Indian

All India Café (431 State St., 805/882-1000, daily 11:30 A.M.–3 P.M. and 5–10 P.M., $15) offers a lunch buffet with over 15 items to choose from; it's always popular, and the Bombay chicken, poached in ginger, onion, and spices, is exceptional—or stick with the shish kebab and other traditional dishes. For a different type of drink try the *nimbu paani,* a lemonade with fresh ginger and lime juice. The decor will remind you of India, though you'll remain squarely on State Street.

Healthy Fare

Don't be alarmed by the word *vegetarian* if you're a carnivore. The 🄲 **Sojourner Cafe** (134 E. Canon Perdido, 805/965-7922,

www.sojournercafe.com, Mon.–Sat. 11 A.M.–11 P.M., Sun. 11 A.M.–10 P.M., $10), or The Soj, as it's called, will make you rethink how good vegetarian can be. Celebrating 30 years in business, they turn out some of the best food in town, with amazingly flavorful smoothies, fresh-baked cookies, and daily specials. The interior needs a face-lift, but that doesn't detract from the polenta royale, their Cobb salad using hominy, or their cornbread supreme, doused with pinto beans, veggies, garlic butter, and cheese.

🄲 **Silvergreens** (791 Chapala, 805/962-8500, www.silvergreens.com, Mon.–Wed. 7:30 A.M.–9 P.M., Thurs. 7:30 A.M.–10 P.M., Fri. 7:30 A.M.–10 P.M., Sat. 8 A.M.–10 P.M., Sun. 8 A.M.–9 P.M., $10) aims for a healthy alternative. But this doesn't mean it's all tofu and sprouts. You can get burgers, cookies, shakes, their excellent pesto pasta salad, or a breakfast scramble as well. Your order comes with a specialized receipt that tracks calories and nutritional information—and the food here tastes really good. Everything is made on-site, and the attention to detail shows. It's directly across from the Paseo Nuevo Mall so you can get out and about and burn those calories.

Spiritland Bistro (230 E. Victoria, 805/966-7759, www.spiritlandbistro.com, Wed.–Sun. 5:30–9 P.M., $25) is more high-end vegetarian, in an intimate dimly lit environment with booths and freestanding tables. They do have some chicken and fish dishes, but their menu identifies which dishes are gluten-, wheat-, and/or dairy-free. The bistro of a dozen tables manages to stay quiet even with lots of guests. They serve dinner only, and the food—like falafel salad, Thai coconut curry, and the very tasty artichoke purée—will make you realize how wonderful healthy can taste. A favorite dessert is the lavender and organic honey crème brûlée.

Mexican

At 🄲 **Chino's Rock & Tacos** (714 State St., 805/741-1888, www.chinosrocks.com, Sun.–Wed. 11 A.M.–10 P.M., Thurs.–Sat. 11 A.M.–11 P.M., $10) the interior has a rock 'n roll vibe: Large paintings of rock stars hang in the narrow space, and there is an upstairs lounge for events. You order at the counter and your food is brought to the table. Everything is made from scratch using fresh ingredients, like their grilled mahi tacos and avocado and chicken salad topped with their signature spicy cilantro dressing. It's a simple premise, and the fresh food has lots of flavor.

La Playa Azul Café (914 Santa Barbara St., 805/966-2860, Sun.–Thurs. 11:30 A.M.–9 P.M., Fri.–Sat. 11:30 A.M.–10 P.M., $18) has been dishing up Mexican fare longer than most Mexican restaurants in town. The best seating is the outdoor patio, facing Santa Barbara Street, covered with red and green umbrellas and red bougainvillea. The interior, too, is ripe with color: Mexican plates hugging the walls creating a festive, spacious, and appealing spot to dine. You'll find tostadas, shrimp and fish dishes, carne asada, and tasty margaritas.

Cheap Eats

Quick and easy is always a good option, especially when it's coupled with good prices.

◖ **D'Vine Café** (205 W. Canon Perdido St., 805/963-9591, www.dvinecafe.com, Mon.–Fri. 8 A.M.–4 P.M., Sat. 11 A.M.–3 P.M., $8) has been crafting sandwiches and salads for years, creating inexpensive, portable food that does not shock your wallet nor offend your taste buds. Insanely popular is their grilled salmon salad, and the chicken salad sandwich is great. They make wraps, and you can customize you sandwich in either a whole or half size. The place is basic to look at—indoor and outdoor seating with lots of plastic chairs. But for made-to-order food at these prices, you won't go wrong.

For pastrami lovers there is **Norton's** (18 W. Figueroa, 805/965-3210, Mon.–Fri. 11 A.M.–7 P.M., Sat. 10:30 A.M.–3:30 P.M., $8), which has the classic feel of a New York deli—small tables in a cramped space turning out food at a rapid pace. There are only four tables and four stools at the bar. Corned beef and pastrami on rye are the favorites here—sloppy, yes, but tasty. They also have standard lunch fare like ham and swiss and tuna melts. It does get busy at lunch time, so plan ahead.

For a more classic Santa Barbara experience, the **Santa Barbara Chicken Ranch** (2618 De La Vina, 805/569-1872, www.sb-chickenranch.com, daily 11 A.M.–10 P.M., $9) is all chicken and tri-tip and nothing else. It is relatively small inside, but there's plenty of outdoor seating. Faded photos line the walls and the distressed wood tables give a Western feel to the wood-toned place. Chicken or tri-tip is usually served as a plate with rice and beans. It's a simple formula and they do it well. You can get a burrito, but that's merely the same ingredients placed in a tortilla.

Bitterman's Deli (5 W. Canon Perdido, 805/965-7500, www.bittermans.com, Mon.–Fri. 8 A.M.–5 P.M., Sat. 9 A.M.–5 P.M., $8) has a thing for the old *Seinfeld* TV show, so much so that a number of sandwiches are named after the characters. One can order the George (smoked ham and swiss cheese on a French roll), the Kramer (a Hebrew national all-beef hot dog), the Elaine (dolphin-safe tuna), and even the Hello…Newman (pastrami and corned beef on rye). There's even a signed cast photo and a TV that runs continuous loops of *Seinfeld* episodes for die-hard fans. It's a great shtick, and the food is good, certainly at these non-union prices.

Breakfast and Brunch

D'Angelo Bread (25 E. Gutierrez, 805/962-5466, daily 7 A.M.–2 P.M., $15) is a hybrid: half bakery, half restaurant. The place is quaint, with tiled floors and cramped bistro tables both inside and outside. Breakfasts get crowded here—the earlier you arrive, the better. D'Angelo is known for their breads, of which they bake no less than 15 varieties every morning, such as rosemary lemon, or try their cream cheese danish, tri-berry scones, or the buckwheat waffle. To spice it up, you can't go wrong with huevos rancheros.

At **Crush Café** (1315 Anacapa St., 805/963-3752, www.crushcakes.com, daily 8 A.M.–5 P.M., $10) the cupcakery has expanded into a full-service restaurant. The old hardwood floors give way to a European country feel (a wood pitchfork is clamped against one wall, for example). It's not elaborately decorated; instead the place prefers simple wood tones. It feels homey, undoubtedly because the 100-year-old place was once a residence. They bake a lot here, including strawberry scones and cinnamon rolls. If you've been out too late the night before, try their Hangover Helper: a grilled breakfast sandwich of eggs, tomato, cheddar cheese, and bacon on sourdough, with a side of fresh fruit. Another favorite is Peace, Love, and Granola: chunky house-made granola over house-made vanilla bean yogurt and drizzled with honey.

Coffee and Tea

There are always the ubiquitous national coffee chains, but since you're in Santa Barbara, go local.

The **Santa Barbara Roasting Company** (321 Motor Way, 805/962-0320, www.sbcoffee.com, Mon.–Fri. 5:30 A.M.–9 P.M., Sat. 6 A.M.–9 P.M., Sun. 6:30 A.M.–9 P.M.) roasts their own style of beans with names like Santa Barbara Blend and Rincon Blend, all in a really cool exposed brick space with free Wi-Fi. They sell a few baked goods too. Locals call it RoCo for short, and it's almost always crowded.

At **The Daily Grind** (2001 De La Vina, 805/687-4966, Mon.–Sun. 5:30 A.M.–10 P.M.), which is one of the most popular places for early morning, the prime seats on the outside deck always seem to be taken, but there is an indoor seating area near the counter as well. This place is so full of locals that you might feel intimidated. Teas, smoothies, and an abundance of coffee drinks and 11 regular coffees are at the ready. They serve a variety of pastries made on-site and breakfast and lunch options. It's cash only.

The **Coffee Cat** (1201 Anacapa St., 805/962-7164, Mon.–Fri. 6 A.M.–7 P.M., Sat.–Sun. 7 A.M.–7 P.M.) gets a more well-dressed crowd due to its proximity to the county buildings. That doesn't mean you won't see flip-flops, shorts, and plenty of laptops at the booths, freestanding tables, or outside—all types come here. The best thing to do is to take your coffee to the Sunken Gardens at the courthouse (kitty-corner from Coffee Cat) and enjoy it outside, surrounded by the grass, trees, and simple beauty of Santa Barbara at its best. If you stay inside, head toward the raised platform with the booths that front the wall, or head to the small exterior space.

Desserts

There has been a surge of cupcake joints in recent years, but **Crushcakes** (1315 Anacapa St., 805/963-9353, www.crushcakes.com, Mon.–Sat. 9 A.M.–6 P.M., Sun. 10 A.M.–5 P.M.) takes the cake. They produce a dozen different varieties of these minicakes each day; their red velvet cake is the most popular. They also bake up a vegan cupcake. At $3 a pop they aren't cheap, but one is all you really need.

Breweries

Santa Barbara Brewing Company (501 State St., 805/730-1040, Sun.–Wed. 11 A.M.–11 P.M., Thurs.–Sat. 11 A.M.–midnight, $15) has TVs, video games, pool, food, and yes, beer. Well established in town, they offer an eclectic assortment of brews, which they make in the back. Their location right on State Street and their 15 years making brews means they have loyal followers. Come for the beer—the Rincon Red and Santa Barbara Blond are two of their best-selling styles—as the food is only so-so.

OCEANFRONT

For better or worse, the oceanfront offers a collection of average restaurants with great views. The food is standard and the service is usually hit and miss. Most visitors want ocean views, understandably. But you may find it's best to search out better food to avoid being frustrated by a bad experience. The ocean is visible from much of Santa Barbara, so save your hard-earned cash and spend it on quality food, then go walk on the beach. Listed here are some of the oceanfront places that shine.

Seafood

Brophy Brothers (119 Harbor Way, 805/966-4418, www.brophybros.com, Sun.–Thurs. 11 A.M.–10 P.M., Fri.–Sat. 11 A.M.–11 P.M.,

$25) is the exception to the oceanfront rule. Located at the harbor, it is eternally busy serving fresh local seafood in a hectic, loud environment. The prime seats are outside on a narrow strip of balcony crowded with people standing at their outdoor bar. A sunset dinner of fresh seafood here overlooking the boats is killer. Their side dishes like salad, coleslaw, and rice seem like afterthoughts, but the entrées are exceptional. They offer a raw oyster bar and the staff, while busy, are efficient. They don't take reservations, so if you arrive late, you'll find yourself in their downstairs bar waiting to be called.

The Boathouse (2981 Cliff Dr., 805/898-2628, www.sbfishhouse.com, Mon.–Fri. 7:30 A.M.–9 P.M., Sat.–Sun. 7:30 A.M.–10 P.M., $16) is located at Hendry's Beach and has clear glass panels along the beach that allow outdoor diners to enjoy perfect views without getting too much wind or ocean mist. From the open bar that looks to the beach, to the take-away window for easy access, the Boathouse feels like home. The interior uses clean lines and a blue and white theme. The white curved monolithic seating allows for views into the kitchen, if that's appealing to you. CAn ahi tuna club sandwich, lobster tacos, and Dungeness crab cakes are just a few of the fish options here.

Shoreline Beach Café (801 Shoreline Dr., 805/568-0064, Mon.–Fri. 10 A.M.–8 P.M., Sat.–Sun. 8:30 A.M.–8 P.M., $15) is, surprisingly, one of the only places where you can dine at a table that sits in the sand. The food is pretty average, but sitting at a table as you watch the kids play in the surf while munching on shark tacos or a salmon salad isn't a bad way to spend the day. They have a to-go window as well for grabbing a smoothie or a quick bite.

Italian

Emilio's (324 W. Cabrillo Blvd., 805/966-4426, www.emiliosrestaurant.com, nightly 5:30–9 P.M., $20) is one of those place off by itself that creates tremendous food, but it seems like only a handful of people know about it. The cramped interior is made to look like a bit of Italy, with rough-hewn beams and shutters on the windows and walls made to look like limestone. Flatbread pizzas, fresh pastas like simple goat cheese ravioli, and seafood with a dash of Italian flair and spices make this a great spot for dinner. The tables are tight together and the service is off a lot of the time, but the entrées and desserts are quite wonderful.

Sandwiches and Burgers

Metropulos (216 E. Yanonali, 805/899-2300, www.metrofinefoods.com, Mon.–Fri. 8:30 A.M.–6 P.M., Sat. 10 A.M.–4 P.M., $10) is a mere block from the beach and is the best place to stop to gather picnic supplies. Get a sandwich or salad to go, or some of the many olives from Africa, Spain, and Italy. Their sandwiches are wonderful, such as their apple ham brie panini on multi-grain sourdough. Ortry a cranberry goat cheese salad with spinach and organic mixed greens. They also have a small wine shop, colorful and creative pastas to cook at home, and a really moist chocolate biscotti. There are a handful of prime outdoor seats.

Union Ale (214 State St., 805/845-8423, www.unionale.com, daily 11 A.M.–midnight, $15) is bar food done right. Flavorful pizzas and juicy burgers are served in a masculine interior—lots of wood and TVs—and the outdoor area, with its retractable roof, is classic Santa Barbara. The purple-potato nachos with gorgonzola sauce are fantastic, as is the thankfully restrained BBQ chicken pizza. They have about 20 brews on tap; though it appears that they make their own brews, they are actually private labeled by Firestone Walker Brewery, the area's best mid-sized brewery.

Fusion

◖ **Santa Barbara City College** has a culinary arts program, and they offer the public the chance to sample their efforts at the on-campus **John Dunn Dining Room** (805/965-0581, ext. 2773, Thurs.–Fri. 5:30–6:30 P.M. seating only, reservations a must, $40). This is a great program and gives you the chance to enjoy a four-course meal, with wine pairing, all prepared and served by the students as part of their training. The menu has a limited number of entrées, possibly steak, seafood, or game. But the beauty is in knowing that you're helping to support future chefs and restaurateurs. The meal will take roughly two hours and they only have one seating. It's a great adventure worth checking out.

Breakfast and Brunch

For 50 years **Sambo's** (216 W. Cabrillo Blvd., 805/965-3269, www.sambosrestaurant.com, daily 6:30 A.M.–3:30 P.M., $12) has maintained this original location of its once well-established chain. But times have changed, and this is the only Sambo's left. The comfortable booths are set against mustard-colored walls in a casual environment. The front half of the restaurant has views to the beach, and black-and-white photos of the restaurant's past hang nearby. The back half is dotted with prints from *The Story Little Black Sambo,* in which an Indian boy who was harassed by tigers in the forest wisely outwits them and somehow turns them into butter. Butter, of course, goes with pancakes, which they offer, along with other popular breakfast fare, such as eggs, french toast, and their very excellent biscuits and gravy. On weekends about 10:30 A.M. there is always a wait.

Nearby is **Beachbreak Café** (324 State St., 805/962-2889, www.beachbreakcafe.com, daily 7 A.M.–2 P.M., $10), with unpretentious old red and burgundy booths and haphazard colorful murals on the walls. The outdoor seating overlooks State Street, and the freeway and train tracks are so close you can almost touch them (when the train whistle blows it might startle you). Breakfasts include the firehouse omelet, which is loaded with chili, cheese, and tons of white onion, and comes with fresh fruit. Though it's called a "firehouse," the chili is not of the four-alarm variety. It is, in fact, the same chili used by Tommy's Burgers in Los Angeles, a local chain of chili-burger joints with an incredible number of die hard fans.

UPPER STATE STREET

Far from the madding crowds—well, not too far—State Street as everyone knows it turns into Upper State, a decidedly different place than what most tourists ever see. It's mainly residential, with some restaurants worth checking out.

Italian

❰ **Via Maesta 42** (3343 State St., 805/569-6522, Mon.–Sat. 8:30 A.M.–9 P.M., Sun. 11 A.M.–5 P.M., $15), so named for the owner's address in his hometown in Alba, Italy, is located in an unremarkable strip mall right next to the post office. But this place turns out delicious, authentic Italian food, including a wide variety of pastas and cured meats. The space is small, with a few outside seats. It gets crowded and the service is a tad slow, but it's worth the wait. You can also buy Italian cheeses, meats, and gelato to go. During truffle season, they import both white and black truffles from Italy for sale to the public can buy, several restaurants in town also purchase their truffles here.

Petrini's Family Restaurant (14 W. Calle Laureles, 805/687-8888, Mon.–Sat. 11 A.M.–10 P.M., Sun. 11 A.M.–9 P.M., $12) is going on 50 years in business in town. It isn't fancy, classy, or pretentious, but they turn out pizza, linguini, and a great manicotti all at prices that won't break the bank. The red and white checkered tablecloths and the walls, painted with Italian countryside scenes, are classic old-time Italian, just like the straw-covered Chianti bottles, but the food is solid and dependable.

German

Brummis (3130 State St., 805/687-5916, Mon.–Fri. 11:30 A.M.–1:30 P.M. and 5–9 P.M., Sat. 5–9 P.M., $20) has an inside decor as simple as spaetzle; all bare bones, with a few posters hanging loosely on the walls. But the restaurant, run by a mother and daughter team from Germany, is as authentic as you can get. A few German beers are available to complement your meal, and it's not uncommon to hear conversations in German taking place around you. Schnitzel, sauerbraten, and kasslerbraten will put the oompah in you if you have a hankering for German food.

In contrast, the **Dutch Garden** (4203 State

St., 805/967-4911, Wed.–Sat. 11 A.M.–8 P.M., $20) feels exactly like it should be located in some small German town, but they speak English here. The interior is surrounded by steins and other German paraphernalia. It's very low-key on most nights, with people barely speaking loud enough to be heard at other tables. The red and white checkered tablecloths add a bit of color. All dinner entrées come with a veggie, cabbage, soup, or salad and a potato variation such as potato salad or potato pancake. Sauerbraten and schnitzel can be consumed with any one of a dozen German beers.

French
Mimosa (2700 De La Vina, 805/682-2272, lunch Mon.–Thurs. 11 A.M.–2 P.M., dinner Tues.–Sat. 5:30–9 P.M., $20) is a 26-year veteran of the city. It has a subdued ambience, with an older clientele and lots of quiet conversation. The blue carpet and tablecloths accent salmon-colored walls and the decor is simple, but the food shines. Chicken *en croute*, Cornish game hen, and pork scaloppini are familiar dishes, but Mimosa keeps true to its French-inspired menu with food that is flavorful and straightforward. Their success is in keeping it simple and uncluttered.

Steakhouse
Tee-Off (3627 State St., 805/687-1616, www.teeoffsb.com, Mon.–Thurs. 5–10 P.M., Fri.–Sat. 5–11 P.M., Sun. 5–9 P.M., $25) is old school meets, well, old school. Tee-Off has been around for 40 years, and very little has changed. It's the kind of place where when you walk in, people immediately know if you're a local or not. (But don't worry, they're still friendly.) This is the place where the waitress will call you "hon" and mean it. Get there early for a choice seat in the red booths that face the bar and pig out on way too much food. Forget the fish or anything else and get the prime rib—that's what the locals do.

Sushi
Ahi Sushi (3631 State St., 805/687-6942, lunch Mon.–Sat. 11:30 A.M.–2:30 P.M., dinner Mon.–Thurs. 5:30–9:30 P.M., Fri.–Sat. 5:30–10 P.M., Sun. 5:30–9 P.M., $20) is one of many sushi joints in town. Their lunch and dinner menus offer a dizzying array of choices, but the Ragin' Cajun roll is the standout. Blackened salmon is wrapped with asparagus and avocado, then a blowtorch seals the spices to the roll. There are plenty of other rolls, plus sashimi, and even a few sakes if you're so inclined. There's a modern Asian feel to the place, and it fills up quickly at lunchtime.

Kyoto (3232 State St., 805/687-1252, www.kyotosb.com, lunch Mon.–Fri. 11:30 A.M.–2 P.M., Sat. noon–2:30 P.M., dinner Sun.–Thurs. 5–10 P.M., Fri.–Sat. 5–10:30 P.M., $20) is on the opposite end of Upper State Street, in a spot that has been a sushi restaurant for 30 years. Eight booths face the four tatami rooms; a separate sushi bar is sequestered behind a pony wall. There's a great price-to-value ratio here, enhanced by their nightly sushi happy hour from 5 to 6 P.M. when the small space gets crowded and 40 rolls and nigiri are half off. For those who don't like sushi there's plenty of tempura and hibachi, served by a family who is genuinely glad you're there.

Breakfast and Brunch
If you've ever been to Paris and eaten a fresh baguette, you know heaven can look like a loaf of bread. Classic French pastries and breads are loaded with real butter, cream, and plenty of calories at **Renaud's Patisserie and Bistro** (3315 State St., 805/569-2400, Mon.–Sat. 7 A.M.–6 P.M., Sun. 7 A.M.–3 P.M., $15), which also has the best croissants in the city. Their classic European breakfast basket containing a croissant and toasted baguette with butter and jam, plus coffee or tea, will transport you to Paris. For those who need something more, quiche lorraine, *pain bagnat,* and cheese ravioletis will satisfy you. Save room for any of their sweets. It's run by a Frenchman, so you know you're getting authentic French food.

Max's (3514 State St., 805/898-9121, daily 7 A.M.–3 P.M., $10) opened up 25 years ago and is still quietly going about their business. They have developed a loyal following; the place is usually filled with regulars who lounge over their breakfast, chatting amicably with the staff. The interior is homey, thanks to a simple country decor, wood wainscoting, and warm golden-hued walls filled works by local artists that rotate every few months. The best breakfasts include the crab and avocado omelet and the smoked salmon scramble; all breakfasts come with home-style potatoes and house-made biscuits or muffins like peach-walnut.

Coffee and Tea
If tea is your bag, then check out **Vices and Spices** (3558 State St., 805/687-7196, Mon.–Sat. 7 A.M.–6 P.M., Sun. 8 A.M.–5 P.M.), which has been quietly brewing teas and making coffee for 35 years. This isn't for the trendy loud-ordering crowd with their fancy names and mocha-whatevers, this is an unpretentious, quiet environment for people who are serious about their coffees and teas—it's the kind of place where you let it steep before you drink it. They offer dozens of loose teas for purchase.

GOLETA
Goleta, no longer Santa Barbara's unincorporated sister, became an incorporated city in 2002. Though the area is predominantly residential, there are more and more restaurants coming in to serve the residents who don't want to make the trek downtown.

Burgers and Pizza
Z's Tap House and Grill (5925 Calle Real, 805/967-0128, www.zodos.com, daily 11 A.M.–11 P.M., $15) is inside a bowling alley—not exactly a place you'd think of for anything besides forgettable food used as fuel to score that perfect game. But Z's classic bar/pub/bowling fare is done surprisingly well. Try Z's super sampler of wings, potato skins, quesadillas, chicken tenders, and onion rings, or go for Thai chicken pizza while you watch TV or check out the bowlers struggling for a spare. There are 40 beers on tap, and you can also play in the extensive arcade or shoot pool. At Z's you'll score a very good meal and have fun to boot.

The decor at **The Nugget** (5687 Calle Real,

805/964-5200, daily 11 A.M.–9:30 P.M., $15) can only be described as Western eclectic, an attempt to provide visual cues to the gold-rush days, with little success. A small bar is at one side, loosely separated by a wall that gives way to freestanding tables and booths hugging the perimeter. There's also a lushly landscaped outside area. People mainly come for the burgers, like the Crunch Burger, served on an English muffin. But they also have terrific ribs and pasta dishes, all at reasonable prices.

Pizza may be ubiquitous, but it's not all the same. And **Gina's Pizza** (7038 Marketplace Dr., 805/571-6300, daily 11 A.M.–10 P.M., $15) serves some of the best in the city. Whether you order a Hawaiian style or a meat lovers or even a vegetarian pizza, what sets this place apart is the copious use of fresh ingredients and an exceptional crust. You can order thick or thin crust, and the sauce is kept to a minimum instead of using ridiculous amounts to cover up faulty ingredients like many other pizza places do. The ingredients are well spaced throughout the pizza so each bite gives you comprehensive flavors. They also have pasta dishes like lasagna, and minestrone soup.

Chinese
Red Pepper (282 Orange Ave., 805/964-0995, Mon.–Sat. 11 A.M.–2:30 P.M. and 5–9 P.M., $15) is a wonderful local Chinese restaurant in Goleta, sitting incongruously right next to a plumber and a locksmith. Though the ambience is sparse and frankly uninteresting—unless you consider the nine-pound koi in the fish tank an intriguing sight—the food makes up for the decor. Their onion pancakes are a great start to any vegetarian or meat dishes, and their hot and sour soup lives up to its name. As you leave you'll get a hug from the owner, but that's nothing unusual.

Mexican
Venturing into what is called IV (for Isla Vista on the UCSB campus) you'll find **Freebird's World Burrito** (879 Embarcadero Del Norte, 805/968-0123, 24 hours, $7), a popular spot that assembles burritos, tacos, nachos, and

quesadillas around the clock. You are just as likely to see college students as you are faculty members and men in ties, in part because everything tastes so good. You order and move down the counter as they put your food together in front of you. The success to Freebird's is their no-frills limited menu and the subtle diversity within that menu. But if the food tastes great and is freshly prepared, then options aren't that crucial. There will be lines out the door at peak times and parking is a problem, but at these prices for this quality, who cares?

Mediterranean
Tucked nearly out of view inside a strip mall is **Mediterra Café** (5575 Hollister Ave., #A, 805/696-9323, Mon.–Fri. 10 A.M.–7 P.M., Sat. 10 A.M.–5 P.M., $9), a small space with metal tables inside and outside. It's quiet and low-key bordering on simple inside, with soft yellow walls and views to the mountains. Olive oils and other sundries including Turkish coffees and hearts of palm line one wall. Taking their cues from the broader Mediterranean region, many cultures are represented including Greece, India, and Italy. Hummus, falafel, and gyros fill their menu, and there's a nice baklava for dessert.

Breakfast and Brunch
Mama's Bakery & Deli (5342-C Hollister Ave., 805/692-1666, Mon.–Sat. 6 A.M.–4:30 P.M., $6) is not your typical sit-down breakfast place. They have one table inside and two outside, but this is more grab and go. The interior is a little off-putting at first, and Mama's certainly won't be featured in *Architectural Digest*. But the food is consistently good and the service is enthusiastic and friendly. They offer four different brewed coffees to go with their one-third-pound chorizo breakfast burrito (or vegetarian option). Or try one of their daily soups, or stick with one of the massively large plain croissants or chocolate croissants.

Coffee and Tea
Java Station (4447 Hollister Ave., 805/681-0202, daily 6 A.M.–9 P.M., $7) offers coffee and smoothies, bagels and pastries in a roomy place with indoor and outdoor seating. Tables and chairs share space with couches, and there's often a fire going. On the weekends lots of cyclists congregate here, and during the week there's a younger college crowd working feverishly on their laptops.

Desserts
The idea of an organic pie or cheesecake might not turn some people on, but **Simply Pies** (5392 Hollister Ave., 805/845-2200, www.simplypiessb.blogspot.com, Tues.–Sat. 11 A.M.–3 P.M.) makes extremely excellent pies that are, in a sense, almost good for you. They offer the option of gluten- and sugar-free crusts as well as a vegan option, and frankly, they taste fantastic—especially the pumpkin cheesecake. Or pick up a strawberry rhubarb pie or chocolate cream. You will be amazed.

MONTECITO
Montecito is not its own city, contrary to what they would like you to believe. This celebrity-frequented wealthy high-end enclave is actually part of the county. Regardless, it's home to Coast Village Road, their own version of State Street. While there are several restaurants in the area, they are pricier than every other area in the entire county.

American
At the east end of Coast Village Road is the **Montecito Cafe** (1295 Coast Village Rd., 805/969-3392, www.montecitocafe.com, daily 11:30 A.M.–2:30 P.M. and 5:30–10 P.M., $15), located at the Montecito Inn. This local favorite gets packed with the Montecito crowd chowing down on fettuccini with lamb sausage, Idaho trout salad, and goat cheese pancakes. It's an older, monied crowd, though the prices here are exceptionally reasonable for this area. The decor is outdated, sort of like an upscale 1970s coffee shop, but it's a lively ambience and good food.

You're in for a treat at the **Plow & Angel** (900 San Ysidro Ln., 805/565-1724, daily 5–10 P.M., $25) is housed at the ritzy San

Ysidro Ranch. Beautiful walls of large stone blocks belie the fact that the space is actually rather intimate, with a fireplace at one side, and a handful of tables and round amber-hued stained-glass windows. Monday–Wednesday is locals' night, when they offer a comprehensive meal of soup or salad, entrée, and dessert for a set price, about $35. Otherwise try their stunning signature macaroni and cheese—it's that good—or the Colorado lamb sliders. The only drawback is that you have to valet your car since this is on hotel property.

Italian
At **Tre Lune** (1151 Coast Village Rd., 805/969-2646, daily 7:30 A.M.–2:30 P.M. and 5:30–10 P.M., $25), white linens rest on wood tables and black-and-white photographs of (one assumes) Italian people line the walls, as do tiny wooden chairs, each with a name plate in honor of regulars and local celebrities. Try a ricotta and spinach calzone or the *insalata* Tre Lune, comprised of arugula, radicchio, and endive topped with grilled chicken. The penne Melchiori has a wild-boar *ragù* that might have you going wild yourself.

Mollie Ashtrand, a native of Ethiopia, came to the United States and founded her eponymous Italian restaurant, **Trattoria Mollie** (1250 Coast Village Rd., 805/565-9381, www.tmollie.com, lunch Tues.–Sun. 11:30 A.M.–2:30 P.M., dinner nightly 5:30 P.M.–close, $25), in 1993. Then Oprah Winfrey raved about the turkey meatballs, and that drew lots of attention. The interior is an open space, simple bordering on sparse in its decoration, with a few forgettable paintings hanging on the tan-colored walls. Yes, the meatballs are good, but they're now overpriced. Instead go for the spinach cannelloni or risotto *gamberi,* and definitely save room for the excellent house-made tiramisu.

THE MESA AND MILPAS
As is true anywhere, once you veer off Santa Barbara's main drag you'll still find good eats, but oftentimes cheaper and certainly with fewer crowds. Areas like Mesa and Milpas offer

very nice food without the hassle of long waits, as is typical on State Street during the summer season. That's not to say off-the-beaten-track restaurants don't get busy, only that if you go, you'll be surrounded by locals and you'll discover terrific food.

Mexican
Mexican Fresh (315 Megis Rd., 805/963-7492, daily 8:30 A.M.–8:30 P.M., $9) serves up cheap, flavorful eats. It looks like a beach joint wedged into a strip mall, and with the furniture askew it looks generally forlorn. The setup is simple: Order at the counter, they make your food fresh, you pick it up and grab plastic utensils, and sit wherever you want. The monster burritos, nearly the size of a football, will keep you stuffed. There are also fish tacos, tortas, nachos, and tostadas.

Los Agaves (600 N. Milpas, 805/564-2626, daily 11 A.M.–9 P.M., $12) is one of the newest in a growing number of Mexican restaurants in Santa Barbara. Just off the Mesa, the interior is a brightly colored space with Saltillo tiled floors. They make nine different salsas to try with your meal, including a smoky and spicy chipotle, the super-hot habanero, and the creamy and mild *aguacate.* Chimichangas, plenty of fish, beef, and pork tacos, and tortas are the usual and customary standard fare, but the place is lively and the food is prepared as fast as the kitchen can manage. Lunches can get packed, translating to a longer wait—something to keep in mind if you're on a tight schedule.

Thai
Meun Fan Thai (1819 Cliff Dr., 805/882-9422, Mon.–Thurs. 11 A.M.–9:30 P.M., Fri.–Sat. 11 A.M.–10 P.M., Sun. 4–9:30 P.M., $15) makes no apologies for the very flavorful and spicy foods served in their spot on the Mesa—let them know if you need a restrained version of your meal. There is a terrific selection here: pineapple fried rice with a bit of curry, drunken noodles with deftly prepared pan-fried noodles, *nam* salad with mint, ginger, red onions, and peanuts on top of rice and lettuce with a healthy

dash of lime juice. The service is well meaning but a little slow, but the food is worth the wait.

Spanish

Alcazar Tapas Bar (1812 Cliff Dr., 805/962-0337, www.alcazartapasbar.com, Mon.–Wed. 5:30–10 P.M., Thurs.–Sat. 5:30–11 P.M., $20) is a lively and energetic narrow restaurant with red and yellow walls, wood tables and chairs, and rotating local artwork. The minimal lighting and abundance of candles create a romantic, moody environment. The small plates include tequila tofu and a wedge of melted brie with apples and onions in a balsamic reduction sauce. Or get a full meal infused with Spanish spices and flavors like chicken enchiladas with mole, or a shrimp or beef dish. They make a number of types of mojitos to wash down the food.

Coffee and Tea

There's nothing like a good cup of coffee, and **The Good Cup** (1819 Cliff Dr., 805/963-8699, Mon.–Thurs. 6 A.M.–8 P.M., Fri.–Sun. 6 A.M.–6 P.M., $8) will give you just that. They're actually better known for their chai teas, but also make an array of coffee drinks, and they have pastries, muffins, and scones at the ready, though they don't bake them onsite (they come from a local bakery). The corner location is bright and airy with tiled floors and wood ceilings; many people come here to camp out for a while, pecking at the keys on their laptops and enjoying the vibe of a neighborhood coffeehouse.

CARPINTERIA

Just south of Santa Barbara, Carpinteria is attempting to assert itself as a dining destination along Linden Avenue, and they are doing quite well.

American

The absolute best spot in all of Carpinteria is **Sly's** (686 Linden Ave., Carpinteria, 805/684-6666, www.slysonline.com, lunch Mon.–Fri. 11:30 A.M.–2:30 P.M., dinner Sun.–Thurs. 5–9 P.M., Fri.–Sat. 5–10 P.M., brunch Sat.–Sun.

9 A.M.–3 P.M., $25) for classic American fare, such as beautifully tender steaks and fresh local abalone and pastas. Chef James Sly built a huge following while he was the head chef at Lucky's in Montecito before starting his own venture—and the people have followed. The interior is high-end retro, with gorgeous wood tones, exposed brickwork, and white tablecloths. And the food is nearly perfect, as long as James is in the kitchen. Order any steak and you'll be happy, or try the spaghetti carbonara. Everything is à la carte here, therefore the amazing creamed corn is an additional charge. Sly's is pricey but worth it.

For a throwback to a long gone dining era, **Clementine's Steakhouse** (4631 Carpinteria Ave., 805/684-5119, Wed.–Sun. 5–9 P.M., $22) is your place. Schmaltzy music plays over the speakers, the older clientele talks quietly, the decor is 1960s country—and you can't help but smile. Burgundy tablecloths are contrasted with pink scalloped napkins, and nearly everyone leaves with leftovers. All entrées come with a crudités plate, house-baked bread, soup, and salad, along with a choice of side dish and finally home-baked pie. It's a tremendous amount of food, and they haven't changed their formula in over 30 years. Steaks, fresh fish, chicken, and pastas plus all those sides will keep you very full.

As you head upcoast you'll pass by little Summerland, where you'll find **Tinkers** (2275 Ortega Hill Rd., 805/969-1970, daily 11 A.M.–8 P.M., $6), whose wood-shingled exterior looks classier than the interior. Don't let that scare you off, though: Tinkers has great, fresh food at unbeatable prices, it's just that it's a true beach dive. You can sit at the small counter, so close to the grill you might just as well cook your own food, or head to the back eating area that does double duty as a storage area. The burgers, fish-and-chips, burritos, and shakes and malts are well prepared, and the staff is helpful.

Wine Country Cuisine

At **Corktree Cellars Wine Bar & Bistro** (910 Linden Ave., 805/684-1400, www.corktreecellars.com, daily 11 A.M.–10 P.M., $15) you can order a full meal, an appetizer, a glass of wine, or a flight of wine. The interior is decked out with wood tables and chairs, a curved bar, comfy leather chairs, and yellow walls with rotating artwork. It's warm and inviting—and yes, they actually have a cork tree. The food is creative and uses diverse ingredients; try the lobster and white truffle macaroni and cheese, the corn bisque, or New England lobster melt panini. Wines can be ordered by the glass or in flights—three different tastes of a particular varietal, like Hailing a Cab with three cabernet sauvignons, or Drawing a Blanc with three sauvignon blancs. All the wine flights show a diversity of places: Santa Ynez, Napa, Argentina, New Zealand, and more.

Just around the corner, the most striking thing about **Zooker's Cafe** (5404 Carpinteria Ave., 805/684-8893, www.zookerscafe.com, Mon.–Sat. 11:30 A.M.–3 P.M. and 4–10 P.M., $17) is the amazing display of orchids of all sizes and colors, which add a beautiful, tranquil quality to the busy eatery, complementing the olive- and mustard-colored walls. Lunches are filled with salads, sandwiches, and a quiche of the day, and dinners veer into fish, beef, and chicken entrées, all sourcing local ingredients. The fruit crisp is the best way to end your meal here.

Barbecue

Santa Barbara has long had a dearth of dependable barbecue joints, so it's great that **The Barbecue Company** (3807 Santa Claus Ln., 805/684-2209, Wed.–Sun. noon–9 P.M., $15) is around. Two flat-screen TVs flanking the faux rustic interior play an endless supply of concert footage, and a musical motif continues in the artwork. All their meats are slow smoked, then finished on the grill and "mopped" with an amalgam of all the sauces they make on-site. Whether you order baby-back ribs, pulled chicken, or pork, you can get a side of cornbread or mac 'n' cheese and feel like you're down home.

Breakfast and Brunch

The Garden Market (3811 Santa Claus Ln., 805/745-5505, www.thegardenmarkets.com, Sun.–Thurs. 7 A.M.–4 P.M., Fri.–Sat. 7 A.M.–5 P.M., $10) has a small interior with a few tables, but most people choose a table on the front patio or on the back patio filled with plants. Either way, you'll enjoy fresh-brewed tea, or coffee drinks made with free-trade beans and organic milk. Their focus is on breakfast sandwiches with ingredients like provolone, tomato, egg, cream cheese, red onion, and fresh basil squished between fluffy ciabatta bread, or muffins and bagels. It's mainly a local's spot, and a great discovery for everyone else.

Coffee and Tea

To get to **Café Luna** (2354 Lillie Ave., 805/695-8780, daily 7 A.M.–6 P.M., $12) you walk through an archway of flowering vines. It's a Thomas Kinkade–style entrance to a laid-back old house turned coffee bar. Café Luna makes very good coffee drinks, not the watered-down versions that proliferate everywhere, and some of the best here are the caramel latte, cappuccino, and Mexican spiced hot chocolate. Scones and muffins share the stage with fun breakfasts like the quesadilla, a flour tortilla filled with eggs, tomato, beans, corn, cilantro, onion, and cheese.

Information and Services

MAPS AND TOURIST INFORMATION

The **Santa Barbara Chamber of Commerce Visitors Center** (1 Garden St., 805/965-3021, www.sbchamber.org, Mon.–Sat. 9 A.M.–4 P.M., Sun. 10 A.M.–4 P.M.) is located directly across from the beach and offers discounted tickets to many restaurants and sights in town.

John Dickson has put together a most comprehensive website, www.santabarbara.com, which includes things to do, and reviews of hotels and restaurant by locals. Though some of the information is out of date, it's still a valuable resource. And www.santabarbaraca.com is the official website for the visitors center, with an up-to-date section of maps you can download, and the latest specials and deals.

EMERGENCY SERVICES

Cottage Hospital (at Bath and Pueblo Sts.) is the only hospital in town, and has the only emergency room. In case of an emergency, call 911 immediately. The **Santa Barbara Police Department** is located at 215 East Figueroa Street (805/897-2335).

NEWSPAPERS

The only daily newspaper in the area is the *Santa Barbara News-Press* a locally owned paper that can be found all over town and at www.newspress.com. Each Friday they publish restaurant reviews and in-depth interviews with musicians and artists who have current shows in town. The Sunday paper includes travel articles, coupons, and information about events. Thursday is the food section, with information about local farmers markets and wine reviews.

The alternative free weekly, publishing on Thursdays, is the *Santa Barbara Independent* (www.independent.com), found everywhere. They have good entertainment listings including shows, concerts, theater, and film. Since it's published weekly not everything is always up to the minute, but they do provide a very good overview of local politics and special events.

LOCAL TV AND RADIO

KZSB AM-1290 is the only local talk radio station, with a variety of local programming, traffic reports, local news, and worldwide news from the BBC. Show topics include gardening, real estate, food, travel, and politics, all with a local perspective.

Channel 18 is the local community access TV channel, with way too much coverage of city hall meetings and various boards and commissions like the architectural board of review. But they also offer some local programming.

KEYT (www.keyt.com) is the main TV station broadcasting from Santa Barbara (it's channel 3 in town), where you can get the latest local, regional, and some national news, as well as local sports and weather. They broadcast from what is called TV Hill, just above the harbor.

POSTAL SERVICES

The main branch of the post office is located at 836 Anacapa Street, one block east of State Street. A second smaller downtown branch is in Victoria Court at 1221 State Street, in the back of the building. For those closer to Upper State, the San Roque station is at 3345 State Street. The main phone number for all three branches is 805/564-2226. What with budget cuts, it is best to phone ahead to check ever-changing hours.

LAUNDRY

If the need arises, you can have your laundry done for you at **Launderland** (2636 De La Vina, 805/687-8380) or use their coin-operated services. They have fast turnaround times and are very professional.

Getting There

Santa Barbara is not really on the way to anything, unless you are looking for the Pacific Ocean.

BY AIR

The **Santa Barbara Municipal Airport** (601 Firestone Rd., Goleta, 805/967-7111, www.flysba.com) is a small airport that currently serves only regional flights from 10 destinations on five airlines. There is an expansion underway to enlarge the runways to accommodate more and larger planes, and the airport will be expanded from two terminals to four, losing some of the charm of the small-town red-tile-roofed airport.

Shuttles

Chances are you'll fly into Los Angeles or San Francisco and then connect to Santa Barbara. If you're coming in from L.A. and not connecting to Santa Barbara by air, the 90-mile drive takes about two hours. There are commercial shuttle vans and buses from L.A., but keep in mind these will also take two-plus hours,

depending on traffic. **Santa Barbara Air Bus** (805/964-7759, www.santabarbaraairbus.com) runs between LAX and Santa Barbara every day and will deliver you in comfort.

BY CAR

By car, the only entrance to Santa Barbara north or south is Highway 101, a two-lane highway that is reasonably traffic free—at least so far. Exits and off-ramps are clearly marked, and you'll know you are getting close when you see the ocean out your window.

BY TRAIN

Amtrak (209 State St., 805/963-1015, www .amtrak.com) pulls into Santa Barbara's 1905 depot right on State Street, one block from the beach.

BY BUS

Greyhound (34 W. Carrillo, 805/965-7551, www.greyhound.com) has a somewhat dingy terminal a block off State Street. It's convenient, though, as this is the main hub.

© MICHAEL CERVIN

If you arrive in Santa Barbara by train, you'll land at this 1905 train station, a block from the beach.

Getting Around

A great resource for bike trails, walking paths, train info, taxi cabs, water excursions, and all manner of transportation is www.santabarbaracarfree.com, which offers downloadable maps and ways to experience Santa Barbara while reducing your carbon footprint.

It's important to make a note about the unusual orientation of Santa Barbara. As you stand at the water's edge near the harbor, it would be easy to assume you are facing west—but you are actually looking southeast. It's a geographical oddity, but it's important to know in order to get your bearings. The city of Goleta is to the west (upcoast), and to the east (downcoast) are the unincorporated areas of Montecito, Summerland, and the City of Carpinteria, which abuts the county line with Ventura.

DRIVING AND PARKING

Laid out in a grid pattern, the city is very easy to navigate, at least the downtown core. Of particular note is that State Street, the defining street, travels from the oceanfront in a northwest direction and then makes a 90-degree bend to run east–west (where it's known as Upper State Street). Eventually State Street turns into Hollister, and by then you are entering Goleta. But all things fan out from State Street, and most directions are given in relationship to State.

The other thing to consider is that although most streets have unique names and there is little possibility of confusing them, three streets can cause a problem: Castillo, Carrillo, and Cabrillo. Here's all you need to know: Cabrillo (think of the *b* as in beach) runs the length of the waterfront. Carrillo (think of the *r* as in running right through town) bisects State Street in the center of downtown. And Castillo (think of the *s* for State) parallels State Street. If you keep that in mind, it should be easier to get around.

In general, parking is pretty easy. There are a number of parking lots in the downtown area and street parking is, mostly, 75 minutes for free. But be advised that parking enforcement is out and about, and they will ticket you should you go over your allotted time; parking tickets are $50.

WALKING TOURS

Seeing Santa Barbara on foot is the best way to experience the city. The **Red Tile Walking Tour** (www.santabarbaraca.com) is a condensed 12-block self-guided tour of all the important buildings in town. You can download either a map version to print, or a podcast version narrated by John O'Hurley (of TV's *Seinfeld*). You'll see Casa de la Guerra, the county courthouse, and the presidio, among other defining buildings.

Or for a more structured tour, **Santa Barbara Walking Tours** (805/687-9255, www.santabarbarawalkingtours.com, $23) has a 90-minute docent-led tour of the visual art and history in town. It combines parts of the Red Tile tour but also shows you some of the beautiful paseos, tile work, and public art that's almost everywhere.

TROLLEY TOURS

If walking just isn't your thing, get an expanded overview of the city by riding through it. The best is the **Landshark** (805/683-7600, www.out2seesb.com, Nov.–Apr. noon and 2 P.M., May–Oct. noon, 2, and 4 P.M., $25 adults, $10 children under 10), which is a live-narrated 90-minute tour on the Landshark, a 15-foot-high amphibious vehicle. You'll see most of the important buildings, though not the mission. On the plus side, in the last portion of the tour the Landshark plunges into the ocean and turns into a boat, going past the breakwater for great views of the coast. It's fun and informative, and you can ask all the questions you want. More likely than not you'll see dolphins and seals at the very least. All Landshark tours depart from the entrance to Stearns Wharf.

The **Santa Barbara Trolley Company** (805/965-0353, www.sbtrolley.com, daily 10 A.M.–5:30 P.M., $19 adults, $8 children under 12) offers another live narrated tour that includes the mission and other great locations like Butterfly Beach in Montecito and the bird refuge. Tours pick up and drop off at 15 different locations every 60 minutes; see the website for a comprehensive schedule.

TAXI CABS

Taxis are not abundant in town, nor are they in much of a rush; it's best to call for one. Assuming you do get a taxi, you're apt to get a leisurely cab ride to your destination. **Santa Barbara Checker Cab** (888/581-1110) is a safe bet.

STATE STREET TROLLEY

For just 25 cents, you can ride the trolley the length of the waterfront, or the length of State Street. Two electric shuttle routes (www.sbmtd.gov) serve the downtown corridor (State St.) and the waterfront (Cabrillo Blvd.) daily every half hour. Children under 45 inches can ride free, and a free transfer is available between the Downtown Shuttle and the Waterfront Shuttle—just ask your driver.

VENTURA AND OJAI

Ventura County has long been considered a stopping-off point on the way from Los Angeles to Santa Barbara and points north—just a section of the state to use as a rest stop before moving on—but the area has much more to offer. Yes, Highway 101 bisects the county as it takes you north out of Los Angeles. But it's also an area rich in natural, cultural, architectural and historical treasures, with rugged transverse mountain ranges and fertile valleys ranging down to a magnificent coastline with offshore islands. In recent years, Ventura has begun to develop a new image, and a unique and solid identity as a place with beachfront access, nearby mountains, thrift shops, a growing and impressive arts scene, and a thriving restaurant landscape. And it even boasts its own wine trail of a dozen wineries, an attempt to intercept day-trippers heading through the area. Ventura is also the gateway to the Channel Islands, a series of five undeveloped islands that still retain their primal beauty, with unique spots to hike, fish, scuba, snorkel, and kayak. Home to one of the most successful missions in the California chain, Ventura County does not have a long history, but it is varied. Despite being so close to Los Angeles, Ventura has retained its seaside charm and indifference for its southern neighbor. There is little pretense in Ventura, where a whole world awaits discovery.

Just 16 miles up the road but a universe away is the small enclave of Ojai, an ideal one-day trip from Ventura or Santa Barbara. Ojai has long been a mecca for the artistic crowd, and anyone who seeks something left of center, and is a hub for meditation, spiritual retreats, and

HIGHLIGHTS

◖ Mission San Buenaventura: One of the most prosperous of the Central Coast missions, San Buenaventura has the prettiest courtyard and is still a viable part of the community (page 102).

◖ Main Street: Ventura is still a classic California beach town, and Main Street is a throwback to a city center that hasn't seen new development for decades. Stores, galleries, and restaurants thrive on this unpretentious boulevard (page 103).

◖ Channel Islands National Park: The Central Coast's backyard is a primal, pristine wonderland of volcanic rock, indigenous flora and fauna, stunning vistas, and clear water (page 105).

◖ Fillmore and Western Railway: Get a glimpse of the past as you ride the rails through the agriculturally rich Heritage Valley just north of Ventura in a historic train (page 109).

◖ California Oil Museum: The region is home to some of the largest natural gas and oil reserves in the country, a fact not lost on oil explorers a hundred years ago. This museum breaks it all down in a compelling manner (page 110).

◖ Heritage Square: A dozen historic Victorian-era buildings were moved and reassembled in Heritage Square to present a unique block of history and an extraordinary visual experience (page 111).

◖ Ojai Avenue: Not much has changed on Ojai's main drag since it was built in 1917. Primarily the vision of one man, this thoroughfare is the heartbeat of Ojai (page 131).

◖ Meditation Mount: This peaceful, quiet spot offers the best visual overview of Ojai, the valley it's nestled into, and the mountains that protect it (page 133).

LOOK FOR **◖** TO FIND RECOMMENDED SIGHTS, ACTIVITIES, DINING, AND LODGING.

CATASTROPHIC FAILURE: THE ST. FRANCIS DAM COLLAPSE

At five minutes to midnight on Thursday, March 12, 1928, the towns of Santa Paula, Newhall, Piru, and Fillmore were undoubtedly peaceful, residents asleep in their warm beds, supposedly safe from harm. But less than three minutes later, all hell would break loose and more than 600 people would be dead. The collapse of the St. Francis Dam was the single worst engineering disaster of the 20th century in the United States, and the second worst in California history. Construction had begun in April 1924; the 210-foot-tall

remnants of the collapse

© MICHAEL CERVIN

teachings. The town was used as the backdrop for the 1930s movie *Lost Horizon,* though these days the once secluded town is anything but hard to find. Summer sees flocks of tourists shopping and dining on Ojai Avenue, doing yoga, getting in touch with their inner self, or just escaping the hectic pace of somewhere else. Similar to Santa Barbara's renewal after the 1925 earthquake, Ojai created its current Spanish Revival appearance after a fire decimated much of the town in 1917. Known as an arts destination, it also hosts annual festivals of playwrights, music, wine, and theater. Nearby Lake Casitas offers plenty of boating, swimming, and camping in a somewhat remote mountain setting.

HISTORY
Ventura

Ventura, now home to more than 100,000 residents, was originally—and sometimes still is—called San Buenaventura, which loosely translated means "city of good fortune" in Spanish. The name is taken from the Spanish

St. Francis Dam located just north of Magic Mountain was to provide a substantial holding reservoir for Los Angeles. Decades later the dam's failure was determined to have been caused by hydraulic uplift, meaning that prior to its demise the base of the dam actually rose up slightly, due to its inherent instability, and began to tip over. Additionally, the rock the dam was anchored to was also inherently unstable, and unbeknownst to engineers or locals, the dubious rock was becoming saturated with water.

At 11:57 P.M. on March 12, 1928, the St. Francis Dam failed and 13 billion gallons of water merged with the Santa Clara River. The initial wall of water was 200 feet high. Of the 70 people that lived just below the dam, only three survived. By the time the water hit Castaic Junction, near Magic Mountain, it was 75 feet high, and Santa Paula faced a torrent still 25 feet high, with trees and broken houses acting like battering rams, obliterating anything in their way. The eventual path of destruction was 54 miles long. In Newhall, a makeshift morgue was set up in the dance hall, which was still festooned with decorations from the dance held there the night before. Five and a half hours after the dam collapsed, it lapped the Pacific Ocean near Ventura Harbor. Driving up Highway 126, it's possible to retrace the nearly exact route the water took through the Santa Clara River. Today it serves as a reminder of how many people can perish so quickly.

The destruction was total, with 600 people dead, plus livestock, and cars, roads, power lines, bridges, train tracks, and farms all washed to the ocean or covered in a blanket of mud, debris, and wreckage nearly 30 feet thick. The numbers are staggering: 1,200 homes demolished, 24,000 acres of fertile land destroyed, almost 11,000 acres of crops laid waste, 140,000 trees uprooted or badly damaged. Upwards of 3,000 volunteers searched for bodies, some of which were recovered as far south as San Diego; others were found weeks later in the isolated canyons along the river, and some have never been found.

After multiple inquires and reports, dam safety legislation changed. California mandated professional registration for engineers, which became the model for the rest of the country. The Los Angeles Department of Water and Power, who oversaw the construction of the dam, established soil compaction tests and acquired a greater understanding of hydraulic uplift. Today the dam site is tangible history. Parts of the dam are still visible, though malformed and eroding. Catherine Mulholland, the granddaughter of William Mulholland who was responsible for constructing the dam, said:

By now we know that Homo sapiens *have plundered the earth. We've dislodged, displaced, and removed forests and oceans. We've flourished and also suffered. When you move water, things get destroyed in the process.*

---

mission that was built here in 1782 by Father Junípero Serra.

Many cultures have inhabited the land where Ventura is now located. The earliest were the Chumash Indians, whose village was called Shisholop. Archaeologists discovered even earlier cultures dating back as far as 10,000 years. The San Buenaventura Mission brought the Chumash Indians under the auspices of the Catholic Church, encouraging them to establish a regimented life, learn new skills, and develop agricultural practices. Mission San Buenaventura, named for Saint Bonaventure, was the most successful and influential of the California missions founded by Father Serra.

Following the Central Coast earthquake of December 1812, the mission began a period of reconstruction to repair damages caused by the quake. Over time, due to diseases and a lack of funds, mission life declined, and in 1866 the City of San Buenaventura officially became part of Santa Barbara County. The majority of the residents were of Spanish, Mexican, and Native American origin. In 1873, Ventura

County was formed and San Buenaventura became a city within the new county.

The Northern California gold rush in 1849 brought many easterners to California, and after the Civil War came another influx of new residents, who bought land from the Mexicans or simply squatted on property. Vast holdings were later acquired by easterners, including railroad magnate Thomas Scott. Scott was impressed by a young employee named Thomas R. Bard who had been in charge of train supplies to Union troops; Bard was sent west to handle Scott's property. Bard is most often regarded as the father of Ventura. The Union Oil Company, located today (as it was then) in Santa Paula, was organized with Bard as president in 1890. The main Ventura oil field was drilled as early as 1914; at its peak it produced 90,000 barrels a day. For most of its history, Ventura has escaped the thrust of immigrating peoples, and has been able to enjoy its own more leisurely, less crowded way of life. At the same time, however, Ventura became prosperous. The city is located between two richly endowed valleys, the Ventura River and the Santa Clara River, and so rich was the soil that citrus grew better here than anywhere else in the state. The growers along these rivers got together and formed Sunkist, now the world's largest organization of citrus production.

For most of the century that followed the incorporation of Ventura in 1866, it was pretty much isolated from the southern part of the state—not that locals seemed to mind. Even from the north, entrance was by way of a single road along the beach, and stagecoach passengers either had to wait until low tide, when the horses could cross on the exposed wet sand at the Rincon, or go up the Ventura River Valley and then cross over the mountains to Santa Barbara via Casitas Pass, which was always a long and difficult trip. Inland, Ventura was hemmed in by Los Padres National Forest, composed of mountainous country, deep canyons, and peaks that rise as high as 8,831 feet, namely Mt. Pinos. Ventura remained quite isolated until a narrow road, the Maricopa

Highway, was built in the 1920s, but even then travel by car was slow and hazardous. Now, there is direct access to the city and the perilous journeys of long ago are forgotten, thanks to the completion of the Ventura Freeway from Los Angeles to Ventura, the last link of which was finished in 1969.

Ojai

Originally called Nordhoff, Ojai was mapped out in 1874, though the Chumash Indians had lived here for thousands of years prior to that. The area was originally part of a Spanish land grant to Fernardo Tico in 1837; Tico sold his vast holdings in 1853 and the land went through a series of land owners until, after some failed oil exploration, many of the settlers decided to form an actual town, and Nordhoff was born. You'll still see the name around town, such as Nordhoff High School. In the early 20th century a businessman from Toledo, Ohio, named Edward Libbey came to Nordhoff and immediately fell in love with the place. In 1914 he unveiled grand plans to create a viable community, a cohesive town rather than the ramshackle stores and buildings that had congregated on the main street. In 1917 he got his chance, when a fire decimated much of the town and Libbey was handed a clean slate. A wealthy man wanting his newly adopted town to be distinctive, he financed much of the civic development to realize his dream. His work gives downtown Ojai its distinctive charm: a Spanish Colonial–style arcade along the main street, a post office tower designed after Havana's Campanile, and a pergola, the official entrance to Libbey Park. Today, Ojai's wealth is mostly apparent in large parcels of land and multimillion-dollar homes. But pretentiousness is not welcomed here, and Ojai retains a modest feel.

The name Ojai (pronounced o-hi) is derived from the Chumash Indian word *awhai*. The word might mean "nest," or it might mean "moon," depending on whom you ask. Much of the literature about Ojai claims one meaning over the other, but frankly there is no definite proof of either.

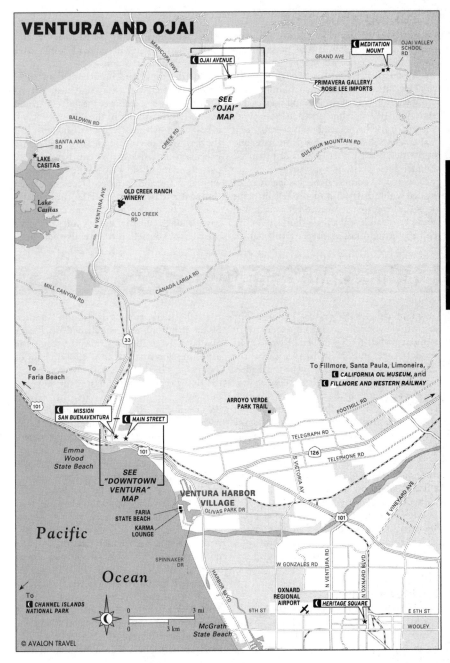

VENTURA AND OJAI

MARICOPA HWY

☾ OJAI AVENUE

GRAND AVE

☾ MEDITATION MOUNT

OJAI VALLEY SCHOOL RD

SEE "OJAI" MAP

PRIMAVERA GALLERY/ ROSIE LEE IMPORTS

BALDWIN RD

SANTA ANA RD

★ LAKE CASITAS

CREEK RD

SULPHUR MOUNTAIN RD

Lake Casitas

N VENTURA AVE

OLD CREEK RANCH WINERY

OLD CREEK RD

MILL CANYON RD

CANADA LARGA RD

33

To Faria Beach

To Fillmore, Santa Paula, Limoneira, ☾ CALIFORNIA OIL MUSEUM, and ☾ FILLMORE AND WESTERN RAILWAY

ARROYO VERDE PARK TRAIL

FOOTHILL RD

101

☾ MISSION SAN BUENAVENTURA

☾ MAIN STREET

TELEGRAPH RD

126

TELEPHONE RD

Emma Wood State Beach

101

S VICTORIA AV

SEE "DOWNTOWN VENTURA" MAP

VENTURA HARBOR VILLAGE

OLIVAS PARK DR

E VINEYARD AVE

101

N VENTURA RD

N OXNARD BLVD

Pacific

FARIA STATE BEACH

KARMA LOUNGE

SPINNAKER DR

W GONZALES RD

Ocean

To ☾ CHANNEL ISLANDS NATIONAL PARK

HARBOR BLVD

0   3 mi

0   3 km

McGrath State Beach

OXNARD REGIONAL AIRPORT

✈

☾ HERITAGE SQUARE

5TH ST

E 5TH ST

WOOLEY

© AVALON TRAVEL

PLANNING YOUR TIME

It is nearly always sunny in Ventura. On average, there are over 250 days of sunshine annually, and 70-degree weather delights nearly year-round. Rain is sporadic, though typically falls November through March. Summers certainly see an influx of people, and the beaches teem with sun-worshippers. The best times to visit tend to be September–November and February–April, when the crowds are fewer and the weather, while perhaps a bit cooler than the summer, is clear, clean, and pristine.

Downtown Ventura can be reasonably experienced within a day. But to also take in some of the outlying areas, a weekend at a minimum would be ideal, if still a little short. If you intend on being outdoors, sailing, hiking, or

heading to the islands, you'll need more time. Also, if you hope to visit Santa Paula, Oxnard, and Camarillo, you will need to factor in drive times to those destinations.

On a day trip, Ojai will enchant you with its small-town feel, walkability, and beautiful setting. But to fully experience the quiet town and absorb the tranquility of the area, a weekend is best. Summertime can get hot and crowded; the best times to visit this peaceful enclave are February–June, when the rains have usually passed and the hillsides are beginning to sprout with new life, and October–December, when the town is festively decorated for the holidays. Yes, it's a bit cooler then, but the crowds will have thinned, and even though you won't have the place to yourself, it will feel like you do.

Ventura and Vicinity

Geographically, water defines Ventura. The Ventura River forms the city's northern boundary, while the Santa Clara River is at its southern edge, and the Pacific Ocean is to the west. The eastern boundary is the Los Padres National Forest. Sandwiched between Los Angeles and Santa Barbara Counties, Ventura has long been the middle child, going about its own business, unaffected by the passage of time. The county itself encompasses many different geographic areas, but downtown Ventura is rather compact and easy to walk around; it's three blocks from the beach and still feels somehow unfettered by "progress." Without scads of new development taking over, the city's personality has remained unchanged. The mission, the beach, parks, riding and hiking trails, and lots of unique stores, shops, and galleries make this an eclectic place.

SIGHTS
Downtown Ventura
◖ MISSION SAN BUENAVENTURA

The Mission San Buenaventura (211 E. Main St., 805/643-4318, Mon.–Fri. 10 A.M.–5 P.M., Sat. 9 A.M.–5 P.M., Sun. 10 A.M.–4 P.M., closed

major holidays, self-guided tour $1 adults, $0.50 children) was established on Easter Sunday (March 31) 1782, and it became the ninth mission founded in the total chain of 21 missions in the state. Like most missions, the first structure, which lasted for 10 years, burned to the ground. In part, the mission prospered due to a seven-mile aqueduct that was constructed from the Ventura River to the mission grounds. This allowed a wide variety of crops to grow, including fruits, vegetables, grains, and even exotic fruits such as bananas, coconuts, and figs. The padres often sold these goods to travelers, which helped greatly with the needed funds to support mission life.

The mission, like most, was built as a complete quadrangle. The church was on the southwest corner, and a cemetery was on the west side of the church. (A grade school now stands where the old cemetery was.) In 1818, the pirate known as Bouchard was seen off the coast of California and began terrorizing Ventura. The mission fathers and the Chumash Indians buried some of their valuables and sacred objects and literally took the rest to the mountains for about a month until the pirate and his

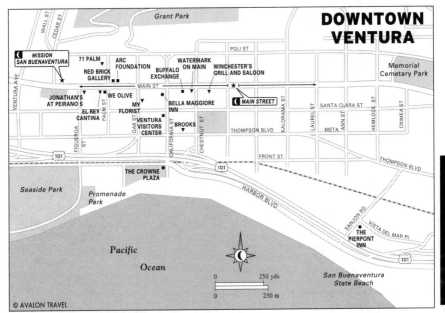

band had gone. The church walls of tile, stone, and adobe are just over six feet thick, built by Indian labor. It's still an active church and one of the most visited sights in Ventura.

To visit today you first pass through the gift shop, with its miniature mission collection and spiritually oriented cards and gifts, then you'll head up a few steps to the very small museum, which holds a few items such as vestments and everyday utensils from the mission period. This is also one of the few missions to still have wooden bells on display. The door then opens to the courtyard, a beautifully landscaped area with a fountain in the center, surrounded by a few benches and interlocking short pathways. The church is across the courtyard. The church itself is long and narrow, a neoclassical-looking arch over the altar giving a more modern feel to the interior. Carpet covers much of the original tile floors, unfortunately, and there's a rather off-putting sign dead center of the altar warning you that you are being videotaped. Behind the church is part of the original brick reservoir, and current housing for the staff.

MAIN STREET

The city of Ventura is, basically, Main Street. Of course there are other arteries that cut through town, and other things to see and do, but the concentration of these few blocks is what Ventura has become—namely, a city undergoing a renaissance. New and trendy restaurants are opening up, the art scene is showing off its talent, and nightlife offerings are improving with a mix of bars, clubs, and live music. Main Street is mainly a collection of one-story storefronts, occasionally punctuated by a few two-story facades, so it keeps a low profile, both literally and figuratively, and in no way feels overwhelming, large, or disproportionate. Unlike other small towns, the city has managed to keep its identity and has not given in to a plethora of corporate chain stores. There are eclectic buildings here forming an amalgam of sorts—brick buildings from the turn of the 20th century, art deco facades, old boarded-up shops next to polished tile-and-glass buildings.

Starting at its westernmost end is the

EL CAMINO REAL, THE KINGS HIGHWAY

As you drive Highway 101 from Ventura up through Paso Robles and beyond, you'll begin to notice signs along the road of what looks like a shepherd's crook with a bell on it, and the words El Camino Real. The signs are peppered along a nearly 600-mile route in California. Here's why: At the same time that the American colonies were rebelling against England, a handful of Spaniards and Mexicans were establishing outposts up the California coast. In 1769, a fortress and the very first mission were established in San Diego. A footpath called the El Camino Real, or the Kings Highway, was created to connect each of the subsequent missions as they were constructed. The missions were situated in areas where large populations of indigenous people lived, and where the soil was fertile enough to sustain a settlement. Each mission was designed to be a day's travel from the next – at least in theory – all linked by El Camino Real. As time progressed and more missions were built, the footpath became a roadway wide enough to accommodate horses and wagons. It was not, however, until the last mission was completed in Sonoma in 1823 that this little pathway became a major road. Ultimately, El Camino Real linked all of California's 21 missions, pueblos, and four presidios, from San Diego to Sonoma. In 1904 the El Camino Real Association was formed to preserve and maintain California's historic road. The first commemorative bell was placed in 1906 in front of the Old Plaza Church in downtown Los Angeles, and by 1915 approximately 158 bells

© MICHAEL CERVIN

had been installed along the Camino Real. The bells were made of cast iron, which encouraged theft, and the number of original bells plummeted to about 75. New bells of concrete were then installed in 1974. Highway 101 loosely follows this original footpath.

mission, then the old thrift shops, eateries, and art galleries; as you move east you find bars, espresso bars, wine-tasting bars, and a brewery. There is no formal plan to Main Street, no overarching idea of how best to experience it. It has a uniqueness that defies interpretation and it's best to just wander down one side, exploring and discovering, then come back on the other side of the street. In the middle of it all you might choose to walk to the beach and soak in the low surf before returning to your amble down Main Street.

VENTURA HARBOR VILLAGE

There are many seaport villages strewn across the California coast, but what makes Ventura Harbor Village (1583 Spinnaker Dr., 805/642-8538, www.venturaharborvillage.com) so unique is the abundance of shops, and that it is also home to the working fishermen's fleets. As you browse the stores, walking right next to the boats, you'll notice the unusual olfactory confluence of just-harvested fish and waffle cones from the ice cream shop. Part working environment, part tourist section, it tries to straddle the

© MICHAEL CERVIN

Downtown Ventura's charming storefronts make it a welcoming place.

line between the two. Some unique spots not to be missed are the dive shop Ventura Dive and Sport and the kid-friendly arcade, which includes plenty of video games as well as a full-size 36-horse carousel. There's also skeeball, race-car driving games, indoor basketball, air hockey, and a large candy counter. The Village is also home to seafood restaurant Brophy Brothers, gift shop Carol's Cottage by the Sea, and kite store Harbor Wind & Kite. The Village faces the harbor, but if you cross the street you can walk out onto the sand and face the Pacific Ocean. There is three-hour free parking.

◀ Channel Islands National Park

At the end of Spinnaker Drive is the artistically unimpressive two-story headquarters for Channel Islands National Park, called the Robert J. Lagomarsino Visitor Center (1901 Spinnaker Dr., 805/658-5730, www.nps.gov, daily 8:30 A.M.–5 P.M., free), that oversees the islands. There are a few displays about native animals and birds that inhabit the islands, plenty of literature, and a few small touch tanks and a very cool 3-D display of all the islands and their topography. Perhaps best of all, you can climb to the second-story observation

deck and look out to sea as well as along the extensive Ventura Harbor. But it's all ultimately all about the islands here.

The Channel Islands National Park is made up of a total of eight islands, though only five of those (Anacapa, Santa Cruz, Santa Rosa, San Miguel, and Santa Barbara) actually border the Central Coast, within sight of the mainland. For just over 30 years these areas have been federally protected. Long before they were tourist spots, they were ranch lands. And even longer before that, archaeological evidence suggests, there were inhabitants on the islands as many as 13,000 years ago. Santa Cruz Island in particular was prime grazing land in the 1800s for cattle and sheep, without the worry of predators as on the mainland. Santa Cruz was also home to a winery, the remnants of which are still there.

The peculiar thing is that, although the islands are relatively close to the mainland, a preponderance of locals from both Ventura and Santa Barbara have never visited this part of their own backyard. To sail there can take three to four hours, and motor boats make the trip even faster, and yet people don't explore. Perhaps it is because the islands look so

© MICHAEL CERVIN

Ventura Harbor Village

SANTAROSEA

The Channel Islands off the Central Coast are identified as five separate islands, but the islands in the northern channel are actually connected to each other and form a large 724-square-mile land mass that existed 200,000 years ago, which scientists now call Santarosea. There have been discoveries of pygmy mammoth bones on the islands as recently as 2009, and scientists believe that Columbian mammoths crossed from the prehistoric mainland to Santarosea in search of food and eventually evolved into pony-sized pygmy mammoths, which roamed the islands until their extinction. A 1959 discovery of human bones on Santa Rosa Island buried 30 feet down in an old stream bed were dated to 13,000 years ago; they are believed to be the oldest human bones in North America.

far away (but Anacapa is only 12 miles from Ventura Harbor). True, San Miguel, the farthest west, is not a short trip, nor is the small rock island of Santa Barbara. But Anacapa, Santa Cruz, and to a lesser degree Santa Rosa can be done as day trips, though only Santa Cruz and Anacapa trips are available year-round. There can be tough weather conditions, and it's often very windy since there's little shelter. These islands are some of the last vestiges of pristine and unadulterated life on the West Coast, retaining a purity we all long for. A visit to Ventura practically begs you to spend a day exploring the islands on land or by sea.

Inexpensive day trips allow visitors to explore, hike, kayak, snorkel, camp, and scuba dive at the islands. Multi-day trips allow for extended camping excursions into the islands' interiors and for visiting several islands.

ANACAPA ISLAND

Anacapa is best known for a geologic formation called **Arch Rock,** which is, well, an arched rock. You can't access Arch Rock by foot, only sail by it, or kayak underneath it,

Arch Rock, Anacapa Island

but this volcanic formation has become an indelible landmark of Anacapa. The entrance to the island is at the tediously named Landing Cove, a small harbor where boats will anchor. You will need to take a zodiac to an old rusted metal ladder to access the island, as the harbor is small and the waters can get rough. There are sheer cliffs almost all the way around Anacapa, and you'll climb 154 steps to reachthe top of the island. Up top the vegetation is sparse and low and there few trees. From the top you can clearly see the "spine" of the island, which curves and bends toward Santa Cruz Island. The stunning volcanic formation almost looks like separate islands, forming a chain that extends for five miles. Anacapa has about 130 sea caves and is also home to the largest brown pelican rookery in the States. You'll discover that fact for yourself once you land, as the stench is obvious in certain spots. Travel time to the island is about an hour, and you're very likely to see dolphins on the way.

SANTA CRUZ ISLAND

Santa Cruz is the largest of the islands, some 22 miles long. There are more old buildings on this island than the others, and there is a day camp near Scorpion Bay where you can pitch a tent, store your food in metal lockers, and explore on foot. There are trees here, as well as old dried-out creeks and former grasslands that are often barren depending on the winter rains. This used to be farm land—hard to believe, but true. Being so far removed from the mainland, the island's cattle operations dwindled out in the 1920s. The elusive and nimble Channel Islands fox is difficult to spot, but there are ravens, beautiful large black birds that make a home here. This is also the only place in the world to see the endemic island scrub jay. Santa Cruz is by far the most popular island to visit, in part because it most closely resembles the mainland and, frankly, it is the most hospitable. Travel time is just over an hour, and once there you'll offload onto a short pier directly connected to shore, though shore landings from a skiff are possible depending on conditions.

Santa Cruz is a large, vast piece of land, and it's best to visit the center of the island if

© MICHAEL CERVIN

There are hundreds of caves like this at Channel Islands National Park.

possible—there the vegetation is thick, dense, and nearly Jurassic Park–like in its appearance. You half expect to find some strange prehistoric animal, calmly eating leaves off a tree. The best way to explore is by kayak or boat, to really get a feel for the inherent beauty of the rock formations, the multicolored strata of the rock, the numerous coves, and tiny beaches that are still relatively unused. Seals and sea lions make their homes in some of these coves, and the craggy rocks are home to oystercatchers, eagles, pelicans, and plenty of animals that crave the security and tranquility of these pockets of land.

SANTA ROSA ISLAND

Parts of Santa Rosa are a bit more forlorn than Santa Cruz, with low grass and some trees in the old water ravines. As with Anacapa, the steep cliffs prohibit landing just anywhere. There are some beautiful white sand beaches, though, and coastal lagoons and places that seem virtually untouched, as if no one has walked these shores before. The vistas from the top of some of the plateaus are beautiful,

with views to neighboring Santa Cruz Island and the California coastline in the distance. Travel time is about three hours by boat; you'll need to climb a 20-foot steel-rung ladder to reach flat land.

SAN MIGUEL ISLAND

San Miguel is available for concession tours during only part of the year. It is often a remote and desolate place, with fierce winds that sometimes prohibit landing. But the stark beauty is enchanting to some, and there are more species of birds, plants, and animals here than on the other islands. Stories abound that Juan Rodriguez Cabrillo, the first Westerner to set eyes on the West Coast in 1542, died and was buried here; there is a small memorial to him in Cuyler Harbor, a white cross planted firmly in the hard earth. It's true that when Cabrillo landed at the islands (not in Santa Barbara, as many believe—he never touched the mainland), he became sick and died. But specifics on exactly where he was buried are a matter of conjecture. Some say his crew buried him at San Miguel; some say they took his

© MICHAEL CERVIN

Santa Rosa Island has some pretty steep cliffs.

body to Catalina Island off the coast near Long Beach. Regardless of historical hypothesis, there is no definitive proof of where Cabrillo's bones remain.

San Miguel was used for cattle and sheep grazing until just after World War II, when it became a bombing range for military practice. Travel time is about four hours. Usually a skiff will run you to shore, though it depends on the weather conditions, which can be hit and miss.

SANTA BARBARA ISLAND
Santa Barbara Island is little more than a small rock in the lonely Pacific, and it's virtually impossible to see from the mainland. There are campsites on these 644 acres, but if you set up camp you might wonder exactly why you're here. Shut off, secluded, and lonely, it's a rare stop for most people, in spite of the occasional lush vegetation that grows here. Travel time is just over three hours; once there, you will not only have to climb a steel-rung ladder from a skiff, you'll then have to laboriously trudge up a quarter mile set of steps to reach the top.

Once there, you won't find any shelter, but you will be on one of the least-visited islands. It's a very cool feeling, to know few people have walked this land before you.

Fillmore, Santa Paula, and Oxnard
Not everything worth seeing on the mainland is within the downtown area. These sights are no more than a 30-minute drive out of town.

◖ FILLMORE AND WESTERN RAILWAY
Trains have become something of a novelty in America, at least to those on the West Coast. In Fillmore, 20 minutes from downtown Ventura, you can ride the rails on the vintage trains at Fillmore and Western Railway (351 Santa Clara St., Fillmore, 805/524-0330, www.fwry.com, call for weekend trains). Many of their trains have been used in film production (*Get Smart* is a recent example), and they offer a wide variety of themed train rides, like the murder mystery, polar express for the holidays, and margarita and wine themes. They typically run two to three different trains for their events. The trains are beautifully restored

and adorned with period furnishings, and it's an experience novice train riders will not soon forget. It should be said that the trains lumber along—you might think you could walk faster than the train, and you might be right. There's no air-conditioning, and the food and beverages are fairly inadequate. But all that aside, it's about the experience of being onboard a vintage train.

LIMONEIRA

In the 1890s someone realized that the area near Santa Paula might make a great orchard, given the nutrient-laden soil, the vast amount of flat land, and the proximity to a viable water source, namely the Santa Clara River. Lemon, orange, and avocado trees were planted, and several companies moved in to grow citrus. Several of the smaller companies banded together to form Sunkist. And then there was Limoneira (1141 Cummings Rd., Santa Paula, 805/525-5541, www.limoneiratours.com, call for tours), created in 1893, which is still a powerhouse in the lemon and avocado business. Nowadays, you can visit their old goods store, which houses a museum chronicling the history of the lemon packing area. Early farming techniques are explained and ancient equipment is on display. The old packing house, which is still in use, has the beautiful scents of lemon in the air, and there are demonstration orchards of 300 citrus trees. Limoneira has incorporated a solar orchard on the property in an effort to reduce waste and harness the sun's energy; it also provides both school kids and adults with an opportunity to learn about green technologies. There are 12 bocce ball courts and places to picnic out among the orchards. It can get windy there with breezes that run the length of the valley, but it's also peaceful and serene. Specialized tours can be arranged, including jeep tours and hot-air balloon rides over the orchards.

◀ CALIFORNIA OIL MUSEUM

It comes as a surprise to most people that Ventura and Santa Barbara are oil-rich lands. In fact, the coast off these two counties, and areas inland in Ventura and Ojai, are home to the largest natural oil and gas seeps in the Western Hemisphere. Seeps are, in essence, natural seepages primarily from the ocean floor of tar and gas emissions. The early Chumash Indians used the naturally occurring tar as a sealant for their wood boats, called *tomols*, which transported them between the Channel Islands and the mainland. Even now you can walk the coastline and occasionally smell the tar seeping up from the ocean. Only a 15-minute drive out of downtown, the California Oil Museum (1001 E. Main St., Santa Paula, 805/933-0076, www.oilmuseum.net, Wed.–Thurs. noon–2 P.M., Fri. noon–3 P.M., Sat.–Sun. 11 A.M.–3 P.M., $3), located in Santa Paula, offers an important understanding of the early years of this area. Included in the museum are overviews of oil exploration and how exactly oil is drawn from underneath the ocean floor, and an amazing display of three different drill bits used to penetrate the ocean's floor. There are exhibits that explain how oil is created, and a number of vintage gas pumps.

The upstairs of this building houses the original 1890s offices, exactly as they were at the turn of the 20th century. The nine original offices of Union Oil Company, each with their own storied past, have been restored to original mint condition, and include ten tiled fireplaces, oak wainscoting, plaster archways, ceiling medallions, stained glass, and vintage lighting, and they are probably the finest 1890s commercial building interior restoration in California. But most interesting of all is the back building, known as the Rig Room, which houses a circa-1900 iron-and-timber full-size operating drilling rig. Noisy and cumbersome, it's a fantastic reminder of the primitive nature of oil exploration and just how far we have evolved as a technological society. Oil exploration these days is done with geo-thermal mapping and computers. But back then it was dangerous, slow, tedious, and dirty work, and the percentage of failure was high. This explains why so many iron horses were installed, still visible and pumping from Ventura to Paso Robles. Being able to access oil was crucial to the growth of the region.

VENTURA AND OJAI

© MICHAEL CERVIN

Heritage Square is Oxnard's best kept secret.

◖ HERITAGE SQUARE

Heritage Square (715 South A St., Oxnard, 805/483-7960, www.heritagesquareoxnard.com, guided tours Sat. 10 A.M.–4 P.M., Sun. 1–4 P.M.) seems like an aberration at first. Just south of Ventura, in a somewhat grimy neighborhood, you'll suddenly come upon 15 Victorian buildings, and you might think you've stumbled upon a mini-mall created as a shopper's paradise. But no, these are fully restored historic buildings, all dating from 1887–1912, that were brought together to preserve the Victorian identity of Oxnard. A winery, a restaurant, a theater, an original quaint wood church from 1902 that holds a tiny historical display, and commercial tenants all call this home. The old houses are meticulously painted, showcasing vintage Victorian design and color. Docents in period dress will take you around the square. Concerts are held during the summer, and occasional special events take place. It's exceptional at Christmas, when the square is lit up and festively decorated. There are no shops to speak of, as this is a strolling place, a great reminder of preservation at its best. The

city partnered with some of the original owners of the old homes and private investors to help create this exceptional square of history.

BEACHES

People come to Ventura as much to walk along the beach as to walk downtown, and the beach is a core element of a visit here. Beach preferences are very personal: Some people like low and flat, some like rocky and wide. Whatever your tast, Ventura has something to offer. Keep in mind, however, that state-run, and some county-run, beaches charge day-use fees averaging about $10.

San Buenaventura State Beach

San Buenaventura State Beach (San Pedro St. and Hwy. 101, 805/968-1033, www.parks.ca.gov, daily dawn–dusk) features swimming, surfing, and picnicking. The beach has two miles of sandy beach, sand dunes, picnic sites, a parking lot, a snack bar, and a shop that rents beach equipment. Bike trails connect with other nearby beaches. The beach is the site for a number of special events, such

© MICHAEL CERVIN

Emma Wood State Beach

as the Pirate Festival, a triathlon, and occasional volleyball tournaments. The 1,700-foot pier has a snack bar, restaurant, and bait shop, and San Buenaventura State Beach offers Wi-Fi, though to pick up the signal you need to be within about 150–200 feet of the lifeguard tower located in the park.

Emma Wood State Beach

Emma Wood State Beach (W. Main St. at Park Access Rd., 805/968-1033 for recorded information, www.parks.ca.gov, daily dawn–dusk) is currently undergoing restoration efforts and offers no facilities. Due to the current budget cutbacks in California, there is no definitive timeline when the facilities will be reopened. Though the main road leading into the beach is closed, you can still park on the access road right off Main Street and Highway 101. The walk is only a few minutes to reach the campground and at the far east side of the parking lot there is a small path leading out to the beach that goes under the train tracks. To your right are views up the coast to the Rincon. The beach itself has many rocks nearly the size of footballs

strewn about. It is a great spot for windsurfing, as the winds come off Rincon Point just up from the mouth of the Ventura River, to create ideal windy conditions. There's a half-mile trail leading through the reeds and underbrush at the far end of the parking lot; though you can hear the surf and the highway, you can't see anything, and you'll feel like you're on safari until you reach the beach where the Ventura River ends.

McGrath State Beach

Just south of Ventura is McGrath State Beach (2211 N. Harbor Blvd., 805/968-1033 for recorded information, www.parks.ca.gov, daily dawn–dusk) is close to Oxnard, just south of where the Santa Clara River meets the ocean. It is known as one of the best spots to watch migratory birds in Southern California, with the lush riverbanks of the Santa Clara River and sand dunes piled along the shore. A nature trail leads to the Santa Clara Estuary Natural Preserve. The two-mile beach is popular with surfers and campers, but adventurous swimmers are advised to use caution due to strong riptides. The tree-shaded campground is spacious, with many spaces for family and group camping; reservations are strongly recommended. It's set back about a five-minute walk from the surf. To get to McGrath, take Highway 101 south from downtown Ventura and exit at Harbor Boulevard. Stay on Harbor; the park will be located on your right about five miles down the road.

Harbor Cove Beach

Harbor Cove Beach (1900 Spinnaker Dr., daily dawn–dusk) is located directly across from the Channel Islands Visitor Center at the very end of Spinnaker Drive. Families with young children prefer this beach because the shelter of the harbor's breakwaters provides safety from the currents, and the sand dunes provide a measure of isolation and protection. The wind can kick up at times, but when it's calm it's perfect. You can also watch sailboats and powerboats come and go through the mouth of the harbor. There's plenty of free parking, lifeguards during peak seasons, restrooms, and foot showers. Harbor Cove is across the street from Ventura Harbor Village, so food and other amenities are close by.

Faria Beach

Further north, the Ventura County–run Faria Beach (4350 W. Hwy. 101 at State Beach offramp, 805/654-3951, daily dawn–dusk) is available for tent camping and has 15 RV hookups. The campground has a playground and horseshoe pits, barbecues, and shower facilities, but it is quite small and very crowded with campers, trucks, and people during nice weather, due to its proximity to the water. You might find you have more companions than you care for, but it's a long flat beach, so you can spread out.

WINERIES

Most people don't think of Ventura as being home to any wineries, let alone a dozen countywide, with more cropping up, often in the least unexpected of places. The official **Ventura County Wine Trail** (www.venturacountywinetrail.com) was developed in hopes of catching some of the wine lovers who are heading

to Santa Barbara and Paso Robles from further south. The grapes used are not grown in Ventura at all, since row crops are far too valuable to ever give way to grapes, but the expanding wine scene is making a big difference in how people perceive Ventura. Two of the wineries are actually in Malibu in Los Angeles County, and two are not open to the public, but there are more being planned.

Two other beverages are currently produced in Ventura as well, though they do not offer a tasting room of any kind and are merely available at bars and clubs, or at shops by the bottle. **The Ventura Limoncello Company** (www.venturalimoncello.com) makes classic *limoncello* with lemons sourced from Limoneira in Santa Paula. And a local optometrist, who owns acreage in Jalisco, Mexico, produces **Tequila Alquimia** (www.tequilaalquimia.com), an all-organic tequila that is heavily distributed in the area. Both are local flavors worth looking for while you're out and about.

Cantara Cellars

Cantara Cellars (126 Wood Rd., Camarillo, 805/484-9600, www.cantaracellars.com, Sat.–Sun. 11 A.M.–5 P.M., tasting fee $7.50) is run by a husband and wife team who started making wine in their garage as amateurs. Fast forward to their opening as an official winery in 2006, and they now ferment 15 different varietals and bottle a dozen different wines. Most of their grapes come from the Lodi area, where a family ranch is located. Among their offerings are chardonnay, petite sirah, and cabernet sauvignon. The name Cantara is taken from the subdivision where the owners live. The tasting room is small, but the warm ocher-colored walls and obvious camaraderie make it irresistible. Everyone is offered a personal tour of their 6,500-square-foot facility, which is most often done by owner Mike Brown himself. Barrel samples from future releases are routinely offered during the winery tour.

Rancho Ventavo Cellars

Rancho Ventavo Cellars (741 S. A St., Oxnard, 805/483-8084, www.ranchoventavo.com,

Fri.–Sun. 11 A.M.–6 P.M., tasting fee $10) has the benefit of being located in a fully restored 1902 home with gorgeous woodwork; you can wander the house as you sip their wines. It's set in Heritage Square, so even if you're not into wine this is a great place to visit. They offer a full portfolio of red wines with fruit sourced from Napa, Santa Barbara, and Paso Robles. The owners will be there to pour for you; they're so likable you might end up staying longer than expected. Former home winemakers, they launched as a professional winery in 2005.

Herzog Wine Cellars

Herzog Wine Cellars (3201 Camino del Sol, Oxnard, 805/983-1560, www.herzogwine-cellars.com, Sun.–Thurs. 10:30 A.M.–9 P.M., Fri. 10:30 A.M.–4 P.M., closed Sat., tasting fee $3–6) is not just a massively large winery, but a kosher winery. The granite countertops of the tasting room are surrounded by warm wood tones. They have a full complement of gift items and make a large portfolio of wines, from dry to sweet, white, red, and blush, in-expensive everyday drinking wines to pricey Napa Valley cabernet sauvignons. Tours that include a tasting cost $10, otherwise you can take a self-guided tour that gives an overview of the process and vistas into their large tank and barrel rooms. It's housed in an industrial complex, where you'd never think to look for a wine-making facility.

ENTERTAINMENT AND EVENTS
Bars and Clubs

As a general rule, the established bars and clubs in Ventura survive, while some of the newer establishments seem to struggle. Those clubs that have tried to emulate Hollywood or Los Angeles clubs are not nearly as successful—Ventura just wants its old-fashioned watering holes.

Winchester's Grill and Saloon (632 E. Main St., 805/653-7446, Mon.–Fri. 4–11:30 P.M., Sat.–Sun. 11:30 A.M.–11:30 P.M.) is just such a watering hole. Maybe it's the 40-foot-long ma-hogany bar, or the rustic wood-toned feel of the place, or the fact that they have the biggest selection of beers on tap between L.A. and San Francisco (about 40), but it's just really fun here. It can get loud and rowdy—people seem to step inside and somehow think they instantly be-come cowboys. Winchester's is open later than many establishments, and their covered patio is more popular than being inside. Wherever you sit, their specialty is game dishes.

Dargan's Irish Pub (593 E. Main St., 805/648-3001, daily 11 A.M.–2 A.M.) is, for the most part, an upscale Irish bar, with traditional food like shepherd's pie and corned beef. Pool ta-bles are close at hand, as is the jukebox. Dargan's can be massively busy and understaffed on big nights like game or fight nights, but at its best it's still a little neighborhood bar.

Karma Lounge (281 W. Main St., 805/641-9090, www.karmaventura.com, Thurs.–Sun. 8 P.M.–2 A.M.) has a sleek Asian feel to the in-terior, with low-to-the-ground seating and a dimly lit bar area. The large outdoor patio will get you away from the music long enough to decide if you want the bottle service, which starts at $150 for just the average beverage. It's still one of the hottest clubs around, with a younger party set.

Card Room

For a bit of card play try **The Players Club** (906 N. Ventura Ave., 805/653-9326, www.player-sclubventura.com, daily 9 A.M.–2 A.M.), which was established as a state-regulated card room in the 1930s and has been under the ownership since 1949. Though the interior looks more like a Social Security office, it's packed with friendly card players playing Texas Hold'em, Omaha, and other variants of poker like Pineapple and Big-O.

Live-Music Venues

The Majestic Ventura Theater (26 S. Chestnut St., 805/653-0721, www.venturatheater.net) is one of the most popular live venues in Ventura. It opened in August 1928, and after decades of showing movies it was closed and converted into a concert venue. The seats on the main floor have been removed to form a pit, and only the balcony seats remain in place. There is a bar in the rear of the main floor and they serve some food, mainly forgettable sandwiches. The old chandeliers still hang in the auditorium and other remnants of the 1920s decor remain, creating a unique vibe unlike most new venues. The bands lean towards the alternative, though some mainstream groups have played here. It's conveniently located close to the bars and restaurants for before or after a concert.

Zoey's Cafe (451 E. Main St., 805/652-1137, www.zoeyscafe.com, cover $5–20) is located at the end of a long dimly lit courtyard, and at first you might not think there's anything back there. They call themselves a listening room and the emphasis is on acoustic music—you won't leave with your head spinning. This is the kind of cozy spot you can bring your kids and focus on the singer-songwriter in front of you. You might also hear folk, country, reggae, or even comedy. There's a full menu and a wine and beer list, as well as coffee drinks.

Bariloche (500 E. Main St., 805/641-2007, www.mybariloche.com, daily 11 A.M.–10 P.M.) is a restaurant focusing on South American food, but every night from 7 to 10 P.M. it offers live music like bossa nova, Spanish guitar, high-energy Cuban music, and more. It's a small space, but the intimacy lends itself to this type of music and people get very involved. You don't need to dine—you can just cozy up to the bar with a glass of Argentinean merlot or a Chilean chardonnay and enjoy the wonderful music.

It's All Good Bar and Grill (533 Main St., 805/647-9681, Mon.–Fri. 2 P.M.–2 A.M., Sat. 11 A.M.–2 A.M., Sun. 11 A.M.–11 P.M.), more commonly referred to as just Good Bar, is unlike most venues in that all types of people tend to show up here. There's live music most nights, and you can hear it from a few blocks away. There's also dancing, cheap shots of cheap liquors, and inexpensive beers, with a vibe like a controlled frat party. You'll hear all manner of music, but it's not a talking place—you're there to party.

Performing Arts

Rubicon Theatre (1006 E. Main St., 805/667-2900, www.rubicontheatre.org) opened in 1998 as a professional theater, with stars like Jack Lemmon and John Ritter. They have presented original works and shows that have gone on to other venues, and have won numerous awards. A night at the theater is a great activity, and this 200-seat space is a wonderful venue in which to see top talent and quality theater at a fraction of the price of Hollywood.

Ventura Improv Company (34 N. Palm St., 805/643-5701, www.venturaimprov.com, $10 adults, $8 seniors and children under 12) is the place to tickle your funny bone. With performances on Friday and Saturdays nights and classes offered throughout the week, there's always something to laugh about. They focus on team comedy improvisation and not solo acts. You can get involved as an audience member and match wits with the county's longest-running comedy group.

Festivals and Events

The **Ventura Music Festival** (805/648-3146, www.venturamusicfestival.org) during the first week of May features live musical acts at a variety of unique and intimate venues throughout the county. Diane Schuur, Pink Martini, and Herbie Hancock are just a few of the acts that have claimed center stage at the festival. In addition to the concerts there are lectures, live talks, interviews, and interaction with schoolchildren to educate them about music.

Ventura Artwalk (www.venturaartwalk.org), held in the middle of April and again in the fall, is a free self-guided walking tour of roughly 200 established and emerging artists at over 80 galleries, studios, and eclectic gallery-for-a day venues all within Ventura's Downtown Cultural District. The event is held just steps from the beach and the Ventura Pier. Participating art venues include restaurants, salons, antiques shops, unique boutiques, and coffee shops—most any place with walls. You might also encounter outdoor multicultural performances, and there is a free shuttle bus to any of the outlying locations. ArtWalk is one of the best ways to check out Ventura's diverse art community.

August's **Ventura County Fair** (Ventura

County Fairgrounds, 10 W. Harbor Blvd., 805/648-3376, www.venturacountyfair.org) has been going strong for well over 100 years. It draws some big-name musicians and comedians, and you can bungee jump, ride the Ferris wheel, and eat cotton candy. The fair maintains that small-town fair atmosphere, with agriculture still a dominant component.

SHOPPING
Shopping Malls and Districts

For traditional shopping, visit the **Pacific View Mall** (at Mills and Main Sts., 805/642-5530, www.shoppacificview.com, Mon.–Fri. 10 A.M.–9 P.M., Sat. 10 A.M.–8 P.M., Sun. 11 A.M.–7 P.M.), with 140 stores and restaurants like Sears, Target, Old Navy, Gap, Ben & Jerry's, and many more. The two-story indoor mall offers Wi-Fi in the food court. Some of the restaurants have improved over typical fast-food joints, and occasionally chair massages are offered. There are several nail places, as well as familiar brand-name stores. It does get crowded on weekends, but it's pretty easy to get around midweek.

Further south in Camarillo are the **Camarillo Premium Outlets** (740 E. Ventura Blvd., off Los Posas Ave., 805/445-8520, www.premiumoutlets.com, Mon.–Sat. 10 A.M.–9 P.M., Sun. 10 A.M.–8 P.M., holiday hours vary), with more outlet stores than should be allowed by law. You can find most anything in this massive complex, including Nike, Banana Republic, Sketchers, J. Crew, Tommy Hilfiger, and Jockey—160 stores in all. Many people spend the entire day here, and they actually bus large groups in. If you're not a shopper, the slow, methodical pace of people meandering from store to store might drive you crazy. If you love to shop, you're guaranteed to find several stores you can't live without.

For non-traditional shopping, **Main Street** in downtown Ventura is home to a surprising number of unique local and specialty stores and has managed to retain a sense of individuality.

Thrift Stores

Though Ventura's long been known for a plethora of inexpensive thrift stores drawing savvy shoppers from multiple surrounding counties, the thrift store scene is changing. Only a handful of stores remain, down significantly from the dozen or so that used to exist here. Many of them were converted into restaurants or bars. Still, there are bargains to be had. It is worth remembering that these thrift stores were originally designed as ways to bring in revenue for charitable organizations; even now the majority still only take cash.

Child Abuse and Neglect Thrift Store (340 E. Main St., 805/643-5956, Mon.–Sat. 9:30 A.M.–6 P.M., Sun. noon–5 P.M.) has a wide selection of donated goods, all in good working condition, including some antiques and furniture. The prices lean a little high and you need to shop carefully, but there are still bargains around the store if you have the time to look.

Treasure Chest Thrift Shop (328 E. Main St., 805/653-0555, daily 9 A.M.–7:30 P.M.) thrives on donations as well and has a larger selection of furniture and modern beach-cruiser bikes. Some pieces are clearly overpriced since they are newer, but you'll find some better deals if you scan the perimeters and especially the back of the store.

Coalition Thrift Store (270 E. Main St., 805/643-4411, Mon.–Sat. 9 A.M.–6 P.M.) has an excess of men's and women's clothing consuming the majority of the front section of the store. Their collectibles section is often neither collectable nor well priced, but their general housewares section is terrific. There's also a decent selection of books, toys, and small appliances located in the very back.

The **ARC Foundation** (265 E. Main St., 805/650-8611, Mon.–Sat. 9 A.M.–6 P.M., Sun. 10 A.M.–5 P.M.) has more clothes than anything else. The perimeter has a few typical thrift items-cheap glassware, old stereos and whatnot, including books and CDs to the right-hand side as you enter. But their clothing selection is varied and quite good, especially for women. The organization's goal is to improve the quality of life for individuals with developmental disabilities, as they have been doing since 1954, so your money is well spent here.

Art Galleries

Ventura is starting to brand itself as a new arts capital, and there are a number of galleries coming into the region. There has always been a strong arts scene here, but it's been overshadowed by Los Angeles, though that is beginning to change.

Red Brick Gallery (315 E. Main St., 805/643-6400, www.redbrickart.com, Sun.–Thurs. 11 A.M.–6 P.M., Fri.–Sat. 10 A.M.–8 P.M.) offers shows that rotate every six weeks. The gallery is, logically, lined with exposed redbrick walls, and represents about 160 artists, all from the West Coast. Here you will find artists working with paint, wood, glass, and photography, even jewelry designers and greeting card–makers. There is a great diversity here and they provide a variety of art classes as well, from watercolor to mosaics.

Sylvia White Gallery (1783 E. Main St., 805/643-8300, www.sylviawhite.com, Wed.–Sat. 11 A.M.–5 P.M.) is a 5,000-square-foot space with a focus on well-known artists. This is museum-quality art by big names, with prices to match.

The two-story **Artists Union Gallery** (330 S. California St., 805/643-3012, www.venturaartistsunion.org, Thurs. and Sun. noon–6 P.M., Fri.–Sat. noon–9 P.M.) hosts fine-art exhibitions and juried shows as well as spoken word, dance, and music performances in a beachfront promenade. Every Tuesday is poetry night, and every Saturday and Sunday from 10 A.M. to 4 P.M. in the plaza overlooking the ocean they sponsor Arts and Crafts by the Sea, which, though small, features all hand-crafted home and garden art, jewelry, clothing sold by the artists. There are a great number of local artists represented here and you can actually converse with them.

Clothing

B on Main (337 E. Main St., 805/643-9309, Mon.–Thurs. 11 A.M.–6 P.M., Fri. 11 A.M.–8 P.M., Sat. 10 A.M.–8 P.M., Sun. 11 A.M.–5 P.M.) is all about beach clothing with a 1950s retro twist. It's a fun store to browse, but can be a little pricey. The fashions and accessories are mainly tailored for women. They also have a full line of retro beach posters, as well as an eclectic collection of gift cards and small gift items like soaps and dishware.

Buffalo Exchange (532 E. Main St., 805/648-6873, Mon.–Sat. 11 A.M.–7 P.M., Sun. 11 A.M.–6 P.M.) sells really cool used clothing, but they have lots of stuff on consignment so the prices may seem a bit high. The majority of the clothes and shoes are of recent vintage and not so wildly out of date that you'd look foolish wearing them. You can also sell your old stuff to them.

At times we all seek a little something special. **Aphrodite's Lingerie and Gift Gallery** (477 E. Main St., 805/652-0082, www.aphroditesonline.com, Mon.–Tues. 10:30 A.M.–5:30 P.M., Wed.–Thurs. 10 A.M.–7 P.M., Fri.–Sat. 10 A.M.–9 P.M.) has a great selection of lingerie, teddies, corsets, stocking, games, toys, body products, and even a few fun costumes, all sold by a knowledgeable staff who can direct you. Women will feel comfortable and men won't feel intimidated.

Blue Moon (600 E. Main St., 805/643-2553, Mon.–Sat. 10:30 A.M.–6 P.M., Sun. noon–5 P.M.) sells both new and used clothing at great prices. Nothing is too formal here; the clothes are pretty casual, including a nice selection of pendants, hats, and shoes. The stock rotates often so there's always something new.

Antiques

Times Remembered (467 E. Main St., 805/643-3137, daily 10:30 A.M.–5:30 P.M.) is packed with antiques, collectibles, and newer vintage items. They have a large selection of books and everything from toys to jewelry. These are mainly small items and some are merely knock-offs of actual vintage items. The interesting stuff tends to be locked in the cases, and you need to wade though the cramped quarters and cluttered shelves in order to unearth some cool finds.

For Your Home (443 E. Main St., 805/641-1919, Mon.–Sat. 10:30 A.M.–6 P.M., Sun. 11 A.M.–5 P.M.) is a large two-story space that carries traditional contemporary, ornate, reproduction, sleek and modern, and lots of Mission and Amish-style pieces. Many are less authentic antique and more reproduction type, but are of very good quality. There are furnishings and accents for every room in your house, including colorful 1950s dinette sets on the 2nd floor.

Home Furnishings

At **Pure Life and Home** (576 Main St., 805/641-2500, Mon.–Wed. 11 A.M.–6 P.M., Thurs. 11 A.M.–7 P.M., Fri.–Sat. 11 A.M.–9 P.M., Sun. noon–6 P.M.) you'll find a collection of things for your home, like tables, chairs, lighting, accent pieces, fountains, and the eclectic, but with a true sense of craftsmanship. What's sold here is high quality without the high prices. The items are simple in their work, not augmented with too much extraneous flair, and have a grounded feel, with a hint of Asian style. Like the name says, they are furnishings, pure and simple.

Gifts

Carol's Cottage by the Sea (1591 Spinnaker Dr., 805/658-8222, Mon.–Thurs. 11:30 A.M.–5:30 P.M., Fri. 11:30 A.M.–7 P.M., Sat.–Sun. 10:30 A.M.–7 P.M.) carries a huge selection of unique gifts and collectibles like Webkinz, Disney, Wee Forest Folk, and Sid Dickens. There are also gifty gifts of home decor, including stained-glass objects, custom gift cards, candles of all types, unique jewelry, music boxes, and a whole lot more oriented to a traditional sensibility. Say hello to Della, the store's mascot dog. The conversation tends to lean towards exactly what breed she is, since no one is really too certain.

Specialty Stores

In the mood for a wee bit of olive oil? **We Olive** (294 E. Main St., 805/648-6166, www.weolive.com, daily 10 A.M.–6 P.M.) has over 40 olive oils ready for sampling. And these are not just California oils, but olive oils from across the globe including the granddaddy of oil producers, Italy. Here you'll be able to discern the subtle and not so subtle differences between

oils. They also offer about 10–20 balsamic vinegars to taste. It's a great stop and an interesting change of pace.

Rosie Lee Imports (673 E. Main St., 805/643-5832, www.rosieleeimports.com, Mon. 11 A.M.–6 P.M., Tues.–Sat. 10 A.M.–6 P.M., Sun. noon–5 P.M.) is all Britain, all the time. A cuppa tea, biscuits, gift items, teapots, cheese and sausages—this fun store is run by a British expat who knows her stuff. If you need a touch of Europe you'll find it here, including English newspapers. Even if you're not related to British ancestry, a stop here might make you wish you were.

Harbor Wind & Kite (1575 Spinnaker Dr., 805/654-0900, www.harborwind-kite.com, Sun.–Thurs. 10 A.M.–6 P.M., Fri.–Sat. 10 A.M.–7 P.M.) has kites literally hanging everywhere. A 20-year veteran of the Village, they have every conceivable type of kite, plus kite accessories including items for kiteboarding and kite buggies. They also carry more kites and wind-oriented toys, like Frisbees and boomerangs, than you can imagine. Since the Ventura coast gets its share of winds, a kite here can go a long way.

Farmers Markets

There are only nine farmers markets spread out over the entire county, which is surprising given the strong agricultural emphasis in Ventura. There are two markets in the downtown core: the **Downtown Market** (Santa Clara and Palm Sts., 805/529-6266, Sat. 8:30 A.M.–noon) and the **Midtown Market** at the Pacific View Mall (Sears parking lot at Main and Mills Sts., 805/529-6266, Wed. 10 A.M.–1 P.M.). These are straightforward farmers markets, so you won't find arts and crafts, roving musicians, or anything like that. People come here to shop for food.

SPORTS AND RECREATION
Golf

Buenaventura Golf Course (5882 Olivas Park Dr., 805/642-2231, www.buenaventuragolf.com, green fees $14–41) is an excellent 18-hole course for beginning and seasoned players, and this course is the most beautiful in Ventura. It is tightly designed but has strong crosswinds, making it more challenging than it looks. The course is a traditional style with undulating bent-grass greens and fairways lined with mature trees. The grounds are very attractive and compact, and all the greens have been re-sculpted using classic Bell designs. It's a heavily played course, with good reason.

Olivas Park Golf Course (3750 Olivas Park Dr., 805/677-6770, www.olivaslinks.com, green fees $20–52) is still a relatively inexpensive course to play, in spite of it being owned by the city. It's located near the Ventura River so you will get some off shore breezes coming in, but usually nothing to affect your game on this par-70 course. Voted the number one public golf course in Ventura County for several consecutive years, it's a links-style course with sculpted fairways, well-placed bunkers, strategic lakes, and excellent greens. About 100,000 rounds of golf are shot each year at this course, which opened in 1969.

Saticoy Regional Golf Course (1025 S. Wells Rd., 805/642-6678, www.saticoy.americangolf.com, green fees $12–14) is a 9-hole, par-35 public course that opened in 1921. It's a well-rounded short, flat course that makes for an enjoyable walk as well. It has small greens but no water hazards, and also offers a 20-stall driving range. Other amenities include a pro shop, snack bar, cart and club rentals, putting green, and driving range. A lighted driving range for late-night golfers is a huge draw.

Horse Racing

If you feel like horsing around, head to **The Derby Club at the Ventura County Fairgrounds** (10 W. Harbor Blvd., 805/653-2533, www.venturacountyfair.org). They offer horse racing live via satellite in three separate rooms. There are food and drinks available, but no one under 18 is allowed in. Rates vary for each room depending on the type of racing.

Hiking Trails

With the Los Padres Mountains as a backdrop, the area has plenty of hiking within a short

drive from downtown. The website www.venturacountytrails.org is a good reference for local hikes with GPS coordinates and photos.

The Arroyo Verde Park Trail (Poli and Day Sts., www.cityofventura.net, daily dawn–dusk) is a moderate hike that covers just under four miles out and back. It runs parallel with a popular picnic area then quickly turns backcountry, with rugged terrain and a 300-foot elevation gain that leads to nice views of the Pacific Ocean and Channel Islands. At first glance, Arroyo Verde Park looks like any manicured city park—with the exception that there are over four dozen different types of trees planted here. A lush green lawn gives way to picnic areas, playgrounds, and a couple of baseball fields. Weekends draw families with young kids. But if you look beyond the edges you'll see hints that there is more to this park than just pretty landscaping. High in the hills surrounding it, you will find hikers and runners making their way through dense chaparral and semi-rugged terrain to viewpoints that overlook the park and the Pacific Ocean. From downtown, drive east on Main Street, turning left on Poli Street near Ventura High School. Poli turns into Foothill, which will take you to the park located on your left-hand side where Poli intersects with Day Street.

Though the majority of the trails at **Grant Park** (Poli Rd. at Brakey Rd., www.serrapark.org, www.cityofventura.net, daily dawn–dusk) are paved, the hiking is a workout, uphill the entire way. Once you reach the summit, you'll have killer views to the ocean and Ventura splayed out before you. A simple up and back is less than three miles, but you can extend that off-road on the smaller trailheads. Near City Hall, off Poli Road is Brakey Road. Park on Poli and walk up, staying on Brakey, which twists and turns. Once at the summit, head left towards the Padre Serra cross (you'll see the sign), with excellent views to the ocean. From Brakey heading further into the interior of this 107-acre park, there are little sub trails, none with actual names—or signs for that matter—but each marked by a simple metal gate. These go off-road and wander the undeveloped hilltop area. There are picnic tables and restrooms as well. Then, get ready to head back down the steep road to your car.

Bike Trails

Pacific Coast Bike Trail (Hwy. 101, Hwy. 1) extends from the Oregon border to the Mexican border. In Ventura the oceanfront highway gives you great scenery, namely the Pacific Ocean. The only drawback is that you're on the highway. Yes, there is a dedicated bike lane, but this route should be used only by experienced riders who want long stretches of uninterrupted road and are already familiar with riding under these conditions.

The **Ventura River Trail** (Main and Peking Sts., www.ventura-usa.com) follows the Ventura River from Main Street just over six miles inland one-way, ending at Fosters Park. From there it joins the **Ojai Trail,** a two-lane bike path that follows Highway 33 into Ojai (16 miles one-way). This trail corresponds to a 100-year-old Southern Pacific rail line that used to run thorough here. At times both of the paths hug the highways, but they also course through beautiful scenery. The elevation gain is close to 1,000 feet, but it's a gentle climb that escorts you through prime agricultural land.

Sulphur Mountain Road (Hwy. 33 and Sulphur Mountain Rd.) is a maintained double-track fire road that extends for a nine-mile ride one-way, climbing about 2,000 feet. Once near the top you have some great views to Lake Casitas and into Santa Paula. Along the way you'll see deer, coyotes, bobcats, and foxes, especially at dusk. Keep your eyes skyward for one of the many red-tail hawks in the neighborhood. There also might be napping rattlesnakes, busy tarantulas, skittish roadrunners, and seemingly bored cattle. This is a very busy trail. Equestrians and hikers use it and have as much right to it as bikers. So pay attention, and be friendly. Also, obey the No Trespassing signs and stay on the trail. From the 101, go north on Highway 33 towards Ojai. About two miles after the divided freeway ends is the turn onto Sulphur Mountain Road, which is clearly marked. The trailhead is a few hundred yards down the road at the gate. Pay attention to any posted No Parking signs.

You can rent a bike at **Cycles-4-Rent** (239 Main St., 888/405-2453), which rents just about anything mobile, including but not limited to bikes, tandems, inline skates, and scooters. **Wheel Fun Rentals** is located right at the pier (850 Harbor Blvd., 805/650-7770) for in-town cruising or meandering along the promenade by the water.

Running Trails

The Promenade, also known as the **Omer Rains Trail,** is a concrete and asphalt route. It's easy to find and is flat and perfect for simply cruising the area and feeling the beach breeze in your hair. From downtown simply head to the ocean at California Street. You can pick up the trail and head up or down the coast. If you turn right at the promenade you'll go towards the county fairgrounds and end near Emma Wood Beach. If you turn left, you'll head towards San Buenaventua Beach, and it will take you straight to the marina. The entire length from point to point is eight miles. It's safe and easy, but it can get crowded during nice days. There are restroom facilities along the way and you'll skirt the ocean for the entire length.

Blanche Reynolds Park to the Harbor (3120 Preble Ave.) is an out-and-back six-mile run that starts at the park and follows Preble Avenue for one block. From there, turn right onto Lemon Grove under the freeway bridge and through the strawberry fields, paralleling Arundell Street to get to the Ventura Harbor. (If you want to cut the run in half, simply have someone pick you up near Ventura Harbor Village.) The fields are low and flat and provide some great views, not to mention the sweet smell of strawberries when in season. The harbor section, along Spinnaker Drive, is great because you have the harbor on your right side and the ocean to your left. This is a moderate run with little elevation gain. To get to Blanche Reynolds Park, from Highway 101 south, exit at Seaward, and cross back over the highway. Turn right on Ocean, then take a right on

© MICHAEL CERVIN

VENTURA AND OJAI

kayaking in the Ventura Harbor

South Bourchard and a left onto Preble; the park is on the right.

Whale-Watching and Harbor Cruises

December–March is the ideal time to see Pacific gray whales pass through the channel off the coast of Ventura. From late June to late August is the narrow window for both blue and humpback whales as they feed offshore near the islands. Most whale-watching trips are about three hours. Sometimes, if you visit the Channel Islands during these times, you'll see whales on your way out or back—sort of a freebie, if you will. But for straight whale-watching trips, these companies will get you as close as possible. Remember, though, that whale-watching is also weather-dependent, so cancellations can and do occur.

Island Packers Cruises (1691 Spinnaker Dr., 805/642-1393, www.islandspackers.com, $23–32) has operated whale-watching cruises for years and is the most experienced. They also run harbor cruises with a variety of options from dinner cruises to group charters.

Their website has all the pertinent details for customizing to get exactly what you want.

Ventura Boat Rentals (1575 Spinnaker Dr., 805/642-7753, www.venturaboatrentals.com) offers sunset cruises and dinner cruises starting at the harbor. They will also rent you a boat, sailboat, surf bike, or paddle boat. Their schedule varies a bit, so it's best to contact them for specific times and rates.

Kayaking Tours

Blue Sky Kayak Tours (805/290-3306, www.blueskykayaktours.com, day trips from $165) will take you to Anacapa and Santa Cruz Islands, where you'll paddle right off the boat in your kayak to explore the abundant sea caves, like Painted Cave, the coast, and cliffs, and some of the sealife that teems beneath you. The great benefit to kayaking with Blue Sky is that owner Matt May, a former firefighter, has a special agreement with The Nature Conservancy (which operates specific areas that are closed to the general public) that allows him to kayak around and land on parts of the islands you can't normally access. He has single and tandem kayaks and does day trips and overnight trips; he also arranges special charters. He also teaches a wilderness first responder and first aid course. Round-trip boat trips to the islands include kayaks, wet suits, instructions, and snorkel gear, should you choose to get in the pristine water.

Channel Islands Kayak (1691 Spinnaker Dr., 805/644-9699, www.cikayak.com, Mon.–Fri. noon–5 P.M., Sat.–Sun. 10 A.M.–5 P.M., $12.50/hour to rent, full kayak tours from $79.95) will rent you single or tandem kayaks and a wet suit if you need one. You can glide around the harbor on your own, or they will take you out to the islands for a guided tour.

Scuba Diving

The quickest way to the Channel Islands (Anacapa Island is the closest), is via Ventura Harbor. There are many charter boats that will take divers to the islands and surrounding areas, but it's always best to go on a dive boat with a divemaster, someone who knows the islands, the surges, the swells, and the water patterns at any given time of year.

Raptor Dive Charters (1559 Spinnaker Dr., 805/650-7700, www.raptordive.com, $110–125) will travel to all five islands (San Miguel is the most distant and difficult to get to, and Santa Barbara is the most forlorn). Their multi-day trips will get you to remote places where most people never dive. They also do night diving and lobster trips. Winter is routinely the best time to dive, as the water is the clearest and there are frequent plankton blooms. Yes the water is colder, but it's worth suffering a little for better visibility.

Peace Boat (2419 Harbor Blvd., 805/650-3483, www.peaceboat.com, $100–135) is a 65-foot dive boat that departs from the harbor for single- and multi-day dive trips; it'll even traverse the waters south to San Nicolas and Santa Catalina Islands. They have a very conscientious staff who know the waters and emergency procedures, and are certified and equipped for Nitrox. Plus, soaking in their hot tub with an ice cream is the perfect ending to a long day of diving.

Ventura Dive and Sport (1559 Spinnaker Dr., 805/650-6500, Mon.–Fri. 10 A.M.–6 P.M., Sat.–Sun. 8 A.M.–6 P.M., $110–125) offers dive classes in their heated pool, dive trips to the Channel Islands, scuba diving lessons, equipment sales and rentals, and a full line of sports apparel, including sunglasses, all best suited to Ventura's outdoor activities.

Surfing

The Rincon (Bates Rd. and Hwy. 101) is Ventura's most famous surfing landmark. The name Rincon describes the actual road that is part of Highway 101, the entire cove, and the surfing area, which is a thin strip of land with a large point, with a long right break. In the early 1920s a road was built to connect Ventura to Santa Barbara, as there was barely any room there since the cliffs plunged directly into the Pacific Ocean. At first the Rincon road was built of rustic logs and then wood planks between the cliffs and ocean, but they kept getting washed away by the pounding surf. Finally Highway 101 was built, the area was extended, and traffic now moves freely, though as you drive it it's clear how little room there is between the cliffs and ocean. But much of the Rincon portion of the highway still abuts the water, and during storms it's common to have the ocean splashing over onto the highway, soaking cyclists and drivers alike.

For surfers, it's a great spot, and now, due to its fame, it's almost always crowded. Wintertime is when the Rincon is at its best as north and west swells sweep in, wrap around the shallow cobble point, and peel off with an almost predictable evenness around the bend. When conditions are ideal, you can ride the waves in Santa Barbara all the way into Ventura, since the Rincon straddles both counties. To access the Rincon, exit at Bates Road from the north or south off Highway 101 and turn towards the beach. There are city and county parking lots, though usually the parking is filled early in the morning. There's a small gate that leads down a path behind several residences, which drops you at the rocky beach. If you head to your right towards the point you can jump in the water.

Surfers hit the waves early.

C Street is the nickname for California Street, which is near what some people call Surfers Point at Seaside Park. For surfers, it's simply referred to as C Street. Early mornings are favored for surfers in this spot close to the pier. There are three distinct zones along this mile-long stretch of beach. At the point is the Pipe, with some pretty fast short breaks. Moving down the beach is the Stables, which continues with the right breaks, with an even low shoulder, and then you have C Street, breaking both right and left. Yes, it gets crowded here, and there are a lot of spectators walking along the concrete boardwalk. But you also have a lot of amenities and some free parking at your disposal.

SURF CLASSES

All things considered, surfing is not as difficult as it might seem—well, reasonably so—while you're at the beach, why not at least get your feet wet? These places can teach you the basics so your time in the water can be a blast.

Surf Class (805/200-8674, www.surf-class.com, $90 two-hour session) meets at various beaches around Ventura depending on weather and swells. They teach everyone from novice landlubbers to rusty shredders. The rates are quite good for their two-hour classes and they limit class sizes for individual attention. They will also teach you surf etiquette and lingo.

Ventura Surf School (607 W. Channel Islands Blvd., 805/218-1484, www.ventura-surfschool.com, $125 two-hour session) can also teach you to surf, and they also offer a weeklong surf camp and kids-only classes.

SURF RENTALS

If you just need gear, swing by **Seaward Surf and Sport** (1082 S. Seaward Ave., 805/648-4742, www.seawardsurf.com, daily 9 A.M.–7 P.M., all-day surfboard rentals $15–50), which is the place to go to buy or rent most anything for the water: bikinis, body boards, sunglasses, wet suits, and everything else. They are a half a block from the beach, so you can rent and then head straight to the water.

At **Beach Break Surf Shop** (1559 Spinnaker Dr., #106, 805/650-6641, www.beachbreak-surfshop.com, daily 10 A.M.–5:30 P.M., all-day

The Rincon is the best-known surf spot in all of the Central Coast.

wetsuit rentals $25), you're already at the harbor, so you can simply cross the street and hit the beach. They rent all manner of surf gear, including long boards and boogie boards. They have a Hawaiian theme and also carry a lot of Hawaiian shirts.

Spas

Ventura is already a relaxing place to be. If you need further relaxation, check out these spas, which provide a variety of different options.

At **Michael Kelley Salon and Day Spa** (1895 E. Main St., 805/648-7743, www.michaelkelleysalon.com, Tues.–Sat. 8 A.M.–8 P.M., spa packages start at $185) you can get a full spectrum of salon services, including Michael Kelley's signature treatment: a two-and-a-half-hour salt-glow exfoliation including a steam, cleanse, scrub, and a final rinse with the Vichy shower (various water pressures flood over you while lying down in a tiled room). Or get your nails done, perhaps have a massage, or mix and match at this colorful and exuberantly decorated day spa.

Lavender Blue (3453 Telegraph Rd., 805/339-0253, by appointment only, individual treatments $15–55) is a small one-on-one space and focuses only on manicures, pedicures, facial waxing, and hair treatments. The decor is slight French in essence, but warm and intimate, just like the service. This is not a large shop with people running everywhere, but individual service and attention.

Yamaguchi Salon and Coastal Spa (1794 S. Victoria, 805/658-7909, www.yamaguchibeauty.com, Mon.–Tues. 8 A.M.–4 P.M., Wed.–Thurs. 8 A.M.–7 P.M., Fri.–Sat. 8 A.M.–5 P.M., individual treatments start at $50) will definitely color your hair, but you can also get massages and wraps. Their prices are reasonable, if just slightly high, and they use their own products. They are also one of the few full day spas in town and they have other salons around Southern California.

The dark floors and beige walls at **Bellissima Salon and Spa** (1786 E. Main St., 805/643-0388, www.bellissimasalonvta.com, Tues.–Fri. 10 A.M.–7 P.M., Sat. 8 A.M.–3 P.M., individual treatments start at $20) make it comfortable and professional-looking. The salon has developed a loyal fan base, mainly for hair coloring and facial treatments.

ACCOMMODATIONS

There are accommodations downtown, of course, but a drawback to most of them is the unfortunate placement of the freeway and train tracks. It can't be helped, but it also can't be ignored, and many hotels will offer earplugs when you check in—or you might want to bring some with you just in case. With your room's window or sliding door shut you usually only hear the vague rumblings of noise, but that's no fun during the summer when you would like the fresh air.

Under $150

Downtown's **Bella Maggiore Inn** (67 S. California St., 805/652-0277, $90–140 d) has a definite European feel. Just three blocks from the beach, the 32 rooms in this charmingly peculiar spot are all configured differently and have a quirky quality, some with built-in drawers and cabinets, others with spas. The furnishings, too, are varied. Some bathrooms have Formica countertops, and some rooms have old chassis TVs—it's definitely a throwback. The hallways are narrow and quiet, and there is an upstairs sundeck. The attached restaurant is actually a fully covered brick courtyard with old vines climbing the walls. The inn almost feels more like a large bed-and-breakfast than a hotel. They are slowly upgrading the rooms, but this isn't the place for state-of-the-art interiors. And for some, that's just fine.

If a chain hotel is more your style, the **Best Western Inn of Ventura** (708 E. Thompson Blvd., 805/648-3101, www.bestwesterncalifornia.com, $130–150 d) is a safe and reliable choice. Less than a half mile to the beach and a half mile to downtown, it's well situated to explore. A heated pool and hot tub, continental breakfast, and microwaves in the rooms round out the offerings of the smoke-free property.

The **Vagabond Inn-Ventura** (756 E. Thompson Blvd., 805/648-5371, www.vagabondinn-ventura-hotel.com, $80–110 d) is another chain hotel that will go easy on your wallet if you want basic accommodations. Pet friendly and centrally located, this spot is one of the least expensive in town. You can't expect too much, except to save money on accommodations so you can spend elsewhere.

The **Country Inn and Suites** (298 Chestnut, 800/596-2375, www.countryinns.com, $139–155 d) has 119 rooms two blocks from the beach. They sit overlooking the freeway, so there will be some residual noise. But they offer a free full hot breakfast, a heated outdoor pool, and free Wi-Fi. The rooms are garden-variety hotel rooms, but they do have microwaves, mini-refrigerators, and coffeemakers. Plus you can easily walk to the beach and downtown.

$150-250

The Holiday Inn Express (1080 Navigator Dr., 805/856-9533, www.hiexpress.com, $150–195 d) overlooking the harbor is a 101-room standard hotel that is more popular with business travelers than with tourists. It's standard fare and nothing exciting, but it will serve you well for the views and proximity to other things to do. The rooms are larger than most of this type, but not all views reach the harbor, so be advised of that issue if you have your heart set on seeing the water from your room.

The **Comfort Inn** (2094 E. Harbor Blvd., 805/563-5000, www.choicehotels.com, $199–239 d) is another chain with 42 standard rooms; it is dependable, clean, and located near the harbor. All of the rooms have microwaves, refrigerators, in-room coffeemakers, Wi-Fi, and a free breakfast at the Denny's next door is included. The rooms are bathed in soft warm wood tones and though nothing out of the ordinary, it's a safe bet.

The **Inn on the Beach** (1175 S. Seaward Ave., 805/652-2000, www.innonthebeachventura.com, $175–195 d) is aptly named, as the hotel is actually pushed up against the sand. The best views are from the 2nd floor, as the 1st-floor views tend to be obstructed by small mounds of sand. Each of the 28 rooms is fancifully decorated with very different antiques. There are parts that could use a face-lift, and it's not the brand-new digs some people may care for, but there's free Wi-Fi, and a lot of repeat customers. It's out of the way, somewhat by itself, but within a block walk of a few restaurants and coffee shops, and downtown is a short drive away.

The **Marriott Hotel Ventura Beach** (2055 E. Harbor Blvd., 805/643-6000, www.marriott.com, $150–220 d) has 270 rooms and 15 suites, which means that you'll probably always have company at this large hotel near the sand south of downtown. Big is sometimes good, in that Marriott is a trusted name and the prices are reasonable (but keep in mind the $10 daily parking rate that is added to your bill). Though there is a large pool and spa with palm trees around them, this is standard hotel fare. Chances are you can more readily find a special deal offered here than at other places.

(The Crowne Plaza** (450 E. Harbor Blvd., 805/648-2100, www.crowneplaza.com, $190–225 d) is beautifully positioned right at the beach. There are great views of the pool and the beach from the upper floors, and you're right at the five-mile boardwalk and just steps from the pier. The walk to downtown, over the freeway and train tracks, is a mere three blocks. Being one of the largest hotels, at 258 rooms, they can provide better pricing. And it is actually a wonderful place to stay. The rooms are very comfortable with a modern feel to them, echoing the overall modern retro feel of the lobby and bar area. There's an in-house restaurant, but you're close enough to downtown that you can find something better within a five-minute walk. There is an outdoor patio that abuts the boardwalk; it's gated and inaccessible to passersby.

The Pierpont Inn (550 Sanjon Rd., 805/643-6144, www.pierpont.com, $145–250) was originally built in 1910, and it still retains its wood shingled exterior and rich Craftsman-style lobby, which looks through to the restaurant and straight out to the ocean. The hotel tends to be frequented by an older crowd, which means that it is quieter here. The 77 rooms also give a nod to the Craftsman style, and there are Tempur-pedic mattresses in all

the rooms. The bathrooms are a bit small, so if you're looking for a long soak, this isn't the place. Unfortunately the freeway is extremely close, making it a little tough to sit outside by the water feature and have a cocktail, but the rooms are relatively quiet. There's a day spa, restaurant, meeting space, and tennis courts on-site, and though it's a few blocks away, you can walk to the beach by heading under the freeway to reach the sand.

(Four Points Sheraton** (1050 Schooner Dr., 805/658-1212, www.starwoodhotels.com, $160–190 d) is located at the harbor, the only full-service hotel there. It is 10 acres of prime coastal land designed by the Frank Lloyd Wright Foundation (not Mr. Wright himself); the hotel was renovated in 2008 and features 102 spacious and well-appointed guest rooms and four suites, most with private balconies and wonderful views of the boats. It's near Harbor Village and freeway access, and it's a short jaunt to downtown.

FOOD

The culinary scene has taken off in the last few years, and Ventura is seeing its share of excellent restaurants claim center stage. You won't see the sophisticated leanings of Los Angeles, but there are more chefs turning to Ventura to avoid the hype and pressure of Hollywood. There is an abundance of fresh local produce, vegetables, fish, and shellfish.

American

One of the best examples of this new culinary scene is **(** Watermark on Main** (589 Main St., 805/643-6800, www.watermarkonmain.com, Tues.–Thurs. 5–9 P.M., Fri.–Sat. 5–10 P.M., $30), housed inside a stunningly and lovingly restored 1928 bank building. Vintage art deco light fixtures, a hand-painted plaster ceiling, and an original mural over the bar share the space with new African mahogany booths—the look is all very sophisticated. In contrast, the upstairs bar known as H2o is all modern, using a blue theme to capture the ocean, which you can just see from the rooftop lounge. The mezzanine is where the old bank vault still sits; it now holds the pricey liquors like single-malt scotches. Signature dishes include the Watermark Chile Relleno with Santa Barbara prawns, cranberries, and summer squash, and free-range Black Angus steaks. This is hands down the most beautiful interior of any restaurant in Ventura. They do have a dress code: no hats or shorts, and men must have a collared shirt.

It's a little more casual at **((Brooks** (545 E. Thompson Blvd., 805/652-7070, www.restaurantbrooks.com, Tues.–Sun. 5 P.M.–close, $25) created by Andy Brooks. It's a little gem of a restaurant in an unremarkable location. The exterior looks like a chain store, but the interior is warehouse chic with 1950s accents. Brooks is known for really cool cocktails, like the tequila-sage blood-orange margarita rimmed with chili salt, or the concoction of Blue Coat gin, St. Germain liqueur (made from wild elderflowers), orange, lemon, and lime juice, rimmed with toasted coriander sugar. The food coming out of the kitchen is excellent: The wild-game chili is earthy, rich, and immensely satisfying, as are the spicy rubbed shrimp. Regardless of what you order, you won't go wrong.

At **Café Zak** (1095 E. Thompson Blvd., 805/643-9445, www.cafezak.com, Mon.–Fri. 11:30 A.M.–2 P.M. and 5:30–9 P.M., Sat. 5:30–9 P.M., $25) you'll find a varied menu from boar to pastas and salads, and rotating fish specials. The converted corner house just off Main Street is removed enough that you feel you're in a special place. Well, a special place that borders a lumberyard. But the food and service are routinely wonderful, and the house-made desserts are worth saving some space for. A much favored local spot, it gets a little cramped on busy nights.

Though it's a fairly new restaurant, **Prime Steakhouse** (2009 E. Thompson Blvd., 805/652-1055, www.primesteakvc.com, Mon.–Sat. 5–10 P.M., $30) is a traditional streak house with an old-school vibe, including low lighting and white tablecloths. With a great selection of side dishes, cocktails, and a wine list, Prime aims for the quintessential beef experience in a sophisticated environment. The menu is compact with little variation, so don't expect to have lots of choices.

((My Florist (76 S. Oak St., 805/653-0003, www.myfloristcafe.com, daily 7 A.M.–midnight) feels like an art deco restaurant wrestling with its identity. There certainly is a throwback feel, with sleek burgundy chairs, couches, a raised performing area with a piano on top, and a very tall silver deco statue that catches the eye. All that might be irrelevant, though, because the food is quite good. Serving breakfast, lunch, and dinner, and offering a full bar and live music, it manages to succeed by being comfortable and slightly sophisticated. The breakfast burrito is a spicy way to begin your day, and all their pastries are baked on-site. The port poached pear and blue cheese salad is a great collection of flavors and textures, as is the miso Meyer lemon salmon. It's one of the few places open early on Sunday mornings, good to know if you're an early riser.

((The Sidecar (3029 E. Main St., 805/653-7433, www.thesidecarrestaurant.com, Tues.–Sat. 11 A.M.–2 P.M. and 5–9 P.M., Sun. 10 A.M.–2 P.M. and 5–8 P.M., $25) has become perhaps best known for their Grilled Cheese and Jazz Night every Tuesday. Housed in a vintage 1910 Pullman rail car, and the restaurant focuses on locally grown, sustainable ingredients and grass-fed beef. Many ingredients used in the entrées are culled from area farmers and farmers markets. The Sidecar has transformed itself into a genuine American bistro phenomenon, with high-brow sensibilities like the carrot risotto, but low-brow satisfaction like the ever-popular iceberg lettuce wedge salad.

Mexican

((Yolanda's Mexican Cafe (2753 E. Main St., 805/643-2700, www.yolandasmexican-cafe.com, Mon.–Thurs. 11 A.M.–9:30 P.M., Fri.–Sat. 11 A.M.–10 P.M., Sun. 10 A.M.–9 P.M., $10) serves some of the best Mexican food in Ventura. They now have four restaurants throughout the county; they're noisy, colorful, and very good food for the price. They turn out food in an efficient manner, but they've been doing so in Ventura since 1984, and now with their multiple locations continue to achieve a remarkable level of consistency and success many restaurants only dream of. You will find the obvious here—burritos, tacos, tostadas, and the like. House specialties include the Shrimp Villa, sautéed shrimp with jalapeños, green onions, and mushrooms and blanketed with melted cheese, and the Ventura Veggie Plate of fresh locally grown veggies sautéed in fajita sauce and served on a bed of rice, avocado, tomato, and green onions.

El Rey Cantina (294 E. Main St., 805/653-1111, www.elreycantina.com, Mon.–Fri. 4 p.m.–close, Sat.–Sun. 11:30 a.m.–1 a.m., $12) offers nearly 100 tequilas for those in search of that perfect margarita. The decor is committed to preserving the memory of the King, with over-the-top velvet Elvis Presley paintings on the semi-arched ceiling. Red Venetian plastered walls are adorned with classic 1950s movie posters, and a bar hugs one wall and booths the other. It's not a large spot, but it's the most unique interior on all of Main Street. The menu is limited, but go with the pozole, the ribs roasted in tomatillo sauce, or the seared ahi burrito. All menu items are under $10.

Joannafina's Mexican Cafe (1127 S. Seaward, 805/652-0360, Mon.–Fri. 11 a.m.–3 p.m. and 5–9 p.m., Sat.–Sun. 9 a.m.–8 p.m., $10) is just a block from the beach but a world away. You can't miss the green and purple exterior with wildly colored accents. The brightly colored interior keeps the theme going. It is a small place with a tiny outdoor patio, but they dish up homemade tamales and have very good margaritas and sangria. Their moles and the albóndigas soup are also quite good.

French

71 Palm (71 N. Palm, 805/653-7777, www.71palm.com, Mon.–Sat. 11:30 a.m.–2:30 p.m. and 5–9:30 p.m., $22) is a 100-year-old historic house with a large exterior deck just up from Main Street. The small tables are spaced far enough apart that you feel you have some room to converse. Though billed as French, it's a loose interpretation of French food; the

kitchen excels at dishes like chicken ravioli with a sage cream sauce, aged New York steak served with a morel sauce, or the Salad Lyonnaise with poached eggs and smoked bacon. They also offer cooking classes on a monthly basis. This is a great spot for quiet conversation and a slow meal. Afterwards you can walk the half block to Main Street.

Italian

Cafe Fiore Restaurant and Martini Lounge

(66 S. California St., 805/653-1266, www.fiorerestaurant.net, lunch daily 11:30 a.m.–3 p.m., dinner Mon.–Thurs. 5–10 p.m., Fri.–Sat. 5–11 p.m., Sun. 5–9 p.m., $20) has become almost more about the martini bar scene than anything else. The seductive bar is usually packed, but the restaurant area is less so. The butternut squash pasta with sage cream sauce and the chicken-stuffed ravioli are favorites.

Mediterranean and Seafood

The brick building that houses **Jonathan's at Peirano's** (204 E. Main St., 805/648-4853, www.jonathansatpeiranos.com, Tues.–Sun. 11:30 a.m.–2:30 p.m. and 5–9 p.m., $25) dates from 1877 and is the oldest brick building in Ventura. It was an Italian grocery for well over 100 years, and now has new life as one of the top restaurants on Main Street. You're just as likely to find paella as steaks, stuffed dates, and pasta, all with a Middle Eastern flair. Start with the hummus or Portuguese crab bisque and move into the eclectic menu. The well-trained staff is always at the ready. You're well positioned after dinner to walk along Main Street.

Like its sister restaurant in Santa Barbara, **◖ Brophy Brothers** (1559 Spinnaker Dr., 805/639-0865, daily 11 a.m.–close, $25) is always loud and always crowded, and has really wonderful fish. With a complete oyster and raw bar and lots of outdoor seating, this restaurant is larger than the one in Santa Barbara. There are still great views to the boats and the Ventura Harbor, and fresh fish is hauled in just steps away. Forget the side dishes—they simply take up space—and just enjoy the fresh, moist fish. This is a quintessential harbor stop as much for the views as for the food.

Near the harbor, **Andria's Seafood Restaurant** (1449 Spinnaker Dr., 805/654-0546, www.andriasseafood.com, Sun.–Thurs. 11 A.M.–9 P.M., Fri.–Sat. 11 A.M.–10 P.M., $15) is known for their clam chowder, fish-and-chips, and an angel shark burger simply called the fish burger. They are also known for their fish market, where you can purchase the same type of fish you may have recently eaten. The line for the restaurant is often out the door, but it does move reasonably quick. You order at the counter and then sit down, more in the fast-food vein. If you sit outside, watch out for aggressive seagulls.

Pub Grub
The **Anacapa Brewing Company** (472 E. Main St., 805/643-2337, www.anacapabrewing.com, Mon. 5 P.M.–close, Tues.–Sun. 11:30 A.M.–close, $15) is the only brew pub in Ventura; they opened in 2000 in a 115-year-old brick building. Your basic IPA and wheat ales are made here, as well as seasonal brews and specialties like the chocolate porter and oatmeal stout. The elongated narrow space and the fully exposed brick walls and fermentors give it that classic pub feel. They serve up decent food, and the outdoor patio, though small, is always packed—it's prime people-watching territory. Try the jambalaya, the black and blue chicken sandwich, or the asiago cheese dip with your brew.

INFORMATION AND SERVICES
Maps and Tourist Information
The **Ventura Visitors Center** (101 S. California St., 805/648-2075, www.ventura-usa.com, Mon.–Fri. 8:30 A.M.–5 P.M., Sat. 9 A.M.–5 P.M., Sun. 10 A.M.–4 P.M.) is packed with everything you could want to know about Ventura. They have a surprisingly large amount of information in their large digs, and the staff is eager to help.

Emergency Services
Community Memorial Hospital (147 N. Brent St., 805/652-5011) has the only emergency room in the area. The **City of Ventura Police Department** is located at 1425 Dowell Drive (805/339-4400). In case of emergency, call 911 immediately.

Newspapers
The only daily newspaper is the *Ventura County Star,* which can be found all over town. The alternative free weekly, published every Thursday, is the *Ventura County Reporter,* also available everywhere. They have good entertainment listings, including shows, concerts, theater, and film.

Local TV and Radio
KTVA on AM 1520 is the local talk radio station, with a variety of local programming, traffic reports, local news and weather, jokes of the day, and national news; it covers the entire county.

Postal Services
The main branch of the post office is located at 675 East Santa Clara Street (805/643-3057). What with budget cuts, it is best to phone ahead for current hours.

Laundry
No one likes to do laundry, but if the need arises you can head over to **Mission Plaza Laundry** (110 Olive St., 805/653-9077). They offer pickup and delivery.

GETTING THERE
By Air
Most people fly to Los Angles and Burbank, the closest major airports to Ventura. But the small and efficient **Oxnard Airport** (2889 W. 5th St., 805/382-3024, www.iflyoxnard.com) might also be an option if you can get a connection. Though there are limited flights, the airport is pretty much hassle free, and there are rental cars. The drive from Oxnard to Ventura is just 15 minutes.

SHUTTLES
Assuming you fly into Los Angeles, the drive is a mere 60 miles, but can take an hour and a half depending on traffic out of the L.A.

area. There are commercial shuttle vans from L.A., but keep in mind that these will take longer than if you drove yourself and are also affected by traffic. The **Ventura County Airporter** (805/650-6600, www.venturashuttle.com) runs their shuttle service to and from L.A. every day of the year. Rates start at $35, which is very reasonable. **Roadrunner Shuttle** (800/247-7919, www.rrshuttle.com) also does the airport route with private vans, town cars, and even limos.

By Car

From the north or south, Ventura sits squarely off Highway 101. You can also access Ventura by car from I-5 (near Magic Mountain), taking Highway 126 through Fillmore and Santa Paula. This area, beautiful in its own right, is the agricultural workhorse of Ventura County, and you'll pass citrus and avocado groves, fruit stands, and probably most of the traffic. But don't exceed the speed limit, which is easy to do on this road.

By Train

Arriving for a day or two in Ventura by train is a great idea, as much of the downtown is so compact. **Amtrak** (800/872-7245, www.amtrak.com) sets you down in a modest Spanish-style building right by the county fairgrounds near downtown. To get to Main Street is a five-minute walk.

By Bus

Greyhound (291 E. Thompson Blvd., 800/231-2222, www.greyhound.com) will bring you to its small station near downtown Ventura from the north or south.

GETTING AROUND
Driving

Ventura is designed on a small grid and the downtown is three blocks to the beach, so if you are concentrating on this area, you really don't need a car: Simply park at your hotel and forget about the vehicle. However, there are many sights outside of the city, and driving is simple as there are three main arteries from

which everything is accessible. Highway 101 runs north–south and is the main transportation route. To access Ojai and the mountains, Highway 33 will take you out of the city into the rural areas, and Highway 126 towards Santa Paula is not only a beautiful and easy drive with rich agricultural heritage, but it eventually connects with I-5 near Magic Mountain.

Parking

Downtown parking on Main Street and the surrounding arteries underwent dramatic changes in 2010, when solar-powered pay stations were installed. Parking used to be free on these streets, but it now costs $1.50 for two hours. The machines accept coin or credit/debit cards.

By Bus

Gold Coast Transit (GCT, 201 E. 4th St., Oxnard, 805/643-3158, www.goldcoasttransit.org) has bus service in western Ventura County, specifically bus lines 6A and 6B, though their main station is in Oxnard. Fares range from $0.65 for seniors to $1.35 for adults, one-way. Fares are in the process of being increased, so check their website for specific pricing when you arrive. The Ojai–Main Street line, route #16, is available seven days a week, except holidays. GCT connects to Metrolink, Amtrak, and Greyhound at the Oxnard Transportation Center.

Taxis

Taxis in Ventura are not exactly ubiquitous; it's best to call a cab company for a taxi. Two of the best companies are **Yellow Cab of Ventura** (805/659-6900) and **Cab4You** (805/850-9200).

Biking

Matt's Cycling Center (2427 E. Harbor Blvd., 805/477-0933, www.mattscycling.com, Tues.–Sat. 11 A.M.–5 P.M.) rents and sells cruisers, mountain bikes, trailers, tandems, hybrids, and children's bikes—most anything with wheels.

The **Ventura Bike Depot** (239 W. Main St., 805/652-1114, www.venturabikedepot

.com, Sun.–Thurs. 9 A.M.–5 P.M., Fri.–Sat. 9 A.M.–6 P.M.) is located right where the bike path towards Ojai starts, and they have lots of free parking so it's very convenient. You can rent four wheelers, tandems, and all the accoutrements.

Walking Tours
Self-guided walking tours of all types are available free at the **Visitors Center** (101 S. California St., 805/648-2075, www.ventura-usa.com, Mon.–Fri. 8:30 A.M.–5 P.M., Sat. 9 A.M.–5 P.M., Sun. 10 A.M.–4 P.M.). You can pick up a map for the **Ventura Historic Walking Tour,** highlighting Mission San Buenaventura and historic adobes from the Mexican Rancho era, or for the aspiring

gumshoe there's **Perry Mason's Ventura Tour,** which leads visitors to sites throughout the city that inspired Perry Mason creator and novelist Erle Stanley Gardner to pen his classic series. For food lovers, the **Ventura à la Carte Tour** highlights Ventura's farmers markets, nearby farms, fine dining, road food, cooking classes, breweries, and more. Pick up a map and get walking.

If a walking tour is too tame for you, consider a **Ghost Tour** (805/658-4726, www.ghoststalker.com) hosted by Richard Senate, who has been studying paranormal activities since 1978. In addition to conducting lectures on the supernatural and leading local ghost tours in Ventura County, he has authored 14 books and appeared on several radio and television programs.

Ojai

The native Chumash considered the Ojai Valley to be deeply spiritual, and today you'll find plenty of folks who have come here to set up meditation centers, practice alternative healing arts, offer retreats, or enjoy every manner of soul-centered activity. This also means that there's a relaxed approach to things, a friendly "hippie" vibe that cannot be disassociated with Ojai. The valley just seems to draw a wide swath of religious thinkers.

Regardless of your belief system, you'll agree Ojai is indeed a beautiful place, the mountains and rich agricultural lands creating a sense of verdant abundance and beauty. The surrounding mountains are capped by Topa Topa, the highest peak, which soars from near sea level to a height of 6,244 feet and occasionally gets a dusting of snow. Hiking within the Los Padres Mountains is as close as a mile away. The original shops, art galleries, and inherently beautiful surroundings make this a getaway for most people to not go and do, but to stay put and detox.

SIGHTS
◀ Ojai Avenue
Ojai Avenue is the main street and the lifeblood

of Ojai. It was created as a boulevard in 1917 with a park on one side of the street, a Spanish-style arcade housing shops on the other, and a single tower; these elements have defined Ojai for generations. Yes, there is the backcountry, the beautiful mountains that flank this small valley, the snow-capped peaks, and stunning sunsets, but without Ojai Avenue, the dream of Edward Libbey in 1914, people would not be flocking to this small town north of Ventura. It is the defining central point that gives residents and tourists alike a sense of cohesion and an introduction to what Ojai is all about.

Ojai Valley Museum (130 W. Ojai Ave., 805/640-1390, www.ojaivalleymuseum.org, Wed. guided tours only, Thurs.–Fri. 1–4 P.M., Sat. 10 A.M.–4 P.M., Sun. noon–4 P.M., $4 adults, $1 children 6–18) is housed in an old Catholic church that was rebuilt in 1918 after the devastating 1917 fire. From the outside you may not think it looks like a church at all. On the inside the small museum with an all-volunteer staff presents permanent and rotating exhibits about the history and livelihood of the Ojai Valley. The interior belies the building's former incarnation until you see the mural of

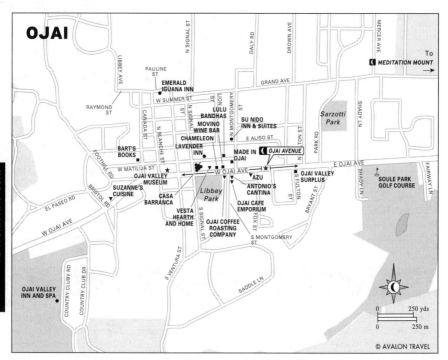

the Sespe Wilderness that serves as a backdrop of the backcountry of Ojai, complete with stuffed wildlife, in what was the church altar. The museum holds a biannual sale of native plants. In the parking lot behind the building they have a small but intriguing Chumash Interpretative Garden of roughly 30 different plants, showing how the Chumash Indians used them for healing, tonics, food, or jewelry.

The Arcade (500 block of Ojai Ave.) comprises much of Ojai Avenue. It is here that locals and tourists meander in and out of stores, making this a social gathering place as well. The Spanish arches shield the sidewalk, providing shade in the hot summers and protection from foul weather.

Krotona Institute of Theosophy

When spirituality and history come together, there's no place more suited for a visit than the Krotona Institute of Theosophy (2 Krotona Hill, 805/646-2653, Tues.–Fri. 10 A.M.–5 P.M., Sat.–Sun. 1–5 P.M.), on a 115-acre wooded site. The Theosophy movement started in the 1870s on the East Coast, and Krotona was located in Hollywood until it migrated to Ojai in 1924. The site has a meditation school, library, and bookstore, and you needn't be a theosophist to visit—all are encouraged to stop in. The mirror pools behind the library are contemplative in themselves, as are much of the grounds. The library in the main building holds over 8,000 titles and is absolutely beautiful; it has a classic 1920s feel with high bookshelves, a fireplace, lots of peace and quiet, and worn comfortable chairs. The library's collection pertains largely to an understanding of spiritual subjects, including astrology, yoga, metaphysics, and reincarnation.

Ojai Olive Oil

The very first olive trees were planted in

THE SPIRIT OF OJAI

It's been suggested that Ojai is to spirituality what Silicon Valley is to technology. From retreat and meditation centers, to spiritual centers, mystics, and shamans, for those who preach enlightenment and those who quietly go about seeking it, Ojai has long been considered ground zero for spiritual awakening and is now a diverse community offering a wide variety of spiritual and religious organizations and centers including the teachings of Krishnamurti (805/646-2390, www.kfa.org), a Jewish temple (805/646-4464, www.ojaitemple.org), a theosophy institute (805/646-2563, www.theosophical.org), a Dharma center (805/646-2102, www.satdharma.org), non-denominational retreat houses, and more than 20 Christian and Catholic churches. But what's in the ground that makes this area so special?

The geologic structure of the Ojai Valley is in fact essential to the charm and the spiritual influence that affects those who live here. The valley, 10 miles long and 3 miles wide, has a unique atmosphere that is apparent to even the first-time visitor; it's due in part to the transverse nature of the surrounding mountains, which lie in an east-west configuration, whereas most of California's mountains run north-south. The sun rising at one end of the valley and setting at the other provides the residents with lingering morning and evening sun and some of the most spectacular sunrises and sunsets available anywhere. Given the fresh air, laid-back pace, and lack of the toxic elements found in many cities, Ojai may not be a healing center, but it is certainly a place to release the stresses of life.

California around 1789 at the mission in San Diego. In Ojai, immigrants planted Spanish olive trees in 1880. Those trees still stand today, and Ojai Olive Oil (1325 Carne Rd., 805/701-3825, www.ojaioliveoil.com) still harvests them. The Asquith Family Farm has planted an astonishing 2,000 olive trees in the last 12 years to complement the old Spanish trees, in Italian, French, and Spanish varieties to maximize flavors and complexities for their oils. Since Ventura County is on the same latitude as Casablanca in North Africa, the Asquiths believe it enjoys an ideal Mediterranean climate in which to grow olive trees. On Saturdays from 10 A.M. to 3 P.M., rain or shine, they welcome visitors to tour the farm's olive grove, explore the working ranch, and to taste their olive oils. Their tour begins outside with the history of the grove; an explanation of the different olive varieties, the maturing process, the harvesting; and a visit to the tree nursery. In addition to the variety of extra virgin oils, there are olive oil soaps and a face cream, balsamic vinegars, and flavored olive oils like rosemary, garlic, and mandarin.

◀ Meditation Mount

Meditation Mount (10340 Reeves Rd., 805/646-5508) has spectacular vistas of the valley and mountains. To get there, drive east about three miles from downtown on East Ojai Avenue and turn left on Reeves Road. Continue through the orange groves until the road becomes a dead end. From there, the hill climbs toward the meditation center; park and look for the signs to the mount. You'll walk down a short path with benches and water features until you reach the end, which is quiet, serene, and contemplative.

WINERIES
Casa Barranca

Casa Barranca (208 E. Ojai Ave., 805/640-1255, www.casabarranca.com, Fri.–Sun. noon–6 P.M., tasting fee $10) is an organic winery. Their tasting room echoes the Casa Barranca house, which was designed by meticulous Craftsman architects Greene and Greene from Pasadena. The tasting room carries the house's motifs into the space with lots of wood and Stickley Mission patterns on the furnishings and bar. There are a few gift items as well,

THE PINK MOMENT

As the sun begins to set in Ojai, people will come outside and gaze upwards, seemingly transfixed. At first you might think that visitors from another galaxy are about to pay a visit, but everyone is actually looking toward the Topa Topa Mountains where, when the atmospheric conditions are right – which usually means a light cloud cover – the bluff above town will turn pink. The phenomenon is called the Pink Moment. When the moment comes, some claim to see the face of Chief Peak (Chief Peak is the high point on the ridge, where some see the head and bonnet, and there is indeed some resemblance to the relief of a sleeping Indian chief). Others say that a few times a year the entire valley, not just the mountains, glows with a pinkish hue. It's a well-documented experience with plenty of professional and amateur photographers attempting to capture the moment. There's even a Pink Moment Press, a novel called *Ojai: The Pink Moment Promises*, a chocolatier who has created Pink Moment Sweets, and doggie T-shirts that promote the pinkness of your pet. There's even a local wine called the Pink Moment Rosé made by Casa Barranca. Photos, trinkets, and anything else that can sell touts the pinkness, and in reality, it's quite a beautiful sight to behold, adding to the allure of Ojai.

and a few tables and chairs in which to sit and relax and sample organic wines like chardonnay, pinot noir, and various blends.

Old Creek Ranch Winery

The small family-owned Old Creek Ranch Winery (10024 Old Creek Rd., 805/649-4132, www.oldcreekranch.com, daily 11 A.M.–5 P.M., tasting fee $10) is located off Highway 33 on the way to Ventura. Turning off the road, you'll drive a few miles as the scenery become more rural and you come upon cherry trees on the winery property. The current winery building is in front of the original winery from the 1880s, still visible but in serious disrepair. The small space has gift items and a small tasting bar offering chardonnay, pinot noir, merlot, and cabernet sauvignon. The tasting bar can get crowded, but the mood is always jovial.

ENTERTAINMENT AND EVENTS
Bars and Clubs

There's not a huge nightlife scene in this town of just over 8,000 people, but a few spots offer a bit of action or a place to grab a drink.

The Hub (256 E. Ojai Ave., 805/646-9182, daily noon–1 A.M.) is a low-key bar that seems half built. One side is lined with bookshelves and round barstools, and there are pool tables in the back. There's a lot of wood paneling and a few games sitting around—it looks like it wasn't quite sure what it wanted to be. But it's definitely old school, reflecting its roots as a bar since its inception in 1948. There's no pretension at the Hub: You don't get fancy drinks here, you get beer in a can. It's comfortable and neighborly, the last of a vanishing breed of bars. Every Sunday morning they offer a Bloody Mary bar along with biscuits and gravy. There's live music on the weekends and some weeknights, mainly locals with a flair for bluegrass, folk, and rock.

Jimmy's Pub (905 Country Club Rd., 805/640-2100, Mon.–Thurs. 3 P.M.–midnight, Fri.–Sun. 11 A.M.–midnight) may sound like a neighborhood watering hole, but it's not. Located at the Ojai Valley Inn, it's as far from a dive bar as you can get. This is an upscale bar, a counterpoint to the Hub. With a wider selection of most everything, Jimmy's is a comfortable and relaxing spot with a selection of food, specialty cocktails, and fine wines.

Movino Wine Bar & Gallery (308 E. Ojai Ave., 805/646-1555, www.movinowinebar.com, Mon. 5–11 P.M., Wed.–Thurs. 5–11 P.M., Fri. 5 P.M.–1 A.M., Sat. 3 P.M.–1 A.M., Sun. 3–9 P.M.) brings together wine, art, and

© MICHAEL CERVIN

Wander around The Arcade, peek into art galleries, and wine taste, all in downtown Ojai.

music. Without the music, the narrow space is quiet and comfortable, and conversation is easy. Add the music and your conversation will evaporate, but the food will still satisfy.

Performing Arts

The 1,200-seat **Libbey Bowl** (200 Signal St., 805/646-3117, www.libbeybowl.org) is the type of open-space amphitheater that people associate with outdoor music events, and it's the performing-arts centerpiece of town. However, due to its failing structure, the bowl was demolished in June 2010 and a new bowl is due to open in June 2011. The Ojai Music Festival is usually held here, as well as a variety of classical concerts and everything from pop to country.

If you need a bit of drama in your life, check out **Theatre 150** (316 E. Matilija St., 805/646-4300, www.theatre150.org), which started in 1997 in a converted pool hall as a venue to present plays, spoken word, poetry, and music. After being embraced by the community it moved to larger digs—they actually converted a mortuary into an 80-seat theater and continue to offer an eclectic schedule of new works Shakespeare,

poets, and musical acts. They also offer acting workshops on occasion.

Festivals and Events

The annual **Holiday Home Look In** (www.ojaifestival.org) benefits the Ojai Music Festival and is held the third weekend in November, right before Thanksgiving. Each year four private homes, works of art in their own right, are spruced up and opened to the public. There are a vast number of beautifully homes in the area, designed by well-known and perhaps less-than-well-known architects. Many of the region's homes are hidden from sight, on vast expanses of land, tucked into hillsides, down mountain sides, or off private roads you'd never suspect held such treasures. There's always a great diversity to the homes—Craftsman, mid-century modern, contemporary, and revivals of every ilk. This is a self-driving tour so you can go at your own pace.

The Ojai Music Festival (805/646-2094, www.ojaifestival.org), held the second week in June, began in 1947. Over the years, this valley of olive trees and art galleries has played host to such distinguished visitors as Igor Stravinsky,

© MICHAEL CERVIN

Meditation Mount has the best views of the Ojai Valley.

Aaron Copland, and the Kronos Quartet. The festival has earned a reputation as a breeding ground for eclectic new music emerging in the world. It's definitely worth a visit if you're in town, or make a special trip if this is music to your ears.

Over the course of 12 days in August, new plays, playwrights, actors, directors, dramaturges, and technicians come together at the **Ojai Playwrights Conference** (www.ojaiplays.org) to rehearse and present new, unproduced works of the theater. Some playwrights are well known, while others are not. Many of the plays developed at the Ojai Playwrights Conference have gone on to productions on stages in Los Angeles, Chicago, Seattle, Boston, and New York. These are works in progress, and that's half the interest for the people attending. There are additional seminars and readings by well-known actors and directors, but the stars are the new works presented to an audience for the very first time.

Each June, the popular **Ojai Wine Festival** (11311 Santa Ana Rd., 800/648-4881, www.ojaiwinefestival.com) is held at nearby Lake Casitas. Over 50 vintners and brewers from all over California offer samples of their creations. Arts and crafts vendors present their works, multiple bands play throughout the one-day event, food is sold, and people break into spontaneous dancing—all of this overlooking the lake in the afternoon. Plus since this is a charity event, well over 30 organizations are helped with the monies raised. It gets crowded with close to 4,000 people showing up, but it's a terrific event.

SHOPPING

There's not much to shopping in Ojai: You walk down Ojai Avenue and you've pretty much covered it all. On one side of the street are a few stores and the park, and the other side is taken up with the arcade, a long row of shops covered by a long archway built in 1917. There are also some shops on the side streets, an easy, brief walk from the main drag.

Clothing

Chameleon (326 E. Ojai Ave., 805/646-2979, call for hours) is the sort of store you walk past and are immediately attracted to by the cornucopia of color. The interior has beautiful

© MICHAEL CERVIN

the open-air Bart's Books

hardwood floors, purple walls and couches, and equally colorful items for sale. From sunglasses and handbags to comfy plush socks to shoes and even local jewelry, there is a wonderful mix of the latest trends, both hip and expressive.

Casa Bonita (311 W. Ojai Ave., 805/646-6200, Tues.–Sat. 10 A.M.–5 P.M., Sun. 9:30 A.M.–3 P.M.), in a small cottage, is one of the first stores you come to as you enter Ojai. It's a fun and different mix of upscale cowgirl clothing including boots and hats, sterling silver and turquoise jewelry, and vintage lighting and antique furniture.

There's plenty of clothing for men and women at **Ojai Surplus** (952 E. Ojai Ave., 805/646-2350, www.ojaisurplus.com, Mon.–Sat. 9 A.M.–6 P.M., Sun. 10 A.M.–4 P.M.), but it tends to be camouflage, jeans, and industrial gear, rugged and definitely a fashion statement. The women's section also has dresses and jewelry. There's a large selection of camping gear as well.

Bookstores

Located next to the library, **Twice Sold Tales** (121 W. Ojai Ave., 805/646-4094, daily noon–5 P.M.) sells used books from the library's collection. Paperbacks are just $0.50 and hardcovers are $2. Though this is a small shop, they have the benefit of a varied selection due to donations from the library. Plus, the proceeds help the library, and who doesn't want that? Local artwork graces the walls.

Just a block off Ojai Avenue, on the corner of Matilija and Canada, is **Bart's Books** (302 W. Matilija St., 805/646-3755, daily 9:30 A.M.–sunset), famous for being a mostly open-air bookstore, with 35-cent specials on a shelf outside, sold on the honor system since 1964 when the original Bart first put out a coffee can to collect his earnings when he wasn't around. The selection is surprisingly large, with paperbacks, hardcovers, and even first editions and antiquarian books. A 400-plus-year-old oak tree shades the property, and there's a handful of tables where you can sit and read.

Specialty Stores

Rains (218 E. Ojai Ave., 805/646-1441, www.rainsofojai.com, Sat. 9:30 A.M.–6 P.M., Sun. 11 A.M.–5 P.M.) is that rare store, the true original department store. The space goes back to 1874 as a hardware store and has since morphed into a department store, but not the kind we think of today. This is not a massive warehouse space with industrial lighting and miles of endless volume, but an intimate store reflecting more simple times. There is kitchenware, local jams and jellies, clothing, appliances, and they still sell hardware as well. It truly is a one-of-a-kind store, unpretentious yet filling a need for the residents of Ojai.

Part art gallery, part crafts store, **Human Arts Gallery** (246 E. Ojai Ave., 805/646-1525, www.humanartsgallery.com, Wed.–Mon. 11 A.M.–5 P.M.) has been in Ojai for over 30 years. Much of what they sell has a whimsical, expressive flair: brightly painted furniture, hand-colored glass, and minutely detailed wood boxes using multiple types of wood. The store itself is like an adult playground, and the items here are creative and energetic. They have some local works here as well.

Made in Ojai (323 E. Matilija St., 805/646-2400, www.madeinojai.com, daily 10 A.M.–6 P.M.) is the store to visit when you want something made locally. They operate as an artists' collective, and everyone who sells items in the store also works there. There's a wide range, including fine art and prints, pottery, handmade teddy bears, custom leather boots, and gemstone jewelry. They also feature local olive oils, teas, lavender lotions, jellies, local honey, handmade soaps, and skin-care products, as well as books and music by local talent, and even hula hoops. It's quite impressive. Interestingly, the store opened in what had been scheduled to be a Subway sandwich shop.

Ojai Beverage Company (655 E. Ojai Ave., 805/646-1700, www.ojaibevco.com, daily 10 A.M.–9 P.M.) offers tastings and wines by the glass on a daily basis. It's not a bar, but they do have a vast selection of over 300 whiskies, 200 tequilas, 750 beers, and more wine than you can imagine. They have a small tasting area in the back and a side patio to lounge and relax. It's not creatively decorated, as this is primarily a store, but they also serve light food and there's a huge selection of things to try.

Farmers Market

Ojai Farmers Market (300 E. Matilija St., 805/698-5555 www.ojaicertifiedfarmersmarket.com, Sun. 9 A.M.–1 P.M.) is a cornucopia of abundance in all seasons. Vendors sell organic produce, eggs, honey, aromatics, homemade tamales, and much more near the Arcade Plaza. The market is also one of the better people-watching spots—you are likely to see a wide swath of humanity represented amidst the small stalls that line the parking lot.

Art Galleries

Primavera Gallery (214 E. Ojai Ave., 805/646-7133, www.primaveraart.com, Mon.–Sat. 10 A.M.–5 P.M., Sun. 11 A.M.–5 P.M.) is without a doubt the largest and most unique gallery in Ojai. They have maintained their ground for more than a quarter of a century and have an impressive collection of glasswork, oil paintings, plein air, incredible woodwork, jewelry, and American crafts. Many of the 100 artists represented have been with the gallery for decades; many also show internationally. This is an expensive place, but the quality of the work is unmatched. There are multiple rooms and much of the work rotates. It's a visual treat and one stop you shouldn't miss.

Trowbridge Gallery (307 E. Ojai Ave., 805/646-0967, www.trowbridgeart.com, Wed.–Fri. 11 A.M.–5 P.M., Sat. 10 A.M.–6 P.M., Sun. noon–5 P.M.) is a rather large two-story gallery with soft almond-colored hardwood floors. There are local artists represented here, as well as regional and national artists, and though there is a preference for plein air and traditional landscapes and still life, the unifying theme is an expressive use of color. The gallery originally opened in 2002 and has been successful due in part to the fine works on display.

Nomad: The Leslie Clark Gallery (307 E. Ojai Ave., 805/646-1706, www.nomadgal.com, Wed.–Mon. 11 A.M.–5 P.M.) has a strong preference for the nomadic imagery of Africa. Posters, original oil paintings, watercolors, and giclées of African and nomadic cultures are mixed with tribal items like masks

© MICHAEL CERVIN

Lake Casitas offers a diverse array of outdoor activities.

and fertility deities, and some Western art. It's an out-of-the-ordinary stop where you can also find hand-embroidered shirts for men and women made by African tribespeople.

Palette (435 E. Ojai Ave., 805/640-8822, www.palette-gallery.com, hours vary) gallery opened in March of 2005, intending to bring an innovative approach to a place where art, music, dance, and performance could converge in Ojai and shake things up a little. Openings are typically boundary-pushing themed events with DJs, stilt-walkers, hula-hoopers, live models, hand-drummers, projected video, performance artists, food, wine—and oh yes, the art. There's a strong L.A. feel in the sculpture, painting, and commissioned work here-showy, but interesting and entertaining.

Aside from a regular exhibition schedule and the permanent collection at **Beatrice Wood Center for the Arts** (8560 Ojai–Santa Paula Rd., 805/646-3381, www.beatricewood.com, Sat.–Sun. 11 A.M.–5 P.M.), there are artist workshops and occasional performances. The center has its history in Ojai dating back to the 1940s. Much of the work displayed is eclectic and modern, infused with an arts and crafts sensibility. There is sculpture, photography, and all form of painting, and some occasional commissioned work. A gift shop is located on the property as well. Workshops vary; contact them for schedules.

SPORTS AND RECREATION
Lake Casitas

Lake Casitas (11311 Santa Ana Rd., 805/649-2233, www.lakecasitas.com) is a 2,700-acre man-made lake with 400 campsites and something for everyone. For decades, Lake Casitas was known for its fishing. The photos at the bait shop near the marina proudly display some of the monster largemouth bass and trout that dedicated and patient anglers have pulled from these waters over the last 30 years. Among fishermen, Lake Casitas has been a favorite spot to land a world-record catch. The lake is also stocked with rainbow trout, perch, and catfish.

But the popularity of sportfishing nationwide has declined, and to make up for the lost revenue in paying visitors, the Casitas Municipal Water District decided to build the

VENTURA AND OJAI

© MICHAEL CERVIN

view of Lake Casitas from Highway 150

Casitas Water Adventure water park and the adjoining **Lazy River,** a winding pool with water jets that push inner-tube riders around a 1,200-foot route. Just inside the park entrance is a spraying jungle gym set inside a large wading pool. A few feet away, a snaking concrete-lined waterway with a mellow current carries inner-tube riders in a circuitous route under waterfalls and cascading showers.

There are also boats for rent, plus camping, hiking, biking, or just the serenity of lounging or strolling by the water's edge. There's also plenty of bird-watching and Frisbee golf. But since this is a reservoir, swimming and wading in the water is not allowed. Amenities include coin-operated showers, on-site boat rental, a café with forgettable food, and a seasonal park store, should you have forgotten something.

What people may not know is that the creation of this reservoir obliterated the Santa Ana Valley, which lies underneath the 80 billion gallons of water and the 32-mile shoreline that is Lake Casitas; the dam that holds the water was completed in 1958. The lake is also a wildlife preserve. The federal government has spent

$25 million to buy up land around the lake from the homeowners who lived there. It will be left as permanent open space to help facilitate a clean watershed. It is home to 65 species of birds, including herons and egrets, and it's not uncommon to see deer, coyote, foxes, and other creatures. In 1984 the lake hosted the Olympic rowing events.

Golf

The 18-hole, par-70 golf course at the **Ojai Valley Inn** (905 Country Club Rd., 800/422-6524, www.ojairesort.com, green fees $180) was originally designed in the 1920s by George C. Thomas Jr., who also designed the Riviera, Bel Air, and Los Angeles Country Club courses further south. He wanted every tee, fairway, and green to offer a different panorama, both beautiful and challenging. This course has hosted seven Senior PGA Tour events, and you won't be bored either by the challenges of the course or the views you'll enjoy while waiting for your opponent to chip out of the trap. The sheer beauty of the course, parts of which sit below the resort flanked by some of the surrounding mountains, is a treat all to itself. There is also a driving range.

The par-71 **Soule Park** (1033 E. Ojai Ave., 805/646-5633, www.soulepark.com, green fees $48–62) is an 18-hole regulation golf course with a medium-length layout that will reward good shots and provide a fun golf outing. It's mildly challenging, but only because of the back-to-back holes at 14 and 15 where you have 400-plus yards into the wind. The fees are reasonable and the views are wonderful. There's a driving range and a small restaurant.

Hiking

Shelf Road (termination of Signal St.) is an Ojai favorite for hiking. It's an easy, wide trail with minimal elevation gains and fantastic views of the valley; out and back is about four miles. You'll see walkers, runners, horses, and cyclists along the path. The trailhead starts high above downtown, nearly a thousand feet above Ojai Avenue. The national forest is on one side, and orange groves are on the other. The high point of the trail is only 150 feet higher than the actual trailhead, but the views open up to both sides of the valley. To get there from downtown, head north up Signal Street and drive about a mile until you reach the end. Parking is available at the trailhead, which is marked by a gate. The trail takes you to another gate two miles away at Gridley. Bring your camera to capture those great views.

At the **Rancho El Nido Preserve** (Rice Rd. near El Roblar Dr.) there are miles of well-marked trails that weave through the Ventura riverbed, which is typically dry. There are a few natural springs on the preserve that run year-round. This is a riparian habitat that abuts the Los Padres National Forest and is home to 300 plant and animal species. Stay near the riverbed for a flat hike, or head up the fire road for a more strenuous workout. The preserve is accessed from the Riverview trailhead off Rice Road: Take Highway 150 towards Lake Casitas; shortly after the split from Highway 33 make a right at Rice Road and look for the preserve signs about a half mile up.

Located in the Sespe Wilderness, **Piedra** **Blanca** is about 20 miles outside of Ojai off Highway 33. You'll need to stop at **Wheeler Gorge Visitors Center** (17017 Maricopa Hwy., 805/640-9060) for a day-use pass. Continue up Highway 33 to the Rose Valley Road turnoff on your right and drive about six and a half miles until it dead ends at the parking lot. The white rock formations of Piedra Blanca will be in front of you just to the north. The trail is relatively flat with an overall elevation gain of 300 feet. It's approximately a mile and a half one-way, mostly through chaparral and manzanita with a few small creek crossings, depending on the winter rains. The landscape then changes from thick brush to smooth sandstone, offering dramatic boulders to climb on.

Bike Trails

The **33 North/Ventucopa** is a challenging bike trail up Highway 33 north, through Meiners Oaks and towards the mountains, a nearly 4,000 foot climb with stunning vistas into the often unseen backcountry of the Los Padres Mountains. You can continue the ride

Rose Valley Falls near Piedra Blanca

© MICHAEL CERVIN

VENTURA AND OJAI

well into the Carrizo Plain in Santa Barbara County, assuming you're fit enough, but that's close to 60 miles one-way. The route vacillates between pine-covered mountains and the dry desert-like stretch toward the north near Cuyama. From downtown, simply take Highway 33 north and you'll be on your way.

West Ojai Avenue will take you toward Lake Casitas, a popular route. Follow Ojai Avenue on the bike trail; once you reach the turnoff to the lake, Highway 150, simply follow the signs. There are some hills, but once outside of town there are vast meadows with panoramic views to the mountains. This can be a long ride—over 40 miles—or short, depending on when you decide to turn back. Chances are that once you pass the lake and begin the mountain ascent you might decide to head back.

East Ojai Avenue runs flat on the opposite end of town toward orchards of citrus trees, then the road begins to climb toward Santa Paula and Highway 126. If you're not into the climbs, simply turn back toward your hotel after about four miles and you'll have a pleasant ride through the valley.

Yoga

LuLu Bandhas (306 E. Matilija St., 805/640-7868, www.lulubandhas.com) features a multitude of teachers, classes, and workshops; it's almost like a small college. If yoga is something new or perhaps even strange to you, then stop in for a single class like Stiff White Guys, for those just getting started. If you're already familiar with yoga, try the vinyasa classes or meditation. They have online classes, DVDs, books, and everything for the soul. Single yoga classes start at just $15.

Spas

Ojai Valley Inn and Spa (905 Country Club Rd., 888/697-8754, www.ojairesort.com) has consistently been rated among the top spas in the country. From traditional spa treatments to water therapy, dry steam rooms, eucalyptus hot tubs, and seasonal body scrubs, they offer everything. If you want aromatherapy,

you'll get it. A facial? No problem. They offer Kuyam, which they claim is the only treatment of its kind in the United States. Kuyam is a Chumash Indian word that means "a place to rest together," and it combines the therapeutic effects of desert clay, dry heat, inhalation therapy, and a traditional Chumash guided meditation. None of this comes cheap of course, but you'll definitely feel pampered.

The Day Spa of Ojai (1434 E. Ojai Ave., 805/640-1100, www.thedayspa.com, Mon.–Sat. 10 A.M.–6 P.M., Sun. 10 A.M.–4 P.M.) is housed in a beautiful old stone home on the outskirts of town. This is also a true day spa; simple hour-long treatments are available, but the usual packages typically last three to four hours and include foot treatments, followed by a massage and then a facial, so you'll likely be here for hours. They also have wooden-barrel saunas and infrared saunas that penetrate more deeply for maximum relaxation. Chances are you'll be blissed out, so it might be best to get a ride so you can continue to relax.

The Oaks at Ojai (122 E. Ojai Avenue, 800/753-6257, www.oakspsa.com) is a traditional spa inside a hotel that caters primarily to women and offers what you'd expect with massages and scrubs. But they go beyond the ordinary with health consultations, acupressure, and a fitness regimen along with food and proper eating techniques, offering a lifestyle approach and not merely an hour-long session.

ACCOMMODATIONS
Under $200

Casa Ojai Inn (1302 E. Ojai Ave., 805/646-8175, www.ojaiinn.com, $150–160 d) is a 45-room eco-sensitive lodging with Craftsman/Polynesian-themed custom-made furnishings and "green" touches like sink aerators, luxury low-flow showerheads, and efficient toilets. If you show up in an electrical or hybrid certified vehicle, they'll knock 5 percent off your stay. Try a refreshing swim in the saltwater pool or enjoy the hot tub, then sunbathe on a spacious sundeck. Guests can enjoy discounts for spa services at the Ojai Day Spa or stay fit with complimentary passes to the Bryant Street

© MICHAEL CERVIN

The Day Spa of Ojai

Gym. The exterior looks more like a two-story motel, but don't let that put you off.

The **Lavender Inn** (210 E. Matilija St., 805/646-6635, www.lavenderinn.com, $125–170 d) is located just off Ojai Avenue in an 1874 single-story building originally used as a schoolhouse and community center. Today it offers intimate charm as a Victorian-style bed-and-breakfast. Each of the nine rooms is uniquely designed and offers mountain or garden views. The rooms are a bit small—or cozy, depending on your perspective. They offer a full breakfast each morning with herbs from their garden, a computer with Internet access for guest use, and a wine and cheese reception each evening. This is the closest accommodations to the center of town.

The **Ojai Cottages** (1434 E. Ojai Ave., 805/646-9779, www.ojaicottage.com, $125–175 d) is a unique property located just outside of downtown that has three distinct lodgings near the Soule Park golf course. The cottage is an 800-square-foot two-story stone structure with a two-person whirlpool tub; it sleeps up to four people. There's a full kitchen, and the knotty pine walls makes it feel like a secluded cabin. The loft has one bedroom and a bath plus a full kitchen and small deck—not as charming as the cottage, but still very nice quarters. The studio is a one-room space, nicely decorated with a small kitchenette. They don't provide any food, but they do have a pool, hot tub, croquet, and horseshoes.

As you enter the **◖ Blue Iguana Inn** (11794 N. Ventura Hwy., 805/646-5277, www.blueiguanainn.com, $159–199 d), the first thing you'll notice is Iggy, a large mosaic iguana fountain out front. The building's exterior has a pueblo feel, and there are a dozen rooms and suites on the property with interiors that range from Spanish Pueblo to Craftsman. There are a lot of oaks on the site, as well as a pool and various decks on which to relax. The inn is close to downtown and right off the highway, so there can be some traffic noise when you're outside.

$200-300

The sister property of the Blue Iguana Inn, the **Emerald Iguana Inn** (110 Pauline St., 805/646-5277, www.emeraldiguanainn.com,

iguana fountain, Blue Iguana Inn

$200–289 d) seems like an upscale tree house. Off Ojai Avenue in a residential area, the stone walls are covered with vines and beautiful old oaks, sycamores, and pepper trees shade the property. In keeping with that theme, the 13 rooms are accented with Craftsman-style furnishings, soft wood tones, and ample space. Additionally they offer one- and two-bedroom cottages that can sleep up to six people for extended stays. The inn caters to adults only, aiming to create a quiet retreat feel.

$300-400

Su Nido Inn & Suites (301 N. Montgomery St., 805/646-7080, www.sunidoinn.com, $309–359 d) features Mission Revival architecture and nine rooms and suites ranging from 600 to 1,000 square feet in size. Even the smaller rooms are palatial, and so beautifully decorated you'll feel like you're on a new home tour. With tiled kitchens and bathrooms, exposed-beam ceilings and plush beds and sofas, this is wonderful luxury. The focused attention of the staff is also exceptional. During the high season a two-night stay is required on weekends.

Ojai Valley Inn and Spa (905 Country Club Rd., 800/422-6524, www.ojairesort.com, $360–625) sits on 800 acres with its own golf course and tennis courts. The inn dates back to 1922, when wealthy Ohio glass manufacturer Edward Libbey commissioned noted architect Wallace Neff to build a country club in a Spanish Colonial style. During World War II, the U.S. Army took over the resort as a training camp, stationing 1,000 troops here until 1944. The next year the navy occupied the resort as a rest and relaxation facility for their officers. The 308-room inn is massive and seems more like a small village. The staff and service are what you'd expect, professional and genuinely friendly and helpful. It features prime Spanish details: tiled fountains and walkways, red-tile roofs, and a voluminous lobby. The rooms vary in size, some being small, though a renovation has upgraded everything and the amenities have improved. It's a great spot for children and teenagers, as there's a lot to keep them occupied here with special classes, and it's not a secluded getaway place—there are a lot of people here.

FOOD
American

Deer Lodge (2261 Maricopa Hwy., 805/646-4256, Mon.–Fri. 11 A.M.–10 P.M., Sat.–Sun. 8 A.M.–10 P.M., www.ojaideerlodge.net, $20) is just three miles from downtown. Since 1932 this rustic log cabin–style animal-head-on-the-wall joint has been making people feel great with live music, lots of beef and game dishes, cornbread, and a pig roast every Sunday. There are a lot of bikers who come here on the weekends, and it's easy to be intimidated by the sheer number of Harleys and other bikes out front. But there is plenty of room for everyone here.

A former lumber yard, **Ojai Cafe Emporium** (108 S. Montgomery St., 805/646-2723, daily 7 A.M.–3 P.M., $10) looks and feels like a down-home diner inside. The choice seats are on the covered patio, which looks out to the parking lot. The views are not very exciting, but the food is. Sunday brunches here are packed and the quiche is a winner, as is their house specialty, the Topa Topa salad of greens, chicken, taco seasoning, kidney beans, corn chips, cheddar cheese, tomato, and avocado tossed with thousand island dressing and topped with sour cream.

Feast Bistro (254 E. Ojai Ave., 805/640-9260, Tues.–Sat. 11:30 A.M.–2:30 P.M. and 5:30–9 P.M., Sun. brunch 10:30 A.M.–3 P.M., $17) is a restaurant; wine, espresso, and tea bar; cooking school; and even small retail space with olive oils and condiment items, all rolled into one. Stop in and see what part of Feast works for you. This is a true bistro, with a tightly packed small space, a lively ambience, and an open kitchen. Wine-tastings, winemaker dinners, and cooking classes are offered intermittently; contact them in advance to see what's coming up. While you're there, try the duck breast, one of their daily frittatas, or a veggie burger, and conclude with their olive oil cake made from local olive oil.

Vesta Hearth and Home (242 E. Ojai Ave., 805/646-2339, www.vestaojai.com, Sun.–Thurs. 10 A.M.–6 P.M., Fri.–Sat. 10 A.M.–8 P.M., $15) is part home accessories store and part restaurant. This former British high-tea spot has kept the formal tea service, but is now also an eclectic spot serving burgers, baked brie, panini, and salads—you can shop for your home, but stay to fill up your belly. The food is reasonably priced and very tasty, and it's one of the few places left on the Central Coast to offer high tea.

Italian

◖ **Suzanne's Cuisine** (502 W. Ojai Ave., 805/640-1961, www.suzannescuisine.com, Wed.–Mon. 11:30 A.M.–2:30 P.M. and 5:30 P.M.–close, $25) has long held the reputation of being one of the best restaurants in town. Their seasonal menu has been bringing customers in since 1992. Part of what makes the restaurant so successful is that the owners make daily trips to Los Angeles farmers markets to retrieve the best produce and freshest foods; the other part of their success is their fierce dedication to service and creating the best dining experience possible. You'll find dishes such as calf liver, pasta dishes such as fettuccini with portobello mushrooms, poached salmon with a dill cucumber sauce, and four-egg omelets. There's a great diversity represented in this country French interior. Reservations are recommended.

Mediterranean

Azu (457 E. Ojai Ave., 805/640-7987, www.azuojai.com, lunch Tues.–Sat. noon–4, dinner daily 5:30–9 P.M., $12) is a tapas and Mediterranean restaurant that creates a variety of distinctive dishes such as Syrian chicken salad on romaine lettuce with marinated artichoke hearts, Moroccan olives, cherry tomatoes, shaved Manchego cheese, and lemon mint vinaigrette, or the seared sea scallops with an English pea butter sauce and crispy *jamón* Serrano. For dessert, they have a great selection of gelato. The hardwood floors and dark wood chairs in contrast with the soft yellow walls and white linens give it a mildly sophisticated look. There are always fresh flowers on the tables, and the staff carries out their duties promptly.

Mexican

For south-of-the-border fare try **Antonio's Cantina** (106 S. Montgomery St., 805/646-6353,

COOKING CLASSES

Ojai Culinary Studio (315 N. Montgomery St., 805/646-1124, www.ojaiculinary.com) is an intimate space for classes like mastering crème brûlée, braising and roasting, and making soups, all taught by visiting chefs and noted cookbook authors. The owner even teaches a class in making multiple meals from five ingredients found at Trader Joe's. Basic classes start at $30; if you've ever fumbled around in the kitchen, this is a great place to start.

Mon. 5–9 P.M., Tues.–Sun. 11:30 A.M.–9 P.M., $12). The interior has 1950s-style semicircular booths, tiled tables, and brightly painted wood chairs. The prime seating is outside by the water feature, the fountain, the fireplace, or the fire pit. They have been dishing up food at this location since 1967. The standard fare of burritos, tacos, and tostadas is served with no real deviation, but it's well-priced and dependable Mexican food.

Los Corporales (307 E. Ojai Ave., 805/646-5452, daily 11 A.M.–8 P.M., $10) is an unpretentious place to hang out for chips and salsa and plenty of tequila shots. The shrimp cocktail is a terrific option, or stick with traditional Tex-Mex food like the chile verde, or one of their inexpensive burritos with your choice of meat. The service is slow at times, but if you sit outside you can view Libbey Park.

Vegetarian

Farmer and the Cook Market and Cafe (339 W. El Roblar Dr., 805/640-9608, www.farmerandcook.com, daily 8 A.M.–8 P.M., $15) is an amalgam of market, café, and farm. It's a tight space to dine in, and not fancy at all— more like a glorified roadside stand. But they have organic, vegetarian, and some vegan options, with a grilled squash quesadilla, handmade tamales, a salad bar, and even a wee bit of pizza and sushi. Or, you can shop for organic fruits and vegetables in the market.

Breakfast

Few eateries open early in Ojai, and serve a hearty early breakfast, but **Eggs 'n Things** (1103 Maricopa Hwy., 805/646-5346, Mon.–Fri. 6:30 A.M.–2 P.M., Sat.–Sun. 7 A.M.–2 P.M., $10) does both. The portions are large and the fried potatoes are the standout. The food isn't overly creative or original, but classic tried and true American breakfasts, served quickly.

Bakeries

The **Ojai Cafe Emporium** (108 S. Montgomery St., 805/646-2723, daily 6:30 A.M.–3 P.M.) has a small bakery fronting the street where you can pick up fresh scones, pastries, breads, and brownies made on-site each day. There's also a coffee bar with half a dozen different coffees each day.

Coffee Houses

The **Ojai Coffee Roasting Company** (337 E. Ojai Ave., 805/646-4478, www.ojaicoffeeroastingco.com, daily 5:30 A.M.–5:30 P.M.) roasts all of their 20 different coffees on-site. You can also order tea to have with your maple scone or other baked good, and there is free Wi-Fi in the cozy, comfortable but increasingly crowded little store. The service is friendly and efficient.

Ice Cream

Ojai Ice Cream (210 E. Ojai Ave., 805/646-6075, daily 11 A.M.–7 P.M.) sells 32 flavors of ice cream made on the premises, including Ojai Orange. They also have yogurt, sorbet, and their own fudge in this small, often crowded store that's been a great stopping point for over 30 years, especially during the summer months.

INFORMATION AND SERVICES
Maps and Tourist Information

Located inside the **Ojai Valley Museum** (130 W. Ojai Ave., 805/640-1390, Mon.–Fri. 10 A.M.–4 P.M.), the tourist information center is oftentimes understaffed. Thankfully, much of the information on Ojai is located in the foyer of the museum, so if the information center is closed, you can still grab all the literature you need.

Emergency Services

The **Ojai Valley Community Hospital** (1306 Maricopa Hwy., 805/646-1401) is the only hospital in Ojai and the only emergency room. In case of emergency, call 911 immediately. The **Ojai Police Department** is located at 402 South Ventura Street (805/646-1414).

Newspapers

The main newspaper is the *Ojai Valley News,* published twice weekly on Wednesdays and Fridays, which can be found all over town. *The Ojai Post* (www.ojaipost.com) is a local blog covering all of what's happening in town.

Postal Services

The main branch of the post office is located on the main drag at 201 East Ojai Avenue (805/646-7904). This is a very small post office, and is also facing budget cuts like many others, so it is best to phone ahead to check hours.

Laundry

For laundry services try **Ojai Valley Cleaners** (345 E. Ojai Ave., 805/646-2745).

GETTING THERE
By Air

Los Angles and Burbank are the closest major airports to Ojai, but the small and efficient **Oxnard Airport** (www.iflyoxnard.com) might also be an option. Though there are limited flights, the airport is pretty much hassle free, and there are rental cars. The Santa Paula Airport is home to small craft only.

SHUTTLES

Chances are you'll fly into Los Angeles or Burbank, or you might have the option of connecting to Santa Barbara. If you're coming in from L.A., the drive is just 60 miles, but it can take perhaps one and a half hours by car. There are commercial shuttle vans from L.A. to Ojai, but keep in mind that these may take two-plus hours, depending on traffic. The ride south from Santa Barbara is only 30 minutes.

By Car

The most logical driving route to Ojai is Highway 33, located off Highway 101 at the coast near downtown Ventura. From Ventura near the coast driving northbound, Highway 33 will take you directly into Ojai. From Santa Barbara, drive southbound on Highway 101, and near Carpinteria take Highway 150, which will eventually place you at Highway 33 where you will turn left to enter Ojai. There are two back routes into Ojai from the interior part of California as well: Highway 126, from Santa Paula, and Highway 33, which traverses the backcountry. Both of these roads are accessed off I-5. These are long, arduous drives and you'll want to avoid them unless you have lots of time to kill.

By Train

There are no trains to Ojai. If you arrive in Ventura by train, you will need to take another mode of transportation to then get to Ojai, either by car or bus.

By Bus

Greyhound (291 E. Thompson Blvd., 800/231-2222, www.greyhound.com) has a small station near downtown Ventura. From there the **South Coast Area Transit** (805/643-3158, www.scat.org) provides service to Ojai.

GETTING AROUND
Parking

Don't be fooled: Small towns are not lazy when it comes to parking. While there is plenty of parking on the side streets, Ojai Avenue gets crowded fast. In summer, it's difficult to find street parking anywhere. The side streets are diligently patrolled, and if you violate your time limit you will get a ticket.

Bicycles

There are plenty of flat streets and gentle climbs about the valley, and a bike is a great way to see more without speeding past in a car. **Bicycles of Ojai** (108 Canada St., 805/646-7736) has a full line of bikes to rent. While at Lake Casitas and the surrounding area, **Lake Casitas Bike**

If you don't feel like walking, take the Ojai Trolley.

© MICHAEL CERVIN

Rentals (1311 Santa Ana Rd., 805/649-6001) has a large selection of bike rentals.

Walking Tours

The **Ojai Valley Museum Guided Historical Walking Tour** (130 W. Ojai Ave., 805/640-1390, $10) is a great way to learn about Ojai's colorful past, get the lowdown on pioneer families, and check out architectural highlights and unique shops in town. The one-hour tours begin at the Ojai Valley Museum, and a local museum docent leads the tour of the downtown area. Times vary, so phone ahead.

By Trolley

The red and green **Ojai Trolley** (www.ojaitrolley.com) operated by the city is hard to miss since it looks like Christmas on four wheels. It runs the length of the small valley, but chances are you won't need to take it as Ojai is a walking town. In case you do walk far enough that you don't feel like walking back, one-way fares are $0.50 for adults and $0.25 for seniors

and children under five, but you need exact change. You can find a printable schedule on their website.

By Taxi

It's easier to find a penny on the ground than a taxi in Ojai. Should you need one, **Ojai Taxi** (100 N. Signal St., 805/646-8294) will do the trick.

By Bus

The **Gold Coast Transit** (GCT, 201 E. 4th St., Oxnard, 805/643-3158, www.goldcoast-transit.org) has bus service in western Ventura County, specifically Route 6, though their main station is in Oxnard. Fares range from $0.65 for seniors to $1.35 for adults, one-way. Fares are in the process of being increased, so check their website for specific pricing when you arrive. The Ojai–Main Street line, route #16, is available seven days a week, except holidays. GCT connects to Metrolink, Amtrak, and Greyhound at the Oxnard Transportation Center.

SANTA BARBARA WINE COUNTRY

At the heart of Santa Barbara's wine country are the towns of Santa Ynez, Los Olivos, Solvang, and Santa Maria. These small farming communities are often overlooked in favor of the surrounding beach communities. But underneath their small-town charm is a big equestrian history, rustic Western lifestyle, and even prohibition-era ideals and temperance movements, ironic for an area with a now-thriving wine industry.

Solvang started in 1911 as a Danish retreat. It is still ripe with Scandinavian heritage as well as a new modern sensibility, though the theme park atmosphere is not lacking in kitsch. In the 1950s, far earlier than other themed communities, Solvang decided to seal its fate by keeping a focus on Danish architecture, food, and style, which still holds an allure nearly 50 years after its conception. An easily walkable town, Solvang is close to the now-famous ostrich farm from the movie *Sideways*. Solvang is also home to Mission Santa Inés, bakeries, miles of rolling paved roads for bikers and cyclists (Lance Armstrong once trained here), oak-studded parks, and the well-known Solvang Theaterfest, an outdoor event and theater venue. The Chumash Casino is nearby if you need your one-armed-bandit fix.

Santa Ynez has always been a laid-back horse and farming community, unaffected by time. That it is now the gateway to the wine region does not detract from its agrarian roots. Los Olivos is an artist's enclave and a wine taster's dream. The central flagpole, sitting boldly on Grand Avenue, is the de facto rallying point for tourists, since there are still no stoplights

© MICHAEL CERVIN

HIGHLIGHTS

◖ Solvang: Long before thematic towns came into vogue, the quaint town of Solvang decided to stay true to its Danish heritage. With Danish bakeries and restaurants, a Danish history museum, and excellent wineries, Solvang is completely unlike any other town on the Central Coast (page 164).

◖ Foxen Canyon: Whether you drive with the top down or ride your bike, Santa Barbara wine country has beautiful scenic back roads. Foxen Canyon Road, beginning in Los Olivos and ending in Santa Maria, is one of the most popular routes, passing green rolling hills, farms, ranches, and vineyards (page 183).

◖ Beckmen Vineyards: Having set the standard for sustainable farming using biodynamic methods, Beckmen Vineyards is one of those places where not only are the wines terrific, but the planet is better off for it (page 184).

◖ Mission La Purisima Concepcion de Maria Santisima: Now a state park sitting on 2,000 acres in Lompoc with access to hiking trails, Mission La Purisima is the most

beautiful, yet the least-visited, mission on the Central Coast (page 194).

◖ Vandenberg Air Force Base: There is very limited access to this active military base, but three-hour tours of the base include a visit to the Heritage Museum and Space Launch Complex. There is also a viewing site for the Vandenberg rocket launches (page 196).

◖ Jalama Beach: The drive to Jalama Beach is worth the trip, but ultimately this beach, a former Chumash Indian village, is ideal for its inherent beauty and remote location (page 197).

◖ Flying Goat Cellars: Pinot noir lovers should not miss a chance to taste the seductive wines at this simple, industrial-like tasting room, where the dedication and focus on the grape is evident in each sip (page 198).

◖ Kenneth Volk Vineyards: Taste award-winning wines, with a focus on chardonnay, pinot noir, and "heirloom" varietals, on 12 acres of serene land along the Tepusquet Creek (page 200).

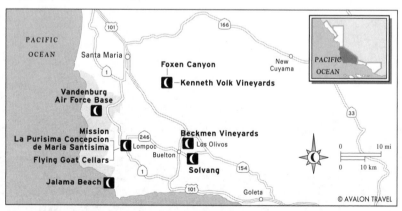

LOOK FOR ◖ TO FIND RECOMMENDED SIGHTS, ACTIVITIES, DINING, AND LODGING.

WINE COUNTRY

in the area. Within a two-block radius of the flagpole are a dozen tasting rooms, half a dozen excellent restaurants, and a few art galleries representing some of the best local artists. Unpretentious and simple, it's a perfect one-day getaway—unless you also use it as a base to explore Lake Cachuma, Figueroa Mountain, or the broader wine region, in which case you'll need several days.

Santa Maria is the workhorse of the agricultural area within Santa Barbara County. Driving through Santa Maria you see fields and vineyards on both sides of the freeway, and it's easy to assume it's merely a farming region, but Santa Maria also has a strong Western history, not to mention the now famous Santa Maria tri-tip barbecue. Though it's now built up with housing, there are still small charming areas like the Far Western Tavern in Guadalupe, the historic Santa Maria Inn, and the single best mission on the entire Central Coast, Mission La Purisima. There is also Vandenberg Air Force Base where you can watch missiles and rockets take off, wineries that produce some of the top-scoring and top-selling wine in the country, and the Santa Maria Valley Strawberry Festival.

PLANNING YOUR TIME

This region has many small towns with distinct personalities and one major city, Santa Maria. Santa Ynez and Los Olivos can both easily be visited within a day from Santa Barbara. Solvang is a five-minute drive from Santa Ynez and Los Olivos, but it is suggested that visitors reserve an entire day for this town. Santa Maria is a 15-minute drive north of Solvang, and because it has a lot more outdoor recreational opportunities, it is best to reserve an entire day for a visit to this area as well. In a weekend, you can get a feel for all of the towns in the Santa Barbara Wine Country, but as always, more time is necessary if you want to really explore these areas in depth.

HISTORY

Today we call it wine country, but this vast expanse in Northern Santa Barbara County is really two valleys—the Santa Ynez Valley and the Santa Maria Valley—and they were not originally known for grapes or wines. Santa Maria was originally farmland, and still is, producing strawberries and broccoli, among many other crops. Between 1869 and 1874, four of the valley's prominent settlers were farming on 40 acres of land where their properties met to form a four-square-mile city that became known as Grangerville, centered on Main Street and Broadway today. It was renamed Santa Maria in 1905; it is the agricultural heart and soul of the county.

The Santa Ynez Valley is made up of Solvang, Santa Ynez, and Los Olivos; these towns were formed more out of necessity, as Los Olivos and Santa Ynez were stagecoach and rail stops. In the late 1800s the stagecoach from Santa Barbara stopped twice a day in Santa Ynez at the College Hotel, then proceeded down Edison Street toward the main stagecoach stop at Mattei's Tavern in Los Olivos, which eventually became a railroad stop. Solvang, which means "sunny fields," developed as a settlement for the Danish who migrated to these sunny fields in 1910. The town fathers bought 10,000 acres and the town was created in 1911. The goal was to create a home away from Denmark; the first building was the Lutheran Church, the second building to be built was a Danish folk school, which still stands today as the Bit O' Denmark restaurant.

Wine History

The first documented viticulture in California dates from 1779 at Mission San Gabriel Arcángel in Southern California, and eventually grapes were grown throughout the mission system. The so-called "mission grape," a hybrid of different types, was high in sugar content, low in acid, and produced a thin sweet wine that by many accounts of the times, wasn't all that good. But this grape dominated the industry until the end of California's Mexican era in the late 1840s. By that time, wine and brandy production was a significant source of income for some of the missions. Old Mission Santa Barbara established a vineyard

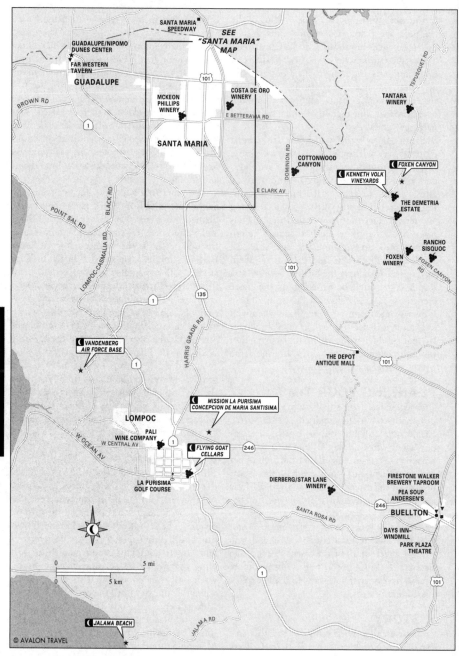

SANTA MARIA SPEEDWAY

SEE "SANTA MARIA" MAP

GUADALUPE/NIPOMO DUNES CENTER

FAR WESTERN TAVERN

GUADALUPE

BROWN RD

MCKEON PHILLIPS WINERY

COSTA DE ORO WINERY

E BETTERAVIA RD

TANTARA WINERY

SANTA MARIA

POINT SAL RD

BLACK RD

LOMPOC-CASMALIA RD

DOMINION RD

COTTONWOOD CANYON

E CLARK AV

FOXEN CANYON

KENNETH VOLK VINEYARDS

THE DEMETRIA ESTATE

RANCHO SISQUOC

FOXEN WINERY

FOXEN CANYON RD

TEPUSQUET RD

HARRIS GRADE RD

VANDENBERG AIR FORCE BASE

THE DEPOT ANTIQUE MALL

MISSION LA PURISIMA CONCEPCION DE MARIA SANTISIMA

LOMPOC

PALI WINE COMPANY

W OCEAN AV

W CENTRAL AV

FLYING GOAT CELLARS

LA PURISIMA GOLF COURSE

DIERBERG/STAR LANE WINERY

FIRESTONE WALKER BREWERY TAPROOM

PEA SOUP ANDERSEN'S

BUELLTON

SANTA ROSA RD

DAYS INN–WINDMILL

PARK PLAZA THEATRE

0   5 mi
0   5 km

JALAMA RD

JALAMA BEACH

© AVALON TRAVEL

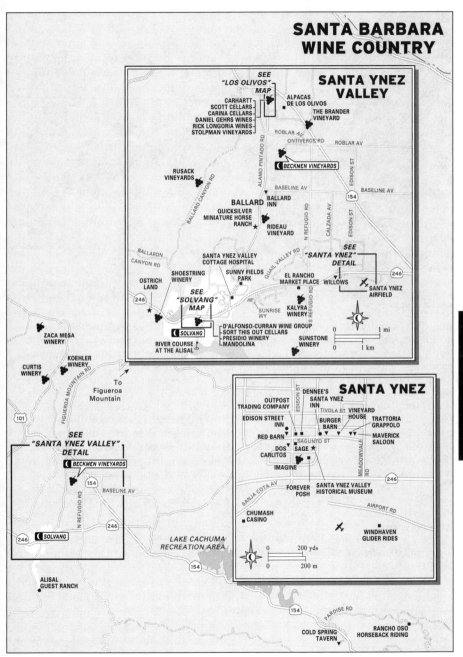

SANTA BARBARA WINE COUNTRY

SANTA YNEZ VALLEY

SEE "LOS OLIVOS" MAP

CARHARTT
SCOTT CELLARS
CARINA CELLARS
DANIEL GEHRS WINES
RICK LONGORIA WINES
STOLPMAN VINEYARDS

ALPACAS DE LOS OLIVOS

THE BRANDER VINEYARD

ROBLAR AV
ONTIVEROS RD
ROBLAR AV

BECKMEN VINEYARDS

RUSACK VINEYARDS

BALLARD CANYON RD
ALAMO PINTADO RD
EDISON ST

BASELINE AV
BASELINE AV

154

BALLARD INN
BALLARD
QUICKSILVER MINIATURE HORSE RANCH
RIDEAU VINEYARD

N REFUGIO RD
CALZADA AV
EDISON ST

BALLARDN CANYON RD

SANTA YNEZ VALLEY COTTAGE HOSPITAL

SHOESTRING WINERY
SUNNY FIELDS PARK

QUAIL VALLEY RD

SEE "SANTA YNEZ" DETAIL

246

OSTRICH LAND

246

SEE "SOLVANG" MAP

EL RANCHO MARKET PLACE
WILLOWS
SANTA YNEZ AIRFIELD

SOLVANG

D'ALFONSO-CURRAN WINE GROUP
SORT THIS OUT CELLARS
PRESIDIO WINERY
MANDOLINA

SUNRISE WY

S REFUGIO RD

KALYRA WINERY

RIVER COURSE AT THE ALISAL

SUNSTONE WINERY

N
0   1 mi
0   1 km

ZACA MESA WINERY

KOEHLER WINERY

CURTIS WINERY

FIGUEROA MOUNTAIN RD

101

To Figueroa Mountain

SEE "SANTA YNEZ VALLEY" DETAIL

BECKMEN VINEYARDS

154
BASELINE AV
N REFUGIO RD

246

SOLVANG
246

ALISAL GUEST RANCH

LAKE CACHUMA RECREATION AREA

154

154

PARDISE RD

COLD SPRING TAVERN

RANCHO OSO HORSEBACK RIDING

SANTA YNEZ

OUTPOST TRADING COMPANY
DENNEE'S
SANTA YNEZ INN
EDISON ST
TIVOLA ST
VINEYARD HOUSE

EDISON STREET INN
BURGER BARN
TRATTORIA GRAPPOLO

RED BARN
SAGUNTO ST
MEADOWVALE RD
MAVERICK SALOON

DOS CARLITOS
SAGE

IMAGINE

SANJA COTA AV

FOREVER POSH
SANTA YNEZ VALLEY HISTORICAL MUSEUM

246

AIRPORT RD

CHUMASH CASINO

WINDHAVEN GLIDER RIDES

N
0   200 yds
0   200 m

WINE COUNTRY

© MICHAEL CERVIN

merlot grapes

and winery around the 1830s. Grapes were used not only to make wine, but also raisins, which were handy food for travelers. But grape production was not limited to the missions. About 1820, San Antonio winery was built in what is now Goleta. The lonely historic adobe winery is still standing nearly 200 years later, though on private property. Another commercial winery, the Packard Winery, was built in 1865, also in Santa Barbara, and in the late 1890s about 200 acres of grapes were being turned into wine on Santa Cruz Island. Near Mission La Purisima grapes were planted in the 1880s as well, and a few of those vines still survive today, though they are now on private property.

When the first commercial grapevine plantings were made after prohibition in the 1960s and 1970s in the Santa Maria Valley, grape growers and vintners planted anything and everything, without regard to the end product. It has taken Santa Barbara nearly 20 years to understand its soil, its climate, and what is best suited for their diverse growing regions and the American Viticultural Area's (AVA) federally recognized grape growing regions. Currently there are 64 different varieties of grapes planted throughout the county on 21,000 acres. Pinot noir and chardonnay are the most widely planted varieties, with chardonnay commanding an astounding 40 percent of that acreage; pinot noir comes in at 25 percent. The wine industry in Santa Barbara County is thriving, in spite of the fluctuations of the economy, transitional markets, fickle consumers, and inconsistent harvests.

Santa Ynez Valley

The wine industry has dominated the region in the last 10 years, even though commercially planted grapes have been here for over four decades. With the success of the film *Sideways*, the area has received additional attention, helping to place a visit to this area on the list of wine lovers across the globe. Some areas, like Happy Canyon, have hotter temperatures and can produce cabernet sauvignon and sauvignon blanc. And cooler growing regions like the Santa Rita Hills benefit from close proximity to the coast. There are cool- and warm-climate plantings of syrah and chardonnay, providing different styles and acid levels, and the diversity of the area is astounding. Every winery is doing something different, and it is this attitude of experimentation that has contributed to its success. It also doesn't hurt that the valley is a beautiful place to spend time.

SANTA YNEZ AND VICINITY

Named The New Town when it was founded in 1882, Santa Ynez retains its historical Western flavor, with some of its old storefronts still intact. By 1889, the town had become the focal point both socially and economically of the entire Santa Ynez Valley, complete with mercantile stores, blacksmith shops, garages, grocery stores, a barber shop, harness shop, millinery shop, and several saloons. The College Hotel was once the area's main lodging establishment, complete with a Victorian design and 16 roof turrets. The hotel, which stood on Sagunto Street just south of Edison Street, hosted guests from all over the world. These days Santa Ynez is a shadow of its former self, no longer the important hub it was, a quiet spot with a handful of businesses. And yet people still come to the valley from the world over to explore the region.

Sights and Drives

Santa Ynez is a very small town. There are only two hotels here, not including the Chumash Casino resort, which is technically in Solvang in spite of being just down the road from Santa Ynez. One of the reasons people choose to stay here is that it makes a good base from which to explore, and it is ultra quiet. If you don't want lots of people around in the mornings or at night, it's ideal. You can walk the length of town in about 10 minutes, and there are a few sights and drives to check out.

Wine country is notorious for long winding roads that pass vineyards, ranches, cattle, and old oaks. These roads are ideal for a drive, a bike ride, or even a run. Make sure you share the road and keep alert, as the beauty and serenity sometime lulls you into a very calm state.

Directly off Highway 154 is an area known as **Happy Canyon,** which is the warmest grape-growing area in the entire valley. To get here, you can take Highway 246 toward Happy Canyon from Santa Ynez. Highway 246 eventually connects with Highway 154 and near the intersection of Highways 154 and 246 is Armor Ranch Road. If you follow Armor Ranch Road for about four miles Happy Canyon Road will be on your left. There are a lot of horses here, and if you take Happy Canyon Road towards the mountains there is some beautiful scenery as it heads deeper into the low, flat region before it begins climbing into the mountains. Or, simply stay on Armor Ranch Road and make a loop back to Highway 154. You'll exit south of where you entered, so turn right back on to Highway 154, then to get back to Santa Ynez turn left onto Highway 246.

Though Santa Ynez is small, the area does have some history to it, admirably presented at the **Santa Ynez Valley Historical Museum and Parks-Janeway Carriage House** (3596 Sagunto St., 805/688-7889, www.santaynez-museum.org, Wed.–Sun. noon–4 P.M., suggested donation $2). There's a good-sized diorama with a narrow gauge train that eeks its way around the track, showing how the train depot near Mattei's Tavern used to look back in the day. It's not high tech, but it is kind of fun. There are also small displays in the Valley

© MICHAEL CERVIN

Edison Street in Santa Ynez

Room showing the original five small towns of Solvang (founded 1911), Santa Ynez (1882), Los Olivos (1887), Ballard (1881), and Buellton (1920). These are short histories, but are part of the great development of the valley. The Pioneer Room is three rooms outfitted with turn-of-the-20th-century furnishings, many from local ranches.

The carriage house is an impressive collection of all types of carriages, surreys, and wagons, including an old popcorn wagon from 1909 that sold nuts and fresh popcorn, as well as an old fire wagon. These carriages are in fantastic shape; it is clear they have been well cared for. There is also a selection of tack and saddles.

Wineries

There used to be a larger contingency of wineries in and near Santa Ynez, but the migration to Solvang and Los Olivos has left only a few. A short drive will get you to some wonderful area wineries.

IMAGINE

Imagine (3563 Numancia St., 805/688-1769, www.imaginewine.com, Mon.–Sat. 10 A.M.–5 P.M., tasting fee $10) is the only tasting room still in town, and it is staffed solely

by the owners. The light wood-toned interior has a classic Victorian feel, and the room is spacious with lots of light. You'll get an average of six tasting samples to ponder, including viognier and chardonnay on the white side, and syrah, zinfandel, pinot noir, and merlot on the red side. The winery is an easy walk from anywhere in town; the space doubles as an art gallery.

KALYRA WINERY

Kalyra Winery (343 N. Refugio, 805/693-8864, www.kalyrawinery.com, Mon.–Fri. 11 A.M.–5 P.M., Sat.–Sun. 10 A.M.–5 P.M., tasting fee $7) is famous for having been featured in the film *Sideways*. The building itself has been home to several other wineries prior to Kalyra moving in, such as the Santa Ynez Valley Winery and Lincourt Vineyards. The partial wraparound deck provides great views of the valley and mountains, and when the sun is setting and the golden hues hit the leafed-out vines, it's truly beautiful. The winery's interior gives a nod to brothers Mike and Martin Brown's Australian roots and love of surfing. They initially started out producing sweet wines but have since expanded their portfolio to include a large number of red and white wines, including some made from Australian grapes.

WINE-TASTING 101

Tasting wine is not a science, but it's not a sport either. There are specific steps to follow in order to have the best possible experience, and to fully enjoy and understand what the winemaker was trying to accomplish with his or her wine.

You may see both wine know-it-alls and sport tasters while you're out wine-tasting, but don't pay any attention to anyone who is arrogant, rude, or intoxicated. Wine-tasting is meant to be enjoyed, not endured. If a tasting room is crowded and there's no room at the tasting bar, move on to another one. If you see limos out front, that might also be a clue to avoid that particular tasting room, as often people hire limos so that they can taste liberally.

1. Swirl: First off, it's important to know that your nose is much more powerful than your taste buds. Swirling the wine in your glass might seem like a ridiculous custom, but this actually releases the esters, the aromatic compounds in the wine. The air interacts with the wine and enhances the scents.

2. Smell: The second step is to smell the wine. Really get your nose in the glass and take a deep breath. Exhale and do it again. This sets the stage for your palate, and will immediately give you clues and ideas about the wine. Frankly, there's no mystery here. It's no different than smelling anything – your food, cologne, whatever – except that wine has many parts and layers that can be detected. Your nose will give you a greater understanding of the wine. As you smell it, ask yourself what specific scents you can identify.

3. Taste: To spit or not to spit? That's a matter of preference. Part of wine-tasting is actually the tasting part, and fully experiencing a wine means swallowing it. As with any wine-tasting, though, most wineries will pour about six wines, and some may pour more than that. In California, the law allows a one-ounce pour. That may not seem like a lot, but if you sample six to eight wines, that's the equivalent of one glass at a restaurant. It's also important to plan out your trip. If you plan on visiting, say, four wineries, visit two, take a food break, and then visit two more. Alcohol is dehydrating, so always keep water with you to stay hydrated. It's easy to forget about water in a fun tasting-room atmosphere. It's also important to try new things. Some people say they only like a certain wine, but every winery produces their wines differently, and there is no standard recipe for anything. Be adventurous and sample. If you don't like it, spit it out. And never let anyone tell you that you should or shouldn't like a wine. It's ultimately a personal preference. Buy what you like, but try everything.

RIDEAU VINEYARD

Rideau Vineyard (1562 Alamo Pintado, 805/688-0717 www.rideauvineyard.com, daily 11 A.M.–4:30 P.M., tasting fee $10) is housed in an 1884 two-story adobe, one of the few remaining in the entire state. The emphasis here is on Rhône varieties, namely syrah, viognier, roussanne, and grenache, as well as blends and other wines like Riesling and grenache blanc. The small gift shop has some New Orleans–inspired items since owner Iris Rideau originally hails from Louisiana, and they have concerts several times each year where you'll find gumbo and other Creole foods being served. It's a beautiful spot to enjoy a picnic on their lush green back lawn and relax. Tastings are done both inside and outside.

BRIDLEWOOD WINERY

As you drive up the long driveway of Bridlewood Winery (3555 Roblar, 805/688-9000, www.bridlewoodwinery.com, daily 10 A.M.–5 P.M., tasting fee $10) you'll come upon a long structure that looks like a mission but is actually a former equestrian center; all Bridlewood's wines have a horse theme. The focus here is on Rhône varieties, such as eight different versions of syrah alone, as well

© MICHAEL CERVIN

Rideau Vineyard's two-story adobe tasting room

as three different viogniers, which they do very well. Tossed in the mix is a bit of chardonnay, port, pinot noir, and zinfandel, from vineyards up and down the state. The tasting room is a large facility that can accommodate big crowds, but you can also head outside and enjoy the surroundings. Being removed from the main road, it's a peaceful spot, perfect for a picnic on their back veranda.

SUNSTONE WINERY
Just a mile from Kalyra Winery is Sunstone Winery (125 N. Refugio, 805/688-9463, www.sunstonewinery.com, daily 10 A.M.–4 P.M., tasting fee $10), which has a Spanish and Tuscan vibe with mottled yellow walls suggesting an old estate in the countryside in Europe—it's not actually an old building, but it feels like it. Since its inception in 1990, the focus at Sunstone has been growing grapes without any pesticides, and they are certified organic growers. Probably best known locally for their merlot, they also produce Bordeaux blends and syrah, and their white wines include viognier and sauvignon blanc. This is a very popular spot and sometimes gets downright crowded.

Entertainment and Events
The land in Santa Ynez was home to the Chumash Indians long before grapes were ever planted. With the advent of the reservation system, the Indian community needed a source of viable revenue and a way to be self sustaining, so the **Chumash Casino** (3400 E. Hwy. 246, 800/248-6274, www.chumashcasino.com, 24 hours) was created. For a long time it was housed in a tent structure, but they eventually petitioned the county to build a proper resort. This was met with local opposition, but they got their casino. Now it is one of the largest draws in the area and one of the few places in the county to draw big-name performers. Additionally, the Chumash have been actively involved in giving back to the community in various ways. The casino itself consists of 2,000 slots, a variety of poker options, including a 24-hour room, bingo large enough for 1,000 players, and blackjack. People are routinely bused in, so expect crowds. There are three restaurants within the casino, a 123-room hotel, a gift shop, and a 1,300-seat entertainment showroom bringing in a solid lineup of performers.

The **Maverick Saloon** (3687 Sagunto St., 805/686-4785, www.mavericksaloon.org, Mon.–Fri. noon–2 A.M., Sat. 10 A.M.–2 A.M.) has hardwood floors, dollar bills hanging from the ceiling, and every kind of sign you can imagine

WINE COUNTRY

© MICHAEL CERVIN

Gamble, eat, and sleep at the Chumash Casino.

tacked to the walls. It gets loud and wild here, especially on nights and weekends when the bar is packed—in part because there's not much else to do in the area. The outdoor patio seating is taken first, then the bar becomes flooded with people. The stage area is a larger space for overflow, unless there's a band playing. Live bands from the region play on Friday and Saturday night 8:30–11:30 P.M., then a DJ spins tunes till closing. A $5 cover charge applies. There's also darts, pool, and a whole lot of that renegade, devil-may-care vibe.

Each May hundreds of people get ready for the **Wine Country Half Marathon** (starts on Sagunto St., www.runsantaynez.com), a 13.1-mile race through the wine country. Both individuals and teams can enter. If you enjoy running, this is a great way to see the valley, as it starts in Santa Ynez, winds through Los Olivos, traverses down Ballard Canyon, and ends in Solvang, passing vineyards and farms along the way. The plants are leafed out in May and the weather is nearly perfect. The post-race festival includes a wine- and beer-tasting, music, food, and awards.

Held at Live Oak Camp each October, the **Chumash Intertribal Pow Wow** (www.pow-wows.com) is open to the public to watch

traditional tribal dances and drumming circles and learn about Native American culture via speakers and literature. There are also native arts and crafts for sale and the chance to expand your knowledge of Chumash and other Indian tribal culture by conversing with members of various tribes. It's free to attend but there is a small parking fee.

Sports and Recreation
LAKE CACHUMA RECREATION AREA
The Lake Cachuma Recreation Area (2225 Hwy. 154, 805/686-5055, www.countyofsb.org, $8 day-use vehicle fee, $5 day-use hiker, $13 if towing your boat) was built in 1953 to provide a reservoir for the region. The lake covers just over 3,000 acres and has 42 miles of shoreline. Being that it is a drinking-water source, there is no swimming allowed, nor any body contact with the water. There is a fully stocked general store that has firewood, canned foods, clothing, even a small selection of magazines and books. There's also a gas station, coin laundry, hot showers, fishing piers, and plenty of hiking and biking trails.

Boating on the lake is simple. You can bring your own boat to the four launch ramps and small harbor located at the marina, or rent a boat on an hourly, half-day, daily, weekly, monthly, or annual basis. They have outboards, rowboats, pontoons, and paddle boats. Daily rental rates range from $30 per hour for a four-passenger rowboat all the way to $385 per day for a pontoon boat accommodating 20 passengers. Early spring mornings are great if you bring hot cocoa and get out on the water before the sun rises to wait for the warmth of a new day to liberate you.

The **Nature Cruises** (located at the marina, $15 adults, $7 children 4–12) are conducted by park employees and are a great way to see the lake and surrounding area without any effort. Two cruises are offered, each two hours long and held on a 30-passenger covered pontoon boat called the *Osprey*. A naturalist is on board and speaks about the environment and wildlife and answers any questions visitors may have. The **Wildlife Cruise** runs March–October and focuses on the animals, such as deer and bears, and plants that make the lake their home. It's a wonderful outing to get an up-close look at the shoreline and learn about the wildlife and history of the habitat, but make sure you bring a wrap as it can get cool in certain parts of the lake. The **Eagle Cruise** runs November–February with a focus specifically on bald eagles and osprey, both of whom live here. You'll also see a greater concentration of migratory birds during these months.

If **fishing** is your thing, Cachuma is a good spot due to the lake bottom's topography of rocks, shallow areas, and aquatic plant beds, all of which make great habitats for fish. During non-drought years the lake supports populations of largemouth and smallmouth bass, crappie, bluegill, red-ear sunfish, channel catfish, and rainbow trout. Normally you'd be able to rent gear at the bait shop in the marina, but the parks department is currently in the process of taking bids on a new concessionaire, so for now it's best to bring your own equipment.

For those who prefer to camp, there are several choices for your **camping** experience. Single-family campsites are first come, first served. More than 400 campsites, 100 with full electrical, water, and sewer hookups, and 30 with electrical and water hookups, can accommodate any size RV. Each campsite contains a picnic table and fire ring, with showers, restrooms, and potable water nearby. An RV dump station is also available. It books up early so you'll need to plan ahead. The County Parks website (www.countyofsb.org) has detailed campsite information to view and download.

And then there are the popular **yurts** (805/686-5050 for reservations, $60–70). A cross between a tent and tepee, the yurts at Cachuma feature platform beds that sleep up to six people. They have a lockable door, inside light and heat, and screened windows. Set on a bluff with access to the lakeshore, they have very nice views.

There are also four **cabins** (805/934-1441, www.centralcoastcabins.com, $135–210 per night) for rent, which are operated independently from the park. One- and two-bedroom cabins are equipped with electricity, full bathrooms, kitchenettes, living rooms, private porches, picnic tables, and fire pits. Simply pack your sleeping bag or bring bedding, plus pillows, towels, toiletries, and groceries (these items are costly at the general store). The cabins can be reserved year-round and up to one year in advance, but the price is high these simple cabins with few amenities.

GLIDER RIDES

Windhaven Glider Rides (at the Santa Ynez Airport, 900 Airport Rd., 805/688-2517, www.gliderrides.com, Sat.–Sun. 10 A.M.–5 P.M., $125–245) offers glider rides over the wine country. It's an amazing experience to float above the region and not only see the vineyards, but get a better understanding of the topography of the land. Windhaven has been operating for 20 years and takes any age, from 4–104 years old. Flights last 15–30 minutes. A plane tows the glider up along with you and a pilot, then drops the tow line so you're soaring above the earth without the noise of engines, making this a relatively quiet and very scenic experience. Of course, everything ultimately depends on the weather.

HORSEBACK RIDING

Sitting on 300 acres and a fair drive from anywhere, **Rancho Oso Horseback Riding** (3750 Paradise Rd., 805/683-5110, www.ranchooso.net) offers a variety of horseback riding options. The one-hour trail ride starts at $40, and though your horse isn't roaming free, it's still a nice, if predictable, ride through the backcountry. You cross streams and will see a few Chumash Indian artifacts (this was a Chumash village site long ago) as you meander the lower canyons. There are longer rides that offer scenic vistas, but the lumbering pace can be annoying after a few hours.

Shopping

The few shops in Santa Ynez are all a stone's throw from each other, so you can browse all the shops in this area easily.

For 15 years **Dennee's** (3569 Sagunto St., 805/686-0842, Mon.–Sat. 9 A.M.–5 P.M., Sun. 11 A.M.–5 P.M.) has provided lots of interesting home furnishings with a country and equestrian motif. The place is packed with large and small items, some from local craftsmen in town, and there's a large diversity of things from leather couches to accent pieces, mirrors, and decorative pieces for your home. Think of it as high-end farm decor with a country twist.

Outpost Trading Company (1102 Edison St., 805/686-5588, Mon.–Fri. 10 A.M.–5:30 P.M., Sat.–Sun. 11 A.M.–4 P.M.) is an eclectic shop that sells Western wear, art, and home furnishings, couture clothing, handcrafted items, and custom-made furniture and woven tack.

Forever Posh (3583 Numancia, 805/688-1444, Tues.–Sat. 10 A.M.–5 P.M.) has trendy clothes and lounge wear for women, custom jewelry, sunglasses, and designer handbags, as well as bridal gifts. The shop is small but offers expert help and a nice assortment of items.

Sage (1095 Edison St., 805/688-0955, Mon.–Sat. 10 A.M.–5 P.M.) features a wide variety of home items and decor, including imported furnishings, table linens, Italian dishware, books, candles, unique lamps, bath products, Egyptian cotton towels, soaps from Provence, wind chimes, and CDs.

Accommodations

$200-300

Four rooms and a guest cottage make up the unique **Edison Street Inn** (1121 Edison St., 805/693-0303, www.edisonstreetinn.com, $230–305 d). It represents the best of the area by combining Victorian and Western themes. The rooms are more home-like than inn-like, detailed, spacious, and comfortable, and all very romantic. A full breakfast at a local restaurant is included. Note that there are no in-room telephones, so make sure to bring your cell.

OVER $300

As you enter the elegant and opulent ◖ **Santa Ynez Inn** (3628 Sagunto St., 805/688-5588, www.santaynezinn.com, $345–495 d) you're transported into a Victorian era. Think of this as a high-end bed-and-breakfast and you get the idea. The average room is about 600 square feet and has a steam shower and heated tile floor. The rooms are large with beautiful antiques, and it's clear they have spent a good deal of time and money to make it all the highest quality they can. Breakfast is served each morning in the parlor, a lushly wood-rich Victorian room that feels more like a museum than an inn. In the evening they offer a wine and cheese reception. There are only 20 rooms here; it's a quiet place in a quiet town to enjoy a quiet experience.

Food

ITALIAN

The immensely popular Italian restaurant **Trattoria Grappolo** (3687 Sagunto St., 805/688-6899, www.trattoriagrappolo.com, lunch Tues.–Sun. 11 A.M.–3 P.M., dinner nightly 5–10 P.M., $25) serves pizzas, fresh fish, and tender roast chicken, all cooked in their wood-burning oven. Of course, there is also pasta, and a nice diverse selection of Californian and Italian wines is presented. The restaurant has a compact interior, so many people opt for the deck instead. It's not uncommon

WINE COUNTRY

© MICHAEL CERVIN

Santa Ynez Inn

to see workers and winemakers from the vine-yards show up in their cowboy boots and hats for authentic Italian cuisine in the sometimes loud space.

MEXICAN

Modern pueblo meets country at Mexican restaurant **Dos Carlitos** (3544 Sagunto St., 805/688-0033, www.doscarlitosrestaurant.com, daily 11 A.M.–10 P.M., $25), which boasts high vaulted ceilings and a nice outdoor patio. The furnishings were made in Mexico and there is an authentic feel to the place, though the authentic Mexican food comes with a steep price tag. Sit at the copper-topped bar and try one of 50 tequilas by the shot. Shots range $25–75.

AMERICAN

Inside the 1907 [Vineyard House (3631 Sagunto St., 805/688-2886, www.thevine-yardhouse.com, Mon.–Sat. 11:30 A.M.–3 P.M. and 5–9 P.M., Sun. 10 A.M.–3 P.M., $20), there is some magic at work. Creative flavorful food comes out of this kitchen on a regular basis. The baked brie is always a treat, as is the crispy

buttermilk chicken and a hearty, thick veni-son chile verde. They make their own soups and salad dressings as well as desserts like the eternally decadent and gooey molten choco-late cake. The interior is homey and intimate, but the prime seating on nice days is the deck overlooking Sagunto Street, where the pepper trees hang languidly over the tables.

You can't miss **Red Barn** (3539 Sagunto St., 805/688-4142, daily 11 A.M.–2 P.M. and 5:30 P.M.–close, $20) since it actually is a red barn. Though the white unmarked door seems like an obscure entrance, once inside it's all down home. A small bar is off to one side and the coun-try wood tables with red and white checkered tablecloths and chairs have the feel of a low-key country diner. People have been coming to Red Barn for its steaks and desserts since 1924. The portions are generous, if a little pricey.

Sequestered from the casino, **Willows** (3400 E. Hwy. 246, 805/686-0855, www.chumash-casino.com, Sun.–Thurs. 5–10 P.M., Fri.–Sat. 5–11 P.M., $30) is unexpectedly elegant, with white tablecloth–clad tables between narrow arches. They have private dining rooms on the

© MICHAEL CERVIN

Rustic and secluded, Cold Spring Tavern is a great spot for food and live entertainment.

outdoor terrace as well. The emphasis here is seafood and beef entrées. Side dishes are extra, so be prepared to throw down some cash. The only drawback is that you have to walk through the casino to get here, but once inside the noise of clanging slot machines quickly fades away.

The no-frills **Burger Barn** (3621 Sagunto St., 805/688-2366, Mon.–Fri. 7 A.M.–3 P.M., Sat.–Sun. 8 A.M.–3 P.M., $8) is known for inexpensive but tasty burgers and salads. Very popular with tourists and locals, in part because of the price, it can get very crowded. The outdoor area has plastic tables and chairs and the interior doesn't fare much better, but it's all about quick and easy food.

◖ Cold Spring Tavern (5995 Stagecoach Rd., 805/967-0066, www.coldspringtavern.com, restaurant Mon.–Fri. 11 A.M.–3 P.M. and 5–9 P.M., Sat.–Sun. 8 A.M.–3 P.M. and 5–9 P.M., tavern daily noon–9 P.M., $20) was a former stagecoach stop when wagons and riders had to traverse the mountains from the valley to Santa Barbara. It was built in 1886 and hasn't changed much since. Rustic and secluded, it hosts live music every Friday–Sunday. A stream runs by the place, situated in a narrow canyon that

can be cool even during the summer months. Motorcyclists, townies, and locals hang out in the bar area and there is often dancing both inside and outside the bar. The on-site restaurant, in a separate building, is the place to find tri-tip sandwiches during the summers months, grilled outdoors over an open flame, as well as wild game, rabbit, venison, boar, and very good chili. A visit to the tavern is as much about the food as it is about enjoying the charming space. There's also an old jail on-site, a one-room wood building that used to hold unruly customers.

Information and Services
MAPS AND TOURIST INFORMATION
Your only bet is the **Santa Ynez Valley Visitors Association** (www.syvva.com), which has a fairly comprehensive website covering much of the valley. Remember that many businesses here still don't have websites, only phone numbers, so getting specific information is often a challenge.

EMERGENCY SERVICES
The **Santa Ynez Valley Cottage Hospital** (2050 Viborg, Solvang, 805/688-6431) offers

emergency services. Should you have an emergency, dial 911 immediately. Police services are contracted with the County of Santa Barbara Sheriff's Department (1745 Mission Dr., Solvang, 805/688-5000).

NEWSPAPERS AND MEDIA
The *Santa Ynez Valley Journal* (www.syv-journal.com) publishes weekly and though small, usually about 30 pages, it has a broad scope. There is a calendar listing current and upcoming events and plenty of local stories and interviews.

POSTAL SERVICES
The post office is located at 3564 Sagunto Street (805/693-9287). Given its limited size it's advisable to call ahead for operating hours and services.

LAUNDRY
There are no laundry services in town; your best bet is St. Paul Cleaners and Laundry, located a few miles down the road in Solvang (1693 Mission Dr., Solvang, 805/688-9618).

Getting There
BY CAR
Santa Ynez is accessed by Highway 246, which cuts through the area. If you're arriving by car from the north you can exit and drive through Solvang, or take Highway 154 exit and drive the back way. Each drive has its advantages. Driving through Solvang is great if you've never seen the town before, but on weekends the road is packed with slow-moving cars, buses and RVs. The back route with scenic rolling hills and a few vineyards can take you through Los Olivos or along Highway 154 until you turn right onto Highway 246. If you're driving from the south, take either Highway 101 up through the Gaviota Pass and exit through Solvang, or drive the San Marcos Pass, Highway 154, which can also be a long drive depending on traffic. Here you'll pass Lake Cachuma, where chances are you'll see deer and cattle strolling about the oak-studded hillsides.

BY AIR
Small craft can land at the **Santa Ynez Valley Airport** (900 Airport Rd., 805/688-8390, www.santaynezairport.com), a tiny airport right near town that serves the entire valley.

Getting Around
There's no secret to getting around Santa Ynez: You walk. There are no trolleys, no tours, no taxis. In any town that's two blocks long and two blocks wide you don't need much, just a decent pair of shoes.

◖ SOLVANG
To some, Solvang might seem like Denmark on steroids, but the colorful and charming village-like town is unlike any other in the area—or the state for that matter; it's a great escape from the tedious mall architecture that dominates much of America.

Solvang originally looked like other towns of the day, with a Spanish theme punctuated by Western stores. The vision to create the Solvang we see today emerged post–World War II. Long before thematic towns or city centers were in vogue, Solvang agreed upon a unifying design theme, and that is part of the allure.

You'll notice storks displayed above many of the stores in town; they're a traditional symbol of good luck. Solvang draws nearly two million visitors each year, and you'll still hear the muted strains of Danish spoken on occasion. During peak summer times and holidays, Solvang can be congested, with people clogging the brick sidewalks, riding rented surreys through the streets, loitering in front of the bakeries and chocolate shops, and it feels uncharacteristic of a small town. Try to visit during off season, when the simple joys of meandering the lovely shops can still be enjoyed. It's at its best in the fall and early spring when the hills are verdant green and the trees in town are beautiful.

Sights and Drives
BALLARD CANYON
Ballard Canyon is not only a great local drive, it's also popular with cyclists and even runners.

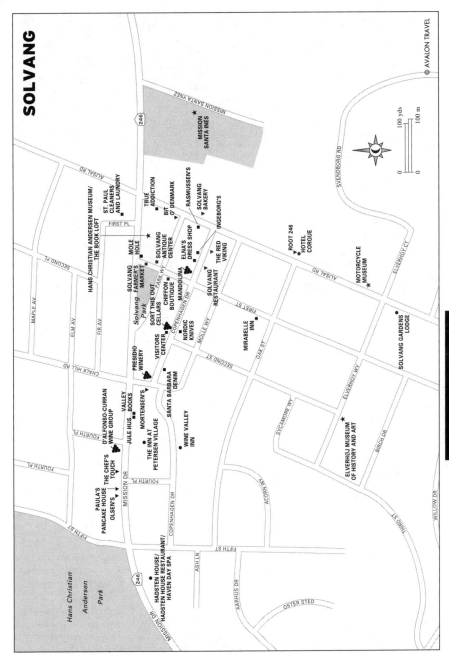

SOLVANG

MISSION SANTA YNEZ

MISSION SANTA INÉS

© AVALON TRAVEL

100 yds

100 m

ST. PAUL CLEANERS AND LAUNDRY

TRUE ADDICTION

BIT O' DENMARK

RASMUSSEN'S

SOLVANG BAKERY

INGEBORG'S

ALISAL RD

FIRST PL

HANS CHRISTIAN ANDERSEN MUSEUM/ THE BOOK LOFT

MOLE HOLE

SOLVANG ANTIQUE CENTER

ELNA'S DRESS SHOP

THE RED VIKING

ROOT 246

HOTEL CORQUE

SECOND PL

MAPLE AV

ELM AV

FIR AV

SOLVANG FARMERS' MARKET

Solvang Park

SORT THIS OUT CELLARS

CHIFFON BOUTIQUE

MANDOLINA

SOLVANG RESTAURANT

MOTORCYCLE MUSEUM

EVERHOY CT

CHALK HILL RD

Park Wy

Copenhagen Dr

NORDIC KNIVES

MOLLE WY

FIRST ST

ALISAL RD

PRESIDIO WINERY

VISITORS CENTER

MIRABELLE INN

OAK ST

SECOND ST

EVERHOY WY

SOLVANG GARDENS LODGE

SANTA BARBARA DENIM

FOURTH PL

D'ALFONSO-CURRAN WINE GROUP

VALLEY

JULE HUS

BOOKS

MORTENSEN'S

WINE VALLEY INN

SYCAMORE WY

ACORN WY

BIRCH DR

WILLOW DR

THE INN AT PETERSEN VILLAGE

ELVERHOJ MUSEUM OF HISTORY AND ART

FOURTH PL

PAULA'S PANCAKE HOUSE

THE CHEF'S TOUCH

OLSEN'S

MISSION DR

MISSION DR

FOURTH PL

FIFTH ST

Hans Christian Andersen Park

HADSTEN HOUSE/ HADSTEN HOUSE RESTAURANT/ HAVEN DAY SPA

COPENHAGEN DR

ASH LN

FIFTH ST

AARHUS DR

OSTER STED

SVENDBORG RD

246

246

WINE COUNTRY

© MICHAEL CERVIN

windmill in Solvang

Just off the main street in Solvang, you can ride, drive, or run the canyon past vineyards, bison, and cattle; the road will drop you out near Los Olivos. What makes this road so wonderful is the combination of straight parts mixed with gentle curves and occasional steep climbs, and of course the bucolic scenery from low in the canyon to high atop the ridge with views to the surrounding areas. To access Ballard Canyon from downtown Solvang, head north on Atterdag. The hill will climb for a while, then drop you down into the canyon. You'll veer right onto Ballard and take that all the way through the canyon to meet up with Highway 246. To your right is Los Olivos; straight ahead is Foxen Canyon Road.

SANTA ROSA ROAD

Santa Rosa Road winds its way through the Santa Rita Hills, the best-known pinot noir–growing region in the county. The two-lane road meanders past a few wineries, old ranch houses, and lots of gentle sloping hills. Both cars and cyclists share this road, which eventually connects with Highway 1 south of

Lompoc. The hills rise to your left; to your right are vineyards and farmland. Early morning and late afternoon are great times to be here as the sun gently bathes the hills and vineyards in a soft golden hue.

OSTRICH LAND

Made popular by the film *Sideways,* the Ostrich Land (610 E. Hwy. 246, 805/686-9696, www.ostrichlandusa.com, daily 10 A.M.–dusk, $4 adults, $1 children under 12) farm is on Highway 246 two miles before you reach Solvang from Highway 101. At first glance it seems somewhat prehistoric; you'll see massive birds wandering through the shrubs in the distance, their thin necks sporting small heads and big eyes. They usually keep their distance and only approach when there is food to be had. Should you decided to feed them, you need to hold the food plate firmly in your hand as they don't eat gingerly, but attack the plate with a fierce determination to get food, so if you have a loose grip on the plate it will fly out of your hand with the first attack for food. Aside from feeding them you can shop

© MICHAEL CERVIN

view from the scenic Santa Rosa Road

for ostrich eggs and ostrich jerky as well as emu eggs and ostrich-feather accoutrements.

MISSION SANTA INÉS

Throughout its 200-plus-year history, Mission Santa Inés (1760 Mission Dr., 805/688-4815, www.missionsantaines.org, daily 9 A.M.–5 P.M., mass daily 8 A.M., $4) has overcome natural disasters, political turmoil, and financial hardships and remains a working church to this day. It is named after Saint Agnes, Santa Inés in Spanish. The town name is spelled Santa Ynez, an anglicization of the Spanish pronunciation. The interior is similar in size to the other missions. A long, tall narrow church, this one is more simply decorated with hand-painted interiors and without much architectural detail. Of note is the large collection of about 500 church vestments held here, dating from the 15th century to the early 1700s. Near the stations of the cross at the south end of the property, there are expansive views to the valley below, which used to be orchards for the mission. There is a back entrance few people seem to know about through a parking lot at

Mission and Alisal Roads in Solvang. Behind the public restrooms, a brick walkway leads into the backside of the mission grounds.

The mission, established in 1804, was designed to be a stopping point between the missions of Santa Barbara and La Purisima in Lompoc. It was devastated by the earthquake of 1812 but was rebuilt; what is visible today is not original, with the exception of part of the original arch toward the south end of the property. The Chumash population was reported to be close to 1,000 at its peak. After Mexican Independence from Spain in 1821, secularization caused the departure of the Spanish missionaries and most of the Chumash and the decline of the mission itself until it was rescued by much-needed attention and money.

ELVERHØJ MUSEUM
OF HISTORY AND ART

To fully understand Solvang, it's important to visit the Elverhøj Museum (1624 Elverhoy Way, 805/686-1211, www.elverhoj.org, Wed.–Thurs. 1–4 P.M., Fri.–Sun. noon–4 P.M., $3)

© MICHAEL CERVIN

Feed an ostrich at Ostrich Land.

which is a delightful and surprisingly cool place. Not only do they offer tabletop and kitchen linens and local crafts, they have a comprehensive history of the area with nostalgic photos of the early settlers. Of particular note is the typical Danish kitchen, hand-painted in green with stenciled flowers everywhere and pine floors, countertops, and tables—it gives an idea of how creative the Danes made their homes, no doubt in an effort to brighten bleak winters. Those winters brightened considerably after arriving in the area, but it was a long journey. The museum also features exhibits of traditional folk art from Denmark like paper-cutting and lace-making, which is clearly evident throughout town. There are displays of wood clogs and the rustic tools used to create them, and they offer rotating exhibits throughout the year that focus on the valley. It would be easy to dismiss the museum as just a novelty, but clearly the passion of the original settlers and their willingness to come to America and continue their way of life from the old country is something we can all learn from.

HANS CHRISTIAN ANDERSEN MUSEUM

The small Hans Christian Andersen Museum (1680 Mission Dr., 805/688-2052, www.bookloftsolvang.com, daily Sun.–Mon. 9 A.M.–6 P.M., Tues.–Thurs. 9 A.M.–8 P.M., Fri.–Sat. 9 A.M.–9 P.M., free) has a few artifacts of Andersen including a bronze bust (a copy of which is in the park on Mission Dr.), first editions of his books from the 1830s in Danish and English, photographs, and a timeline chronicling his life and work and his impact on literature. It's easy to overlook Andersen as simply the writer of fairy tales, but Andersen also wrote novels, plays, and other works. Even a short visit will enlighten you about the prolific work of Andersen.

MOTORCYCLE MUSEUM

The Motorcycle Museum (320 Alisal Rd., 805/686-9522, www.motosolvang.com, Sat.–Sun. 11 A.M.–5 P.M., weekdays by appointment, $10) is truly a unique and interesting stop. Along the self-guided tour 95 motorcycles, vintage and new, are on display. Each bike has a description and some are downright beautiful,

WINE COUNTRY

© MICHAEL CERVIN

Mission Santa Inés

polished, and lovingly restored. There are bikes from the 1930s and 1940s, the earliest from 1903, and some are so cool that you'll want to strap on a helmet and take a ride. After 10 years in this spot they have amassed quite the private collection with Ducati, Crocker, Matchless, Nimbus, and many more. Admission is not inexpensive compared to other things to do in town, but if motorcycles are your passion, you need to visit.

HANS CHRISTIAN ANDERSEN

Hans Christian Andersen came into a poor family, which certainly influenced a lot of his later writings. So, too, did his slow rise to fame and the feeling that he never quite fit into the upper echelons of society. He left home at age 14 in 1819 to try his hand in theater in Copenhagen. Although he was unsuccessful, Andersen was tied to the theater for the rest of his life, as the author of numerous plays and as the translator and adapter of foreign plays. During these years in Copenhagen (1819-1822), he tried in vain to find success as a ballet dancer, actor, and singer. Finally, he tried his hand as a playwright, which was also unsuccessful, at least at first. His first work was published in 1829, but it was a novel in 1835 that saw him achieve real success. Surprising everyone, Andersen became the most widely traveled Danish writer of his day. His literary fame grew rapidly from the mid-1830s, when his novels enjoyed widespread circulation, mainly in Germany. From 1839 onwards, though, it was the fairy tales that solidified his reputation in both England and America. Andersen never married – he apparently had the desire to, but his affections were never returned. This experience also made its way into his writings. His best-known works live on: *The Emperor's New Clothes, The Little Mermaid, The Princess and the Pea, The Red Shoes,* and *Thumbelina.* Hans Christian Andersen wrote more than 160 fairy tales, which have been translated into more than 100 languages.

QUICKSILVER MINIATURE HORSE RANCH

It's free to stop by the Quicksilver Miniature Horse Ranch (1555 Alamo Pintado Rd., 805/686-4002, www.qsminis.com, daily 10 A.M.–3 P.M.), a ranch that specializes in miniature horses for a growing list of customers from across the globe who desire these horses as pets. If you drive by the farm on most any spring day, you may catch a glimpse of 25–30 newborn foals, measuring 20–21 inches tall, testing out their new legs as they attempt to leap and bound on the grass. Visitors can get up close with the newborns and the adults, but should remember that this is not a petting zoo, it's a working ranch. There are usually about 90 horses on the ranch at all times.

Wineries

There are no actual vineyards in Solvang per se, but there are tasting rooms, and they're all within walking distance of each other. Many people overlook Solvang tasting rooms because they assume that since it's a tourist spot, the wineries located here might be, shall we say, not as serious. Well, that's definitely not so. There are some excellent wines represented locally, and you would do well to seek these out.

PRESIDIO WINERY

Presidio Winery (1603 Copenhagen Dr., Ste. 1, 805/693-8585, www.presidiowinery.com, daily 11 A.M.–6 P.M., tasting fee $8) is one of the few wineries in all of the Central Coast to be certified as a biodynamic winery. You'll see a small label on the back of the bottles that identifies the wine as having been approved by Demeter, the authoritative body that governs this farming method. Biodynamic is beyond organic and employs, ideally, a closed-loop farm system. Simply put, it's farming the best way to insure non-intrusive outside elements don't interfere with a healthy respect for the land. That aside, owner Doug Braun's wines are quite good, and his style of winemaking is more restrained than most others in the area. Chardonnay, pinot noir, syrah, and late-harvest wines are on offer at his tasting room on Copenhagen Drive at Mission

Drive, in the heart of Solvang, a great place to begin your education about local wines and biodynamic farming methods.

MANDOLINA

Winemaker Megan McGrath-Gates produces some terrific white wines at Mandolina (1665 Copenhagen Dr., 805/686-5506, www.mandolinawines.com, daily 11 A.M.–5:30 P.M., tasting fee $8–12), a bright and airy tasting room with exposed beams on the ceiling and a copper-topped wood bar. The focus here is on Italian varietals including pinot grigio, barbera, nebbiolo, dolcetto, malvasia bianca, and sangiovese. There's a delicate touch to the wines due to Megan's sensibilities, and she's studied in Italy to understand their winemaking process—reflected in the wonderful wines she makes. The wines, especially the whites, are quite good and sold at very reasonable prices.

D'ALFONSO-CURRAN WINE GROUP

A merger between a husband and wife team, the D'Alfonso-Curran Wine Group (1557 Mission Dr., 805/688-3494, www.curranwines.com, Mon.–Fri. 11 A.M.–5 P.M., Sat.–Sun. 10 A.M.–5 P.M., tasting fee $15) now has their own tasting room. Both winemakers have long been well known in the local wine industry and have worked as winemakers for respected names like Sea Smoke and Sanford. They have always crafted their own wines as well, and this tasting room is dedicated to their own small-production labels. The zinc-topped bar and cool, minimalist interior belies the beauty of their wines, chardonnay and pinot noir on the D'Alfonso side, and grenache blanc, sangiovese, and syrah on the Curran side. The tasting fee is a little pricey, but it's a worthwhile stop.

SHOESTRING WINERY

Shoestring Winery (800 E. Hwy. 246, 805/693-8612, www.shoestringwinery.com, Fri.–Sun. 10 A.M.–4 P.M., tasting fee $10) is on the main road into Solvang, just before you reach the town. This winery started out when the owners migrated from Baltimore, Maryland, and bought 65 acres. Formerly adept at training

THE *SIDEWAYS* UP EFFECT

The movie *Sideways* was released in 2004; it was nominated for five Academy Awards, and won one for best adapted screenplay. In the 30 weeks the movie was in theaters, gross domestic ticket sales topped $70 million, with worldwide sales reaching more than $100 million, making it the 40th highest-grossing movie of that year.

In spite of the off-putting behavior of the two main characters, it showcased the Santa Barbara wine country like no film ever had, and soon visitors were showing up in the valley's towns toting *Sideways* maps, enamored with the wine country vibe and the images of lush leafy vines, clear blue skies, beautiful valleys, and soft rolling mountains, looking to re-create the film's experiences for themselves. And they kept coming. Many local businesses saw a net increase in business of 20-30 percent after the film came out.

In a well-known scene, one of the characters, Miles, tells his friend that he won't drink merlot (using more colorful language than is appropriate here), and also praised the virtues of pinot noir. That registered in the minds of a fickle public, and sales of pinot noir increased approximately 15 percent, while the maligned merlot dropped about 2 percent in sales. Was it just the result of a line in a movie? Well, yes and no. Merlot had been over-planted in California to begin with, and there was a surplus of inadequate merlot flooding the market. But pinot noir did see an impressive rise in sales as a direct result of the film. Merlot producers across California were frustrated by the merlot bashing, and wine writers only added fuel to the fire by dissing merlot. Rex Pickett, author of the novel *Sideways* on which the film was based, was the featured speaker at a "Merlot Fights Back" dinner. The success of the film even spawned a Japanese-language remake, changing the location to Napa from Santa Barbara.

Regardless, the film generated traffic for the wine country. In Santa Barbara County, wine is a $360 million industry that produces more than one million cases annually. More than a quarter of those bottles come from the Santa Ynez Valley, which is home to over 100 wineries and roughly 5,000 acres of vineyards. The county is best known for its pinot noir and chardonnay – and yes, there is merlot produced here too. In 2008, nearly 17 percent of the over eight million visitors to the county said they came for the wine. *Sideways* produced an up effect, and the ripples are still being felt.

racehorses, they still have a few on the property, but the focus is on wine. The early days were tight financially and a shoestring budget allowed them to plant more and more vines. They still have a small production, but they offer merlot, syrah, sangiovese, rosé, and pinot grigio. The tasting room, in an old barn with a really cool floor made from wood posts, is more farm feeling than polished and glitzy.

SORT THIS OUT CELLARS

Michael Cobb, owner of Sort This Out Cellars (1636 Copenhagen Dr., 805/688-1717, www.sortthisoutcellars.com, Sun.–Thurs. 10 A.M.–7 P.M., Fri.–Sat. 10 A.M.–10 P.M., tasting fee $5–15), decided to create a new type of winery that doesn't own any vineyards, land, or actual grapes, but instead simply buys the fruit. After all, you don't need a plot of land to make wine. The retro tasting room was inspired by an old photograph of the famed 1960s Rat Pack outside the Sands Hotel in Las Vegas. It has low-back bar stools at the tasting counter, lots of shiny chrome, and pin-up girls on the wine labels. The ambience just might make you feel cool enough to sample their cabernet sauvignon, merlot, syrah, sangiovese, sauvignon blanc, chardonnay, muscat, and a super Tuscan blend.

RUSACK VINEYARDS

Rusack Vineyards (1819 Ballard Canyon, 805/688-1278, www.rusackvineyards.com, daily 11 A.M.–5 P.M., tasting fee $9) is one of the best picnic spots in the valley. Bring your lunch and

© MICHAEL CERVIN

Solvang Theaterfest puts on four plays each summer in a beautiful outdoor venue.

pick up a bottle of their sauvignon blanc, sangiovese, pinot noir, or their flagship Bordeaux wine called Anacapa, and lounge under the old oaks on the side deck. Ballard Canyon is, for the most part, a quiet canyon, and the views of the other vineyards from the outside patio are wonderful. Around Halloween the canyon is dotted with bright pumpkins, and you'll occasionally see bison roaming the hills.

Entertainment and Events

It's important to understand that this part of the valley rolls up the sidewalks pretty early. There are events that take place, but bars and clubs are nearly nonexistent, unless you head to a restaurant bar. For a full-on bar and club scene, you'll need to either drive 30 minutes south to Santa Barbara, or 20 minutes north to Santa Maria. Businesses don't stay open late, and you'll be hard pressed for things to do when the sun goes down.

CINEMA

Keeping in mind this is small town USA, there's only one movie theater in the area, serving the southern part of the valley. The **Park Plaza Theatre** (515 McMurray, Buellton, 805/688-7434, $9) is located right off Highway 101 between Buellton and Solvang, sandwiched between the Marriot and the McDonald's. It has five small screens and comfortable seating. You're likely to find the latest films here, and few crowds.

FESTIVALS AND EVENTS

The **Solvang Theaterfest** (420 2nd St., 805/688-1789, www.solvangtheaterfest.org) features semiprofessional theater, with both professional actors and local talent, at a beautiful outdoor venue. The Solvang group puts on four plays each year between June and October in a 700-seat venue originally built in 1974. There is a focus on musicals and lighter fare, and there has been great support for live theater in this small town. In a small compound of Danish-style architecture and beautiful old oak trees, this is a great summertime tradition.

Danish Days (www.solvangusa.com), held the third weekend in September, is a big draw. Started in 1936, it features clog-wearing Danes dancing in the streets, pastries and coffee everywhere, and even an *aebleskiver* (pancake)-eating contest. It's Solvang's annual salute to its cultural heritage and local women dress in traditional skirt, apron, and cap, despite the heat of the season. The men too wear their clogs and traditional outfits. The festival is also referred to as Aebleskiver Days on occasion, and it has been a tradition for locals to serve *aebleskiver* from pans set up in the streets.

The food and wine event **Taste of Solvang** (www.solvangusa.com), held the third weekend in March, has been in existence for 18 years and it keeps growing and becoming more sophisticated each year. It starts with a dessert reception, and considering the pastry and sweets history among the Danes, that's enough right there. Following that is the walking smorgaasbord, which features roughly 40 stops in town where you pop in and sample what they might be serving, usually Danish food, though some restaurants and stores offer non-Danish food samples. Ten tasting rooms pour their vintages into your souvenir glass, and there's live entertainment in the park where many people bring a picnic and relax. It's a three-day event that immerses you in the local culture and customs and the new crop of wineries.

The Solvang Century (562/690-9693, www.bikescor.com) is the best-known cycling race in the entire valley. Well, technically it's not a race, but a fundraiser, but you still can't help but compete. They added a half-century race to accommodate riders who prefer the shorter distances, but there is still some pretty serious elevation gain at a minimum of 2,000 feet, making this a challenging course. The money raised benefits heart-related diseases since the founder of the event used cycling as a way to promote health after his own heart surgery.

Shopping
BOOKSTORES
Valley Books (1582 Mission Dr., 805/688-7160, daily 9 A.M.–7:30 P.M.) sells predominantly used books with a small section of new books. There's an abundance of paperbacks, but also magazines, newspapers, and hardcovers. You can sit outside, or inside in comfy chairs, and read, sip coffee or tea, and enjoy a Danish pastry. This place is made to lounge. The have Wi-Fi and there's a small kids' section with little tables and chairs. It's a quiet respite from all the shopping.

The Book Loft (1680 Mission Dr., 805/688-6010, www.bookloftsolvang.com, Sun.–Mon. 9 A.M.–7 P.M., Tues.–Thurs. 9 A.M.–8 P.M., Fri.–Sat. 9 A.M.–9 P.M.) sells mostly new books, though there's a small section of used books as well. This 35-year-old two-story store has a vast very well-organized selection of authors, including locals. The wood stairs creak as you venture upstairs to see even more books. It has the feel of an old bookstore, not sanitized with fancy shelves—in fact these shelves were all handmade. They also have a nice selection of antiquarian books, and upstairs is the Hans Christian Andersen Museum.

ANTIQUES
The **Solvang Antique Center** (486 1st St., 805/686-2322, www.solvangantiques.com, daily 10 A.M.–6 P.M.) is home to some incredible antiques. In addition to a stellar collection of magnificent gilded antique clocks, there are music boxes, jewelry, watches, and gorgeous vintage telephones from old candlestick models to the 1930s and 1940s models. They also have artfully restored antique furniture. The 7,000-square-foot showroom has over 65 specialty dealers from around the globe. It is an expensive place, but has such diversity that any antiques lover should stop in, even if just to browse one of the finest stores in the Central Coast.

In Los Alamos, 10 minutes north of Solvang, is a massive space filled with a vast collection of antiques, priced much lower than the Solvang Antique Center. **The Depot Antique Mall** (515 Bell St., Los Alamos, 805/344-3315, Mon.–Sat. 10 A.M.–5 P.M., Sun. 1–4 P.M.), once the depot for the Pacific Coast Railway, now holds over 60 antiques vendors in three large rooms. Prices are reasonable on everything from vintage posters to an abundance of furniture to collectibles, and it's worth the short drive. Some items are knockoffs, but the wide

Inexpensive antiques can be found at The Depot Antique Mall.

selection rotates often, especially the larger furniture pieces.

CLOTHING

Elna's Dress Shop (1673 Copenhagen Dr., 805/688-4525, daily 9:30 A.M.–5:30 P.M.) is the place to go for handmade Danish dresses and costumes, as well as more contemporary but conservative and non-Danish-themed dresses for women. If you're searching for that perfect Danish outfit for a young one, you'll find it here. Aprons, caps, and brightly colored simple dresses, some with beautiful lace, are available off the rack, or they will make one for you. They have only a few Danish pieces for young boys, and they're pretty darn cute.

True Addiction (485 Alisal Rd., 805/686-2868, Thurs. 9:30 A.M.–6 P.M., Fri.–Mon. 9:30 A.M.–7 P.M.) sells hip and trendy clothing for a younger crowd including a large section of shoes, boots, and jewelry. Their stock rotates frequently and in spite of being situated in a tourist area, they have very reasonable prices and contemporary fashions.

Santa Barbara Denim (1608 Copenhagen Dr., 805/688-5458, daily 10 A.M.–6 P.M.) has fashions for both men and women at greatly reduced prices. The women's clothing is front and center while the men's is relegated to the back upstairs portion. The store was formerly called Beach Bumz, but the name change hasn't affected their focus on providing quality clothes at a discount. The fashions lean toward modern and hip, and there are a lot of silk shirts for men. Their stock rotates with the seasons.

SPECIALTY STORES

Mole Hole (1656 Mission Dr., 805/688-7669, www.moleholesolvang.com, daily 9:30 A.M.–5:30 P.M.) is a gift shop with an emphasis on miniature collectibles, as well as decidedly feminine and romantic items, many with a fairy theme or lots of lace. There is an upstairs humorous section of gifts for men—well, men heading over 50. They are extremely helpful here, which has contributed to their success.

You'll feel a little better from the moment you enter **Jule Hus** (1580 Mission Dr., 805/688-6601, www.solvangschristmashouse.com, daily

Typical Dutch dresses like these can be found at Elna's Dress Shop in Solvang.

© MICHAEL CERVIN

9 A.M.–5 P.M.), where it's the holiday season all year long. They offer hand-carved wood ornaments, blown-glass ornaments, traditional Scandinavian ornaments, and stand alone decorations, as well as a huge selection of nutcrackers. There are also traditional Danish quilts and lace items and plenty of trees fully decked out. Jule Hus has celebrated the Christmas spirit since 1967, and there are always people milling about searching for that ideal ornament. Other stores in town have small sections of Christmas items, but here it's all they have.

Rasmussen's (1697 Copenhagen Dr., 805/688-6636, www.rasmussenssolvang.com, daily 9 A.M.–5:30 P.M.), opened in 1921 and still going strong five generations later, is everything Scandinavian, a one-stop shop for gifts, books, souvenirs, Danish packaged food items, and kitchen items.

Nordic Knives (1634 Copenhagen Dr., 805/688-3612, www.nordicknives.com, daily 10 A.M.–5 P.M.) has more knives than you've probably ever seen in one place, including expensive high-end custom-made knives by well-known knife makers, and jeweled, engraved,

and one-of-a-kind knives. Many of them are very impressive. There are also hunting and kitchen knives with prices that are much lower than the custom blades. The shop has been in Solvang nearly 40 years, and they know their knives. Whether you need a simple knife or a traditional Swiss Army knife, they'll have it. The display case on the right-hand side as you enter is worth a look, with beautiful knives of all types and pedigree.

Ingeborg's (1679 Copenhagen Dr., 805/688-5612, www.ingeborgs.com, daily 9:30 A.M.–5:30 P.M.) has been making traditional Danish chocolates for nearly half a century. Over 70 varieties of chocolates are here, handmade on the premises. It isn't cheap, but it is Danish chocolate made by Danes. They also carry hard-to-find Dutch chocolates. Grab a seat at one of the six round red barstools and enjoy their ice cream.

Every Wednesday year-round, rain or shine, fresh fruits, veggies, flowers, and local items from surrounding farms make an appearance at the **Solvang Farmer's Market** (Mission Dr. and 1st St., 805/962-5354,

It's Christmas year-round at Jule Hus.

WINE COUNTRY

summer 4–7 P.M., winter 3–6 P.M.). This is not a major farmers market and takes up only two blocks, but they close off the street next to the park and you can find fresh food harvested from local farms, many of which are within a mile of town. It's hard to get much fresher than that.

Sports and Recreation
PARKS
At 15 acres, **Hans Christian Andersen Park** (500 Chalk Hill Rd.) is the largest park in the area. Enter through a castle gate and you're amidst pine and oak trees. Then you come to the skate park, which has cavernous half pipes and is actually well designed, though there are more bikers who use it than boarders. There is a small wooden playground behind the skate park for the younger ones. If you continue driving through the park you'll come to another playground with tall chute slides embedded in the sand. There are plenty of trees and picnic tables, all well groomed. If you drive all the way to the end, there are four tennis courts right next to a beautiful gnarled

old oak tree. There are restroom facilities and drinking fountains.

Sunny Fields Park (900 Alamo Pintado, 805/688-7529) is almost a pint-sized Solvang. There's a Viking ship, swings and slides, and monkey bars, plus a gingerbread house, a faux windmill, and plenty of things to climb around on. Trees offer shade, as it gets hot during the summer. This is a great spot for little kids and it's reasonably quiet, being just outside of town. There are drinking fountains and restrooms, plenty of parking, and a large grassy flat ball field.

GOLF
The 18-hole, par-72 **River Course at the Alisal** (150 Alisal Rd., 805/688-6042, www.rivercourse.com, green fees $60–70) was featured in *Sideways*. It's a beautiful course on the banks of the Santa Ynez River, punctuated with magnificent oak trees. Challenging and beautiful, it features four lakes, open fairways, tricky hazards, and large, undulating greens accented by native sycamore trees. Elevated tees reveal some vistas and occasional vineyards, so bring your best game and your camera.

SPAS
Haven Day Spa (1450 Mission Dr., 805/686-1264, www.hadstenhouse.com, daily 9 A.M.–5 P.M., basic one-hour massage $110) is hidden behind antique Asian doors. Beyond the doors the day spa reveals a quiet soft-toned interior for a mix of facials, massage, body wraps, and even a tuning-fork therapy that utilizes strategically placed tuning forks to bring harmony and balance back to the nervous system, muscles, and organs. The staff here is knowledgeable and ready to accommodate.

Chiffon Boutique (475 1st St., 805/686-1155, www.chiffonboutique.com, Wed.–Fri. 11 A.M.–6 P.M., Sat. 10 A.M.–6 P.M., Sun. noon–5 P.M., basic one-hour massage $70) is all about facials, waxing, nails, and haircuts, color, and styling. This small shop has quickly gained a reputation for having nice and trustworthy staff who listen. They contract out for massage services

© MICHAEL CERVIN

© MICHAEL CERVIN

River Course at the Alisal

Accommodations

UNDER $100

Days Inn-Windmill (114 E. Hwy. 246, Buellton, 805/688-8448, www.daysinn.com, $70–90 d) was featured in the film *Sideways*—you can even stay in the same room where the main characters stayed in the film. The 108 rooms here are pretty standard and basic, with the best feature being the outdoor pool. It's right off Highway 101 and you can't miss its namesake windmill. It's best to avoid the rooms fronting the freeway and go for an interior room to cut down on the noise. There are no views to speak of, but the prices are good.

$100-200

(**Solvang Gardens Lodge** (293 Alisal Rd., 805/688-4404, www.solvanggardens.com, $169–199 d) is a 24-room delight just on the edge of town. It feels like a small village. There are stone fireplaces and marble bathrooms, and each room is unique and different. Some are decorated with a more modern theme, some have a traditional feel, but all are very well appointed. Beautiful gardens in both the front and center of the property give you a peaceful green space. The local owners will do everything they can to ensure your stay is the best it can be. It's quieter here since it's not on the main drag. In the morning you can walk into town or down to the dry riverbed.

$200-300

Wine Valley Inn (1465 Copenhagen Dr., 800/824-6444, www.winevalleyinn.com, $209–359 d), with 56 rooms and six cottages, is larger than it looks, and the rooms are spacious as well, with interiors bathed in soft tones. Some of the rooms have wood-burning or artificial fireplaces. The inn is right downtown, so you can get around without a car.

(**Hotel Corque** (400 Alisal Rd., 800/624-5572, www.hotelcorque.com, $279–309 d) was originally a very Danish hotel, but an extensive renovation morphed it into a sleek and sophisticated hotel catering to a younger crowd. It feels like it belongs in a major city, not a rural area, and that's part of its appeal. Though the 100 rooms and 17 suites are a tad small and the amenities are nothing unique, there's no

Located in downtown Solvang, The Inn at Petersen Village is a classic Solvang accommodation.

disliking the decor—if you're looking for cool digs, you've found them.

Hadsten House (1450 Mission Dr., 805/688-3210, www.hadstenhouse.com, $205–255 d) is a nonsmoking property, and one of the best places to stay in Solvang. French-style furnishings with custom mattresses, dark-toned furniture, and ample space pulls you out of the Danish mentality and into a contemporary and sophisticated setting. A full breakfast and nightly wine and cheese are offered, as well as a heated outdoor pool and hot tub. It's one of the closest hotels to the 101 and the first you come to as you enter Solvang. Set in a square horseshoe pattern, it offers no views, except across the street to another hotel. Regardless, these are comfortable, well-appointed rooms with a European flair.

The 42-room **The Inn at Petersen Village** (1576 Mission Dr., 805/688-3121, www.peterseninn.com, $265–295 d) is unusual in that the rates include dinner and breakfast at their in-house restaurant. The decor is traditional, maybe even a little stuffy, but it is also right on Mission Drive, so you simply walk outside into the thick of things. The inn has been around a long time, and it sees its share of return guests.

Mirabelle Inn (409 1st St., 805/688-1703, www.solvanginns.com, $250–295 d) is run by well-seasoned veterans of the hospitality industry. The 10 medium-sized rooms decorated with antiques and lace are much more Victorian bed-and-breakfast in their feel; many have four-poster beds and a few have sleigh beds. It's located in the heart of Solvang, so you can leave the vine-covered walls and go explore, then return to this other world. They have an in-house restaurant that serves wonderful food.

OVER $300

The **Alisal Guest Ranch** (1054 Alisal Rd., 805/688-6411, www.alisal.com, $495–650 d) dates back to 1946. The 73 rooms at this ranch retreat are all very large and have a strong Western and pueblo feel to them. Full breakfasts and dinners are included in the rates. And since this is considered a retreat, there are no TVs or telephones, but you do have access to Wi-Fi, tennis courts ($20 per hour), fishing in their lake (guided three-hour trip starts at $180), horseback riding ($50 per hour), and even archery ($35 per hour). The secluded and luxurious environment makes it possible for

WINE COUNTRY

© MICHAEL CERVIN

© MICHAEL CERVIN

Wine Valley Inn is a great choice for a romantic getaway.

complete relaxation. But if you need to, you can walk into town.

Food

There are many places in town that serve traditional Danish food, which doesn't typically conjure up images of innovative global fare. But as Solvang is growing, with new hotels and wine-tasting rooms opening up, restaurants are looking to stand out from the traditional in what is becoming, albeit slowly, a true destination with farm-fresh food and innovative ways of preparing it. But if you are looking for the traditional, you'll find it here too, occasionally with an accordion player outside the front door, enticing you to come in.

AMERICAN

The Chef's Touch (1555 Mission Dr., 805/686-1040, www.thechefstouch.com, Mon. and Wed.–Sat. 11 A.M.–4 P.M., Sun. 9 A.M.–3 P.M., $12) is one of those hybrid places—restaurant, wine shop, kitchen store, and cooking class central. The outdoor seating gives you people-watching views to the main street in Solvang,

but the interior lets you watch a variety of foods being prepared. The paninis are excellent, and their pizzas and salads are infused with fresh ingredients. The Roman artichoke is a deep-fried artichoke dusted with parmesan, garlic, salt, and pepper and is a great start to any meal. The prices are perfect for a quick bite or a cappuccino. If you're in town for a while, consider one of their cooking classes.

Hadsten House Restaurant (1450 Mission Dr., 805/688-3210, www.hadsten-house.com, Sun.–Thurs.5–9 P.M., Fri.–Sat. 5–10 P.M., $25) entered the dining scene in 2008 but immediately elevated the local culinary perspective. Dark and moody inside, it has a central fireplace that creates a hip urban environment, more metropolitan than rural. The short ribs have a demi-glace that will send your mind reeling, and the warm spinach salad is perfectly balanced. Or go for the Hadsten burger, which is piled with everything—including an egg. It's best to make reservations for this small space producing some very fine food.

Sleek and sophisticated, **Root 246** (420 Alisal Rd., 805/686-8681, www.root-246.com, daily 5:30–10 P.M., $30), one of the newest additions to the dining scene, has upped the ante. It looks like it belongs in Hollywood, not in rural Solvang, but that's part of the evolution of Solvang and wine country cuisine. Chef and consultant Bradley Ogden has started over 10 restaurants and knows how to create exciting food. The menu rotates often depending on seasonal ingredients. You'll find oysters, organic mushroom flatbread, and a variety of fish and game dishes. The crowd is young and urban—you don't see a lot of old-school Danish residents here.

DANISH

Year after year, **(Paula's Pancake House** (1531 Mission Dr., 805/688-2867, daily 6 A.M.–3 P.M., $10) is the top spot for Danish food. It can get very crowded, especially on the patio, so be prepared to wait during peak times. Their three-page breakfast menu is replete with huge plate-size pancakes of all types including the Danish apple. Or go Dutch and try the Dutch sausage omelet. They serve breakfast and lunch, but not dinner. Lunches include traditional Danish foods as well as some Americanized versions. The interior is casual, with more of a coffee shop feel, but it's also slightly Scandinavian.

Bit O' Denmark (473 Alisal Rd., 805/688-5426, daily 11 A.M.–9 P.M., $15) is known for their traditional smorgaasbord as well as roasted duck and Monte Cristo sandwiches. It is the oldest restaurant in Solvang, housed in one of the very first buildings the original settlers built in 1911.It became a restaurant in 1929 and continues to cook up Danish ham, Danish pork, roast beef open-faced sandwiches, and their extensive smorgaasbord, which includes *medisterpolse* (Danish sausage), *frikadeller* (meatballs), *rodkaal* (red cabbage), *spegesild* (picked herring), and an array of cold salads. The room to the left as you enter is the best, with large curved booths.

Solvang Restaurant (1672 Copenhagen Dr., 805/688-4645, www.solvangrestaurant.com, daily 6 A.M.–3 P.M., $10) is well known for their *aebleskivers,* round doughy concoctions topped with jam; don't be surprised to see a line out the door. This little diner also dishes up breakfasts in a quaint environment. The overhead wood beams are decorated with Danish proverbs.

(The Red Viking (1684 Copenhagen Dr., 805/688-6610, daily 8 A.M.–8 P.M., $10) rolls out Danish dishes such as *hakkebof* (chopped sirloin and onion topped with a fried egg), Weiner schnitzel (veal cutlet), and authentic Danish smorgaasbord, and a line of Danish cheeses, hams, and beers. They are one of the top Danish food stops.

Pea Soup Andersen's (376 Avenue of the Flags, Buellton, 805/688-5881, www.pea-soupandersens.net, daily 7 A.M.–10 P.M., $15) is the granddaddy of Danish restaurants, first opened in 1924. They serve American food, like burgers and milkshakes, and of course, pea soup in a bread bowl. There's a small gift shop, a bakery with fresh daily sweets and fudge, a small art gallery upstairs, and best of all, a mini-museum about Rufus T. Buell (as in Buellton), how he started the town, and how Andersen's came into being. It also chronicles some of the changes in the dining scene locally. It's just outside of Solvang proper, located right off Highway 101, and has the feel of a coffee shop. And there are plenty of cans of soup for sale.

BAKERIES

Mortensen's (1588 Mission Dr., 805/688-8373, Mon.–Fri. 8 A.M.–5:30 P.M., Sat.–Sun. 7:30 A.M.–6:30 P.M.) is one of the stalwarts of the Danish bakeries. It's best to visit the low-key interior for a strudel or éclair and a pot of tea or coffee and relax in the subdued environment. The Danish decor is not over the top, but it's still good Danish, and this is a great place to start your day.

Olsen's (1529 Mission Dr., 805/688-6314, www.olsensdanishbakery.com, Mon.–Fri. 7:30 A.M.–6 P.M., Sat.–Sun. 7:30 A.M.–7 P.M.) was established in Denmark way back in 1890, though this location isn't quite that old. They've been turning out homemade breads like grain pumpernickel, sunflower seed pumpernickel, and Swedish cardamom, as well as cookies and all manner of sweets, for three decades.

Solvang Bakery (460 Alisal Rd., 805/688-4939, www.solvangbakery.com, Sun.–Fri. 7 A.M.–5 P.M., Sat. 7 A.M.–6 P.M.) is a bright open space in a blue and white shop with an eye-catching array of gingerbread houses, Danish waffles, almond butter rings, and plenty more. They have been baking in Solvang for 30 years. Their onion cheese bread is a signature loaf.

GROCERIES
El Rancho Market Place (2886 Mission Dr., 805/688-4300, www.elranchomarket.com, daily 6 A.M.–10 P.M.) is an upscale supermarket and features an old-fashioned full-service meat counter, fresh local organic produce, and a complete selection of local and international wines, champagnes, and spirits. They have very good hot and cold entrées, salads, and fresh baked bread and pies—perfect for putting together a picnic. If you want something quick and easy, they have a great selection. There's some outdoor seating near the entrance and on occasion they grill tri-tip outside.

Information and Services
MAPS AND TOURIST INFORMATION
The Solvang Visitors Center is located at 1639 Copenhagen (800/468-6765, www.solvangusa.com) and is staffed by locals wearing red vests. They have comprehensive information on not just Solvang, but the entire valley as well.

EMERGENCY SERVICES
The Santa Ynez Valley Cottage Hospital (2050 Viborg, Solvang, 805/688-6431) offers emergency services. Should you have an emergency, dial 911 immediately. Police services are contracted with the County of Santa Barbara Sheriff's Department (1745 Mission Dr., Solvang, 805/688-5000).

NEWSPAPERS AND MEDIA
The *Santa Ynez Valley News* covers the local angle and is published each Thursday. For more countywide coverage, the *Santa Barbara* *News-Press* and the *Santa Maria Times* are both dailies available for purchase.

POSTAL SERVICES
The post office is located 430 Alisal Road (805/688-9309). Given its limited size, it's advisable to call ahead for operating hours and services.

LAUNDRY
If you need to do laundry on your trip, try **St. Paul Cleaners and Laundry** (1693 Mission Dr., 805/688-9618).

Getting There
BY CAR
Highway 246 bisects the town. Known as Mission Drive while it runs through town, Highway 246 connects to Highway 101, which is the primary freeway on the Central Coast, and the small but still well-traveled Route 154, which connects to Santa Barbara in the south and Highway 101 further north. It's important to note that Solvang gets crowded on weekends, and getting in and out can be a slow proposition. But, since you have little choice but to wait it out, just remind yourself of how good a Danish cookie will taste when you finally arrive.

BY BUS
The **MTD Valley Express** (805/683-3702) is a regional commuter line running Monday–Friday between Santa Barbara, Buellton, and Solvang.

BY TRAIN
Amtrak will connect to the valley via motorcoach. The bus stop is located at 1630 Mission Drive in Solvang, but trains stop only in Santa Barbara and San Luis Obispo. Travel times for the coaches is approximately one hour.

Getting Around
Solvang, while the largest of the small towns in the area, is still a very navigable town and can easily be explored on foot in less than a day.

BY TROLLEY
A horse-drawn trolley traverses the streets of

horse-drawn trolley in Solvang

Solvang, taking willing participants on a narrated tour on the Honen Streetcar, which is a replica of either a late 1800s or 1915 streetcar, depending on whom you choose to believe. Two large horses will pull you around town as you learn the history and noteworthy spots of Solvang. The tours last about 25 minutes and run every 35 minutes Thursday–Monday noon–6 P.M. Board at the visitors center at Copenhagen and 2nd Streets. Cost is $9 adults, $7 seniors, $5 children.

BY TAXI
Solvang Taxi (805/688-0069) operates 24 hours a day. You'll need to call them, however, as you rarely see a taxi in town. They also offer, like everyone else, wine transportation. **Promenade Cab Company** (805/717-8400) also operates in Solvang.

BY BUS
The **Santa Ynez Valley Transit** (805/688-5452, www.cityofsolvang.com) is a scheduled minibus serving Ballard, Buellton, Los Olivos, Santa Ynez, and Solvang, operating Monday–Saturday starting at 7 A.M. The Chumash Casino also offers a shuttle service (800/248-6274) serving Solvang, Buellton, Santa Barbara, Goleta, Santa Maria, and Lompoc. Riders with a Club Chumash gaming card get preferred seating.

LOS OLIVOS
Tiny Los Olivos is marked by a flagpole that sits dead center on Grand Avenue, acting as a roundabout. Most of the shops and other venues here are within two blocks of the flagpole, which is often used as a marker when locals are giving directions.

Los Olivos began as a town in 1861 with the establishment of the Overland/Coast Line Stage Station at Ballard. Actually, at the time it was more a loose aggregate of residences; it wasn't until 1887 when Swiss-Italian immigrant Felix Mattei, anticipating the arrival of the Pacific Coast Railway, opened a hotel to accommodate rail and stage passengers making both north and south connections in Los Olivos that a semblance of an actual town began to form. The local streets were leveled by

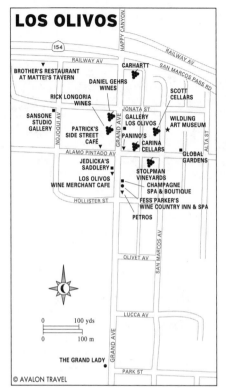

LOS OLIVOS

HAPPY CANYON
154
RAILWAY AV
RAILWAY AV
SAN MARCOS PASS RD
CARHARTT
BROTHER'S RESTAURANT
AT MATTEI'S TAVERN
DANIEL GEHRS
WINES
SCOTT
CELLARS
RICK LONGORIA
WINES
JONATA ST
GRAND AVE
SANSONE
STUDIO
GALLERY
GALLERY
LOS OLIVOS
WILDLING
ART MUSEUM
PATRICK'S
SIDE STREET
CAFÉ
PANINO'S
NOJOQUI AV
CARINA
CELLARS
ALTA ST
ALAMO PINTADO AV
JEDLICKA'S
SADDLERY
GLOBAL
GARDENS
STOLPMAN
VINEYARDS
LOS OLIVOS
WINE MERCHANT CAFE
CHAMPAGNE
SPA & BOUTIQUE
HOLLISTER ST
FESS PARKER'S
WINE COUNTRY INN & SPA
PETROS
SAN MARCOS AV
OLIVET AV
0   100 yds
0   100 m
LUCCA AV
GRAND AVE
THE GRAND LADY
PARK ST
© AVALON TRAVEL

Chinese workers from the railroads, and following the first whistle of the engine in November 1887, Los Olivos, while still small, was finally placed on the map. Though the town is reasonably new, the Keenan-Hartley home from 1882 is the oldest wooden home in Los Olivos and is a Santa Barbara County landmark. The house has undergone several additions and is now the Wildling Art Museum.

Sights and Drives
🄲 FOXEN CANYON
If there is any drive or ride that's important to Los Olivos, it's Foxen Canyon. It's the site of a wine trail but worth checking out even if you're not into wine; Foxen Canyon is a beautiful, meandering road, immensely popular with cyclists and perfect for tooling about with the top down. Where Alamo Pintado Road ends

and turns into Highway 154 at the northern end of Los Olivos, Foxen Canyon Road Begins. You can take Foxen Canyon Road just south to Los Alamos or continue all the way into Santa Maria. Typical of these areas, there are wineries, ranches, and farms populated with oak trees, cattle, deer, and hawks.

FIGUEROA MOUNTAIN
Figueroa's 4,528 foot crest is one of the shortest drives you can take to get the furthest away from what is the typical valley topography of chaparral-covered hills and lots of oak trees. Yes, this is also where Michael Jackson's Neverland Ranch is located, but you can't see anything, just a rather nondescript gate. As Figueroa Mountain Drive peels off from Route 154 near Los Olivos and you make your way toward the foothills, the oak trees begin to be replaced by pine trees, wildflowers, and more pronounced rock formations. From the lookout tower located on top of the mountain, 360-degree views of much of the county greet you. The Santa Ynez Mountains are to the south, appearing as a sheer mountain wall from this perspective. On a clear day, typically between February and April, the Channel Islands shimmer on the horizon.

The foreground of this view is the Santa Ynez Valley. Above and to the west is Point Conception, a land revered by the Chumash, the place of the setting sun, where these Native Americans believed they would travel to in the life that comes after death. You can descend the way you came, or if you're adventurous (and depending on the type of car you have), you can continue on some bumpy roads and over streams to eventually merge with Happy Canyon Road, making this a 30-plus-mile loop. This is not a short drive, but offers some spectacular scenery.

WILDLING ART MUSEUM
The genesis of the Wildling Art Museum (2928 San Marcos Ave., 805/688-1082, www.wildlingmuseum.org, Wed.–Sun. 11 A.M.–5 P.M., $3) was a desire to showcase the West and its expansive beauty in landscapes, flora, and fauna.

© MICHAEL CERVIN

Foxen Canyon is one of the most scenic drives in Los Olivos.

There's an educational center, research library, and a large museum gift shop where the books and other items feature wilderness art. Each year they mount four large exhibitions, which include lectures on art but also the preservation of the diminishing western lands. Once a month they offer a free Friday night movie, again with the theme of the wilderness and the inherent beauty it possesses. The museum is housed in the 1882 Keenan-Hartley house, the oldest frame-constructed house in the area, which was moved to its present location in 2000. The house, a Santa Barbara County Historical Landmark, is the perfect backdrop for an arts museum whose views are to the very mountains from which it draws inspiration.

CLAIRMONT FARMS

Clairmont Farms (2480 Roblar, 805/688-7505, www.clairmontfarms.com, daily 10 A.M.–6 P.M., suggested donation $3) is a family-owned and -operated working organic lavender farm that has five acres of lavender, as well as 175-year-old olive trees originally planted by the Catholic fathers (it's part of the grove that gave Los Olivos its name). Visitors can observe the process of distilling lavender and learn all the ways this herb is being used, in essential oils or as a cooking herb. They sell oils, teas, honey, soaps, and more, all infused with lavender; there's even lavender shampoo for your dog. Not only is it informative, but you'll leave feeling totally relaxed.

Wineries

Los Olivos has become a hub of wine-tasting rooms. Not long ago the area was mainly full of art galleries and just a few wineries. Now with 20 wine-tasting rooms, Los Olivos has become a convenient stop to taste and shop for all things wine. This tiny hamlet can become quite packed during the high season: Parking is at a premium, tasting rooms can be full to overflowing, and there are often waits at the few restaurants in town. Plan your trip to avoid the high season and you'll have a much better time.

◖ BECKMEN VINEYARDS

You'll need to drive to Beckmen Vineyards (2670 Ontiveros Rd., 805/688-8664, daily 11 A.M.–5 P.M., tasting fee $10–15), since it is located in the middle of a residential district. The tasting room is small, plain, and uneventful, but there are several lattice-walled picnic booths that overlook a small pond and the surrounding soft hills covered with vines. It's peaceful out here, and that's the point. Their grapes are biodynamically farmed, using no chemicals whatsoever, on a plot of land called Purisima Mountain. You'll see this name at many wineries in the valley; the Beckmen fruit is very popular and sold to other wineries. Sauvignon blanc, cabernet sauvignon, marsanne, a killer grenache, and a variety of syrahs are available to taste. This is one of the best wineries in the area, and they excel at most every wine they make.

Carhartt has the smallest tasting room in the valley.

CARHARTT

Carhartt (2990 Grand Ave., 805/693-5100, www.carharttvineyard.com, daily 11 A.M.– 5 P.M., tasting fee $10) is the smallest tasting room in the entire valley, but the winery makes big wines. Their tasting room, which looks like a wood shack, can comfortably hold maybe six people, but it does have an outdoor area allowing for some elbow room—though people seem to like crowding themselves inside. Their signature wines, merlot and syrah, come from their very own 10-acre estate, a former cattle ranch, and they buy fruit to produce sauvignon blanc, sangiovese, and petite sirah from both Santa Barbara and Paso Robles.

CARINA CELLARS

Carina Cellars (2900 Grand, 805/688-2459, www.carinacellars.com, daily 11 A.M.–5 P.M., tasting fee $10) has made a name for themselves with syrah, specifically syrah coming from the well-regarded Colsen Canyon vineyard. But they also have a blend, Iconoclast, that merges Napa Valley cabernet sauvignon with Santa Barbara syrah. Other wines in their portfolio include viognier, petite sirah, and red Rhône blends. Their tasting room also features rotating art on the rustic-looking walls. They have expanded to two tasting bars inside to handle the influx of people. Located right in downtown Los Olivos, this is one of the best and most consistent wineries.

STOLPMAN VINEYARDS

Stolpman's (2434 Alamo Pintado Ave., 805/688-0400, www.stolpmanvineyards.com, daily 11 A.M.–5 P.M., tasting fee $15) tasting room, in a late-1800s building with a red-painted board-and-batten exterior with white trim, was originally a private residence. The tasting room's interior was designed using recycled materials and features two tasting bars. These days, lawyer turned vintner Tom Stolpman remains steadfastly focused on syrah and syrah blends as their flagship wines, but also includes sangiovese, malbec, and white Rhône blends. The tasting room also has a selection of crystal decanters and their very own estate olive oil. They produce outstanding wines, though a little on the pricey side.

© MICHAEL CERVIN

© MICHAEL CERVIN

Stolpman Vineyards is one of the premier wineries in Los Olivos.

DANIEL GEHRS WINES

Housed in a 100-year-old home, Daniel Gehrs Wines (2939 Grand Ave., 805/693-9686, www.danielgehrswines.com, daily 11 A.M.–6 P.M., tasting fee $10) was a residence, then a doctor's office, long before it became a wine-tasting room. There are several rooms packed with gift items, a small tasting bar in the front, and a nice patio in the back where they conduct wine-tastings during the summer months. Dan Gehrs has long been a fixture in the wine scene and was one of the first winemakers in the valley. Among their offerings are Riesling, pinot noir, ports made with traditional Portuguese grapes, sangiovese, gewürztraminer, and a few of Dan's daughter's wines under the Vixen label.

RICK LONGORIA WINES

Like Daniel Gehrs, Rick Longoria has been involved in the wine industry for decades, and his winery (2935 Grand Ave., 805/688-0305, www.longoriawine.com, daily 11 A.M.–4:30 P.M., tasting fee $10) is right next door to Daniel Gehrs Wines. The small, narrow tasting room, originally a machine shop from the turn of the 20th century, carries chardonnay, pinot noir, and tempranillo, and Rick's locally well-known Blues Cuvée, a blend of predominantly cabernet franc with the addition of merlot and cabernet sauvignon. Their Blues series of wines features labels portraying famous blues artists. The winery has a little partially shaded side patio with a few tables, and you can hear the two water fountains on the patio as you sample the wines.

KOEHLER WINERY

The Koehler Winery (5360 Foxen Canyon Rd., 805/693-8384, www.koehlerwinery.com, daily 10 A.M.–5 P.M., tasting fee $10) seems to have it all: They produce cabernet sauvignon, syrah, viognier, sauvignon blanc, and other wines in a very pretty hillside location. There are picnic tables outside, and since it's pulled back from the main road, it's quiet and serene here. They also make pinot noir, which they don't grow on-site but source from the Santa Rita Hills. Koehler wines have received outstanding scores from the national press.

ZACA MESA WINERY

The Zaca Mesa Winery (6905 Foxen Canyon, 805/688-9339, www.zacamesa.com, daily 10 A.M.–4 P.M., tasting fee $10) is one of the oldest wineries in the county and the very first to plant syrah way backing the 1970s, long before anyone even knew what syrah was. This has given them a leg up on working with the variety. Viognier, chardonnay, roussanne, grenache, and mourvedre round out the offerings at this winery, which has a very cool large-scale chess set on the property. It's a great spot to picnic, as it's off the beaten path. The tasting room is midsized, meaning it can get crowded at peak times.

SCOTT CELLARS

Owner Peter Scott does almost everything himself at Scott Cellars (2933 San Marcos Ave., 805/686-5450, www.scottcellars.com, Wed.–Mon. 11 A.M.–5 P.M., tasting fee $7), including building his own tasting bar. With production of less than a thousand cases, this is a small operation, but a dream come true for Scott, a self-taught winemaker who started out with a tiny winery in Ventura before it shut down. His wines include sangiovese, pinot noir, syrah, pinot gris, and chardonnay. He's usually there, brimming with enthusiasm, and will talk as along as you stay at the tasting bar. The interior is simple and uncluttered and there is one table off to the side.

CURTIS WINERY

Curtis Winery (5249 Foxen Canyon, 805/686-8999, daily 10 A.M.–5 P.M., tasting fee $10) has a thing for Hawaiian shirts, and that's pretty much the vibe here: low-key and fun. The emphasis is solely on Rhône-style wines like grenache, mourvedre, syrah, roussanne, and viognier. They were actually one of the first wineries to focus on these grapes. They routinely turn out some very fine wines that showcase the area, which leans toward bright expressive fruit. They also have a lot of gift items and books, and a grassy area fronting the main road with picnic tables and views to the vineyards across the street.

THE BRANDER VINEYARD

The Brander Vineyard (2401 N. Refugio Rd., 805/688-2455, daily 10 A.M.–5 P.M., tasting fee $10) facility looks like a small wine château

in Europe—well, except for the pink walls. Surrounded by flowers and poplar, cottonwood, and redwood trees, and a rustic courtyard with picnic tables, this is a place known for sauvignon blanc. Brander is the undisputed king of that varietal in this area, having been making it since the 1970s. Equally impressive is a cabernet sauvignon—remarkable considering that this is not the prime growing area for it. Chardonnay, syrah, and merlot round out the offerings.

Festivals and Events

The annual **Quick Draw and Art Auction** (805/688-1222, www.judithhalegallery.com) is held right across from the flagpole each August. Local artists race against the clock to complete a drawing, painting, or sculpture within 45 minutes. The works are then auctioned off in a live auction, and you can walk home with something hot off the press. There's also a silent auction and a barbecue in the park, and artists have demonstrations as all the local galleries stay open late. They've been doing this for over a quarter of a century.

Shopping

CLOTHING

Jedlicka's Saddlery (2883 Grand Ave., 805/688-2626, www.jedlickas.com, Mon.–Sat. 9 A.M.–5:30 P.M., Sun. 10 A.M.–4:30 P.M.) is all cowboy, all the time. Jeans, hats, boots—whatever you might need for actual cowboy work or pretend cowboy work is all here. Jedlickas's first opened in 1932 on the site of the town's turn-of-the-20th-century blacksmith shop. Western and English clothing, gear, and tack and a large selection of clothing for kids keeps people coming back.

SPECIALTY AND GIFTS

Global Gardens (2477 Alamo Pintado Ave., 805/693-1600, www.oliverevolution.com, daily 11 A.M.–5 P.M., tasting fee $3) uses mainly organic pesticide-free ingredients in their line of extra virgin olive oils, fruit vinegars, appetizer spreads, glazes, snacks, and sweets. They import Greek oils as well, and a tasting at the

WINE COUNTRY

© MICHAEL CERVIN

Alamo Pintado Avenue in Los Olivos

small wood-framed store will open your eyes to the vast differences in oils. If you've had enough wine, opt for olive oil.

Alpacas de Los Olivos (2786 Corral de Quati, 805/688-5748, www.whyalpacas.com, Sat. 11 A.M.–3 P.M., or by appointment) is a private ranch dedicated to alpaca, the smaller cousins of llamas and camels. Their rustic gift shop is stocked with items made from the soft, durable alpaca fibers, including sweaters, vests, ponchos, blankets, and even dresses. Additionally they'll give you a brief education about the animals, which are pretty darn cute, and you can see them up close.

ART GALLERIES

What once was an art destination with a dozen galleries has dwindled down to just two galleries now, and the Wildling Art Museum.

The largest gallery in town these days is **Gallery Los Olivos** (2920 Grand Ave., 805/688-7517, www.gallerylosolivos.com, daily 10 A.M.–5 P.M.), which acts as an artists' co-op, with the artists themselves running the show. They present regional artists from within Santa Barbara County working with wood, acrylic, ceramic, and pastels to create original traditional and abstract works of art. They rotate monthly solo shows. The space is larger than you'd expect, with a lot of first rate work.

At **Sansone Studio Gallery** (2948 Nojoqui Ave., 805/693-9769, www.sansonestudio.com, daily 11 A.M.–5 P.M.), Joel and Pamela Sansone use the medium of vitreous enamel on copper to create vibrant work. Vitreous enamel is applied to a copper surface, then kiln fired. The powdered glass becomes molten and fuses to the copper, making the colors extremely rich and deep. Their work is abstract in theme and their small off-the-beaten-path studio is worth seeking out just to see their unique pieces.

Spas

Champagne Spa & Boutique (2860 Grand Ave., 805/686-9202, www.fessparker.com, Mon.–Sat. 10 A.M.–5 P.M., Sun. 11 A.M.–4 P.M.) is housed near the pool at the Fess Parker Inn, and you don't need to be a guest of the inn to partake of their services. Check out the deep-tissue massage or grapeseed-oil massage, or the full line of waxing and manicures. They also offer facials for women, men, and kids.

Accommodations
$200-300
It's easy to pass by **The Grand Lady** (2715 Grand Ave., 805/686-5762, kspurbeck@verizon.net, $250), which bills itself as a cottage and vacation rental. But they also rent out a 700-square-foot space located above the garage next to the beautiful Victorian home for single-night guests. There are two rooms that can sleep

up to four people, a full kitchen, a washer and dryer, and you can easily walk the one block into Los Olivos. This is an upstairs unit private deck, and you have access to owner Kathy and Gerry Spurbeck's lovely back garden. The decor is simple, but it's a nice change from a hotel and you'll feel like you're a world away. They do not provide any amenities like food or morning coffee, but that's easy to find in town. Should you consider this option it's best to contact them in advance, as they sometimes rent the space for as long as several months.

OVER $300
Fess Parker's Wine Country Inn & Spa (2860 Grand Ave., 805/688-7788, www.fessparker.com, $395–520 d) was built by Fess Parker (who played Davy Crockett and Daniel Boone in the early TV shows), whose mini-empire included his own winery. Parker, who passed away in March 2010, was smart enough to get into land and real estate after his television days, and he was long a fixture of the valley. There's a wine store and a restaurant on the premises, and the feel of this traditional inn is changing to adopt a more modern feel, letting go of the older Victorian decor and replacing it with hipper and sleeker decor. But it still retains the elements people come here for: small-town hospitality, easy access to the wine country, and a Victorian and Western motif. The rooms are comfortable and large, and they surround a garden courtyard. This is the only hotel in Los Olivos, but Santa Ynez and Solvang are a short drive away.

Food
At **(Patrick's Side Street Café** (2375 Alamo Pintado Ave., 805/686-4004, Wed.–Fri. 11:30 A.M.–4 P.M. and 5–9 P.M., Sat.–Sun. 11:30 A.M.–3 P.M. and 5–9 P.M., $25), owner Patrick is something of a prickly pear. If he doesn't like you, you're out. If you want a meal cooked a certain way and he doesn't agree, he'll let you know. But the man knows how to cook—trust him. The rustic, unpretentious space has artwork adorning the walls, local wines, a dedicated clientele, and fierce food.

The warm duck salad is worth having, as is the paella. Be advised that it is a pet-friendly restaurant, meaning any and all animals are welcome, both inside and on their outdoor deck.

(Panino's (2900 Grand Ave., 805/688-9304, daily 10 A.M.–4 P.M., $10) is all about sandwiches and salads. A small chain in the county, this outpost does very well. It's the perfect choice when you don't want a full sit-down meal but a quick bite to eat, maybe something to take on the road. Their sandwiches and salads are made to order, and there is a good selection of vegetarian options. The roast turkey and brie sandwich is a favorite, as is the avocado and provolone with fresh basil and honey mustard.

(Ballard Inn (2436 Baseline, Ballard, 805/688-7770, Wed.–Sun. 5:30–9 P.M., $28) is one of those restaurants where you keep thinking, How did they end up here, of all places? Chef-owner Budi Kazali has transformed Ballard into a destination—well, actually, it's the only reason to stop in Ballard, which is sandwiched between Solvang and Los Olivos. There are only a dozen tables in this intimate space, and on busy nights (most any weekend), it can get loud. The menu rotates often to take advantage of the freshest ingredients Kazali can find. Most all the vegetables come from local farms, and the seafood from Santa Barbara. On any given night you might find crispy barramundi, truffled cauliflower soup, or a beef dish. Whatever is presented on the small menu, you can be sure it will be artfully prepared and exceptionally good.

Brother's Restaurant at Mattei's Tavern (2350 Railroad Ave., 805/688-4820, www.matteistavern.com, daily 5–10 P.M., $30) is part history lesson, part restaurant. It was built in 1886 right across from the railroad, which was where the highway is now. The narrow gauge would stop here and folks would head to Mattei's for food and rest—and they still do. With prime rib, lots of beef and fish entrées, it's a wonderful stop, and the old wood interior is lined with photos of times gone by and original paintings done by the original owner's son. Eternally popular with locals and tourists, Mattei's offers a well-priced and versatile wine list to complement their food.

© MICHAEL CERVIN

Brother's Restaurant at Mattei's Tavern has been serving weary travelers since 1886.

The current restaurant is run by actual brothers Jeff and Matt Nichols, who have been creating fine dining in the valley since 1996. **Los Olivos Wine Merchant Cafe** (2879 Grand Ave., 805/688-7265, www.losolivoscafe.com, Mon.–Fri. 11:30 A.M.–9 P.M., Sat.–Sun. 11 A.M.–9 P.M., $20) has been plying their trade since 1995, and always did well. But *Sideways* really cemented their popularity, and now it's nearly always packed. You can sit outside on the deck, inside at the tables, or at the bar. They have a wall of wine as part of their offering, so if you find something you'd like to have with your lunch or dinner you can buy a bottle, or take one home with you. It gets noisy and the service is usually strained because of capacity crowds, but they prepare wonderful food like cage pot roast, and their excellent housemade bread dipping oil is sold by the bottle.

Petros (2860 Grand Ave., 805/686-5455, www.petrosrestaurant.com, Sun.–Thurs. 7 A.M.–10 P.M., Fri.–Sat. 7 A.M.–11 P.M., $25) is located inside the Fess Parker Inn. The Greek restaurant has a stunningly modern and hip decor in contrast to the conservative inn and the town, and is a culinary change of pace unlike anything in the valley. They bake their own pita, make fresh yogurt, and serve predominantly small plates, which is perfect since there is an abundance of things to try like the sesame-crusted feta and spanakopita. There are full entrées as well, and many of the seasonings used are imported from Greece.

Los Olivos Grocery (2621 W. Hwy. 154, 805/688-5115, www.losolivosgrocery.com, daily 7 A.M.–9 P.M.) is part grocery store and part deli. With an impressive selection of cheeses and a decent wine department, they also have a full deli for picnic foods or will assemble one for you. Get the red-pepper hummus or their Happy Canyon club, or grab a breakfast burrito to go. All their produce in sourced from the area, and they have terrific sandwiches and salads to eat there on the covered patio, or to take with you as you explore wine country.

Information and Services
The website www.losolivosca.com is the best source of information about the town, though it is by no means comprehensive.

© MICHAEL CERVIN

Patrick's Side Street Café

EMERGENCY SERVICES

The Santa Ynez Valley Cottage Hospital (2050 Viborg, Solvang, 805/688-6431) offers emergency services. Should you have an emergency, dial 911. Police services are contracted with the County of Santa Barbara Sheriff's Department (1745 Mission Dr., Solvang, 805/688-5000).

NEWSPAPERS AND MEDIA

The *Santa Ynez Valley News* covers the local angle and is published each Thursday. For more countywide coverage, the *Santa Barbara News-Press* and the *Santa Maria Times* are both dailies available for purchase.

POSTAL SERVICES

The post office is located at 2880 Grand Avenue, Suite B (805/688-4573). Given its limited size, it's advisable to call ahead for operating hours and services.

LAUNDRY

Since there are no services of this type in town, your best bet is **St. Paul Cleaners and Laundry** (1693 Mission Dr., 805/688-9618), a few miles down the road in Solvang.

Getting There

Los Olivos is best accessed off Highway 154 near the 101, as it sits directly off the highway. The Santa Ynez Airport accepts small craft, and the Santa Maria Airport is within a 20-minute drive.

Getting Around

Just like Santa Ynez, Los Olivos is a walking town. Only three blocks by two blocks, it is simple to get around. Some of the side streets don't have sidewalks, so be careful. It's also a small enough town that people simply wander the streets and cross whenever they feel like it, which is not a good idea—peak times get busy with traffic, and it's important to obey the traffic rules.

Santa Maria Valley

The Santa Maria Valley used to be a stretch of lonely land populated with sagebrush, deer, bears, and rabbits stretching from the Santa Lucia Mountains toward the Pacific Ocean. Today, Santa Maria is agriculture central. As you pass through on Highway 101, you see fields and vineyards coupled with new housing developments. Most people readily assume this is all farming, but Santa Maria has a strong Western history, and its namesake food, the Santa Maria–style tri-tip. Though it doesn't have the idyllic charm of other towns along the Central Coast, it is the gateway to the wine industry, beaches, and some fabulous under-the-radar restaurants.

The Chumash Indians made their homes here, and in 1769 the Portolá exploration party came through the Santa Maria Valley, signaling the advent of Mission San Luis Obispo de Tolosa in 1772 and Mission La Purisima in 1787. Settlers soon followed, looking for the possibility of free land. By the time of California statehood in 1850, the Santa Maria River Valley was one of the most productive agricultural areas in California, and it's still a key component of the economy.

The Santa Maria Valley saw its share of oil exploration beginning in 1888, leading to large oil discoveries by the turn of the 20th century. In 1901, William Orcutt urged his company, Union Oil, to lease more than 70,000 acres. For the next eight decades, thousands of oil wells were drilled and put into production, facilitating growth for the city. By 1957 there were almost 1,800 oil wells in operation in the Santa Maria Valley, producing $60 million worth of oil. The city remained just four square miles until 1954, when annexations increased the city's size to about 22 square miles. You can still see some of the old wells, but more than likely you'll see vineyards and row crops, and chances are you'll eat and drink the bounty of Santa Maria wherever you dine.

SIGHTS
Santa Maria Museum of Flight
The Santa Maria Museum of Flight (3015 Airpark Dr., 805/922-8758, www.smmof.org, Fri.–Sun. 10 A.M.–4 P.M., $5 adults, $4 seniors, $3 children 12–18, $1 children 6–12) features displays of WWII and present-day aircraft and artifacts. The small but interesting museum is presided over by an all-volunteer staff. There are two hangars and a few old planes, as well as a 3,000-volume library on aviation. Their yearly air show, Thunder Over the Valley, is a huge draw each August. This is not a large museum, but the dedication of a few individuals makes this a great visit for aviation lovers.

Santa Maria Valley Discovery Museum
Santa Maria Valley Discovery Museum (705 S. McClelland St., 805/928-8414, www.smvdiscoverymuseum.org, Mon.–Sat. 10 A.M.–5 P.M., $8) is a place for kids, and the emphasis is on education. They have a lot of small hands-on exhibits such as how a tractor works, and information about agriculture, how saddles are made, a boat and its terminology, and a 3,000-gallon tank with—you guessed it—sharks! If you're traveling with younger kids, this is a great stop. They do an admirable job at this museum, with a diversity of things for kids to be involved in. The interior is brightly colored, allowing for a lot of stimulation.

Guadalupe/Nipomo Dunes Center
Guadalupe/Nipomo Dunes Center (1055 Guadalupe St., Guadalupe, 805/343-2455, www.dunescenter.org, Thurs.–Sun. noon–4 P.M.) is housed in a 1910 Craftsman house, still beautiful inside with built-in bookshelves that hold the research library. Staff can guide you as to how best to explore the 18 miles of coastline and the 22,000 acres that broadly encompass the dunes complex, whether you're a bird-watcher or an off-roader, or you just want to walk the beach. Upstairs is a small exhibit space including a vertebrae from a whale, a brief history of the area and dunes, and most visited of all, the history of the set of the 1923

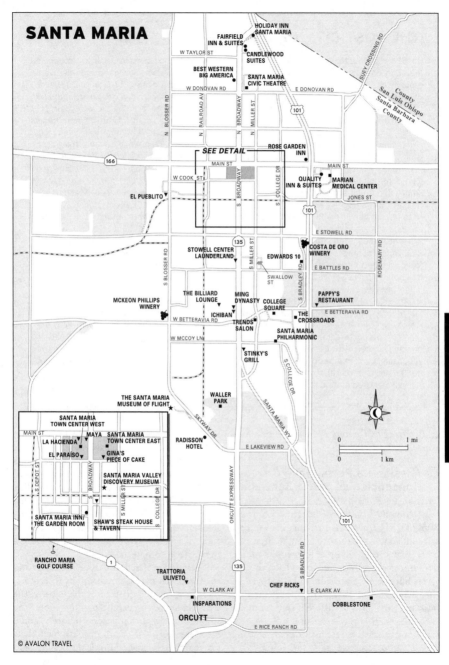

SANTA MARIA

HOLIDAY INN
SANTA MARIA
FAIRFIELD
INN & SUITES
W TAYLOR ST
CANDLEWOOD
SUITES
BEST WESTERN
BIG AMERICA
SANTA MARIA
CIVIC THEATRE
W DONOVAN RD
E DONOVAN RD

N BLOSSER RD
RAILROAD AV
N BROADWAY
N MILLER ST

101

SUEY CROSSING RD

San Luis Obispo County
Santa Barbara County

166

SEE DETAIL

ROSE GARDEN
INN

MAIN ST
MAIN ST

W COOK ST

EL PUEBLITO

S BROADWAY
S COLLEGE DR

QUALITY
INN & SUITES
MARIAN
MEDICAL CENTER

JONES ST

101

E STOWELL RD

135

STOWELL CENTER
LAUNDERLAND

S MILLER ST

EDWARDS 10

COSTA DE ORO
WINERY

E BATTLES RD

ROSEMARY RD

SWALLOW
ST

MCKEON PHILLIPS
WINERY

S BLOSSER RD

THE BILLIARD
LOUNGE

MING
DYNASTY

COLLEGE
SQUARE

PAPPY'S
RESTAURANT

E BETTERAVIA RD

ICHIBAN
W BETTERAVIA RD

TRENDS
SALON

S BRADLEY RD

THE
CROSSROADS

W MCCOY LN

SANTA MARIA
PHILHARMONIC

STINKY'S
GRILL

S COLLEGE DR

SANTA MARIA WY

THE SANTA MARIA
MUSEUM OF FLIGHT

WALLER
PARK

SKYWAY DR

WINE COUNTRY

SANTA MARIA
TOWN CENTER WEST
MAIN ST
MAYA   SANTA MARIA
TOWN CENTER EAST
LA HACIENDA
EL PARAÍSO
GINA'S
PIECE OF CAKE
SANTA MARIA VALLEY
DISCOVERY MUSEUM

S DEPOT ST
BROADWAY
S MILLER ST
S COLLEGE DR

SANTA MARIA INN/
THE GARDEN ROOM
SHAW'S STEAK HOUSE
& TAVERN

RADISSON
HOTEL

E LAKEVIEW RD

ORCUTT EXPRESSWAY

0   1 mi
0   1 km

101

RANCHO MARIA
GOLF COURSE

1

TRATTORIA
ULIVETO

135

W CLARK AV

CHEF RICKS

S BRADLEY RD

E CLARK AV

INSPARATIONS

ORCUTT

COBBLESTONE

E RICE RANCH RD

© AVALON TRAVEL

THE LOST CITY OF DEMILLE

In 1924, film director Cecil B. DeMille made an epic film, one that was intended to be the most epic of all films – The Ten Commandments. Well, by the standards of the day, it was epic. The year before filming began he constructed the largest set in movie history, called The City of the Pharaoh, in the dunes at Guadalupe. When filming was completed, DeMille ordered that the entire set be dismantled and buried by the fast-shifting sands. He allegedly had concerns that his set might be used for cheap knockoffs. And it stayed there, forgotten, for the next 60 years.

In 1983, a one-line clue in DeMille's posthumously published autobiography suggested what he had done, and the hunt was on to find the remains of the set. In 1988, what came to be called the Lost City of DeMille site passed into the hands of The Nature Conservancy, which endorsed efforts to save the set. In 1990 Bank of America got in on the act. The Bank's original founder, A. P. Giannini, had helped DeMille complete The Ten Commandments when the film's producers threatened to sever DeMille's funding for the costly drama. To honor that relationship, Bank of America provided $10,000 for an archaeological survey of the dunes. The survey used ground-penetrating radar to confirm the existence of what was suspected beneath the sand. Initially the team discovered the probable location of 12 buried sphinxes. And slowly they tried, mostly in vain, to bring the set to the surface. Since it was constructed of plaster of Paris, it was brittle and sections simply fell apart. A few items have been recovered, however, and they are on display at the Dunes Center. The rest of the old set lives up to its adopted name, merely a lost city, now gone forever. To some, an old Hollywood set may not be that impressive. But here are the facts behind the set of The Ten Commandments.

The set was approximately 120 feet high and 720 feet wide; about 1,500 workers constructed it using a half a million feet of lumber. They built 300 chariots and had 75 miles of reinforcing cable to steady the massive structure. 125 cooks turned out 7,500 sandwiches and other meals for 3,000 actors, who also consumed 5,000 apples and oranges each day. This doesn't take into account the 5,000 animals on the set. Of the items recovered, more cough syrup bottles were pulled out than anything else. After all, this was during Prohibition, and cough syrup was just about 13 percent alcohol. There's no commandment that says you can't drink.

film *The Ten Commandments,* which was filmed at the dunes.

◖ Mission La Purisima Concepcion de Maria Santisima

Mission La Purisima Concepcion de Maria Santisima (2295 Purisima Rd., Lompoc, 805/733-3713, www.lapurisimamission.org, self-guided tours daily 9 A.M.–5 P.M., free one-hour guided tours daily at 1 P.M., $6 adults, $5 seniors) was founded on December 8, 1787, but the first mission was destroyed in the earthquake of 1812. The fathers then rebuilt the mission in a different spot, and it is that mission that a quarter of a million visitors enjoy today as a state historic park. Sitting inside 2,000 acres are trails for simple hikes

and walks, and many people bring a picnic. When you visit you can examine the five-acre garden that shows native and domestic plants typical of a mission garden, including fig and olive trees and a wide variety of plants like sage and Spanish dagger. There are also mission animals typical of the times, such as burros, horses, longhorn cattle, sheep, goats, and turkeys, which are displayed in a corral located in the main compound.

The mission is actually three buildings and there are well over a dozen rooms to explore, including sleeping quarters of the soldiers, the weaving shop, the candle-making room, the simple church, chapel, priest's quarters, and a lot more. Many of the rooms still have their original dirt floors, and this is the best mission

© MICHAEL CERVIN

Mission La Purisima is one of the most beautiful missions on the Central Coast.

to visit to truly get a feel for daily life back then. There are also a few conical huts that the Chumash used to live in. This is one of the only missions that does not have church services, now that it's a state park.

In 1785, Sergeant Pablo de Cota, stationed at Mission San Buenaventura in present-day Ventura, was ordered to find a location for a new mission, which was to be roughly equidistant between the missions at San Luis Obispo and Santa Barbara. The Mission of the Immaculate Conception of Most Holy Mary was dedicated and construction began in the spring of 1788, after the winter rains. It was constructed in the traditional quadrangle shape, and the converted Chumash lived outside the mission walls in their traditional huts.

On the morning of December 21, 1812, a major temblor stuck the coast. Two shock waves virtually destroyed the mission, and what was left of the shattered adobe walls dissolved in the heavy winter rains. When they decided to rebuild the traditional design was abandoned and the new mission was built in a linear design, making it unique among California missions.

But this mission, too, would fall into ruin, a victim of the passage of time and simple neglect. In 1824, La Purisima was at the center of a failed Chumash revolt. Soldiers guarding the mission were poorly paid, and the mission was waiting to receive monies owed them from Spain. Spain didn't pay, and the soldiers turned their frustrations out on the Indian population. The friction between the military and the missions exploded as the Chumash Indians of the three Santa Barbara missions rose up in armed revolt. Soldiers from the presidio at Monterey took the La Purisima mission by force; the attack left 16 Chumash Indians dead and several wounded. One of the fathers negotiated surrender terms for the Chumash Indians, but seven Chumash Indians who surrendered were executed, and 12 others were sentenced to hard labor at the Santa Barbara presidio.

Secularization in 1834 was the final nail in the coffin for La Purisima. Church services ceased in 1836, and buildings fell into disrepair. By 1845 the mission was sold for a little more than $1,000, and the church was stripped of its roof tiles and timbers. The walls, exposed to the

© MICHAEL CERVIN

Public tours are a must at Vandenberg Air Force Base.

elements, crumbled. Eventually, the building was used as a stable. It was rescued in 1934, when the site was deeded to the State of California. A resulting restoration project became one of the largest of its kind in the nation.

◖ Vandenberg Air Force Base

The tours at Vandenberg Air Force Base (Hwy. 1 at Black Rd., 805/606-3595, www.vandenberg.af.mil) take visitors by bus through the base and include a tour of the Heritage Museum, which provides mock-ups of missile silos, an old missile control station, and decommissioned rocket engines, as well as a visit to Space Launch Complex 10, an old still-intact launch area for missiles from the 1960s to the 1980s. They do offer private tours for 15 or more people. Tours last nearly three hours, in part because the drive time around this massive military installation will consume over an hour of that. Remember that this is an active military base and joking about national security is seriously frowned upon. Public base tours are offered through the Public Affairs office the second Wednesday of each month. Reservations are required at least two weeks in advance.

Information on **Vandenberg rocket launches** is available by calling the oddly named Launch Update and Rumor Control Hotline at 805/606-1857. Launch days and

times are released three to five days in advance. The public viewing site for Vandenberg launches is off Corral Road near Vandenberg's main gate. To access the area, take Highway 1 to the Santa Maria Gate and proceed on Casmalia Road. At the barriers, turn right onto Corral Road and bear left to the top. Most launches are held in the very early morning hours. Due to weather, visibility might be hindered.

Once a haven for wild game and cattle grazing, some 86,000 acres of open lands in the Lompoc, Guadalupe, and Santa Maria area came under the control of the United States Army in 1941. Originally called Camp Cooke, it was a training center for armored and infantry troops during World War II. Unknown to many, German and Italian prisoners of war were sent to Camp Cooke. To help alleviate the severe labor shortage in the commercial market created by the war, some of the German prisoners also worked in local communities, mainly in agricultural jobs. A maximum-security army disciplinary barracks was constructed on the property in 1946 specifically for military prisoners from within the army, and today serves as the United States Penitentiary at Lompoc.

It was then transformed into the nation's first space and ballistic missile training base in 1957 and renamed Vandenberg Air Force Base after General Hoyt S. Vandenberg. The base

© MICHAEL CERVIN

Jalama Beach

is the only military base in the United States from which unmanned government and commercial satellites are launched into polar orbit. It is also the only site from which intercontinental ballistic missiles are test fired into the Pacific Ocean; they land at the Kwajalein Atoll near the Marshall Islands. The base's coastal location, in addition to its size, remoteness from heavily populated areas, and moderate climate that afforded year-round operations, allows these missiles to be launched without any negative impact over populated areas. Today, Vandenberg is the third largest air force base in California.

⟨ Jalama Beach

This 23-acre Santa Barbara County park (9999 Jalama Rd., Lompoc, 805/736-3504, www.jalamabeach.com, day-use fee $8) near Jalama Creek, once a Chumash Indian settlement called Halama, maintains 98 campsites, all overlooking the ocean. Each site has a picnic table and barbecue pit, with hot showers, restrooms, and potable water nearby; 29 sites offer electrical hookups, and dump stations are available. It's easy to think that since Jalama is so remote it would be off the radar, but it can actually be a busy place on holiday weekends. From Highway 101, take Highway 1 toward Lompoc. After 14 miles you'll see the sign for Jalama. This road is another 14 miles to the

beach. It's a stunning drive and amazingly quiet, starting with low rolling hills and a few barns, and as you climb and drop over the first small range, you are suddenly shaded by canopies of oak trees, quail running in front of your car, and hawks catching the thermals above you. Finally you crest a hill and the Pacific is displayed in front of you.

Once you reach Jalama Beach you'll see so many RV and tents you'll think you've arrived at a camping convention. Thankfully the campsites, which fill very fast, are well spaced apart. Groceries, sundries, firewood, fishing bait and tackle, ice, and beer and wine can be purchased at the Jalama Store. Other services include mail and video rentals. The store and its popular grill are open daily starting at 8 A.M. Day-use picnic areas provide tables and raised fire boxes. Additional activities include surfing, horseshoes, whale-watching, birdwatching, nature photography, and fishing the surf or rock outcroppings for perch, cabezon, kelp, bass, or halibut, and there's a play area for the kids. You probably won't get cell service out here. Many protected California native plants like sand verbena, saltbush, and sea rocket grow within the park. There's a lot of powerful surf at Jalama, so be careful if you get in the water. It also tends to be blustery, but the views to the coastline, all green cliffs and blue water, are fantastic.

WINE COUNTRY

WINERIES

The wineries in the Santa Maria area are spread out, requiring a car to visit even a few of them. Some are in industrial sections of the city, and some are among vineyards. Unlike Solvang, Los Olivos, and Santa Ynez, where it's easy to find several wineries along one road or right in the middle of the town, you have to plan your trips to these wineries. A great initial resource is www.santamariawines.com.

◖ Flying Goat Cellars

The focus is on pinot noir at Flying Goat (1520 E. Chestnut, Unit A, Lompoc, 805/736-9032, www.flyinggoat.com, Thurs.–Sat. 11 A.M.–4 P.M., tasting fee $10). In addition to several iterations of beautifully seductive pinot noir, they are locally well known for Goat Bubbles, a light, delicate pinot noir sparkling wine. Owner Norm Yost goes for an uncommon restrained style with his wines, allowing the lush cherry and raspberry elements of the pinot noir grapes to express themselves and not be overwhelmed with too much oak. These are consistently excellent wines and avoid the bombastic and overripe characteristics that many pinot noirs tend to exhibit. As Norm has said, Why spend $4,000 a ton buying pinot noir fruit only to mask it behind oak? Ultimately he makes wine he would like to drink, and Norm steadfastly adheres to his principles. His tasting room is nothing more than a table at his small winery. This is a working facility and not a spot to lounge and look at pretty vineyards. In fact the only wildlife you'll see will probably be Norm's dog.

Foxen Winery

Foxen Winery (7600 Foxen Canyon Rd., 805/937-4251 daily 11 A.M.–4 P.M., tasting fee $10) is known for its rustic wood tasting room that looks like a run-down shed. But the wines are a far cry from that image. In addition to chardonnay, syrah, cabernet sauvignon, and pinot noir, the winery is one of the few to produce chenin blanc, an underappreciated grape. Foxen has a long-standing reputation of producing some of the finest wines in the area,

and the Foxen name goes back six generations. Their 10-acre vineyard is the only dry-farmed vineyard in the area, meaning that there is no irrigation, they simply rely on what Mother Nature provides.

Cottonwood Canyon

Cottonwood Canyon (3940 Dominion Rd., 805/937-8463, daily 10 A.M.–5:30 P.M., tasting fee $10) started in 1988, and though it's just 10 minutes from downtown Santa Maria, this winery has managed to keep under the radar, though after trying their wines you'll wonder why you haven't heard of them. With a standard portfolio of wines including six iterations of chardonnay, they also include a couple of sparkling wines and a dessert-style syrah as well as several pinot noirs. They farm 78 acres with the San Rafael Mountains as a backdrop. Winemaker Norm Beko also loves food, and many weekends he's grilling up something to share.

McKeon Phillips Winery

McKeon Phillips Winery (2115 S. Blosser Rd., 805/928-3025, daily 11 A.M.–6 P.M., tasting fee $8–13) is part tasting room and part art gallery and studio, where you can sip wines while examining rotating works of art including the winemaker's own impressionistic creations. Chardonnay, nebbiolo, cabernet sauvignon, and some delicious thick ports come out of here. This is another winery that has a low profile; when you drive to their tasting room located in a small industrial warehouse you may initially think that you might be in the wrong spot. There are no pretty views here, but a broad portfolio of wines and good conversation.

Tantara Winery

A dozen different pinot noirs are the flagship wines at Tantara Winery (2900 Rancho Tepusquet Rd., 805/938-5051, www.tantarawinery.com, by appointment only). There is also chardonnay, but that's it. These wines are sold directly at the winery since they have no tasting room, which is located at Bien Nacido Vineyards. The winemaking team of Jeff Fink and Bill Cates is focused on small

WHAT'S IN A NAME? THE STORY BEHIND SOME WACKY WINERY NAMES

A quick glance at the wine industry reveals that the majority of wineries are named after people. There's certainly nothing wrong with naming a winery after yourself: Foley, Babcock, Melville, Rusack, Beckmen, Mosby, Huber, and many other wineries are named after their owners. But some winery names go beyond a mere surname.

Mike Brown named his winery Kalyra, which loosely translated from Australian Aboriginal means "a wild and pleasant place." Sea Smoke in the Santa Rita Hills sounds seductive, through most folks don't realize that the name refers to the ocean fog climbing over the mountains. Lincourt Winery refers to the names of two daughters of the owner, Lindsey and Courtney.

Bill Cates, co-owner of Tantara Winery, owned a horse named Tantara when he lived in Virginia, and she led a charmed life. When Tantara got on in years, Bill sent her to live out her days with other mares. But after a while Bill realized she wasn't getting around very well, and made the difficult decision to put her down, and arranged for a vet to euthanize her. About a month later he went back to visit Tantara's grave site. As he stood there, tears in his

eyes for the loss of his beloved horse, something bumped him from behind. It was Tantara. The vet had put down the wrong horse! After that, Bill says, he let Tantara live out her days on her own terms.

Kathy Joseph, owner of Fiddlehead Cellars, already had two different vintages aging in barrels, but still had no idea what to call her new winery. One day, while working in her fern bed, it struck her – she'd call the project Fiddlehead, the word for the coiled tip of a fern frond. The fiddlehead emerges once a year into a very elegant leaf, just like her vintages, and is considered a delicacy; the name was perfectly playful, matching her approach to making wine.

You may have never seen a goat fly, but Norm Yost, owner of Flying Goat Cellars, has. Apparently he had pygmy goats on his property, and he built a little house for them. A few of the goats would climb on top of the house and jump off the roof. A perfect name for his pinot noirs, he thought. In fact, many people try his wines based solely on the label and name. Norm says, "Names are powerful and I wanted to create some levity in the wine business."

lots of exceptional fruit, and they source pinot noir from some diverse growing areas along the Central Coast and Monterey and produce various expressions of those spots. Often they will pull barrel samples for visitors to taste. Their wines are not on the cheap side, but this is the place if you're looking for beautiful high-end pinot noir.

Demetria Estate

The Demetria Estate (6701 Foxen Canyon Rd., 805/686-2345, www.demetriaestate.com, by appointment only) features stellar beautifully crafted pinot noir, syrah, pinot blanc, chardonnay, and a Rhône white blend, though these are not inexpensive wines. They biodynamically farm their vineyard, which was formerly

the site of a vineyard that made merely average wines—apparently the farming techniques make all the difference. The care given the vines is expressed in these wines. Their facility is a yellow mottled Tuscan-looking building set on a hill overlooking the vines and is impressive enough, but even more so coupled with the wines. Bring some food and relax.

Dierberg/Star Lane Winery

Dierberg/Star Lane Winery (1280 Drum Canyon Rd., Lompoc, 805/739-0757, www.starlanevineyard.com, daily 11 A.M.–5 P.M., tasting fee $10) has vineyards located in Happy Canyon, one of the warmest spots in the valley, hence the reason they can make exceptional cabernet sauvignon. Their green and red barn tasting room is on the opposite side of the valley, however, and a little off the beaten path, but worth the drive for any serious wine lover. The Dierbergs operate three wine labels: Star Lane, their estate wines called Dierberg, and Three Saints. All of these wines, at various price points, are excellent. The Star Lane sauvignon blanc is terrific, and the value-priced Three Saints wines, including merlot, cabernet sauvignon, and pinot noir, are best bets.

Pali Wine Company

Pali Wine Company (1036 W. Aviation Dr., Lompoc, 805/736-7200, www.paliwineco.com, Fri.–Sat. 11 A.M.–4 P.M., Sun.–Thurs. by appointment, tasting fee $10) is located out in a warehouse-looking building in Lompoc, where you taste the wines next to the barrels, stacked cases of wine, and stainless steel fermentation tanks. Pinot noir from multiple vineyard sites across California is their specialty, showcasing how a single grape type can be so different depending on where it was grown. They also make a killer grenache, chardonnay, and cabernet sauvignon. It's a younger winery, but they have produced impressive wines in part because they are dedicated to not taking shortcuts with their wines.

◖ Kenneth Volk Vineyards

The owner of Kenneth Volk Vineyards (5230 Tepusquet Rd., 805/938-7896, www.volkwines.com, daily 10:30 A.M.–4:30 P.M., tasting fee $5) was not initially into wine. At college in San Luis Obispo he pursued a degree in fruit science, imagining a future in an orchard or greenhouse. But in 1981 he established Wild Horse Winery & Vineyard in Templeton, and over the next two decades production soared from 600 to 150,000 cases. In 2003, Ken sold Wild Horse, and in 2004 he formed Kenneth Volk Vineyards in Santa Maria. He wins countless awards, and makes damn good wines using as many diverse aspects of winemaking as possible. "Just as a rich stew or curry creates a more vivid culinary experience when it includes a complex combination of ingredients that harmonize, we seek

to bring together complementary flavors for a richer wine experience," he says. In addition to the standard offerings like chardonnay, pinot noir, viognier, cabernet sauvignon, and merlot, he's been a champion of what are called heirloom varieties, funky, wonderfully oddball wines like cabernet pfeffer, négrette, verdelho, and Aglianico. You won't regret the long trek to get to the tranquil 12-acre property along the Tepusquet Creek, surrounded by oak and sycamore trees.

Costa de Oro Winery

Costa de Oro Winery (1331 S. Nicholson Ave., 805/922-1468, www.cdowinery.com, daily 10 A.M.–6 P.M., tasting fee $7) started off as a farming operation with row crops; they then decided to plant grapes on a patch of land that wasn't working right. Well, the grapes thrived, and now pinot noir and chardonnay are the main wines they produce from their 20 acres. Friday nights and Sundays there's usually something musical happening at the tasting room, which is also the outlet for their produce operation. Today the tasting room, which opened in 2006, sits on the site of the Gold Coast strawberry stand, where you can also pick up fresh veggies and fruits in season. The wines offered at Costa de Oro include sauvignon blanc, three different versions of chardonnay, and three different versions of pinot noirs, among others.

Rancho Sisquoc

Rancho Sisquoc (6600 Foxen Canyon Rd., 805/934-4332, www.ranchosisquoc.com, Mon.–Thurs. 10 A.M.–4 P.M., Fri.–Sun. 10 A.M.–5 P.M., tasting fee $8) is one of those spots where you really have to want to go there. Located out in the boonies, it's a beautiful spot, and is probably best enjoyed by bringing a picnic. Their wood-sided tasting room is rustic but comfortable, more like an upscale barn. Grab a bottle of their sylvaner, chardonnay, sangiovese, or merlot and sit outside with some food and enjoy wine country, looking out to a vast field with low hills in the distance. This is definitely a quiet place!

ENTERTAINMENT AND EVENTS
Nightlife
For a little pool, check out **The Billiard Lounge** (1931 S. Thornburg, 805/925-3780, daily 11 A.M.–2 A.M., $9/hr), which has plenty of regulation pool tables and a jukebox with old songs you thought you left in high school. Try karaoke if your pool game is off. There tends to be a younger crowd here, as the beers are cheap.

Performing Arts
Like its cousin in Solvang, the PCPA Theaterfest (800 S. College Dr., 805/922-8313, www.pcpa.org, tickets $15–30) is housed on the campus of Allan Hancock College and has been producing theater for 40 years. They offer two stages: The Seversen Theatre is a theater in the round with seating on all sides, and the larger Marian Theatre has a traditional stage. They offer mainly musicals and comedies, light-hearted theater to keep you happy.

Just up the road is the **Santa Maria Civic Theatre** (1660 N. McClelland, 805/922-4442, www.smct.org, tickets $14) is an intimate 100-seat theater operating since 1959; though nonprofessional it has kept a high standard of quality. Some of the shows are well-known theater pieces, from the likes of Agatha Christie, while other works are less known. They run shows on Friday and Saturday nights only.

The **Santa Maria Philharmonic** (605 E. McCoy Lane, 805/925-0142, www.santamariaphilharmonic.org, tickets $30 adults, $25 seniors, $12 students) presents various classical music performances at a variety of venues, so it's best to check with their website to see where they might be. Primarily they perform at a local church, but they also offer free concerts at the malls, and travel out of county as well.

Cinema
The **Edwards 10** (1521 S. Bradley, 805/347-1164) shows first-run films on 10 screens. Overall the seats are comfy and the drinkholders work. The screens are a little small, but standard. Unfortunately, standard ticket prices are $10.50, steep by comparison to other areas. Another movie theater is being planned but details are not concrete yet.

Festivals and Events
Strawberries are a big crop here, and for over two decades they have celebrated the berry with more strawberries than you've ever seen at the **Santa Maria Valley Strawberry Festival** (Santa Maria Fair Park, 937 S. Thornburg, 805/925-8824, www.santamariafairpark.com, $6 adults, $4 seniors and children 6–11, $5 parking), held over three days in April each year. There are food booths, rides, live bands, an old-fashioned carnival, and the chance to sample different strawberry varieties and strawberry desserts while you learn about the strawberry industry, the valley's number one crop. This is one of the most attended festivals in the county.

The **Celebration of Harvest** (Rancho Sisquoc Winery, 6600 Foxen Canyon Rd., www.sbcountywines.com, 1–4 P.M., $75) is an annual event held each October. In fact the Chumash also had a harvest ceremony, known as the Hutash, which lasted for several days. Now, it's a time to drink wine, listen to bands, bid on silent auction items, see local artists, sample local food, and bask in the outdoor beauty of Rancho Sisquoc. The winery itself is located here, but it's also one of the few fields around that's large enough to accommodate 3,000 people. Most every winery shows up and frankly there's no way to sample everything. But if you're on the hunt for certain wines or varieties, this is a great place to get a feel for all of Santa Barbara County's wines.

SHOPPING
Santa Maria is mainly a mall town. Sure, there are still small shops that dot the main arteries, but most everything is relegated to strip malls—quite lovely and large strip malls with a Spanish flair, but malls nonetheless—and new versions are popping up all the time.

Shopping Centers
Santa Maria Town Center East (142 Town Center East, 805/922-7931, www.santamariatowncenter.com, Mon.–Fri. 10 A.M.–8 P.M.,

WINE COUNTRY

The Santa Maria Town Center East is the largest indoor mall on the Central Coast.

Sat. 10 A.M.–7 P.M., Sun. 11 A.M.–7 P.M.) is the largest spot to shop in Santa Maria and the largest indoor mall on the Central Coast with over 60 stores. Anchored by Sears and Macy's, it's your basic mall with standard shops like Bath & Body Works, Doc Burnstein's Ice Cream Lab, Payless Shoes, Subway, and Foot Locker. There are plans for a movie theater with 10 screens, but that's still in the works. The interior is pleasant enough, light, bright, and airy, and there's free parking in a covered parking lot. You'll be able to find coffee, sushi, and cookies here as well.

Across the street is **Santa Maria Town Center West** (at Stowell and Broadway), which is a mix of older stores, like one of the few remaining JCPenneys, and places like Big Lots, Subway, Starbucks, and a few Mexican restaurants. With the construction of the new mall, Santa Maria Town Center East, this original site has been somewhat neglected, but new storefronts have been put up in parts that stand in stark contrast to the old portion of this outdoor strip mall. It's not nearly as frequented as the other malls, but there's also plenty of parking to be found.

The Crossroads (2104 S. Bradley) is where Costco, Wal-Mart, and Home Depot all sit on what were once fields of beans. You can't miss the shopping center, as it is directly off Highway 101 at Betteravia. It is a long mall, and is also home to heavyweights like Best Buy, Staples, and TJ Maxx. It's certainly well designed and attractive as malls go, with a series of roundabouts on Bradley Road to connect to the various parking lots. It gets very busy simply because of the diversity of stores here.

College Square (540 E. Betteravia) is home to Panera Bread, who has the best spot, dead center inside this strip mall. It is joined by Jamba Juice, Starbucks, Cycle Star Bicycles, See's Candies—all stores that you've probably seen before. But there's also a nail salon, yogurt shop, and pizza joint. It's still under construction, with new tenants coming in to this more gentrified-looking mall with close access to the highway. It's not nearly as cumbersome as Crossroads, but it's also more limited.

Farmers Markets

There are two farmers markets in Santa Maria. On Wednesday from 12:30 to 4:30 P.M. at 100 South Broadway at Main Street (location of the original town site), there are the usual veggies and breads, pastries, plants, flowers, and lots of bee products including pollen and honey. In Orcutt there is a market on Tuesday from 10 A.M. to 1 P.M. at the corner of Clark and Bradley.

SPORTS AND RECREATION
Parks

Bounded by residential communities, **Waller Park** (3107 Orcutt Rd., 805/934-6211, daily 8 A.M.–sunset) is one of the loveliest parks you

© MICHAEL CERVIN

The Crossroads is Santa Maria's largest outdoor mall.

will encounter in Santa Maria. There are two beautiful lakes with fountains, and 153 acres of grassy lawn, shady picnic areas, playgrounds, basketball and volleyball courts, and even a disc golf course, as well as barbecue grills and picnic tables, horseshoes, a small playground, and restrooms. A three-acre off-leash dog park is within the greater park and has canine drinking fountains.

Cobblestone (Clark and Stillwell Rds., 805/934-6123, daily 8 A.M.–sunset) is less park and more two acres of open space. There's a lot of lush grass and a small playground. There aren't very many trees and it can get downright hot in summer, but it's quiet here and not often busy. There are no facilities, however.

Golf

La Purisima Golf Course (3455 E. Hwy. 246, Lompoc, 805/735-8395, www.lapurisimagolf.com, daily 6:30 A.M.–dusk, green fees $40–91) is an 18-hole, par-72 course designed by Robert Graves, who also designed Sandpiper in Santa Barbara and Hunter Ranch in Paso Robles. It's moderately priced and there

is a small grill for food and a pro shop. This is a tough course, with more hills than most any course, and brisk, cool winds in the afternoon—in other words, "challenging" is an understatement. But if you're up for it, it will be worth your effort, in spite of its rather remote location. Like many courses on the Central Coast, there is an abundance of oak trees to contend with.

Rancho Maria Golf Course (1950 Casmalia Rd., 805/937-2019, www.ranchomariagolf.com, daily 6:30 A.M.–dusk, green fees $22–35) is a rather unknown 18-hole, par-72 course even more secluded than Purisima. Though there are no parallel fairways and no houses to be seen on this remote course, there are a lot of trees and a short elevation gain. They have a small coffee shop, putting green, and practice bunkers. The pricing is quite good for a municipal course.

Car Racing

Santa Maria Speedway (1900 Hutton, Nipomo, 805/922-2232, www.racesantamariaspeedway.com) is located just off Highway 101 and is home to not only car races, but also tractor pulls—all of it loud, fast, and out of control. They also host occasional concerts. The third-mile oval clay track has been operating since 1964, and though it's not large, it does see a steady stream of races. The crowds get pretty rowdy here, as there's nothing else like it in the area.

Spas

InSpaRations (130 E. Clark Ave., Orcutt, 805/934-8682, www.insparations1.com, Tues.–Sat. 9 A.M.–7 P.M.), located just south of Santa Maria in Orcutt, will do your hair or give you a pedicure, manicure, or massage. The bright, cheery space is enhanced by the sincere and knowledgeable staff.

Trends Salon (338 E. Betteravia Rd., 805/349-9031, Mon.–Fri. 8 A.M.–7 P.M., Sat. 8 A.M.–4 P.M.) is more about trendy hair than anything else, though they perform manicures and pedicures and an esthetician is on staff as well.

WINE COUNTRY

ACCOMMODATIONS
Under $100

The **Rose Garden Inn** (1007 E. Main St., 805/922-4505, $70–85 d) is for the budget conscious. The place is a little worn but offers a great value compared to most hotels in Santa Maria. You won't find too many amenities here—but then if you don't need them, why pay for them? Coffee is located in the lobby, as is Wi-Fi. They are a little further from the shopping malls so you'll need to drive to them, or most anywhere else.

At the **Quality Inn & Suites** (210 S. Nicholson, 805/922-5891, www.quality-inn.com, $90–105 d), a complimentary breakfast is served each morning. In addition to an outdoor pool they provide a spa tub and a children's pool, Wi-Fi, a coffee shop, and outdoor barbecue grills. There are 64 guest rooms in this two-story property, and the standard rooms feature refrigerators and coffee- and tea-makers.

$100-200

Santa Maria Inn (801 S. Broadway, 805/928-7777, www.santamariainn.com, $139–169 d), constructed in 1917, now has 164 good-sized rooms and 18 suites. You can choose to stay in the historic part of the hotel, or one of their newer rooms. Either way they keep the feeling of the turn of the 20th century in the decor and Victorian-style furnishings. Located centrally in Santa Maria, the pet-friendly inn has an in-house restaurant and an old tavern on the premises. The rooms have coffeemakers and hairdryers, and there are five acres of grounds for you to walk with your pet.

Candlewood Suites (2079 Roemer Ct., 805/928-4155, www.candlewoodsuites.com, $135–164 d) is a newer 72-room hotel located on the outskirts on town, which means you'll need your car to get around. Located in a more industrial area next to a few other hotels, it does benefit from close freeway access north of town. There's a fitness area and laundry facility, as well as a small business center. It's clean, comfortable good-value accommodations.

Radisson Hotel (3455 Skyway Dr., 805/928-8000, www.radisson.com/santamariaca,

$135–195 d) is located near the airport and the southern portion of town. It's another standard hotel, though the rooms have been given a face-lift with brighter colors. There's an outdoor pool and an in-house restaurant, which looks to the airstrip. Basic amenities and good pricing make this a worthwhile choice if you're searching for a reliable name.

The **Holiday Inn Santa Maria** (2100 N. Broadway, 877/859-5095, www.holidayinn.com, $135–195 d) offers some rooms with kitchenettes, which is why it's big with business travelers and for extended stays. The four-story hotel was renovated in 2008 and has 415 rooms and suites, which are the standard rooms you'd expect from Holiday Inn—nice, but nothing out of the ordinary. They have free Wi-Fi, a fitness room, and a swimming pool on the premises.

Fairfield Inn & Suites (2061 Roemer Ct., 805/925-8500, www.marriott.com, $129–209 d) is a four-story newer hotel that has 89 rooms from a trustworthy name. The rooms are nicely decorated, going for an upscale corporate feel. There's an indoor pool and continental breakfast, but it's a pretty basic hotel. It does not accept pets, but is completely smoke free. The entire hotel is wired for Internet as well as Wi-Fi.

With an eye toward what they call early-American furnishings, **Best Western Big America** (1725 N. Broadway, 805/922-5200, www.bigamerica.com, $125–145 d) is one of the top-rated places to stay in Santa Maria. The 106 rooms, while a little dull and of the standard hotel type, are still large and clean, and there are a lot of amenities, including a 24-hour pool and hot tub and a continental breakfast each morning. It is located downtown right in the thick of things. They have an on-site restaurant, and provide shuttle service to the airport.

FOOD
American

Firestone Walker Brewery Taproom (620 McMurray Rd., Buellton, 805/686-1557, www.firestonewalker.com, daily 11 A.M. to 9 P.M., tasting fee $6.50, food $20) features four Firestone Walker beers in addition to four

TRUE TRI-TIP

Everyone seems to have heard of tri-tip, but most people don't know exactly what tri-tip is. Santa Maria barbecue has its roots in the mid-19th century, when the rancheros gathered to help each other brand their calves each spring. The host would then prepare a Spanish-style barbecue as a thank you. The meal included barbecued sirloin, salsa, Pinquito beans (which are native to the area), toasted French bread, and green salad. The present Santa Maria-style barbecue grew out of this tradition, and further developed about 60 years ago when locals began to string their beef on skewers and cook it over the hot coals of a red-oak fire. The meat, either top block sirloin or the triangular-shaped bottom sirloin known as a tri-tip cut, is rolled in a mixture of salt, pepper, and garlic just prior to cooking. It is then barbecued over red-oak wood, giving the meat a hearty, smoky flavor. The only condiment used is fresh salsa. Barbecue, however needs to be understood in its proper context, which in this case means that the meat is grilled low and slow, close to the flame for an extended period of time – this does not refer to a sweet barbecue sauce, as real tri-tip has no sauce. Tri-tip is everywhere these days, even for sale in supermarkets across the country, but if you want the real deal, you need to stop in Santa Maria and try authentic tri-tip for yourself at a place like **The Garden Room at the Santa Maria Inn** (801 S. Broadway, 805/928-7777, www.santamariainn.com, daily 6 A.M.-2 P.M. and 5-10 P.M., $25) or **Shaw's Steak House & Tavern** (714 S. Broadway, 805/925-5862, lunch Mon.-Fri. 11:30 A.M.-4 P.M., dinner nightly 5-9 P.M., $20).

alternating beers on tap. You can get it by the pint or mug, or try a sampler of four beers. They also offer food like pork chops, steaks, and burgers, and beer-battered fish-and–chips. Firestone Walker is the best brewery on the Central Coast and right off Highway 101, just north of Buellton. Grab a brew, and if your picky friend wants wine, well, they'll pour Firestone wines by the glass.

Chef Ricks (4869 S. Bradley Rd., 805/937-9512, www.chefricks.com, Mon.–Sat. 11 A.M.–9 P.M., $25) has long been regarded as Santa Maria's best restaurant, certainly its most dependable. There's a low-key approach to the menu, which is filled with salads, sandwiches, and entrées. There is a Southern influence to much of the food, like the Louisiana blackened halibut salad. But there are also straightforward dishes like the smoked turkey burrito or Black Angus steaks. Decorated with brightly colored paintings, it's festive without being pretentious.

Stinky's Grill (2430 S. Broadway, 805/614-9366, www.stinkysgrill.com, daily 11 A.M.–10 P.M., $15) is your loud, noisy sports bar, stuffed with all kinds of sports decorations and way too much testosterone. But if you like a true sports bar that serves food, here it is. There are 15 different beers on tap and the garlic fries, sliders, and St. Louis ribs are all home runs here. They also have a great happy hour with inexpensive drinks and food.

The Garden Room at the Santa Maria Inn (801 S. Broadway, 805/928-7777, www.santamariainn.com, daily 6 A.M.–2 P.M. and 5–10 P.M., $25) is located on the 1st floor of the hotel. White tablecloths, lots of old wood, and a proper environment—like your grandparents' house, it's a little stuffy inside but worth a stop, if only for the ridiculously decadent Vermont french toast. Tri-tip is on the menu, as is their very good signature tortilla soup. On nice days they serve on the back patio, a sunny little spot away from the noise on the main street.

Pappy's Restaurant (1275 E. Betteravia, 805/922-3553, Mon.–Thurs. 6 A.M.–11 P.M., Fri.–Sat. 6 A.M.–1 A.M., Sun. 6 A.M.–10 P.M., $15) is more truck stop than sit-down formal. It opened in 1959 and, frankly, not much has changed with the place. Old cowboy photos line the walls, and it's very casual, with a counter facing the kitchen and basic booths

WINE COUNTRY

and furniture. It's also one of the few places open late. They make a great tri-tip and their home fries are terrific. It's right off the freeway, and the large parking lot is convenient if you're towing something.

Steakhouses

The **((Far Western Tavern** (899 Guadalupe St., Guadalupe, 805/343-2211, www.farwesterntavern.com, Mon.–Sat. 11 A.M.–close, Sun. 9 A.M.–close, $25), out in Guadalupe, is one of those places where you can scarcely believe it hasn't changed since it was originally built as the Palace Hotel in 1912. Modern restaurants can only try and emulate the authenticity of this very cool place. Old leather booths, animal heads on the walls including a massive bull moose, red velvet wallpaper, and hides acting as drapes—this is classic old-school steakhouse dining. They grill their meats over red oak, which lends a beautiful smokiness to them. Best known for a 14-ounce bull's-eye steak, this is a great throwback.

At **Shaw's Steak House & Tavern** (714 S. Broadway, 805/925-5862, lunch Mon.–Fri. 11:30 A.M.–4 P.M., dinner nightly 5–9 P.M., $20) old black-and-white photos line the walls of the heavy wood interior. Your main courses are prepared in plain sight, meaning the oak-wood grill sits behind a window and is visible from just about every table. Best known for their tri-tip, this is the kind of comfortable place where you're tempted to kick off your shoes and get totally relaxed. Shaw's has been a locals' spot for years, in part because the portions are large, and the tavern is often packed.

Italian

Housed in a little cottage, **Trattoria Uliveto** (285 S. Broadway, Orcutt, 805/934-4546, www.trattoriauliveto.com, Tues.–Sun. 11:30 A.M.–2:30 P.M. and 5–10 P.M., $18) has warmth and charm from its hardwood floors to its soft wood and exposed-beam ceilings. Yet it still feels slightly sophisticated. The food is dependable and authentic, and it's one of the few Italian places in the area.

Chinese

Ming Dynasty (2011 S. Broadway, 805/928-6881, Mon.–Thurs. 11 A.M.–9 P.M., Fri.–Sat. 11 A.M.–10 P.M., Sun. 11 A.M.–9 P.M., $12) is a hugely popular restaurant most notable for its buffet. Yes, it's kind of Americanized and has that usual Chinese decor that seems just slightly old, but it is great value, fresh and flavorful food, and it gets crowded. They do have à la carte options, but most everyone heads for the all-you-can-eat lunchtime buffet.

Sushi

It seems stunning to most everyone that in the midst of steaks and tacos is **Ichiban** (2011 S. Broadway, 805/614-9808, daily 11:30 A.M.–2 P.M. and 5–9 P.M., $20), a very good, though pricey, Japanese restaurant in the middle of Santa Maria. They offer attentive service, and the quality of the fish is uniformly very high. They survive because they serve some of the best sushi on the Central Coast.

Mexican

((El Paraíso (241 Town Center West, 805/614-2883, Mon.–Sat. 11 A.M.–10 P.M., $12) is a little mom-and-pop place with a fanatical following. The deep ocher walls and the multicolored tablecloths make it bright and festive inside. The owners, Gus and Rosie, will greet you by name, and if they don't know you when you arrive, you'll be on a first-name basis by the time you leave. Try the pozole, the flan—well, most anything. Their food is fresh and lacking heavy ingredients, and they will make vegetarian options if you like. The carne asada is tremendous, using lean thin beef. The chips and salsa and perfect, with crisp chips and a spicy house-made salsa. They are located on the opposite side of the Town Center Mall behind the defunct Mervyn's department store.

El Pueblito (603 S. Blosser, 805/349-1088, daily 6 A.M.–10 P.M., $10) has solid, dependable Mexican food, made with real ingredients. Sometimes the food can be a little greasy, but the shrimp fajitas are excellent. The restaurant is small but spacious enough, and the prices are lower than most other spots.

© MICHAEL CERVIN

Santa Maria has dozens of Mexican restaurants, but El Paraíso is one of the best.

The hefty wood tables and chairs at **La Hacienda** (312 W. Main St., 805/349-8820, daily 10 A.M.–8 P.M., $12) are spaced out so they seem like they fit inside this spacious restaurant. The food here is so authentic that you see lots of Mexicans, some wearing boots and cowboy hats. They have a few breakfast items like the Chilaquiles Don Jose, a mix of fried tortilla chips, eggs, onion, rice, beans, chicken, and salsa that will get your morning started off right. They also serve burgers and fries for those who don't like Mexican food—yes, there are a few!

Maya (110 S. Lincoln, 805/925-2841, Mon.–Thurs. 7 A.M.–9 P.M., Fri.–Sun. 7 A.M.–10 P.M., $12) has been faithfully serving Mexican food since 1966. The brightly painted wood chairs and tiled floors make it feel festive as well as intimate. In addition to the standard Mexican fare they offer a lot of fish dishes like the *pescado a la diabla,* a fillet with a bacon, ham, and onion sauce. They also have a great senior menu—a typical Mexican item, which includes rice and beans, for about six bucks.

Bakery

Voted the best in the area, **Gina's Piece of Cake** (307 Town Center East, 805/922-7866, www.ginaspieceofcake.com, Tues.–Fri. 7:30 A.M.–7 P.M., Sat. 7:30 A.M.–6 P.M., Sun. 7:30 A.M.–5 P.M. $3) is that great bakery where you can smell the sweet icing used for all the cakes they make. But more than just beautiful custom cakes, they bake brownies, cookies, muffins, éclairs, bagels, and breads in their little pink shop.

INFORMATION AND SERVICES
Maps and Tourist Information

The **Santa Maria Valley Chamber of Commerce and Visitor & Convention Bureau** is located at 614 South Broadway (800/331-3779, www.santamariavisitor.com).

Emergency Services

The **Marian Medical Center** (1400 E. Church St., 805/739-3000) offers emergency services. Should you have an emergency, however, dial 911. The **Santa Maria Police** are located at 222 East Cook Street (805/925-0951).

Newspapers and Media

There are two newspapers that compete for attention. The *Santa Maria Times* (805/739-2200, www.santamariatimes.com) is the daily paper available throughout Santa Maria. The *Santa Maria Sun* (805/347-1968, www.santamariasun.com) is the free alternative weekly, which publishes on Thursdays.

Postal Services

There are two post offices within the city (201 E. Battles Rd., 805/922-0321, and 142 Town Center East, at the Town Center Mall, 805/922-2972). Due to budget cutbacks, it's advisable to contact each office for specific hours and services.

Laundry

Check out **Stowell Center Launderland** (1511 S. Broadway, 805/922-2628) or **Paramount Cleaners and Laundry** (400 W. Main St., 805/922-7734). Both of these are on main thoroughfares.

GETTING THERE
By Car

If you're driving, Santa Maria is located directly off Highway 101. The major streets that have access from both north- and southbound Highway 101 are Betteravia, Main, and Stowell.

By Bus

An unstaffed stop for Amtrak motor coaches connecting to Amtrak trains in Santa Barbara and Hanford is located in Santa Maria at the International House of Pancakes (205

Nicholson Ave. at Main St.), just off Highway 101. Neither tickets, nor baggage, nor package express shipments are handled here. The nearest stations to Santa Maria offering these services are either north in San Luis Obispo or south in Santa Barbara.

By Train

The Amtrak Surfliner does not stop in Santa Maria. The closest train stops are 10 miles south in Guadalupe, or 10 miles north in Grover Beach in San Luis Obispo County.

By Air

The Santa Maria Airport (SMX, 805/922-1726, www.santamariaairport.com) is quite small, but a few airlines do fly here. It might be worth looking into if you can get a commuter connection from Los Angeles or Las Vegas.

GETTING AROUND
By Taxi

As spread out as Santa Maria is, you might find yourself in need of a taxi. **Santa Maria Yellow Cab Co.** (1125 E. Clark Ave., 805/937-7121), the **Yellow Cab Company of Santa Maria** (805/939-5454), and **Santa Maria Valley Taxi** (805/937-1121) are all available on short notice.

By Bus

Bus services are provided by the **Santa Maria Area Transit** (805/928-5624), which can accommodate both bikes and wheelchairs. For a complete schedule visit www.santa-maria.ca.us. Basic one-way fares are $1.25 and exact change is required.

SAN LUIS OBISPO AND PASO ROBLES

Locals call San Luis Obispo by its nickname, SLO, and a visit to the city will immediately impress upon anyone that slow is the order of the day. But the secret is out, and a bourgeoning wine industry and excellent quality of life means that SLO is starting to speed up. With a beautiful downtown fronted by Higuera Street and the accompanying river walk, San Luis Obispo is beginning to receive attention for its idyllic way of life, proximity to the ocean and mountains, wide-open tracts of land, and nearly ideal weather.

Paso Robles, 30 minutes north of San Luis Obispo off Highway 101, is the heart of the wine industry in San Luis Obispo county, and this cowboy town, home to fewer than 30,000 people, is garnering worldwide acclaim for its wines. Paso Robles is also a hop, skip, and a jump from the coast, where nearly a million people flock to the tiny hamlet of San Simeon on the rugged Pacific Coast to visit Hearst Castle. But El Paso de Robles, known simply as Paso by locals, is slowly eking its way out of its Western roots and embracing a more cosmopolitan vibe. Artisanal cheese makers, abalone farmers, high-end restaurants and wineries, and a thriving (if competitive) olive oil industry share the downtown with renegade dive bars and local mom-and-pop venues. You're just as likely to see a tractor heading through town as you are a limo packed with eager wine tasters.

PLANNING YOUR TIME

Since San Luis Obispo is called SLO, that's really how it should be explored, slowly. You can get the feel of SLO in a weekend, but a

© MICHAEL CERVIN

HIGHLIGHTS

Higuera Street: Many of the original turn-of-the-20th-century buildings are still in operation on this main boulevard in San Luis Obispo. Creek-side restaurants and shops make this the ideal Central Coast street (page 212).

Bubblegum Alley: To some, this alley covered with used chewing gum that's been there since the 1960s is urban pop art. Make a statement and add your chew to the collection (page 214).

Madonna Inn: The flamboyant decor is the highlight at the Madonna Inn, which is overrun with pink kitsch. It's a unique place to stay, but also a fun spot for lunch, dinner, or even just a photo op (page 215).

Paso Robles Downtown Square and City Park: This Norman Rockwell-esque grassy one-block town park and square complete with mature trees, picnic tables, horseshoes, a gazebo, and a 1910 historic museum at its center is ground zero for all things social in Paso Robles (page 236).

Hunt Cellars: Hunt Cellars owner David Hunt is legally blind, which has aided in his winemaking and blending abilities. His lavish, textured wines are not to be missed (page 242).

Denner Vineyards: Stellar architecture and wines come together at Denner Vineyards. A gracefully modulated tasting room complements the layered and inviting wines, all with beautiful views of rolling hills of vines (page 243).

Eberle Winery: Eberle Winery was the harbinger to the Paso Robles wine industry when it opened its doors in 1973. The most-

LOOK FOR **(** TO FIND RECOMMENDED SIGHTS, ACTIVITIES, DINING, AND LODGING.

awarded winery in the nation, it continues to produce wines that showcase the best of the region (page 245).

Ancient Peaks Winery: Their vineyard was planted in an upraised ancient ocean-floor bed, where the ocean's inherent minerals and nutrients aid the complexity of their wines, providing nuanced flavors (page 248).

SAN LUIS OBISPO

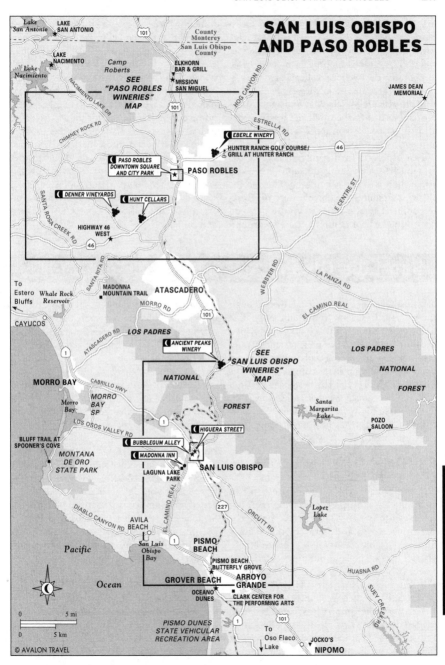

SAN LUIS OBISPO AND PASO ROBLES

Lake San Antonio
LAKE SAN ANTONIO
LAKE SAN ANTONIO
101
County Monterey
San Luis Obispo County
ELKHORN BAR & GRILL
LAKE NACIMIENTO
Lake Nacimiento
Camp Roberts
MISSION SAN MIGUEL
HOG CANYON RD
JAMES DEAN MEMORIAL

SEE "PASO ROBLES WINERIES" MAP

NACIMIENTO LAKE DR
101
ESTRELLA RD
EBERLE WINERY
46
CHIMNEY ROCK RD
HUNTER RANCH GOLF COURSE/ GRILL AT HUNTER RANCH

PASO ROBLES DOWNTOWN SQUARE AND CITY PARK
PASO ROBLES
E CENTRE ST

SANTA ROSA CREEK RD
DENNER VINEYARDS
HUNT CELLARS
HIGHWAY 46 WEST
46

SANTA RITA RD
WEBSTER RD
LA PANZA RD

To Estero Bluffs
Whale Rock Reservoir
MADONNA MOUNTAIN TRAIL
ATASCADERO
MORRO RD
EL CAMINO REAL

CAYUCOS
1
ATASCADERO RD
101
LOS PADRES
ANCIENT PEAKS WINERY
SEE "SAN LUIS OBISPO WINERIES" MAP
LOS PADRES

MORRO BAY
CABRILLO HWY
MORRO BAY SP
NATIONAL
FOREST
NATIONAL
Santa Margarita Lake
FOREST

Morro Bay
LOS OSOS VALLEY RD
1
FOREST
POZO SALOON

BLUFF TRAIL AT SPOONER'S COVE
MONTANA DE ORO STATE PARK
HIGUERA STREET
BUBBLEGUM ALLEY
MADONNA INN
LAGUNA LAKE PARK
SAN LUIS OBISPO

DIABLO CANYON RD
AVILA BEACH
EL CAMINO REAL
227
ORCUTT RD
Lopez Lake

Pacific
San Luis Obispo Bay
1
PISMO BEACH
HUASNA RD

Ocean
PISMO BEACH BUTTERFLY GROVE
GROVER BEACH
ARROYO GRANDE
SUEY CREEK RD

0   5 mi
0   5 km
© AVALON TRAVEL
OCEANO DUNES
CLARK CENTER FOR THE PERFORMING ARTS

PISMO DUNES STATE VEHICULAR RECREATION AREA
1
To Oso Flaco Lake
JOCKO'S
NIPOMO

SAN LUIS OBISPO

long three-day weekend is even better to explore and get into the groove of this laid-back town, stroll the streets, and see the variety of sights. The summer months see more tourists, but because the two local colleges aren't in session then there are actually fewer people. Ideal times to visit are March–May and September–November due to the moderate weather that allows you to play outdoors, hiking, biking, and just hanging out at the beach.

Paso Robles is further inland, making the area much warmer during the summer months; triple-digit weather is common. Conversely, the winter months dip down toward the freezing point. The best times to visit, unless you prefer the heat of summer, are also around March–May and September–November. Keep in mind that September in Paso Robles is harvest time for the wineries. It's still usually quite warm, and oftentimes you can be where the winemaking action is as the wineries are busy crushing grapes. Paso Robles can best be explored over a weekend. If wine is a focal point, however, you'll want to visit for at least three or four days—or do a one-day wine tour for a quick overview of the wineries in the area. Weekends are the most crowded at the tasting rooms, so you may want to visit wineries on a weekday since many tasting rooms are open seven days a week. If you have a particular winery you're especially eager to visit, plan ahead and find out their hours.

San Luis Obispo

San Luis Obispo is not a coastal town, though the water is less than 10 minutes away. The beauty of its location is that it offers everything within a 15-minute drive: great restaurants, access to hiking and biking trails, wineries, wide-open space, and an ideal climate. Since it is inland, if it's foggy at the beach, more often than not San Luis is warmer and sunny. If it's in the triple digits in Paso Robles, San Luis tends to be cooler. It's just one of those spots with great weather.

SIGHTS
(Higuera Street
Higuera Street is the defining street in San Luis Obispo, and pretty much everything revolves around it. Mature trees flank the charming street, and many of the historic turn-of-the-20th-century storefronts are still in place. There are no large buildings on Higuera Street, which creates a very open and walkable space. It's also a one-way street, which means traffic and congestion are reduced. The street follows the same path as San Luis Creek, making Higuera Street an ideal spot for dining and strolling. Shops and restaurants overlook the creek, and during the spring and summer

months these are the best spots to be. The creek is accessible from several points and kids often play in the freshwater. Bubblegum Alley is on the 700 block, and just across the creek is the mission. Higuera itself even has a book written about it, *San Luis Obispo: 100 Years of Downtown Business: Higuera Street,* which was published in 2007. It shows how much the surroundings have changed, but how little the storefronts have changed.

Mission San Luis Obispo de Tolosa
The Mission San Luis Obispo de Tolosa (751 Palm St., 805/781-8220, www.missionsanluisobospo.org, daily 10 A.M.–4 P.M., suggested donation $3) was founded in 1769. On September 7–8 of that year Gaspar de Portolá and his expedition party traveled through the San Luis Obispo area on the way to rediscover the Monterey Bay. The expedition's diarist, Padre Juan Crespi, recorded the name given to this area by the soldiers as Llano de los Osos, or "the bear plain," as there used to be a preponderance of bears in the area. In fact, Los Osos, just west of San Luis Obispo, still holds that name. In 1770, Father Serra founded the second mission, San Carlos Borromeo, in

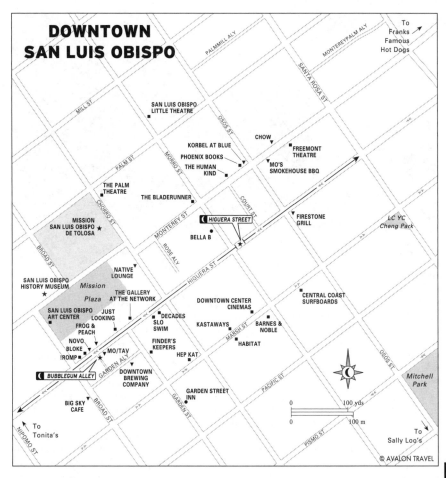

DOWNTOWN SAN LUIS OBISPO

Monterey, which was moved to Carmel the following year. As supplies dwindled in 1772 at the four missions in existence at the time, the people faced starvation. Remembering the bear plain, a hunting expedition was sent to San Luis Obispo to bring back food in the summer of 1772, and over 25 mule loads of bear meat was sent up coast to the waiting mission. It was after this that Father Serra decided that San Luis Obispo would be the ideal place for a fifth mission. The region had abundant supplies of food and water, the climate was mild, and the local Chumash were very friendly. Given these conditions, Serra set out on a journey to reach the bear plain and on September 1, 1772, he celebrated the first mass with a simple cross erected near San Luis Creek.

After Father Serra left, the task remained to actually build the mission, which was accomplished primarily by the hard work of the local Chumash. The church and priest's residence were built by 1794, and other structures made up the primitive mission in the early days, namely storerooms, residences for single women, barracks, and mills. The mission also used the land for farming and raising livestock, since the

© MICHAEL CERVIN

Higuera Street

mission padres, soldiers, and indigenous people depended upon any and all produced goods, including vegetables, fruits, nuts, and meats, for their survival. Expansion proceeded for a few years due to the prosperity of the mission, but those days were numbered and Mission San Luis, like all the other missions, gradually fell into disrepair. When Mexico won her independence from Spain in 1821, the missions were secularized and often mission lands were sold off. Governor Pio Pico sold the San Luis Obispo Mission to Captain John Wilson for a mere $510 in 1845. The building served multiple functions, including jail and first county courthouse.

Today the mission fronts Mission Square, facing the creek, and Higuera Street. The courtyard is a popular place for small gatherings and festivals. The interior of the mission is minimally decorated, mainly hand painted, and is long and tall. Still an active church, it holds mass each day. While the church itself is modest looking, the interior grounds, also rather simple, are quite pretty, with flowers and hedges and a small arbor. The museum portion includes black-and-white photographs and a limited collection of furniture and accessories from mission life.

◖ Bubblegum Alley

Bubblegum started mysteriously appearing on the walls of Garden Alley, on the 700 block of Higuera Street, in the 1960s, with a few people defacing the exposed brick with their chewed-up bubblegum. Some assumed it was college kids disposing of their used-up wads. Fast forward to today, and Bubblegum Alley is a sticky and unusual landmark in San Luis Obispo.

It doesn't resemble anything but what it is: tens of thousands of wads of multicolored chewing gum squished one on top of another in a masticated mosaic some 70 feet long and 15 feet high. At the top of the brick-walled alley, the gobs have been blackened by age and weather. This might be sickening to some, to others it is urban pop art, a unique expression of individuality. Some people seek to make a statement, spelling out their love or their hopes, while others merely press tasteless gum onto the wall. It's not uncommon to hear people walk by and use adjectives like "disgusting" and "gross" to describe the alley. There are gum dispensers on either side of the alley; for a mere 25 cents, you can get a piece of gum to add your own chewed-up message.

© MICHAEL CERVIN

Bubblegum Alley

C Madonna Inn

The Madonna Inn (100 Madonna Rd., 805/543-3000, www.madonnainn.com) is a one-of-a-kind sight. It would be considered kitschy if it was planned today, but it wasn't: The first 12 rooms were completed in December 1958. An additional 28 rooms were quickly built, making a total of 40 rooms available to travelers. Pink was the color of choice when the inn was built.

Today there are 110 unique rooms, each decorated wildly differently to suit many individual tastes. There are rock rooms, waterfall showers, rock fireplaces, European fixtures, and fine furnishings, to name a few features. It's truly an experience to stay here and shouldn't be missed, in part because the service is routinely excellent.

The Madonna Inn sits on approximately 2,200 acres, and the large rocks used in the construction came from these surrounding acres. Some of the larger rocks weigh in excess of 200 tons each and are clearly visible on the exterior and in some of the rooms. Then there is the well-known men's bathroom downstairs,

where the urinal is built out of rock and a waterfall flushes away the waste. Men routinely stand guard so their mothers, sisters, wives, and female friends can go in to gawk at the unusual bathroom. The leaded glass work throughout the inn and the etched-glass windows in the coffee shop were custom made. The leaded-glass inserts in the windowed area facing the large fireplace illustrate each of the various Madonna enterprises of construction, lumber, and cattle. The hand-carved marble balustrade in the Gold Rush dining room came from Hearst Castle. All the copper and brass items were etched from original designs and fabricated on-site. The 28-foot gold tree fixture in the main dining room was made from electrical conduit left over from building projects, as well as from left-over remnants of copper. Several wood carvers were brought in for the specialty work of hand carving the doors, beams, railings, and the many other carved adornments you see everywhere.

And then there is the pink, pink everywhere—it was Alex Madonna's favorite color. The gregarious Alex Madonna made his money in the construction business, something he learned when he served in the Army Corps of Engineers. After he left the service he built much of Highway 101 along the Central Coast. He was known to be flamboyant, effervescent, and larger than life, and he never shied away from the bold use of pink. Nowhere is this more robustly expressed than the beyond Vegas-style dining room. Of course it's crazy, but it's also unique, and has been a landmark since the day it opened. Most people who visit the Madonna don't stay here, which is a shame, since it's a really cool place to stay. But they stop by to marvel at the over-the-top decor, maybe have lunch or dinner, get their photos taken, and head on their way. It's worthy of a stop, however brief, and you won't soon forget it.

San Luis Obispo History Museum

The San Luis Obispo History Museum (696 Monterey St., 805/543-0638, www.slochs.org, Wed.–Sun. 10 A.M.–4 P.M., free) is housed in a Carnegie Library from 1904, and was designed

© MICHAEL CERVIN

the kitschy Madonna Inn

by the same architect who designed the Carnegie Library in Paso Robles. The museum itself is pretty simple, with a few artifacts and lots of photographs detailing the visual history of the area. Just behind the building on Broad Street is a small portion of wall, the only remaining original wall from the mission dated to 1793. It's covered with moss now, but gives an idea of how the original buildings were made.

Pismo Beach Butterfly Grove
The Monarch butterfly grove in Pismo (Hwy. 1 just south of North Pismo State Beach Campground, 805/473-7220, www.monarch-butterfly.org, daily 24 hours, docents available 10 A.M.–4 P.M.) sees the return of butterflies each November–February, when tens of thousands of Monarch butterflies migrate to this small grove of eucalyptus trees near the beach to mate. On average there are about 30,000 of these silent winged creatures, and the trees are often transformed into brilliant shades of orange after their 2,000-mile journey to get here. This is the largest of the four gathering spots for the Monarchs in California. Docents staff the area

between 10 A.M. and 4 P.M. and give brief and fascinating talks about the butterflies and their very unique but short lives. Talks are given daily at 11 A.M. and 2 P.M. during season. It's free to walk into the grove and free to hear the docents, and there's a short boardwalk that leads to the beach near a large picnic area near the low sand dunes and cypress trees near the water's edge. Parking is along the side of the road, so use caution when crossing the busy street.

BEACHES
Avila Beach
Avila Beach (San Miguel and Front Sts.) has a nice pier and large wide, flat beaches, and tends to have a more family vibe, probably because of the swing sets right on the sand facing the ocean. There are restroom facilities on the beach side of the street and plenty of food and coffee options in the sherbet-colored buildings on the other of the boardwalk. The bay is protected, therefore the water tends to be warmer and gentler, and the weather here is almost always nicer than any other place on the Central Coast.

© MICHAEL CERVIN

The 1904 Carnegie Library is home to the San Luis Obispo History Museum.

Pismo Beach

Pismo Beach (Pomeroy and Cypress Sts.) is how we imagine classic 1960s California: friendly people, great waves, low-key and easygoing. Pismo still has that allure and the beaches, best accessed by heading down Pomeroy straight towards the pier, are flat, long, and wide stretches of sand. There are plenty of restrooms, food, and parking nearby, and the pier is the focal point of this beach.

Oceano Dunes

Just south of San Luis Obispo and Pismo Beach are the Oceano Dunes (928 Pacific Blvd., 805/473-7220, www.parks.ca.gov), vast sand dunes that stretch for 18 miles from Pismo Beach south to Guadalupe in Santa Barbara County. This is one of the few places left in America with this amount of dunes covering so great a distance. And some of these are not small dunes, but large and domineering, reaching 20 feet or more. The benefit to visiting Oceano Dunes is that it's relatively uncrowded and there are flat, wide beaches. It can be breezier here at times, but there is also a moonscape beauty to the beaches.

THE PISMO CLAM

Pismo Beach was once nearly synonymous with the word *clam*, as there used to be a thriving clam industry here. Even before the arrival of the Europeans, the Chumash Indians made use of the clams, using the meat for food and the shells for decorative arts.

From the turn of the 20th century until about World War II, the clam industry as defined by Pismo Beach, part of Morro Bay, and into Monterey was substantial. And though the clam population is smaller these days, due to over-fishing and natural predators like otters, the Pismo clam still has good years and bad years. But clamming isn't what it used to be, and though Pismo Beach has its share of clam chowder, few people recall the association between Pismo Beach and its clams.

SAN LUIS OBISPO

The Oceano Dunes are also home to a vehicular recreation area, meaning you can actually drive on the beach in certain parts, though you do need a State of California license for an Off-Highway Vehicle. There are very specific rules and regulations for this section of beach, and it's best to visit www.parks.ca.gov for detailed information.

WINERIES

Though Paso Robles is the undisputed leading wine region in the county, the San Luis area, which includes the Edna Valley and Arroyo Grande, has a diverse number of wineries. Don't dismiss this region, thinking that Paso is the end all, be all. There are some excellent wines coming out of this area, and any exploration of the wine region needs to include San Luis Obispo.

Wood Winery

Taste wine and watch the sunset at the Wood Winery (480 Front St., Avila Beach, 805/595-9663, www.wildwoodwine.com, daily 10:30 A.M.–6 P.M., tasting fee $5) on Avila Beach boardwalk. They are licensed to sell wines by the glass, and they offer cheese plates and patio seating. There's a love of syrah here, but also a wide selection of sangiovese, cabernet sauvignon, chardonnay, and zinfandel. The vineyards are at the foot of the Cuesta Grade, just north of downtown San Luis. The tasting room is one of the few oceanfront tasting rooms in the entire state, and from the tasting bar you can simply turn around to enjoy the views. The room is decorated in soft aquatic tones and local artwork hangs on the walls. It's so relaxing here you may not want to leave.

Per Bacco Cellars

The Per Bacco Cellars (1850 Calle Joaquin, 805/787-0485, www.perbaccocellars.com, daily 11 A.M.–5 P.M., tasting fee $5) tasting room, located on a historic ranch property, sits a stone's throw off the 101 freeway near San Luis Obispo. It isn't your typical well-appointed tasting room. In fact, it's not really a tasting room at all, but is the actual winery,

filled with barrels and fermentation equipment. They have added a small bar area to serve guests and tacked a few paintings on the walls, but the surroundings are still very industrial. The focus is on a restrained style of winemaking, one that allows the nuances of the grape to shine through. Small batches of pinot noir, chardonnay, syrah, petite sirah, and pinot grigio come out of this well-regarded winery.

Edna Valley Vineyards

A stalwart of the area, Edna Valley Vineyards (2585 Biddle Ranch Rd., 805/544-5855, www.ednavalleyvineyard.com, daily 10 A.M.–5 P.M., tasting fee $5–10) benefits from its namesake region. The large tasting room and panoramic views to the hills (dormant volcanoes known as the Nine Sisters) in the distance with near views to the vineyards are stunning. They have a sizable number of gift items for sale in the large tasting room. There's also a demonstration vineyard out front, a place to examine different trellising techniques and how those methods affect how the grapes grow. Zinfandel, chardonnay, syrah, and pinot noir are the main wines produced here.

Talley Vineyards

The name Talley has been associated with farming in San Luis Obispo County since 1948. As you drive towards Lopez Lake you'll immediately notice Talley Vineyards (3031 Lopez Dr., 805/489-0446, www.talleyvineyards.com, daily 10:30 A.M.–4:30 P.M., tasting fee $8–15) on your left. The Mediterranean/Tuscan-style tasting room sits squarely in the middle of flat cropland, the surrounding hillsides covered in vines. A three-tiered fountain stands like a sentinel in the courtyard. The interior of the spacious tasting room features floor-to-ceiling glass, a horseshoe-shaped tasting bar, and high vaulted ceilings. You can often purchase some of the fruit and vegetables that grow on the property, including bell peppers, zucchini, tomatoes, and spinach. Pinot noir, chardonnay, syrah, cabernet sauvignon, and pinot gris are the main wines here, but they are most well known for producing excellent chardonnay

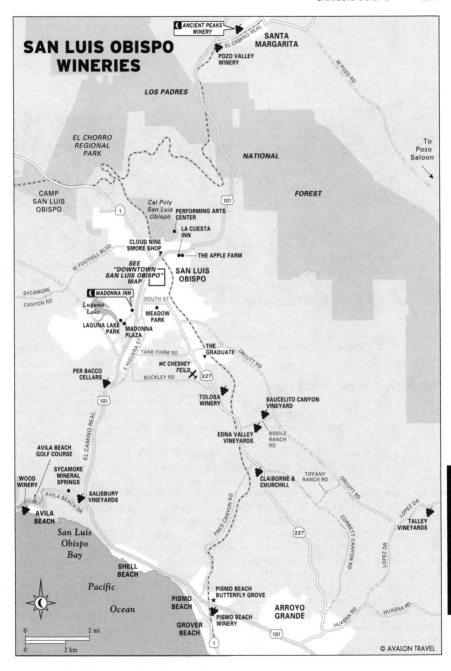

SAN LUIS OBISPO WINERIES

ANCIENT PEAKS WINERY

EL CAMINO REAL

SANTA MARGARITA

POZO VALLEY WINERY

W POZO RD

LOS PADRES

EL CHORRO REGIONAL PARK

NATIONAL

To Pozo Saloon

CAMP SAN LUIS OBISPO

FOREST

101

Cal Poly San Luis Obispo   PERFORMING ARTS CENTER

LA CUESTA INN

CLOUD NINE SMOKE SHOP

THE APPLE FARM

W FOOTHILL BLVD

SEE "DOWNTOWN SAN LUIS OBISPO" MAP

SAN LUIS OBISPO

SYCAMORE CANYON RD

MADONNA INN

SOUTH ST

Luguna Lake

MEADOW PARK

LAGUNA LAKE PARK

MADONNA PLAZA

TANK FARM RD

THE GRADUATE

ORCUTT RD

PER BACCO CELLARS

MC CHESNEY FEILD

BUCKLEY RD

227

101

S HIGUERA ST

TOLOSA WINERY

SAUCELITO CANYON VINEYARD

EDNA VALLEY VINEYARDS

BIDDLE RANCH RD

EL CAMINO REAL

AVILA BEACH GOLF COURSE

SYCAMORE MINERAL SPRINGS

CLAIBORNE & CHURCHILL

TIFFANY RANCH RD

ORCUTT RD

WOOD WINERY

SALISBURY VINEYARDS

AVILA BEACH DR

PRICE CANYON RD

227

CORBETT CANYON RD

LOPEZ DR

TALLEY VINEYARDS

AVILA BEACH

San Luis Obispo Bay

LOPEZ DR

SHELL BEACH

Pacific Ocean

PISMO BEACH BUTTERFLY GROVE

ARROYO GRANDE

PISMO BEACH

PISMO BEACH WINERY

HUASNA RD

HUASNA RD

GROVER BEACH

1

101

0   2 mi
0   2 km

© AVALON TRAVEL

Saucelito Canyon Vineyard

and pinot noir. Talley also has a second label, Bishop's Peak, a line of very good-value wines for under 20 bucks.

Saucelito Canyon Vineyard

Saucelito Canyon Vineyard (3080 Biddle Ranch Rd., 805/543-2111, www.saucelitocanyon.com, daily 10 A.M.–5 P.M., tasting fee $6) has one of those unique stories better suited to the History Channel than the pages of a guidebook. The parcel of land, located past Lake Lopez down a three-mile gated road, is so far removed from anything, that during Prohibition federal agents could never shut the winery down simply because they couldn't find it. The three acres of zinfandel originally planted in 1880 are still producing fruit to this day. The tasting room is small, and though it's not made for more than 15 people, it has the necessary ingredients for a good time, namely a friendly staff, very good wine, and a relaxed, intimate environment. There are even old photos from the turn-of-the-20th-century showing the old vine zinfandel and homestead. Outside there are a few tables for relaxing. Zinfandel is

king here, though they are making other varieties such as sauvignon blanc, tempranillo, merlot, and cabernet sauvignon. They open their historic vineyard property about once a year for the public to view the centuries-old vines. The canyon is remote, beautiful, and serene, and pulsates with the history of men and women working the land.

Tolosa Winery

Imagine James Bond creating a tasting room, and you'll get an idea of what the interior of Tolosa Winery (4910 Edna Rd., 805/782-0500, www.tolosawinery.com, daily 11 A.M.–5 P.M., tasting fee $5) is like: cork floors, stainless steel ceilings, glass bar, wood panels, and back lighting, all sleek and sophisticated. A plasma screen displays pictures of recent events and the winemaking process, while the LCD screen displays up-to-date specials and wine club information. There's even ambient music playing throughout the tasting room, patio, halls, and bathroom. The tasting room looks out over the fermentation tanks of gleaming polished stainless steel. Guests can take a self-guided tour through the facility as well. Stay and picnic at their tranquil outdoor picnic area, or play a round of bocce ball as you soak in the peaceful surroundings. The focus is on chardonnay and pinot noir, but you'll also find merlot, syrah, viognier, and even grenache blanc.

Salisbury Vineyards

This 103-year-old schoolhouse, now a tasting room and art gallery, underwent a historic interior renovation and opened in the spring of 2005 with a new lease on life. As you enter the tasting room at Salisbury Vineyards (6985 Ontario Rd., 805/595-9463, www.salisburyvineyards.com, daily 11 A.M.–6 P.M., tasting fee $5), you're immediately struck by the openness of the space and the copious amount of wood, most notably the original hardwood floors. A sign by the front door warns that stiletto heels can have a detrimental effect on their old floors, and to walk gently, but that everyone is still welcome. Salisbury is aiming for the schoolhouse to serve a multitude of diverse functions, not simply as a tasting room. It's also part art gallery, presenting artwork from around the globe that rotates every 8–10 weeks. Chardonnay, syrah, zinfandel, and cabernet sauvignon are the main wines produced here.

Claiborne & Churchill

Claiborne & Churchill (2649 Carpenter Canyon Rd., Edna Valley, 805/544-4066, www.claibornechurchill.com, daily 11 A.M.–5 P.M., tasting fee $5) winery was started in 1983, inspired by the wines of Alsace, France, even though these types of wine were not often made in California, let alone San Luis Obispo County. Claiborne & Churchill decided to specialize in premium dry wines made from Riesling, gewürztraminer, and pinot gris grapes, as well as pinot noir from nearby vineyards. Not wanting to limit their portfolio, they also produce small lots of other wines, including a dry muscat, chardonnay, syrah, cabernet sauvignon, sparkling rosé, and a port-style wine. Claiborne & Churchill is still a small family-owned winery, and their facility

is constructed out of straw bales and covered in plaster, making it unique among wineries in the United States. Using these sustainable materials has greatly reduced their cooling costs. However, when you visit the winery, you won't notice, as it looks like any interior. They do have a small section of part of a wall that shows how the bales fit together and gives more information about this unique architectural approach.

Pismo Beach Winery

It took nearly 10 years for the dream of two brothers to become a reality when Pismo Beach Winery (271B Five Cities Dr., 805/773-9463, www.pismobeachwinery.com, daily noon–5 P.M., tasting fee $10) finally opened its doors. Located across from the outlet mall, this urban winery is making about 1,500 cases of wine; their portfolio consists of chardonnay, cabernet sauvignon, zinfandel, barbera, pinot noir, and petite syrah. This is a small, family-owned operation, and the corrugated metal exterior belies what's inside. The tasting room is bright and open, with soft yellow walls and wood door trim and tasting bar, and views into the barrel room. There's a low-key vibe here, and usually someone from the family is behind the counter pouring their wines.

ENTERTAINMENT AND EVENTS
Nightlife
BARS AND CLUBS

San Luis is a college town, and the college bar is **Frog & Peach** (728 Higuera St., 805/595-3764, daily noon–2 A.M.), a narrow, small space that's usually packed on the weekends. When the bands start playing it gets warm, but the outside patio overlooking the creek is a way to cool down and escape the throngs. Though they call themselves a pub, it's more a pure bar, with basic worn wood and booths that face the long bar. Tuesday evenings are pint nights. If you're looking for a younger crowd, this is the spot.

Koberl at Blue (998 Monterey St., 805/783-1135, www.epkoberl.com, daily 4–11 P.M.) has white tablecloths, exposed brick walls, and more sophisticated flair than Frog & Peach. There are still beers—a wide variety of European brews, in fact—and a stellar wine list. But they are most well known for their martini options—locals know it's one of the best places to grab a signature martini after work.

Mo/Tav (725 Higuera St., 805/541-8733, www.motherstavern.com, daily 11:30 A.M.– 1:30 A.M.) used to be called Mother's Tavern, but this is not your mother's tavern. In addition to bottle service and a dance floor, they have karaoke every Sunday and Monday and DJs spinning dance tunes the rest of the week. The long wood bar with a massive round mirror echoes the upscale saloon feel of this very popular place.

Native Lounge (1023 Chorro, 805/547-5544, www.nativelounge.com, Tues.–Sun. 10 P.M.–2 A.M.) is one of the hippest looking places in SLO, with sleek lines and minimalist furnishings. It's the trendy place for the younger crowd. DJs spin nightly and the place crackles with bottle service and cool drinks. The patio fronts the creek, for those needing some air or just wanting to be seen.

LIVE-MUSIC VENUES

The Graduate (900 Industrial Way, 805/541-0969, www.slograd.com, cover $5–10) is aimed, as the name implies, at the college and post-college crowd. There's College night on Wednesday, salsa and merengue on Friday, country on Thursday and various other events in between, and a large dance floor with a bar and restaurant. Live bands as well as DJs provide a a cool place to hang out.

The **Pozo Saloon** (90 W. Pozo Rd., 805/438-4225, www.pozosaloon.com) is one of the best venues for live music on the entire Central Coast. The problem is, it's not near anything—seriously. Seventeen miles off the highway in the all but forgotten town of Pozo, you'll come across this 3,000-seat outdoor venue. It may seem unknown to most, but many big-name acts have performed in Pozo, like the Black Crowes, Ziggy Marley, and Merle Haggard. If you decide to go with general admission, you need to bring your own

chair or blanket. Cell phones don't work out here and there's only one restaurant. It gets packed, in part because it's such a cool venue, away from everything, out among low hills and oak trees. Always check the schedule, as you don't want to head all the way out there on the wrong day.

For a step back in time, the Madonna Inn's **Gold Rush Steakhouse** (100 Madonna Rd., 805/784-2433, www.madonnainn.com) has live music and dancing Thursday–Monday beginning about 7:30 P.M. There is no cover, and they have mainly swing and ballroom music. There's an older crowd here, but it's festive and everyone's in a good mood, in part because it's hard to be unhappy in the vibrant pink interior. You don't have to dance, of course—just watch and listen if you like.

At the **Downtown Brewing Company** (1119 Garden St., 805/543-1843, www.dtbrew.com) there is an actual stage, with the best acoustics in town. They showcase a diverse range of music here, including acoustic, rock, country, and blues. They serve food in the upstairs portion, and there are pool tables, while the downstairs acts like a true entertainment venue; it holds 300 people. Shows begin at 8 P.M. and run most nights of the week. When they do have cover charges, which is dependent on the band, they run about $5.

Performing Arts

The **Performing Arts Center** (1 Grand Ave., 805/756-7222, www.pacslo.org) is a catch-all title for an arts complex that houses a concert hall of just under 1,300 seats, a pavilion, and a smaller theater of just under 500 seats. The complex is located on the edge of the Cal Poly campus and is the stop for concerts, theater, the San Luis Obispo symphony, and performances by Cal Poly students.

The **San Luis Obispo Little Theatre** (880 Morro St., 805/781-3889, www.slolittletheatre.org) is, indeed, a little theater of about 100 seats. It's one of the oldest continuously running community theaters in the nation. In 1947 they began with the oft-staged *Blithe Spirit,* and continue to perform well-known

the Performing Arts Center in San Luis Obispo

musicals and dramas as well as some original works. Over 400 productions later, having used more than 20 locations around the county, they finally found a home in the former SLO County Public Library. Ticket prices average $35.

Clark Center for the Performing Arts (487 Fair Oaks Ave., Arroyo Grande, 805/489-9444, www.clarkcenter.org) consists of two state-of-the-art theaters, the 617-seat Forbes Hall and the 120-seat Studio Theatre. Though it's on the high school campus, it's not what you might think—this is a sophisticated theater. Big names come here, in part for the intimacy, including jazz, comedy, and theatrical productions.

Cinema

The Palm Theatre (817 Palm St., 805/541-5161, www.thepalmtheatre.com) is the independent and foreign film theater here, located in what was the Chinatown portion of the city. It's the only locally owned theater left in town and, as a side note, it's solar powered.

For traditional films in a traditional setting, the seven-screen **Downtown Center Cinemas** (888 Marsh St., 805/564-8600) are located below the mall. This is the spot for current releases and blockbusters.

The Fremont (1025 Monterey St., 805/541-2141) is a great 1940s-vintage theater, but the ticket prices head towards $10, making it the most expensive place in town. There's an emphasis on re-releases here and not current films.

Festivals and Events
SPRING

Each March in Pismo Beach, the **World of Pinot Noir** (805/489-1758, www.worldofpinotnoir.com), an all pinot noir event, is held on the bluffs overlooking the ocean. This three-day event is filled with seminars about growing conditions and regions, and there's a vintage tasting and a chef's challenge. The pinot noirs are not exclusive to California; every year pinot producers come from Oregon and Europe as well. It's a great focused time on one varietal and there are plenty of tastings in which to educate your palate.

If wine is not your thing, there is the **California Festival of Beers** (www.hospiceslo.org, tickets

The Fremont is a great place to see vintage films.

$75–200) held each May at the Avila Beach Resort. For over two decades, this collection of nearly 50 brewers from the West Coast and beyond has gathered near the ocean in Avila Beach to celebrate all things beer. Get your pretzel necklace, enjoy the live music and the golf tournament, and know that the proceeds from the event support Hospice of San Luis Obispo. This event always sells out.

SUMMER

Similar to its cousin in Santa Barbara, the **I Madonnari** (805/541-6294, www.aiacentralcoast.org) festival appears each year in September at the plaza of the Old Mission downtown, which is transformed with colorful large-scale street paintings. The 200 squares are divvied up and the labor-intensive work of chalk painting commences. Festival hours are daily 10 A.M.–6 P.M., and admission is free. Street painting has a long tradition in cities in Western Europe and probably started in Italy in the 16th century. The artists who use chalk to draw on the street are known as *madonnari,* or "Madonna painters,"

because they originally reproduced icons of the Madonna.

FALL

It's no time to clam up at the annual **Pismo Beach Clam Festival** (195 Pomeroy St. at the Pismo Beach pier, 805/773-4382, www.pismochamber.com) each October. The parade comes first, then clam digging in the sand, and, of course, the clam chowder cook-off, where local restaurants strenuously attempt to defeat whoever was top clam the year before. There's live music and vendors with arts and crafts and wine-tasting. This has been going on for over six decades, and the Pismo namesake is both celebrated and eaten.

The **City to the Sea Half Marathon** (www.citytothesea.org) is still the best running event in SLO. It starts in downtown SLO and heads all the way to the ocean in Pismo Beach each October when the weather is just about perfect for a long run. This is one of the largest races in the area and draws all manner of runners, from experienced to novice, to attempt the 13-mile route.

© KATHY GRUVER

author Michael Cervin at the City to the Sea Half Marathon

The Central Coast is home to lots of writers, and once a year they get to showcase all things literary at the **Central Coast Book and Author Festival** (805/546-1392, www.ccbookfesti-val.org). This festival is by no means just local writers, however. In addition to public readings for kids and adults, the one-day fall event takes over Mission Plaza with dance performances and even cooking demonstrations. There are seminars by authors and illustrators, used and new books for sale, and booths to browse and meet your new favorite writer. It's free to attend.

WINTER

Restaurant Month (800/634-1414, www.san-luisobispocounty.com) is a month-long culinary celebration in which about 40 restaurants throughout the county participate in showing off their styles. For 30 days, each restaurant serves a three-course meal for just 30 bucks. It's a great way to explore new dining options and has been a huge success. If you're visiting in January and you happen to like food, you'll have a breadth of options to explore at reasonable prices.

SHOPPING
Shopping Malls
Madonna Plaza (221 Madonna Rd., 805/544-3900) has all the big-name stores, including Kohl's, Starbucks, Best Buy, Borders, Sears, Bed Bath & Beyond, Forever 21, and others, all set in an architecturally friendly upgrade from the tedious malls that dominate California, with plenty of parking.

Prime Outlets (333 Five Cities Dr., Pismo Beach, 805/773-4661, www.primeoutlets.com, Mon.–Sat. 10 A.M.–9 P.M., Sun. 10 A.M.–7 P.M.) features many outlet store with recognizable names: Nike, Tommy Hilfiger, Calvin Klein, Harry and David—123 stores in all. Perhaps the best thing to be said for this type of shopping is that you're on the Central Coast, and therefore you've got pretty good weather. It's a close drive to the beach and very good restaurants after a day of shopping.

Bookstores
Many bookstores in San Luis Obispo have closed, but **Phoenix** (990 Monterey St., 805/543-3591, Mon–Sat. 10 A.M.–9 P.M., Sun.

SAN LUIS OBISPO

11 A.M.–9 P.M.) still has a large selection of used books. It's actually two stores joined by a doorway, with wall-to-wall books, and some just stacked on the floor. The upstairs section has world histories like Ireland and Wales, suggesting a good selection in any category. There is one small case of rare books, and you're more likely to hear NPR than music on the radio.

Other than the Phoenix bookstore, the only other options in the area for your literary needs are large blockbusters like **Borders** (243 Madonna Rd., 805/544-8222, www.borders.com, Sun.–Thurs. 10 A.M.–9 P.M., Fri.–Sat. 10 A.M.–10 P.M.) at the Madonna shopping center, or downtown's **Barnes & Noble** (894 Marsh St., 805/781-8334, www.barnesandnoble.com, daily 9 A.M.–11 P.M.).

Clothing and Shoes

Bella B (1023 Morro St., 805/547-8700, www.bellab.com, Sun.–Thurs. 10 A.M.–6 P.M., Fri.–Sat. 10 A.M.–8 P.M.) sells comfortable dresses, sandals, and active wear that reflect the San Luis Obispo casual lifestyle in loose fitting, free-flowing fabrics that are easy to care for and colorful enough that they're simple to accessorize.

Head to **!Romp** (714 Higuera St., 805/545-7667, www.rompshoes.com, Mon.–Sat. 11 A.M.–6 P.M., Sun. 11 A.M.–5 P.M.) for hand selected, handmade Italian footwear that isn't carried most places. Owner Karen English offers an exclusive collection of fashionable footwear for women that's worth seeking out. There are also handbags, belts, and some jewelry. The stylish store also carries some styles for men, including boots, sneakers, and loafers.

Hep Kat (778 Marsh St., 805/596-0360, www.hepkatclothing.com, daily 11 A.M.–8 P.M.) has a focus on 1950s clothes, hats, and accessories, but these retro Rat Pack–style looks are not true vintage but brand-new modern renditions of men's and women's fashions from that period. Though the store is small, there's a lot to look at here, including Bettie Page–style dresses and hair pomade.

Decades (785 Higuera St., 805/546-0901, daily 11 A.M.–5:30 P.M.) is a large thrift shop crammed with used, mostly vintage, clothes for men and women. There's also a good selection of Hawaiian shirts for men plus kitschy memorabilia like a giant Homer Simpson doll, shark heads, lunch boxes, and other oddball items. But they predominantly sell clothes, shoes, and hats.

Finder's Keepers (1124 Garden St., 805/545-9879, Mon.–Sat. 10 A.M.–5 P.M.) is a high-end women's consignment store carrying mostly name-brand items from some of the bigger names in fashion like Gucci, Donna Karan, Prada, True Religion, and many others. The stock rotates often in this small space and since it works on consignment, you can sell your fancy shoes or purses to the shop and then choose something else in exchange.

SLO Swim (795 Higuera St., 805/781-9604, daily 10 A.M.–5:30 P.M.) sells bathing suits and swimwear with an emphasis on full-figured women. There's a tiny selection of suits for men, but not much. Shopping for swimwear can be taxing as it is, but here they'll find something that actually fits your body type, especially if you're a hard to fit type.

Kastaways (778 Marsh St., 805/610-3153, Tues.–Sun. 10 A.M.–5 P.M.) is an upscale re-sale store featuring men's and women's clothes, some vintage, but most just older items. There are accessories as well, such as jewelry, belts, and hats, even a few shoes. Books and housewares round out the offerings.

Bloke (716 Higuera St., 805/542-0526, daily 11 A.M.–5:30 P.M.) is a men's store that caters to gents the way most clothing stores cater to women. Designed for an attractive interior with soft green walls and leather chairs, it feels more like a salon. A few animal heads dot the walls, overseeing trendy urban clothes and name-brand designers.

Specialty Stores

The SLO life can be best summed up at these cool stores. **Cloud 9 Smoke Shop & Hookah Lounge** (584 California Blvd., 805/593-0420, www.cloud9slo.com, Mon.–Wed. noon–10 A.M., Thurs.–Sat. noon–2 A.M., Sun. noon–8 P.M.) has two parts. The first is the smoke shop, with beautiful high-end water pipes and accessories, and next door, through the black curtain, is a surprisingly nice hookah lounge with black leather couches and chairs and interesting artwork on the walls. Though it's near campus, it's not child's play here, and they have strict regulations about everything. There's a great diversity of flavored tobacco for the hookahs but minimal snack items, mainly candy and chips. It's one of the few hookah lounges between Los Angeles and San Francisco, and they do a nice job keeping it clean and inviting. Hookah prices start at $6 per person.

At **Central Coast Surfboards** (855 Marsh St., 805/541-1129, www.ccsurf.com, daily 10 A.M.–7 P.M.) you'll find the classic surfboards and boogie boards with which this 30-plus-year institution originally made a name for itself. There are wet suits upstairs, and downstairs are swimsuits, skate shoes, and a wide selection of clothing including backpacks for the skater, surfer, or wannabe. They have a huge selection of Ugg boots.

Habitat (777 Marsh St., 805/541-4275, Mon.–Sat. 10 A.M.–6 P.M., Sun. 11 A.M.–5 P.M.) sells furniture and home accessories, and they use lots of recycled wood and old roots polished into beautiful tables, some capped with metal. There is a Polynesian and Balinese theme and a few antiques mixed in, and all in all some really cool and unique pieces you may not have seen before.

The Human Kind (982 Monterey St., 805/594-1220, www.humankindslo.org, Mon.–Sat. 10 A.M.–6 P.M.) is a nonprofit store that deals with fair-trade products like clothing, home accessories, books, toys, and jewelry. It's all certified as fair trade, so you can shop with confidence knowing that your purchase will directly benefit the person who made the item.

Art Galleries

It's no surprise that this area inspires artists to create, and more galleries are turning up all the time. The choices here will give you a great overview of the art scene in town; check out www.sanluisobispogalleries.com for more information on SLO galleries.

Group and solo exhibitions feature Central Coast artists at **San Luis Obispo Art Center** (1010 Broad St., 805/543-8562, www.sloartcenter.org, Wed.–Mon. 11 A.M.–5 P.M., closed July 4–Labor Day), but they also occasionally feature artists from across the United States. Four small galleries show new exhibits each month. They also offer lectures and art workshops, including stained glass, working with silks, printmaking, and a variety of other media. Plans are in the works to eventually turn this into a museum, but that's years away. For now they continue to occupy their space near Mission Plaza and the river walk.

Just Looking (746 Higuera St., 805/541-6663, www.justlookinggallery.com, daily 10 A.M.–5:30 P.M.) is the oldest gallery in SLO, having opened its doors in 1984. They represent well-known artists from across the globe and do not have a focus on local artists, which is unusual for the area. Also unusual is that many of their clients are tourists to the city, who "discover" these international artists while visiting downtown. That's not to suggest that locals are not interested in what is currently hanging on the walls. In fact, it's a great way to be exposed to artists from around the United States and Europe. You just won't find anything made in the county.

The Gallery at The Network (778 Higuera St., Ste. B, 805/788-0886, www.galleryatthenetwork.com, daily 11 A.M.–6 P.M.) features about 35 artists, some local and some regional, that work with glass, pottery, oil and pastel, wood, and ceramics. The gallery is inside a small indoor mall, which can be easy to miss since there's no storefront on Higuera Street. If you're looking for local art, this is a good stop.

Farmers Market

Every Thursday night year-round, a great farmers market kick-starts the weekend. Around 5 P.M. local farmers set up stands along the four blocks of Higuera Street downtown to sell seasonal fruits, specialty herbs, organic vegetables, fresh flowers, and barbecue tri-tip sandwiches. Local musicians provide much of the entertainment, setting up concerts on adjoining streets, and many of the stores and shops extend their hours for the evening. It's more than a farmers market, it's a social and cultural event that has drawn tourists, college kids, and locals for years.

SPORTS AND RECREATION
Parks

With all the natural beauty in San Luis Obispo, it's hard to imagine you'd need to visit a park, but there are a few that provide more than just respite.

Laguna Lake Park (Madonna Rd. at Dalidio Dr.) is 375 acres, and the large lake takes up one side of the park. There is Frisbee golf, a dog park, and lots of trails that meander around, as well as volleyball nets, barbecue stands, and a brightly colored playground with slides and chutes in bold primary colors. You can fish at the lake, though few do anymore, and if you have a kayak or small boat you can access the water from an old ramp.

The **Meadow Park** (corner of Meadow and South Sts., near Broad St.) features 14 acres with individual and group picnic/barbecue areas, two horseshoe pits, two sand volleyball courts, multiuse basketball courts, a softball field, playground, and a fitness course and walking trails, not to mention a large expanse of grass. The trees do not provide shade for the large grass area, but they do cover the picnic spots.

The **LC YC Cheng Park** (corner of Santa Rosa and Marsh Sts.) is tranquility central—a place for contemplation, not recreation. On the former site of an auto repair shop, a pagoda sits over a small body of water and two stone Chinese lions stand at the entrance. There are six benches that hug the perimeter and, when the traffic is at a low rumble, you can hear the creek nearby.

Golf

The **Avila Beach Golf Course** (6464 Ana Bay Dr., Avila Beach, 805/595-4000, www.avilabeachresort.com, green fees $56–70) is an 18-hole, par-71 public course. The front nine holes are situated within oak-lined valleys, peaceful and serene. The back nine traverse a tidal estuary. Try not to let the views distract you from the task at hand. There are elevated tees and the course is a little tight, but certainly readable. Just don't underestimate it. There's a pro shop and a very good grill on-site.

Monarch Dunes (1606 Trilogy Pkwy., Nipomo, 805/343-9459, www.monarchdunes.com, green fees $30–78) is an 18-hole, par-71 public course, fairly new to the Central Coast. Their 12-hole challenge course is becoming a favorite because you can play a little more after the regular course, or just this one if you're short on time. But it's tough, as in some cases you're hitting directly into the wind, and there are five lakes that actually serve as storage water for the nearby housing development. The layout of the course uses the natural sand dunes as a road map to create a rugged and raw course.

Hiking

With so many hills in close proximity, there are great hiking trails to try out. The **Oso Flaco Lake** two-mile round-trip trail (Oso Flaco Rd. off Hwy. 1, north of Guadalupe, www.dunescenter.org) is more of a walk than a hike. The trail is on a boardwalk that crosses the lake and reaches the top of the dunes overlooking the ocean, with killer views of the coast. It has a very large number of birds, best seen in the morning hours. White pelicans, cormorants, herons, snowy plovers, and California least terns are a few of the birds using the lake. In all, about 200 species have been spotted. Parking is $5; walk down the tree-shaded causeway and turn left onto the boardwalk. There are benches on the boardwalk over the lake.

Walk the **Bluff Trail at Spooner's Cove** (Montana de Oro, Pecho Valley Rd.), where you will get excellent views of the ocean and back to Montana de Oro State Park. Spooner's Cove is on the right about four miles in from the official park entrance. There's a parking lot at Spooner's Cove, which is clearly labeled. The trail hugs the blufftop and cliffs and the low, flat vegetation allows killer views of the ragged short cliffs and rock. Out and back is about two miles, but there are inland trails that

© MICHAEL CERVIN

the small, tranquil LC YC Cheng Park

connect to Rattlesnake Flats Trail, so you can be out much longer if you wish.

The **Estero Bluffs** (Hwy. 1 at San Geronimo Rd.) is a four-mile stretch of relatively new state park coastline just north of Cayucos. Access the trail by any of several pullouts on the west side of Highway 1. A trail follows the bluff the entire way, and you can often find short scrambles down to the rocky beaches. It's a great place for seeing sea otters and is mainly level except for heading down to and back from the beach areas. The northern half has better access to beaches and good tidepooling at low tide. Reach the area just one half mile past North Ocean Avenue as you leave Cayucos on Highway 1. Park at any of the pullouts and head towards the bluff. There you'll find the trails and low sparse vegetation.

Bike Trails

There's no shortage of cyclists in SLO. The **San Luis Obispo Bicycle Club** (805/543-5973, www.slobc.org) organizes weekly rides and has a wealth of information on local routes.

Bob Jones City to the Sea (Hwy. 101, exit at Avila Beach Dr.) is undoubtedly one of the most popular and well-traveled routes, in part because it's separate from the main road and is fully paved, wandering through pretty trees and shrub-lined areas until it terminates at the ocean. It follows an old railroad line, and this out-and-back three-mile course also follows San Luis Obispo Creek. From Highway 101, exit at Avila Beach Drive and take that a quarter of a mile, then turn right on Ontario. About another quarter mile up you'll see the dirt parking lot. The trailhead is across the street.

Barranca Trail Loop (access via Pecho Valley Rd.) is part of the Hazard Peak Trail in Montana de Oro Sate Park and has ocean views and some elevation gain depending on how far you ride. This is a dirt single-track. Access the trail off Pecho Valley Road, and turn left towards Horse Camp, which puts you on the Hazard Canyon multiuse road. The road is gated, so you'll need your bikes at this point. You'll ride about a half mile on the road, then it turns dirt and becomes the Manzanita Trail for another half mile before you pick up Barranca Trail, which if you take it to the end is a little over two miles one-way. If you're feeling frisky, you can access the Hazard Trail through the interior portion of Montana de Oro to elevation gains of a thousand feet.

In town there is **Madonna Mountain** (Maino Open Space at Marsh St.), also known as San

Luis Mountain, which has short steep trails that are great for a fast, hard bike workout. The wide fire road is two miles to the top of the hill, which gives you great views back toward San Luis and of the surrounding hills. The trailhead is accessed at the Maino Open Space at the termination of Marsh Street at Fernandez Lane on the west side of Highway 101.

Spas

Sycamore Mineral Springs (1215 Avila Beach Dr., 805/595-7302, www.sycamoresprings.com, daily 8:45 A.M.–8:45 P.M.) is best known for its private hot tubs built into the hillside and fed by natural mineral waters. The spa, located near the tubs, is a Tuscan-looking building with treatment rooms facing a central pool. You can get a massage, facial, body wrap, anything you want—and incorporate a mineral soak as well. Or take a yoga class, or simply stroll the grounds and use the labyrinth to detox. This is a one-stop place to find something to soothe you.

The Bladerunner (894 Monterey St., 805/541-5131, www.thebladerunner.com, Mon.–Sat. 9 A.M.–6 P.M., Sun. 11 A.M.–4 P.M.) is a spacious full-service salon and spa with tranquil green walls and a very competent staff. You can have everything done here, from facials to waxing to a cut and color. They also offer chair massage in 15-minute increments if you need a quick de-stress. They are right downtown for easy access and have a little waiting area should someone come with you.

ACCOMMODATIONS

In spite of being so close to the beach, there are still relatively inexpensive places to stay in town. Prices are higher at places near the water.

Under $150

Inn at Avila Beach (256 Front St., 805/595-2300, www.hotelsavilabeach.com, $115–130 d) is known locally as the pink hotel because of its faded pink walls. A Mexican theme runs throughout this 32-room property, with tiled walkways and decent-sized rooms, some of which face the beach. The rooms are a little

older looking, and some are more decorated than others. The beach is right out the front door of the hotel, and even if you're not at the beach you can hear the surf. The sun deck is a favorite hangout with semi-private cabanas with couches, TVs, and hammocks overlooking everything. There is no air-conditioning here, but chances are you won't need it. They also have a collection of 300 movies you can rent for in-room entertainment for those nights when you might be wondering what to do since Avila shuts down early.

La Cuesta Inn (2075 Monterey St., 805/543-2777, www.lacuestainn.com, $90–120 d) offers great pricing, and although the place is average in appearance, it hardly matters since you'll be spending most of your time outside anyhow. This 72-room property is set near the hills and in the afternoons they serve tea, coffee, and cookies. The rooms are comfortable and nicely decorated, but nothing out of the ordinary, and a great choice if you're not picky about views. It's a mile to downtown, with a heated outdoor pool and hot tub and free Wi-Fi.

$150-250

Embassy Suites (333 Madonna Rd., 805/549-0800, www.embassysuites.com, $200–240 d) offers comfortable rooms, standard in size and decor; the suites provide more room for a longer stay. They offer a wide range of packages, including golf, wine, and Hearst Castle. There is a nice indoor pool and hot tub, and next door is the fitness room. The lobby is a central courtyard with rooms facing the voluminous space. The restaurant is there, as well as a coffee bar, and they provide a cooked-to-order complimentary breakfast. Pets are welcome. It's at the south end of the shopping mall and near Laguna Lake Park, though you'll need to drive to downtown.

The Apple Farm (2015 Monterey St., 800/255-2040, www.applefarm.com, $150–180 d) has 104 rooms spread out over a large area, and the Victorian-country theme and dainty decor draws big crowds because it feels like a hotel your grandmother might run. There tends to be an older clientele here, and the service is very focused. Fireplaces, large shower tubs, and the daily newspaper are available, and they also have an extensive gift shop and in-house restaurant with early-bird dinner specials for seniors. They are right off the highway just north of downtown and near the site of the very first motel in California. Though it's near the freeway, it's relatively quiet here.

Best Western Royal Oak Hotel (214 Madonna Rd., 800/545-4410, www.royaloakhotel.com, $150–190 d) has 99 rooms that are larger than most hotel chain rooms and thoughtfully decorated. There is the usual and customary continental breakfast, pool, and hot tub, and it's close to downtown (though you'll need to drive); you can walk to Laguna Lake Park. This is an independently owned property and there is a level of service here that exceeds many Best Westerns.

Garden Street Inn (1212 Garden St., 805/545-9802, www.gardenstreetinn.com, $179–199 d) is a 13-room bed-and-breakfast right downtown, so you can walk anywhere. It was built in 1887, and though the kitchen has been remodeled, the rest remains pretty much original. The floor-to-ceiling wood-paneled library on the 1st floor has lots of books to read, and a full breakfast is served each morning. Every evening the inn offers a wine and cheese reception. The rooms are very nicely furnished, all with an eye toward creating a sense of authenticity, even if the room phones are push-button models.

$250-350

The **C Dolphin Bay Resort and Spa** (2727 Shell Beach Rd., Pismo Beach, 805/773-4300, www.dolphinbay.com, $270–320 d) has undoubtedly one of the best locations on the entire Central Coast, perched just yards from the cliffs that drop dramatically down to the Pacific Ocean. From oceanview suites to their wellknown Lido Restaurant, the resort not only boasts magnificent views, but has proximity to much of what the Central Coast offers. You can bike (bikes are provided for all guests), kayak, fish, shop, or simply bask in the golden hues of sunsets. The one-bedroom suites, at nearly 1,000 square feet, have full kitchens, fireplaces, and flat-screen plasma TVs. All guests have access to the pool and 24-hour workout room. Cooking classes are available throughout the year, and on Tuesday nights there's a wine-tasting featuring local wineries. If you are traveling with little tykes, they offer a Saturday afternoon educational exploration of the beach's tide pools and sealife, along with lunch, so the adults can have some time off to play.

The **C Avila La Fonda** (101 San Miguel St., Avila Beach, 805/595-1700, www.avilalafonda.com, $280–320) has a Spanish hacienda feel. A walled waterfall greets guests as they enter. The lobby was patterned after Mission San Miguel in both size and height. If you look at the front of the hotel you'll see it's meant to resemble a Mexican village, with the mission set in the center. A hospitality suite to the right of the lobby always has chocolate chip cookies, coffee, and tea, and a full spread of cheeses and wine 5 to 6:30 P.M. And there is the chocolate pantry, open 24 hours, if you get a craving for something sweet, all at cost to guests. The 28 rooms feature large, deep whirlpool tubs, towel warmers, fireplaces, and wide flat-screen TVs. Some rooms have tiled floors and some are carpeted; the colorful walls and Mexican accents like pottery and paintings do a good job of creating a modern hacienda interpretation. Some rooms are spa rooms, some are studio rooms with a kitchen, and they can be opened to each other to form a full-size master suite. There is covered parking. Costco members can save 30 percent off their bill.

Each of seven rooms at **The Sanitarium** (1716 Osos St., San Luis Obispo, 805/544-4124, www.thesanitariumspa.com, $290–350 d) is different, though each has a deck, a wood-burning stove, and a Moroccan tub. This bed-and-breakfast in a residential neighborhood of well-tended Craftsman houses was founded in the 1880s as an actual sanitarium. The owner whitewashed the wood-sided building inside and out and filled it with paintings and sculptures. Breakfasts are made from local produce and include basics like pancakes, French toast, and scrambled eggs served with fresh organic fruit, unusual jams, fresh-squeezed juice, and coffee.

SeaVenture Resort (100 Ocean View Ave., Pismo Beach, 800/662-5545, www.seaventure.com, $290–320 d) has oceanview and mountain-view rooms, all just steps from the sand. There's covered parking, and an in-house restaurant on the 2nd floor with uninterrupted views to the ocean. There are fireplaces in the rooms, and some have private balconies, and a continental breakfast is delivered to your room when you want it. The rooms are intimate and very comfortable, with dark green walls accented by white beach-type furniture with a country flair. You're within walking distance to the center of Pismo Beach and the pier, but you'll need to drive 10 minutes to reach San Luis. But with these views, you may not want to leave.

FOOD
Steakhouses
Jocko's (125 N. Thompson, Nipomo, 805/929-3565, daily 8 A.M.–10 P.M., $25) is out of the way in Nipomo, and off to the east several miles in an unremarkable building, something like a 1950s Elks lodge that never caught up to the present day. They're known for their oak-grilled steaks and their decor, which is comprised of stackable banquet-type chairs, inexpensive tables, and frankly rather cheap silverware—it's all part of the experience. The steaks and grilled meats are all prime quality, cooked and seasoned by people who know how to grill. On weekends, and often on weeknights as well, there are notoriously long waits. Make reservations, though that doesn't mean you won't still wait.

The ◖ **Gold Rush Steakhouse** (100 Madonna Rd., 805/543-3000, www.madonnainn.com, daily 5–10 P.M., $25), located inside the Madonna Inn, is an old-school steakhouse with over-the-top decor. There aren't too many places like this around: The pink booths, surrounded by golden cherub angels hanging from the ceiling and red velvet wallpaper, might make you feel like you're in a

David Lynch movie. Dine on prime beef grilled over red oak, with salad and a baked potato wrapped in gold foil. They do offer chicken and fish as well. The service is attentive, and the blue cheese dressing is dynamite. Finish the meal with a slice of pink champagne cake and you'll be close to heaven.

Just down from the Madonna Inn is **Tahoe Joe's** (485 Madonna Rd., 805/543-8383, www.tahoejoes.com, Mon.–Thurs. 11 A.M.–10 P.M., Fri.–Sat. 11 A.M.–11 P.M., Sun. 11 A.M.–9 P.M., $20), where big booths and big portions are the name of the game. It is a small chain, but this is the only coastal location, and they serve excellent prime rib and steaks, not to mention some of the best garlic mashers. It's a hugely popular spot and you may have to wait on weekends, but if you're hungry, this is your stop.

American
◖ **Mo's Smokehouse BBQ** (1005 Monterey St., 805/544-6193, www.smokinmosbbq.com, Sun.–Wed. 11 A.M.–9 P.M., Thurs.–Sat. 11 A.M.–10 P.M., $18) is the spot for barbecue. Forgo the salads and sandwiches, and go for the pork and beef ribs with their special barbecue sauce, which you can purchase on-site (and you'll want to), and get a side of onion rings. All their meats are smoked on-site and they use hickory wood. The walls are covered with photos of barbecue joints all across the country, an homage to those unsung heroes who create mouthwatering barbecue each and every day.

The **Custom House** (404 Front St., Avila Beach, 805/595-7555, www.oldcustomhouse.com, Sun.–Thurs. 8 A.M.–9 P.M., Fri.–Sat. 8 A.M.–10 P.M., $15), situated on the boardwalk, provides copious seating, both indoors and out, with views to the beach. It's certainly popular, and there is often a wait on weekends. The interior has a nautical theme, with dark wood and large wide windows. For breakfast, they have excellent eggs Benedict with a large slab of ham and creamy hollandaise sauce. For lunch their mahi mahi fish-and-chips can be served either tempura style or breaded. Dinner has six different steaks, fresh fish, and barbecue dishes with their house-made sauce.

At the **Firestone Grill** (1001 Higuera St., 805/783-1001, Mon.–Wed. 11 A.M.–10 P.M., Thurs.–Sat. 11 A.M.–11 P.M., Sun. 11 A.M.–10 P.M., $12), it's all about the tri-tip sandwich. There's a heavy college contingency, and game days can be cumbersome and loud. Most any weekend means lines out the door that may move quickly, but seating is at a premium. Don't be alarmed by the wait, but do be prepared for it.

At **Franks Famous Hot Dogs** (950 California Blvd., 805/541-3488, daily 6 A.M.–9 P.M., $5), the real highlights are the chicken strips and breakfast burritos, not the hot dogs. Crowded because it's pretty cheap, it's also not an overly attractive place, but hey—it's a hot dog stand. For something slightly different, order what the owner calls the pigpen, a hot dog and bun chopped up then doused with chili, cheese, and onions.

Gardens of Avila (1215 Avila Beach Dr., 805/595-7365, www.sycamoresprings.com, Thurs.–Sun. 5–9 P.M., $25) is tucked into the Sycamore Mineral Springs. The small space has a large glass wall that looks onto the stone wall holding up the back hill, so it feels intimate, almost cave-like. The best spot, however, is a one-table balcony overlooking the dining room. The menu is limited, but the selections cover a wide range of flavors from Niçoise tuna tartar and local snapper to duck confit and traditional steaks. They also always provide a vegetarian option. For breakfast, the sour cream banana pancakes are terrific. They provide complimentary corkage on local wines.

International Fusion

Novo (726 Higuera St., 805/543-3986, www.novorestaurant.com, daily 11 A.M.–2:30 P.M. and 5 P.M.–close, $20) was originally a cigar factory in the 1890s. Their brick building is located downtown across from the Mission Plaza and has a fully heated terraced patio overlooking the creek. In the center of the deck an oak tree provides shade and a bit of tranquility. Downstairs, the Cellar is truly a unique subterranean room;

once home to the Old Cigar Factory safe it's now a must-see wine cellar. Novo specializes in international cuisine, pulling spices and flavors from Brazil, Asia, and the Mediterranean with entrées like lavender lamb chops with sea salt and roasted spring onions, and *sopes* with slow-roasted carnitas.

Italian

Café Roma (1020 Railroad Ave., 805/541-6800, www.caferomaslo.com, lunch Mon.–Fri. 11:30 A.M.–2 P.M., dinner Mon.–Sat. 5–9 P.M., $20) offers a casual dining experience with upscale decor featuring yellow mottled walls with red accented carpet and drapes and white tablecloths. There's a separate bar and a large outdoor patio for those slow summer evenings, with views to the trains just across the way. Stick with the pasta dishes, like the pumpkin ravioli with sage sauce or the orecchiette with Hearst Ranch beef Bolognese, which is what they do best, and everything will be all right. If pasta isn't quite your thing, they offer fish, chicken, and beef dishes, all with an Italian flair.

Asian

Chow (1009 Monterey St., 805/540-5243, Mon.–Sat. 11 A.M.–3 P.M. and 5 P.M.–close, Sun. 5 P.M.–close, $20) specializes in California-Asian cuisine featuring house-made noodles, farmers market produce, and fresh fish specials. Try the Chinese chili crab or the five-spice roast duck breast. The duck is served with fresh crepes for rolling the duck medallions with scallions and hoisin sauce. Located next to the historic Fremont Theater in downtown San Luis Obispo, Chow's hip sky-lit bistro interior highlights all the bamboo and Asian furniture. It's bright and open, with red booths hugging the walls.

Organic and Farm Fresh

It's not all vegetarian at homey **Sally Loo's** (1804 Osos St., 805/545-5895, Tues.–Sun. 6:30 A.M.–6:30 P.M., $12), but they certainly focus on healthy natural organic ingredients in dishes like strawberry and black pepper scones or goat cheese and asparagus quiche.

They occasionally feature live music and even tango lessons. The venue feels like it belongs in San Francisco and has a community vibe, with communal tables, worn couches, and funky art on the walls. You'll see Sally Loo there too: Just keep your eyes peeled for the content pit bull. **Big Sky Cafe** (1121 Broad St., 805/545-5401, www.bigskycafe.com, Mon.–Fri. 7 A.M.–9 P.M., Sat.–Sun. 8 A.M.–10 P.M., $15) supports a farm-to-table mentality and offers organic-only dishes like roasted eggplant lasagna, as well as dishes like marinated catfish, braised lamb, and a full selection of salads. The ambience is pleasant and service is very friendly. The wood tables and chairs can be a bit uncomfortable after a while, but after a salad and some organic bread you really don't mind.

Mexican

Tonita's (1024 Nipomo St., 805/541-9006, daily 9 A.M.–3 A.M., $7) is very small with only four tables inside and a tiny counter for ordering. They have a basic menu with flavorful Mexican favorites like burritos, albóndigas soup, and carnitas. Expect to pay extra for chips and salsa. The restaurant sits over a creek and features an outdoor patio. It usually gets packed with the late-night crowd on weekends, looking for something to do after the bars close.

Seafood

Steamers of Pismo (1601 Price St., 805/773-4711, www.steamerspismobeach.com, daily 11:30 A.M.–3 P.M. and 4:30–9 P.M., $25) is all about seafood, with dishes like cioppino, Chilean sea bass, and a very good clam chowder. They are also well known for their cocktails, including the (local) award-winning apple-coconut mojito martini. Their small bar area with great views of the water is available during lunch and for early dinners. If you want a table that looks directly to the Pacific, make reservations. This is a popular spot for tourists because of the excellent views, and the service and food are equally good.

Splash Cafe (197 Pomeroy, Pismo Beach, 805/773-4653, www.splashcafe.com, daily

8 A.M.–9 P.M., $10) is the place to go for cheap eats by the beach. This is classic Pismo—bright, airy, and rambunctious, with plastic chairs and tables and crudely painted walls with old surfing photos and other surfing paraphernalia. They are best known for their thick, chunky, and creamy clam chowder, which has recently been picked up by Costco. The fish-and-chips and fish tacos are also worth trying. Burgers and shakes are also served. It does get crowded, so plan to get there early.

The oft-crowded **Cracked Crab** (751 Price St., Pismo Beach, 805/773-2722, www.crackedcrab.com, Sun.–Thurs. 11 A.M.–9 P.M., Fri.–Sat. 11 A.M.–10 P.M., $25) is *the* place to crack open crab, lobster, and other shellfish in a cafeteria-style environment. Old black-and-white photos of fishing days gone by line the walls. Perhaps it's the plastic bibs that give it away, but this is a hands-on joint. They will dump the shellfish right on your table so you can get to work.

INFORMATION AND SERVICES
Maps and Tourist Information

The tourist center (1037 Mill St., 800/634-1414) is located right in downtown. They have maps and specific guides for restaurants, wineries, and the like, but nothing authoritative of the area, unless you purchase a guide for about four bucks.

Emergency Services
HOSPITALS

There are two hospitals that serve San Luis Obispo. **French Hospital Medical Center** (1911 Johnson Ave., 805/543-5353, www.frenchmedicalcenter.org) has been in the area for 60 years and has 209 beds. The smaller 165-bed **Sierra Vista Regional Medical Center** (1010 Murray Ave., 805/546-7600, www.sierravistaregional.com) has also been in SLO for 60 years. If you have an emergency, however, call 911 immediately.

POLICE

For police services there is the City of San Luis Obispo Police Department (1042 Walnut

St., 805/781-7317) and the San Luis Obispo County Sherriff's office (1585 Kansas Ave., 805/781-4550). If you have an emergency, call 911 immediately.

Newspapers and Media

The *San Luis Obispo Tribune* is the second largest daily paper on the Central Coast and is widely distributed. The *New Times* is the free alternative weekly, which appears every Thursday. *Central Coast Magazine* (www.centralcoastmag.com) makes a monthly appearance and covers a variety of subjects including shopping, restaurants, wineries, and profiles of local businesses from Monterey down through Santa Barbara, but with an emphasis on San Luis Obispo.

Postal Services

The main post office (893 Marsh St., 805/541-9138) is located downtown, while the other post office (1655 Dalidio, 805/453-2605) is further south near the Madonna Plaza center.

Laundry

For those unexpected moments, there's **Laguna Village Launderosa** (1338 Madonna Rd., 805/546-9274, www.launderosa.com, daily 7 A.M.–10 P.M.) and their other location, **Cal Poly Launderosa** (552 California Blvd., 805/544-8266, www.launderosa.com, daily 6 A.M.–11 P.M.) just uptown where the freeway crosses California Street.

GETTING THERE
By Car

As with most towns on the Central Coast, Highway 101 cuts through the town, and access is off this main artery. Traveling north or south, the main exits are Broad and California Streets. You can also reach town by driving south from Morro Bay via Highway 1, which will place you right in downtown.

By Bus

Amtrak Thruway Motorcoach Service (www.amtrak.com) travels between Oakland in the north and Santa Barbara in the south,

with stops in Paso Robles, San Luis Obispo, and Grover Beach. The specific bus routes are 17, 21, and 36, and one can connect to the Pacific Surfliner as well.

By Train

The **Pacific Surfliner** (www.amtrak.com), one of Amtrak's coastal trains, travels between San Luis Obispo in the north and San Diego in the south, with stops in Los Angeles, Goleta, Santa Barbara, Grover Beach, and smaller towns in between, while the **Coast Starlight** (www.amtrak.com) travels between Seattle in the north and Los Angeles in the south, with local stops in Paso Robles, San Luis Obispo, and Grover Beach. This has sleeper cars and can be a great way to reach the area from the Pacific Northwest.

By Air

Located just two miles south of the city of San Luis Obispo, the **San Luis Obispo County Regional Airport** (903-5 Airport Dr., 805/781-5205, www.sloairport.com) serves areas as far north as southern Monterey County and as far south as northern Santa Barbara County. The airport offers dozens of flights daily; it's currently served by four commercial airlines with flights to Las Vegas, Los Angeles, Phoenix, Salt Lake City, and San Francisco.

GETTING AROUND
By Car

Unless you're staying just within the downtown core, you'll need a car. San Luis Obispo is on a grid system with its main street, Higuera, a southbound one-way street; Marsh is one-way heading north. Two-hour parking is the norm except on Sundays, when there is free parking all day on city streets.

By Taxi

If you need to move about on someone else's wheels, **234-Taxi** (872 Morro St., 805/234-8294, www.234taxi.com) is a good bet. They serve the area and take all major credit cards. There's also the **SLO Cab Company** (202 Tank Farm Rd., 805/544-1222).

By Trolley

The brown and green **Downtown Trolley** costs a mere $0.25 to ride. The loop goes from the hotels on the north end of Monterey Street, near Highway 101, to Mission Plaza, down Higuera Street, back up Marsh Street, and back to Monterey at Osos Street. It runs every 15–20 minutes on Thursday 3:30–9 P.M., Friday–Saturday noon–9 P.M., and Sunday 10 A.M.–3 P.M.

By Bus

The San Luis Obispo Regional Transit Authority (179 Cross St., 805/781-4472, www.slorta.org, Mon.–Fri. 6 A.M.–9:45 P.M., $1.25–2.75) covers all of the county. All the buses are wheelchair accessible and have bike racks. As a general rule they do not operate on major holiday, so it's best to contact them for specific schedules. Exact change only.

Paso Robles

El Paso de Robles, meaning "the pass of the oaks," is just called Paso around here. Part Western outpost, part sleepy town, it's emerging as a destination for wine and food lovers. Though it's still a small town, with a population under 30,000, there are many who believe it will grow to become larger than the county seat, San Luis Obispo. That may or may not happen, but Paso still has an easygoing charm and its own unique feel. You'll still see farmers in cowboy boots and tractors driving along the roads, due to the area's very viable farmland. Though it's spread out, the downtown is on Spring Street, accessed right off Highway 101, and this is where most people find themselves.

To the west are the Paso Robles wineries, as well as Morro Bay, Cambria, and Hearst Castle, a 30-minute drive from downtown Paso Robles. San Luis Obispo is a 30-minute drive to the south. And heading north is undeveloped land stretching towards Monterey.

SIGHTS
◖ Paso Robles Downtown Square and City Park

Mature oaks and sycamore trees dot the interior of the one-block square and City Park in downtown Paso Robles, the focal point of the city. There is a gazebo, playground, horseshoe pit, and plenty of grass to stretch out on. Free concerts are offered, and a majority of festivals and the farmers market are held here. In the center

is the old original Carnegie Library, which has a sister in San Luis Obispo. Between 1883 and 1919, philanthropist Andrew Carnegie spent a vast sum of his money to help fund libraries all across the globe, nearly half located in American towns. Now the library has new life as a fully restored and beautiful history museum. Most everything fans out from the City Park: wine-tasting rooms, restaurants, lodging, bars, a movie theater, antiques stores, and clothing stores. It's easy to spend an entire day within the few blocks that make up this downtown area.

Mission San Miguel

Founded on July 25, 1797, as a stop between San Luis Obispo and Mission San Antonio, Mission San Miguel (775 Mission St., San Miguel, 805/467-2131, www.missionsanmiguel.org, daily 10 A.M.–4:30 P.M.) is one of those missions that's not near a major city and therefore became something of an outcast. Like many of the other missions on the Central Coast, it went through periods of disrepair and secularization, but it retains a stark beauty. Though not on most people's radar, it is worth a visit if you're in Paso Robles.

Just after 11 A.M. on December 22, 2003, the Central Coast was rocked by a 6.5-magnitude earthquake, the largest to strike the region in over 50 years. Though the mission was located 35 miles from the epicenter, it was especially hard hit. Numerous cracks appeared

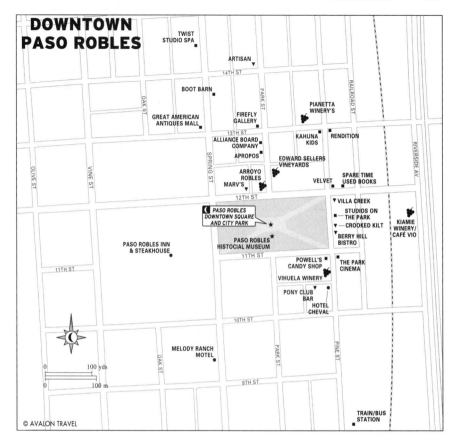

DOWNTOWN PASO ROBLES

in many of the old walls, and entire sections of plaster fell apart, exposing the vulnerable adobe. The entire mission complex was closed to the public for a three-year renovation costing nearly $15 million.

Today the church looks much the way it has for hundreds of years, in fact the inside of the church has never been repainted, and you can still see the handiwork of the early Salinan Indians who painted it. The interior is long and narrow, as was common at the time it was built, and the hand-carved beam ceiling is actually the most interesting part of the simple structure. The extravagantly painted church is a contrast from the subdued interiors of other missions of the Central Coast. The exterior has been shored

up and kept true to its original design of multiple arches fronting a quadrangle. It's located directly off Highway 101, the most accessible of all of the missions in Central California.

The Paso Robles Historical Museum

Dead center in City Park, the Paso Robles Historical Museum (Spring St. btwn. 11th and 12th Sts., 805/238-4996, www.pasorobleshistoricalsociety.org, Thurs.–Tues. 10 A.M.–4 P.M.) is housed in a former library built in 1907 that underwent a long renovation and seismic upgrade in order to become the historical museum. It's been worth the wait, as the interior is beautiful, with wood column supports and

JAMES DEAN: DEATH ON THE HIGHWAY

In the 1950s, James Dean was fast becoming a well-known movie star, and he loved making films. He also loved his car, a silver Porsche 550 Spyder that he nicknamed Little Bastard. In the early afternoon of September 30, 1955, Dean and Porsche factory mechanic Rolf Weutherich were on their way to an auto rally in Salinas, California. Dean was pulled over for speeding by a Bakersfield police officer, who issued a citation for driving 65 in a 55 zone and cautioned Dean to slow down and be careful. Dean and his companion continued on their way towards Paso Robles, with plans to spend the night, then leave the next morning for Salinas.

Around the same time, 23-year-old Cal Poly student Donald Turnupseed was heading home in his 1950 Ford Tutor. He made a left turn at the intersection of Highway 41 onto State Route 466 (later named State Route 46), unaware of the Spyder approaching. Contrary to reports that have since stated Dean's speed was in excess of 80 miles per hour, California Highway Patrol officer Ron Nelson, one of the first law enforcement officers on the scene, said the wreckage and the position of Dean's body "indicated his speed at the time of the accident was more like 55 mph." The two vehicles met nearly head on. Little Bastard crumpled and spun around, coming to rest near a telephone pole about 15 feet off the road. Rolf was thrown from the car and suffered a broken leg and serious head injuries, though he would survive. Amazingly, Donald Turnupseed escaped the accident with only a gashed forehead and bruised nose. But James Dean suffered fatal injuries, including near decapitation. The coroner listed Dean's injuries as broken neck, multiple fractures of upper and lower jaw, multiple fractures of the left and right arm, and other internal injuries caused by the two-car collision. James Dean was 24 years old.

In 1977, a James Dean memorial was erected near the site of the crash. The stylized sculpture is composed of concrete and stainless steel around a tree in a place called Cholame. Today the Jack Ranch Café sits nearby, all

© MICHAEL CERVIN

the James Dean memorial in Cholame, designed by Japanese artist Seita Ohnishi

that's left of the little town of Cholame. The sculpture was made in Japan and transported to Cholame, accompanied by the project's benefactor, Seita Ohnishi. Ohnishi chose the site after examining the location of the accident, now little more than a few road signs and flashing yellow signals. This is not the exact spot where the crash occurred; it was 900 feet northeast, before the highways were realigned. In September 2005, the intersection of Highways 41 and 46 in Cholame was dedicated as the James Dean Memorial Highway as part of the commemoration of the 50th anniversary of his death. Donald Turnupseed went on with his life, forming a fairly successful electrical contracting business and trying to avoid the spotlight, refusing all interview requests. He died in 1995. The site still draws visitors and curiosity seekers, though not as many as it used to. Dean only made three films, *Rebel Without a Cause*, *East of Eden*, and *Giant*, but his legacy lives on.

GHOSTS OF THE COAST

You may be a believer, or you may not be. Either way, most everyone loves a good ghost story. In and around Paso Robles are three long-standing ghost stories. You can visit these spots and decide for yourself. At the **Adelaida Cemetery** (near the intersection of Chimney Rock and Adelaida Rds.) there is apparently a woman in white who stands by a grave. The woman is believed to be Charlotte Sitton, a Mennonite woman who took her life at age 19 after her two children died from diphtheria. Allegedly she has been seen laying flowers on the grave sites of her children, buried next to her own grave, and. Many people have reported seeing other paranormal activity at the old cemetery, including apparitions of boys playing.

Just south of Paso Robles in Arroyo Grande, the old **Rose Victorian Inn** (789 Valley Rd.) was believed to be the death site of a young girl named Alice. There was apparently no foul play relating to her death – some say it was pneumonia, some say an adverse reaction to a bee sting. Regardless, a little girl's laughter is said to be heard coming from the nursery of the building, which is no longer an inn. These days the property is used for weddings and special events. Perhaps you might hear her too as you pass by.

At **Mission San Miguel,** just north of Paso Robles, there was a bloody killing rampage in 1848. John Reed, who bought the mission after secularization, turned the church into a tavern. Apparently Reed had amassed quite a fortune and liked to brag about his hidden wealth. One night a group of men, some say pirates, came into the tavern and heard Reed boasting of his buried treasure. They left the tavern and doubled back and went on a killing spree, murdering everyone in the mission, 11 people in all, to find the loot. They didn't find anything, and the law eventually caught up with the killers in Santa Barbara. Cold spots have been reported in the chapel, and there have been many reports of ghosts wandering the mission grounds, ghosts who may resemble John Reed and his wife. No one knows if the treasure was for real, or if it was ever found.

cases, old books and photographs, memorabilia, and period furniture. There's even an 1810 harmonium, an early reed organ from Wales. You don't need a lot of time to explore the exhibits here, so it's easy to add this sight to your itinerary. There is also a small gift shop as well as maps of the downtown area and wineries.

WINERIES

That Paso Robles has become known for being an important wine region should not be surprising. That it's taken this long is the real stumper. Things are changing quickly, but there are still a number of small family-owned wineries with tasting rooms that are simple and unpretentious and perhaps even a little inglorious, and that's part of the charm. Often you'll find the winemaker pouring your wines. As the area has grown there are more of the large and flamboyant Napa-style tasting rooms, which might make you forget you're in a small farming town.

Downtown

Within the downtown area, meaning only a few blocks, you can walk to over a dozen tasting rooms, making wine almost as ubiquitous as food.

EDWARD SELLERS VINEYARDS

Edward Sellers wanted to make wine, in spite of his moniker. (Yes, that's his real name, not a marketing gimmick.) With a production of 5,000 cases and using exclusively Paso Robles fruit, the Edward Sellers (1220 Park St., 805/239-8915, www.edwardsellers.com, daily 11 A.M.–6 P.M., tasting fee $6) winery specializes in viognier, rosé, syrah, and various blends, and these are uniformly some of the best Rhône-style wines coming out of Paso Robles. The tasting room is simple and uncluttered with minimal

Located in City Park, The Paso Robles Historical Museum was built in 1907.

accessories. Winemaker Amy Butler possesses an uncanny ability to make her wines both lush and restrained. In fact she gets many compliments from fellow winemakers. With wines like these you don't need much else.

VIHUELA WINERY
Vihuela (840 11th St., 805/226-2010, www.vihuelawinery.com, Sun.–Mon. 11 A.M.–4 P.M., Wed.–Sat. 11 A.M.–7 P.M., tasting fee $5) only makes one white wine so far, a chardonnay; they mainly focus on syrah and cabernet sauvignon. They plan a white Rhône blend of marsanne, roussanne, and viognier to round out their white offerings, but the two best friends who formed this winery still prefer big reds and Bordeaux varietals. Their signature blend, called Concierto del Rojo, meaning "concert of red," is an unorthodox blend of syrah, merlot, and petite verdot. The tasting room shares an unpretentious and frankly uninteresting space with Vivant Fine Cheese. But there is an outdoor patio in which to enjoy the wines and cheese.

PIANETTA WINERY
The tasting room for Pianetta Winery (829

13th St., 805/226-4005, www.pianettawinery.com, Wed.–Mon. noon–6 P.M., tasting fee $5) is charming, clean, and inviting. The theme is that of a ranch house, and there are wooden arbors set against the walls and old family farming photos hanging in close proximity. In keeping with the theme, and honoring tradition, at the front of the tasting room is the very pump that the owners' grandfather used when making his homemade wine. Wood tones dominate the space; the old hardwood floors remind you that this is one of the older buildings in Paso Robles, the Grangers Union Building, which dates to the late 1880s. Wines include sangiovese, syrah, cabernet sauvignon, petite sirah, and several blends that will win you over with lots of up-front fruit and balance.

KIAMIE WINERY
Kiamie Winery (1111 Riverside Dr., 805/226-8333, www.kiamiewines.com, Thurs.–Mon. 11 A.M.–6 P.M., tasting fee $5) is a newer addition to the Paso Robles wine scene. Their tasting room is downtown, though just off the downtown square near the train tracks, and is simple and unpretentious. The salmon-colored

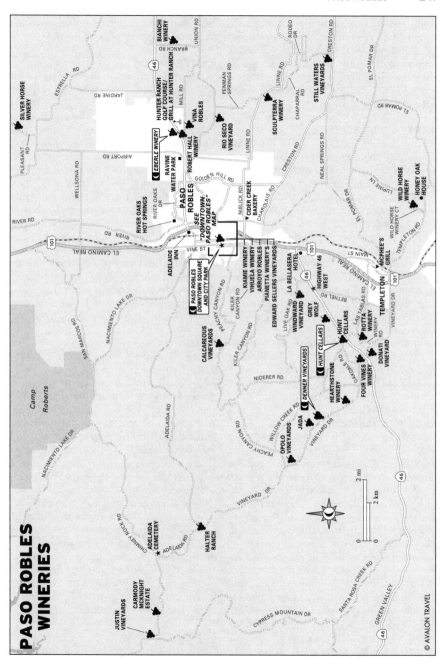

PASO ROBLES WINERIES

SILVER HORSE WINERY

BIANCHI WINERY

HUNTER RANCH GOLF COURSE/ GRILL AT HUNTER RANCH

VINA ROBLES

EBERLE WINERY

ROBERT HALL WINERY

RAVINE WATER PARK

RIO SECO VINEYARD

SCULPTERRA WINERY

STILL WATERS VINEYARDS

HONEY OAK HOUSE

WILD HORSE WINERY

PASO ROBLES

SEE "DOWNTOWN PASO ROBLES" MAP

RIVER OAKS HOT SPRINGS

ADELAIDE INN

CIDER CREEK BAKERY

PASO ROBLES DOWNTOWN SQUARE AND CITY PARK

VINE ST

KIAMIE WINERY

VIHUELA WINERY

ARROYO ROBLES

PIANETTA WINERY'S

EDWARD SELLERS VINEYARDS

LA BELLASERA HOTEL

HIGHWAY 46 WEST

MCPHEE'S GRILL

MAIN ST

TEMPLETON

CALCAREOUS VINEYARDS

WINDWARD VINEYARD

GREY WOLF

HUNT CELLARS

ROTTA WINERY

DONATI VINEYARD

HUNT CELLARS

DENNER VINEYARDS

HEARTHSTONE WINERY

FOUR VINES WINERY

JADA

OPOLO VINEYARDS

Camp Roberts

ADELAIDA CEMETERY

HALTER RANCH

CARMODY MCKNIGHT ESTATE

JUSTIN VINEYARDS

2 mi

2 km

© AVALON TRAVEL

walls hold a few pieces of artwork, but aside from that it's all about the wines. The emphasis is on Rhône and Bordeaux blends. Their grapes come from the Westside region, and all the vineyards they source are within close proximity to each other, lending to the balanced nature of their wines.

ARROYO ROBLES

Arroyo Robles (739 12th St., 877/759-9463, www.arroyorobles.com, daily 11 A.M.–7 P.M., tasting fee $5) is located directly across from Paso Robles' downtown historic City Park. Arroyo Robles offers wine, of course, but also a plethora of other items in their well-stocked tasting room, including books, gift items, and maple syrup and pancake mix, a sort of homage to a property they owned back in Vermont. Even now they offer a pancake breakfast before all the major wine festivals in town. A broad portfolio of wine is made here, including the standard offerings like chardonnay, zinfandel, and syrah, but they have also branched off into viognier, tempranillo, two rosés, and several ports. Not willing to rest on their laurels, they also produce two sparkling wines, one of which is a sweet almond sparkler.

Highway 46 West
◖ HUNT CELLARS

David Hunt was diagnosed at a young age with a degenerative retinal disorder; his sight has eroded over four decades and is now all but gone. For many people that may seem like a handicap, but for Hunt, it has honed his sense of taste and smell, and his wines benefit tremendously from his acute ability. "Blindness in some ways helps me in making wine," he says. He claims he can actually sense the weight and texture of a wine by its sound. The timbre changes as it pours into a glass, explains this ex-musician. A full line of wines, predominantly reds, all velvety and seductive, are available at Hunt Cellars (2875 Oakdale Rd., 805/237-1600, www.huntcellars.com, daily 10:30 A.M.–5 P.M., tasting fee $5–10), but they are not inexpensive. You'll find cabernet sauvignon, barbera, zinfandel, petite sirah, and tremendous ports and dessert wines.

HALTER RANCH

A long drive on curved roads under a canopy of oaks leads up to the old property known as Halter Ranch (8910 Adelaida Rd., 805/226-9455, www.halterranch.com, daily 11 A.M.–5 P.M., tasting fee $5). The 1880 Victorian house and old silo and barn seem perfectly suited to the spot. By contrast, the tasting room, built in 2005, is modern, with a curved bar, warm wood tones, and hip track lighting embedded in the wood beams. Halter Ranch is a 960-acre ranch with 150 acres of grapes, mostly dedicated to cabernet sauvignon. They also make rosé, sauvignon blanc, and syrah. A selection of cheeses, cured meats, dipping oils, and crackers are for sale and are perfect for a spontaneous picnic outside under the olive trees, or near the outdoor fireplace on the flagstone. Fresh bread is brought in on Fridays. Halter Ranch honey is also available.

JADA

Wines at Jada (5620 Vineyard Dr., 805/226-4200, www.jadavineyard.com, Thurs. noon–5 P.M., Fri.–Sun. 10 A.M.–5 P.M., tasting fee $10) go by unique names like XCV, a white blend of viognier, roussanne, and grenache blanc; Mirror, a mix of syrah and petit verdot; Hell's Kitchen, another blend of syrah, grenache, mourvedre, and tannat; and Jack of Hearts, a Bordeaux blend of cabernet sauvignon, petit verdot, and merlot. The stacked stone walls and arched iron gate that fronts the highway will lead you alongside a line of mature purple-leafed plum trees. Inside the tasting room, the ceiling narrows down, forcing the eyes to the windows behind the tasting bar with beautiful views to the vineyards. The viewing deck, an expansive area of tables and chairs, also provides views of the vines and nearby properties. The facility has a hip modern design, which juxtaposes the earthy, laid-back rolling hills.

DONATI VINEYARD

All of Donati Vineyard's (2720 Oak View

view from Highway 46

Rd., 805/238-0676, www.donatifamilyvine-yard.com, daily 11 A.M.–5 P.M., tasting fee $5–10) wines come from Paicines, a place most people have never heard of in a remote part of Monterey County. The majority of their production is red wine, especially cabernet sauvignon, which is made into a single varietal wine and which is also blended into their claret, Meritage, and merlot. There are also limited quantities of syrah, cabernet franc, and malbec. As for the white wines, they produce pinot blanc, chardonnay, and pinot grigio. The tasting room is housed in a European-looking white building off Highway 46 west. The interior is modern with a sleekly styled tasting bar, in contrast to the Old World feel of the exterior. They make some wonderful wines and it's a worthy stop.

GREY WOLF

Grey Wolf's (2174 Hwy. 46, 805/237-0771, www.greywolfcellars.com, daily 11 A.M.–5:30 P.M., tasting fee $5) tasting room is inside a restored 60-year-old farmhouse, a great backdrop for tasting their wines. Grey Wolf was established in 1994 with the goal of mainly red wine production. They use only French and American oak in their barrel program, which supports their big reds like zinfandel, syrah, petite sirah, cabernet sauvignon, and their

excellent Meritage blend. They have one or two white wines, but those are produced in small quantities and usually sell out quickly.

◖ DENNER VINEYARDS

At Denner Vineyards (5414 Vineyard Dr., 805/239-4287, www.dennervineyards.com, daily 11 A.M.–5 P.M., tasting fee $10), it's all about Rhône-style wines, with the lone exception of zinfandel. Syrah, mourvedre, grenache, viognier, and roussanne are the grapes of choice, blended into seamless plush and sensuous wines. It's a state-of-the-art modern winery with a curvilinear design to match the rolling hillside. The tasting room, with expansive views to the surrounding vineyards, feels more like Napa Valley than Paso Robles. But it's all wonderfully executed, and from the wines to the building it is a sophisticated and beautiful experience.

CALCAREOUS VINEYARDS

Calcareous Vineyards (3430 Peachy Canyon Rd., 805/239-0289, www.calcareous.com, daily 11 A.M.–5 P.M., tasting fee $5) is named for the calcareous limestone soil that is rich with calcium and magnesium and pretty much defines this region's dirt. With over 400 acres they are able to make an impressive array of wines, from cabernet sauvignon and petit verdot to pinot

SAN LUIS OBISPO

noir, chardonnay, viognier, and lots of blends. Their beautifully manicured lawn at the front and back of the tasting room gives nice views to the mild hills that surround them, and they have tables to relax at.

WINDWARD VINEYARD

Windward Vineyard (1380 Live Oak Rd., 805/239-2565, www.windwardvineyard.com, daily 10:30 A.M.–5 P.M., tasting fee $10) is something of an anomaly. Normally pinot noir grows better in cooler weather, often near coastal influences. Windward is in Paso Robles, which is hot in the summer and downright cold in the winter. But this small parcel of vines is situated down in a pocket of land that protects it. All they make is pinot noir, and they usually have several vintages out for tasting to compare and contrast. They sit among other vineyard neighbors, and their wood-paneled tasting room, though small, occasionally carries artwork tacked to the wall.

FOUR VINES WINERY

Four Vines Winery (3750 Hwy. 46, 805/227-0865, daily 11 A.M.–6 P.M., tasting fee $10) burst onto the wine scene in 2002 with an edgy attitude and wines like the Heretic, a petite syrah; the Biker, a zinfandel; and a Naked chardonnay, meaning it is fermented in stainless steel and therefore retains a crisp acidity. They also offer barbera, syrah, and dessert wines. Most of their grapes are sourced from Paso Robles, and some from the Sierra Foothills. They make a lot of wines, about 60,000 cases, so this ain't no small-town winery. It's popular and the small tasting room does get crowded, so arrive early.

ROTTA WINERY

Rotta Winery (250 Winery Rd., 805/237-0510, www.rottawinery.com, daily 10 A.M.–5 P.M., tasting fee $5) is a small tasting room with views into the fermentation and barrel room. The Rotta family goes back to the early 1900s in San Louis Obispo County and is the oldest family-operated winery on the Central Coast. Their wines are well priced, most under $20, including chardonnay, zinfandel, merlot, and

their black monukka, a dessert wine from an obscure grape that's done tremendously well for them.

OPOLO VINEYARDS

Opolo is the name of a blended rosé-style wine found on the Dalmatian Coast bordering the Adriatic Sea. Yes, it's a far cry from Paso Robles, and Opolo Vineyards (7110 Vineyard Dr., 805/238-9593, www.opolo.com, daily 10 A.M.–5 P.M., tasting fee $10) doesn't even make the opolo wine. They do, however, make lots of other wine, nearly 40,000 cases of 30 different wines, including the standard offerings of zinfandel, cabernet sauvignon, chardonnay, merlot, and syrah. But they also produce lesser-known wines like roussanne, malbec, grenache, and petite verdot. There are also three walking trails that meander through the vineyards, so everyone can experience first hand the beauty and tranquility of the vines. Tables are placed strategically along the trails for impromptu picnics.

HEARTHSTONE WINERY

At Hearthstone Winery (5070 Vineyard Dr., 805/260-1945, www.hearthstonevineyards.com, Thurs.–Mon. 11 A.M.–5 P.M., tasting fee $5), the tasting room, in a modest building in some of Paso's prime wine-growing region, has postcard views from the back deck of the verdant rolling hills the area is known for. The warm, earthy tones of the interior make you feel like you're safe and secure, like being protected by rock and earth, which is exactly what the name Hearthstone was meant to imply. The 40 planted acres have a shallow clay top layer, perfect for stressing the vines, and is dotted with chunks of limestone rocks everywhere. One particular wine called Slipstone, a blend of syrah and grenache, received its moniker when the earthquake that hit Paso Robles in 2003 dislodged a large limestone rock that tumbled down the mountain and hit up against the grenache vines. It's still there to this day. Cabernet sauvignon, sangiovese, syrah, pinot noir, roussanne, and rosé round out the offerings.

CARMODY MCKNIGHT ESTATE

The Carmody McKnight Estate (11240 Chimney Rock Rd., 805/238-9392, www.carmodymcknight.com, daily 10 A.M.–5 P.M., tasting fee $10) is one of those spots you just don't want to leave. As you're tasting the wines, you look out onto a little pond with a small boat in it, and you know you could get in it and lounge away the day. And then there's the art gallery located inside the tasting room; much of the art finds its way onto the labels, and most of it is done by the owner himself. The wines are wonderful, restrained, balanced, and elegant. You will find pinot noir, cabernet franc, and four versions of chardonnay, among others.

JUSTIN VINEYARDS

Up the road from Carmody McKnight Estate is Justin Vineyards (11680 Chimney Rock Rd., 805/238-6932, www.justwine.com, daily 10 A.M.–6 P.M., tasting fee $10). Justin has become known as one of the best wineries in the area, crafting Bordeaux blends like Isosceles and Justification that almost always score well in the national wine press. Once inside the tasting room, the plush rich wood tones of the bar and remote setting make it hard to leave and drive back down the mountain.

Highway 46 East

Though the majority of wineries are concentrated on the west side of Highway 101, the east side has a number of wineries as well. Since the region is warmer, there are different expressions of the wines.

◖ EBERLE WINERY

Gary Eberle is the father of Paso Robles wine—that much is undisputed. He arrived from Pittsburgh and realized the potential of the area, and with a few investors bought 160 acres in 1973. Today his Eberle Winery (3810 Hwy. 46 East, 805/238-9607, www.eberlewinery.com, daily 10 A.M.–5 P.M., free) is the single most-awarded winery in the United States. Rub the boar statue out front for good luck before you enter the tasting room. All money tossed into the fountain is collected and given to a local charity. Don't mind the friendly black poodles that will come up next to you as you sip the wines; they are part of the Eberle family. Once inside, the long wood bar allows plenty of space to see the countless ribbons they have won. There are gift items and views to the outside vineyards. Tours of the winery and their wine caves are offered free of charge. Eberle reserve cabernet sauvignons are top-notch. Other wines in the portfolio include viognier, sangiovese, barbera, zinfandel, chardonnay, and too many others to list. One of the reasons they are so good is that the wines are uniformly consistent. Bring a picnic and relax on the deck, as this is a great spot to soak up the visuals of the vine-covered hills. The majority of Eberle wines are priced under $25.

ROBERT HALL WINERY

Robert Hall Winery (3443 Mill Rd., 805/239-1616, www.roberthallwinery.com, daily 10 A.M.–5 P.M., tasting fee $10) is a massively large complex; as you enter the tasting room you realize how small you are by contrast. The chandelier alone is huge. The tasting bar sits in the center, and the perimeter is full of products and gift items. They offer a wide selection of wines, from everyday inexpensive wines like their chardonnay and sauvignon blancs, to their higher-end reserve syrah, cabernet sauvignon, and vintage ports. Robert Hall wines are widely distributed. Part of that is marketing, but part of that is due to the talent of winemaker and Texas native Don Brady. The grapes are sourced from the Paso Robles region in part to show off how wonderful a region like Paso Robles is. Robert Hall made enough money doing diverse entrepreneurial things to be able to secure a prime plot of land in the early 1990s. Today they are one of the largest wineries in Paso Robles and stalwart promoters of the area.

VINA ROBLES

At Vina Robles (3700 Mill Rd., 805/227-4812, www.vinarobles.com, summer daily 10 A.M.–6 P.M., winter daily 10 A.M.–6 P.M., tasting fee $5–12), the centerpiece of the

SAN LUIS OBISPO

© MICHAEL CERVIN

vineyards on Highway 46 East, Paso Robles

tasting room is the large fireplace surrounded by comfy sofas. This is a voluminous space with stone walls and eclectic artwork. The massive arched window looks out to the vineyards and small lake. The wines consist of cabernet sauvignon, petite sirah, zinfandel, petite verdot, and blends of these grapes as well. Their estate wines are well priced, most being under $20, and they source fruit from other counties as well, notably Monterey County. They also offer summer concerts held on their expansive lawn. They're becoming quite popular, as are weddings, due to their large location.

BIANCHI WINERY

The tasting room at Bianchi Winery (3380 Branch Rd., 805/226-9922, www.bianchi-winery.com, daily 10 A.M.–5 P.M., tasting fee $10), off Highway 46 east, has a small lake that hugs the exterior patio, surrounded by vines. The interior is beautifully designed, a melding of natural stone, expansive windows, and an inviting fireplace. The curved bar has an etched glass countertop and the vibe inside is modern and hip, a juxtaposition to the rural surroundings. Bianchi produces about

15,000 cases and has the standard offerings of pinot noir, chardonnay, cabernet sauvignon, and others, with a nod to Bianchi's Italian heritage with wines like sangiovese, barbera, and refosco, an obscure oddball grape from Northern Italy.

STILL WATERS VINEYARDS

Still Waters Vineyards (2750 Old Grove Ln., 805/237-9321, www.stillwatersvineyards.com, Thurs.–Mon. 11 A.M.–5 P.M., tasting fee $5) produces very small lots of wine, at most 200 cases per wine of chardonnay, viognier, merlot, malbec, and cabernet sauvignon at their out-of-the-way property. Since there was a 100-year-old olive grove on the property, they naturally decided to make olive oil too, something becoming more common in the Paso Robles area. A somewhat under-the-radar winery, they make some very nice wines.

SCULPTERRA WINERY

At first glance, Sculpterra Winery (5125 Linne Rd., 805/226-8881, www.sculpterra.com, Fri.–Sun. 10 A.M.–5 P.M., tasting fee $10) seems more like a gimmick than a serious winery. Huge sculptures like a 10-ton puma and an 8-ton mammoth, all designed by local Atascadero artist John Jagger, greet visitors. The gardens are great for picnicking near these pieces after you've sampled mourvedre, merlot, petite sirah, and chardonnay. While you're visiting, try the pistachios that grow on the property. Their wines are well balanced, achieving acidity with fruit ripeness, and their blends are quite nice.

RIO SECO VINEYARD

At Rio Seco Vineyard (4295 Union Rd., 805/237-8884, www.riosecowine.com, daily 11 A.M.–5 P.M., tasting fee $5), you'll realize that baseball has nothing in common with wine—unless you're owner Tom Hinkle. Tom was a baseball scout, visiting high school, college, and semi-pro games to find the best young talent throughout America. Then he retired and went into the wine business. The tasting room is unimpressive, a metal and wood building whose former owner was growing marijuana in the barn, but the wines Tom makes, like zinfandel, viognier, cabernet sauvignon, and syrah are inexpensive and unpretentious, just the sort of wine you'd have with pizza or burgers.

SILVER HORSE WINERY

The first thing you notice as you step out of your car onto the blufftop tasting room of Silver Horse Winery (2995 Pleasant Rd., San Miguel, 805/467-9463, Fri.–Mon. 11 A.M.–5 P.M., tasting fee $7) is how quiet it is. Then you notice the views of a vast sky with simple rolling hills that begin to dissipate in the distance. The Silver Horse portfolio includes only one white wine, albariño, as well as cabernet sauvignon, merlot, petite sirah, and several blended wines. The interior of the Spanish-style tasting room is comfortable with a vaulted ceiling, wood-burning fireplace, and leather club chairs. Autumnal tones and Southwest art creates a warm, relaxed vibe. On either side of the tasting bar, window cutouts allow for views into the barrel room. Outside are bocce ball courts and, fittingly, horseshoes.

WILD HORSE WINERY

Wild Horse Winery (1437 Wild Horse Winery Ct., 805/788-6310, www.wildhorsewinery.com, daily 11 A.M.–5 P.M., tasting fee $5) has long been one of the leading wineries on the Central Coast. They produce nearly 200,000 cases each year, and few wineries in California source fruit from such a broad spectrum of vineyards, which has allowed Wild Horse to select grapes from the specific areas they feel best showcase a particular wine. For example, they produce a pinot noir from one growing region in San Luis Obispo and two distinct growing regions in Santa Barbara. Viognier, chardonnay, and their malvasia bianca, which is a perennial favorite, are just some of their white wines. Syrah, sangiovese, cabernet sauvignon, merlot, and their flagship variety, pinot noir, are on tap for the reds. When you visit be certain to try the heirloom varietals they have become known for like negrette, blaufrankish, and grenache blanc. When in season, the grapes hanging from the arbor at the entrance are tantalizing fruit that you're encouraged to sample. There are plenty of picnic tables out front on the grass. The tasting room is small with a low bar on one side of the room, and frankly isn't interesting. Like many tasting rooms, the decor is not really the point, it's the wines. They are located near Templeton, and it's a quiet drive through rolling hills to get there.

POZO VALLEY WINERY

Pozo Valley Winery (2200 El Camino Real, Santa Margarita, 805/438-3375, www.pozovalley.com, Fri.–Sun. noon–5 P.M., tasting fee $5) is not located specifically in Pozo Valley, which might arguably be a good thing. The town of Pozo is 18 miles southeast of Santa Margarita, whereas the Pozo Valley Winery tasting room is merely a mile and a half off Highway 101 in Santa Margarita. The tasting room is rustic, much more of a cowboy feel than the flashy architecture of Napa Valley. An old wooden wine press sits in the corner, a reminder of earlier days. Viognier, zinfandel, cabernet sauvignon, and merlot are the inexpensive offerings, and they work well with food.

Ancient Peaks Winery tasting room

© MICHAEL CERVIN

⬛ ANCIENT PEAKS WINERY

Ancient Peaks Winery (22720 El Camino Real, Santa Margarita, 805/365-7045, www.ancient-peaks.com, Thurs.–Mon. 11 A.M.–5:30 P.M., tasting fee $5) is located just a mile off Highway 101 in Santa Margarita. Their vineyards are located at the southernmost part of the Paso Robles growing area and their unique soils, comprised of ancient ocean floor, is what makes their wines different, as well as the talent of the winemaker. The nutrients found in this uplifted sea bed is like nothing else in the entire region. You really need to sample the wines yourself to understand their uniqueness. Their tasting room is all polished wood with a pleasing rustic charm, and they pour sauvignon blanc, merlot, cabernet sauvignon, syrah, and zinfandel with bottle prices usually under $20.

ENTERTAINMENT AND EVENTS
Nightlife

This is still a growing area, and there are not very many nightlife options yet. The **Pony**

Club Bar (1021 Pine St., 866/522-6999, Sun.–Thurs. 5–9 P.M., Fri.–Sat. 4–11 P.M.) at Hotel Cheval is like an old-school clubhouse: wood toned, sophisticated, and centered around a zinc-topped horseshoe bar. They serve light appetizers and many local wines. You don't need to stay at the hotel to pony up to the bar and sample Central Coast wines.

Crooked Kilt (1122 Pine St., 805/238-7070, www.thecrookedkilt.com, daily 11 A.M.–9 P.M.) offers live music Thursday–Sunday, with Tuesday night always devoted to Irish music, at their courtyard stage in their back patio with a blarney stone at the foot of the stage. Times vary, so you'll need to call ahead. A classic neighborhood tavern, it has a new section through the small doorway at the back that loses the woody bar atmosphere and has a more upscale feel. From either place, however, you can hear the music. Local bands with a rock sensibility perform here, as well as out-of-county bands.

Café Vio (1111 Riverside Dr., 805/237-2722, www.cafe-vio.com, daily 6:30 A.M.–6 P.M.) is a cozy coffee shop, Internet café, art gallery, and live music joint, where people like hanging out because it's just so comfortable with stuffed chairs and relaxing wood tones. Every Friday they have live music, and every Saturday evening is open mic night. The first and third Wednesday of each month is devoted to jazz with a local band.

Just up the road from Café Vio in San Miguel is one of the oldest operating bars in the entire state of California, originally started in 1853. **Elkhorn Bar & Grill** (1263 Mission, San Miguel, 805/467-3909, Mon.–Thurs. 10 A.M.–midnight, Fri.–Sat. 9 A.M.–2 A.M., Sun. 9 A.M.–midnight) has friendly bartenders and a rowdy but enjoyable local crowd. Animal heads share the walls with beer signs and sports paraphernalia without covering up the old walls. There are pool tables, a jukebox, free Wi-Fi, and large-screen TVs, and Pabst Blue Ribbon is always on tap.

Cinema

The Park Cinema (1100 Pine St., 805/227-2172) is directly across from the City Park is the only movie theater in town. It has six screens and shows the latest releases. For more selection, or art-house films, you'll need to drive into San Luis Obispo.

Festivals and Events

SUMMER

The Western spirit is alive at the **California Mid-State Fair** (2198 Riverside Ave., 805/239-0655, www.midstatefair.com, $8 adults, $5 children 6–12) held each July–August. In addition to big-name musical talent performing at one of the multiple stages, the Western-themed fair has horse events, pig races, and of course a carnival. But as this is now wine country, there are special winemaker dinners around town, the Central Coast Wine Challenge judged by professional wine judges to find the best wines, and an olive oil competition. A state-of-the-art culinary center hosts cooking demonstrations to show off the many local farmers and growers. This is a great family event at a great price.

The **Winemakers' Cook-Off** (800 Clubhouse Dr., 805/238-4600, www.winemakerscookoff .com, $75), which began in 1998, and is held

each August, raises money for local charities. The event, open to the public, pulls in 30 winemakers, all of whom personally grill up their best dishes to match their wines. It's a feast for the senses, and more food than you can possibly consume. The live band adds to the festive environment as the public chooses their favorite wine and food pairing too. The event has raised over a quarter of a million dollars and has become one of the must-attend events in the region. Don't be surprised to see people sneaking around with beers and tequilas—after all, with that much wine, you might want something different.

SPRING

Not very family oriented, but nonetheless fun, the **Zinfandel Festival** (2198 Riverside Ave., 805/239-8463, www.pasowine.com, $60–85), held the third weekend in March, is all about California's signature grape. About a dozen local restaurants pair foods to match the big jammy zinfandel characteristics of this area. The main draw is the all-zinfandel tasting held on Saturday night, when four dozen wineries pour their zins and zin blends and a dozen local restaurants showcase food to match. There's a silent auction, live music, and all weekend long local wineries offer special deals at their tasting rooms.

If you enjoy wine and food but are concerned about the toll on the environment, then the **Earth Day Wine & Food Festival** (held the weekend closest to Earth Day, 805/369-2288, www.earthdayfoodandwine.com, $75) is right up your alley. About a thousand people attend this very fun event. Recyclable and compostable plates, bowls, forks, and spoons are used, and a team of volunteers manages a constant effort of both recycling and composting. Event programs and information guides are produced using only post-consumer recycled materials, and even the entertainment stage is solar powered. About 200 producers of sustainably grown food and wine gather to let you sample dishes sourced from locally grown fruits, vegetables, meats, cheeses, olive oils, and wine. There is live music, a silent auction, and

© MICHAEL CERVIN

Firestone Walker Brewing Co. sponsors Oaktoberfest every fall.

the chance to kick back and meet farmers and vintners who are committed to sustainability.

FALL

Oaktoberfest (held at River Oaks, 800 Clubhouse Dr., 805/238-2556, www.firestone-walker.com, $35)—no, that's not a misspelling—is sponsored by Firestone Walker Brewing Co. This version of Oktoberfest is given a California twist and is held outside near the oaks. In addition to the beer Olympics, which include a keg-tossing contest (they actually use what's called a firkin, an empty 11-gallon stainless steel keg), the barrel roll, and stein racing, there's lots of German food and music, horse-drawn carriages, and people dressed up as beer maidens, with most of the guys wearing silly hats. The mayor taps the first keg and though this is about beer, there are a few wines present too. The proceeds benefit Hospice of San Luis Obispo.

SHOPPING
Clothing

Alliance Board Company (1233 Park St., 805/238-2600, Mon.–Sat. 10 a.m.–6 p.m.,

Sun. 10 a.m.–5 p.m.) is the place to buy surf, skate, and snow accessories and gear. It's a large shop, comprehensive in its inventory, with plenty of street clothes. Wet suits, ski gear, sports watches, and footwear like Vans and flip-flops round out the offerings. The staff is young, and very helpful and nice.

Apropos (1229 Park St., 805/239-8282, Mon.–Thurs. 10 a.m.–6 p.m., Fri.–Sat. 10 a.m.–8 p.m., Sun. noon–4 p.m.) caters to an older clientele for women's retail clothing, with predominantly dresses, pant suits, wraps, and jewelry. The clothes are a bit more traditional, though within that context they have some pieces with an urban flair.

By contrast, **Velvet** (801 12th St., 805/237-7372, Mon.–Sat. 10 a.m.–6 p.m., Sun. noon–4 p.m.) has hip boutique clothing with a wide selection of styles, from sleek and sexy dresses to coats, tops, shoes, and even a few hats, all set in a relaxed but fun environment looking out to the park.

As soon as you walk into **Boot Barn** (1340 Spring St., 805/238-3453, Mon.–Fri. 9 a.m.–7 p.m., Sat. 9 a.m.–6 p.m., Sun.

11 A.M.–5 P.M.), the heady scents of leather greet you. Boots, hats, belt buckles, and all types of jeans, shirts, and coats are ready for trying on to get into the cowboy mentality. Paso is still a Western town at its heart, and there are plenty of boot-wearing farmers walking around. This has been a staple outfitter for the area for a long time. You can't miss the store—just look for the faded plastic horse high atop the sign.

For the latest and hippest fashions for the cool little one in your life, drop by **Kahuna Kids** (840 13th St., 805/237-9497, www.kahunakidspasorobles.com, Mon.–Sat. 10 A.M.–6 P.M., Sun. 11 A.M.–5 P.M.), which has clothes for toddlers and infants. The owners come from a surf background, so there's a lot of skater-type baby clothing, as well as baby carriers and blankets.

Art Galleries

Studios on the Park (1130 Pine St., 805/238-9800, Thurs. noon–6 P.M., Fri.–Sat. noon–7 P.M., Sun. noon–6 P.M.) is a warehouse-sized space with a series of studios that are home to two artists each. There's a silversmith, pottery throwers, and others that create right in front of your eyes. You can watch, ask questions, and get intimately involved with the two dozen local artists. Their finished works are presented for sale.

The **Firefly Gallery** (1301 Park St., 805/237-9265, daily 11 A.M.–5 P.M.) is a mother-daughter team who left the constraints of Los Angeles to open this unique space. Downstairs is jewelry, clothing, crafts, handmade dishes, and accessories, and upstairs is an art gallery. There are a number of local artists represented, not just with the upstairs art, but with the crafts downstairs as well. Most of the items are handmade, some from recycled materials.

Specialty Stores

The **Great American Antiques Mall** (1305 Spring St., 805/239-1203, daily 10 A.M.–5 P.M.) has 40 vendors who are ready to buy sell and trade. Virtually everything is here—kitchen furniture, kitsch, glassware, silver, collectibles, and both new and vintage in a comfortable

9,000-square-foot space. It's well organized and makes intuitive sense as you walk around. This isn't high-end antiques, but a very good selection of well-priced items.

Powell's Candy Shop (840 11th St., 805/239-1544, Mon.–Sat. 10 A.M.–9 P.M., Sun. 10 A.M.–8 P.M.) has all sweet things vintage. From the pressed-tin ceilings to the candy you assumed they stopped making years ago, it's all here, including a lot of novelty candy like bacon-flavored mints. They also carry gelato and hand-dipped truffles, jelly beans, and bulk candy. If you are looking for that gum you always chewed as a kid, chances are you will find it here.

Rendition (1244 Pine St., 805/238-2433, www.renditioninterior.com, Mon.–Sat. 10 A.M.–6 P.M., Sun. 11 A.M.–4 P.M.) sells lots of big furniture. They have a plethora of wrought-iron sconces, chandeliers, and beautiful hefty wood pieces for the dining room, kitchen, and bedroom. Not afraid to be bold, these are pretty masculine works with a handcrafted feel.

Spare Time Used Books (945 12th St., 805/237-1140, Mon.–Sat. 10:30 A.M.–5 P.M.) sells predominantly paperback books with only a small fraction of hardbacks. As you enter you can clearly smell the paper and print of old books. The prices for most of the paperbacks are $2–5.

Shopping Malls

There are two malls in three sections near downtown. Nibblick Road, right off Spring Street and Highway 101, bisects **Woodland Plaza** (180 Nibblick Rd.), which is technically on both sides of Nibblick Road. This large outdoor mall includes Kohl's, Staples, Big 5, a pharmacy and grocery store, JCPenney, Wal-Mart, the usual food joints, smaller specialty stores like investment places and insurance companies, and plenty of parking. Right across the street where Nibblick and South River Road meet is the smaller **The Highlands** (Oak Hill and Nibblick Rds.), which includes Cider Creek Bakery, a church, Taco Bell, and a coffee store. This regional shopping area,

Powell's Candy Shop

including Woodland Plaza, is the most prominent in Paso Robles.

SPORTS AND RECREATION
Lakes

Even though Paso is located about 30 miles from the coast, you can still get a water fix nearby. **Lake Nacimiento** (10625 Nacimiento Lake Dr., 805/238-3256, www.nacimientoresort.com), or "Nassi" as it's called locally, is 165 miles of shoreline, with a year-round general store, a full-service marina, over 350 campsites, and basketball courts, volleyball, rentals of water skis, wake boards, kayaks, and pontoon boats, and 120 rental boat slips, all just 15 miles from Paso Robles. Kayak rentals start at just $5 per hour and you can move up to a 24-foot pontoon boat. Semi-rustic lodge accommodations are available as well. It's only 20 minutes up a curvy road to reach the lake; the area looks like a small village. There's a housing community called Heritage Ranch here as well, so the infrastructure is good.

Lake San Antonio (74255 San Antonio Rd., 805/472-2311, www.lakesanantonioresort.com) is the smaller sister lake with just 65 miles of shoreline on its 17-mile length, but with over 2,000 campsites. It's further north from Paso Robles and Lake Nacimiento. For fishing, the lake is stocked with largemouth and smallmouth bass, striped bass, crappie, catfish, bluegill, and squawfish, as well as other varieties. If you bring your own boat, the slip fees are just $15 each night, much less expensive than the cabins, which range $160–250 nightly. The south shore general store is open year-round, but leans towards expensive. There is water skiing and boat rentals as well. The lake is accessed from Highway 101 north or south by taking the Jolon exit west to New Pleyto Road, then following signs to the lake.

Water Park

Considering it gets into the triple digits in Paso during the summer, a cooling ride in some clean pure water might be just the thing. At **The Ravine Waterpark** (2301 Airport Rd., 805/237-8500, www.ravinewaterpark.com, summer daily 10:30 A.M.–6 P.M., hours can vary—phone ahead, from $19.95 adults, $14.95 under 48",

THE SULPHUR SPRINGS

Paso Robles used to be considered a health resort, much like Santa Barbara. In 1864 the *San Francisco Bulletin* commented that Paso Robles was the spot for natural springs and mud baths, and by 1868 people were coming from as far away as Oregon, Nevada, Idaho, and even Alabama to take the waters. Besides the well-known mud baths, there were the Iron Spring and the Sand Spring, which bubbled through the sands.

In 1882, Drury James and the Blackburn brothers issued a pamphlet advertising "El Paso de Robles Hot and Cold Sulphur Springs and the Only Natural Mud Baths in the World." By then there were first-class accommodations in Paso Robles, a reading room, a barber shop, a general store, a top-of-the-line livery stable, and comfortably furnished cottages for the tourists. Visitors could stay in touch with the rest of the world since mail was delivered twice each day. There was also a Western Union telegraph office and a Wells Fargo agency. As the springs became more and more a destination of the well-to-do as a place to socialize and be seen, the original purpose of the springs, to heal, became peripheral.

A bathhouse was erected over the sulphur spring in 1888, with 37 bath rooms, and a plunge where water is piped in from the springs. The following year, work began on the large Hot Springs Hotel, which was completed in 1900 but burned down 40 years later before being rebuilt as the Paso Robles Inn. Since the privileges of using the baths were restricted to guests of the hotel, and many people who desperately needed its healing powers couldn't afford the rates of the fashionable hotel, a few businessmen in Paso Robles made arrangements for the right to bore for sulphur water on a private lot. A sulphur well was reached, a bath house built, and baths offered at an affordable rate of 25 cents. The establishment was later offered to the City, and is currently the site of the Municipal Pool. The main spring was originally located at 10th and Spring Streets.

$10 seniors) you can take a 325-foot flume ride into a bed of water, grab an inner tube and simply let the current take you leisurely around the water creek, or splash in the wave pool. It's great for younger kids, but the truth is there are a lot of adults here too. It's probably the best way to cool off and have fun at the same time.

Golf

Hunter Ranch Golf Course (4041 Hwy. 36 East, 805/237-7444, www.hunterranch-golf.com, daily 6:30 A.M.–dusk, green fees $50–100) is surrounded by oak trees with views to vineyards. It's directly off the highway and this 18-hole, par-71 course might lull you into a false sense of security. You earn each shot here, and familiarity with the course beforehand will definitely help you. They have a full-service restaurant, pro shop, and three tee boxes and driving range.

River Oaks (700 Clubhouse Dr., 805/226-7170, www.riveroaksgolfcourse.com, daily 8:30 A.M.–dusk, green fees $10–12) is a six-hole course, so three go-rounds gets you to 18. It was designed in part as an instructional course, and there are plenty of ways to utilize it, either with a golf pro, or if you simply want to get in a quick short round. It's a par 19 with three tees for each hole providing different approaches for each shot.

Bike Trails

Highway 46 West to the Coast is not an official route or anything like that, it's just a very popular stretch of road. Assuming you pick up the route near Highway 101, it's about 24 miles one-way. But the best parts are at the back end, closer to the coast, for sweeping vistas of beautiful multiple rolling hills. About 13 miles in you can park off York Mountain or Apple Roads and unload your bike there. The elevation at the top of the pass, before it drops down towards Cambria and Highway 1, is about 1,700 feet, and on clear days the views extend to the

SAN LUIS OBISPO

The outdoor hot tubs at River Oaks Hot Springs offer serene views.

lush green hills, Morro Rock, and the Pacific Ocean.

Vineyard Drive can be accessed directly off Highway 46 or further south off Highway 101. This is a two-lane road with moderate climbs and lots of twists and turns taking you by old vineyards, farms, and moss-covered oaks that hang languidly over the road. You can even plan to stop by a winery as part of your ride. You do need to keep an eye on the traffic, as chances are they've been visiting the area wineries, and with little wiggle room on this road it's always best to be vigilant.

Spas

Service with a twist is what **Twist Studio Spa** (1421 Spring St., 805/239-3222, daily 9 A.M.–5 P.M.) is impressive from the moment you walk in, with its dark wood tones, slate-tile floors, and open feel. You can get a haircut or color in the front, then head to the back where there is a narrow café serving sandwiches and salads. They also have a mini–wine bar that features a different winery each week. Spa packages can be up to five hours for full-day

treatment. There are private massage and esthetician rooms and the dark woods, exposed trusses, and earthy-looking environment makes this feel more like a really cool cabin.

For a more traditional approach, the **River Oaks Hot Springs** (800 Clubhouse Dr., 805/238-4600, www.riveroakshotsprings.com, Tues.–Sun. 9 A.M.–9 P.M.) has massage and the usual list of services like waxing and facials, but the best part of their offerings is the outdoor hot tubs with Paso Robles' natural water being fed into them at 102 degrees. Each tub is surrounded by wood latticework for privacy, and the serene environment lets you view the oaks on the low sloping hillsides. You can even bring your own bottle of wine for a $10 corkage fee. If that's too outdoorsy, you can experience the same waters inside in a private room. The outdoor tubs start at $16 per hour, but the views to trees and the pastoral scents of the short grasses are all free.

ACCOMMODATIONS
$100-200

The **Melody Ranch Motel** (939 Spring St., 805/238-3911, $80–90) is a classic California motor court with all rooms facing the center. It's easy to miss the low building as you drive by it. It's close to downtown and is kept well cleaned, but remember this is not a new property. There is an outdoor pool and though not fancy, it's probably the best bargain in town. From here it's a five-block flat walk to the City Park, the hub of the action.

The **Best Western Black Oak Motor Lodge** (1135 24th St., 805/238-0726, www.bestwestern.com, $129–140 d) has 100 rooms that are larger than those at most hotels, and three dedicated for folks with disabilities. They have a heated pool, hot tub, sauna, and free Wi-Fi. Each of the renovated rooms is decorated differently, but certainly in a traditional style. They don't provide breakfast, but do provide a $5 voucher for breakfast at the nearby diner. Downtown is a 10-block walk from here, otherwise a very brief drive is inevitable.

The rooms at **La Quinta** (2615 Buena Vista, 805/239-3004, www.lq.com, $139–150 d) are all a pretty standard size, but the main features are the fitness room, their 5:30–7 P.M. wine reception, the in-room 32-inch flat-screen TVs, and the outdoor pool and hot tub. Since it is just on the west side of Highway 101 there's less traffic noise and plenty of privacy. This also makes for a closer drive if you're spending time over at Cambria or Morro Bay.

At the **Holiday Inn Express** (2455 Riverside Dr., 805/238-6500, www.hixpaso.com, $150–170 d) there are 91 very nicely appointed guest rooms with in-room coffeemakers, free Wi-Fi, free local phone calls. A hot breakfast is also included, and you are reasonably close to downtown, though you will need to make a short drive to get there. There's a small fitness room too, and the rooms, while nothing spectacular, are comfortable and spacious.

The **Hampton Inn** (212 Alexa Ct., 805/226-9988, www.hamptoninn.com, $160–180 d) is right off Highway 101 just south of the Spring Street exit, which makes it very convenient. The 81 rooms are garden variety, but they are clean. There's a lovely lobby with a sofa and a fireplace and they have a gift shop, safety deposit boxes, and a coin laundry. Located on the west side of Highway 46, it's also next door to a shopping mall with a few food places and coffee outlets.

Adelaide Inn (1215 Ysabel, 805/238-2770, www.adelaideinn.com, $99–119 d) has been family-owned and -operated for 45 years. The rooms are very spacious and well appointed, and the staff is very friendly. There's an outdoor pool and hot tub. For the price, this is an exceptional value. Rooms include a work desk, refrigerator, coffeemaker, microwave, free high-speed DSL, and large bathroom and dressing area. Frankly, many places in the area charge more for less than you get here. You have quick access to Highway 101 and though you're not near downtown, there are restaurants and coffee places within walking distance.

At **Seven Quails B&B** (805/237-2598, www.sevenquails.com, $160–200 d), four rooms are tucked into the middle of nowhere, except that you have views to the vineyards from each room. Quiet and serene, it's removed from downtown and the noise, and with so few rooms you won't see too many people. The owners make their own wine, which they will share with you; their hospitality is excellent. You're already near many of the wineries on the Westside and only a 20-minute drive to the coast.

$200-300

Paso Robles Inn (1103 Spring St., 805/238-2660, www.pasoroblesinn.com, $230–250 d) is the brick building on Spring Street across from the park and has been an institution for years. The interior portion is beautifully landscaped with brick walkways, a koi pond, and a heated outdoor pool. The rooms are a bit small since this is an older property, but you can walk to the majority of downtown shops and restaurants from the hotel. They offer in-room coffeemakers and double-vanity bathrooms, and the attached restaurant serves breakfast, lunch, and dinner.

Honey Oak House (2602 Templeton Rd., Templeton, 805/434-5091, www.laraneta.com, $200–250 d) is located at Laraneta Winery,

© MICHAEL CERVIN

The Honey Oak House is a quiet retreat.

where owners Bill and Melinda Laraneta have opened up two rooms in their home and a free-standing room off the main house as a bed-and-breakfast. The owners are nice, friendly people, and they make excellent wine. The added bonus of staying here is that it's not a corporate hotel, nor a hotel at all. All three rooms have their own bathrooms, and the up-stairs unit has a balcony with serene, peaceful views of the vineyards right below. The sep-arate cottage is so peaceful you might think you're the only one left on earth. All rooms fea-ture queen beds and there are no visible street lights from the property. This accommodation is a bit remote, yet not that far from downtown; it is a good place to relax.

The **Courtyard by Marriott** (120 S. Vine, 805/239-9700, www.courtyardpasorobles.com, $200–230 d) has 130 rooms, with an on-site restaurant and fitness center. One of the newer hotels to be built in Paso, it has great views of the city from the top floors. It's not in down-town, but it is within walking distance to the Woodland Shopping Mall. They have a 24-hour business center and outdoor heated pool and hot tub, as well as same-day laundry ser-vice and large in-room flat-screen TVs. The rooms are a bit small, but the suites are more spacious. Since you're on the west side of the freeway, it offers faster access to the Westside wineries and the coast.

$300-400

⚫ Hotel Cheval (1021 Pine St., 805/226-9995, www.hotelcheval.com, $300–450 d) is hands down the nicest place to stay in Paso Robles. There are 16 large rooms with wood-burning fireplaces and private balconies or patios, de-pending on which floor you are on. The inte-rior courtyard is hewn stone with fireplaces for an intimate setting and umbrellas to shield the heat. You're close enough to walk to the City Park, shopping, restaurants, and downtown wineries, and they have a horse-drawn carriage to take you about if you don't feel like walking. It's a classy place with service to match, and their bathrooms and showers are quite large. A con-tinental breakfast is served to your room and there's in-room free Wi-Fi and CD/mp3 play-ers, plus a complimentary morning paper. This is one of those pampered getaways that's plush enough you just don't want to leave.

At the **La Bellasera Hotel and Suites** (206 Alexa Ct., 805/238-2834, www.labellasera.com, $199–399 d), many of the rooms start at over 400 square feet, so space is not even an issue.

Hotel Cheval

The 60 rooms, some with whirlpool tubs, are all nicely appointed and comfortable, with a hint of an Italian theme running throughout. The place doesn't feel large and that's part of its success-that and the exceptional attention to service. There's a pool, a fitness room, an on-site restaurant, and free Wi-Fi, and you're right at Highway 46 for easy winery or coastal access.

FOOD
Breakfast and Bakeries
If you want a filling, tasty meal that's not complex, try **House of Bagels** (630 1st St., 805/237-1818, www.centralcoastbagels.com, Mon.–Fri. 6:30 A.M.–3:30 P.M., Sat. 7 A.M.–3 P.M., Sun. 7 A.M.–2 P.M., $6). The beauty of a bagel sandwich is the large selection of bagels to choose from: whole wheat, plain, sesame seed, and plenty of others. They add turkey for lunch, or egg and ham for breakfast. The service is quick and efficient, and this is a great to-go stop, right off Highway 101 where Spring Street exits, so you can grab and go. They do have a few tables inside and a few outside should you decide to stay.

Across Highway 101 is **Cider Creek Bakery** (205 Oak Hill Rd., 805/238-4144, Mon.–Fri. 7 A.M.–6 P.M., Sat.–Sun. 7 A.M.–3 P.M., $6), which started out as a small bakery on the Westside of Paso Robles. Then they started making wine—just one wine actually, a zinfandel. Then they expanded to the Eastside and added sandwiches and soups. But it's still a bakery at heart, and their store is packed with muffins, cookies, breads, pastries, and the best snickerdoodles in town. They also have their own line of preserves like peach amaretto and plum butter, and make their own salsas. There are a few tables inside for when that heady sugar rush makes you weak in the knees.

American
When you enter the **Good Times Café** (1104 Pine St., 805/238-3288, Sun.–Thurs. 11 A.M.–8 P.M., Fri.–Sat. 11 A.M.–9:30 P.M., $10), you walk into the 1950s. Photos of Elvis, James Dean, old license plates, and 45s cover the walls, and music from the 1950s and 1960s fills the air. They serve milk shakes and cook up old-fashioned burgers like the Duke, with

© MICHAEL CERVIN

THE NEW GOLD: PASO ROBLES OLIVE OIL

In 1849 the gold rush brought thousands of people to California. These days, wine has replaced gold nuggets to draw people in. But there is a new gold that is actually close to gold in color — olive oil — and Paso Robles has become a huge producer of estate olive oils. As the Franciscans marched north establishing missions in California in the late 1700s, they also planted olive groves. Southern California probably saw the very first olive trees at Mission San Fernando. The olive is native to Asia Minor and spread from Iran, Syria, and Palestine to the rest of the Mediterranean basin about 6,000 years ago. It is among the oldest known cultivated trees in the world. It was being grown on Crete by 3,000 B.C. and the Phoenicians spread the olive to the Mediterranean shores of Africa and Southern Europe. Olives have been found in Egyptian tombs from 2,000 B.C. The olive culture was spread to the early Greeks then Romans. As the Romans extended their domain they brought the olive with them. These days local wineries like **Laraneta, Carmody McKnight, Jada,** and **Halter Ranch** are turning out small batches of olive oil along with dedicated producers like **Pasolivo,** who has its own press. The gold is still in the hills, only now it's hanging from the trees.

© MICHAEL CERVIN

olives ready to be pressed

bacon, onion rings, and melted cheese and slathered with barbecue sauce, which is no frills but very satisfying.

The Grill at Hunter Ranch (4041 E. Hwy. 46, 805/237-7440, daily 7 A.M.–4 P.M., $12) has great views to the Hunter Ranch golf course, set in a beautiful Craftsman-style restaurant with ample outdoor seating. The food here is basic grilled food, perfect whether you golf or not. Their BLT is a great choice for lunch, as is the chicken-fried steak for breakfast. Pleasant and away from the rush of most restaurants, it's a nice deviation from the norm.

⟨ McPhee's Grill (416 S. Main St., Templeton, 805/434-3204, www.mcphees.com, daily 11:30 A.M.–2 P.M. and 5 P.M.–close, $20) is consistently rated as one of the top restaurants in the area, and Ian McPhee has created a true dining destination in little Templeton. Locals love it, tourists keep coming back for more, and the food and service have not suffered because of it. Best known for their Kobe beef burger, duck and cheese quesadilla, and spicy Kung Fu ribs, the modest tavern exceeds expectations in its upscale yet rustic ambience with wood-paneled walls.

Artisanal Cheeses

Vivant Fine Cheese (840 11th St., 805/226-5530, www.vivantfinecheese.com, Sun.–Thurs. 11 A.M.–5 P.M., Fri.–Sat. 11 A.M.–7 P.M., $11) does offer a few sandwiches and flatbread pizza, as well as an organic soup each day, with produce farmed at Cal Poly. But it's the cheese that brings people here. There are local artisanal cheeses made in Paso Robles, like Rinconada Dairy, as well as cheese from places across the globe such as France, Spain, and Italy. This tiny spot smells absolutely heady as you walk in. They offer large and small cheese plates that include delectable Marcona almonds and other items. They are right off the City Park, so you don't have to go too far.

Pizza

It's all about the pie at long-standing pizza joint **Marv's** (729 12th St., 805/238-1851, daily 11 A.M.–9 P.M., $15). Located just across from the City Park, they turn out excellent traditional crust pizzas like their vegetarian, or meat combination, both of which are loaded with toppings. The interior is exactly what you'd expect a pizza place to be, basic and utilitarian with TVs bolted to the walls and clunky furniture as well as a few arcade games. If you're staying locally, they will deliver to your hotel room.

Organic and Local

⟨ Artisan (1401 Park St., 805/237-8084, www.artisanpasorobles.com, Sun. brunch 10 A.M.–2:30 P.M., lunch Mon.–Sat. 11 A.M.–2:30 P.M., dinner Sun.–Thurs. 5–9 P.M., Fri.–Sat. 5–10 P.M., $28) showcases locally grown organic produce and foods that are seasonally grown, wild caught, or sustainably farmed, with no growth hormones or antibiotics. That's been part of their success. The other part is that they serve excellent food. You'll find organic chicken, Arctic char, lamb, and Hearst Ranch grass-fed beef, all artfully prepared and executed. This is a destination restaurant for most visitors to the area, and it does Paso Robles proud. The feel is upscale with its white linens, but still comfortable and not pretentious. It's also immensely crowded, so make reservations.

Villa Creek (1144 Pine St., 805/238-3000, www.villacreek.com, nightly 5:30–10 P.M., $20) excels with natural and organic ingredients in their dishes, be that their butternut squash enchilada or their poblano chile stuffed with oxtail. They have an extensive wine list and separate bar area, and when the windows are opened to the City Park it has an expansive feel. There's a small back patio for something a little more intimate.

Eclectic

Berry Hill Bistro (1114 Pine St., 805/238-3929, Sun.–Thurs. 11 A.M.–8:30 P.M., Fri.–Sat. 11 A.M.–9:30 P.M., $15) is located right off the City Park. This friendly spot is Mediterranean in its feel with mottled walls, colorful accents, and plants, and it gets loud when crowded. But the food shines, and their seasonal menu has dishes like raspberry chipotle chicken panini and crab wontons. There are a few outdoor

Artisan is one of the best restaurants in Paso Robles.

seats, prime in summer, when you can watch everyone in the park.

INFORMATION AND SERVICES
Maps and Tourist Information
A visit to the **Paso Robles Visitor's Center** (1225 Park St., 805/238-0506, Mon.–Fri. 8:30 A.M.–5 P.M., Sat.–Sun. 10 A.M.–2 P.M.) will provide you with all the necessary materials to make your stay perfect.

Emergency Services
Twin Cities Community Hospital (1100 Las Tablas Rd., Templeton, 805/434-3500) is the nearest hospital to Paso. The **Paso Robles Police Department** is located right downtown at 1220 Paso Robles Street (805/237-6464).

Newspapers and Media
Paso Robles Press (www.pasoroblespress.com) comes out every week and also has a digital version. It's all local information, with high school sports scores and local politics. The *San Luis Obispo Tribune* is the daily paper that covers the county.

Postal Services
The U.S. Post Office is located at 800 6th Street in Paso Robles (805/237-8342).

Laundry
The **6th Street Laundromat** (719 6th St., 805/237-9255, daily 6 A.M.–10 P.M.) has an attendant on duty and provides fluff-and-fold services as well as coin-operated machines.

GETTING THERE
By Car
Paso Robles is directly off Highway 101 as you traverse a north–south route. Additionally, from the central valley (Fresno and Bakersfield), Paso Robles is accessed via Highway 46, which leads directly into the city. It's a two-lane road with a few passing lanes; if you get stuck behind a camper, RV, or someone towing a boat, which is very common, simply enjoy the ride and pass when it's safe to do so.

By Bus
The City of Paso Robles is the official agent for the Greyhound depot (805/238-1242,

www.greyhound.com), which is located within the Transit Center Facility at 800 Pine Street along with other modes of transportation. Greyhound operates Monday–Saturday 8:30 A.M.–4:30 P.M.

By Train

Amtrak's Coast Starliner makes northbound and southbound stops at 800 Pine Street, but only two stops daily. There are no ticket sales here; you'll need to buy in advance from Amtrak (800/872-7245, www.amtrak.com).

By Air

The **Paso Robles Airport** (4912 Wing Way, 805/237-3877, www.prcity.com) sits just on the outskirts of town. There is no scheduled commercial airline service at Paso Robles, but there are charter services available.

GETTING AROUND
By Car

A car will be important while you're here, unless you plan to stay and explore only in the downtown area. Should you want to visit any wineries or even head to the beach, a car will be a necessity. Getting around Paso Robles is simple and easy.

By Taxi

Paso Robles Cab (805/237-2615) has rates at about $3 per pickup and $2 per mile.

By Bus

The local bus, the **Paso Express** (805/239-8747, www.pasoexpress.com), is a fixed-route bus operating along designated routes within the city. It's available to the general public and provides low-cost transportation. Paso Express can be picked up at any designated bus stop in the city and the buses are lift equipped to serve those with disabilities; they also feature bicycle racks. Then there is **Dial-A-Ride** (805/239-8747, www.pasoexpress.com), an on-demand public transit service that provides curb-to-curb service anywhere within city limits. These too are lift equipped. One-way fares for both buses are $1.50, but they offer a variety of passes that will save money in the long run.

By Shuttle

The Wine Line (805/610-8267, www.hoponthewineline.com) is one of the few companies to offer a hop on, hop off option. For about $50 they'll pick you up at your hotel, then you can use three vans that operate on essentially a figure-eight route between downtown and both east and west wineries, running about every 40 minutes. They provide water and small bags of chips; you'll need to get more substantial food on your own. This is not a tour, but merely a shuttle service operating to and from some of the wineries. The best part? At the end of the day, they'll drop you back at your hotel.

Breakaway Tours (179 Nibblick Rd., 800/799-7657, www.breakaway-tours.com), on the other hand, is a full-service operation that will cover wine-tasting, basic ground transportation, airport shuttle, groups—virtually anything. They'll even head all the way down to Los Angeles to get you from the airport. They've been operating for 15 years and know the area well. They're happy to customize a day or weekend event for you. Frankly, anything you throw at them they can handle. They also operate out of San Luis Obispo and Santa Barbara.

CAMBRIA, SAN SIMEON, AND MORRO BAY

As the soft wide beaches of Santa Barbara and the San Luis Obispo region begin to dissipate as you travel north, the coastline becomes more rugged. This is clearly evidenced in the coast that runs through Morro Bay, Cambria, and San Simeon as it works its way up into Big Sur. The roads twist and turn, there's much more open space, and you begin to see pine trees. Though the coastline has changed, these coastal cities and towns have remained relatively unspoiled. Morro Bay still looks much like it did decades ago, a small beach community that fronts the Pacific Ocean, its namesake Morro Rock standing guard at the mouth of the bay. Cambria still has so many 1880s storefronts and a feel of yesteryear that you forget where you are. And San Simeon, a small outpost, hasn't grown much since the turn of the 19th century. These are the final towns for miles and miles, before the stunning and scenic Highway 1 crawls up towards Monterey. These are indeed some of the smallest towns along the coast and they have managed to remain unspoiled not only in their natural beauty, but in the simplicity of the shops that adorn their streets.

These three beachside communities, as well as Harmony and Cayucos, which are sandwiched in between them, are all directly off Highway 1. The hills to the east make this coastal region unique from the inlands area. But that doesn't mean they have constantly cool and foggy climates. Certainly there is a marine influence, but summers can get downright hot.

© MICHAEL CERVIN

HIGHLIGHTS

◖ **Hearst Castle:** Opulent, erratic, and ultimately all-American, this massive, lavish compound built on a remote hill is the closest thing to a true castle in California. Media mogul William Randolph Hearst spared no expense to construct the ultimate expression of grandiose dreams as a playground for the wealthy elite and socially connected. Original artwork and parts of European buildings were stitched together to create a truly unique but disjointed homage to the American home (page 266).

◖ **Nitt Witt Ridge:** Cambria's early version of recycled home construction, made from junk and found materials, is the unusual solution for one man with no money who, like William Hearst, desired to build his dream home (page 273).

◖ **Elephant Seal Rookery:** Every winter elephant seals show up on the beaches north of San Simeon to birth their pups. The males loudly fight and spar with each other, the females begin to wean the newborns, and the public gets a free show (page 274).

◖ **Abalone Farm:** The quintessential California shellfish, abalone is farmed in this low-tech operation that has been raising the sea snails for over 40 years. Tours allow you to understand the life span of these most sensitive of mollusks (page 275).

◖ **Moonstone Beach:** This stretch of beach is perfect for walking, thinking, strolling, and absorbing the beauty of this rugged area, with an accessible boardwalk on the cliffs just above the beach. There are as many otters and sea lions as tourists (page 275).

◖ **Morro Rock:** Primal, austere, energetic, and endlessly photogenic, this ancient dormant volcano defines Morro Bay and is a refuge for endangered falcons, home of native Indian lore, and a tourist's delight (page 289).

◖ **Black Hill:** Black Hill is the single best spot to view the entirety of Morro Bay, the other dormant volcanoes, and the valleys lead-

LOOK FOR ◖ TO FIND RECOMMENDED SIGHTS, ACTIVITIES, DINING, AND LODGING.

ing into San Luis Obispo. The soaring views are unforgettable (page 289).

◖ **Montana de Oro State Park:** This 8,000-acre park is one of the most diverse parks in the entire state. With access to the coast and beaches, scrub brush valleys, and rugged mountain terrain forested with canopies of trees, it offers walking, hiking, biking, and picnicking (page 292).

PLANNING YOUR TIME

One day and a night is enough time to get a feel for Cambria and San Simeon. Similarly, one day and a night can be perfect for just Morro Bay. The village of Cambria can be scouted out in a day, and you'll leave with an appreciation for the area, though you'll undoubtedly desire to return. Morro Bay and nearby Cayucos also can be explored relatively well in a day and a night. But these places beg for leisure time, the ability to wander the beaches, the hillsides, and the streets with no agenda. To fully absorb the natural setting, two days is an ideal time frame.

Most visitors attempt to include Cambria and Hearst Castle as well as a trip to Morro Bay, but realistically that requires a weekend. There's no advantage to planning a night specifically in Morro Bay or Cambria, since they are only 15 miles apart. It's more an issue of your final destination. Heading north, it makes sense to spend the day in Morro Bay and work your way up the coast, finding accommodations in Cambria, and the reverse is true when heading south.

The ideal weekend can include both towns, and should, as they are very different from each other in look, tone, and feel. You simply can't cover it all in a weekend; if that's all you have, a day for Cambria and the castle and another day in Morro Bay will suffice, though you will miss out on the finer points of both places.

HISTORY

Surprisingly, in 1880 Cambria was the second largest town in San Luis Obispo County. But by 1894, the railroad cut through San Luis Obispo, bypassing Cambria and shifting the economic base inland. The town continued on, however, as a quiet, isolated farming community. The advent of the automobile in the 1920s caused improved roads to be built to Cambria, which in turn brought land developers. The Cambria Pines Lodge was built so that prospective land buyers would have a place to stay as they scoped out potential building sites. Then, in 1958, Hearst Castle became a state park and opened its doors to the public.

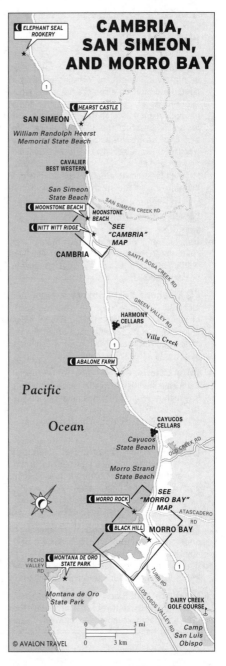

CAMBRIA, SAN SIMEON, AND MORRO BAY

ELEPHANT SEAL ROOKERY

HEARST CASTLE

SAN SIMEON

William Randolph Hearst Memorial State Beach

CAVALIER BEST WESTERN

San Simeon State Beach

MOONSTONE BEACH

SAN SIMEON CREEK RD

MOONSTONE BEACH

NITT WITT RIDGE

SEE "CAMBRIA" MAP

CAMBRIA

SANTA ROSA CREEK RD

GREEN VALLEY RD

HARMONY CELLARS

Villa Creek

ABALONE FARM

Pacific

Ocean

CAYUCOS CELLARS

OLD CREEK RD

Cayucos State Beach

Morro Strand State Beach

SEE "MORRO BAY" MAP

MORRO ROCK

ATASCADERO RD

BLACK HILL   MORRO BAY

PECHO VALLEY RD

MONTANA DE ORO STATE PARK

TURRI RD

Montana de Oro State Park

LOS OSOS VALLEY RD

DAIRY CREEK GOLF COURSE

Camp San Luis Obispo

© AVALON TRAVEL

0   3 mi

0   3 km

THE WRECK OF THE *MONTEBELLO*

It's easy to assume that California in general, and the Central Coast in particular, were not affected by any wars, least of all World War II. Yet Santa Barbara was actually shelled by the Japanese in 1942, though to no effect. A 440-foot oil tanker called the *Montebello* left Avila Bay in 1941 on December 23 around 4 A.M., loaded with three million gallons of oil. That same morning, around 5:30 A.M., a Japanese submarine fired and hit the *Montebello*'s pump room and a storage area in the fore section of the ship. Damage was done and the ship began to take on water, though the oil was intact. The *Montebello* started a very slow descent, allowing time for all the crew to abandon ship.

The submarine began firing on the soldiers as they boarded their life rafts; fortunately, none of the 36 crewmen were hit, though the experience was harrowing nonetheless. Poor visibility caused the submarine to eventually peel off. The wounded *Montebello* came to rest in 900 feet of water, just six miles off Cambria's Moonstone Beach. The wreck has been surveyed twice, in 1996 and again in 2003. There's been some thought about recovering the oil before the ship finally gives way to the forces of nature and releases all that oil. But for now the ship rests peacefully, almost fully intact except for a part of the bow, in a lonely grave near Cambria.

This brought throngs of tourists and gave quiet Cambria a new life, though it has managed to remain unspoiled.

San Simeon was once a vital whaling port, specifically around where the pier was built. There were homes near the point and plants to process the harvested whales. After the decline of the whaling industry and in spite of mining in the area, San Simeon slowed down. Today it's a service-oriented area that predominantly serves visitors to Hearst Castle.

Morro Bay was first spotted by Westerners when Juan Rodriguez Cabrillo explored the area and called the rock El Morro. It's always been a fishing village, and abalone were abundant here and in neighboring Cayucos until over-fishing took its toll and depleted the resource. Even today fishing and tourism are the main economy of the town. The layout for Morro Bay was planned as far back as 1872, and the town began to take a formal shape. There's a bit of drama too, as during Prohibition out-of-work fishermen turned to running Canadian whisky near the rock. The Embarcadero, today the most popular spot in the city, didn't exist then; it was created on landfill from World War II that the navy filled in. These days people flock here to spend time in the mild weather and enjoy the views, the rock, the shopping, and perhaps get a drink or two.

Cayucos has always been a small town. Established primarily as a shipping port, this old Spanish land grant has never really grown much. Part of its lack of growth was due to its being so secluded and hard to get to from land. With the advent of the Pacific Coast Highway, people came, but they tended to drive right by, either staying in Morro Bay or heading to Hearst Castle. Even now it's uncrowded, though there are a surprising number of second homes here, as virtually every residence in this tiny enclave has views to the water.

Cambria and San Simeon

Cambria, originally known as Slabtown, retains nothing of its original if uninspired moniker. Divided into east and west villages, it is a charming area of low storefronts, easily walkable with moss-covered pine trees as a backdrop. Typically you'll see tourists meandering in and out of the local stores, browsing art galleries or combing Moonstone Beach for souvenirs like moonstone rocks. The really great thing about Cambria is that, aside from the gas stations, you won't find any chain stores—not one—in town, and Cambrians, and most visitors, like it that way. It truly is an idyllic spot, even during bustling summer months when the crowds swell dramatically. Many of the buildings are original, dating to the 1880s.

San Simeon, on the other hand, is less of a town and more of a stopping point. Stores, hotels, and restaurants flank both sides of Highway 1 with no center of activity, and frankly there's not much activity at all. This is the last stop before Hearst Castle, and many people stay here due to its location just two miles from the castle. If there's any strolling to be done, it's along the bluffs or on the rocky beaches. Set amidst incredible open space between the hills and the ocean, San Simeon is truly a paradise of natural beauty, with stunning coastlines. Sunsets are gorgeous as the amber light casts its warm tones on the craggy rocks at the surf line.

SIGHTS
◖ Hearst Castle

It's virtually indescribable, this mammoth compound on a remote hill on a remote stretch of coastline, in a remote part of the state. Nearly 700,000 people flock here each year to experience the grandeur of long ago. Hearst Castle (750 Hearst Castle Rd., 805/927-2020 or 800/444-4445 for tour info, www.hearst-castle.org) is a uniquely American experience.

Main Street in Cambria

© MICHAEL CERVIN

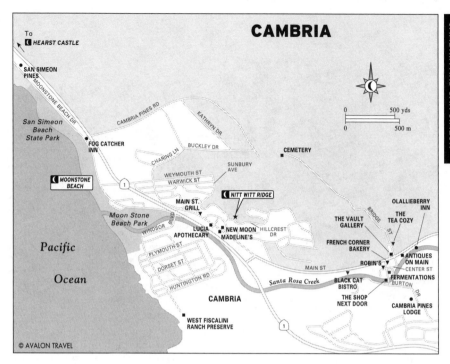

William Randolph Hearst was born to wealth and inherited 270,000 acres in and around San Simeon. Hearst was the very first media mogul, operating 26 newspapers, a movie studio, and other endeavors, which he oversaw from his center of operations, Hearst Castle, during his zenith in the 1920s and 1930s. As gargantuan as the property was, the home Hearst built for himself was also gargantuan. The numbers are staggering: 38 bedrooms, 61 bathrooms, 19 sitting rooms, and 41 fireplaces, all housed in a 90,080-square-foot complex of buildings: a massive main house and three guest "cottages" ranging in size from 2,200 to 5,800 square feet. A fourth and fifth cottage were planned but never built. There are two swimming pools, tennis courts, a private zoo, an airstrip (originally located where the visitors center is now), movie theater, and four enormous vaults in the basements that housed guests' valuables including mink coats and artwork. A bowling

alley and grand ballroom were also planned but never constructed. It may surprise most people to hear that the castle was never completely or formally finished. Hearst slowly ran out of money, and you'll see unfinished portions of the exterior to the west side of the main house, a tedious grey concrete that juxtaposes the gloss and detail of the rest of the building.

Certainly you can experience the castle in one day and with one tour, but that only tells part of the story. It's advisable to visit the castle twice, with at least two different tours. You can easily do one, two, or even three tours in a day, but it can be over-stimulating and make for a long day. If you have the time, it's best to visit over two days, which allows time to explore the rest of the coast and keep things at a reasonable pace. It's impossible to absorb everything on any one single tour, there's simply too much detail, both visually and audibly. And since each of the tours are designed to showcase certain

© HEARST CASTLE/CALIFORNIA STATE PARKS

aerial view of Hearst Castle

portions of the estate, you would need to take every tour to fully comprehend the castle in its entirety. There are no discounts for purchasing multiple tours however.

Things you won't see on the tours include architect Julia Morgan's minuscule wood-shed office, located in the back of the main house. (You might ask if you can see it, though it's not on the usual tours.) You also won't see the vaults in the basement, with original hand-carved doors, and stuffed with statuary and other historical artifacts undergoing restoration. Pricing for all the tours is $24 for adults and $12 for children 6–17. The evening tour is slightly higher at $30 for adults and $15 for children 6–17. The first tour is at 8:20 A.M. and the last tour leaves the visitors center at 3:20 P.M.

The visitors center is nearly a sight in itself. The large parking lot, operated by the state, provides free parking, but that's the only deal you'll get here. The large domed building houses restrooms and a food area that serves pizza and Hearst Ranch beef hamburgers. There's a patio outside with tables. The airstrip and the airstrip hangar were originally located

here. The current airstrip is a mile north of the visitors center and is still used by the Hearst family. The nearby theater shows a film about Hearst, his past, and how the castle came to be. It's about 40 minutes long and very well done; it is worth seeing if you don't know much about the Hearst history. At the very back end of the visitors center are two doors that lead outside to a small viewing area with a few tables and chairs and telescopes to view the castle that stands in the distance. On your way to the viewing area you'll pass by a few exhibits including the 1940s fire truck that was once used on the property.

A high-end gift shop sells replica items from the castle, as well as everything you can imagine with a Hearst logo on it, even things that have no relation to the castle at all. You'll have your photo taken against a background of the main house, like it or not, but you don't have to buy the photos. Then you'll board the bus and be driven up the winding road while recorded narration gives some preliminary information about the property. The ride up and back is about 30 minutes and needs to be factored into

THE HEARST LEGACY

William Randolph Hearst: The name conjures images of wealth beyond belief. And with great wealth comes great responsibility. The William Randolph Hearst Foundation was established by its namesake, publisher William Randolph Hearst, in 1948 under California nonprofit laws, exclusively for educational and charitable purposes. Since then, the Hearst Foundations have contributed more than $735 million in the areas of education, health care, social services, and the arts in every state.

Since Hearst owned 26 newspapers at the height of his power, the foundation has always had a strong affinity for the written word. The **Hearst Journalism Awards Program** was founded in 1960 to provide support, encouragement, and assistance to journalism education at the college and university level. The program awards scholarships to students for outstanding performance in college-level journalism. The 50th annual program offered more than $550,000 in awards and consists of six monthly writing competitions, three photo-

journalism competitions, four broadcast news competitions (two in radio and two in television), and a multimedia competition.

Hearst also had political ambitions and his father was a state senator, thus the foundation also funds programs for service in the public interest. The **United States Senate Youth Program** was established in 1962 by U.S. Senate Resolution, and is a unique educational experience for outstanding high school students interested in pursuing a career in public service. Two student leaders from each state, the District of Columbia, and the Department of Defense Education Activity spend a week in Washington, D.C., experiencing their national government in action. Student delegates get the chance to hear major policy addresses by senators, cabinet members, officials from the Departments of State and Defense, and directors of other federal agencies. The students are also allowed to participate in a meeting with a Justice of the U.S. Supreme Court.

© HEARST CASTLE/CALIFORNIA STATE PARKS

Even on a cloudy day the castle stands alone.

JULIA MORGAN: A WOMAN OF INDEPENDENT MEANS

Best known for designing and building Hearst Castle over a 21-year period, architect Julia Morgan designed more than 700 buildings in an illustrious career that spanned nearly 50 years. At 5 foot, 2 inches she was a small woman, but never one to be underestimated. On a cool spring morning in 1919, William Randolph Hearst swaggered into Julia Morgan's office in San Francisco. "Miss Morgan, we are tired of camping out in the open at the ranch in San Simeon and I would like to build a little something," Hearst said in his high-pitched voice. And that set in motion events that would catapult her into architectural history.

Julia Morgan never married; she was devoted to her work and she carved out a lasting legacy for women everywhere. She was the first woman to graduate from the prestigious Ecole des Beaux-Arts in Paris and was one of the first (man or woman) to graduate from U.C. Berkeley with a degree in civil engineering. Her notable California projects included not only the enduring Hearst Castle, but also the Bavarian-style **Wyntoon,** also for W. R. Hearst; **Asilomar,** located in Pacific Grove; the **Los Angeles Herald Examiner Building** in Los Angeles; the **Margaret Baylor Inn** in Santa Barbara; and a plethora of commercial buildings, as well as YWCAs, private residences, apartments, churches, and educational facilities.

Julia Morgan ultimately gave hope to women and girls everywhere, living a life that proved to them that their vision could someday be realized. Today the **Julia Morgan School for Girls,** an all-girls middle school in Berkeley, California, provides girls with education and empowerment. Morgan passed away in 1958 at the age of 85. In 1957, Morgan granted her one and only press interview, stating simply and succinctly: "My buildings will be my legacy. They will speak for me long after I am gone."

---

your schedule. If you go on multiple tours in one day, you will still have to return to the visitors center each time and start all over again with the next tour, as there are no waiting facilities up at the castle.

THE TOURS

There are four daytime tours available and an evening tour. There is no sitting, except for on the bus rides; you'll be standing or walking the entire time. All tours require visitors to climb stairs; the tour descriptions here and in the sight's website and pamphlet note how many stairs are on each tour and how much distance is covered. All tours arrive at the Neptune outdoor pool, a magnificent Greco-Roman style pool that features unparalleled coastline views from the hilltop, and all tours end at the Roman indoor pool, decorated from ceiling to floor with one-inch-square mosaic tiles, many of which are covered in gold. How the time in between is spent depends on which tour you choose.

You'll leave the castle feeling like you've missed seeing things. And you have. There's simply no way to assimilate all the visuals, and the information given, on any tour. And there's really no solid plan that allows you to see more, either. The best approach is probably to just let yourself gravitate towards the visuals that you find appealing, maybe the hand-carved ceiling, the peculiar statuary, the furnishings or artwork. No tour guide will touch on everything, but there is time for questions, so speak up. Ask about that object that you want to know about—otherwise the tours are overwhelming and leave you understanding very little of not only the building, but why it's important today, and why it was important in its time. (To this end, the film shown at the visitors center does provide useful background information.)

Tour One (170 steps, two thirds of a mile) is recommended for first-time visitors, as it provides a broad overview of the many facets of Hearst Castle and it is the least physically

© HEARST CASTLE/CALIFORNIA STATE PARKS

the Neptune Pool at night

demanding of the tours. Tour duration is 1 hour and 45 minutes, which includes the bus ride to and from the castle. The tour takes visitors to one of the most beautiful sections of the grounds, featuring marble sculptures and flowers in season. Hearst planted many flowering plants and fruit-bearing trees, in part because he liked the color palette, not so much because he wanted the fruit. This is clearly evident when the gardens are in bloom and the myriad colors interact with their surroundings. You'll also see Casa del Sol, which is an 18-room guesthouse facing the majestic Pacific Ocean. On clear days you can see the vast stretch of ocean and land before you. Casa del Sol, like all the other cottages, is replete with massive fireplaces, beautifully sculpted furnishings, and more ornate decorations than you can imagine.

The main stop on Tour One is the main house, or Casa Grande. Five rooms on the ground floor are shown, including the Assembly Room, which is the largest of the four sitting rooms and was once a gathering place for Hearst's guests as they waited for dinner. Interestingly, even as massive as this room is, there's little light coming from the two windows flanking the room or the main entrance. The Refectory is the single dining room at Hearst Castle, with an unbelievably long table with silver utensils and a massive hand-carved and intricate ceiling. The Morning Room is a magnificent sitting room filled with Spanish antiques and Flemish tapestries, and the Billiard Room is a game room featuring two 1920s billiard tables and a Gothic tapestry. Leaving there, you enter the theater, where Hearst used to show the movies his film company produced.

Tour Two (404 steps, three quarters of a mile) focuses on the architectural elements and vast art collection in the main house. Featured rooms on this tour include the Doge's Suite, a Venetian-style room with an open balcony,

the Gothic Suite

and the Cloisters, four guest rooms flanked by open walkways. The library is classic wood-paneled walls with nearly every inch given to books, almost 4,000 books in fact, and a collection of rare Greek and Roman antiquities. The Gothic Suite, which occupies the entire 3rd floor and includes Hearst's impressive private suite, library, and office, is the size of a small house in itself. Lastly you'll see the huge kitchen, which has heated countertops, something new back then.

The castle's North Wing is featured on **Tour Three** (343 steps, three quarters of a mile), which treats visitors to three floors of guest suites completed during Hearst's final years. These rooms exhibit more modern and spacious interiors, and there is a lot of art deco influence in some of the furnishings and accent pieces. The 1940s bathrooms blend efficiency and glamour, as in a beautiful black-and-white marble example on the 2nd floor. There are also antique Spanish ceilings in the rooms. Pay

special attention to the lamps and clocks here, all unique and original reflections of the period. You'll also visit Casa del Monte, one of the guesthouses that overlooks the Santa Lucia Mountains and includes 10 rooms lavishly decorated with tapestries, antique furniture, and pieces from the castle's vast art collection.

Tour Four (240 steps, one mile) not only concentrates on the beauty of the botanical gardens, but also provides a glimpse into some of the less familiar aspects of Hearst Castle; it is offered April–October only. You'll start with the Neptune Pool men's and women's dressing rooms, upstairs from the pool, which are nicely adorned. You'll also get a little time on the patio, where you can imagine a summer party with eye-catching views to the mountains and ocean. You'll then slip into Casa del Mar, which is the largest and most elaborate guesthouse and includes sweeping views of the Pacific Ocean. It was in Casa del Mar that Hearst himself spent his final years at

© HEARST CASTLE/CALIFORNIA STATE PARKS

Fountains and statuary punctuate the grounds.

the residence before finally leaving the property because of poor health. Then comes the Esplanade, and all of the estate's gardens, terraces, and walkways. Included here is the so-called hidden terrace, which was a remnant of early construction and includes a staircase, pond, and terrace completely concealed by later construction; it was rediscovered during modern restoration. An up-close look at the wine cellar showcases old bottles, ports, and French wines, but compared to the rest of the grandeur it's a basic room, unadorned and, frankly, a little dull. But hard-core wine lovers will no doubt find labels that interest them.

Tour Five: The Evening Tour (308 steps, three quarters of a mile) is a special tour that allows visitors to experience the castle at night as one of Hearst's own guests might have. The evening tour is available October–December and features highlights from Tour One, Tour Two, and Tour Four. Docents in period dress and a newsreel shown in the theater add a touch of authenticity to the magnificent surroundings and take visitors back to the castle's 1930s heyday. It's similar to a reenactment: You'll peer into the great rooms to see "guests" dressed in their finest socializing and preparing themselves for dinner. In the kitchen you'll

see cooks, though they're not actually cooking anything. The docents are not allowed to communicate with the tour groups. It's actually a fun way to spend the evening, adding a unique dimension to touring the castle. It's important to note, however, that since this is an evening tour, there's a different feel to the interiors, bathed in the amber glow of the lamps instead of the sunlight that normally illuminates many of the spaces. The Evening Tour takes approximately 2 hours and 10 minutes, including the bus ride to and from the hilltop.

There is also an **Accessibly Designed Tour,** which is an option for visitors who have difficulty climbing up and down stairs, or who have difficulty with standing or walking for lengths of time. Companions of anyone with accessibility needs are also welcome to join this tour. Visitors are allowed to use their own wheelchairs, providing those chairs can fit through doorways 28 inches wide. Visitors may also borrow wheelchairs at no extra charge. A specially equipped bus takes visitors to the castle for the tour and, trams are then used to escort visitors along the tour route.

◖ Nitt Witt Ridge

Called the poor man's Hearst Castle, Nitt Witt Ridge (881 Hillcrest Dr., 805/927-2690, by appointment only, $10 adults, $5 children) is a "mansion" of found materials, in stark contrast to Hearst Castle. Starting in 1928 and continuing for 51 years, Arthur Harold Beale, also known as Capt. Nitt Witt, collected junk, trash, and recycled goods to use in building his classic American folk-art home. A favorite material was old Busch beer cans, which were always in supply it seems. He also used washer drums, car tire rims, shells from the nearby beaches, tile, car parts, old stoves, and toilet seats as picture frames—just about anything people wanted to throw out. Beale claimed that some of the materials he used just washed up on the beach, or that he found discarded junk at construction sites.

This is a far cry from a sanitized residence or museum, and it's been left mostly to the devices of nature, so it might not be what you expect.

© MICHAEL CERVIN

Nitt Witt Ridge

In reality the place is in disrepair, in spite of it being on the National Historic Register. But it is definitely worth a stop to see the dedication one man had to constructing a home out of the abandoned materials of society. Tours are not offered at regular times and it might take some persistence to get hold of the current owners to give you a tour, so you'll need to plan ahead. It's on the hill just behind the west village so it's not a far drive.

◖ Elephant Seal Rookery

The Elephant Seal Rookery (four miles north of Hearst Castle entrance on Hwy. 1, www.elephantseal.org) is 12 miles north of Cambria or just 4 miles north of San Simeon. Don't worry about missing it—you will notice the brown Elephant Seal Viewing Area signs, along with a horde of people staring down at the beach over a low wood fence, not to mention the parked cars, buses, and vans. No one is certain why the seals keep showing up here, but they do. Elephant seals have been known to choose a spot to breed for many years, then leave and find something else. It's still one

of those mysteries that scientists can't specifically explain. They started appearing on these protected beaches in the early 1990s and haven't left yet. It's believed they like this cove for the protection it offers from the rough seas and predatory wildlife, plus the easy accessibility for pregnant females to get on land.

In the winter months the seals come here to breed, and in the summer months they molt. Winter is the best time to view the males, females, and newborn pups. They might seem lazy, sprawled across the sand, but they can dive up to 3,000 feet and swim at three miles an hour, carrying all that blubber with them. The males will spar for territorial rights and the females appear like they'd prefer to be left alone. The seals are around all year, though not in the great quantities of summer and winter. The docents, with Friends of the Elephant Seal emblazoned on their blue jackets, are there all year too. Ask them anything. The information is free, the show is free, and you might spend more time here than you ever expected.

Crowds gather to view the elephant seals at the Elephant Seal Rookery.

◖ Abalone Farm

Tucked into 18 bluff-top acres nearly hidden from view between Cayucos and Cambria, the Abalone Farm (805/995-2495, www.abalone-farm.com, by appointment only) has farm-raised abalone and is one of the largest producers of red abalone in California. Call ahead to schedule a tour that shows how they grow the abalone from eggs with pumped-in ocean water so the abalone are in their most natural habitat. Abalone grow notoriously slow, about an inch each year, and most abalone served in restaurants are 3–4 inches—do the math. If you can arrange a tour, this is a fantastic stop to see how a decidedly low-tech operation is producing one of the Central Coast's most delectable foods. The farm is not open to the public and you cannot purchase abalone from them simply by driving by, but many Central Coast restaurants get their abalone here. At the very least, their website has a video tour that is well worth watching.

BEACHES

The wide sandy beaches of the Central Coast end here, giving way to more rugged beaches with lots of rocks and minimal sand. These are prime areas for tide-pooling. You will occasionally see dolphins and whales from the shore, but you're most likely to see sea otters, seals, and many water birds.

◖ Moonstone Beach

Moonstone Beach (accessed off Highway 1 at either Windsor Dr. to the south or near Moonstone Gardens at the north end) is a mile-long boardwalk on the bluffs with occasional beach access; it is ideal for strolling, and is also wheelchair accessible. This is the beach that most people associate with Cambria. You can park anywhere along the beach side of the road at the pullouts—it's all free and there is no time limit. This is a more rugged beach, with less flat sand and more washed-up wood, seaweed, and yes, moonstones. At high tide there's little to no room to walk on the beach, but at low tides there's ample room to tide-pool, watch the otters and the seals, and sit on the wood benches along the boardwalk. These benches were all made by locals, and a dedicated group of locals keeps the area clean,

© MICHAEL CERVIN

Sunsets in Cambria are serene.

so please do your part by disposing of trash properly. If you look closely you'll find some areas removed from the boardwalk where you can rest. You'll also notice the ground squirrels who pop out from under the boardwalk, hoping you'll give them food. Feeding them is frowned upon, but they are adventurous and curious. Though hotels claim the other side of the road, there are no public facilities here. The closest are at Leffingwell Landing, a boat and kayak launch ramp at the north end of Moonstone Beach Drive, or at Shamel Park at the south end.

West Fiscalini Ranch Preserve

West Fiscalini Ranch Preserve (Windsor at Hwy. 1) is at the opposite end of town from Moonstone Beach and though technically there's no beach access, there are boardwalks that grace the property on the low rolling blufftop. Much less crowded than Moonstone, this is where the locals go, and where you can absorb the sheer beauty of the coastline in relative tranquility. The cliffs drop down to the water and there is precious little place to walk even if

you wanted to. To access West Fiscalini, turn south on Windsor at Highway 1 and the entrance to the west village, and follow it through a residential section until the road ends. You can park directly in front of the wood fence and access the trailhead. Turn to your right and follow the boardwalk to the ocean.

Little Pico

There is actually no official name for this beach, but locals simply call it Little Pico (Pico St. at Hwy. 1) because the Little Pico Creek meets the ocean here. It sits on a dead-end street; to access it you simply turn west on Pico Street directly off Highway 1 and park. Concrete steps will take you down to the shore. Typical of the area, it's not a sandy beach, but pulverized rock, sometimes dense and hard, and other times loose enough that you'll sink into it by a few inches. The sunsets, casting an amber glow everywhere, are what bring people out. At low tide you can walk down coast for a long time. Walking upcoast towards the creek and the weathered hills and rocks for tide-pooling on the other side is fine at low tide, but it becomes more difficult at high tides or after rains, when the creek becomes almost impassable because of the water streaming down from the hills. But there are little hidden places for sealife in the craggy rocks, and the muddy soil by the mouth of the creek is a great spot for bird-watching.

William Randolph Hearst Memorial State Beach

On the opposite side of the entrance to Hearst Castle is William Randolph Hearst State Beach (750 Hearst Castle Rd., 805/927-2020, www.parks.ca.gov, daily dawn–dusk). The old pier is still there, and the beach sits in a small cove with lots of trees on the nearby bluffs. A creek wanders into the ocean and at low tide it's easy to cross and make your way to the rock formations on the north side, which are teeming with starfish. Though this sits across from the entrance to Hearst Castle, it's relatively unused, and happily so. There are picnic sites, restrooms, and barbecue grills. Fishing from the San Simeon pier is allowed without a license. As with many state-run parks, funding could be cut and you may find these services unavailable.

SHOPPING

Part of the draw to Cambria are its shops dotting Main Street. You'll notice that there are no chain stores here, and that is by design. Stores and shops are family-run small businesses, which makes shopping here an adventure—you're never exactly sure what you'll find.

Antiques

Antiques on Main (2338 Main St., 805/927-4292, Sun.–Thurs. 10 A.M.–5 P.M., Fri.–Sat. 10 A.M.–8 P.M.) has, among other things, the best selection of vintage and novelty lamps and lighting, including 1930s vanity bullet lamps. The basement contains lots of garden furniture, and the upstairs has even more clothes, books, and accessories—just under 10,000 square feet in all. You'll find vintage furniture pieces here, as well as non-vintage merchandise like rocks and minerals and a collection of sport knives, and lots of women's clothes.

Literally two doors down is the smaller **Country Collectibles & Antiques Mall** (2380 Main St., 805/927-0245, daily 10 A.M.–5 P.M.), which has vintage LPs, sheet music, and books, as well as newer items. There are also coins, glassware, and fruit crate labels in abundance, some Central Coast labels as well. Furniture and accent pieces tend to rotate out quickly.

Art Galleries

Seekers Glass Gallery (4090 Burton Dr., 800/841-5250, www.seekersglass.com, daily 10 A.M.–10 P.M.) has an impressive array of all things glass—beautiful vases, sculpture, paperweights, bowls, jewelry, and lamps, as well as decorative pieces, infused with deep rich colors. These are not inexpensive glass works, but master works by well-known glass workers and artists from around the world. If you're seeking high-end glassware, then Seekers needs to be on your radar.

When you walk into **The Vault Gallery** (2289 Main St., 805/927-0300, www.vaultgallery.com, Thurs.–Tues. 10:30 A.M.–6 P.M.), you just might want to buy everything. An incredibly diverse and eclectic group of artists from Santa Barbara and San Luis Obispo Counties is represented here. Modern sculpture, photography, painting—there is an edginess to many of the works, forgoing the traditional landscapes and pretty beach scenes. It's worth checking it out to see some really cool pieces of art. Fitting with the name, a few of the works are even displayed in the vault, since the building was formerly a bank.

The **Teresabelle Gallery** (766 Main St., 805/927-4556, daily 11 A.M.–5 P.M.) is more of a stop to see local artists, though it is by no means limited to just that. The paintings are predominantly of local nature scenes, seascapes and landscapes, and are located in the small upstairs area. But there are also lots of beaded jewelry, handcrafted visual arts, and even some beautiful wood watches and garden ornamentation.

The **Artifacts Gallery** (775 Main St., 805/927-4465, www.artifactsgallery.com, daily 10 A.M.–5 P.M.) is one of those places where animation reigns supreme; it's an authorized dealer of Disney animation cells and artwork. These include hand-painted and highly collectible pieces, which share space with various sculpture pieces, some traditional bronze and some more whimsical ceramics, as well as oil paintings and limited-edition prints. To say there is diversity represented here would be an understatement. They also have a frame shop on-site.

Wine
Fermentations (4056 Burton Dr., 800/446-7505, www.fermentations.com, Fri.–Sat. 10 A.M.–9 P.M., Sun.–Mon. 10 A.M.–7 P.M., tasting fee $5) used to be a private residence; the cottage is now a wine shop and tasting bar. They feature local wines, but often have non–Central Coast wines as well. Where the tasting bar is now used to be the kitchen of the residence. In addition to pouring a wide variety of wines, they have a large selection of all things wine including shirts, gift baskets, and wine accessories, and issues of well-known wine publications. They also sell a line of their own olive oils and vinegars and specialty food items like their wonderful zinfandel mustard.

Black Hand Cellars (766 Main St., 805/712-9463, www.blackhandcellars.com, Sat.–Sun. 11 A.M.–5 P.M., tasting fee $5) is only open on the weekends. Their production facility and vineyards are located in Paso Robles, but they decided to place their tasting room in Cambria, and there's certainly less competition here. The emphasis is really on syrah, but there's also a lovely rosé and Bordeaux blends. This is a small-case production with some limits on the number of bottles you can buy, but it's an intimate spot, perfect for people-watching.

Home Furnishings
The Shop Next Door (4063 Burton Dr., 805/927-9600, www.squibhouse.net, Sun.–Thurs. 10 A.M.–6 P.M., Fri.–Sat. 10 A.M.–9 P.M.) predominantly sells Amish-crafted furniture. They feature beautiful custom-made handmade rocking chairs, dressers, dining tables, and game tables made to individual specifications. Some works have a distinct early-American feel; others are Craftsman in their approach. Woods used include ash, oak, and cherry, and many people sit in the rocking chairs and don't get up for a long time. They also carry other house accessories, but it's the finely crafted furniture that is the main draw.

The Garden Shed (2024 Main St., 805/927-7654, www.cambriagardenshed.com, daily 10 A.M.–5 P.M.) has a ton of garden accessories to complement your house, inside or outside. There are pots, of course, and fountains, whimsical figurines, birdhouses, tools, and aprons. The shop, which opened in 1999, has a beautifully landscaped back patio loaded with items, also worth a stop. You can get advice on making your green thumb a little greener.

Clothing and Accessories
At **New Moon** (791 Main St., 805/927-4496, daily 10 A.M.–6 P.M.) you'll find women's clothing with a kind of upscale gypsy feel. It's comfortable, non-constraining clothing that has a slightly new age twist, with patterns that incorporate woven elements and muted colors. There is accompanying jewelry like earrings, necklaces, and even leather jackets.

The **Down Under Trading Company** (604 Main St., 805/927-7069, www.downundertrading.com, Thurs.–Tues. 11 A.M.–5 P.M.) has lots of clothing, including the ubiquitous Ugg boots, traditional Australian work boots, and plenty of pants, shirts, and hats, all imported from Australia. Even the socks are imported, so you can get suited up for a walkabout and hike the trails in style. There are even a few food items, like the Aussie candy bar Violet Crumble.

Gifts
Wampum Trading Post (9190 Castillo Dr., San Simeon, 805/927-1866, daily 9:30 A.M.–5 P.M.) is the place for souvenirs of the nearby Hearst Castle like postcards, key chains, and non-castle merchandise such as Indian jewelry, artifacts, kachinas, and pottery. On the more mundane side, there are sunglasses and even snacks.

For a decidedly different approach to gifts, the **Cambria Music Box Shoppe** (734 Main St., 805/927-3227, www.cambriamusicbox.com, daily 10 A.M.–6 P.M.) has not only a multitude of music boxes of every kind and shape (including some with Central Coast scenes on the covers), but they offer wind chimes, wall art, musical wall clocks, and CDs as well.

Bath and Beauty
Stop in **Lucia Apothecary** (746 Main St., 805/927-1831, www.luciacompany.com, Mon.–Tues. 11 A.M.–5 P.M., Thurs.–Sat. 11 A.M.–5 P.M., Sun. noon–4 P.M.) for bath products like body scrubs, soaps, body oils, bath salts, and fragrances, each inspired by places along the Central Coast and with names like Obispo, Ojai, Cambria, Barbara, Montecito, and Robles. You can take part of the coast home with you, and remind yourself of your trip every time you wash.

At **Heart's Ease** (4101 Burton Dr., 805/927-5224, www.heartseaseshop.com, daily 10 A.M.–5 P.M.) you can find hand and face lotions, soaps, potpourri, and about a hundred different essential oils in a true 1870 homestead, one of the oldest in the village. They have a large and lovely garden out back and dried flowers hang from the rafters inside. They also have some garden gift items and books and a well-stocked selection of fresh and dried herbs.

Farmers Market
The **Cambria Farmer's Market** (1000 Main St., Veterans Hall, 805/927-3624, 2:30–5:30 P.M.) is held each Friday at the Veterans Hall. There's a multitude of flowers, fruits, veggies, and nuts from farms all along the coast. You'll also find cookies and pies and a very laid-back environment.

SPORTS AND RECREATION
Lawn Bowling
You're not required to wear white to participate, but you might want to consider stopping at the **Cambria Lawn Bowls Club** (950 Main St., 805/927-2585, Mon., Wed., Fri., and Sat. at 8:45 A.M.) to check out all the fuss. You'll get free lessons in the nuances of lawn bowling, and you can't beat hanging out with the locals and engaging in rolling a ball around. It's right on Main Street, so you can wander the town when you're done.

Hiking
For a short burst of activity, the **Burton Drive Trail** on East Lodge Hill is less than a half mile each way. You can start at the Cambria Nursery (2801 Eton Rd. at Burton and Eaton Drives) and head down the hill toward Santa Rosa Creek. The short trail, which follows the road, is on the opposite side of the guardrail, so you don't need to worry about traffic. A large shaded and immensely green wooded and vine-covered ravine is to your left. This trail will take you into town once you cross over the creek. Of course, this is the easy part—then you need to walk back up. The trail is pretty steep, so it's a hearty workout.

Near Burton Drive is the **East Fiscalini Ranch Preserve,** which is accessed via a pedestrian bridge near the Bluebird Motel (1880 Main St.). The interconnecting trails here vary between unimproved steep dirt paths and flat, wide easy paths. The area is full of moss-covered trees and lush green chaparral. Just beware of poison oak, and don't veer off the paths. There aren't the typical views to the ocean, but this short two-miler is more forest covered and secluded, giving a great idea of how forested Cambria actually is.

Bike Trails
For those looking for a challenge and with time to spend, the biking route along **Highway 1 North to Ragged Point** will satisfy you. From Cambria or San Simeon, simply start at Highway 1 and begin pedaling north. The route, all along the highway, is a mere 15 miles, but once you're past the low rolling hills near San Simeon you begin the long ascent up to Ragged Point. The road twists and turns past stunning drop-offs and old trees hugging the cliffs—this is the beginning of the spectacular and scenic drive towards Big Sur. Once at Ragged Point you have jaw-dropping vistas of the coast. You can also refuel at the Ragged Point restaurant (19019 Hwy. 1, 805/927-5708, www.raggedpointinn.com), then coast most of the way back.

For an easy ride, **Highway 1 South to Harmony** is a good route. It also follows the

© MICHAEL CERVIN

lawn bowling in Cambria

highway, but once you hit the down slope out of Cambria it's flat and wide, and the grass-carpeted hills are dotted with cattle and the rock formations are gorgeous. Simply take your bike to Highway 1 and pedal south from anywhere. You can pedal to the town of Harmony on your left-hand side, do a wine-tasting at **Harmony Cellars** (3255 Harmony Valley Rd., Harmony, 805/927-1625, www.harmonycellars.com, daily 10 A.M.–5 P.M., tasting fee $3), and then continue on towards Cayucos, which is 13 miles out of Cambria one-way, or return to Cambria.

Spas

The **Moonstone Day Spa** (7432 Exotic Garden Dr., 805/927-5159, www.moonstonedayspa.com, daily 9 A.M.–7 P.M., and by appointment) is located in the beautiful Hamlet at Moonstone Gardens just north of town. They offer facials, glycolic peels, face and body waxing, massages, body polishing, manicures, pedicures, and makeovers, many featuring mineral products. They also carry a full line of professional beauty and body-care products.

The **Sojourn Healing Arts & Spa** (2905 Burton Dr., 805/927-8007, www.sojourn-spa.com) is located at the Cambria Pines Lodge. They have been practicing since 1988 and offer warm stone massage, Swedish massage, deep-tissue work for those knots, Reiki energy balancing, and facials and body treatments that include mud, salt-glow, and pumpkin peels. Perhaps better still, they'll work on your hands and feet. They offer side-by-side couples massage, and they have a spa, sauna, and outdoor pool available for use as well.

ENTERTAINMENT AND EVENTS
Nightlife

Being a small town, Cambria has limited choices for things to do at night.

Cambria Pines Lodge (2905 Burton Dr., 805/927-4200, nightly 8–11 P.M.) is one of the few places to offer entertainment seven nights a week; the majority of talent is local. There are karaoke nights and small acoustical sets, but ultimately it's about the environment: The fire in the massive stone fireplace, the semi-rustic environment with worn but comfortable couches and chairs, and the laid-back musicians make this a mellow place to relax and hear tunes. There's no charge to sit and listen, but since the bar is right there you can curl up with a drink and make a night of it.

There's always live music at **The Hamlet at Moonstone Gardens** (7432 Exotic Gardens Dr., 805/927-3535, www.moonstonegardens.com). The jazz concerts began at the Hamlet way back in 1991. Currently there are usually two concerts each month. They are always on Sundays and there are two separate performances on concert nights by the same group. The first begins at 4 P.M. and consists of two sets of music with an intermission and ends around 6:30 P.M. or so. The first show costs $15 per person. The second show begins around 7:15 P.M. (usually a little after because the first show can run long) and consists of one long uninterrupted set that ends around 8:30 P.M. This costs $12. The cost for both performances is $20. You'll have views to the ocean and sunset while dulcet tones relax you.

If something more upbeat is your preference, **Las Cambritas** (2336 Main St., 805/927-0175, daily 11:30 A.M.–8 P.M.) has live music on Sundays only; on good weather days they set up on the outside patio and the strains drift over the rooftops. Usually it's a local solo or duo act, but occasionally a three-piece band will show up, performing music with a Latin feel.

Performing Arts

The **Pewter Plough Playhouse** (824 Main St., 805/927-3877, www.pewterplough-playhouse.org) is a small proscenium stage community theater that produces about four shows each year. Usually two are well-known plays while the others are new works. They also present a series of readers' theater throughout the year, where actors read from their scripts and there is little to no set. There is no hard and fast formal schedule, so it's best to contact them about performances while you're in town. Shows usually run Friday and Saturday nights, with an occasional Sunday matinee.

Festivals and Events

The **Cambria Art and Wine Festival** (805/927-3624, www.cambriaartwine.org, $15–85) is a January weekend of shopping deals, demonstrating artists, and lots of art for sale throughout the village. The wine-tasting main event is on Saturday from 1 to 4:30 P.M. and includes an art show of well over 30 local artists, and there's a silent auction, wine-tasting, gourmet food, and demonstrations with local artists showing a variety of techniques. There are about 25 wineries that participate. Businesses are open the entire weekend and feature different foods and wines at their stores to lure you in. Tickets can be purchased for the entire weekend, or for separate art and/or wine events.

ACCOMMODATIONS

While there are quite a few places to stay in Cambria and San Simeon, beachfront lodgings are the most popular. Peak summer months fill up quickly, as does Thanksgiving to New Year's. Plan ahead to get the hotel you want.

Under $100

Value is important, and if you're passing through San Simeon and Cambria for just one night, you might consider the following budget-friendly lodgings.

The **Silver Surf Motel** (9390 Castillo Dr., 805/927-4661, www.silversurfmotel.com, $70–90, d) has 72 rooms on three acres across the street from the beach. There is also a small grass area for pets or the kids, and you have very easy access to Hearst Castle for a morning tour. The rooms are slightly bigger than standard hotel rooms, and they offer an indoor pool and hot tub as well as Wi-Fi.

Just down the road is the **San Simeon Lodge** (9520 Castillo Dr., San Simeon, 805/927-4906, www.sansimeonrestaurant.com, $80–95 d), a 60-unit motel near Hearst Castle and the beach. It's a very good value, though the accommodations are simple and basic. If you're just around for a night and aren't planning on hanging out too much in the room, it's a fine stay. The rooms are clean and practical and there is an outdoor pool. There is a small restaurant (San Simeon Beach Bar & Grill) next to the front desk that has karaoke, a pool table, and a small bar.

$100-200

San Simeon Pines (7200 Moonstone Beach Dr., 866/927-4648, www.sspines.com, $119–140 d) is all by itself at the far end of Moonstone Beach Drive, nestled among pine tress on eight acres. San Simeon Beach is right across the street, as is the western entrance to the Moonstone Beach boardwalk. The building itself is a single-story ranch style and the rooms, while standard in size, have a country feel to them. One of the best parts of staying here is that a two-night minimum is not required. They offer real wood-burning fireplaces, a pool, Wi-Fi, a shuffleboard court and croquet area, and a 9-hole, par-3 golf course—they'll loan you clubs to boot.

The **Ⓒ Olallieberry Inn** (2476 Main St., 805/927-3222, www.olallieberry.com, $135–180 d), built in 1873, is a homey nine-room bed-and-breakfast. The floors creak in certain spots, and the rooms with period furniture are larger and laid out differently than standard accommodations. There's a wine reception each evening from 5 to 6 P.M., which also includes a variety of light foods. Sherry in a glass decanter is available in the front hallway whenever you need it. Three rooms are located upstairs, two with detached bathrooms, and three rooms are downstairs. The second house has three rooms. The property abuts Santa Rosa Creek, and during the summer months you can lounge outside and watch it go languidly by. Homemade breakfasts are served at 8 A.M. and 9:15 A.M. and include olallieberry jam. Occasionally, cooking classes are available in their very large kitchen, and you're close enough that you can walk to shops in Cambria. The service is beyond gracious—you'll feel like you're the most important person in the world.

At **Moonstone Landing** (6240 Moonstone Beach Dr., 805/927-0012, www.moonstonelanding.com, $150–175 d) there are only 29 rooms; the 10 facing the ocean are the more expensive, meaning that the value for the non-ocean rooms is quite good, at least for Moonstone Beach Drive. There's a continental breakfast and a hot tub, and though the standard rooms are nothing to write home about, you can access the beach by simply walking across the street. Staying here allows you to spend your money elsewhere, and that's a good deal right there.

Another great value is **Dreydon House** (1979 Dreydon Ave., 800/799-7704, www.dreydonhouse.com, $109), which is inside an actual home, so the two rooms feel, well, homey. It's located in a residential area, a bit out of the way, so it's quieter here, and just a short drive into town. Chances are you'll see deer in the backyard as you sip your morning coffee. There's Wi-Fi, books to read and DVDs to watch, and both rooms have private entrances. A cooked-to-order breakfast is yours in the morning. They only have specific dates they rent out the rooms, so it's best to contact them in advance for availability.

The very comfortable **J. Patrick House** (2990 Burton Dr., 800/341-5259, www.jpatrickhouse.com, $165–185 d) has only six rooms, beautifully decorated with dark woods and unique 1800s antiques so there's an authenticity to the decor. It's located away from the beach in a residential area, but only a 5-to-10-minute walk to the east village. They have a lovely back garden area in which to enjoy fully cooked breakfasts that might include blintzes, soufflé, and homemade bread. Cookies and milk are presented before bedtime, and it's a classic bed-and-breakfast where you end up spending time with other guests.

Even further removed is **Fog's End Bed and Breakfast** (2735 Main St., 805/927-7465,

© MICHAEL CERVIN

Lodgings located on Moonstone Beach Drive offer relaxing views to the ocean.

www.fogsend.com, $175–195 d), which is located on eight acres just outside of the east village. It's a short 10-minute walk to the east village, but seclusion is part of the charm at the three-room house. You can play bocce ball or walk along Santa Rosa Creek Road, which heads back to orchards in a valley. Breakfasts are served in a formal dining room and the house has gorgeous hardwood floors; the rooms are comfortable and inviting. This isn't an older house that's been converted, but a newer building, so it has some modern amenities.

$200-300

C **Cambria Pines Lodge** (2905 Burton Dr., 805/927-4200, www.cambriapineslodge.com, $209–325 d) has everything rolled into one: large and small suites and cottages, many with fireplaces, all with Wi-Fi. The lodge is set in 25 acres, most of it woods and hanging moss, and they are well known for their manicured gardens. The very best parts of the lodge are the gardens and the bar. The bar area is filled with old couches and stuffed chairs, a few wicker chairs, and a beautiful floor-to-ceiling

fireplace made of large round river stones with an old wood hearth. The wide plank floors and knotty pine ceilings make this rustic comfortable. This is an ideal place to hang out and hear live music, or just relax with a glass of local wine. They also offer an in-house restaurant for breakfast and dinner. On nice days you can eat outside, facing the small lawn and hedges. The rock grotto is a fairly recent addition to the lodge and provides some seclusion. The rooms are generally quite large and the furnishings keep with a mountain and wood theme. Some of the older cottages are rather spartan, whereas some of the newer ones, with private balconies or patios, have more modern touches.

The Lodge is also home to **Sojourn Healing Arts & Spa** (2905 Burton Dr., 805/927-8007, www.sojournspa.com), which offers massage, sauna, energy balancing, and facials. The spa is in a renovated cottage right near the indoor pool. This makes it very easy to take advantage of their services if you're staying there, though non-guests can book services too.

The **Fog Catcher Inn** (6400 Moonstone Beach Dr., 805/927-1400, www.fogcatcherinn.com,

$279–299 d) has an English country motif and a yellow Tudor-style exterior with a classic thatch roof, making it look more like it belongs in the countryside of Wales or England. A continental breakfast is enhanced with eggs cooked to order. Like every accommodation on Moonstone Beach Drive, the beach is right across the street. The rooms are outfitted with refrigerators and microwaves and lots of space; the feel here is kind of upscale rustic, with knotty pine and earthy tones to the furnishings. Outside there is a heated pool and spa, from which you can see the ocean, and there are always cookies at the front desk. The staff is universally helpful.

Best Western Cavalier Oceanfront Resort (9415 Hearst Dr., San Simeon, 800/826-8168, www.cavalierresort.com, $219–319 d) was built in 1965 and is still a family-run operation. The best rooms face directly to the ocean; it's one of few hotels where you can simply open your sliding door and hear the beautiful rumblings of the Pacific—for this reason, some of these choice rooms are booked over a year in advance. They also have real wood-burning fireplaces, though they use a compressed-wood-pulp disc. There are 90 rooms on-site, some without direct ocean views; each room has binoculars, plus cedar-lined drawers for your belongings. There's an on-site restaurant offering room service for all three meals. There are two pools, a hot tub, and three outdoor fire pits right on the bluffs.

The 34-room **El Colibri Hotel** (5620 Moonstone Beach Dr., 805/924-3003, www.el-colibrihotel.com, $219–239 d) is one of the newest additions to Cambria. At the far end of Moonstone Beach Drive, this is the most modern and hip of accommodations in the area, with a clean traditional European design. The hotel is situated near the creek and wildlife area and the rooms facing that, with small balconies, have views to the riparian area. You're close enough to walk into the village, or head down Moonstone Beach Drive. The sleek rooms all have deep soaking tubs, and afterwards you can head to the wine bar in the lobby and hang by the fireplace. This is a far cry from most every other place to stay in Cambria.

Also on Moonstone Beach Drive is the **Sea Otter Inn** (6656 Moonstone Beach Dr., 800/966-6490, www.seaotterinn.com, $239–279 d), which touts a fireplace in each room—it's actually a gas unit, but still nice. There are in-room coffeemakers and there is an outdoor heated pool. The rooms vary; ocean-view rooms include whirlpool tubs, and rooms with a garden view look onto a basic interior courtyard, but with the beach just across the street it's not a big deal. The rooms lean towards the feminine side, with soft pastel tones, and they are a decent size for the price. You can save money by foregoing the ocean view.

Sand Pebbles Inn (6252 Moonstone Beach Dr., 800/222-9970, www.sandpebblesinn.com, $214–299 d) is actually rather unremarkable from the exterior, sort of boxy and blue-gray. But don't let that turn you away, as the quality and comfort are terrific. Afternoon tea is served daily from 3 to 6:30 p.m., and a full continental breakfast is available each morning. They offer a decent DVD collection, and who doesn't like bedside chocolates? There are also coffeemakers and mini-microwaves in all the rooms. The rooms are a standard size and frankly aren't too interesting in the decor department, but they are comfortable, and the beyond helpful staff will accommodate you in every way.

$300-400

Driving by the **Pelican Cove Inn** (6316 Moonstone Beach Dr., 805/927-1500, www.moonstonehotels.com, $350–400 d), you can't miss the yellow clapboard siding of this hotel. The inn's balconies face the ocean and the room interiors are reminiscent of English cottage decor, including soft glowing woods and slightly overstuffed furniture. The inn has a fitness room, heated pool, cooked-to-order breakfast, and Wi-Fi. In the evenings the inn offers free coffee and dessert from 7:30 to 9 p.m., and prior to that a wine-tasting reception from 3 to 5 p.m. They offer a multitude of packages, including wine-tasting, romance, and garden-lover retreats.

The **Blue Dolphin Inn** (6470 Moonstone Beach Dr., 800/222-9157, www.cambriainns.com, $329–349 d) offers that full-on oceanfront experience you crave, with a view of the ocean from a beautifully appointed room. Amenities include a breakfast picnic to go, yes, to go, at the time of your choosing. There's also free Wi-Fi, 32-inch flat-screen TVs, in-room coffeemakers, microwaves, and refrigerators, and luxurious bedding and robes that make you feel pampered. The rooms are large and all different in style, each with a loose beach theme incorporating American and Asian influences. If you want the full treatment, this might be your spot.

FOOD

Cambria has its share of touristy places with average and standard food, and then there are some wonderful restaurants that take you by surprise.

Breakfast and Brunch

Though it's kept quiet, the **Cambria Pines Lodge** (2095 Burton Dr., 805/927-4200, www.cambriapineslodge.com, Mon.–Fri. 7:30–10 A.M., Sat.–Sun. 7:30–11 A.M., $8) offers breakfasts to non-guests of the hotel for just $8. They have a buffet-style setup, with eggs, biscuits, yogurt, bacon, coffee, and the like. You'll be seated in one of three rooms that looks out to the gardens. You won't get a better value than this, and the breakfast, while limited, is pretty good.

Linn's Fruit Bin (2277 Main St., 805/927-0371, www.linnsfruitbin.com, daily 8 A.M.–9 P.M., $15) serves breakfast items like omelets and paninis, but is most famous for the pies they have been baking for over 20 years. You'll also find Cobb salads, beef stroganoff, and house-made pot pies, but it's still about the fruit pies, including strawberry-rhubarb, Dutch apple, and olallieberry. The interior is down-home country, and since this is such a popular place, a wait can be expected. They also have a small gift shop where you can purchase whole pies and canned fruit.

OLALLIEBERRIES

You'll see the name olallieberry around Cambria, perhaps spelled differently each time. Part logan berry, part raspberry, this berry grows in and around Cambria, but it was actually created in a science lab. The original cross was made as early as 1935 as a joint project between Oregon State University and the U.S. Department of Agriculture. Selected in 1937 and tested in Oregon, Washington, and California and referred to as Oregon 609, it was eventually named Olallie and released in 1950. While developed in Oregon and planted there, it has never been very productive in that environment, and is therefore primarily grown in California. It has usually been marketed as olallieberry, just as Marion is sold as marionberry. "Olallie" means berry in Native American languages. The taste and structure is similar to a blackberry but a little milder. Make sure you try it around town, or pick up a jar to take with you to impress your friends, who chances are, have never heard of it before.

Cheap Eats

The **Main St. Grill** (603 Main St., 805/927-3194, daily 11 A.M.–8 P.M., $7) serves simple food, done well. It has more of a bar-and-grill feel; you order at the counter and they call your number to pick up your food. There are three flat screens to watch the game, a small bar, and copious indoor and outdoor seating. It is usually crowded. The chicken tenders and onion rings are consistently good, all prepared while you wait. This is one of the last places to get very good food at good prices before you head off towards Big Sur.

Sebastian's (442 San Simeon Rd., 805/927-3307, Tues.–Sun. 11 A.M.–4 P.M., $10) is an amalgam of small restaurant, tiny general store, and post office dating from 1852. The same family has owned it since 1914, and they used to serve the fishermen who docked at the once-busy port in San Simeon. These days it's less busy, and still a world away. The original

Sebastian's in San Simeon has been family-owned since 1914.

old wood floors are worn and beat up, a nod to a long history of service. As you leave Hearst Castle, this is the closet food you'll find. They make a mean French dip sandwich, and meatloaf, using Hearst Ranch beef. You can hang out on the side deck, with distant views to the castle, then head down to the pier.

Pizza

Moustache Pete's (4090 Burton Dr., 805/927-8589, www.moustachepetes.com, daily noon–10 P.M., $15) is part Italian and all pizza. There's a sports bar on the main level, and if you come in with kids you might think you're in the wrong spot at first. But upstairs is a bright, open restaurant that serves à la carte dishes including manicotti, salads, pizzas, calzones, and spaghetti and meatballs. There is an outdoor dining area for those with dogs or who just want to soak up the Cambria sun.

Mexican

You can't miss the dark salmon-colored **El Chorlito Mexican Restaurant** (9155 Hearst Dr., 805/927-3872, www.elchorlito.com, daily

11 A.M.–9 P.M., $10), the only Mexican place in San Simeon, which has held its ground for over 30 years. They have indoor and ocean-view patio seating with a moderate Mexican decor. House specialties include homemade vegetarian salsa and lamb shanks in a mild tomato sauce, and they dish up menudo (tripe stew) on Saturday and Sunday. They'll gladly substitute tofu in any meat dishes. It's a fun, simple spot.

At **Medusa's Taqueria** (1053 Main St., 805/927-0135, Mon.–Sat. 7 A.M.–8 P.M., $10) in Cambria, there are a mere half a dozen tables inside their colorful eatery. Though small, it turns out food with big flavors. The chile relleno, fish tacos, and huevos rancheros are some of the best dishes. The chips and salsa are made on-site and the service is friendly and attentive. It's easy to drive right by this tiny spot, but it's worth a stop.

Cafés and Tea Rooms

At local haunt the **French Corner Bakery** (2214 Main St., 805/927-8227, daily 6:30 A.M.–6 P.M., $10), the five tables are often occupied by people sipping coffee, reading the

© MICHAEL CERVIN

morning paper, and discussing current events. It's a great stop for a cappuccino or espresso and a baked good like the chewy cinnamon twists. There are also scones, croissants, breads, sandwiches, and plenty of cakes and cheesecake.

The Tea Cozy (4286 Bridge St., 805/927-8765, www.teacozy.com, Wed.–Sun. 11 A.M.–5 P.M., $15) has been serving up British tea and scones since 1999. The interior of the small old cottage is all plank wood, a bit rustic in contrast with the idea of a high tea, but the service and food make up for this oversight. They also carry a selection of true British foods like Yorkshire pudding mixes, water crackers, and butterscotches, as well as an assortment of loose teas. They will also dish up soups and sandwiches for those whose appetite needs more than tea and bread.

The **Cambria Coffee Roasting Company** (761 Main St., 805/927-0670, www.cambriacoffee.com, daily 7 A.M.–5:30 P.M., $7) not only roasts its own blends, with over 30 years of roasting experience, but they have scones, muffins, and pastries as well. Locals keep their mugs there on a separate shelf. The interior is small, so most people sit out front along Main Street, or head up a flight of stairs to a little sundeck to read the paper, chat, and enjoy the morning.

American

Though the name doesn't imply fine dining, the **(** **Sow's Ear** (2248 Main St., 805/927-4865, www.thesowsear.com, daily 5–9 P.M., $20) has been creating fine food for years, with an eye toward comfort food like beef stroganoff, lobster pot pie, and chicken and dumplings. The interior has wood paneling that ties in with the wood chairs and brick fireplace, though it feels a tad heavy in this very small space fronting the street. But it's intimate and romantic and consistently good.

Madeline's (788 Main St., 805/927-4175, www.madelinescambria.com, Thurs.–Tues. 5–9 P.M., $28) shares its space with a wine bar. Both ventures are fairly new to the dining scene in Cambria, though the spot has been a restaurant for many years. There is a surprisingly diverse menu here compared to

other places in the village, with dishes such as wild boar piccata, butternut squash ravioli, and even a Louisiana seafood gumbo. The wine list, while not extensive, is well priced, and the small space is accented with ocher-colored walls and white linen tablecloths.

The interior of the **(** **Black Cat Bistro** (1602 Main St., 805/927-1600, www.blackcatbistro.com, Thurs.–Mon. 5–9 P.M., $20) feels like a 1920s bungalow with vintage light fixtures and hardwood floors; next to the fireplace is the best seating. It's all dim lighting, mustard-colored walls, and tables set close together. The chef's mom decorated the interior and made the cushions on the benches, and the chef herself used to be a producer in TV before bolting out of L.A. She did it backwards, starting the restaurant first, then going to culinary school, but she prepares excellent food. The menu features mostly American dishes with a global influence, like soup with roasted corn, crab, cilantro, and bacon; crispy potatoes with a chipotle butter; and seared ahi with crispy mushrooms and shallots. There's a great focus on textures here, presented by a staff that knows exactly what they're doing.

Asian

Wild Ginger (2380 Main St., 805/927-1001, www.wildgingercambria.com, Fri.–Wed. 11 A.M.–2:30 P.M. and 5–9 P.M., $17) is wildly small, with six tables inside and three on their patio, but they dish up Pacific Rim food that is flavorful and mixes creative dishes such as smoked salmon–cream cheese wontons with standard Asian cuisine like Hunan beef and spicy calamari. They also offer a decent selection of vegetarian options and make their own sorbets. It's cramped inside, so if you're claustrophobic sit this one out. Otherwise, you're in for a treat.

Eclectic

(**Robin's** (4095 Burton Dr., 805/927-5007, www.robinsrestaurant.com, daily 11 A.M.–9 P.M., $18) is one of the best places to eat in Cambria. The restaurant is in a 1920s cottage that was the home of a construction supervisor for Hearst

Castle. The interior is cozy and intimate with a small fireplace. The outdoor enclosed patio is a great spot with views to the garden and is surrounded by a 30-year-old red trumpet vine. The ingredients are fresh and flavorful, with a focus on healthy ingredients. The lobster enchiladas are terrific, as are the espresso-rubbed short ribs. You'll find an eclectic selection of food here like cumin black bean nachos and portobello and spinach lasagna. They have vegetarian food and even some vegan dishes as well. Reservations are a wise idea for weekends and holidays, as they get packed quickly.

INFORMATION AND SERVICES
Maps and Tourist Information
The **Cambria Chamber of Commerce** (767 Main St., 805/927-3624, www.cambriacham-ber.org, Mon.–Fri. 9 A.M.–5 P.M., Sat.–Sun. noon–4 P.M.) is probably the best resource for information on the area. They also provide a free yearly publication that lists many of the stores, restaurants, and lodgings in the area. Do be certain to pick up a trail guide for additional hikes and walks—Cambria has great places to roam and you don't want t miss them. The **Cambria Public Library** is at 900 Main Street (805/927-4336, Tues.–Sat. 11 A.M.–5 P.M.). They offer additional information and local history, including a map for a self-guided historical walking tour.

Emergency Services
Cambria is served by three facilities: **Twin Cities Hospital** in Templeton (25 miles inland), and **Sierra Vista Regional Medical Center** and **French Hospital,** both in San Luis Obispo (37 miles south). Being that this is an unincorporated area, Cambria and San Simeon are served by the **San Luis Obispo Sheriff Department** (800/834-3346). If you have an emergency, please dial 911.

Newspapers and Media
The Cambrian (2442 Main St., 805/927-8652) is the local paper, published each week on Thursday. It costs $0.50. KTEA FM-103.5 is the local radio station.

Postal Services
There is a post office (4100 Bridge St., 805/927-8610) that is currently open Monday–Friday 9 A.M.–5 P.M., or there is the small post office in San Simeon at **Sebastian's General Store** (444 S. San Simeon Rd., 805/927-4156, Mon.–Fri. 9 A.M.–5 P.M.).

GETTING THERE
By Car
Cambria and San Simeon are located directly off Highway 1 and are only accessible from this route, whether you're coming from Monterey or Morro Bay. You can access Highway 1 from the 101 by scenic Highway 46 west, which will place you at Highway 1 just south of Cambria.

By Bus
The regional bus system, the **RTA** (805/541-2228, www.slorta.org), runs between San Luis Obispo, Morro Bay, Cayucos, Cambria, and San Simeon. Fares range $1.25–2.50.

By Train
The Amtrak train station is located in San Luis Obispo, 35 miles south of Cambria; there is no direct train service to Cambria or San Simeon. Car rentals are available in San Luis Obispo, or the county bus runs between San Luis Obispo and Cambria (RTA, 805/541-2228, www.slorta.org).

By Air
Flights to the region arrive at the San Luis Obispo County Airport, which is 35 miles south of Cambria.

GETTING AROUND
By Bus
The **Cambria Otter Bus** is a red and green trolley that runs through Cambria Friday–Sunday 10 A.M.–5:52 P.M. It runs the length of Main Street and heads out to Moonstone Beach Drive. Each ride costs $0.50. The regional bus system, the **San Luis Obispo RTA,** can get you from Cambria to Morro Bay and other cities closer to San Luis Obispo. Exact

timetables and fare information are available at 805/541-2228 or www.slorta.org.

By Car

The only driving you'll need to do in Cambria, really, is between the east and west villages, out to the coast, or towards Hearst Castle. Aside from these brief drives, you won't need to use the car much. Having said that, a drive up towards Ragged Point, 15 miles north, is worth the drive. And if you use Cambria as a base to explore the Paso Robles wine area, or even down into Morro Bay (also about 15 miles), a car will be important. But should you stay exclusively within Cambria, you can go carless.

By Taxi

The only available cab service is **Cambria Cab** (4363 Bridge St., 805/927-4357).

Morro Bay and Vicinity

Visitors come to Morro Bay for a slice of coastal California that seems to be vanishing. They want to stroll along the Embarcadero, looking at the boats gently undulating in the calm waters of the bay. They want to hear the call of the sea lions, flit into stores and shops, snack on saltwater taffy, and languidly pass the time in an environment that has not been overbuilt with trendy shops and hotels. And that's exactly what they will encounter. It's not fancy nor pretentious here, and you're just as likely to see veteran fishermen walking about as you are visitors from all over the world.

The residential section uptown (a few blocks off the Embarcadero) is an odd collection of houses, some new and polished, others from the 1950s, and still others like mobile homes. But Morro Bay still has its original beach vibe intact, unlike the now-swanky Carmel and Monterey. There is plenty of public access to the water's edge, and nearer to the smokestacks there's a boardwalk, which turns into a concrete sidewalk in the center of town. There are also multiple benches off the main drag where you can sit quietly over the water with a fish taco or saltwater taffy and watch the boats. Morro Bay is also home to a large number of vacation or second-home properties, which undoubtedly helps to sustain its image—people want it to stay as it was.

The bay tends to have nice weather because it's pulled back from the open waters. Just south of Morro are the small towns of Los Osos and Baywood Park; though not technically part of the city, they are part of the bay. Similarly, just north of Morro is the small town of Cayucos.

SIGHTS
◖ Morro Rock

The defining geographical feature of Morro Bay is the impressive ancient volcanic and sacred Chumash Indian site called Morro Rock (www.slostateparks.com, daily 24 hours, free). The rock itself is a collection of nine ancient volcanoes, also known as the Nine Sisters (or seven sisters, depending on who is counting). Morro Rock is one of those spots of incalculable beauty, a sheer rock face with low vegetation running up parts of it. If you're standing at the base, or if you're in the harbor, there's nearly a palpable energy, a primal beauty, to this ancient volcano. You cannot climb on it, since it's the home to endangered peregrine falcons. It used to be completely water locked, but now there's a causeway, built mainly from rocks and boulders that fell off of Morro Rock or were quarried from it. To access Morro Rock, take Embarcadero Drive north to its termination point. You can park at the base of the rock for quick accessibility. The breakwater wall connects to the rocks as well, and during storms it's an impressive place to be as the ocean tosses wave after wave over the breakwater.

◖ Black Hill

The second visible volcano in Morro Bay is Black Hill (Morro Bay State Park off State Park Rd., 800/777-0369, www.parks.ca.gov, daily

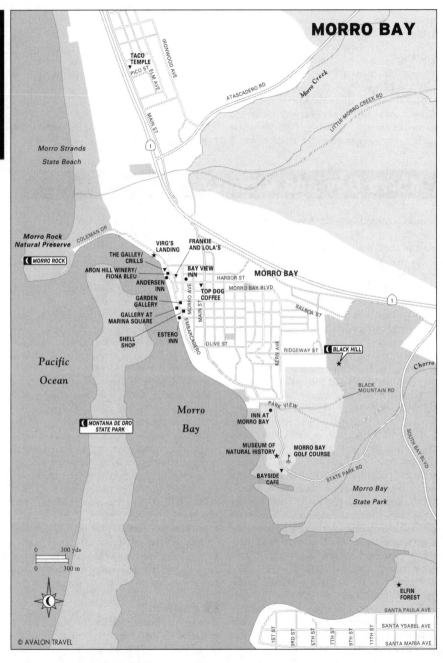

MORRO BAY

© AVALON TRAVEL

THE NINE SISTERS

The Nine Sisters are extinct volcano peaks, or *morros*, that run in an approximate straight line for 12 miles, stretching from Morro Bay to San Luis Obispo. These peaks separate the Los Osos and Chorro Valleys and are approximately 21 million years old, so the geologists tell us. Davidson Seamount, not considered part of the chain, but the actual termination point of the final volcano after Morro Rock, is submerged about two and a half miles offshore from Morro Rock. To see the chain in its entirety is an impressive sight. From the ocean, or the Elfin forest in Los Osos, you can clearly see the chain. Most times, however, you're too close for it to be obvious.

The chain is a big happy family of ancient dormant volcanoes, including:

- **Black Hill** (elevation 665 feet) is located in Morro Bay State Park and is best viewed from the back bay; it provides an overlook to the city of Morro Bay and the estuary.

- **Cabrillo Peak** (elevation 911 feet) was named after Juan Rodriguez Cabrillo, who sailed these waters in the 1450s. It is located within the section of Morro Bay State Park bordered by Turri Road, South Bay Boulevard, and Chorro Creek.

- **Hollister Peak** (elevation 1,404 feet) was named after the family that used to live at its base in 1884. This is the only peak that has a spring located at the base. It is the most majestic looking, and has religious significance to the native Chumash Indians.

- **Cerro Romauldo** (elevation 1,306 feet) was named in honor of the Chumash Indian Romauldo, who received a land grant for the property. It was also a quarry site. Cuesta College lies between this peak and Hollister Peak.

- **Chumash Peak** (elevation 1,257 feet) was given its name by Louisianan Clayton Dart in 1964, in honor of the Chumash Indians who lived in the region. This peak was quarried for rock to be used in foundations of new buildings at Cuesta College.

- **Bishop Peak** (elevation 1,559 feet) was named for a bishop's miter, or hat. This is the highest peak in the chain and its quarries were the source of rock for foundations, curbing, and buildings in downtown San Luis Obispo.

- **Cerro San Luis** (elevation 1,292 feet) is privately owned by the Madonna family and is sometimes referred to as San Luis Mountain, as it was named in honor of Mission San Luis Obispo de Tolosa. It's also known as Madonna Mountain and is visible from Highway 101 near the Madonna Inn.

- **Islay Hill** (elevation 777 feet) is located near the county airport and is a somewhat unremarkable round grassy hill – if you didn't know it was part of the *morros*, you'd think nothing of it. Most of the area around it has been developed.

sunrise–sunset, free), which offers stunning panoramas of Morro Rock, the estuary, and up the coast towards Cayucos and down the coast into Baywood Park, a small residential community. It is accessed by heading into Morro Bay State Park off State Park Road, which is a continuation of Main Street. Immediately after you enter the park you'll turn left, following a sign that says Black Hill Golf Course. This road will pass through the course and wind its way up the hill, where it dead-ends. There's a small parking area and the trail splits off two ways.

Take the left side, which works its way to the summit on a wide path. Once at the top, you'll have views that are close to jaw-dropping. You can see the other nearby *morros* (hills), the Nine Sisters, all of Morro Bay, and the surrounding area. Head to your left, where the path quickly turns into barely a trail as you traverse rocks and chaparral, hugging the side of Black Hill. This rugged route is for the adventurous type, those who don't need a clearly marked path. It will circle around Black Hill, but it is slow going. Bring a camera, as on a clear day you will want

Morro Rock is Morro Bay's defining feature.

to remember this. Non-adventurous types can head back the way they came.

Montana de Oro State Park

It's nearly impossible to describe the inherent beauty of Montana de Oro State Park (805/528-0513, www.slostateparks.com, daily sunrise–sunset, free). Access the park via Los Osos Valley Road off Highway 101. This road turns into Pecho Valley Road and takes you directly into the park. This glorious many-faceted 8,000-acre park has spectacular scenery. As you first enter the park, you're surrounded by a few trees and views to the ocean. But soon you're plummeted into a eucalyptus forest that gets more and more dense. If you stop for just a moment, you can easily inhale the rich aromas of these trees. There are pullouts where small trails wind through the forested section. As you continue on you're suddenly pulled out of the forest and into broad daylight along blufftop roads, the ocean to your right and forested hills to your left. Within Montana de Oro there are trails nearly everywhere, for hiking, walking, and biking. **Spooner's Cove** (805/528-0513, www.parks.ca.gov) is one of the more popular places because of its wide deep cove of ancient

rocks, sandy protected beach, and blufftop trails that lead up from the beach. The visitors center and park headquarters are also located here at the old Spooner Ranch House (3550 Pecho Valley Rd., 805/528-0513, ranger hours vary, call in advance). The beauty of this park is its diversity, with groves of trees, beaches, rocks, and low chaparral. All of this is coupled with tremendous views in a pristine coastal environment. If you do nothing else, drive through this park. Better yet, get a map at the visitors center and spend the day exploring one of the last great coastal regions in the entire state.

Museum of Natural History

The Museum of Natural History (20 State Park Rd., 805/772-2694, daily 10 A.M.–5 P.M., $2 adults, free children under 16) has a great location in the back bay, near the marina. It's a small museum, built on a volcanic point known as White Point, and the front portion of the facility is very kid friendly with lots of touch exhibits about sand, waves, and animals. The back portion has a good assortment of stuffed birds, like the peregrine falcon, so you can get a feel for what you'll see in the area. Best of all,

© MICHAEL CERVIN

the view of Back Bay from Black Hill in Morro Bay

there's an albatross dangling from the ceiling, its massive wing span covering you like a shelter. There's also a full-size skeleton of a minke whale on the outside deck overlooking the bay. They also offer occasional lectures. It's a worthy stop to learn more about the area.

Embarcadero

Chances are you will be on the Embarcadero while in Morro Bay. This is the main street that faces the ocean, where many of the restaurants and shops are. You can walk all the way to Morro Rock, about a mile away, stopping to get saltwater taffy, watch the fishermen unload their catch, shop for clothes, check out an art gallery, and even rent a kayak. It gets crowded in the summer months, understandably so, since everyone wants to be near the water's edge.

BEACHES

There are six miles of flat, uninterrupted sandy beach between Morro Bay and Cayucos, where tide-pooling is a viable sport, at least at low tide. The general catch-all name for this area is **Morro Strand State Beach.** Access is off Highway 1,

anywhere there are pullouts. The main stopping point is Highway 1 and Toro Creek Road, where there is a large parking area, but this long stretch of beach does not have any facilities until you reach the town of Cayucos. The beach continues past the Cayucos pier and suddenly disappears; then it's all straight cliffs. There are a few spots however on this long stretch that offer more, such as **North Point** (Highway 1 at Toro Lane), which has a grassy area for dogs to roam, and picnic tables, but offers no restrooms. A short stairway takes you to the sand, and at low tide some of the rock formations are exposed. The **Cloisters** (San Jacinto and Coral Sts.) is actually a park set back from the sand, with restrooms, barbecue areas, picnic tables, and a playground. The drawback is that there are no trees for shade. A short path offers direct beach access so you can cool off in the water.

WINERIES
AronHill Vineyards

From the bar of the small, quaint tasting room at AronHill Vineyards (845 Embarcadero, Ste. F, 805/772-8181, www.aronhillvineyards.com,

biking through Montana de Oro State Park

daily noon–6 P.M., tasting fee $5), there are near-perfect views of Morro Rock. There's a small patio outside where you can taste wine in full view of Morro's namesake. Actually there's just one table outside, but the owner, Judy Aron, is happy to serve you there if you don't feel like standing at the bar. The sauvignon blanc, chardonnay, cabernet sauvignon, and primitivo she grows come from a plot of land in Paso Robles.

Morro Bay Wine Seller
Just down the street from AronHill Vineyards is Morro Bay Wine Seller (601 Embarcadero, 805/772-8388, www.morrobaywineseller.com, daily 10 A.M.–6 P.M., tasting fee $5), which is a wine store with a diverse collection of over 300 wines, many of them Central Coast wines, as well as regional and international wines. If you're looking to taste a variety of different wines, or to shop for wine gift items, this is the spot.

Cayucos Cellars
Cayucos Cellars (131 N. Ocean Ave., Cayucos, 805/995-3036, www.cayucoscellars.com,

Wed.–Mon. 11 A.M.–5:30 P.M., tasting fee $5) is a family-owned winery, and when you walk into the tasting room one of the family members will be there pouring the wines. Chardonnay, syrah, cabernet sauvignon, pinot noir, and zinfandel are made in their old dairy barn in the hills near Cayucos, but the tasting room is downtown, in an artful little space a block from the beach.

Harmony Cellars
In between Morro and Cambria in the minute town of Harmony (population about 15) is the aptly named Harmony Cellars (3255 Harmony Valley Rd., Harmony, 805/927-1625, www.harmonycellars.com, daily 10 A.M.–5 P.M., tasting fee $3). Their white Riesling is one of their most awarded and best-selling wines, but they also have chardonnay, merlot, zinfandel, and several others. The town of Harmony may seem like an afterthought, and really, it's not a place locals hang out much. But the tasting room, founded in 1989 by Chuck and Kim Mulligan, is one of the main stopping points. Kim's great-grandfather, who owned the land that the winery now

ROCK STARS: THE FALCONS OF MORRO BAY

The peregrine falcon is among the most famous and admired birds of prey. It is also one of the swiftest, having been clocked at a stunning 175 mph in a dive. And a group of them decided that **Morro Rock** would be their home.

Because of its speed, agility, and ability to be trained, the peregrine has been highly prized in the sport of falconry for centuries. In Europe, in the Middle Ages, the peregrine was flown by royalty. It is a strikingly beautiful bird, regal and fierce in appearance, with long pointed wings and tail that visually separates it from all other hawks, except falcons, from which it differs in size. It feeds off live game and prefers to catch it in the air. It is swift enough to overtake the fastest flying bird.

Peregrine falcons prefer to nest on a ledge, in holes in cliff walls, or on high promontories in remote areas. At one time in the mid 1930s, it was estimated that there were 1,000 nesting pairs in the United States and Southern Canada. Now, in all of the United States, outside of Alaska, there are perhaps 50 pairs that mate, lay eggs, hatch, and fledge their young each year. The California State Fish and Game Commission placed the American peregrine falcon on the endangered species list in 1973, where it still sits today, unfortunately. But at least Morro Rock is an ecological reserve dedicated to their protection, so all people can view these remarkable creatures.

---

sits on, was a founder of the old creamery cooperative of the late 1800s, so there's a lot of history here. Sitting atop a hill, the picnic facility looks out on meadows that flank the town. Cattle leisurely meander around, giving little thought to the cars heading to the winery or flashing by on Highway 1.

ENTERTAINMENT AND EVENTS
Nightlife

Every night at the **Otter Rock Cafe** (885 Embarcadero, 805/772-1420, www.otterrockcafe.com, Sun.–Thurs. 10 A.M.–close, Fri.–Sat. 10 A.M.–midnight) there's something musical happening in their rock-themed interior. Every Tuesday–Wednesday is karaoke night, and they claim to have over 5,000 songs to choose from. The rest of the evenings feature musicians from around the Central Coast bringing in a mix of jazz and middle-of-the-road rock. It's always festive and upbeat, and you can dance with an eye to the water.

Legends Bar (899 Main St., 805/772-2525, daily 11–2 A.M.) has cribbage games, over 60 tequilas, a jukebox, and even a moose head squarely centered over the wooden bar. It's small, but has a large selection of drinks.

There's also a pool table and shuffleboard court. They don't serve food, but you can order food from **Sabetta's Pizza** (897 Main St., 805/772-0200) next door. You don't even have to leave the bar: There's a take-out window in the wall! Never mind the goofy statues out front, just head in. On occasional weekends there is live music, usually a local band with a blues/rock feel.

The **Bay Club Lounge** (60 State Park Rd., 805/772-5651, Fri.–Sat. 7–10 P.M.), located at the Inn of Morro Bay, has views of the bay and weekend live music. It's a good low-key nightlife option. They play more traditional lounge music and covers of well-known songs. The pace is slower here, and the primary clientele are guests of the inn.

On Board Nautical (805/771-9916, www.onboardnauticalevents.com, docked in the 700 block of the Embarcadero) offers custom dinners, wine-pairing dinners, and harbor cruises on the yacht *Papagallo II,* with live entertainment. The yacht was built in 1964 and was considered the Rolls Royce of yachts at that time. The old-school yacht has beautiful teak wood and plenty of interior and exterior space. Prices start at $65 per person, which is a fantastic deal considering it includes a

© MICHAEL CERVIN

On Board Nautical offers custom dinners and harbor cruises with live entertainment.

meal, which is prepared on board. On a perfect day, you can lounge near the bow and watch the world go by while eating sumptuous food like pancetta-roasted scallops, or coffee-and-peppercorn-crusted sirloin steak. Chef-owner Leonard Gentieu trained at the Culinary Institute of America and is a top-notch chef.

Cinema

There's only one movie house in town, the **Bay Theatre** (464 Morro Bay Blvd., 805/772-2444), and it has only one screen, so you're pretty limited unless you drive 20 minutes south into San Luis Obispo.

Festivals and Events

WINTER

The **Winter Bird Festival** (866/464-5105, www.morrobaybirdfestival.org, $35–70) is held the middle of January each year and brings out patient bird lovers from all over. Morro Bay is well regarded as one of the premier spots in the nation for bird-watching due to the bay and the large estuary. There are cruises, hikes, photo-hikes, kayaking, and bird searches during the

three-day event. But it's not limited simply to Morro Bay: There are bird events in Santa Barbara County as well, including much of the Central Coast and inland areas. So get your field list and start counting.

The January 1 **Polar Bear Dip** (Cayucos Pier, www.cayucoschamber.com) has been tradition since 1970. Every year on January 1 more than 3,000 people plunge into the Pacific Ocean at noon—and then there is a massive retreat to the pier about 12:01 P.M. Some of the brave souls dress up in costumes, others wear nothing but a swimsuit, but no wet suits are allowed. It's all free, and for some it's fun and the ideal way to start the new year.

SPRING

Every April the **Morro Bay Kite Festival** (1157 Embarcadero, Coleman Park, 805/772-4467, www.morrobay.org) transforms the skies around the bay with colorful kites undulating in the breezes. Kites up to 100 feet long and of every size and shape are welcome. The festival starts off with the ceremonial Blessing of the Wind by local Chumash Indians, and there are displays, vendor booths, even choreographed kite ballets. It's free to attend. Bring a kite, or buy one there, and join the festivities.

SUMMER

The **Cruisin' Morro Bay Car Show** (www.morrobaycarshow.org) takes over the small town each Labor Day weekend. This car show is all about pre-1974 cars of every type such as hot rods, woodies, vintage passenger and commercial cars and trucks, totaling 500 entries from California and beyond. Trophies are given out on Sunday, and they do actually cruise the streets. There's also an ice cream social. It's crowded beyond belief, but it's also a gas.

The **Avocado and Margarita Festival** (714 Embarcadero, 805/772-4467, www.morrobay.org, free) is a yearly September event that may seem like it doesn't fit with the context of Morro Bay. But there are actually about 30 avocado farms within the county, where the climate gives the avocados a longer growing season of 14 months. The majority of avocados from San Luis Obispo County and elsewhere in California are the Haas variety. A prolonged growing season means that the avocados are creamier and have more oils developed in the fruit. That means better-tasting guacamole. Combine it with margaritas, contests, and live music, all within view of the bay, and you've got yourself a classic California festival.

Since 1970 people have done the **Rock to Pier Run** (805/772-6278, www.morrobay.ca.us/rocktopierrun, $20–40), held each July. The six-mile beach run begins at Morro Rock and heads upcoast to the pier in Cayucos, all by the water's edge. The friendly race starts at 7:45 A.M. and has uninterrupted views of the ocean; if you're not concerned about your time, you can run even if you haven't registered.

SHOPPING

Morro Bay is made for leisurely wandering in and out of stores. There are many stores on the Embarcadero, and many people limit their time to the waterfront, but remember that there are shops three blocks up from the beach along Main Street as well.

Gifts and Accessories

It might seem an odd combination, but **De Winkel Shoes and Gifts** (701 Embarcadero, 805/772-4592, daily 10 A.M.–5 P.M.) has a large selection of imported shoes like Clarks and Dansko, should you need comfortable walking shoes or clogs as you wander the Embarcadero, plus collectibles such as the Harbour Lights Collection of collectible lighthouses, and the Mission de Oro Collection of the state's 21 missions. They also have a few souvenir items and postcards as well as themed Morro Bay shirts.

Somewhere in Time (601 Embarcadero, 805/772-8513, daily 10 A.M.–5 P.M.) is packed with collectibles such as Department 56, Historic American Lighthouse Collection, Dreamsicles, and many others. You'll also find porcelain dolls, teddy bears, collector plates, and teapots with matching teacups. There is also a selection of small antique furniture items scattered throughout, usually with other things on top of them. There are postcards and a few souvenirs from the area. They'll love to chat with you about Morro Bay.

At **Zephyrine Jewelry** (601 Embarcadero, 805/772-1810, daily 11 A.M.–7 P.M.) you'll find one of the largest selections of nautical and marine-life themed jewelry. If you need a dolphin ring or pendant, maybe a pair of earrings, or something with a whale, anchor, or sailboat on it, they'll have it. Their jewelry is both gold and sterling silver, and most people who stop in end up buying a gift for someone else. They can also replace your watch battery.

Home and Garden

From the looks of the exterior of the old wood-shingled building, the **Garden Gallery** (680 Embarcadero, 805/772-4044, Mon.–Fri. 10 A.M.–5 P.M., Sat.–Sun. 11 A.M.–5 P.M.) seems like it has been here for years. Well, it has. It opened in 1965. There is an abundance of garden and home decor, kitchenware, and garden ornamentation. The surprisingly large space is home to succulents in terra-cotta pots, and other pots as well, including bonsai, and plenty of things to make you think about your home and garden design.

Clothing

Wavelengths (998 Embarcadero, 805/772-3904, daily 9 A.M.–6 P.M.) has all you'll need for surfing at the beach, skating on the Embarcadero, or just looking cool enough that you look like you belong here. They have a huge selection bathing suits, swim trunks, and all types of beach attire including wet suits, and they also provide skate clothes, shoes, and boards and accessories. If you forgot your flip-flops, they have a large selection of those, too.

Similarly, at the **Dolphin Shirt Company** (715 Embarcadero, 805/771-9580, daily 9:30 A.M.–7 P.M.) you'll find all manner of summer wear, with a large selection of T-shirts, Crocs, Hawaiian shirts, sandals, and even outerwear for if the weather turns colder. And as the name suggests, you can find plenty of shirts with dolphins on them and clothing stitched with the name Morro Bay. They also have a decent selection of postcards.

At **Le Petite Boutique** (317 Morro Bay Blvd., 805/772-2361, Mon.–Sat. 10 A.M.–5 P.M., Sun. 11 A.M.–3 P.M.), not only are there ladies' sizes from petite to XL with a casual resort/beach feel to them, but there is a large selection of jewelry as well. The clothing here is aimed more at an older demographic. They also have a nice selection of Balinese dresses and wraps.

For the men, there is the **Aloha Shirt Shop** (458 Morro Bay Blvd., 805/772-2480, www.alohashirtshop.com, daily 10 A.M.–4 P.M.). Not that you are required to wear a Hawaiian shirt in Morro Bay, but if you should want that tropical feel, this store has plenty to choose from in their 4,000-square-foot shop, including well-known brands like Tommy Bahama, and Paradise Found. It's pretty much all shirts, with bright colorful patterns and some more restrained designs.

Antiques

The aptly named **Remember When Antique Mall** (152 N. Ocean, Cayucos, 805/995-1232, daily 10 A.M.–5 P.M.) will have you remembering when a lot of the items they sell weren't considered antiques! There's a wide variety of collectibles in this space and they have a large selection of fossils and minerals, all at reasonable prices.

Just a few doors down is **Rich Man-Poor Man Antique Mall** (146 N. Ocean, Cayucos, 995-3631, daily 10 A.M.–5 P.M.), which is an astounding 13,000 square feet and two stories where 70 different dealers show off everything from figurines to collectibles and furniture to vintage housewares, posters, and art. The basement contains a lot of the furniture. There's no real theme, just a lot of stuff to browse.

Brenda Sue's Consignment (248 Morro Bay Blvd., 805/772-7226, daily 10 A.M.–5 P.M.) has vintage furniture, in very nice shape, as well as clothes and vintage and modern jewelry. Since much of this is consigned pieces, the quality tends to be better, though it also tends to be more expensive. Her stock rotates fairly frequently so there's usually something new. There are also a few dealers with traditional antiques set against the back wall, many with larger furniture pieces.

Art Galleries

Fifty artists, many local, some regional and national, operate the **Gallery at Marina Square** (601 Embarcadero, 805/772-1068, www.galleryatmarinasquare.blogspot.com, daily 10 A.M.–5 P.M.) as an artists' co-op, which opened in 2003. With that many people involved there's a variety of work, such as beautiful photography, sculpture, painting, wood craft, and fabric art in the two-story complex. Once each month, a guest artist is featured. But since a majority of the artists here are local, you can find works relating to Morro Bay itself.

Fiona Bleu (900 Embarcadero, 805/772-0541, www.fionableu.com, daily 10 A.M.–6 P.M.) veers way off the standard gallery offerings. In addition to their line of recycled light fixtures, made on the Central Coast, they have artists who create mobiles, clocks, paper art, and sculpture with an eye towards a more expressionistic view. There are lots of creative things here, most with a modern vibe.

© MICHAEL CERVIN

Morro Bay's Shell Shop

Specialty Stores

If you see sea shells near the seashore, you're probably standing in the **Shell Shop** (590 Embarcadero, 805/772-8014, daily 9:30 A.M.–5 P.M.) The old faded shell sign out front and low building aren't overly inviting, but this store is great for shell lovers and it has been catering to shell enthusiasts since 1955. There are the standard shells you can find anywhere, and shell accented pieces for your home like shell mirrors, but they also have a vast selection of unique shells like the murex salmonea from Mozambique, a glorious little shell the size of your pinky fingernail, and the large New Zealand red abalone shells, coral, and nautilus shells.

Across the street is the **Native Spirit Gallery** (699 Embarcadero, 805/772-1321, daily 10 A.M.–5 P.M.), which has been selling Native American arts and crafts since 1995. As you walk in you feel a peacefulness—maybe it's the energy of the artists and craftsmen represented. They have a small section of books and CDs, as well as crafted jewelry from Indian silversmiths, pottery and woven rugs from native craftspeople, and gourds and baskets as well.

Farmers Market

The **Morro Bay Farmer's Market** (corner of Main St. and Morro Bay Blvd., 805/602-1009) is held each Saturday. 3–6 P.M. The streets are blocked off and you can find a variety of fruits and veggies, as well as coffee, fudge, kettle corn, and even a few clothing items.

SPORTS AND RECREATION
Whale-Watching and Boat Tours

Though no one can promise you a whale sighting, you'll get pretty close with **Virg's Landing** (1215 Embarcadero, 805/772-1222, www.virgs.com, Dec.–Apr. Fri.–Sun. 9:30 A.M.–noon, $29–39). The gray whales pass through Morro on their way to the warmer waters of Baja California. Though the grays are the most commonly sighted, there are 30 species of whales in the waters at various times of the year. Virg's boat is not a luxury cruising-type boat, it's a fishing boat—but no, there's no dead fish laying around, and it doesn't smell. But this is a working vessel, so don't think you'll be lounging in a recliner. Trips last just under three hours and you need to be alert, as sometimes a whale comes right alongside the boat. They also provide sand-dab fishing trips and other sportfishing trips.

For a different take on exploring the water, look into **Sub Sea Tours** (699 Embarcadero, 805/772-9463, www.subseatours.com, $14 adults, $11 seniors, $7 children 3–12), where you can look into the water from their glass-bottomed boat. This is a Coast Guard–approved boat that mainly stays within the bay or close to the breakwater to see fish, kelp, sea lions, and otters. Of course you can see a lot from the deck too, but the point is to peek below the water's surface. The tours last under an hour.

Kayaking

The best way to experience Morro Bay is to get out on the bay. **Central Coast Outdoors** (888/873-5610, www.centralcoastoutdoors.com) does an amazing job of guiding you to the best spots to view otters, seals, and sea lions and the plethora of birds in and around the bay and providing excellent factual information. Owner John Flaherty and his wife are passionate about what they do, and it clearly shows. They offer a variety of kayaking trips from half day to full day to dinner on the dunes. But you can also hike, bike, and walk on other outdoor adventures—they will customize a tour to best fit what you want. But even their standard kayaking trip gets you up close and personal with the bay's wildlife and gives you a chance to explore the sand spit, something most people never do. Half-day kayak tours start at $65. You can add a lunch option, go for a full day, or plan a weekend of adventurous travel. They are one of the best, most professional, and knowledgeable tour companies on the Central Coast.

Bird-Watching

The **Morro Bay Estuary** (best accessed via State Park Rd., www.mbnep.org), also known

bird-watching with a spotting scope

as the Back Bay, is an 800-acre salt marsh that is one of the prime spots to find birds. A spotting scope is a necessity, or at least very good binoculars, as much of the estuary is muddy and inaccessible. There are a huge diversity of birds in Morro Bay, some 250 species at last count; there are 300 different species along the Central Coast, which means the greatest concentration of birds is right here. You'll see songbirds, raptors, white pelicans, herons, egrets, plovers, warblers, and more in the shallow waters of the estuary and all along the back bay and into the bay proper. But it is the undisturbed estuary that sees the greatest concentration of fowl.

Hiking

A word of warning to potential hikers: January–June is tick season. It's not a big deal, really, as long as you check your clothing after a hike and knock them off. Lighter clothing makes it easier to see the annoying pests.

Cayucos through Montana de Oro is an area

© MICHAEL CERVIN

The Elfin Forest has excellent views to Morro Bay's estuary.

ripe with great hiking, both moderate walks and hefty mountain hikes.

The **Elfin Forest** (11th–17th Sts., Los Osos, www.slostateparks.com, daily dawn–dusk) is a stunted-growth area including 90 acres on Morro Bay's back bay where poor, acidic soil has truncated the growth of these plants, including oak trees. A former Chumash site, it is more chaparral looking than forest, and there are hundreds of species of plants here, not to mention excellent views to the estuary for birds. You can also get a good feel of the Nine Sisters, as Black Hill is directly in front of you, Morro Rock in the distance, and the other mountains behind you. There's about a mile of wide boardwalk, so it's great for wheelchair accessibility. From this vantage point you might notice a few fishing boats in the back bay that don't seem to go anywhere. Chances are they're oyster boats, growing oysters in the waters beneath them. Oysters have been harvested here since the 1950s. From South Bay Boulevard in Los Osos, head west on Santa Ysabel, then turn right on 14th Street. The street will end at the trailhead into the preserve. There are no restroom facilities here.

The **Chumash Trail** begins a half mile past South Bay Boulevard on Turri Road. It starts with a gentle course through grasslands, coastal sage, and native wildflowers within view of Black Hill and the Elfin Forest, and connects with the Crespi and Park Ridge Trails. Out and back is less than a mile, but you can connect with the other trails for a longer hike.

The **Valencia Peak-Bluffs Trail** in Montana de Oro is about 5.5 miles through low scrub and wildflowers, and though there's an elevation gain of over a thousand feet it's not overly strenuous, though there is a bit of loose shale here and there. From the top of Valencia, you have 360 views and can see as far north as the Piedras Blancas lighthouse in San Simeon. From Highway 1 in Morro Bay, take the South Bay Boulevard and follow the signs into Montana de Oro. Once you pass the official state park sign it's just over five miles to the turnout for the Valencia Peak Trail, located on your left.

The **Dune Trail,** also in Montana de Oro, is an easy one-mile round-trip hike. Less than half a mile north of Spooner's Cove on Pecho

Valley Road is a small gravel parking lot located on your right, which is the trailhead for the Dune Trail. This half-mile sandy trail crosses through low, dry vegetation towards the ocean. The trail ends at the top of a cliff looking over the ocean. You can access Spooner's Cove from here as well. It's a steep decline to the cove, but the views are terrific. This is a great spot when it's sunny or when it's foggy.

Golf

Morro Bay Golf Course (201 State Park Rd., 805/782-8600, www.slocountyparks.com) has some pretty stunning views to the bay and is surrounded by oaks and eucalyptus trees; you can see the ocean for six of the holes. It gets windy at times on this 18-hole, par-71 course, but that merely ups your game. During twilight hours it is half price to golf, though of course it's also more difficult to see. The course is located in Morro Bay State Park. Green fees start at $36. There is a clubhouse, driving ranges, and a restaurant.

Just slightly inland is **Dairy Creek Golf Course** (2990 Dairy Creek Rd., 805/782-8070, www.slocountyparks.com, daily 6 A.M.–dusk), which is a beautiful links-style 18-hole, par-71 course with lots of elevated tees in a serene and wide-open valley. They have a pro shop, a restaurant, and a teaching facility on-site. Green fees start at $42.

ACCOMMODATIONS

Some people may assume that it's better to stay in a larger city like San Luis Obispo, but staying in Morro Bay has its own rewards. For starters, you're at the water's edge, and assuming you're not driving all over, Morro Bay is very walkable, so you can leave your car and get out and explore.

Under $100

It may seem hard to believe, but indeed you can stay at the **Sundown Motel** (640 Main St., 805/772-7381, www.sundownmotel.com, $99) for less than any other place in Morro Bay. Yes, this is a true motel, with no amenities except for a coffeemaker in the room and a Wi-Fi signal.

But for those on a budget, you won't go wrong here. The rooms are standard size and minimally decorated, but clean and comfortable.

$100-200

The **Embarcadero Inn** (456 Embarcadero, 805/772-2700, www.embarcaderoinn.com, $130–160 d) is a 33-room hotel at the farthest point from Morro Rock where children under 12 stay free. Half of the average-looking rooms are equipped with fireplaces and there are some views to the bay, though you're across the street and there are other buildings in the view corridor. There's a small continental breakfast served, otherwise you're on your own for food. There's no fitness facility, but they have a deal with Fitness Works in town for a $5 day pass, which is a very good deal. They also have covered parking, something you don't always see.

The **Bay View Inn** (225 Harbor St., 805/772-2771, www.bayviewinn.net, $149–189 d) is a 22-room property set back from the waterfront so you actually have great views. They are only a block from the bay, and they boast Wi-Fi, fireplaces in most of the average-sized rooms, and a nice decor that is part country, part modern. They also have two sundecks in case you want to avoid the sand. This is an older property, so don't expect the newest furnishings and amenities. It is a great value, though, and less expensive than any place right on the Embarcadero.

The **Cayucos Beach Inn** (333 S. Ocean Ave., Cayucos, 805/995-2828, www.cayucosbeachinn.com, $145–195 d) is a 36-room very pet-friendly hotel north of Morro Bay in Cayucos, just a block from the beach. The very large rooms come with refrigerators, microwaves, DVD players (though you have to rent their DVDs, unless you have your own), and a 12-cup in-room coffeemaker. They have a dog-washing area and an outdoor picnic area, and you're close to the beach. There is no breakfast offered and the rooms are pretty standard in decor. If you're not a dog person, you probably shouldn't stay here.

The **Baywood Inn** (1370 2nd St., Los Osos, 805/528-8888, www.baywoodinn.com,

$130–180 d) has 18 rooms, each thematically unique but with an overall Victorian and French country feel with lots of quilted bedding. Located just south across the back bay, it's a short drive to downtown Morro Bay. Though billed as a bed-and-breakfast, they don't actually serve you breakfast but give you a voucher for either La Palapa (1346 2nd St., 805/534-1040) or Good Tides Coffee House (1399 2nd St., 805/528-6000), both of which are right next to the hotel. The rooms are clean and pleasant and the prices are a very good value. Amenities include a microwave and small refrigerator.

Just two blocks away, the **Back Bay Inn** (1391 2nd St., 877/330-2225, www.backbay-inn.com, $175–195 d) has 13 rooms overlooking the water with in-room binoculars, coffeemaker, and refrigerator. The majority of rooms are surprisingly large, and the downstairs rooms have semi-private patios accessed by French doors. They will charge you extra if you have a third person in your party, as they cater to rooms with two guests only—one of the reasons it's relatively quiet. Breakfast is included in the form of a voucher for Coffee 'N' Things (1399 2nd St., 805/528-6000), located next to the property. There's a wine and cheese reception from 5 to 7 P.M., but they don't serve local wines.

$200-300

Dead center in Morro Bay and right on the Embarcadero is **(Andersen Inn** (897 Embarcadero, 805/772-3434, www.ander-soninnmorrobay.com, $259–299 d), an eight-room property that places you squarely in the middle of everything. Three rooms directly facing the water, called the premium rooms, come with fireplaces and deep hot tubs. The other rooms don't directly face the water but have side balconies, so you're not missing anything. A restaurant called the Galley sat here for 46 years, then was torn down to make room for the Andersen Inn and a new Galley restaurant. The inn is clean and sophisticated without being over the top. The soft yellow walls contrast nicely with the wood-toned

furnishings. There are large showers, large closets, large flat screens, Wi-Fi, very comfy beds, and plenty of space in the rooms. And when you step out the door you're in the thick of things on the Embarcadero. Leave your car in their covered parking lot and go explore. They have lots of repeat guests and a large European contingency.

At the other end of the Embarcadero is an eight-room property that opened in 2009 called the **(Estero Inn** (501 Embarcadero, 805/772-1500, www.esteroinn.com, $209–299 d). Designed and owned by a general contractor, it has an abundance of attention to detail. Each room has a different layout and the furnishings are different, some with a Polynesian theme, others with a Mission feel to them, but all with thoughtful appointments. For example, one of the upstairs suites (both have partial wraparound decks) has an angled wall so that when laying in bed, you have a clear view of Morro Rock. They've used triple-pane glass, so it's remarkably quiet. A lot of care and attention went into building the place and that continues with the service.

Removed from the waterfront by only two blocks is the **Ascot Suites** (260 Morro Bay Blvd., 805/772-4437, www.ascotinn.com, $199–259 d), which has a Tudor-looking exterior, unusual for Morro Bay. There are only 32 rooms, though it seems much larger, and rates include a free breakfast, in-room coffeemakers, and a 4th-floor roof garden. The rooms are large, fully wallpapered, and busy with patterns, but with a palatial feel. There's an hour-long wine reception each evening, and though the hotel is not on the Embarcadero, you actually have better views of the bay because it's slightly elevated. It's a short walk to the waterfront.

The **Cass House Inn** (222 N. Ocean, Cayucos, 805/995-3669, www.casshou-seinn.com, $250) is designated a luxury inn, and that's what you'll get, just across the street from the beach in Cayucos. Five rooms with exceptional detail are for those who desire an intimate, pampering experience. It's definitely removed from the hub of activity, but you can get to anything you need to see in 15 minutes. Staying here is not intended to be in the thick of things, it's intended to rejuvenate you. Herbs are pulled from the organic garden to be used in the evening meal.

If you're looking for some quiet, away from the busy Embarcadero, the **Inn at Morro Bay** (60 State Park Rd., 805/772-5651, www.innat-morrobay.com, $230–270 d) is a good choice. Its 98 rooms are situated within the state park, far from the crowds. The French-country decor is pleasant, with lots of overstuffed furnishings. There are two restaurants on-site that both have views of Morro Bay and parts of the back bay. They offer a pool on-site, feather beds, CD players, and most rooms have a fireplace. They charge for Wi-Fi.

At the **La Serena Inn** (990 Morro Ave., 805/772-5665, www.laserenainn.com, $209–289 d) there are 38 rooms and suites with a variety of decor, but most closely resembling French country. The inn is three blocks from the waterfront. Included with the standard-sized rooms is a basic continental breakfast, sparkling cider and cookies in the evenings, and use of their 3rd-floor sun terrace and a dry sauna. The rooms come with in-room coffee-makers, microwaves, and refrigerators.

FOOD

Most people equate Morro Bay with seafood, which is understandable, with fresh fish just a stone's throw away. While here, definitely seek out local fish dishes, but also make sure you diversify your culinary experiences to include non-fish items since Morro Bay has a number of excellent eateries.

Desserts

The **Brown Butter Cookie Company** (250 N. Ocean, Cayucos, 805/995-2076, www.brown-buttercookies.com, Tues.–Sun. 10 A.M.–5 P.M., $5) started when two sisters opened a specialty food store that did reasonably well, but the cookies they made on the side became the real stars. So they opened a bakery, which sells just hand-rolled cookies, made with browned butter and finished with a dash of sea salt. They

literally melt in your mouth, and you'll nearly faint they're so good. They hand-roll over 2,000 cookies a day and ship nationwide. Stop in and get a bag, or two or three.

Crills (903 Embarcadero, 805/772-1679, Mon.–Fri. 8 A.M.–9 P.M., Sat.–Sun. 7:30 A.M.–10 P.M., $4) is the original place that started making and pulling saltwater taffy over 40 years ago. The blue low building has two counters to order from. In addition to nearly two dozen varieties of taffy, they also have home-made fudge, peanut brittle, ice cream, and cotton candy. There is a second Crills (847 Embarcadero) down the road closer to the center of town, but this is the original, right near the smokestacks.

Mexican

Taco Temple (2680 Main St., 805/772-4965, Wed.–Mon. 11 A.M.–9 P.M., $10) is, from the exterior, just another average-looking stop, just outside of downtown Morro Bay. The image doesn't improve a whole lot as you walk in, but that's not the point. They're known for their fish taco, heaped with plenty of ingredients. The fish is moist, spicy, and quite excellent. They also have large burritos and tostadas, but given the name, go for the fish tacos. It's cash only and there's no ATM on-site.

Lolo's Mexican (2848 Main St., 805/772-5686, $10) has plenty of traditional Mexican choices, but they recently added pasta dishes like salmon pasta as well. But most people are here for the fresh house-made chips and salsa, the huevos rancheros, and cheese enchiladas for the kids. They also have menudo and pozole and plenty of à la carte items if you're not as hungry. The interior is so brightly decorated that it might hurt your eyes, but Lolo's has a huge fan base.

Cafés

Top Dog Coffee (857 Main St., 805/772-9225, www.topdogcoffeebar.com, Mon.–Sat. 6 A.M.–8 P.M., Sun. 6 A.M.–7 P.M., $7) is the spot for coffee and Wi-Fi. Not only do they roast their own coffee, but they also sell a small selection of baked goods, breakfast bagels, soups, and sandwiches. No computer? No problem, they have a few computers always at hand. The space gets busy though, and tables are hard to find. If you head to the back, you'll discover a little Zen garden and a little more space in which to work.

At **The Rock Espresso Bar** (275 Morro Bay Blvd., 805/772-3411, daily 6 A.M.–5 P.M., $5) you can see Morro Rock, but you're also off the Embarcadero and more amongst the locals. They roast their own coffee here and turn out pastries, muffins, and scones daily. There are a few computers to check email while you sit on chairs upholstered with old coffee-bean bags. The outdoor patio gives you sun and more glimpses of the rock.

Pizza

The **Nibble Nook Pizza Parlor** (410 Quintana, 805/772-3990, Mon.–Sat. 10 A.M.–8 P.M., $8) is near the highway and not near the water, so it tends to be more locals who come here. Of course the pizza is the best in town, made fresh and served right out of the oven, but there are also pastrami sandwiches and salads and a salad bar, and usually half a dozen soups you can taste before ordering. There are also arcade games and coloring books to occupy the kids. This isn't fancy, it's your basic pizza joint—with better-than-average pizza.

Thai

Noi's Little Thai Takeout (1288 2nd St., Los Osos, 805/528-6647, Mon.–Sat. 10 A.M.–7 P.M., $10) is a 10-minute drive into Los Osos, but it's worth it. This is truly a takeout stand, and the word "little" in the name should give you a clue—there are only four tables that are located outside near the order counter. There is no sit-down service here. Fresh vegetables and generous portions make this very popular Thai food. The pad Thai noodles are suburb and they excel at curry dishes. There can be a very long wait—but you can and should order in advance on weekends by phoning ahead by at least one hour. They don't take credit cards, so bring cash.

Breakfast and Brunch

Frankie and Lola's (1154 Front St., 805/771-9306, www.frankieandlolas.com, daily 6:30 A.M.–2:30 P.M., $10) serves breakfast and lunch in a small, deliberately low-key space with corrugated wainscoting and marine-influenced lighting fixtures to represent the waterfront. They are one of the few places to open early, should you need breakfast before you leave town. Like most everywhere, you can see the rock while you enjoy the creative food, like French toast that is dipped in crème brûlée and mixed with whole nuts, then baked and served in a bowl—it's excellent and not overly sweet—or tri-tip chili, which is rich and earthy.

The **Coffee Pot Restaurant** (1001 Front St., 805/772-3175, daily 7 A.M.–1:30 P.M., $15) has been around a long time. Unpretentious and dated with its decor, it's not aiming to impress. But then, you're here for breakfast. Chances are there will be a wait, as there are few breakfast choices in town, but they'll bring you coffee while you wait. Their vast menu includes veggie omelets and plenty of meat choices, as well as biscuits and gravy, though the service suffers a bit.

Vegetarian

At **Shine Café** (415 Morro Bay Blvd., 805/771-8344, Mon.–Fri. 11 A.M.–5 P.M., Sat. 9 A.M.–5 P.M., Sun. 11:30 A.M.–4 P.M., $10) is located inside the Sunshine Health Foods Market. Nothing is over ten bucks, and it's all vegetarian and vegan, with gluten-free options. They have an array of smoothies, as well as tempeh tacos, spring rolls, and fresh daily soups, most of which are vegan. Everything is artfully prepared and a feast for the eyes.

American

The **Bayside Cafe** (10 State Park Rd., 805/772-1465, Mon.–Wed. 11 A.M.–3 P.M., Thurs.–Sun. 11 A.M.–9 P.M., $15) is located in Morro Bay State Park at the marina near the back bay. For over a quarter of a century this fun and funky little place with both indoor and outdoor seating with views to the boats has brought in a steady clientele. It's out of the way and is more

© MICHAEL CERVIN

Hoppe's Bistro is one of the best restaurants in Cayucos.

a word-of-mouth place, with a huge following from the Central Valley. They feature a winery of the month with very reasonable by-the-glass prices. There's nothing over $15 for lunch or dinner, and you'll find an eclectic menu with burgers, salads, sandwiches, pot roast, vegetarian options, and burritos.

Dinner at **Cass House Restaurant** (222 N. Ocean, Cayucos, 805/995-3669, www.cass-houseinn.com, Thurs.–Mon. 5–9 P.M., $60) is one of those top-notch experiences that takes a full night to enjoy. They offer a four-course menu that changes daily, depending on what fresh ingredients can be sourced. This is really the antithesis of fast food. The space is tiny and somewhat unremarkable in its appearance, but reservations are highly recommended since the restaurant is inside the Cass House Inn and most of the tables go to guests. Menus have included ponzu-marinated kingfish, abalone from the Abalone Farm up the street, and garlic-and-thyme-roasted lamb.

Just a block down the street from Cass House Restaurant is the highly regarded **Hoppe's Bistro** (78 N. Ocean Ave., 805/995-1006, www.hoppesbistro.com, Wed.–Sun. 11 A.M.–10 P.M., $25), which was the first restaurant to really place Cayucos on the culinary map. The dabbled yellowish walls and white tablecloths are pretty standard decor, but this restaurant has proved to be creative and innovative with its cuisine, like abalone from the local Abalone Farm, local grilled quail, a portobello burger with chick peas, or their excellent selection of cheeses, some of which are also local. On nice days, head to the back patio, a secluded little vine-covered spot many people never venture to. Afterwards, stroll down the pier or the beach.

Seafood

Morro Bay has a multitude of great seafood restaurants to choose from.

The Galley (899 Embarcadero, 805/772-7777, www.galleymorrobay.com, daily 11 A.M.–2:30 P.M. and 5 P.M.–close, $25) sits underneath the Andersen Inn and directly over the water, staring right out at the rock. There's a modern Scandinavian feel to the interior but with the clean lines of an Italian design. Multiple semicircle booths face outward and freestanding tables front the windows. The current owner started at the original Galley restaurant as a busboy. Many years and a brand-new restaurant later, the Galley is better than ever. Pan-seared scallops in a beurre blanc capped with shallots is their signature dish, as are the naked fish dishes, like swordfish, ahi tuna, and ono, all simply prepared and served with sauces on the side, so the inherent flavor and quality of the fish come through unhindered. There's a small bar here as well.

Dockside (1245 Embarcadero, 805/772-8100, www.bonniemarietta.com, Sun.–Thurs. 11 A.M.–8 P.M., Fri.–Sat. 11 A.M.–9 P.M., $18) is all about ocean-to-boat-to-table seafood. They have their own fishing boat that hauls in the catch, then they cook it up. You can sit dockside on plastic chairs and under green umbrellas, which is the best way to experience the place, overlooking the boats. Best known for their barbecue oysters, which are huge in size (and not barbecued in the sauce sense but slow grilled with garlic and butter), they also have lots of crispy fried foods. This is low-key dining but with some of the freshest seafood around.

Ciao Bella (725 Embarcadero, 805/772-7175, www.ciaobella-trattoria.com, Mon.–Fri. 5–10 P.M., Sat. 11:30 A.M.–3 P.M. and 5–10 P.M., Sun. 9 A.M.–3 P.M. and 5–10 P.M., $17) overlooks the bay in a 1968 building with some really cool custom-made nautical light fixtures. They serve seafood with an Italian flair and straight-up pasta dishes. The sand dabs are locally caught, as is the sole. There are the usual steamed clams and mussels, or stick with a chicken or beef dish. The bar downstairs, under the same ownership, is a great little spot for a drink or to unwind. Unpretentious and not updated, it's a great throwback to the 1970s.

Dorn's Original Breakers Cafe (801 Market Ave., 805/772-4415, www.dornscafe.com, daily 7 A.M.–9 P.M., $25) is a traditional, more formal dining experience with low lighting and a slightly sophisticated environment. Perched on the hill up from the water, they have exceptional views. Their clam chowder has been a favorite since the restaurant opened in 1960 and

they provide a large selection of fresh seafood. There are also non-fish entrées, which are all very good, but you should go for the fish. They also open early for breakfast.

INFORMATION AND SERVICES
Maps and Tourist Information
The **Morro Bay Chamber of Commerce** (845 Embarcadero, Ste. D, 800/231-0592, www.morrobay.org) has a wonderful visitors center overlooking the bay at the end of a small boardwalk. They have a vast array of printed material you can take with you.

Emergency Services
French Hospital Medical Center (1911 Johnson Ave., San Luis Obispo, 805/543-5353, www.frenchmedicalcenter.org) is the closest hospital. If you have an emergency, please dial 911. The local police offices are located at 870 Morro Bay Boulevard (805/772-6225).

Newspapers and Media
The *San Luis Obispo Tribune* is the widely available daily paper covering the county, while the *Bay News,* is a local weekly paper that appears free each Thursday.

Postal Services
To access the post office you'll need to leave the Embarcadero area and head uptown to 898 Napa Avenue (805/772-0839).

Laundry
American Cleaners & Laundry has two locations in Morro Bay at 365 Quintana Road and at 1052 Main Street. Their phone works for both locations, 805/772-6959. They'll provide pickup and delivery.

GETTING THERE
By Car
As with most towns on the Central Coast, Highway 101 cuts through Morro Bay. If you're traveling south from San Francisco, take Highway 101 south to Atascadero. Then take Highway 41 west, and head south on Highway 1. Exit at Main Street in Morro Bay. If you're

traveling from Los Angeles, the best route is Highway 101 north to San Luis Obispo, then head north on Highway 1 to Morro Bay and take the Morro Bay Boulevard exit into town.

By Bus

There is no direct bus service to Morro Bay, though Greyhound travels along Highway 101 and stops in San Luis Obispo. From there you'll need to connect with the **Regional Transit Authority** (805/781-4472, www.slorta.com) to get into Morro Bay. There are various weekday and weekend lines to choose from.

By Train

Likewise, **Amtrak** (800/872-7245, www.amtrak.com) travels along the highway and stops in San Luis Obispo.

By Air

There is a small airport with limited service in San Luis Obispo (903-5 Airport Dr., 805/781-5205, www.sloairport.com) and also Santa Maria (3217 Terminal Dr., 805/922-1726, www.santamariaairport.com), but nothing is offered commercially in Morro Bay.

GETTING AROUND
By Car

You don't really need a car in Morro Bay. Certainly the Embarcadero is walkable, though can be tiring as it's quite long, and if you decide to walk to the rock, that only extends your time. To get uptown, while only a few blocks, might require a car, and a visit to the golf course, the back bay, or the museum

will require a drive. If you use Morro Bay as a base to explore Hearst Castle or Paso Robles you will definitely need a car. But if you arrive in Morro Bay without a car, be aware that there are no car rentals in town. The closest car rentals are in San Luis Obispo (Avis: 805/595-1464, www.avis.com; Enterprise: 805/545-9111, www.enterprise.com) 15 minutes south.

By Taxi

Bay Services (805/528-1201) is a 24-hour flat-fee taxi and limousine service. The **Bay Taxi** (1215 Embarcadero, 805/772-1222) provides water-shuttle service.

By Bus

A door-to-door general public transit system, **Dial-A-Ride** (535 Harbor St., 805/772-2755, Mon.–Fri. 6:45 A.M.–6 P.M.) operates within the city limits and was established in 1977.

By Trolley

The **Morro Bay Trolley** (595 Harbor Way., 805/772-2744, Mon. 11 A.M.–5 P.M., Fri.–Sat. 11 A.M.–7 P.M., Sun. 11 A.M.–6 P.M.) operates three routes. The **Waterfront Route** runs the length of the Embarcadero, including out to Morro Rock. The **Downtown Route** runs through downtown (as in uptown) area all the way out to Morro Bay State Park. The **North Morro Bay Route** runs from uptown through the northern part of Morro Bay, north of the rock, along Highway 1. An all-day pass (not a bad idea if you plan on seeing a lot of sights) is $3; one ride is $1 for anyone 13 years or older, and $0.50 for children 5–12.

BACKGROUND

The Land

GEOGRAPHY

California's diverse coastal communities are the result of many different natural forces. Tectonic and volcanic activity, which occurred over the past 250 million years, created our coastal mountain ranges. The Channel Islands are the result of a similar geologic process. Coastal streams and rivers, along with wind and rain, helped shape and tear down these mountains through constant erosion. The beautiful though powerful ceaseless waves of the Pacific Ocean also cut into the coastal mountain ranges and helped carve vertical cliffs, terraces, and bluffs into the rock. Elsewhere along the California coast, debris from wave erosion and sand deposited by streams and rivers began to accumulate and form the one thing we all seem to love, California's sandy beaches. Even inland, where wind-blown sand from the beaches collects, you can find fragile systems of coastal dunes, unlike anything else in all of California. Coastal rivers and streams eventually meet with the salty waters of the Pacific and create marshes, lagoons, and estuaries that constitute the Central Coast's prime coastal wetlands. In other areas, abrasive sand and wave motion cut grooves and pockets into the rock where

© MICHAEL CERVIN

TEXAS TEA NEAR THE SEA

In 1989 a routine soil test in Avila Beach for a proposed new construction project happened upon the discovery of a black viscous substance buried deep in the earth. Everyone immediately knew what it was. For over a hundred years, oil pumped from fields in central and coastal California, as far away as several hundred miles, was piped to huge tanks atop a bluff overlooking Avila Beach, at the time a tiny place with a population of less than 800 people. Crude oil, gasoline, and diesel fuel flowed downhill from that storage facility, through pipelines underneath the town, and out to waiting tanker ships. Apparently, over time the pipelines had leaked, and a huge spill of petroleum products, approximately a half million gallons in fact, was sitting under the small town of Avila Beach and inching toward the ocean.

Lawsuits were immediately filed, and Unocal Oil conceded that its underground pipes had been leaking over the preceding decades. Oil had always been integral to this unincorporated San Luis Obispo County community, which had blossomed as a company town in the early 1900s and during World War II was a fueling station for the Pacific fleet. But oil was about to reinvent Avila in ways no one could have imagined. Unocal officials believe no one has ever done what they did, which was to tear down a town, clean it up, and then reconstruct it. The demolition included cafés, biker bars, and shops, and some homes. Approximately 300 residents had to vacate their homes temporarily due to possible liability issues related to the reconstruction of the town. Tons of contaminated soil were trucked to a dump, and the beach was dug up and replaced with new sand. What remains is now a brand-new Avila. Unocal completed one of the industry's biggest cleanups ever and spent more than $100 million on the cleanup and settlements with agencies and individuals.

The funky little beach businesses and everything that made the old town unique have vanished, but the town's new business district has risen from the ashes. Residents were given wide latitude in determining what their reborn town would look like, from the type of trees on the streets to restrooms in the park at the end of the road next to the beach. Along Front Street, Unocal replaced the worn sidewalk, which was constantly covered in sand, with a trendy, shiny promenade, replete with nautical-themed light posts, palm trees, mosaic tile artwork, benches adorned with fake starfish, and a water fountain that simulates a tide pool. Nowhere else has anything like this been done for an environmental disaster. While the case never went to court or set any legal precedents, it did establish an industry standard. An improbable band of engineers from a diverse array of specialties and responsibilities joined with residents to win a massive environmental battle and a town, once contaminated, now has new life.

intertidal communities and tide pools formed. And even below the Pacific Ocean's waters, geologic forces continued to act, through many of the same processes, on the sea floor.

CLIMATE

Santa Barbara, Ventura, and San Luis Obispo Counties all have a semi-arid climate, moderate and pleasant year-round. Summer at the coast means just a handful of triple-digit days, with temps otherwise in the low to mid-70s. But the valleys, however, like Paso Robles and Santa Ynez, will see much hotter weather for a longer period of time, though when the sun sets it cools off quickly.

In the fall and winter it's still nice, with temperatures averaging in the mid-60s. Most of the rain falls between November and April; historically, the region sees less than 15 inches each year.

ENVIRONMENTAL ISSUES

In January of 1969, an environmental disaster occurred in the Santa Barbara Channel when an offshore oil platform suffered a blowout and 200,000 gallons of crude oil escaped into the ocean over a period of 11 days. The oil created an 800-square-mile slick that impacted all of the northern Channel Islands and mainland beaches along the Central Coast. Thousands of seabirds and marine mammals died. Concurrently, scientists were becoming aware of a serious decline in the breeding success of California brown pelicans: The prehistoric-looking birds were unable to nest successfully because their eggshells were too thin to withstand the incubation period and were crushed in the nest. For several years, the pelicans suffered a near total reproductive failure. In 1970, only one chick was successfully raised on Anacapa Island, an island that had historically been the largest breeding colony for California brown pelicans on the entire West Coast. The exact cause of the failed pelican breeding was determined to be the pesticide DDT. High levels of DDT residue caused the eggshells to become thinner over time, and DDT similarly affected bald eagles and peregrine falcons.

Fortunately, the American public and the government reacted reasonably swiftly to the loss of wildlife, and to the egregious pollution of the environment. Many consider the publicity surrounding the Santa Barbara oil spill and the fate of the California brown pelican a major impetus for the environmental movement. Just one year later, in the spring of 1970, Earth Day was born. Ever since then, Santa Barbara has been a leading proponent for conservation. At a minimum, State Street is offers green recycling cans so you can properly dispose of your water bottles and other recyclables.

Beyond the simple importance of personal responsibility, it would appear that the region, with its proximity to the ocean, would be hyper-responsible, especially in light of the aforementioned incidents. But clean creeks remain an issue here—or rather, dirty creeks are the issue. And in all the counties, most notably Santa Barbara, they are bad, very bad. There are creek and beach clean-up days in all three

counties, which you may be able to participate in while you're here. Disturbingly, people still leave their debris all along the beaches, in the creeks, and in parks, though ironically, State Street is cleaner than most of the natural riparian corridors. Tainted creeks, unfortunately, lead to beach closures, which does happen on occasion. Signs will be posted at various beaches if there are extreme unsanitary conditions.

Beach water samples are collected weekly at Central Coast beaches and examined to identify any microbes that could pose a threat to swimmers and beachgoers. As a general rule, it's always best to avoid swimming in the ocean, especially near creek terminations, within 72 hours after rains, as that water will probably contain higher levels of bacteria washed into the ocean from the creeks that fan out through the Tri-Counties.

Water is the other major ecological issue facing the Central Coast. There simply isn't that much of it, which is surprising since the population would not seem to be a factor given that the entire population of the Santa Barbara, San Luis Obispo, and Ventura Counties does not exceed 900,000 people. The reality is that this is a semi-arid climate with below-average rainfall two out of every three years. In Cambria, water is so tight that businesses can get fined for going over their allotment. Historically, urban centers have been located along the area's coastal lowlands, with agriculture concentrated in valley-floor areas and grazing and natural lands occupying the surrounding foothills. But as more people discover the Central Coast and decide to relocate here, population pressures increase, and growth and development have expanded from urban centers to adjacent farmlands and rural areas both on the coast and in the interior sections. Along with population growth, the greatest threats to regional wildlife diversity are expansion of intensive types of agriculture, invasions by exotic species, and overuse of regional water resources.

Flora

TREES
The California Oak
The Central Coast is home to the protected California Oak, the singular signature tree that defines the region. There are 20 species of oaks native to California, roughly one third of the 60 species scattered throughout the United States. But mainly you'll see the two species of massive oaks that grow on the valley floors, hillsides, and ridgetops: the Valley Oak *(quercus lobata)* and the Blue Oak *(quercus douglasii)*. The leaves of Valley Oaks are gracefully sculpted into a series of deep, rounded lobes, much like those hanging from our ears. Leaves on Blue Oaks have scalloped edges. Both trees can grow straight and tall; some have a classic vase shape while others spread wide, with wandering horizontal branches. The mighty oak lives upwards of 200 years, though it grows sparsely and independently, unlike traditional thick forests. As you drive Highway 101, or even travel the region by train, you'll see the oak, twisted and fierce against a backdrop of agriculture and development, virtually everywhere. The oak tree is a sacred tree, at least to the area's indigenous people, who plucked the acorns from the oaks to create flour. They used rock grinders (you can still see many natural grinders in rock formations around the area) to break open the acorns and grind the kernels, and would then rinse the meal to wash away its bitterness.

Eucapyptus
In addition to the sparse beauty of oak trees, the eucalyptus *(Eucalyptus globulus)* grows along much of the Central Coast. In the 1850s, eucalyptus trees were brought to California during the gold rush by Australians, since much of California has similar climate to parts of Australia. By the early 1900s, thousands of acres of eucalyptus trees were planted and even encouraged by the state government. It was hoped these trees would provide a renewable source of timber for construction, furniture making, and more importantly, railroad ties. It was soon discovered, however, that eucalyptus was particularly unsuitable for rail use, as the ties made from the trees had a tendency to twist and buckle while drying, and the dried ties were so tough that it was nearly impossible to hammer rail spikes into them. One way in which the eucalyptus proved valuable in California was as a windbreak for highways, orange groves, and farms in the mostly treeless central part of the state. There are spots along Highway 101 where this is clearly evident.

Avocado
One of the Central Coast's most populous trees, the avocado *(Persea americana)* is grown in orchards and backyards everywhere. Avocados were introduced to California sometime in the 19th century and today the majority of avocados for sale in the United States come from California. Carpinteria has a yearly avocado festival to celebrate all things avo.

Pine
As you move north, the pine tree becomes more prevalent. It is the Monterey pine *(Pinus radiate)* that is the most common tree in Paso Robles and Cambria, usually covered with moss, giving it an almost Southern look. There is even a subspecies of the Torrey pine *(Pinus torreyana insularis)* that grows only on Santa Rosa Island.

FLOWERS
The poppy *(Eschscholzia californica)* is the California state flower, and in periods with a lot of rain you'll see the small simple orange/gold flower everywhere. Near the Santa Ynez Valley they can fully populate entire hillsides. They are also very coastal, and Montano de Oro State Park has lots of poppies as well. The poppy is also durable, reaching to elevations as high as 6,000 feet.

Fields of lupine *(Lupinus)* are also everywhere on rolling hills and the coastal Fiddleneck *(Amsinckia menziesii)* is another species found throughout the region. Many people consider it to be a weed, but its tiny yellow flowers add a dash of color to the region.

Fauna

MAMMALS

Red-blooded creatures inhabit much of the Central Coast, and not just on land. In the ocean, the Pacific gray whales *(Eschrichtius robustus)*, often misidentified as California gray whales, are the most common whales you will see December–March on whale-watching exhibitions. Summer often brings the humpback whale *(Megaptera novaeangliae)*, orcas *(Orcinus orca)*, blue whales *(Balaenoptera musculus)* and their cousin, fin whales *(Balaenoptera physalus)*, which are less visible. Overall there are 30 different species of whales that ply the waters of the Central Coast. Getting to see one is mostly a matter of opportunity and awareness, constantly scanning the horizon for that tell-tale sign of water shooting up from the surface. Nearly every year there is a whale, usually a baby, that loses its way through the channel and comes very close to shore in Santa Barbara.

Beyond whales, there are dolphins, porpoises, California sea lions *(Zalophus californianus)*, elephant seals *(Mirounga angustirostris)*, harbor seals *(Phoca vitulina)*, northern fur seals *(Callorhinus ursinus)*, and adorable sea otters *(Enhydra lutris)* that all are part of the vast circle of life. They're less visible in Ventura, and as you move upcoast there tends to be a greater concentration of them.

SEALIFE

Unless you dive into the temperate waters, chances are that any fish you see will be in a book or dead on a pier with a hook through its lip. Oddly, there are no great aquariums here. The two best are in Long Beach and Monterey, which book-end the Central Coast. Regardless, if you scuba or snorkel, chances are you'll see the Garibaldi *(Hypsypops rubicundus)*, which is the California state marine fish. Bright orange and similar in size to bass, they are curious and very territorial. Garibaldi are actually harmless if you see them while scuba diving, though they will come right up to you to protect their turf, acting all macho. Even while kayaking at the Channel Islands, where pristine water allows 30–40 feet of visibility, you will see them.

The area is also home to spiny lobster *(Panulirus interruptus)*, crab, and ridgeback shrimp, all of which will probably end up on your plate for lunch or dinner. There are far too many fish to list here, but when diving you can reasonably expect to see sheepshead, halibut, sea urchins, and sea bass. There are also sharks in the waters, and occasionally they come reasonably close to shore.

BIRDS

You can't miss the water birds along the Central Coast, like the brown pelicans *(Pelecanus occidentalis)*, cormorants *(Phalacrocorax auritus)*, seagulls *(larus californicus)*, sandpipers, cranes, blue herons *(Ardea herodias)*, and sanderlings *(Calidris alba)*, which scurry about in mass groups around the tides on the beach. There are a plethora of loons *(gavia immer)*, egrets *(ardea alba)*, and mallards *(Anas platyrhynchos)*, which are everywhere and seem to dominate the skies. Over 300 species of birds have been identified along the Central Coast, hugging the coastline and meandering through the sloughs and inland waterways, and the coastal birds also help to define the region. The Black Phoebe *(sayornis nigricans)* is amazing to watch as it catches insects in midair.

As you move inland you'll see red-tail hawks *(Buteo jamaicensis)* often sitting above the freeway on an exit sign or languidly floating on thermal air pockets, searching for food. There are Turkey Vultures *(Cathartes aura)* in abundance

© MICHAEL CERVIN

Garibaldi, the California state marine fish

as well. Near Lake Cachuma there are small pockets of Bald Eagles *(Haliaeetus leucocephalus)* and Osprey *(Pandion haliaetus),* though they are somewhat shy and it takes a lot of patience to find them. Morro Rock is a known peregrine falcon *(Falco peregrinus)* nesting area. The state bird, the California Valley Quail *(Callipepla californica),* occasionally runs across the roads, mainly in northern Santa Barbara County and up into San Luis Obispo County, though predominantly on forested back roads.

Then there is the funky oddball bird like the black oystercatcher *(Haematopus bachmani),* which is a stunning sight to see when you first lay eyes on one. They are black with a long bright orange beak and they frequent beaches and the Channel Islands. There are far too many crows *(Corvus brachyrhyncos),* but should you get to the Channel Islands you'll get the chance to see quite a few common ravens *(Corvus corax).* There is a vast world of birds on the Central Coast, and even if you're not a bird-watcher, a little understanding of these magnificent creatures will go a long way.

REPTILES

Snakes have always been a part of California, and there are 10 snakes in particular that make their home on the Central Coast. Most snakes such as the gopher *(Pituophis melanoleucus catenifer)* and garter *(Thamnophis atratus)* are harmless, even though they are about 3–4 feet in length. It is the Western Rattlesnake *(Crotalus viridis viridis)* that is venomous and potentially dangerous. The distinctive horny rings on the end of their tails and that unmistakable rattle sound mean that you should immediately leave the area. When you're out and about in wild areas, like Black Hill in Morro Bay, More Mesa on the bluffs above Santa Barbara, or along Moonstone bluffs in Cambria, you will probably come across snakes. They love to bask in the warm sun, so you're likely to cross paths with a snake when it's hot out, whether on a coastal trail, a mountain trail, or even in downtown parks. Care should always be used. There is nothing to be afraid of, and most snakes have no more interest in you than you have in them. The bottom line is to leave them alone and move along.

© MICHAEL CERVIN

a Muscovy duck at Laguna Lake Park in San Luis Obispo

You will also see the ubiquitous Western fence lizard *(Sceloporus occidentalis)*.

INSECTS AND ARACHNIDS

One of the beauties of the Central Coast is that we don't see too many pesky insects that torture innocent travelers with copious bug bites. Fall is spider season on the Central Coast and in many other areas of California as well. The most obviously active spiders during this season are the garden spiders, which weave large circular webs between bushes, trees, and vines to catch insects. Known generally as Orb-weavers *(Neoscona crucifera)*, this group contains over 1,500 species. Female spiders make the webs to catch insects so they can produce a sac containing several hundred eggs before they die in early winter. Garden spiders make enough venom to kill their prey, but there is no threat to people. These spiders tend to be shy and will quickly retreat to a hiding place when encountered. Keep in mind that spiders are beneficial insects, as they eat moths, wasps, flies, and other flying insects. If the spider is spinning its web in an inconvenient location, catch it and move it to an out-of-the-way spot where it can weave another web without being in your way. There are also tarantulas, which belong to the group of primitive spiders called *Mygalomorphs*. These beautiful large and hairy spiders are often seen in the mountain regions, scrambling across the asphalt along the wine country back roads.

Butterflies of all types are common on the Central Coast, specifically the Monarch *(Danaus plexippus)*, which has groves in Goleta just north of Santa Barbara, and in Pismo Beach. Both of these locations are eucalyptus groves. In addition to the Monarch, there are hundreds of swallowtails *(Papilionidae Lepidoptera)*, skippers *(Hesperiidae Lepidoptera)*, and the radiant whites and sulphers *(Pieridae Lepidoptera)*. The Santa Barbara Natural History Museum runs an occasional program called Butterflies Alive, a highly successful exhibition devoted to these beautiful winged creatures. Despite its rather hideous name, the California Dogface Butterfly, the state insect, is in reality a beautiful yellow and black butterfly.

AMPHIBIANS

The Central Coast is desirable for animals who want to spend time in the water and on land, and there are many amphibious creatures abound here. Of particular note are the tiger salamander *(ambystoma californiense)*, a four-inch-long black-coated guy with yellow spots and bars who lives primarily underground, and the red-legged tree frog *(rana draytonii)*, also measuring about five inches or so. Their abdomen and hind legs are, you guessed it, red. There are other frogs, toads, and newts present, but these two amphibians in particular have the ability to halt progress in the area, specifically development. Since the tiger salamander and red-legged tree frog are federally protected by the United States Fish and Wildlife Service, the sighting of one of these little critters will bring out conservationists and there will be delays and possibly lawsuits regarding any proposed construction sights.

History

Many people mistakenly believe that California has a limited history and that true U.S. history is all based on the East Coast. Certainly, the early settlements like Jamestown are all back east. But while our forefathers wrestled with democracy, the West Coast and the Central Coast was experiencing its own history.

NATIVE AMERICANS

Prior to the arrival of the Spanish, roughly 15,000 Chumash Indians inhabited the coast, interior valleys, and the Channel Islands from Malibu, north of Los Angeles, to just north of San Luis Obispo. The Salinan Indians lived in parts of Paso Robles and north of Morro Bay. These two tribes were hunter-gatherers, not warriors, and were oriented toward the ocean for their livelihood. They were an advanced people and friendly (much to their ultimate demise), and were known to make the arduous channel crossing in *tomols,* plank boats they constructed. Leadership of their autonomous villages was hereditary. The Chumash were known for the quality of their tools and baskets, woven tight enough to hold water, and it was this type of handiwork that is reflected in

the construction and detailing of the missions, since the majority of these buildings were built by hard-working indigenous people.

THE SPANISH PERIOD AND THE MISSIONS: 1769-1821

Beginning in 1769 the Spanish, who had claimed this region as far back as the 1500s, established four royal presidios—forts, really—and founded 21 Franciscan missions along the California coast. In part, these establishments were built to ward off Russian traders who were working their way down the coast and in fact had established Fort Ross, north of Bodega Bay in Northern California. The very last presidio was dedicated in Santa Barbara on April 21, 1782, by Governor Felipe Neve, Father Junípero Serra, and Captain Jose Francisco Ortega, who was the first commander of the presidio. There were a mere 42 soldiers with them at the time. Spain ruled the area, both in terms of a military presence and in terms of the socioeconomic and spiritual presence. The missions were the sole industries of Alta California and trade with ships of all nations eventually began, especially in hides, tallow, grain, brandy, olive oil, and leatherwork. New England merchants became the biggest customers for trade with the missions by the 1820s and 1830s, thus facilitating news of this area back to the East Coast.

THE MEXICAN PERIOD: 1821-1849

In 1821, Mexico achieved its independence from Spain, but the political unrest didn't go away easily. In 1829, Mexico passed a law abolishing slavery, which was directly aimed at stemming the missions power and freeing the Native Americans. By 1833, a law was finally passed in Mexico that secularized the missions entirely. This meant that the lands held in trust for the Native Americans were to revert immediately to them, which in reality did not happen. Unscrupulous men and women took advantage of the difficult-to-enforce laws, as this region was still a far cry from Mexico and its authority. Mexico struggled to maintain control over the vast expanses of land they had inherited from Spain following their own long war. But lacking the resources to settle much of the territory and suffering from internal political divisions, Mexico blinked.

The United States, fueled by technological breakthroughs and innovation and inspired by the concept of Manifest Destiny, was expanding its territories westward. Between 1846 and 1848, these two neighbors, the United States and Mexico, went to war. It was a defining event for both nations, transforming a continent and forging a new identity for its peoples. By the end of the war, Mexico had lost nearly half of its territory, the present American Southwest from Texas to California, and the United States had become a major power. The Central Coast did not see bloodshed or fighting during the war, but certainly felt its effects.

THE YOUNG STATE: 1850-1920

In 1848 gold was discovered at Coloma in Northern California, and a huge influx of Americans came to settle or make their fortunes in California. By September 1850,

California was a state. By acts of Congress, the United States returned some of the mission lands and buildings to the Catholic Church in the 1850s and 1860s. But the old missions began to fall into disrepair, and struggling parishes sold off buildings, which were turned into inns, stores, bars, and stables. The tile roofs were sold off to pay debts, which opened the adobe walls of the buildings to deterioration from rain and moisture.

And so California and the Central Coast became part of the United States. As easterners made their way here, two spots in particular caught their attention: Santa Barbara and Paso Robles, which were recognized as places for natural healing. With the arrival of the railroad in the late 1880s, wealthy easterners bought up land at rock bottom prices to create vast estates as is evidenced in Santa Barbara's Montecito and Hope Ranch communities. These were second homes for many of the landowners and few of them actually lived here year-round. But the Central Coast remained an aggregate of sleepy little towns for the most part, while Los Angeles and San Francisco continued to grow. In part, that was due to the fact that even though the railroad allowed access to the area, the Central Coast still suffered from its lack of proximity to larger metropolitan cities where goods could be obtained cheaply and conveniently.

THE EMERGING CENTRAL COAST: 1920-PRESENT DAY

When the 1930s dust bowl began to decimate much of the Midwest, many people came to California, especially to the Central Coast, where farming and agriculture was still widely practiced, to seek out new opportunities. When the Rincon portion of Highway 101 was built in the 1930s, it marked the first time you could actually drive to Santa Barbara along the coast, though it did little to increase commercial or residential development. World War II was uneventful for this area, with the exception of a Japanese submarine that actually fired on Santa Barbara (though nothing happened), not to mention the sinking of an

THE DUNITES

It requires a stunning degree of shortsightedness to build anything on shifting sands, but that is exactly what was attempted on the **Guadalupe-Nipomo Dunes** at the turn of the 20th century. The area was to be the "future Atlantic City of the Pacific" with a boardwalk, a hotel, and a pavilion, and venture capitalists were enthralled with the possibility of resort-style living on the sand dunes facing the ocean. But the wind-blown sand wouldn't stay put and inevitably won the battle. By 1917, the few foolishly grandiose buildings were abandoned, their lumber scavenged by the dune-dwellers, an eclectic group of nomads and misfits who built their own new lives in the dunes.

The dunes had long been the home of a drifting population of vagrants and eccentrics, but it was in the 1920s that the people who became known as the Dunites claimed the transitory area for their own. **Edward St Claire,** a Spanish-American war veteran turned poet, was one of the first to claim residence. Then came **George Blais,** a reformed alcoholic turned evangelist and a naturist, who dressed in a loincloth and bandana to go into town but otherwise lived naked in the dunes. One of the most illustrious and flamboyant Dunites was astrologer, writer, and socialite **Gavin Arthur,** grandson of United States president Chester A. Arthur who "had it all" by the standards of the day, but opted out of society. Probably the most well-known resident of the makeshift dune neighborhood was the artist **Elwood Decker.**

The Dunites even published their own magazine, distributed nationally, called the *Dune Forum*, with contributions by photographers such as **Ansel Adams.** The magazine was heavy on intellectual style and expensive for the time at 35 cents. The publication ran for five issues before it too succumbed to forces greater than itself. Eventually the Dunites left their bohemian life on the sands, perhaps recognizing that dunes simply cannot be controlled. To this day, the sands shift where they will.

oil tanker off the Cambria coastline by another Japanese submarine.

In he 1990s land prices began to rise exponentially and people began to realize how desirable the area was. And with the realization that there is only so much oceanfront property available, prices climbed rapidly and demand exceeded available housing. Part of the region's success is that it has remained small and not overbuilt. Many people moved here because they wanted out of hectic and congested metropolitan cities.

Part of the area's growth can be attributed to the wine industry. Prohibition shut down nearly all of the wineries operating along the Central Coast, and it wasn't until 1962 that Santa Barbara Winery (805/963-3633, www.sbwinery.com) planted its first commercial grapevines, which eventually led to the beginnings of a new industry that now brings in over a millions tourists to the Central Coast annually.

Today the Central Coast is widely recognized for what it has long been: a beautiful landscape flanked by oceans and mountains with a relaxed way of life that is envied by many.

Government and Economy

The form of government throughout the Tri-Counties is really no different than other communities in the United States. Republicans and Democrats hold the majority of elected offices, with a handful of independents. In broad terms, the city of Santa Barbara tends to be more liberal with a greater concentration of democratic leadership, while there is more of a balance between conservatives and liberals in the rest of the Central Coast's cities and towns.

The greatest issue these counties struggle with is growth, and that is the dominating political issue most anywhere. The Central Coast has limited natural resources, and though it doesn't appear that way, chief among them is water. These counties have historically been slow- or no-growth oriented. After all, it's the lack of congestion that people love about living here, the lack of crowds and the lack of problems inherent in too many people occupying too little space. In once sense people want to limit growth as much as possible to retain the way of life everyone seems to enjoy; the NIMBY (Not In My Backyard) effect is alive and well, and the local populace will frequently turn up to contest new development. On the other hand, without growth there is limited economic expansion, and that can lead to long-term economic problems. Part of the issue is that many people who choose to live here have plenty of money, and therefore no vested interest in anything changing at all. For the rest of the population, who depend on this area for their livelihood, the goal is intelligent growth that properly lays out a future for the region and the limited resources we all must share. It's

a simple truth that not everyone who wants to can find a place here.

Therefore the economy on the Central Coast is defined by tourism, the wine region, and agriculture. Tourism is by far the major economic thrust of the region. Santa Barbara, the wine regions, and Hearst Castle are important tourist draws, and a predominance of tourists live within a few hours' drive of the Central Coast. Second to that, European travelers flock here in droves. The common experience is to fly into Los Angeles or San Francisco, drive the California coast, and fly out of the airport at the opposite end. Because the Central Coast is unlike the major metropolitan areas of San Francisco and Los Angeles, and is known for its sublime coastline and intact towns, this area is often visited by people who desire a unique and quintessential California experience.

The wine regions are booming, bringing in not only agricultural dollars, but tourist dollars. In retrospect, the wine regions of Santa Barbara, Paso Robles, and to a lesser degree San Luis Obispo, the Edna Valley, and Ventura, have been flying under the radar. But that is changing, and there is a strong demand for a wine country experience.

Education is also big here, with major educational institutions such as Cal Poly San Luis Obispo and University of California–Santa Barbara (UCSB) in the area, as well as smaller but equally important institutions like Santa Barbara City College, Brooks Institute, and Westmont, all in Santa Barbara; Allan Hancock College in Santa Maria; Cuesta College in San Luis Obispo; and Ventura College and Channel Islands College in Ventura.

People and Culture

Though there are quite a few people living on the Central Coast, it's safe to break down the majority into two broad ethnic groups, Caucasian and Mexican. The region is still dominated by these two groups, and there is not a melting-pot phenomenon here as there is in other areas of the country. There are always small pockets of other ethnic groups, specifically Chinese and Japanese, but there is not a wide diversity of people represented here. The effects of tourism, agriculture, and economics means that most farming jobs and much of the service industry is comprised of Mexican workers. The Central Coast is not an inexpensive place to live, and certainly housing follows the California trend of being overpriced. All that has has created an even greater divide between those who can easily afford to live here and those who struggle to make ends meet.

Regardless, the people who live in the Central Coast tend to be very accepting. There isn't the rushed pace of life here, and that equates to people pretty much going about their business and allowing you to go about yours.

RELIGION

The Central Coast, like most other areas, has a broad spectrum of faiths represented, including Catholic, Muslim, Buddhist, Mormon, Christian, and Jewish, though due to Mexican influences, there is a preponderance of people who claim Roman Catholicism as their belief. Religion is often hotly debated in many places, yet this area seems to be very tolerant of differing religious beliefs. One has to wonder if the subdued climate and easygoing pace simply makes people feel more kindly toward each other.

LANGUAGE

It goes without saying that English is the dominant language along the Central Coast, but it is also worth noting that Spanish is the other language you will hear frequently.

Given the heavy agricultural thrust of the area, and that the majority are Mexican workers, roughly 30 percent of families speak Spanish in their homes. In a number of restaurants you will notice this more than other places. So if you speak Spanish, you can get along quite well.

THE ARTS

Santa Barbara, in particular, has a thriving arts scene. In part that's because the money is here to support artistic endeavors. Opera, the symphony, live-theater venues, concerts, art galleries, and lectures are supported by a public with deep pockets, and also helped in part by UCSB and their Arts & Lectures Series, which encourages talent to appear and perform here. Following behind that, San Luis Obispo and Ventura have notable arts representation, with venues like the Rubicon Theatre (805/667-2912, www.rubicontheatre.org) in Ventura, and the Clark Center for the Performing Arts (805/489-9444, www.clarkcenter.org) in Arroyo Grande.

Literature

The Central Coast, specifically Santa Barbara and San Luis Obispo, has long been a haven for writers. The area seems to be the ideal environment in which to write, due to inspiring natural surroundings and so many local things to actually write about. Sue Grafton (*A is for Alibi, C is for Corpse*) has used Santa Barbara as a backdrop for her alphabet series featuring the character Kinsey Millhone, who lives in the fictional Santa Teresa. Multiple prize winner T. C. Boyle (*The Road to Wellville, Tortilla Curtain, Riven Rock*) also resides in Santa Barbara, and actually lives in a Frank Lloyd Wright–designed home. Other well-known area writers include Fannie Flagg (*Fried Green Tomatoes*) and Ross MacDonald, whose Lew Archer crime novels *The Moving Target* and *The Drowning Pool* were both made into films starring Paul Newman. Erle Stanley

Gardner, who created Perry Mason (*The Case of the Velvet Claws,* and well over 40 others) resided in Ventura. Jack Kerouac lived in San Luis Obispo in 1953, during what some claim was the beginning of his best creative period, though you might be hard-pressed to believe that working on the railroad prompted his creativity. Lesser-known writers and journalists carve out great stories each week for the local newspapers and for regional magazines such as *805 Living* (www.805living.com), *Central Coast Magazine* (www.centralcoastmag.com), and *Santa Barbara Magazine* (www.sbmag.com).

Visual Arts

Public art is supported in Santa Barbara, Ventura, and San Luis Obispo, which is not to say everyone likes what they see, but at least it creates discussion. The Central Coast has long been a haven for artists and there are hundreds of art galleries showcasing plenty of local art. Wherever you go in the area, you'll most likely see painters setting up canvases near the missions or along blufftops near the ocean to capture the mountains at sunset. Mission scenes are ubiquitous in local art, as are vineyard scenes, but there are also pockets of experimental and contemporary art.

Santa Barbara Visual Arts (www.sbva.org) lists most every gallery in the entire county on a very comprehensive website. Additionally, the arts district is centrally located (for the most part) on the 800–1200 blocks of State Street in Santa Barbara. Santa Barbara has long had rotating public art displayed on State Street (www.sbartscomission.org), sometimes to rave reviews.

In San Luis Obispo there is no specific arts district, but there are galleries dotted throughout the city, and the San Luis Obispo Art Center website (www.sloartcenter.org) links to a wide variety of artists working in the area. Ventura's ArtWalk held each April (www.venturaartwalk.org) has over 200 artists represented and shows off what is happening art-wise countywide. The Ventura Public Art Program (www.cityofventura.net) was started in 1991 and a seven-member board oversees projects in a variety of media. A map of current public art can be downloaded from their website. Similarly, the Cambria Chamber of Commerce (www.cambriachamber.org) has a fairly comprehensive listing of artists working in the small enclave.

Music and Dance

It's a simplistic notion to assume that small towns produce small talent; nothing could be further from the truth. Aside from well-known musicians who got their start on the Central Coast, including Katy Perry, Dishwalla, and The Mad Caddies, there is a strong dance community, covering hip-hop, flamenco, ballet, folklórico, and much more. Rhythm Dance and Fitness Studios is Tamarr Paul's nearly packed studio for hip-hop and more in Goleta (805/965-0444, www.dointhemost.com). The Linda Vega Dance Studio (805/963-0073, www.vegaflamenco.com) is well known for flamenco and has been one of the premier dance studios in Santa Barbara; students routinely perform at Old Spanish Days Fiesta each August.

The Arlington Theatre (805/963-4408, www.thearlingtontheatre.com) and the Lobero (805/963-0761, www.lobero.com) in Santa Barbara are home to traveling musical and dance shows, as is the Clark Center for the Performing Arts (805/489-9444 www.clarkcenter.org) in Arroyo Grande, and the Performing Arts Center (805/756-2787, www.pacslo.org) located in San Luis Obispo. The Majestic Theater (805/683-0118, www.venturatheater.net) in Ventura sees lots of musical acts too, though not as much dance.

Architecture and Design

Santa Barbara, and to a degree Ventura and San Luis Obispo, are predominantly defined by Spanish Colonial architecture. In large part that is due to the Spanish who thrived here and brought with them a mix of traditional Spanish and Persian designs. Most of downtown Santa Barbara, parts of San Luis Obispo, and Ventura still have Spanish Colonial Revival as their identifying architecture, and this is what people expect to see when they visit.

In contrast are the Western towns like Paso Robles, Cambria, Arroyo Grande, Santa Ynez, and Los Olivos that are identified by their Western-style storefronts. And then there are pockets that are uniquely different from anything else in the area, like Solvang's Danish village and Santa Maria's blocky big-box stores.

ESSENTIALS

Getting There and Around

While not exactly remote, the Central Coast has the distinction of being sandwiched between two major cities that get all the attention, which is actually just fine with many locals. Highway 101 slices through parts of the Central Coast, but that by no means suggests that getting to your ultimate destination is as easy as getting off a plane and hopping in a taxi.

BY AIR

Los Angeles International Airport (LAX, 310/646-5252, www.airport-la.com) and San Francisco (SFO, 800/435-9736, www.flysfo.com) are the two major airports that bring people to

the Central Coast. The current expansion of the Santa Barbara Airport (SBA, 805/681-4803, www.flysba.com) will allow the airport to receive more commercial traffic, and San Luis Obispo is slowly adding more flights to its limited and small airport.

BY CAR

The most effective way to get around the Central Coast is by car. Driving is simple here, and there's not much that could make you get lost. It's important to note that at peak summer times, all three of the main streets—Main Street in Ventura, State Street in Santa Barbara,

© MICHAEL CERVIN

RAILROADS: THE TIES THAT BIND

The Central Coast was made, in large part, because of the railroads. When California became a state in 1850, much of the coastal areas were difficult to reach, and travel by stagecoach was laborious and slow. But plans were made to connect all of California by rail. It used to be that the rails only ran through the Santa Ynez and Santa Maria Valleys, so travel to Santa Barbara and Gaviota was by stagecoach from the stations in Ballard and Los Alamos. But then the railroads changed course, abandoning the interior route for a coastal route. Since several different competing railroads were building track, nothing was ever fully completed or consistent.

The Pacific Coast Railroad Company planned construction of a narrow-gauge railroad from the southern terminus of the San Luis Obispo & Santa Maria Valley Railroad to Santa Barbara, a distance of 80 miles. By 1882 the route had proceeded 11 miles toward its destination, to Los Alamos, and in that year dueling rail companies merged to form the Pacific Coast Railway Company. In 1883 the Pacific Coast Railway Company and the Pacific Coast Steamship Company passed to the control of the Oregon Improvement Company of Seattle, which would later become the Pacific Coast Company. The narrow-gauge rails reached Los Olivos on November 17, 1887. Up north, in October 1886, long-awaited rail service was brought into San Miguel coming from the north. Two weeks later the line was completed to the El Paso de Robles Resort Hotel (located today near Spring and 10th Streets in Paso Robles), and construction track was laid through to Templeton. It was a time-consuming process and continued not out of a desire to support local communities, but out of fear that the other railroad would finish first.

The railroads could not have been built without Chinese laborers, who originally arrived to work in the silver and gold mines, predominantly in Northern California. As the gold rush ended, the railroads on the Central Coast expanded and the Chinese workers moved south. That the Chinese contributed greatly to the success of the Central Coast is largely forgotten, though there were viable Chinatowns in both Santa Barbara and San Luis Obispo, remnants of which are still visible today.

These days, there is a desire by some to revive the railroad as a way to get across the state. For decades California has been wrestling with the idea of a high-speed train connecting San Francisco and Sacramento with Los Angeles and San Diego. In fact, the federal government allocated $2.25 billion for a high-speed rail in California in early 2010.

Powered by electricity, the high-speed trains would be part of the state's effort to mitigate climate change. The system would eventually use 100 percent renewable energy sources, with little or no CO_2 emissions, and use only one-third of the energy of a conventional airplane trip. Trains would travel at 220 mph, reaching Los Angeles from San Francisco in 2 hours and 40 minutes. And yet they would not pass through the Central Coast at all, but divert to the Central Valley through Fresno. And whereas high-speed rail would definitely benefit the Central Coast, perhaps ultimately it's best to not be connected, and to allow the beautiful beach communities to remain unspoiled by too much progress.

getting around via the Santa Barbara shuttle

and Higuera Street in San Luis Obispo—can get congested (although Higuera less so, as it's a one-way street). Aside from that, drives from community to community are easy. The 101 freeway can and does get backed up most afternoons about 4 P.M. as traffic heading south from Santa Barbara toward Ventura, along with freeway construction, slows things down, but it's usually only a 10-minute slowdown that picks up quickly.

Car Rentals

Renting a car is easy on the Central Coast, and a good idea since driving is the best way to see the sights. It's always best to compare rates of course. If you do rent a car, make certain it includes unlimited mileage; the drive from Los Angeles to Ventura is 90 miles, but if you plan on getting to the far reaches of Cambria, for example, you'll start to rack up those miles. Some of the major car rental carriers are: Enterprise (www.enterprise.com) in Ventura (805/648-2882), Santa Barbara (805/966-3097), and San Luis Obispo (805/545-9111); Avis (www.avis.com) in Ventura (805/339-2260), Santa Barbara (805/965-1079), and San Luis Obispo (805/595-1464); Hertz (www.hertz.com) in Ventura (805/654-0828); and Budget (www.budget.com) in San Luis Obispo (805/541-3977).

BY BUS

Greyhound (www.greyhound.com) is the most common way of arriving in the Central Coast by bus. There are major stops in Santa Maria, downtown Santa Barbara, downtown San Luis Obispo, and Paso Robles. Oddly, there isn't a Greyhound stop in the city of Ventura; the closest stop is in Oxnard, 25 minutes south of Ventura. To access beach areas like Lompoc, Guadalupe, Morro Bay, or Cambria you will need to take a regional bus once you get off the Greyhound bus.

The bus systems on the Central Coast are well designed and help you move around within a given city. The South Coast Area Transit (SCAT, 805/643-3158, www.scat.org) has bus service in western Ventura County as well as a connection to Ojai and is available seven days a week, except holidays. In Santa Barbara, you can ride the length of the waterfront, or the length of State Street, for just 25 cents, on two daily electric shuttle routes (www.sbmtd.gov).

WALKING THE COAST

It's no secret that the Central Coast in particular, and California in general, has a stunning coastline. People flock here to be by the coast and to explore the best of what it has to offer. But we are not the first to explore the area. The **Portola Expedition,** led by Gaspar de Portolá of Spain in 1769, marked the first overland journey by any Europeans along the California coast. This was followed in 1775-1776, as the Declaration of Independence was being signed, by the expedition led by Juan Bautista de Anza. This latter effort is now commemorated by the **Juan Bautista de Anza National Historic Trail,** which shares part of its route with the **California Coastal Trail.**

In 1910 and 1911, J. Smeaton Chase explored the California coast by horseback. His record of this journey, published as *California Coast Trails,* describes the pleasure of traveling "within sight of the sea and within sound of its wise, admonitory voice." More recently, in 1996, a determined band of folks from the nonprofit group Coastwalk, hiked the entire California coast to demonstrate that it was possible to do so – despite many impediments along the way.

The California Coastal Trail is one of the great trails not only of California and the Central Coast, but of the nation as well. Once the trail is finally completed, it will extend 1,200 miles through 15 counties, from the Oregon border to the Mexican border. While informal trails along the coast have been used for centuries, the trails' more recent history began in 1972 when California passed Proposition 20, recommending that a trail system be established along or near the coast. Today, roughly half of the California Coastal Trail is complete. At its best it is a network of public trails for walkers, bikers, equestrians, wheelchair riders, and others along the sublime California coastline. You may not choose to visit Ventura, Santa Barbara, and San Luis Obispo Counties in this way, but the option is there.

The Santa Ynez Valley Transit (805/688-5452, www.syvt.com) is a scheduled mini-bus serving Ballard, Buellton, Los Olivos, Santa Ynez, and Solvang. The San Luis Obispo Regional Transit Authority (805/781-4472, www.slorta.org) covers the entire county.

BY TRAIN

Amtrak (www.amtrak.com) is the only train service that operates within the Central Coast. The Pacific Surfliner runs from San Diego to San Luis Obispo, with stops in Ventura, Santa Barbara, Santa Maria, San Luis Obispo, and Paso Robles, but you cannot take the train to the coastal areas of Morro Bay and Cambria.

You might want to consider using the train for part of your trip. Stops in Santa Barbara, Ventura, and Paso Robles mean you can get off the train and walk to the downtown areas. The Santa Barbara stop lets you off on State Street a block from the beach. The Paso Robles stop is a two-block walk to the downtown square. San Luis Obispo's stop is a bit farther from downtown, so you'll need a car or taxi. Taking the train can make for a great day trip if you're short on time. For example, you could hop the train in San Luis Obispo and head to Paso Robles to explore the downtown, and then return to SLO by train, leaving your car parked all day.

BY BIKE

Getting around on a bike is very easy, and all three counties have well-integrated bike lanes and paths. Plus, there's nothing like cruising along the beachfront or on country back roads. Contact Traffic Solutions (805/963-7283, www.trafficsolutions.info) to obtain a copy of the free and most excellent Santa Barbara County bike map. You can rent bikes in Santa Barbara at Wheel Fun Rentals (23 E. Cabrillo Blvd., 805/966-2282, www.wheelfunrentals.com). Be advised that the law in Santa Barbara County is that any cyclist under the age of 18 not wearing a helmet is subject to a $70 fine.

For a great ride in Ventura along the promenade head to Matt's Cycling Center (2427 E. Harbor Blvd., 805/477-0933, www.mattscycling.com), who rents all types of bikes, and in Ojai, try Bicycles of Ojai (108 Canada St., 805/646-7736). For a languid ride in Santa Ynez wine country, check out Surrey Cycle Rentals (475 1st St., Solvang, 805/688-0091). San Luis Obispo offers Art's SLO Cyclery (2140 Santa Barbara St., 805/543-4416) and in Morro Bay, Mark's Baywood Cyclery (2179 10th St., 805/528-2453) will do the trick. Cambria Bicycle Outfitters has stores in Cambria (1602 Main St., 805/926-2230 www.cambriabike.com) and Paso Robles (1645 Commerce Way, 805/221-2602, www.cambriabike.com).

Biking Safety

Maybe it's the alluring near-perfect weather and sunshine, but far too many cyclists ride around here without a helmet. Not a good idea. The Central Coast is a very bike-friendly region, which is good, but sharing the major roads with cars without being protected is not good—though it's not just cars that are a danger. Helmets save lives. If you rent a bike, rent a helmet, or head to a cycle shop and buy one. At the very least check out Play It Again Sports (www.playitagainsports.com), which has stores in Ventura, Santa Maria, and Santa Barbara and sells used sports equipment, including helmets—it's better than having nothing on your head.

Though you'll see people riding bikes without helmets, the police, normally pretty laid-back in these areas, will write citations for those offenses. The congested State Street in Santa Barbara is an area you particularly need to abide by the rules. Within Santa Barbara County, any cyclist under the age of 18 is required by law to wear a helmet. There's a $70 fine if you don't.

TAXIS

Taxis are not prevalent on the Central Coast, and in fact they are few and far between once you leave Ventura and the city of Santa Barbara, though every city has them. In Santa Barbara, Checker Cab (888/581-1110) is a safe bet. In the Ventura and Ojai region there is Yellow Cab of Ventura (805/659-6900), and Ojai Taxi (100 N. Signal St., 805/646-8294). Serving the entire Santa Ynez Valley, Solvang Taxi (805/688-0069) operates 24 hours a day. In San Luis Obispo and Paso Robles there is the SLO Cab Company (202 Tank Farm Rd., 805/544-1222) and Paso Robles Cab (805/237-2615). Along the coast there is Cambria Cab (4363 Bridge St., 805/927-4357) and Bay Taxi (1215 Embarcadero, 805/772-1222) in Morro Bay.

Tips for Travelers

BUSINESS HOURS

For all of its seeming dependence on tourism, it's an interesting phenomenon that all of the Central Coast, including larger towns like Santa Barbara and Ventura, still has a small-town feel. It's not uncommon for businesses to step away during "regular business hours" and place a hand-written note on the door saying they'll be back in a few minutes. A large number of business don't really have set hours; they might stay open later, or close early—it all depends on variables only they know. If there is someplace you absolutely need to visit, it's advisable to call first to make certain they will be open.

ACCESS FOR TRAVELERS WITH DISABILITIES

Several years back, a certain individual took it upon himself to frequent Central Coast wineries, hotels, and restaurants with the sole aim of suing anyone who was not in compliance with the Americans with Disabilities Act (ADA). Though perhaps he was right in broaching the issue, his aim was to extort money from small business in the area. Sadly, several business were forced to close down due to unreasonable demands and legal fees, and ultimately he filed more than 40 lawsuits, not to effect change but to line his own pockets.

ETHICAL TRAVEL

There are basic principles that apply no matter where you travel, and the Central Coast is no exception. Consider the following ideas as you explore the Central Coast, as doing so will enhance your experience.

• **Minimize your environmental impact:** Travel and camp on durable surfaces, dispose of waste properly, and recycle. There are green recycle bins all along State Street in Santa Barbara. Make sure your hotel recycles too. Respect wildlife and don't feed animals. Feeding wildlife damages their health, alters natural behaviors, and exposes them to predators and other dangers. Always follow designated trails, especially when on the Channel Islands. Do not disturb animals, plants, or their natural habitats. Learn about and support local conservation programs and organizations working to preserve the environment.

• **Leave what you find:** Take only photographs. Leave only footprints. The impact of one person may seem minimal, but the global effect of removing items from their native place can be decimating. This is certainly true of beachcombing. People always seem to want to take souvenirs from the beaches on the Central Coast, but the beaches, and the Channel Islands, should be left to their natural state.

• **Support the local economy:** Be aware of where your money is going by supporting locally owned businesses. To avoid buying products made from endangered plants or animals, see Know Before You Go at www.cbp.gov for the U.S. Customs list of restricted items. Bargain fairly: Remember the economic realities of your new currency. When bargaining, do so with respect to the seller and decide on a mutually beneficial price. Doing so contributes to the local economy, while an unfair price may contribute to a region's poverty.

This copyrighted information has been reprinted with permission from the Leave No Trace Center for Outdoor Ethics. For more information or materials, please visit www.lnt.org or call 303/442-8222.

Eventually a federal judge put a stop to his egregious actions.

On the positive side, the region has become more aware of ADA issues, and that has made traveling along the Central Coast easier for anyone with a disability. All buses are wheelchair accessible, for example, and on major streets there are audible pedestrian signals and tactile guide strips for the visually impaired. The Braille Institute (www.brailleinstitute.org) has great programs in the Central Coast; in Santa Barbara and Ventura Counties, contact the local field services coordinator at 805/682-6222, and in San Luis Obispo County phone 805/462-1225. Accessible Journeys (www.disabilitytravel.com) has great pointers and information about traveling with a disability and can put you in touch, through their network of resources, with the right help to fit your needs.

TRAVELING WITH CHILDREN

Assuming your kids like the outdoors, there's plenty to keep them busy with bike paths, hiking, plenty of parks, and tons of beach activities, and it's all relatively inexpensive. Consider a surfing class, tide-pooling, kayaking, and definitely think about a day trip to the Channel Islands. The Central Coast has children's museums and other spots like natural history museums to keep little ones occupied without boring them. In Ventura there is Gull Wings Children's Museum (418 W. 4th St., Oxnard, 805/483-3005, www.gullwings.org). In San Luis Obispo there is the San Luis Obispo Children's Museum (1010 Nipomo St., 805/544-5437, www.slocm.org), located just off Higuera Street downtown. Santa Maria has the Santa Maria Valley Discovery Museum (705 S. McClelland, 805/928-

8414, www.smvdiscoverymuseum.org) and Paso Robles offers the Paso Robles Children's Museum (623 13th St., 805/238-7432, www.pasokids.org). For a comprehensive list of parks, beaches, petting zoos, and much more for the littlest tourists, check out www.central-coastkids.com.

WOMEN TRAVELING ALONE

For both males and females, traveling alone has its perks and its downsides. In general, people along the Central Coast are friendly, and they're likely to offer help if you look like you need it. Women traveling by themselves will find a helpful public. The website Journeywoman (www.journeywoman.com) is a site devoted to women traveling solo, and offers some great advice.

Of course, it's always best to use common sense and to listen to your gut reaction if something or someone seems amiss. There have been reported at area clubs and bars cases of dosings (the act of slipping some kind of drug, such as the "date rape" drug, into your drink when you're not looking), so it's always important to be alert and never, ever leave your purse or drink unattended. If there is a problem, ask for help.

SENIOR TRAVELERS

The Central Coast is a fantastic spot for seniors to visit. The roads are flat and walkable in every community, with very few hills.

The website Senior Journal (www.seniorjournal.com) offers senior travel tips, suggestions, and even itineraries. The locally based website Silver Years (805/405-3164, www.silveryears.net) also provides more detailed regional information. There are often senior discounts available at sights and events; fewer hotels and restaurants offer senior discounts, but it never hurts to ask. Most movie houses offer senior discounts, as do the buses and trolley.

GAY AND LESBIAN TRAVELERS

The Central Coast is a mix of liberal areas like Santa Barbara and pockets of more conservative values. That said, there are virtually no issues between the gay and straight communities here and people tend to coexist very peacefully. In Santa Barbara, the Pacific Pride Foundation (www.pacificpridefoundation.org) has been around since 1974 and is an invaluable resource when visiting the area. The Ventura Rainbow Alliance (www.lgbtventura.org) was established in 1993 and provides excellent information. In San Luis Obispo, the Central Coast Gay and Lesbian Alliance (www.ccgala.org), which became incorporated as a nonprofit in 1994, covers that county. The Pacific Pride Festival (www.pacificpridefestival.org) is held in Santa Barbara each July and is the largest gathering of its kind in the Tri-Counties.

Do keep in mind that the Central Coast is still a small-town region. Outside of the major cities of Ventura, Santa Barbara, and San Luis Obispo, the communities are relatively isolated. However, the upside of areas that rely on tourism is that businesses rarely discriminate against anyone.

TRAVELING WITH PETS

Pet-friendly hotels and establishments are abundant along the Central Coast, as are dog parks. Not all beaches and parks, however, have off-leash areas, so it's important to note the signs posted at each recreation spot. Citations for not leashing your dog can and will be assessed, so pay attention. After all, it's best to play by the rules. Many restaurants will allow pets on their patios, and a few establishments even allow pets inside. Patrick's Side Street Café in Los Olivos, for example, allows animals to join their owners inside the restaurant, and many do. And it's not uncommon to see a plethora of dogs on any major street, be it Main Street in Ventura, State Street in Santa Barbara, and Higuera Street in San Luis Obispo. The website www.dogfriendly.com is a fairly comprehensive source for pet-friendly accommodations, though not everything is listed. If you're not sure about a hotel, it's best to call in advance and find out their pet fees and restrictions.

Health and Safety

HOSPITALS

These are the main hospitals within the Central Coast. For emergencies always call 911.

- Cambria: Twin Cities Community Hospital (1100 Las Tablas Rd., Templeton, 805/434-3500)

- Morro Bay: Twin Cities Community Hospital (1100 Las Tablas Rd., Templeton, 805/434-3500)

- Ojai: Valley Community Hospital (1306 Maricopa Hwy., 805/646-1401)

- Paso Robles: Twin Cities Community Hospital (1100 Las Tablas Rd., Templeton, 805/434-3500)

- San Luis Obispo: French Hospital Medical Center (1911 Johnson Ave., 805/543-5353)

- Santa Barbara: Cottage Hospital (Bath and Pueblo Sts., 805/682-7111)

- Santa Maria: Marian Medical Center (1400 E. Church St., 805/739-3000)

- Santa Ynez Valley: Cottage Hospital (2050 Viborg, Solvang, 805/688-6431)

- Ventura: Community Memorial Hospital (147 N. Brent St., 805/652-5011)

PHARMACIES

These are the main pharmacies within the Central Coast. The Cambria Village Pharmacy (2306 Main St., 805/927-4236) is right downtown. There's a Morro Bay Rite Aid (704 Quintana, 805/772-6198, www.riteaid.com) right off the 101 freeway, and the Ojai Village Pharmacy (202 E. Ojai Ave., 805/646-7274) has been around over 100 years. In Paso Robles there's a CVS (187 Nibblick Rd., 805/238-2815, www.cvs.com). In San Luis Obispo there is a CVS (3960 Broad St., 805/783-2903) and in Santa Barbara there is a Rite Aid (825 State St., 805/966-2760) right on State. In Santa Maria there is a Rite Aid (345 Town Center West, 805/925-1167) in the Town Center Mall. Serving the Santa Ynez Valley,

there's a Rite Aid in Solvang (616 Alamo Pintado, 805/686-0016) in the Neilson's Shopping Center. The Ventura Rite Aid (131 W. Main St., 805/643-1121) is in the Mission Plaza shopping center.

EMERGENCY SERVICES

These are the main police contacts listed for the Central Coast. In an emergency call 911.

- Cambria–San Luis Obispo Sheriff's Department (800/834-3346)

- Morro Bay Police Department (870 Morro Bay Blvd., 805/772-6225)

- Ojai Police Department (402 S. Ventura St., 805/646-1414)

- Paso Robles Police Department (1220 Paso Robles St., 805/237-6464)

- San Luis Obispo Police Department (1042 Walnut St., 805/781-7317)

- Santa Barbara Police Department (215 E. Figueroa St., 805/897-2335)

- Santa Maria Police Department (222 E. Cook St., 805/925-0951)

- Santa Ynez Valley: County of Santa Barbara Sheriff's Department (1745 Mission Dr., Solvang, 805/688-5000)

- Ventura Police Department (1425 Dowell Dr., 805/339-4400)

WATER SAFETY
Riptides

Remember that the ocean is a force greater than yourself, and there are occasional riptides and undercurrents along the calm, serene beaches of the Central Coast. Signs are posted when weather conditions warrant it. It's always best to swim with a buddy, or at the very least have someone waiting on shore for you.

Sailing

Sailing is a fantastic way to spend the day, but sailing requires wind. During the summer months the wind is predominantly from the west to northwest. The winds tend to be funneled around Point Conception, where the coast line turns north, and are accelerated along the north side (mainland facing) portion of the Channel Islands. This area is referred to as "windy lane" and it can get extremely windy here, as the name suggests. This effect is strongest towards the west end of the channel and decreases as you move east. The winds tend to blow strongest in the afternoon and evening.

Be aware that this is a shipping channel, and many tankers and cargo ships move briskly through the waters. They have the right of way. They are huge, but they move fast, over 20 knots. So if you're heading to or back from the islands and you see a tanker in the water, know they probably can't see you—and even if they can, it's impossible for them to change course; they'll be near you faster than you can imagine. Never try and outrun one of them.

Also be on the lookout for dive flags while you're sailing or boating. Divers are required to post a flag that sits atop a buoy; it is a red block with a white line through it. If you see one, avoid the area, as you could inadvertently cut an oxygen supply line. Also keep in mind that in the water, boats under sail have the right of way over motorboats.

EARTHQUAKES

Should a temblor occur while you are visiting, remain calm and follow these instructions.

If you are inside, take cover by getting under a sturdy table or other piece of furniture, and wait until the shaking stops. If there isn't a table or desk near you, cover your face and head with your arms and crouch in an inside corner of the building where the building supports are the greatest (freestanding walls fall easily). Stay away from glass, windows, outside doors and walls, and anything that could fall, such as light fixtures or furniture. Use a doorway for shelter only if it is in close proximity to you and you know that it's a strongly supported, load-bearing doorway. Stay inside until the shaking stops and it's safe to go outside. Research has shown that

most injuries occur when people inside buildings attempt to move to a different location inside the building or try to leave altogether. Be aware that the electricity may go out or the sprinkler systems or fire alarms may turn on. Do not use the elevators!

If you are outside, stay there, move away from buildings, streetlights, and utility wires, and wait until the shaking stops. The greatest danger exists directly outside of buildings. Many of the 120 fatalities from the 1933 Long Beach earthquake occurred when people ran outside, only to be killed by falling debris from collapsing walls. Ground movement during an earthquake is seldom the direct cause of death or injury.

If you're driving, stop as quickly as safety permits and stay in the vehicle. Avoid stopping near or under buildings, trees, overpasses, and utility wires. Proceed cautiously once the earthquake has stopped. Avoid roads, bridges, or ramps that might have been damaged by the earthquake.

CRIME

Crime in Ventura, Santa Barbara, and San Luis Obispo Counties is relatively low according to recent reports by the Office of the Attorney General for the State of California. By comparison to the other 58 counties in the state, the Central Coast falls in the lower middle. However, it's an interesting trend that overall crimes were higher in Ventura County, decreasing in Santa Barbara County, and decreasing even further in San Luis Obispo County. Draw what conclusions you will. Always lock your car and never leave valuables in plain sight; items such as a GPS, cell phone, laptop, or camera should either be taken with you or locked in the car's trunk.

There has been an increase in gang activity unfortunately, and it is clearly charted as being worse in Ventura, and lessening as you move upcoast. Santa Barbara has had several high-profile gang stabbings and incidents, one in particular in broad daylight right on State Street. Task forces have been set up to grapple with these problems.

HOMELESSNESS

It's a sad commentary on our culture that we have allowed the homeless issue to be ignored.

In all three counties you will see panhandlers, with a greater concentration in Ventura and Santa Barbara. Task forces have been set up to deal with this issue too. Local businesses don't want potential customers accosted on State Street or Main Street, but it does happen, and it will continue to occur. Most panhandlers are not aggressive, though there has been an increase in the public's complaints about their assertive practices.

TRAINS

Given the fact that the train runs through all three counties, it's important to know that incidents of people walking along the tracks and/or trying to outrun an oncoming train have been increasing. Granted, many of the deaths are of homeless men and women who are under the influence of drugs and alcohol, but there have also been cases of people just not paying attention. The trains that run are not sequestered in any form, meaning that anyone, including children, can walk onto the tracks at virtually any point in the Tri-Counties. Always use caution when crossing train tracks. If the crossing arms are down and the red lights are flashing, do not attempt to save time by cutting across the tracks before the train passes.

Information and Services

MONEY

All prices within the Central Coast are in U.S. dollars. Current sales tax rates range 8.25–8.75 percent depending on where you go. For example and not surprisingly, Santa Barbara is at the top at 8.75 percent, but most of Ventura County, with the exception of the naval areas, is 8.25 percent. Similarly, in San Luis Obispo, the county overall is at 8.25 percent, but the cities of Morro Bay and San Luis Obispo are at the high end with 8.75 percent. It may not seem like much, but a half percent can add up, depending on the length of your trip. If you spend $2,000 on your trip that half percent is $10—and that's lunch!

All major banks will change money, and they tend to have better rates than small outfits. In Santa Barbara you might consider Santa Barbara Bank & Trust, Montecito Bank & Trust, and American Riviera Bank. In Ventura there is Community West Bank and in San Luis Obispo there is San Luis Trust Bank. There are of course larger banks like Bank of America and Rabobank as well.

For international travelers, www.xe.com will provide exchange rates relating to your specific currency. Always check rates prior to your arrival to avoid unnecessary costs and fees.

COMMUNICATIONS AND MEDIA
Phones and Area Codes

Many visitors to the Central Coast are surprised that there is just one area code for all three counties; it's 805.

Internet Services

Most every hotel on the Central Coast, and an abundance of coffee shops, now offer free wireless Internet (Wi-Fi) connections. Additionally, it's becoming increasingly easier to pick up random signals in a variety of areas. If you don't have a computer, many hotels have a business area with one or two computers for guest use. Another option is to use the public computers at the libraries.

Mail Services

The U.S. Postal Service (www.usps.com) currently delivers mail six days a week. With budget cuts impending, it is advisable to phone the nearest post office to check operating hours in case you need to buy stamps or mail something on a certain day. The main branches of the area's post offices are as follows: In Ventura (675 E. Santa Clara St., 805/643-3057), Ojai (201 E. Ojai Ave., 805/646-7904), Santa Barbara (836 Anacapa St., 805/564-2226), in the Santa Ynez

Valley (430 Alisal Rd., 805/688-9309), in Santa Maria (201 E. Battles Rd., 805/922-0321), San Luis Obispo (893 Marsh St., 805/541-9138), Paso Robles (800 6th St., 805/237-8342), Cambria (4100 Bridge St. 805/927-8610), and in Morro Bay (898 Napa Ave., 805/772-0839).

Newspapers and Periodicals

Major daily newspapers include the *Santa Barbara News-Press,* the *Ventura County Star,* and *San Luis Obispo Tribune.* The weekly free alternative papers, which also provide good coverage of events and some insightful articles on local politics, include the *Ventura County Reporter* in Ventura, *The Santa Barbara Independent* in Santa Barbara, and the *New Times,* covering San Luis Obispo and Paso Robles. These papers publish each Thursday and are free at a multitude of locations.

Radio and Television

Keeping abreast of current events is important when visiting. The main radio stations that will provide you with important information in terms of local politics, talk, and current events are: In Ventura KVTA-AM-1520; in Santa Barbara KZSB AM-1290; in the Santa Maria Valley KSMA AM-1240; for San Luis Obispo KYNS AM-1340; and for Paso Robles, Morro Bay, and Cambria, KKAL FM-92.5.

Local television in the area does pick up channels from Los Angeles, most notably KNBC. But for local news, weather, sports, and events, the three best stations are KEYT (www.keyt.com), which has the most comprehensive media coverage of the Central Coast, followed by KCOY (www.kcoy.com) and KSBY (www.ksby.com).

MAPS AND TOURIST INFORMATION

The Santa Barbara Chamber of Commerce Visitors Center (1 Garden St., 805/965-3021, www.sbchamber.org, Mon.–Sat. 9 A.M.–4 P.M., Sun. 10 A.M.–4 P.M.) is located directly across from the beach and offers discounted tickets to many restaurants and sights in town. They have books and maps on the area as well.

Ventura Visitors Center is located right downtown (101 S. California St., 805/648-2075, www.ventura-usa.com, Mon.–Fri. 8:30 A.M.–5 P.M., Sat. 9 A.M.–5 P.M., Sun. 10 A.M.–4 P.M.) and is packed with everything you could want to know about Ventura. They have a surprisingly large amount of information in their large digs and the staff is eager to help.

Located inside the Ojai Valley Museum, the Ojai Valley Chamber of Commerce (130 W. Ojai Ave., 805/640-1390, www.ojaichamber.org, Mon.–Fri. 10 A.M.–4 P.M.) is oftentimes understaffed, but much of the information on Ojai is located in the foyer of the museum, so if they are closed, you can still grab all the literature you need.

The Solvang Visitors Center (1639 Copenhagen, 800/468-6765, www.solvangusa.com) is staffed by locals wearing red vests. They have comprehensive information not just on Solvang, but on the entire valley as well, including quarterly publications, local newspapers and newsletters, and maps.

Though Los Olivos is just small enough that it doesn't have a visitors center, there is a small but functional website: www.losolivosca.com.

The San Luis Obispo Visitor Center (1039 Chorro St., 805/781-2777, www.visitslo.com, Sun.–Wed. 10 A.M.–5 P.M., Thurs.–Sat. 10 A.M.–7 P.M.) is located right downtown. They have maps and specific guides for restaurants, wineries, and the like.

The Paso Robles Visitor's Center (1225 Park St., 805/238-0506, Mon.–Fri. 8:30 A.M.–5 P.M., Sat.–Sun. 10 A.M.–2 P.M.) will provide you with all the necessary materials to make your stay perfect.

The Cambria Chamber of Commerce (767 Main St., 805/927-3624, www.cambriachamber.org, Mon.–Fri. 9 A.M.–5 P.M., Sat.–Sun. noon–4 P.M.) is probably the best resource for information on the area.

The Morro Bay Chamber of Commerce (845 Embarcadero, Ste. D, 800/231-0592, www.morrobay.org, Mon.–Fri. 9 A.M.–5 P.M., Sat. 10 A.M.–4 P.M.) has a wonderful visitors center overlooking the bay at the end of a small boardwalk. They offer a vast array of printed material you can take with you.

RESOURCES

Suggested Reading

NON-FICTION

Beilharz, Edwin A. *Felipe de Neve: First Governor of California.* San Francisco: California Historical Society, 1971. This long-forgotten book gives a great historical account of the formation of California in the 1770s, including Father Serra and the missions up and down the coast, with a special emphasis on Santa Barbara. It's a tad dry in parts, but is comprehensive in its understanding of the Spanish and their impact upon the Central Coast.

Boutelle, Sara Holmes. *Julia Morgan, Architect.* New York: Abbeville Press, 1988. With projects in Santa Barbara, San Luis Obispo, and San Simeon, Julia Morgan had a major impact on the look and feel of the Central Coast. This definitive study of the reclusive Morgan is replete with color photos and drawings and has an abundance of information on Hearst Castle.

California Coastal Commission. *Beaches and Parks from Monterey to Ventura.* Berkeley: University of California Press, 2007. This covers 310 coastal beaches, with color photographs as well as topographical maps and other useful information.

Castle, Rodger, and Gary Ream. *Morro Bay: Images of America.* Mount Pleasant, SC: Arcadia Publishing, 2006. Written by members of the Morro Bay Historical Society, this book gives a comprehensive history of this seaside town. The old photographs provide visual cues to how the town has changed.

Dana, Richard Henry. *Two Years Before the Mast.* New York: Barnes & Noble Classic Series, 2007. This personal journal chronicles Dana's life aboard a sailing trade ship in 1836. He visited Santa Barbara and other ports in California and talks about trading with the missions and the Indian way of life and gives an excellent look into the Mexican period on the Central Coast. Perhaps the best line, given the current boom in the Central Coast, is, "The Californians are an idle, thriftless people and can make nothing for themselves." If only he could revisit today.

Gardner, Theodore Roosevelt. *Lotusland: A Photographic Odyssey.* Santa Barbara: Allen A. Knoll, 1995. Packed with colorful photographs, this book lays out the rich botanical history of Lotusland in stunning visual detail. Once you see the photos you'll want to visit.

Gray, Mary Taylor. *Watchable Birds of California.* Missoula, MT: Mountain Publishing, 1999. This is one of the most definitive guides to bird-watching, broken down by seacoast, inland, freshwater, and high-country birds. It has color photos to help with identifying.

Gruver, Kathy. *The Alternative Medicine Cabinet.* West Conshohocken, PA: Infinity Publishing, 2010. Santa Barbara author Kathy Gruver uses area parks and agriculture as a springboard to discuss natural health issues common to the Central Coast and to everyone else, including avoiding pesticide-laden foods and searching for healthy alternatives.

Masson, Kathryn. *Santa Barbara Style.* New York: Rizzoli, 2001. Santa Barbara never looked so good. This book includes photos of many Santa Barbara landmarks and Montecito estates, both interiors and exteriors, and shows all the details of what good decorating can do for a home.

McElrath, Clifford. *On Santa Cruz Island.* Santa Barbara: Caractacus Corporation, 1993. This is not an easy book to locate, but it has a wealth of knowledge about the Channel Islands. The author supervised ranching operations on Santa Cruz Island in the early 1920s, and his memoir of those days gives an unprecedented look at island life.

Various Authors. *Ventura County—Looking Back: The Early Years.* Seattle: Pediment Publishing, 2009. More than 350 historical black-and-white photos are presented in this coffee-table book spanning from the 1870s to 1920s that shows how Ventura weathered many changes. This book celebrates the good and the bad and the everyday.

Wilmer, Thomas C. *Romancing the Coast: Romantic Getaways Along the California Coast.* Ashland, OR: RiverWood Books, 2005. Veteran travel writer Tom Wilmer writes in such a way that you want to immediately start searching for a romantic spot to escape to, even if it's just a weekend on the Central Coast. This is a well-written and informative book for those searching for a more intimate Central Coast adventure.

FICTION

Boyle, T. C. *Riven Rock.* New York: Penguin Books, 1998. T. C. Boyle's seventh novel transforms two characters straight out of Montecito history. The people and place are real, and Boyle blends them into a complex novel about a mentally ill millionaire locked up in his own Santa Barbara estate in the early 1900s.

Cervin, Michael. *Generous Fiction.* West Conshohocken, PA: Infinity Publishing, 2009. Many of the poems in this unusual poetry book were inspired by experiences in Santa Barbara that are specifically given credit as they relate to each poem. For example, a Long Island Iced Tea on Stearns Wharf prompted one poem, a walk at the Santa Barbara Mission rose garden was the genesis of another.

Grafton, Sue. *Q is for Quarry.* New York: Ballantine, 2003. The murder in this book, part of the Kinsey Millhone series, was based on a real homicide that occurred in Santa Barbara in 1969, and unfortunately is still unsolved, but other characters in this particular book are also based on people in the sheriff's department, one of whom went on to become the police chief of San Luis Obispo.

Internet Resources

Researching any city before you visit is imperative. Take some time and use these websites to help hone your itinerary.

TOURISM INFORMATION
Cervin It Straight
www.cervinitstraight.com
"No ratings, no hype, just straight talk about wine, food and travel." This book's author covers the Central Coast and beyond, offering his top picks for places to dine, where to stay, and suggestions for some of the best wines, beer, and spirits in the area. New information is being added all the time.

San Luis Obispo Visitors and Conference Bureau
www.sanluisobispocounty.com
The site is also available in Spanish, German, and French. You can sign up for their monthly newsletter before you go to get a feel for the area.

Santa Barbara Conference and Visitors Bureau
www.santabarbaraca.com
This is a terrific comprehensive website that covers everything you can think of and offers many Internet specials and deals on lodging and food. The website provides information about the Santa Ynez Valley as well.

Ventura Visitors & Convention Bureau
www.ventua-usa.com
A comprehensive site about Ventura with a nice collection of photographs and videos. They also have a very cool virtual tour set up to explore different parts of the city, giving a complete 360-degree view of specific points in town.

WINERIES
The Paso Robles Wine Country Alliance
www.pasowine.com
The single best website for researching the wines of Paso Robles. If only all wine websites were like this one. You can search for a specific wine, grape, or winery, or search by acreage. It's intuitive, easy to navigate, and very well planned.

The San Luis Obispo Vintners Association
www.slowine.com
This site covers the reasonably small area south of Paso Robles including the Edna Valley.

The Santa Barbara County Vintners Association
www.sbcountywines.com
The authoritative website for most of the wineries and growers in Santa Barbara County also lists upcoming special events at each winery and downloadable maps.

The Santa Barbara Urban Wine Trail
www.urbanwinetrailsb.com
Though this is a small area in downtown Santa Barbara and not in the grape-growing region of the valley, the Urban Wine Trail is thriving. This website can send GPS coordinates for the wineries directly to your iPhone. Since most of them are within walking distance of each other, though, you'll be fine even without the GPS.

Index

List of Maps

Acknowledgments

Any book, no matter what kind, is equal parts isolation and cooperation. Writers toil away in seclusion, only to come out of their dark hovel to blink at the sun briefly and obtain help from countless people who make their job easier. Many people have suggested to me, or reminded me, of some of the wonderful places throughout the Central Coast that have ended up in this book. And to those folks, thank you.

I would like to thank my editor Erin Raber for her editorial input, graphics coordinator Darren Alessi for his photographic input, and map editor Albert Angulo for all his help with the maps. All three stepped up to the plate during a difficult time to collectively make this book a reality and they deserve my utmost thanks for working diligently behind the scenes.

Linda Parker Sanpei at Parker Sanpei & Associates has been an incredible help in dealing with the San Luis Obispo County section of this book and her help and generosity have been invaluable.

Most importantly however, I need to thank my wife, Kathy, who endured ruthless torment over many months while I was either absent (both physically and mentally) or stressed to the point of nearly calling several nice large men wearing white jackets to come rescue me during looming deadlines. Her patience and willingness to endure solitary hours while I hammered away at a keyboard has been frustrating for her, but helpful and necessary for me.

Though I never thought I would include this, our cats, Uther and Lilith, provided much comfort during lonely hours at home. A resonant purr from a loyal friend has incalculable benefits.

Additionally, sanity comes in many forms, and for me, the simple joys of running at the beach in Santa Barbara, specifically More Mesa—a place I dearly love and included in these pages—has been a great respite from a complicated schedule.

And, lastly, thanks to you, the reader, who uses this resource to make your visit to the Central Coast a memorable one. If it were not for you, I'd be working in an office somewhere doing something with Post-Its and paperclips. I hope you plunge into the Central Coast and that your time there is filled with fond memories and immeasurable joy.

www.moon.com

DESTINATIONS | ACTIVITIES | BLOGS | MAPS | BOOKS

MOON.COM is ready to help plan your next trip! Filled with fresh trip ideas and strategies, author interviews, informative travel blogs, a detailed map library, and descriptions of all the Moon guidebooks, Moon.com is all you need to get out and explore the world—or even places in your own backyard. While at Moon.com, sign up for our monthly e-newsletter for updates on new releases, travel tips, and expert advice from our on-the-go Moon authors. As always, when you travel with Moon, expect an experience that is uncommon and truly unique.

MOON IS ON FACEBOOK—BECOME A FAN!

JOIN THE MOON PHOTO GROUP ON FLICKR